LISTEN

COMMENTARY ON THE SPIRITUAL
COUPLETS OF MEVLANA RUMI

LISTEN
COMMENTARY ON THE SPIRITUAL
COUPLETS OF MEVLANA RUMI

by
Kenan Rifai

Translated by Victoria Holbrook

FONS VITAE

Table of Contents

Table of Contents, continued

Table of Contents, continued

Bismillahirrahmanirrahim
(In the Name of Allah, Most Gracious, Most Merciful)

Foreword to the English Edition of Commentary on *The Spiritual Couplets*

Praised as "*the pith of the Koran,*" the immortal *Spiritual Couplets* of the thirteenth-century Sufi thinker Mevlana Jalal al-Din Rumi has for centuries been an indispensible book of the East, taught at Mevlevi cloisters, read in mansions and palaces and taken as the subject of commentaries for seven centuries. When the poet Yahya Kemal was asked how the Turks occupied themselves in times past, he said: "They ate pilaf and read the *Spiritual Couplets.*"

The book you hold in your hand is a commentary on the first volume of the Spiritual Couplets, the exceptional work whose mysteries the eminent twentieth-century Sufi and perfect spiritual guide Kenan Rifai grasped and expounded from within a spiritual world which can only be comprehended by those aware of that mystery. Select students of his took notes on the *Spiritual Couplets* lessons he gave weekly at the Ümm-ü Kenan Cloister (the Altay Cloister), where he served as Shaykh during the years 1908-1925, and a group of writers made up of Samiha Ayverdi, Safiye Erol, Sofi Huri, Nihad Sami Banarlı and Nezihe Araz, after much meticulous work over long years, at last prepared those notes for publication, offering them for the benefit of all mankind.

Mevlana, who let flow the mighty waters of the love of God and the thrill of faith upon the suffering, needy, discontented masses, who rescued mankind from the slavery of animal instinct, opening his embrace in boundless tolerance to those seeking freedom of conscience and the purity of an examined spirit with the invitation, "Come, whoever you may be, come," has been speaking the mysteries of creation for centuries.

Everyone who examines himself, wondering "What am I, where did I come from and where am I going?" will find in this work answers for the most tortuous of problems and comprehend the meaning of life.

We thank for their service the esteemed researcher Professor Victoria R Holbrook, who translated the book from Turkish to English; Nefes Publications, which covered the costs of the project; and everyone who contributed their efforts to the preparation of the English edition.

Kubbealtı Academy
Culture and Art Foundation

Preface

The *Masnavi* is the interpretation of the Qur'an wherein Rumi explains his own Reality (*Haqiqa*), that is, the *haqiqa* of the Completed Human Being.

It begins with "Listen from the *Nay* (reed flute)." The reed flute is the symbol of the Prophet Muhammad and his spiritual descendants who do not speak from themselves. They only relate the reality (*haqiqa*) of Allah by reflecting it from their non-existent Beings.

I am grateful to Allah that I have been blessed with the slightest role in the introduction of this book to the world. This is a book that we are listening to from the heart of one who enlightens the 20th century in the example of the reed flute, my teacher, Kenan al-Rifai.

I am leaving you now with the *Masnavi*, the truest and most valuable work that you could ever read to understand your own meaning and to know your own Truth.

Cemalnur Sargut, Chair
Turkish Women's Cultural Association
Istanbul branch
October 22, 2011

Preface

It is remarkable that the Persian poetry of Jalal al-Din Rumi (d. 1273) has emerged as one of the most popular literary successes of recent years. To be sure, scholars of Middle Eastern and Islamic culture have recognized the central importance of Rumi's literary work for a long time. Rumi is the author of one of the largest collections of mystical lyrics in the history of Persian poetry (the *Divan-i Shams*, some 35,000 lines), as well as the great epic of the *Masnavi-i Ma`navi* (or *Spiritual Couplets*, in 27,000 lines). It is universally acknowledged among specialists in Islamic mysticism that Rumi is one of the most important figures in this tradition. In particular, Rumi's six-volume *Masnavi* is recognized as a classic of the mystical epic, which employs narratives in verse form to convey the terms of spiritual experience. But early scholarly treatments of Rumi's poetry, such as R. A. Nicholson's edition and translation of the *Masnavi*, were not user-friendly; in fact, for non-specialists they were nearly unreadable.[1] Although some scholars such as A. J. Arberry produced versions that were somewhat more accessible, it was not until the 1990s that popular audiences began to respond to Rumi's verse, primarily through literary adaptations made by contemporary poets like Coleman Barks.[2] As publicized by TV journalist Bill Moyers, Rumi was recognized as the best-selling poet in America.

While it was doubtless a considerable accomplishment to bring the Persian poetry of the 13th-century Sufi to the attention of contemporary readers, criticisms have been made about the popularization of this dense mystical poetry in terms of New Age spirituality. Rumi has frequently been treated as a unique figure who was unassociated with any particular religious tradition; from some of these presentations, one would be surprised to learn that Rumi was actually a Muslim. A number of scholars have pointed out that these literary versions of Rumi's poetry employ a selective approach that leaves out much of the religious and philosophical context that makes it so rich.[3] Fortunately,

---

1. *The Mathnawí of Jalálu'ddín Rúmí*, edited from the oldest manuscripts available, with critical notes, translation and commentary by Reynold A. Nicholson (8 volumes, London: Luzac & Co., 1925–1940). Nicholson made it clear that his painfully literal translation was intended only for students of the Persian text.

2. *The Essential Rumi*, translated by Coleman Barks with John Moyne (San Francisco: Harper Collins, 1996). Arberry conceded that his own translations from Rumi were "as literal as possible, with a minimal concession to readability" (*Mystical Poems of Rumi*, trans. A. J. Arberry, ed. Ehsan Yarshater [Chicago: University of Chicato Press, 2008], p. 32).

3. Sample criticism of some Rumi translations may be seen at Ibrahim Gamard's website on Rumi's poetry <http://www.dar-al-masnavi.org/corrections_popular.html>. A sharp critique of Barks' versions is provided by Majid Naficy, "Coleman Barks and Rumi's Donkey," Iranian. com, December 2006 <http://www.iranian.com/NaficyMajid/2006/December/Barks/Images/Barks.pdf>. For a more balanced perspective, see Ryan Croken, "Found in Translation: How a Thirteenth-Century Islamic Poet Conquered America," in Religion Dispatches, January 28, 2009 <http://www.religiondispatches.org/books/979/found_in_translation%3A_how_a_thirteenth-century_islamic_poet_conquered_america>.

new translations of Rumi's works by accomplished scholars have begun to appear.[4] And in 2009, publication began of a new academic journal devoted to Rumi, the *Mawlana Rumi Review.*[5]

Nevertheless, it must be admitted that Rumi's poetry, particularly in the *Masnavi*, is not easy; for this reason, over the centuries it has been typically read through the medium of a commentary. As Franklin Lewis has pointed out, there is a long history of commentary on the *Masnavi* in multiple languages (Persian, Turkish, Arabic, and Urdu).[6] As is typical in commentary literature, it is designed to explain to the reader not only the grammatical and narrative structure of the text, but also literary references to the Islamic texts and mystical teachings of Sufism that Rumi had in mind. Readers who seek a deeper appreciation of Rumi's *Masnavi*, still have only one resource at this point: Nicholson's two volumes of commentary, a good deal of which is in Persian and Arabic and quite inaccessible to the general reader. No other English commentary on Rumi's *Masnavi* is available in print.

The present volume is a late Ottoman commentary on the Persian text of the *Masnavi*, translated into fluent English. The author, Kenan Rifai (1867-1950), was a major figure in late Ottoman Sufism who navigated the transition from the Ottoman caliphate through the Republican period into the era of Turkish secularism. He can be viewed as a traditionally educated but modernizing figure, who combined an expertise in Arabic and Persian texts with an interest in modern French literature. He supervised the transformation of his branch of the Rifai Sufi order into a spiritually oriented civil society movement that includes prominent women leaders.[7] His Turkish commentary on the *Masnavi* was published posthumously in 1973.[8] His other writings include essays on the *Masnavi* (*Mesnevi hatiralari*, 1952), lectures (*Sohbetler*, 1992), collected poems with accompanying musical score (*Ilâhiyât-i Kenan*, 1974), a biography of the twelfth-century Sufi master Sayyid Ahmad al-Rifa`i (1924), and several other volumes on Sufi thought and ethics.

Like a number of earlier commentators on the *Masnavi*, Kenan Rifai covers only the first volume of the text, which is certainly the most frequently read portion of this lengthy epic. He follows to a certain extent in the footsteps of the great Ottoman commentator, Ismail Ankaravi (d. 1631), whose work was considered by Nicholson to be the most useful of all the commentaries. It is interesting to observe that it was among the Ottomans that the commentary tradition on Rumi was most highly developed; it is for

---

4. Jalal al-Din Rumi, *The Masnavi*, translated by Jawid Mojaddedi, Oxford World's Classics Series (Oxford University Press, 2004-7), of which two volumes have appeared out of a projected six; Jalaloddin Rumi, *Spiritual Verses: The First Book of the Masnavi-ye Manavi*, trans. Alan Williams (London: Penguin, 2006).

5. For details on this periodical, see <http://socialsciences.exeter.ac.uk/iais/research/centres/cpis/rumireview/>.

6. Franklin Lewis, *Rumi, Past and Present, East and West: The Life, Teaching and Poetry of Jalal al-Din Rumi* (Oxford: OneWorld, 2000), pp. 475-81.

7. Information on the biography of Kenan Rifai is available on the website of one of his successors, Cemalnur Sargut <http://cemalnur.org/content/view/19/42/lang,en/>.

8. Kenan Rifai, *Şerhli Mesnevi-i Şerif* (Kizilay, Ankara: Hülbe, 1973; reprint ed., Istanbul: Kubbealtı Neşriyâtı, 2000), 750 pp.

that reason that Ankaravi's Turkish commentary has been translated into Persian.[9] Kenan Rifai's approach is not, however, dependent on Ankaravi's sometimes overzealous application of the metaphysical theories of Ibn `Arabi (d. 1240) to the understanding of Rumi. He clarifies the narrative line, comments on symbolic implications, and connects Rumi's verse to passages from the Qur'an, the hadith of the Prophet Muhammad, and the sayings and poems of Sufi masters in Arabic, Turkish, and Persian. It is this rich multilingual texture that gives Kenan Rifai's commentary its particular flavor. That is, his explanation conveys the multiple levels of reference and allusion that were typically brought to bear in the study circles where Rumi's verses were recited and discussed. Indeed, there is a certain informality in the style of this commentary that distinguishes it from the more scholastic of its predecessors. It is not so much a technical demonstration for scholars as it is a close transcription of how a learned Ottoman Sufi would have explained the significance of the *Masnavi* to an audience of students in oral conversation. Kenan Rifai had a particular interest in those passages of the Masnavi where Rumi is interacting on a personal level with his spiritual comrade, Shams-i Tabriz, and his leading disciple, Husam al-Din; these sections would have resonated vividly for his students.

Probably the most important contribution of this volume will be to offer a window on how Rumi's poetry was read in the land where he composed it. While we know that Rumi's poetic works were widely appreciated from the Balkans to Iran, Central Asia, Bengal, and southern India, it was in the Anatolian heartland of the Ottoman Empire that the Sufi tradition most associated with him took root (the Mevlevi order, the so-called "whirling dervishes"). In addition to the Mevlevis, members of other Ottoman Sufi orders such as the Malamatis and the Rifa`is held the *Masnavi* in special reverence. In view of the controversy over the "New Age" versions of Rumi, it is important to understand the role of this kind of mystical poetry in its own cultural and religious context. Rather than treating Rumi as an isolated figure who transcends all cultural and religious identities, this commentary situates him in terms of the main Sufi traditions, and it presents him as his principal heirs understood him.

This English translation of Kenan Rifai's commentary on the *Masnavi* has been prepared by Dr. Victoria Holbrook, a distinguished scholar specializing in Ottoman studies. As one of the most experienced and sophisticated English-speaking experts on Ottoman Sufi culture today, she is the ideal translator for this work; her grasp of the original Persian of Rumi's text is complemented by her thorough expertise in Arabic as well as the full range of Turkish from Ottoman times until today. Dr. Holbrook has translated not only the entire Ottoman Turkish text of the commentary, but also the original Persian of Rumi, resulting in an independent translation of the original text. It is necessary for her to translate the Persian base text separately from the Ottoman commentary, both in order to avoid the problem of double translation, and because existing English translations of the *Masnavi* (even when they are readable) would not be consistent with the vocabulary in a way that would match this particular commentary. The result is an exceptionally valuable scholarly contribution. The annotation is relatively light, chiefly clarifying the quotations from the Qur'an that may not be obvious to English-speaking readers. The translation is, moreover, extremely readable in a way that only a skilled and experienced translator can produce. In short, this volume is an exceptional contri-

---

9. Ismail Ankaravî, *Sharh-i kabir-i Anqaravi bar Masnavi-i Mawlavi*, Persian trans. Akbar Bihruz (Tabriz: Kitabfurushi-i Hikmat, 1970).

bution to the understanding of a key figure in Islamic mysticism, Jalal al-Din Rumi, as seen in the Ottoman Sufi legacy culminating in Kenan Rifai. Both the translator and the publisher are to be congratulated for making this important book available to the public. In addition, thanks are due to Cemalnur Sargut, President of the Istanbul branch of the Turkish Women's Cultural Association, whose tireless efforts to support this project were essential to its completion.

Carl W. Ernst
William R. Kenan, Jr., Distinguished Professor of Religious Studies
The University of North Carolina at Chapel Hill
October 3, 2011

Translator's Note

There is a vast Turkish literature, written over the course of five centuries, of commentaries on Mevlana Jalal al-Din Rumi's Spiritual Couplets. This early 20th-century commentary by Kenan Rifai on volume one of Mevlana's work is the first example of that literature to be translated into English. The Glossary at the end of this book explicates general items of Islamic and Turkish culture and literature found in the text, but there is a larger vocabulary of terms key to Sufi thought, Islamic philosophy, theology and intellectual history in general which is best understood in context and can be tracked by way of the index.

This translation comes at a time of renewal in translation of Arabic and Persian classics of Sufi thought, especially into English. Great care is being taken to consistently render the terminology which underpins that thought. In keeping with this effort, I have conformed to what I consider the most integral renderings in contemporary translation usage—and by "integral" I mean renderings which also take into account the connotations and resonance of terms; I have given the Turkish in brackets following such vocabulary on first occurrence or when a distinction is being made, so that those interested in the long view of the tradition may trace the development of key terms in a major example of later Turkish usage. There are also a few terms I did not translate, but defined at first appearance and in the Glossary. In most cases where a word has become fairly common in English usage, I gave the most commonly-used English spelling ("murshid" for *mürşit*).

Kenan Rifai's text was published posthumously and there is no author's preface. The source of the Turkish translation of Mevlana's Persian *Spiritual Couplets* provided in the book was not named by the editors. My translation of *Spiritual Couplets* is done from the original Persian. Several English translations of Mevlana's first volume exist, but I did not have one reprinted here because none of them consistently renders key vocabulary, and because the translation here must be in accord with Rifai's commentary. I used R. A. Nicholson's Persian edition, but dropped the very few verses which do not exist in the Turkish translation. I included the several verses present in the translation which are given in Nicholson's text only as variants in footnotes, and I translated from the Turkish a very few others for which I did not find a Persian source. Where Mevlana used Arabic, my translation is italicized. My numbering follows the Kubbealtı edition.

My translation of Mevlana's verses follows the original meter in syllable count; it is not possible to exactly duplicate *aruz* meters in English. I use mostly imperfect (either vowel or consonant) rhyme, as does my translation of verses by Turkish poets Rifai quoted. Where there is no such rhyme in my translation of Turkish verses, there is no rhyme in the original. In my opinion non-versified translation of such works lacks verisimilitude. However, if I have to choose between form and accuracy of meaning, which in my opinion also includes readability, I choose meaning.

A very few verses of Turkish translation of the *Spiritual Couplets* appear to have been missed in the Kubbealtı edition, though not in its numbering (525-527, 2926), and

Rifai provided commentary on these verses which does not make sense without them. I matched his commentary to the corresponding verses in Nicholson and inserted them into the text of my translation in brackets. I have taken the liberty of shifting verse 747 to its subsequent heading (as Nicholson did).

My translations of quotations from the Koran are based on a range of existing translations from the Arabic, but in particular that by Yusuf Ali, which I modified to maintain consistency with Rifai's commentary. Rifai referred to chapters of the Koran by their Arabic names in modified Turkish spelling, but in my translation I referred to them by chapter number, as transliterations and translations of Koranic chapter names vary widely and if English readers wish to look up quotations in a text of the Koran they will find it easier to locate them by chapter number. No citations for the hadiths and other Arabic sayings Rifai quoted exist in the Kubbealtı edition, and if I did not know the source, or the Turkish translation brought out an unusual emphasis relevant to his commentary, I translated from the Turkish. Rifai's commentary contains very free paraphrases of Mevlana's work and other texts, including Koran and hadith, given within quotation marks or presented in bold print, and I have translated these as is.

Some scholars may wonder why, when giving original terms in brackets, I used the Turkish spellings of Arabic and Persian loan-words in Turkish rather than following the widespread practice of using transliterations of Arabic and Persian spellings. Transliteration is often not useful here because even if a reader understands transliteration, is able to figure out from it what the Arabic spelling of a Turkish word is and look up the Arabic word in an Arabic dictionary, he may not find a definition helpful to understanding this text (and if the reader is unfamiliar with transliteration, he will often not be able to look up the word in dictionaries), because usage of loan-words evolves over time and is often different from that of the source languages. The Arabic word *wujūd*, for example, which is usually translated from classic Arabic texts into English as "being" or "existence," appears in Turkish as *vücût*, most often meaning "body," indeed identified with matter [*cisim*]. Like Persian *vujūd*, *vücût* can mean bodily or material existence, as well as a less precisely defined state of created existence. In Rifai's text *vücût* is contrasted with spirit [*rûh* or *cân*], soul [*nefis*], which arises from the joining of spirit with body, and with *varlık*, the Turkish term used to translate Arabic *wujūd* in the sense of "being" (as *yokluk* translates *'adam*, "non-being" or "non-existence"). So, the meanings of Turkish *vücût* may not coincide with those of Arabic *wujūd* (or at least not with the conventional translation of Arabic *wujūd*). Indeed, what emerges from the usages of Rifai's and most other Turkish texts is an identification of *vücût* with body in contradistinction to spirit, soul and being. For example (page numbers are to the Kubbealtı text):

The beautiful concubine's body [*vücût*] seeks worldly pleasures, while her spirit [*rûh*] longs to be free of worldly filth and return to its real homeland (p. 26).

It is enough that this love is not a bodily [*vücût*] lust or an illness of the soul, in short, a mistaken or perverted desire (p. 27).

In short, in the path of divine oneness you will so lose the flavors of your own body [*vücût*], your duality of spirit and body [*rûh ve vücût*], that you will not be able to see your body even in the clearest and most highly polished mirrors... (p. 87).

We have so melted away from our bodies [*vücût*] and souls [*nefis*] that our being [*varlık*] has become the colorless, immaterial light of the level of oneness (p. 7).

However, *vücût* can be taken to include both body and soul:

> If your body [*vücût*] prospers, your world is powerful; if it is ruined, your faith is powerful. Only here is the word 'body' [*vücût*] correct in both of its meanings. The second meaning of 'body' is 'soul' [*nefîs*]. The soul is the body [*vücût*] which is the source of the disease of duality. If your being [*varlık*] is divested of that body [*bu vücûttan harap olursa*], that is, of that soul, the dark powers in your body are defeated and you are prepared for the potential of the powers of light (p. 52).

In this more inclusive meaning of *vücût*, the bodily existence of human spirits in the created world is contrasted with their subsistence as immutable entities prior to God's creation of the world:

> God made these immutable entities fall in love with Him in pre-eternity before they'd yet had scent of body [*cisim*] and created existence [*vücût*] (p. 92).

Finally, there is the issue of the spiritual transformation of the body:

> The day that the human body [*vücût*] reaches the station of annihilation [*yok olma*] by the hand of love, the eternal body [*ebedî vücût*] takes the place of the mortal body [*fânî vücût*]. That is why love is the physician of all bodily [*cismânî*] and even spiritual [*rûhanî*] maladies, love purifies the heart and does away with the faults of the soul (p. 9).
>
> Just as water and clay were transformed into a bird of paradise when the breath of Jesus touched them with the breath of God's affection and love and knowledge of reality, the human body [*insan vücûdu*] made of clay and water escapes its materiality and takes wing to God" (p.120).
>
> But the bodies [*cisimler*] of God's arrived have become light, their bodies have with divine love and attraction transcended the requirements of their own materiality and have entered a state of pure spirituality although they appear to be material [*madde*] and bodies (p.464).

I did not distinguish in translation between Rifai's usages of "Allah" and "Tanrı," both of which I translated as "God," or between "Hakk" and "Cenâb-ı Hakk," both of which I translated as "God the Truth" or simply as "God" when much repetition made that cumbersome. In my judgment these variations in Rifai's usage are rhetorical and do not indicate distinctions in meaning.

The status of the Turkish text is a final issue I will mention. The author died in 1950 and his book was first published in 1973. According to my inquiries, no manuscript of the text is extant. The preface to the 1973 edition, by an anonymous editor, tells us that the book was "prepared" for publication by a group of Rifai's "choice students," and that "the participation of our valued litterateur and literary historian Nihad Sâmi Banarlı from the start in this effort, and his unstinting help with the language and vocabulary of the work, must be remembered here with our profound respect and gratitude." Banarlı was no longer living when I did my translation in 2007-2009, nor was any member of the group of students who could say what the preparation of the manuscript entailed.

Listen!
Commentary
on the Spiritual Couplets of
Mevlana Rumi

1. Listen to this reed flute as it tells its tales
   Complaining of separations as it wails:
   "Since they cut my stalk away from the reed bed
   My outcry has made men and women lament
   I seek a breast that is torn to shreds by loss
   So that I may explicate the pain of want
   Everyone who's far from his own origin
   Seeks to be united with it once again

5. I have cried out in the company of all
   I sought out the good and sought the bad in all
   Everyone supposed that he was my close friend
   No one tried to find my secrets hid within
   My inner life is not far off from my cry
   But the light to see is not in ear or eye
   Spirit's not hid from flesh nor flesh from spirit
   But none is granted leave to see the spirit."
   It's not wind, it's fire, this reed-stalk's wailing song
   Anyone who doesn't have it, won't live on

10. What has struck the reed-stalk is the fire of love
    What has struck the wine is deep passion of love
    Anyone who's lost a friend, the reed's with him
    Its wails tear apart the veils that keep us in
    Who has seen a poison or cure like the reed?
    Who has seen a lover or mate like the reed?
    It's the reed tells of the road that runs with blood
    It's the reed tells tales of madman Majnun's love
    Only to those without sense is such sense known
    Yet the ear has no customer but the tongue

15. In our grief our days have passed by suddenly
    Searing pangs have kept our life's days company
    But though days pass by, say, "Go!"—there's naught to fear
    You but stay, You who unlike all else are pure
    His water sates all but the fish of the sea
    Without daily bread the day goes by slowly
    The states of the cooked can't be grasped by the raw
    So the less talk the better, farewell for now!

Mevlana Jalal al-Din Rumi begins his *Spiritual Couplets* with the word "Listen!" This opening appears not to conform to traditions of Islamic civilization-era religious literature. Works of Islamic religion and Islamic literature begin with the name of God, as do the verse narratives *Garibnâme* [*Book of the Stranger*] by Aşık Paşa, *Feleknâme* [*Book of the Heavens*] by Gülşehri and the *Mevlid* [*Nativity*] by Süleyman Çelebi, some of the earliest important works of our religious literature in Anatolia. The first of these begins with the verse:

> Let us recite the name of God first of all

The same beginning is found in the *Felekname*:

> Let us begin speech with "In the name of God"
> Let us make entreaty with the name of God

And again as the first verse of Süleyman Çelebi's *Mevlid*:

> Let us mention the name of God first of all

It is worthy of note that the *Spiritual Couplets* does not begin in this way. Perhaps the poet was free-thinking, and took pleasure in having his "rising verse" be however it came to him. It may also be that Mevlana thought everything said with love of God has the sanctity of the *besmele* formula, "In the Name of God."

At the same time, *Spiritual Couplets* specialists have sought other reasons why Mevlana began with "Listen" [*bişnaw*] instead of with the *besmele*. They conclude that the word *bişnaw* may hold the place of the *besmele* because both begin with the letter B. For B is among the letters sacred to Islam. Hazret Ali indicated that by saying: "Whatever is in the Koran is in the Fâtiha [first chapter], and whatever is in the Fâtiha is in the *besmele*, and whatever is in the *besmele* is in the letter B." He continued: "Whatever is in the letter B is in the dot under the [Arabic] letter. I am the dot under the letter B." In this way he adorned the sanctity of the letter B with a deeper meaning.

In this view, Mevlana uttered the *besmele* with the first letter of *bişnaw*. And the act of beginning the *Spiritual Couplets* with the word *bişnaw*=listen has other meanings as well. Again according to *Spiritual Couplets* specialists, God indicated in His Koran that listening has greater virtue than seeing. He spoke specifically about the virtue of listening in the Koran. Also, it is considered evidence of the importance of the hearing faculty in humans that none of the messengers sent by God were deaf. By beginning his *Spiritual Couplets* with "listen," Mevlana communicated the sensitive nature of his wish to make his words heard.

Spiritual Couplets specialists have doubtless thought long and hard about the meaning and virtue of this uncommon beginning.

The second important word in this first verse is "reed." The reed pen is dipped in ink for writing and the reed flute is an esteemed musical instrument. But the reed is also a symbol of the spiritually arrived [*erenler*]. The arrived are people united with God. But they are also people who have experienced the countless suffering of exile in distance from God and countless torments of loss before arriving at their station. The arrived, also called "the friends" [*velîler*], communicate their torments of loss in burning tones like the reed flute in order to awaken people who are complacent. That is why the reed flute, with its burning cry heard throughout the *âyin* music accompanying the whirling ceremonies of the Mevlevi dervish order, has performed the sublime office of bringing countless hearts to feel divine love.

Furthermore, to be in the world, in the cage of the flesh [*ten*], is to be in a state which presents obstacles to union [*visâl*] with God. To be sure, for those who know the mystery [*sır*] of being one with God, and who have grasped the infinite sublimity of it, such obstacles are the cause of a profound sense of exile and longing.

Therefore:

With "Since they cut my stalk away from the reed bed / My outcry has made men and women lament," the reed is saying that it used to be in a reed bed. This refers to our being in the same realm with God, the state in which the Creator, who said, "I was a hidden treasure and I loved to be known," is one single substance [*mücevher*] in that hidden treasure, and we are the same substance [*cevher*] with Him.

The creatures came to manifestation because the Creator sought eyes to see and hearts to love His beauty [*güzellik*]. There was no "you" or "I" prior to the visible state of beings. There was only "He." Everything consisted in "He." The person who today cries out like a reed flute was with Him too. Every spirit [*rûh*] that comes into manifestation said "Yes" in reply to God's "Am I not your Lord?" in that realm. That reply was the first step in spirit's adventure of becoming visible in the form of fire, air, water earth, vegetation and animals, and becoming human. The spirits left that gathering of *Alast* [Am I not . . .] and flowed to this realm as women and men. They became eyes and hearts with the ability to see and love the beauty of God, but they also fell into the torment of the most dreadful of separations, that of separation from Him.

Now the reed says: "Hey, you who are left in this world like the reed, imprisoned in the body [*vücût*]! You who are deprived of that state of "being together" [*birlikte oluş*] in that reed bed of old! I seek a heart that can hear my words. A heart in a breast torn to pieces by the fire of separation, a heart to which I can tell all the longing I feel for that sublime God."[1] The reed has come from that presence of God to this mortal [*fânî*] world, and has in the human body [*beden*] tasted and brought others to taste the greatest of all longings.

To be sure, a person far from his origin and true [*hakîkî*] homeland in God's presence will feel pangs of homesickness for that truest [*en sahîh*] homeland of all; he will long for the time when he will be reunited with his homeland again one day.

The human [*insan*] comes into bodily existence [*vücût bulur*] at the point where the divine substance [*cevher*], having set out from God on the arc of descent and passed through the levels of fire, air, water, earth, vegetable and animal, takes its first step on the arc of ascent. The human is the manifestation [*görünüş*] of the divine substance at that point.

After reaching that point, a person is able to return to his origin, that is, to reach God, in two ways: If he passes away with death, having completed the flow of his lifetime, he will not gain much from this, will not have covered much ground. If he never knew what he was in this realm, his condition in the next world is one of ignorance also.

But if a person meets a Perfect Human [*üstün insan*] in this world, that is, if a murshid, a spiritual guide, awakens him and he comes to recognize his own substance, he will understand what the object of the profound longing he feels is. He finds God first in the external world and then in himself. The state in which God's being comes to be sensible within a person is called "self-disclosure" [*tecellî*]. A person who attains to self-disclosure has attained the secret [*sır*] of looking at creation with God's point of view and seeing God wherever he looks. This is the state of a person's being re-acquainted with his God. But it is still not a complete union. A person feels longing for his origin even when he reaches the station of perfection, but it is a sweeter kind of longing.

---

1. Rifai habitually used quotation marks for his very free paraphrase of the text.

That is why the reed, that is, the Perfect Human [*kâmil insan*], pir or murshid, tells the secret [*sır*] of the reed bed. He is among the people, feels profoundly intimate with both the good and the bad among them, and treats them kindly. Because a human, whatever his level, has achieved a degree in the path of reaching God. And that is why people, according to the degree of self-knowledge and insight they possess, seek out these Perfect Humans, befriend them and struggle to achieve their inner states.

I have told the secrets of reality [*hakîkatin sırları*] to people of all levels, but they have approached me only according to their own suppositions. They did not seek a way to know my inner secrets and attain the goal. But in order to be able to take the path of the arrived, one must abandon the path of supposition. In short, divine reality can not be known by way of supposition. Truths [*gerçekler*] are reached only by means of certain [*yakîn*] knowledge, that is, only after having left all doubt and hesitation behind.

This is the only way it is possible to see the light in the treasuries of the hearts of the arrived and reach the meaning hidden in their speech.

The reed says: I was once in a reed bed. My root and my heart were in water and earth. There I swayed with caprice, I conformed to every passing breeze. But the day came when they cut me away from the reed bed. They dried my body with the fire of love and put holes in me. They made wounds in my body. They put me in the hands of someone with sublime breath. His hot breath of love passed through me, clearing out of me everything that was not love. My lips were pressed to the lips of my beloved. Now I was wailing and crying out. The cries that came from within me and passed through me were telling all that was hidden within me, singing of the reality and felicity I'd attained.

In short, my secrets are words that acquire sound in my body. But the light to see these secrets of mine and the inner state to understand the truths [*hakîkatleri*] I speak has not become manifest in people whose eyes are fogged over and whose ears do not hear.

Humans have two states, spirit [*cân*] and flesh. Flesh is a person's visible side, his apparent state. This is the thing that is visible, that has solidity and density.

As for spirit, there are two kinds of spirit in humans. There is one we must call the animal spirit, which is found in other living things and is the power [*kudret*] that keeps a living thing going, that makes it alive. But there is another spirit, the divine substance [*cevher*] in humans, which can self-disclose only in humans. This spirit, unlike the other one, is not mortal. It is eternal [*ebedî*] spirit. It is a substance uniting light and power, and is not visible to every eye. One can also call it the self-disclosure of God's breath in the human. This is the spirit alluded to in the following verse attributed to Yunus Emre:

There is inside me an "I" within my "I"

We can call this divine spirit [*ilâhi rûh*] .

The spirit [*can*] in humans is being [*varlık*], as beautiful as it is transparent, and exists [*mevcut*] in almost every part and particle of the body [*beden*]. It is because of the beauty of the spirit in the flesh that divine spirit loves it so profoundly. Divine spirit sometimes manifests its divine beauty in body and flesh by means of that spirit [*can*].

That is why those possessed of gnosis [*irfan*] recognize people who display divine beauty outwardly in their bodies and behavior.

And that is why Hazret Mevlana says spirit is not hid from flesh nor flesh from spirit; but not everyone is permitted to see the spirit; and in order to reach this reality, that is, in

4

order to see the divine spirit in the flesh, one must like the reed abandon earth and water, and again like the reed, have a breast torn to shreds with the fire of love and separation.

The sound of the reed flute is celestial, like revelation [*vahiy*] and inspiration [*ilhâm*]. That is why it is hot and scorching like flame, like fire. The only recourse for someone who does not feel this fire, someone who touches this fire and is not burned, is non-existence [*yokluk*].

To be non-existent in this way is to become freed from the bonds of material existence [*maddî varlık*] and give the spirit in the flesh over to the hands of love. In short, to cease to exist in the desires and passions of the soul [*nefis*].

Only then will a person understand how and why the sound of the reed flute is scorching. The sound the reed flute makes is the sound of the voices and words of the arrived. A person must listen to these words with the ear of the heart [*gönül*] and grasp the best of prayers in their saying, "Be not" [*Yok ol*]. For ceasing to exist [*yok olmak*] in the soul ends with being [*var olmak*] in divine oneness [*ilâhi birlik*].

A Perfect Human is a person who sees divine wisdom and divine beauty wherever he looks and in whatever he sees. It is impossible to see such beauty and not be struck by the most searing states of love.

That is why the reed, which represents the arrived who are burned by the fire of love, is the instrument whose breast burns with such a love.

As for wine, it is the representation of divine love itself. The arrived are those who have been able to drink of this wine. There comes a day when they pour the wine of love within them into the cup of words and serve it to people who have the preparedness [*istidad*] to drink this wine, the people of love [*aşk ehli*]. Those who have the capacity for love and approach the arrived become drunk on the wine of speech and meaning served to them, and that is why they run to the wine-house, that is, the cloister [*dergâh*], of the friend who serves them that wine.

The reed is the intimate of a person whose created nature [*yaratılış*] is such that he can break away from all material [*maddî*] desires and consorts of the soul. The tones of the reed flute give voice to such persons. Its voice and notes of mystery tear the veils of multiplicity and obscurity which block us from seeing reality and leave us in darkness or a dazzling, raw brightness. It leaves us face to face with the true beloved. In sum, the reed flute is the breath of the Perfect Human, the friend, who will bring us to reach that mystery, that felicity.

The great veil spread between God and His bondsman is not that of the levels of earth [*yerler*] and the heavens [*gökler*]. It comes more from the soul's seeing itself as a being [*varlık*] separate from God. It is when a person attains the secret of dying prior to death, that is, when he matures enough to annihilate the bad and ugly states of his soul, that the veil of heedlessness [*gaflet*] of God is removed. Love of God is the force [*kuvvet*] that brings a person to attain such maturity and superiority. It is when the heart is filled with this greatest love, without shadow or self-interest, that the divine forces in a person overcome the forces of bodily existence [*vücût*] and matter. He loses that love of the world which is love of merely material pleasures and love of all beauty which is mortal and showy. Spirit begins to comprehend [*idrak*] the incomparable pleasure of nearness to God. It is at such a moment that the reed, like an elixir and salve, provides all of spirit's [*rûh*] spiritual needs [*mânevî ihtiyaçları*].

The reed speaks; the reed tells of all its longing for the great being [*büyük varlık*];

and as it speaks, spirit senses [*hisseder*] with profound happiness that its deep wound is being healed and its endless loneliness done away with by the presence of the greatest friend. The Perfect Humans who serve up the love of God like a remedy to spirits are His closest friends, His beloveds.

But the path taken by the arrived who attain the secret of "giving their heads" in the path of God's love, that is, who abandon their claims to their own selfhood [*benlik*] and strive with all their hearts, runs red from end to end with the blood of their wounds and severed heads. However, the pain of those wounds is sweet, and because the shedding of that blood gives eternal life, being able to go down that road is a joyful, pleasurable thing which makes them drunk.

Thus the reed sounds with the breath of Perfect Humans, telling tales of that road red with blood. Its burning notes tell the story of Majnun, the greatest lover of all, who was driven mad by the pain of love and roamed the desert begging God to increase his pain.

Intelligence [*akıl*] transfers itself only to those who are granted a share of it. You should give counsel [*akıl*] to those who have passed away from intellect [*akıl*], who have lost their minds [*akıl*] in the intoxication of love. It is they who have lost their minds who understand sense [*akıl*].

You should give of your love to those capable of love, your speech to those capable of listening, and your voice to those capable of hearing.

Some people perform only prescribed worship in order to reach Him. They are the zahids. Some sense Him by means of emotions in their hearts. They reach him by the path of love. They are the lovers, and have lost their minds because of love, or in other words, have surpassed intellect. This is the state of ascending beyond intellect. The light of truth arises in the consciousness [*şuûr*] of a lover, and mysteries become evident only to him.

So many days have passed in sorrow. We have lost so much time. But it is worth all the days spent in vain if we have had one moment of awakening and begun to grasp a share of "unveiling" [*perde açılma*].

O my heart, do not grieve for the days spent in vain, for we have attained the greatest degree of divine maturity [*ilâhi olgunluk*] we can attain, we dove into the sea of oneness [*birlik*], we were His companion in the sacred palace of oneness. His beauty self-disclosed before our gaze. We melted away from ourselves in a sea of black light and we reached union [*visâl*] with Him . . . We have so melted away from our bodies [*vücût*] and souls that our being [*varlık*] has become the colorless, immaterial light of the level of oneness. If we do not appear in even the shiniest mirror, it is because like Him, we have attained the secret of invisibility, and its humility.

Once we have arrived at this point, or are about to, why should we feel anxious about days in the past spent in grief and separation, for we no longer have either sorrow for the past or fear for the future.

Yes, let us not grieve over the spent days of our lives, since they will end in reaching Him, in union with Him. Since that is the case, let our days pass. O You who are purest, most beautiful, who never die! Stay! You who have no before or after. You will take us to the expanse of before and after, and give us the most desired beloved, Yourself.

And O, Perfect Human! You who know this mystery and this truth, show us the way! Open the light and the way of felicity to that purest, most beautiful one, make it clear to us!

Those on Your path are varied classes of people. There are many of the kind who are not satisfied by any mortal beauty as they seek union with You, many who, in sum, cannot do without You.

They are like fish in the expanses of love of God, and even the waters of love in which they swim can not sate them.

Their thirst will be slaked only with you, they will be sated only by the Kawsar of reaching you.

There is another class of people who know nothing of these things; no share of this destiny has been allotted to them. They are like starving people who cannot find anything to fill their bellies. The days and nights of their sorrowful lives seem very long to them. Even when they mistakenly suppose themselves to be enjoying a transitory pleasure, enthusiasm or joy, they are bound up in a dense and dark lack.

But you should only speak to people according to the degree and level of their understanding. Do not address everyone according to your own station! If they cannot understand what you understand, the fault is yours. Illuminate their way by descending to their level, and bring travelers on the path of heedlessness out to the open space of reality little by little. Set them alight with even the fire of love gradually. So that they, like a reed that is warmed and dried in the sun and one day attains the status of a flute which can bring forth sound, will burn silently and in time mature. O reed, it is you who will show them the way to becoming and finding. O Perfect Human, there is no other way you can get raw folk to taste becoming, to taste maturity.

This is the sum of it, and the reason why talk must be kept short. Farewell!

****

Be free, O my son, loosen and shed your chains
How long will silver and gold keep you in chains?
20.   If you try to pour an ocean in a jar
How much will it hold? A day's worth and no more
The jar of greedy men's eyes is never full
Till the oyster is content it has no pearl
Anyone whose robe has burst apart with love
Is purified of avarice and all fault
O sweet love, be joyful, passion fine of ours
O physician of all maladies of ours
Remedy for our false pride and our good name
O you who are our Plato and our Galen
25.   Earthy body soared to the skies out of love
The mount rose nimble and dancing out of love
Love was, O lover, the spirit of Sinai
Moses swooned when he beheld a drunk Sinai
Were I lip to lip with one who breathes with me
I would tell all that should be told, like the reed
Anyone parted from those who speak his tongue
Though he may know a hundred songs, has no tongue
When the garden fades and the rose is no more
You will hear the nightingale's story no more

30.   All is the beloved, the lover a screen
        The beloved lives, the lover's a dead thing
        When there is no appetite for love in him
        He is left there like a bird without a wing
        How should I sense what's before me or behind
        When my friend's light is not there fore or behind
        Love desires that this I say should be brought out
        What's a mirror if it won't bring secrets out?
        Do you know why your mirror's not indiscreet?
        There's so much rust that you cannot see its cheek

In a verse of the Koran it is said that satanic desires and passions of the soul are a lock fastened on the hearts of those enslaved to love of the world. So you must be freed of the greed that draws you to the world.

The heart will in time come to worship whatever it is fond of. When fondness for gold and silver comes to the point of worship, you cannot get free of it.

Don't spend your lifetime playing with gold and silver like a child playing with pebbles and mud. Ponder the real substance [*gerçek cevher*] beyond all mortal, deceptive values. Seek a guide who will take you to that! Feel love for that!

If you do not break the jar of existence [*varlık*] with the stone of non-existence [*yokluk*], the water-drop of the body [*vücût*] cannot join the sea of oneness [*birlik*] and you will not reach the goal. Let's say you have collected together everything there is in the world and emptied the ocean of foodstuffs into the jar of greed. How much will that jar hold? If you have spent your lifetime piling up gold, if your spirit has not been enriched by any spiritual [*mânevî*] wealth, what are you going to bring with you when you leave here?

Hazret Ali says: "An avaricious person is a pauper. A person contented with what he has is considered rich." Voracity has no end. The eyes of stingy, avaricious people are never sated. Most importantly, there is no room left in their hearts for sincerity and the jewel [*cevher*] of divine love. People who spend their lifetimes hoarding worldly goods, closing their eyes to the jewel of divine and spiritual beauty, end up disappointed. They leave the world with three longings: First, they are not satisfied with what they've had. Then, they haven't found what they'd hoped for. Finally, when they set foot on the road to eternity [*sonsuzluk*], they are deprived of every kind of sustenance for the heart, for gnosis [*irfan*], and for spirituality [*mâneviyat*].

Love of God is the only force that can burst through the shirt of selfhood, wickedness, and non-existence which clothes the human body [*insân vücûdu*]. Those whose soul-shirts are rent by divine love are purified of all faults of the body and of greed.

Those who are buried in the earth without having been purified of these faults are wrapped in veils of materiality, they become earth and remain enslaved and condemned to earth. The day that the human body [*vücût*] reaches the station of annihilation [*yok olma*] by the hand of love, eternal body [*ebedî vücût*] takes the place of mortal body [*fanî vücût*]. That is why "love" [*aşk*] is the physician of all bodily [*cismânî*] and even spiritual [*rûhanî*] maladies, love purifies the heart and does away with the faults of the soul [*nefsânî ayıpları*].

Love is the precious cure for all our faults and physical [*maddî*] and spiritual [*mâ-*

nevî] ills. It is a mistake to suppose that its force does away only with inner sorrows, with sufferings of the spirit and the heart. Love has the power to rid the body of physical suffering. That is why Hazret Mevlana addresses love as the remedy for all our maladies, calling out excitedly, "Be joyful!"

The two great Greek philosophers Plato and Galen were also physicians. They worked to find cures for both the physical and spiritual ills of humanity. Hazret Mevlana believed that both Plato and Galen had rendered great spiritual service to humanity. Especially Plato, who was the representative of ancient Greek pantheism [*panteizm*] .

He was the first great thinker to sense and express the love between humans and God. The Sufis [*sofiler*] called the love they believed in Platonic love because there is a similarity between the two types of divine love. Thus when Hazret Mevlana addressed love, "O you who are our Plato and our Galen," he was adorning the love he believed in by remembrance of these two names.

Moses was summoned by God to Mount Sinai and in his excitement there called out, "My Lord, give me vision that I may gaze upon Thee!" God said to Moses, "*Lan tarānī*," that is, "You cannot see Me!" [2]

What God said to Moses had the meaning: "You cannot see Me as long as you are you. It will only be possible for you to see Me when you have conquered your soul and annihilated your selfhood. And then it will still not be you who sees, it will be I. Because then you will be in Me [*bende*]."

So, the body [*vücût*] created of earth virtually sprouts wings and rises to the heavens when love touches it. Even a mountain can move when love touches such a mountain as Sinai. It virtually dances, moving with all its parts in profound ardor.

For when Moses insisted, God said to him, "Gaze upon the Mountain!" The instant Moses looked, his eyes were dazzled and his spirit burned. Moses swooned. Because the mountain could not bear the reflection of the great beauty [*büyük güzellik*] and broke into pieces in a state of cascading light and fire.

Here the ascension of a human to the heavens does not have the aspect [*çehre*] of metaphor [*mecaz*], but of reality [*hakikat*]. Love of God, in various ways and for various reasons, raised the Messengers Hazret Muhammed, Enoch, and Jesus to the heavens. The mountain danced because of divine self-disclosure. Messenger Moses fainted with that self-disclosure. With that same self-disclosure the mountain was swept away in an ecstasy [*vecd*] never seen before.

When God the Truth self-disclosed, Moses no longer remained, he had become annihilated [*fânî*] in God. Love was the great creator [*yaratıcı*] of all these miracles of spirit and life [*hayat*]. Love was the power taking Moses away from himself and bringing the mountain to dance.

If I had only friends for companions; if those keeping company with me were all friends who could understand me, if non-intimates were not included in our conversations, what secret mysteries I would tell you of the treasuries of the Unseen, mysteries which have never been put into words. I would say and I would tell. But if there is no confidante able to bear my secrets, it is right for me to remain silent. You should speak to people according to the degree of their understanding.

To speak of wisdom and gnosis [*marifet*] to those who don't understand states of consciousness and mysteries is in itself to do wrong to wisdom. Our Messenger says: "If

---

2. Koran 7:142.

you give wisdom to others than its people, you wrong it. If you forbid it to its people, you wrong them."

The mysteries of love are in reality God's trust. Perfect Humans, the friends, are the trusted of God the Truth. Since God commands that trusts be given to their owners, those who give wisdom and gnosis to the people of wisdom and gnosis do right, while those who give them to others have strayed from the right path.

They say an eye that cannot see cannot distinguish light, and a thirsty person knows the value of water. If a person cannot find an acquaintance, friend or intimate who knows his language, what can he say to others? Even if they be possessed of a hundred varieties of knowledge, thought, and gnosis, persons in such a position cannot impart them to ignorant people to whom such knowledge does not belong. That is the meaning of "Anyone parted from those who speak his tongue / Though he may know a hundred songs, has no tongue."

Those who bring the people of the heart to sing like nightingales are friends like roses. Any place that is far away from such friends is silent and empty of joy like gardens out of season. The sounds of the stories of rose and nightingale known to the people of the heart are not heard there. Perfect Humans who have reached God the Truth only speak of the stories of their own hearts in the presence of loved ones who are like roses.

In the this adventure of divine love people see only the lovers, not the beloveds. Those who view it from outside see, instead of the great Beloved, a virtual screen woven of those who love Him, and the true beloved remains hidden behind that screen.

But the ones whom they see as lovers are in a sense beloveds. Because it is He who has being [*var olan*], who is real [*hakîkat olan*] and who never passes away. The lovers in this divine love have in fact melted in His love and His eternalness, they have been annihilated, they have left behind their own souls, their I-ness and their dualistic states, they have arrived.

Just as it is for those who view the adventure from outside, from behind the screen of lovers, who cannot see anything, so it is for those who cannot see the great Beloved from behind the veils of their very own selfhood. Only on the day such people reach the point of being able to sense God within themselves, and succeed in seeing the beloved in their own hearts, will they have torn apart the veil of their own being [*varlık*] and be free of the veil of this mortal being [*vücût*].

How unfortunate are they who never hear of taking wing with love and remain tied to water and earth, in sum, to the world.

If a person condemned to soul and imprisoned in that cage has not been able to free himself from his own deceptive being, has not annihilated that mortal and false being [*varlık*], he cannot take wing to God's being and the eternal beauty of God.

However much God may be comprehended by "intellect" [*akıl*], still it is God's light that gives light to the intellect. Only by God's light can a person comprehend the value of the sublimity of the reward of union, and sense and find God.

The place we have come from is called "the origin" [*mebde*], and the place we turn back in order to reach is called "the point of return" [*meâd*]. A person knows this place we come from and go to in so far as his intellect has been illuminated with the light of God. What are "oneness," "multiplicity," and "annihilation in multiplicity"? These too can only be understood when a person is illuminated by that light.

Those who want to attain this mystery must drink the wine of annihilation and abandon their souls. Then will a person's selfhood be melted in the fire of love and self-disclosure. A person arrives at the point where he senses and sees God both within himself and in everything he looks at. He sees the beauty of oneness in the midst of the multiplicity which has surrounded him of old, and in the mirror of that multiplicity, and no longer sees anything else. In this respect the only thing confronting a person is that absolute beauty, and the only thing within him is "the greatest love" felt for beauty. So, what resolves mysteries is not intellect, it is love. And it is by means of love's guidance that divine speech becomes meaning in the mirror of spirit, that is, that realities [hakîkatler] are fully understood.

It is only in a mirror of spirit that has been cleaned of the dirt of the world, a mirror whose mysteries become illuminated as every kind of rust is erased, that the face of meaning and reality can be fully seen.

Whatever and however much has been shown to us of the "Unseen realm," where divine being [ilâhi vücût] and divine meaning are found, the sole instrument which can reflect it is a shiny mirror of spirit cleaned of all dirt and rust by the hand of love.

The purity of that mirror of spirit is made possible by the purification of the soul from spiritual pleasures and worldly rust. The soul's spiritual training and health depends on the love felt for people who have reflected God's beauty in themselves. With this condition that eye and heart see in those beauties not "the one seen," but the divine beauty self-disclosing in "the one seen," and know how to love it.

And so when you arrive at that state, that greatest Beloved will look into your light-filled heart and see His own beauty in the mirror of your heart. And that will be when you, whose heart is purified of worldly dirt, will be lover and beloved! You will then understand what it is to be human, and understand the human virtue of ascending to God.

****

THE STORY OF HOW A PADISHAH FELL IN LOVE WITH A GIRL AND BOUGHT HER

35.   Listen now, O friends, to this tale I'll relate
        Truly it is the coin of our inner state
        There was once a Shah who lived in times of old
        With dominion of religion and this world
        As it happened he was out riding one day
        With his close advisors in pursuit of game
        When upon the Shah's highway he saw a girl
        And the Shah's spirit was enslaved to the girl
        The bird of his spirit fluttered in the cage
        He spent of his wealth to buy the girl that day
40.   When he'd bought her and attained felicity
        That girl fell ill by decree of destiny
        A man had a donkey but no saddle pad
        By the time he found one, wolves had got his ass
        He had a pitcher but no water at hand
        He found water, but the pitcher now was smashed
        From left and right the Shah gathered physicians
        "The lives of us both," he said, "are in your hands
        My life's naught, my spirit's spirit is the girl

I am suffering and sick, she is my cure
45.   Whosoever finds my spirit's remedy
Will take my corals and pearls and treasury."
They all told him, "We will stake our very lives
We will pool our knowledge and work side by side
Each of us is messiah of his own realm
Each science has a salve that is in our palm."
In their conceit they did not say "If God wills,"
So God showed them how helpless the creature is
Hardness of heart made them drop the saving phrase
The words are mere accident to the real state
50.   How many have not pronounced the saving clause
While their spirits match the spirit of the clause
The more medicines and cures that they applied
The pain increased, these were not what was required
Illness made that girl as skinny as a hair
The Shah's eyes flowed like rivers of bloody tears
Destiny made oxymel bring forth her bile
Oil of almonds just made her condition dry
Citrus brought constipation, she'd no release
Like naphtha, water made fever's flame increase

Hazret Mevlana begins the first great tale of the *Spiritual Couplets* with: "Listen to this tale, friends! Because in truth it is the story of our inner state." This tale truly does relate the great and wisdom-filled adventure experienced by the human spirit after it leaves the land of God.

The separation of the spirit from God, its fall into this realm of multiplicity, its development in this realm by means of the soul's reformation, and return back to the divine being's [*ilâhi varlık*] realm of oneness are narrated in the events of the tale.

There was a padishah called spirit who was prior to the creation of the body [*vücût*]. This padishah was sultan of both the domain of religion and the domain of this world [*dünya*].

One day the padishah spirit mounted the steed of solicitude [*himmet*] and led the armies of knowledge [*ilim*] to rise through the stations of being [*varlık mertebeleri*] and hunt the prey of gnosis. Finally his path led him into the world and there he saw an intellect-dazzling beauty known as the concubine soul [*nefis câriyesi*].

She was such a beauty that she would not leave anyone's intellect intact. She made him forget his real aim [*asıl maksat*], and even made him think she was his real aim. So much so that even the greatest of padishahs, padishah spirit, was also duped by this illusion. He fell madly in love with the concubine soul. He fell into a state of slavery to her. In short, he became the slave of his own soul in a state of captivity to worldly desires and worldly ambitions.

When the Padishah saw the girl he lost his head. He spent great wealth to buy the beautiful girl. But the wealth he spent for her was actually the wealth of the heart, and he forgot that what that wealth is in reality [*hakîkatte*] for is not mortal beauty but beauty that is true and eternal.

And just so, as soon as he obtained his desire by buying the girl, she fell ill with a disease that had no cure.

Although this event demonstrated how faithless are the beauties and pleasures of this world, the Padishah didn't know that and stood by helplessly while his beloved concubine faded away day by day.

Just like the villager who had no saddle for his donkey, and when he left the donkey to go find a saddle, a wolf ate it.

Or the man who had a pitcher but no water, and he found water but then his pitcher broke.

That was the padishah spirit's situation. The moment he got possession of the beautiful girl, she began to fade away with a merciless illness. The Padishah had physicians brought from the four corners of the earth. He asked them to heal her. He said whoever healed her would also heal him, because he was also sick with her illness.

Thus the sanctified [*mukaddes*] spirit entering into the cage of flesh, amidst mortal, alluring worldly desires and deceptive worldly beauties, falls in love at the very first instant with the body [*vücût*] it has entered into. This love, meaning the excessive enslavement of the spirit upon entering the body, along the lines of the body's life and forms, the beauties of its color and flesh, and finally its desires and requirements, is the state of the spirit when, deluded by worldly pleasures and obedient to bodily commands, it strays from its own safe and sound path and, in short, falls sick.

This state makes the spirit suffer. That is why the padishah spirit sought relief of his own suffering in the illness of his concubine. The padishah spirit even sensed that as long as he was not liberated from the error into which he had fallen, he would not be able to find the true path and not be able to reach the spiritual degrees to which spirit should ascend.

That is why the padishah spirit told the physicians he brought from East and West to hurry and show their skills, and told them that the cure for the reality [*asıl*] in him, that is, the spirit, was in their hands, as well as the cure for the body [*vücût*] to which he now was enslaved and loved madly, that is, the soul.

Who were these physicians? What, whom, did they represent? We will understand that further on; but none of these physicians thought such an illness would be difficult to cure. Each of them thought he was the Aristotle of his time and supposed he would find the cure for this great spiritual illness.

Each of them thought he was a messiah, like Messenger Jesus who was called Messiah because he healed the sick by touching them with his hand, and even raised the dead in the same way. In their soul-pride [*nefis gururu*] they believed they could make the patient well. But their efforts were in vain because they did not give themselves over to the divine will, thinking they would succeed without it, or rather because they did not know of such a will. They could not cure the patient.

Their pride even made them forget to say, "If God permits, we will do this work." It did not even occur to them to say "If God wills." For a person is considered to have asked for God's permission when he says "If God wills" within himself, with the words of the heart, without saying it aloud in words. By the same token, someone who says it out loud without believing it inwardly cannot succeed. Because the phrase and the belief are for that great will which can never be deceived.

This truth is enunciated in the hadith of Hazret Muhammed, who said, "God looks not at your forms, nor at your deeds, but He looks at your hearts."

To say "If God wills," whether inwardly or outwardly, means in reality that the deeds of a person accept God, His oneness and greatness, in short, know God.

For a person to know God's power, His qualities, and govern his behavior accordingly is to work at one with the great Creator, and God's aid is according to such deeds and the degree of faith within such deeds.

This is expressed by the hadith of Hazret Muhammed: "That which God willed, happened, that which He did not will, did not happen." In short, it is as in the degree of "To be God with God" in the faith of the Sufis. In "If God wills" there is a degree we can call "to be if God wills," a reality [*hakîkat*] bringing a person to success as if he were collaborating with God.

It is that reality of which the physicians were unaware, and they remained distant from divine aid and their medicines were of no benefit.

As the concubine got thinner, becoming skinny as a strand of hair because there was no cure for her illness, the padishah spirit also suffered profoundly.

The reason is evident: Materialists suppose that the effect of every medicine on a living thing, even the effect of every substance on another, comes from its own nature [*tabiat*], its own composition. According to them oxymel, a syrup made of honey and vinegar, works to reduce bile, and its effect is due to the special effects of honey and vinegar, to the special qualities proper to them.

In the same way almond oil has a softening effect. Because almond oil has this capacity in its nature, its structure, its composition.

The materialists do not consider that all of these things, all of these substances and medicines, only have effect when there is collaboration with divine will. So much so that if divine will is not united with them, actions and effects contrary to their natures occur. For example, a mixture of honey and vinegar begins to increase bile, or almond oil produces hardness, firmness, instead of softness.

In short, the real [*hakîkî*] agent in every thing is God, not substances or things.

****

THE INABILITY OF THE PHYSICIANS TO CURE THE GIRL BECOMES EVIDENT TO THE PADISHAH AND HE TURNS TO THE COURT OF GOD AND DREAMS OF THE FRIEND

55.   When the Shah saw those physicians at a loss
       He left and went running barefoot to the mosque
       He came in and, facing toward the niche of prayer,
       In prostration drenched with tears the place of prayer
       When he awoke from self-annihilation
       His lips parted in praise and adoration:
       "O You whose least bounty is world dominion
       What shall I say when You know what's hid within?
       In our every need You are constant resort
       We have lost our way upon the road once more
60.   But You've said 'Although your secret's known to Me
       You should hasten to declare it outwardly.'"
       When he brought forth from his spirit such a cry
       The sea of mercy stirred and began to rise

As he wept he was overtaken by sleep
And an ancient sage came to him in his sleep
"Good news, O Shah," he said, "your suit is received
If a stranger comes tomorrow, he's from me
A physician keen of mind will come to you
Know him to be trustworthy, for he is true

65.   In his healing behold magic absolute
In his temperament, the power of God the Truth."
When the promised hour arrived and the day dawned
And the sun rose in the East burning the stars
The Shah waited in the belvedere to see
The one who'd been shown to him mysteriously
He saw a person of substance and virtue
A sun amidst shadow coming into view
Like a crescent moon approaching from afar
Non-existent, but in form imaginal

70.   Images seem non-existent in the soul
But a world all made of images behold
Their peace and their war are all imaginal
Their pride and their honor are imaginal
Those imaginal forms which ensnare the friends
Are reflecting the moon-faced in God's garden
The imaginal form the Shah saw in sleep
Was appearing now to him in the guest's cheek
He did not send out his men, he went himself
To meet his own guest from the Unseen himself

75.   Both of them could swim, they both were sailor men
Both were spirits sewn together without thread
"It was you I loved," he said, "it was not her
But in this world one thing becomes another
I am your Umar, my Mustafa is you
I have girded up my loins for to serve you."

The padishah spirit saw that the physicians he consulted were incapable and he ran barefoot to the mosque, that is, he freed his feet of "the clogs." This action, which the ancients called "doffing the two clogs" [hall-ı na'leyn], is when the spirit brings itself, while in a state of passing away [fânî] from the ties of this world and the next, or from the limitations of physicality and spirituality, to a degree of freedom from a kind of body-cage [vücût kafesi].

In such a spiritual state, the Padishah lowered his head in prostration and began to weep. He took refuge in the greatness of God. He spoke first with his tongue, and then when he could not find words for the cries within him, his heart. He made his supplication to God.

He said: "My God! I made a mistake in requesting aid from others helpless like myself. You who set our spirits off from Your own realm and, putting us through various tests, finally brought us to the degree of being human. You gave us the capacities to see

You, hear You, and have faith in You. Thus You saved us from our first error and our first choice of the wrong path. Now we are in error again. Again it is You who know how we may be freed.

"To be sure, you know what is within us. You have said in Your Koran (20:7) that You do. But it is also You who wanted us to declare it openly and tell You by means of our prayers."

And thus, just as wind is necessary to make waves in the sea, prayer from the spirit is enough to stir up the sea of God's mercy.

God speaks with persons either by means of inspiration, or by speaking from behind a screen, or by showing Himself in events. Or He kindly sends a messenger to his creature. And just so, He sent such a sage to padishah spirit when he dropped off to sleep and had a dream.

The sage said to the Padishah, "Tomorrow a person will come to you from far away. He is pure and holy, far from every kind of deception. If you wish eternal life, wrap yourself tightly in the skirt of that light of God!"

He continued: "How does God cure? Behold. For he sees with God, hears with God, he is strong with God and powerful with God. In his being and with his help you will see these powers of God the Truth's."

Finally the dawn arrived, and as the skies filled with the light of the sun the stars became invisible. The padishah spirit set to waiting for the sage promised to him in the dream.

The murshid he waited for appeared before him like a body [*vücût*] of light. His form was the form of a man and his body [*beden*] was as if of light. It is natural that it should be so. Because this personage has annihilated his own existence [*vücût*] in God's being [*varlık*], that is, he has reached the degree of annihilation in God.

In Sufism, reaching this degree is called "Fenâfillah." It is the degree where the creature annihilates his in fact mortal, even illusory existence [*vücût*], that is, his soul, rising above all the ambitions of the soul.

It is after a person has reached this degree that he arrives at a higher station called "Subsistence in God" [*bekābillah*]. At this station he senses the self-disclosure of God within himself. Before his gaze burns the light of God.

The murshid who arrived was like that: The various trials he had undergone to reach the station at which he arrived had made his body [*vücût*] slender as a crescent, but the light of the station at which he arrived had put that body in a luminous state like a crescent moon.

Here the image [*hayâl*] appearing to be barely there, slender as a crescent moon, is in once sense the image of Shams of Tabriz. Like a crescent moon which takes its light from the sun, Shams of Tabriz took his light from God and performed the function of a mediator between God's being [*varlık*] and Hazret Mevlana.

Moreover, there were those who heard from Mevlana himself that before meeting Shams of Tabriz he received a sign in a dream that he would meet him.

For the spirit annihilated in divine being there is neither image nor imagining [*tahayyül*]. For there the spirit encounters reality. The image realm [*hayâl âlemi*] is the realm where we are. This realm where we are is the self-disclosure of God's being in non-existence; from end to end, it is all imagery [*hayâl*] of the divine realm.

Between these two realms there is a third called the realm of likeness [*âlem-i misâl*].

The likeness realm, between the realm of spirits and the realm of bodies [*cisimler âlemi*], is a unique [*özge*] realm which has gathered within itself the formal beauties of bodies and the translucent beauties of spirits. Spirits come to this mortal realm of ours by passing through the likeness realm. The likeness realm, like the realm seen in dreams, is full of the most beautiful images of beings [*varlıklar*]. In that realm there are the images of things, but no bodies.

In the final analysis, both the likeness realm and our mortal realm, whether of translucent beauty or visible to our eyes in the state of bodies which have density, are nothing but imagery of the realm of reality [*gerçek âlemi*]. Try to see as a flow of imagery every realm which is not one of the realms existing [*mevcüt*] in God. Reality is at the other end of that flow.

A person will see reality to the degree he comprehends being annihilated in the divine realm and moves toward being annihilated in it; only those who in the midst of worldly cares arrive at the great thought [*büyük düşünce*] find reality.

We said that there is a realm of meaning and likeness stretching between the realm of spirits and the realm of bodies. This realm is in a sense the gardens of God, and moon-faced beauties stroll in those gardens. Those moon-faced ones are the prophets, who are illuminated with the light of God and who reflect real knowledge, realities, to us. In a sense, all the images in the realms of likeness and bodies are the names and attributes of God the Truth, and in the end, God the Truth Himself. That is why these images attract the arrived to themselves, and enslave the arrived to their beauty and sublimity. The arrived walk on to God, that is, to reality, in the pleasure and felicity of slavery to such beauty.

In short, the images which people see are the beautiful ones in the likeness realm and the beauties on the face of the earth. The images which the friends see are all "He" Himself: Beauty itself. And the padishah spirit sees in the face of the old man who comes to him as a guest all the lights and reflections of that image he saw in his dream who announced he would come to see him.

The Padishah goes out to meet his guest with infinite joy, and in one instant they reach an understanding like that of two spirits, rather than two bodies [*vücût*]; it is as if they have become one spirit. It is understood that this encounter expresses the profound unity of spirit enjoyed by Hazret Mevlana and Shams of Tabriz.

Thus a sea of spirituality in Rum, that is, Anatolia, melds with a second sea coming to Anatolia from Fars and they are transformed into one boundless ocean. They become each other's light.

Here padishah spirit represents Mevlana, who has an infinite capacity to be drawn toward divine light; in Shams of Tabriz shines that light itself.

That shining will perform the function of a bridge to the light and take Mevlana to his Lord [*Mevlâsı*]. The great reality is beyond that bridge.

But just as the faith of Islam was strengthened, even honored by Umar's embrace of it, Shams of Tabriz's sun of arrival was strengthened by Mevlana Jelaleddin. People couldn't know that Shams of Tabriz was a great murshid of his time. Shams was illuminated only, or most of all, by the light of Mevlana's love, and he became legendary with Mevlana's poetry. For Mevlana composed many of the lyrics and quatrains in his Divan-ı Kebir out of love for his great murshid. He did this because he grasped in the most profound way the states of love and respect between disciple and teacher; to put it most briefly, this came through his "observation of right conduct" [*edebe riâyeti*]

****

BESEECHING THE LORD, WHO IS GUARDIAN OF SUCCESS, FOR SUCCESS IN OBSERVATION OF RIGHT CONDUCT IN EVERY CIRCUMSTANCE, AND EXPLICATING THE GRAVE CONSEQUENCES OF A LACK OF RIGHT CONDUCT

> In right conduct let us seek success from God
> Those without it are deprived of grace of God
> With bad conduct it's not just oneself one harms
> No, one sets a torch to all the horizons

80.
> When tables of food descended from the sky
> Without effort or the need to sell or buy[3]
> Individuals from the tribe of Moses
> Rudely asked, "Where are the garlic and lentils?"[4]
> The heavenly bread and dishes were cut off

There was toiling to sow with scythe and mattock

> Then when Jesus interceded, God the Truth
> Sent a table laden with various foods[5]
> The insolent men were ill-mannered and rude
> Like beggars they came and carried off the food

85.
> Jesus entreated those persons, saying "This
> "Is constant on earth and will never grow less."
> To harbor bad faith and rush forward in greed
> Is infidelity at dominion's feast
> Because they were dog-faced and blinded by greed
> The gate of compassion rose beyond their reach
> If the alms tax is withheld no rain clouds come
> Fornication sends a plague on everyone
> Whatever befalls you of sorrow and gloom
> Comes of not fearing God and of being rude

90.
> Whoever does not fear God on the friend's path
> Preys upon men and he himself is no man
> What filled up these skies with light is right conduct
> What made angels blameless and pure, right conduct
> The sun is eclipsed because of insolence
> Azazil[6] was barred because of insolence

Ismail Ankaravi explicates the subject of right conduct [*edep*] and its observation thus: In right conduct all beautiful character traits become embodied, they come into play. Learning the shariat, completing one's acquisition of knowledge and the path—all are made possible by right conduct.[7]

---

3. Koran 2:57, 7:160.
4. Koran 2:61
5. Koran 5:115-118.
6. Azazil was the name of Satan before God barred him from Heaven.
7. *Mesnevî-i Şerîf Şerhi*, vol I, p. 64.

On this subject Hazret Muhammed said: "My Lord trained me in right conduct and made my conduct beautiful." And on the same subject, Abu Hafs said: "Sufism is from end to end right conduct. At every time, in every circumstance, in every place, right conduct."

Here is recalled the Koranic verse, *Wa'ttaqū fitnatan* . . . : "And fear the mischief which strikes not only those among you who do wrong" (8:25).

This means that even if those who are distant from right conduct and fairness intend to punish only oppressors, they hurt not only them. The oppressed are also hurt by the ignorant, irregular behavior of such people.

You know the story of the *mâide* that descended from heaven. The term means a table laden with varieties of food. Such tables came down from the sky to the tribe of Hazret Moses, as a miracle of his, without their having to work for them. But it was only one kind of food. The tribe reproached Moses on that account, asking for a variety of foods. Some of them asked, "So where are the garlic and lentils?" Then the food stopped descending from the sky and people had to toil with the sweat of their brows if they were not to starve.

Many years later, with the intercession of Hazret Jesus, tables laden with varieties of food came down to the same tribe. But those lacking in right conduct this time carried off the food and hoarded it.

Hazret Jesus said to them, "This bounty is perpetual. Do not fall into doubt regarding God's bounty or doubt that He will send it." But he could not make the greedy listen, and of course the laden tables from heaven were cut off.

The incident occurred in the following way: Jesus had twelve companions called Apostles who attained the distinction of fellowship with him. They were fortunate enough to seek instruction from him and they learned religion from him. They asked Jesus, "Does your Lord have the power to send down laden tables?" Jesus found this question a violation of right conduct. He did not find it beautiful to have either his Lord or his own messenger-hood tested. He told them that if they believed in God and in him, they should not ask such things of God the Truth. But the Apostles insisted on witnessing divine power. For they had not yet reached the level of being able to believe without seeing with their own eyes. Having no other choice, Jesus begged God and one Sunday the laden table came down. The Christians recognized Sunday, the day divine power self-disclosed, as their religious holiday.

But soon Jesus's community, fearing that God would one day hold back this bounty descending from heaven, began to hoard it. Their great fault was to doubt God, and it came from their lack of right conduct. Those of Jesus's tribe who doubted and strayed by this deed were immediately punished. They were put into the forms of monkeys and pigs, and died after living in those forms for three days.

In short, whatever catastrophe befalls humans, whether it descends from heaven or rises up from earth, it comes from not knowing one's limits and being so far from human humility as to try to violate God's frontier [*Allah'ın hududu*].

If a society has little faith and its spirituality has been exhausted, if people no longer love one another or help one another, it is natural that catastrophes should occur. For there is a profound connection between the spiritual realms [*mâneviyat âlemleri*] and this realm of bodies which appears to us in material form [*madde şeklinde*]. Moreover, several screens can intervene between the realm of bodies and the spiritual realms and leave our world in darkness, as if the light of the sun were cut off. Heaven's mercy may not be seen. Greed, self-interest, lust and fornication become more and more common on the earth. Moral distortions spread across the world, envy, lust, disaster. However many people may be killed by plague in a city, these ferocious perversions destroy the love of God in the habitations of the heart, they destroy gratitude and contentment, in sum, all the virtues which make a person human.

When people fall from joy into torment, from wealth into poverty, and from health into sickness, it is punishment for their own sins and wrongs. That is the meaning of God's words: "Whatever of evil befalls you is from your own soul" (4:79).

A person who goes astray leads others away from right conduct as well. The nine heavens have since their creation revolved according to the manner and path their nature [*yaratılış*] commands them, without straying one iota from their axis. It is for that reason that God decorated the heavens with moons and stars and illuminated them with the sun.

Likewise does the heaven of the spirit, the heart of a person who walks the path of right conduct, that is, who is filled with love of God, fill with stars of gnosis. Such a person is witness to God's light in the heavens of his heart.

****

THE MEETING OF THE SHAH WITH THE DIVINE PHYSICIAN WHOSE COMING HAD BEEN ANNOUNCED TO HIM IN A DREAM

> The Shah embraced his guest with wide open arms
> Receiving him like love in spirit and heart
> He began kissing him on his hand and brow
> And inquired of his journey and his home now
> 95.   Asking questions thus he led him to the dais
> And said, "In patience I've found treasure at last
> O gift of God the Truth and defense from grief
> Meaning of 'Patience is the key to relief'
> In your face every question is answered
> You solve difficulties without need for words
> You translate all that we have within our hearts
> You extend a hand to those stuck in the marsh
> Welcome, chosen, elected one, without you
> *All that's vast will shrink, divine decree ensue*
> 100.   *You are lord of the tribe, whoever does not*
> *Wish for you is lost, and if he desist not . . . "*
> When that meeting and feast of kindness were done
> He took his hand and brought him to the harem

The padishah spirit embraced the awaited physician with profound longing. He wished to take him within himself and keep him in his heart like a beloved secret.

He took him by the hand. Touching his hand in order to kiss it meant that he wanted his help and wished to be initiated by him. The padishah spirit had now conformed to the pir and chosen his path. As one does when two people meet and ask after each other's health, he asked such questions as where he has come from and where he lives.

20

What these questions really mean is: "What have you done, since the spirits replied 'Yes,' in order to return to divine oneness? What stations have you passed through? What station have you now reached in the divine ascension [*ilâhî yükseliş*]?"

As the Padishah removed worldly filth from his heart, it filled with love of God, a love represented here by the divine physician. This love in the human heart is a great treasure with which no other value can be compared. The padishah spirit understood that he had attained this divine treasure thanks to "patience" [*sabır*]. Now he is finally happy. His heart has filled with the light which comes of taking the right path and finding the truth.

The padishah spirit spoke to the divine physician out of this love and happiness, saying:

> You are the light of God filling me. Now I know that all difficulties will be overcome with patience; freedom from duality will also be possible with patience. You taught me this! Because you are also patience itself, which increases a person's strength!
>
> That is why to see you is to be freed of all difficulties. We can reach the great reality only with you. Without my asking and without your answering, we illuminate mysteries without words.
>
> O Pir! You are the truth filling the heart. Your light saves a person who has lost his way in darkness. We cannot be without you, or we will be in loss. If you leave us, leave our people, it will bring disaster upon us; vast wildernesses will become narrow.
>
> You are lord of every tribe. You, your light, will save us from the abyss into which we have fallen and bring us back up to the heavens, in short, show us the way back from where we have come to.

Thus between the padishah spirit and the divine physician there was a silent, wordless meeting. The polite questioning ended with a complete understanding and a complete knowledge, each of the other. Then the Padishah took the physician who would cure his great pain and brought him to the harem, the place where his beloved concubine was, that is, inside his spirit, into the depths.

****

THE PADISHAH BRINGS THE PHYSICIAN TO THE PATIENT'S BEDSIDE SO THAT HE MAY SEE HER CONDITION

> He spoke of the sickness and of the sick girl
> Then he sat him down in front of the sick girl
> He observed her urine, pulse and complexion
> He listened to her causes and her symptoms
> "All the remedies they have applied," he said
> "Have brought on ruination, not improvement
> 105. They had no knowledge about the inner state
> *I seek God's refuge from what they fabricate*."
> He saw sickness and discovered what was hid
> But he did not tell the Shah and kept it hid
> Black or yellow bile was not cause of her pain
> From its smoke the scent of every wood is plain

21

From her weakness he saw she was weak in heart
The flesh was well, but she was enslaved at heart
Love is known by a malady of the heart
There's no illness like the illness of the heart
110.   The lover's is unlike other maladies
Love is the astrolabe of God's mysteries
Love can rise from this world or from the other
But at last it is our guide to the other
Whatever exposition I make of love
I'm ashamed of it all when I come to love
Though the tongue's commentary is luminous
Yet love without tongue is still more luminous
Though the pen speeds on while writing about love
The pen splits upon itself coming to love
115.   Intellect sinks like an ass into the mud
Only love explains the lover and his love
The proof of the sun is in the sun itself
If you need proof, don't turn from the sun itself
Although shadow is a sign that he is there
Shams[8] gives off spiritual light everywhere
With shadow, like talk by moonlight, sleep will come
But *the moon is clove asunder*[9] when Shams comes
Like the sun there's nothing in the world so strange
The spirit's sun subsists with no yesterday
120.   Although the sun out there may be singular
One may fashion of its likeness a picture
The sun of the spirit, beyond the ether
Has nor in the mind nor outside it a peer
Where in fancy is there room for his essence,
That there should come into fancy his likeness?
When news of the face of Shamseddin arrived
The fourth heaven's sun withdrew its head inside
Now his name's come up it's obligatory
To expound upon his gifts allusively
125.   At this moment spirit's tugging at my skirt
He has caught the sweet perfume of Joseph's shirt
"By right of the long years we've been together
Tell again of those states you had together
So heaven and earth may laugh and multiply
Hundredfold in intellect, spirit and eye"
"Do not burden me, my self has passed away
My understanding is dull, I cannot praise
Anything one may say while not wide awake
Is not worthy, be it forced or vain mistake

---

8. The name Shams means "sun." In Mevlana's usage here, the word may be read as both.
9. The Prophet Muhammed's miracle of splitting the moon (Koran 54:1).

130.   What shall I say, not one vein of mine has sense
         To interpret that friend for whom there's no friend
         To interpret this liver's blood, this exile
         Ask another time, let it go for a while."
         "*Feed me now,*" he replied then, "*for I am starved*
         Hurry up, for surely time's a keen-edged sword
         The Sufi is the son of time, O comrade
         To say tomorrow is not rule of the path
         You, are not you yourself a true Sufi man?
         By delaying payment you'll lose what you have."
135.   I told him, "The friend's secret is better clothed
         Hearken to it within a story enclosed
         It is preferred that the secrets of lovers
         Be related through the stories of others."
         He said, "Tell it unveiled, naked, without fraud
         Leave out superfluities, don't put me off
         Lift the veil up and recount it nakedly
         I don't wear a shirt when my love lies with me."
         I said, "If he were naked before you plain
         Nor you nor your sides nor middle would remain
140.   Make your request, but consider what you ask
         You can't pierce a mountain with a blade of grass
         If the sun which illuminates all the world
         Were to come a little closer, all would burn
         Don't go seeking mischief, bloodshed and turmoil
         Don't ask about Shams of Tabriz anymore"
         This has no end, begin from the start again
         Go back and relate the story to the end

He showed the divine physician his patient. He asked him to cure his patient's illness, making entreaty as Hazret Ali did when he said, "I've not been able to find anyone among Your creatures to cure my pain, I've come to you, my God."

The physician examined the patient. At the same time he tried to find in the Padishah's face the traces of the illness, and understand the reasons for it from what he said.

He realized where the physicians who came earlier to treat the concubine had gone wrong. They were swept up in their pride and, supposing they understood the illness and could treat it, lied to themselves and fell into error. The divine physician sensed the malady in the beautiful concubine's inner world, and he realized what her secret was, but he did not tell. In this way he showed how keen and perceptive a doctor he was. For he sensed what he did by means of intuition. He paid attention to the outward signs of the illness and arrived at the truth that this malady was not any bodily illness but an illness of the heart.

The beautiful concubine's body [*vücût*] seeks worldly pleasures, while her spirit longs to be free of worldly filth and return to its real homeland. The profound, searing pain the concubine feels is the pain of such homesickness; it is an attraction to the great whole of which she is a part, it is love.

It is not possible to cure such a malady with medicines used for bodily illnesses. The cure for that malady is simply the beloved, the beloved's beautiful and faithful countenance.

Love is like the instrument called the astrolabe, which was used in ancient astronomy to study the realm of the stars. Just as the mysteries of the stars, their positions and movements, are understood by means of the astrolabe, the spiritual stars—the true beauties, divine beauty, God's acts [*işlemleri*] and attributes—are only seen and understood through love. Just as a better and superior instrument in needed in order to know and understand the stars, one needs a deeper, truer love in order to know divine mysteries and see the light of truth. Thus love's cure is love itself, the emotion which draws lovers a bit closer to the beloved each moment, which makes them seek and long for the beloved more with every passing moment, the state of love and its torment of longing that increases with time.

Love, of every form and kind, is the path that brings us to the beloved. The intended meaning here is that whether love is of the common, metaphorical type between two people, or at the level of true love between God and man, the result is the same.

When a person falls in love with the divine beauty shining in another person, the beauty he loves, whether he knows it or not, is still God's beauty, its reflection in beings and people.

Since metaphor is a bridge to truth, the human love called metaphorical may one day bring a person to love of God. It is enough that this love is not a bodily lust or an illness of the soul, in short, a mistaken or perverted desire.

Not every person has the capacity to feel, let alone understand, divine love. For that reason, love between persons is a preparation for feeling and living in real love. Many people's spirits grow accustomed to the great and true love in this way, they begin in this way. Gnosis [*irfan*] is the great step on the path of knowledge of God, the path of knowledge of truth, and when it begins to bring a person to sense realities, the individual begins to feel that great love to the extent of annihilating his own duality with true love. So the cure for love is love, true love is experienced as a remedy which cures the torments of metaphorical love.

Silence is also appropriate when it comes to the subject of love. Because no matter how much is said, no matter how much one wants to explain, it is not possible to fit love into a descriptive statement. To be sure, intellect finds ways to express many mysteries and meanings in description of love. But if a person who tries to explain love by means of intellect reaches the point of plunging into the sea of love one day, he looses consciousness in the pleasure and joy of love. He understands that none of the things he's said before in explanation of love could describe it. Then he is ashamed of the incapacity and insufficiency of what he has said and prefers to remain silent.

To be sure, language is a magical instrument when it comes to overcoming difficulties and illuminating mysteries. But the greatest of loves is the love which can't be spoken, and when a person cannot speak, the love he feels is better understood from his state. In short, the language of a person's state speaks more openly, more clearly in the expression of great love than the language of words.

Even the pen treads more easily when writing about other subjects. When it comes turn to write about love, it stops walking.

The hand presses down so hard on the reed pen while writing about love that the delicate slit cut in the tongue of the pen to ensure the steady flow of ink tears and the pen splits down the center.

The human intellect is like that too. It understands and describes all beings, but when it comes to love, it's as if tongue-tied.

That is why the Angel Gabriel, who accompanied Hazret Muhammed as far as the Sidre tree during the Miraj, said when they passed the frontier of intellect and came to the frontier of love: "O Messenger of God! I cannot go on, if I take one step further I will catch fire and burn up!"

The intellect is incapable of explicating love. Love is an event of the heart and the conscience [*vicdan*]. It is love to the extent that it is purified of actions and factors trying to explain it. Love is known by feeling, not by explaining, by being dyed the fiery color of love, in short, by burning.

We know the sun exists because we see its light. You will think that love is like the sun, but the lights of love appear in the arrived, in the countenance and behavior of Perfect Humans [*kâmil insan*]. It is the arrived, whose faces are the mirrors of their hearts, who reflect divine light in that mirror. If you want to see with your eyes what divine love is, look into the faces of the arrived. It is because of the light of love in their hearts that day by day the arrived grow old as people whose faces are filled with light.

There is an allegory [*temsîlî hikâye*] told on this topic. Every term in the story is a symbol [*remiz*]. An old man named "Intellect" enrolls a child named "Pauper" in a school called "Love." The child is unable to learn even one letter of the alphabet there. But one day when he senses that he must go to the school as "heart," not as "thought," he throws his book-bag aside and finds the path of love.

While shadow is evidence of the existence of the sun, it is not the sun itself. Both the intellect and the things to which intellect pays attention and has recourse are in this regard just like shadows.

The sun is like God the Truth Himself. Therefore the shadow called intellect is merely evidence of the existence and light of the love of the divine sun. What gives intellect understanding and knowledge is the light of spirit. When intellect is illuminated by that light, it tries to comprehend love and the beloved. In short, if the eye of intellect were not illuminated by the light of gnosis, neither could it know love, nor would its strength suffice to comprehend the great beloved.

Just as the light of the moon is invisible once the sun has risen, or no longer has sufficient brightness to illuminate, if the light of truth rises and the heart is illuminated by love of God, the moon called intellect becomes invisible. The eye can no longer see the things it has tried to comprehend by means of intellect up to that point. Even if it does see them, these things now make a person lethargic, like bed-time stories heard before sleep, and they fade away and are erased as he heavy eyelids close.

A stranger [*garip*] is in reality someone who has broken off from God's being and landed far away. Like people separated from their homelands, who wander miserably in foreign lands, spirits have landed far away from the one true homeland, the land of God, and they sense their alienation, whether slightly or keenly.

The sun is such a stranger too. It wanders in the unlimited vastness of space. The only sun that subsists [*bâkî*] without setting is the sun of spirit. The sun of spirit is the attributes of God the Truth; it is His self-disclosure; it is "the arrived human" in whom God the Truth has disclosed Himself.

However unique the sun may be in its appearance, painters have succeeded in making pictures of it. But the sun of spirit cannot be pictured. Although it was born in the created universe, it is not possible to see it or draw it, perhaps because its light is so dazzling. The sun of spirit is God, His self-disclosure, it is the mystery or reality called "the reality of Muhammed."

It is that flame of spirit which Şeyh Galip described in his verse:

The candle of spirit has such a flame
It cannot fit inside heaven's lampshade

Hazret Ali said: "Every thing the intellect knows and pictures is a creature created by God." In that case, to see God Himself and His love with the eyes is beyond the dimensions of intellect's knowledge and comprehension.

How beautiful it is to think of the connection between shams [the sun] and Shamseddin! For Shams of Tabriz is the sun of spirit. The light in his face is divine light itself. And so for the sun to withdraw behind a cloud, at this moment, has great meaning: Confronted by divine light, the sun goes out of sight like an arrived person joining the sea of oneness, as if understanding the non-existence of his own material being [*vücût*]: The sun sees the light in Shams of Tabriz's face.

Since we have mentioned Shams, let's reveal a secret here: When the messenger Jacob, who had been blind for years, rubbed the shirt with Joseph's scent on it over his eyes, his eyes opened and he began to see again. And we here mention Shams of Tabriz, who like a shirt of light brought us the scent of truth. While we were mentioning him, the same shirt touched the eyes of Çelebi Husameddin. Just as Joseph's shirt was a sign of the reality of Joseph, Shams's shirt announced divine reality. That is why "spirit," in other words, Husameddin, is tugging at my skirt, making a request.

"Tell us about Shams," he is saying, "tell us about one of your conversations with Shams! Tell us, so that the earths of our souls and the heavens of our hearts may be filled with his light!"

But I am in no state to talk about this. Because I am in a state of the joy of non-existence (*yokluk, fenâ*), and I am bewildered in that state. To taste non-existence is the state of tasting the pleasure and joy of being naught in the sea of God the Truth's oneness, along with all beings [*varlıklar*].

Once a spirit reaches that state, it no longer has anything to say, nor anyone to praise, nor the strength to speak or praise. That state is like the state of one who has not spoken openly since the creation. It is a state of vast silence in which everything is said without tongue, without words, silently; what can the tongue say in such a state of senselessness, especially about that matchless beloved?

Even though we said we should leave the matter of lifting the veil from Shams of Tabriz's light-filled face, that is, talking about his companionship and love, to another, soberer time, Husameddin was already aflame with the attraction of his light and love. With the determination of a gnostic who knows the value of time, he said:

I am hungry! I am in need of the food of meaning and truth! You must serve me from the table of gnosis and the wine of divine love! Because a lifetime does not bear promises for future payment.

Hazret Muhammed has said: 'Prepare yourself for this world as if you were never going to die, and for the hereafter as if you were going to die immediately.' This is the truth upon which all the greats of the faith are unanimous! If you are able to do a thing today, do not leave it for tomorrow! Tomorrow could come, and you not be in the world.

A true Sufi is a child of time. He puts past and future aside and knows the value of the time he is in; he believes in the virtue of making the most of every moment he lives. Until he becomes an arrived gnostic [*ârif-i vâsıl*]![10] Once a spirit has become an arrived gnostic, that is, once he is not dominated by time but dominates it himself, time no longer has any importance for him.

"Mevlana! You are among the arrived who dominate time. But I am only a master of time's son-of-time, your son of time. Don't put me off till a future time. Fill me with meaning and gnosis within the time I am in."

I said: "I am telling you the story of the arrived. I am showing the most beautiful beloved to you within veils. The veils do not show the beloved to those who are deprived of the grace of seeing him. They will think these stories are only things that happened to so-and-so. But the gnostic understands the meaning of the stories hidden under the veils. I am telling you that meaning within the stories of the arrived or of others."

Husameddin, whom I love like my life, still insisted: "Lift the veil when you tell me, one cannot be united with a beloved wearing a shirt. Show me the mysteries unveiled!"

I said: "One cannot attain the great mystery all at once. You will rise to it degree by degree. Wait for the time when instead of being crushed by those mysteries, you will be able to bear them without even realizing it!

"The sun of truth is like the sun that illuminates the world. It burns those who come close to it. Each spirit can approach it according to the measure of its preparedness [*istidad*] and potential for it. It is not possible for the spirit to reach the great light without passing through the necessary stages.

"Remember that when Gabriel reached the Sidre tree on the night of the Miraj, he said, 'If I take one step further I will burn up!' Dear Husameddin, don't rush!

"Dear Husameddin! When the mountain was suddenly struck by the self-disclosure of God the Truth's light, it broke into pieces. Moses fell in a swoon. It's a pity when those who haven't the patience to approach the truth of His light gradually try to skip stages and burn because they are unable to bear it.

"Shams of Tabriz's great meaning is not understood, his secret is not reached and his value is not known. If his mysteries were spoken openly, there would be mayhem, so many heads would roll, so much blood would be spilt. So do not make me say more, don't expect manifestations of truth whose time has not come.

"Not everyone can comprehend the station of annihilation. Don't forget the strife that broke out in Konya because Shams of Tabriz was not understood, the turmoil and

---

10. This is the meaning of the Sufism saying, *ibnü'l-vakt = son of time*. It is a natural duty for Sufis who have not yet reached the degree of non-existence (*fenâ*) to make the most of every instant of time. However, there are non-existents called *arrived gnostics* who have been freed from time and place and attained the degree of subsistence in God [*Allah'ta bâkî olma*]. Because they have reached the reality of time, they have become friends who are freed from domination by time and even dominate time themselves. In Sufism those who attain this degree are called *ebu'l-vakt = father of time, lord of time.*

suffering."

Let us return to our tale. The mysteries of Shams are in the meaning of this story. For Shams of Tabriz is the divine physician in the tale, and the other arrogant, crude doctors are the luckless whose enlightenment is not yet possible, they are those whom the light of gnosis has not reached.

****

THE FRIEND ASKS THE PADISHAH IF HE MAY BE ALONE WITH THE GIRL IN ORDER TO DISCOVER THE CAUSE OF HER AFFLICTION

He said, "O Shah, I ask you to clear the house
Whether they be strangers or kin, put them out

145.   There should be no one eavesdropping from the hall
While I am engaged in questioning the girl."
The house was emptied and no one left within
Other than the patient and the physician
"What city are you from?" he gently asked her
"For each city's people there's a different cure.
And who is there in that city close to you ?
What is there of yours and related to you?"
With his fingers on her pulse he asked again
Of the injustices of fortune one by one

150.   When a person has a thorn stuck in his foot
He lifts it across his knee and puts it up
With a needle he keeps searching for the tip
Moistening the needle with his tongue and lip
If to find a thorn in the foot is that hard
Tell me, what about a thorn inside the heart?
If just any rogue could perceive the heart's thorn
How could sorrow lay a hand on anyone?
Someone sticks a thorn under a donkey's tail
The ass can't get rid of it and jumps and flails

155.   But his bucking makes the thorn more firmly stuck
To extract it takes a thinking intellect
To expel the thorn, the ass in burning pain
Bucks and kicks out at a hundred different things
Master at removing thorns, that wise doctor
Laid his hand on her, here and there, to test her
And he asked again if she would tell to him
The stories and circumstances of her friends
She revealed to the physician many things
Of positions and masters, cities and friends

160.   His ear listened to her story as she spoke
While his mind was on the beating of her pulse
So that if her pulse beat fast at any name
He'd know who in the world was her spirit's aim
She recounted the names of friends in her home

Then spoke of another city not her own
He said, "After you had left the town you're from
In what city did you then reside most long?"
She named one city and then named another
But there was no change in her pulse or color

165.   She spoke of masters and cities one by one
Of the bread she'd broken and places she'd been
City after city and house after house
None made her face go pale nor sped up her pulse
Her pulse stayed calm, there was nothing out of hand
Till he asked about candy-sweet Samarkand
Her face paled and then blushed and her pulse beat swift
For she'd parted from a Samarkand goldsmith
Finding out this secret from the sickly girl
He'd found out the root of her pain and trouble

170.   "What is the neighborhood where he lives?" he said
"Top of the Bridge, in Gatafar Street," she said
He said, "I know what your illness is, and soon
I will work magic arts to deliver you
Be carefree and glad and know this to be true
What rain does for the fields, I will do for you
Do not fret yourself, leave all worries to me
Not a hundred fathers watch more tenderly
But tell no one this secret, be sure not to
Even though the Shah may much inquire from you

175.   When the heart is tomb of that secret of yours
You will more quickly reap that desire of yours."
"He who keeps a secret," said the Messenger
"Is soon wed to the object of his desire."
When seeds are buried under the earth down deep
What's inside of them becomes the garden's green
If gold and silver were not hid from the eye
How would they be nurtured deep inside the mine?
The physician's promises and his kind words
Made the sick girl feel she was from fear secure

180.   There are true promises soothing to the heart
And borrowed promises which bring disquiet

The divine physician told the Padishah: Empty your heart's house of strangers! Let none but myself and the concubine remain within. Because as long as the house of the heart is open to other than love of God, the diseases of the soul are and their causes will not be understood. One must keep strangers and even friends away from this house and the roads near it.

The house is evacuated; neither friend nor foe remain within. This means that no alien feeling or thought will come between the one who is entering upon the path of God the Truth and the one who is showing the way. The murid will be stripped of everything he knows before the murshid; he will ask to be annihilated in the murshid's gnosis and will.

Left alone with the patient, the divine physician asked her gently and sweetly what city she was from; thus he opened the subject of the concubine's original homeland. The original homeland is the land of God. But from what city does one set out in order to reach it? One needs to know that. Because the disease of the people of every city differs according to the material and spiritual climate of that city, and has a different cure.

In short, every country has a different atmosphere and there is a different cure for the disease of every climate.

The physician asked the concubine about her kith and kin and the people she knew in that city so that he could learn to whom and to what her inner tendencies inclined.

He put his finger on the concubine's pulse. His intention was to measure the effects of his questions on her pulse. Which questions will most upset her, which will make her pulse beat faster?

Thus Hazret Mevlana has recourse even at that date to the most important and supposedly modern methods of psychology.

To be sure, a murid does not need to bring a murshid's weaknesses, avidities, and various spiritual states out into the open in order to understand the disease of his heart. But it is not the accepted method for a spiritual trainer [*rûh terbiyecisi*] to act outside of the laws of nature. It is the murshid's duty to put forth with earthly methods the truths he knows by the light of gnosis.

Any spiritual doctor has need of a diagnosis performed by observation of behavior.

Everyone knows what a person who has a thorn stuck in his foot will do in order to get the invisible thorn out.

It takes attentiveness and knowledge even to extract a thorn that is hurting the body [*vücût*], so of course it is not easy to extract a heart's thorn, which cannot be grasped with the hand.

If just anyone were able to find and extract that spiritual thorn stuck in the heart, people would easily rid themselves of worldly filth and worldly desires would have no place in their hearts.

A mischief-maker stuck a thorn under a donkey's tail, and the more the animal kicked in pain the deeper the thorn dug in.

Like the innocent donkey who cannot find the solution for his trouble, there are on the face of the earth so many heedless people unaware of the cure for their troubles of spirit and heart. If someone has a thorn stuck in his heart, if worldly filth has dirtied his heart, in order to get it out he must put his heart in the healing hands of a Perfect Human.

The divine physician was experienced at finding those heart thorns. He spoke with the concubine, always gently, about her former friends.

For one must know about the people close to a person, those he has spent most time with, in order to understand him. One must know what people he likes, what people have left deep impressions upon him. Again Hazret Ali has a saying on this topic: "Tell me who your friends are, and I will tell you what kind of person you are."

When the concubine saw the spiritual intimacy and deep sympathy the divine physician showed her, she set about telling him the story of her whole life.

She told him memories of her former homeland, her masters, and the cities where she had lived.

The physician was listening to the concubine, but his mind was on her pulse. It was clear that the concubine was heartsick, but mention of which place and which name would upset her most?

Questioning at length and mention of many a friend and city had no effect on the concubine's pulse. Given that the concubine was far from her original homeland, what were the places her spirit had passed through, where did she settle, and what degree did she rise to there? One must know these things.

Finally he asked the concubine about Samarkand, the most beautiful city in the Turkish old country, and he sensed her pulse jumped at that, and her face paled and blushed.

The divine physician understood that the concubine soul gave her heart to a goldsmith in Samarkand and became ill and despairing due to loss of him. It is not by accident that the concubine soul is obsessed with a goldsmith. For the goldsmith represents the desires and addictions of the soul; he knows well not only how to please but to steal hearts with his rich, colorful and shiny jewelry.

The patient's complaint was now known to the divine physician. The master physician has understood that the concubine is in love with a goldsmith, that is, with worldly desires, the desires of the soul, and the lush, colorful, deceptive beauties which make a person lose his head in this world. He asked the concubine what neighborhood in Samarkand the goldsmith lives in. Here what is meant by "neighborhood" is the world. The place where spirit is in a cage of flesh, in love with the body [vücût] that envelops it and sick with the bodily desires it seeks to fulfill.

The divine physician comforted the concubine. He gave her strength and courage by means of inculcation and methods used by a psychologist to heal his patient with the most inspiring and convincing words. The divine physician knew very well that not only spiritual but also physical illnesses can be cured by the peace of heart created by convincing promises of health and well-being.

He also knew very well that he must save her from the darkness of despair and the spiritual and physical collapse brought on by hopelessness, which are the greatest dangers for people whose spirits have erred and who suffer from diseases of the soul. That is why one must especially give them glad tidings of spiritual health.

Mothers and fathers only cause the spirit to have a mortal existence [vücût] in the world. That is the service they render, giving spirit a human body and human degree. But religious teachers and murshids perform a duty even more valuable than that of mothers and fathers by giving that same spirit the training and inculcation which will ensure that it becomes great spirit [büyük rûh].

It is the duty of trainers and murshids to give immortality [ebedîlik] to the spirit, to render the service of mother-father of everlasting [ebedî] life. This is demonstrated by the noble hadith: "The best of mothers and fathers are those who educate you." It is also for this reason that the divine physician feels the need to tell his beautiful patient that he will be kinder to her than a hundred fathers.

He told her: "Keep this secret in the vault of your heart! It is dangerous to reveal secrets to others. You will be well to the extent that you keep secrets."

When the spirit is freed from diseases of the soul and reaches degrees on the path toward becoming a Perfect Human, several mysteries become clear to it. One must conceal such mysteries from even those closest to one and not tell secrets before the proper time or tell them to people who cannot digest them.

In short, the most suitable box in which to hide the jewels of mystery is the vault of the heart. It is enough that this vault comprehends the value of the jewels.

That Hazret Muhammed gave glad tidings to those who keep secrets is another indication of this. Keeping secrets is a beneficial act which unites their owner with his desire.

And such is also the case with seeds hidden in the earth which only come alive in abundance of greenery at the proper time.

The virtue of concealment is also shown by the fact that substances with the capacity to become gold or silver are refined after remaining hidden like secrets for ages inside the earth.

The divine physician relieved the patient with promises soothing to the spirit and heart. Because the heart is the best touchstone for separating the true and false among promises. The spirit prepared for sublimity chooses the true among promises.

****

THE FRIEND UNDERSTANDS WHAT THE ILLNESS IS AND PRESENTS THE MATTER BEFORE THE PADISHAH

> After that he rose to go and see the Shah
> He revealed only a small part to the Shah
> He said, "In the interests of curing this pain
> My advice is we have that man here conveyed
> From that far-off city summon the goldsmith
> With gold and robes of state give false hopes to him"
> 185. When the Sultan heard what the physician said
> He embraced his advice in heart and spirit

The divine physician told the Padishah only as much about the beautiful concubine's illness as he could. When the Padishah asked, "What is the cure for her trouble," he said, "The thing to do is to have the goldsmith brought here."

This is a method of training in keeping with tarikat principles. Murshids know that people desire all the more things which have been forbidden to them, and so do not suddenly remove people from the addictions they are devoted to. It is necessary to bring erring spirits to a state in which they will understand the evil and ugliness of their avidities and addictions. It is right to bring them face to face with the emptiness and ugliness of the displays they love; to bring them to a level from which they themselves will see this emptiness and ugliness and despise it, be disgusted by it. A spirit is saved by comprehending the addictions into which it has fallen, and if the body [*vücût*] sheds these, its cure is complete, its health ensured.

That is why the divine physician wanted to bring the concubine face to face with the reality of the goldsmith. A spirit swept up by a reality whose bright and shiny image seizes the eye and heart but whose ugliness comes into view when its shine falls away can only become safe and sound by union with it.

The murshid said to the Padishah: "Bring the goldsmith here from Samarkand! It is true that Samarkand is very far. But if you promise lots of gold and robes of honor, a goldsmith will be beguiled; however far it may be, he will run wherever gold shines."

The Padishah embraced the murshid's advice with heart and spirit.

****

THE SHAH SENDS MESSENGERS TO SAMARKAND TO FETCH THE GOLDSMITH

The Shah sent to that country two messengers
Men perceptive, equitable and clever
When those two emirs arrived in Samarkand
With the Shahinshah's glad tidings for the man
They said, "Kind master perfect in artistry
Your skill is renowned in many a city
Know that for your mastery in goldsmith's art
You have been chosen by such-and-such a shah

190.   Take this robe of honor, this silver and gold
Come and be a shah's favorite at the court."
The man saw the riches and beautiful robes
He was duped and left his children and his home
He set out upon the journey gay and blithe
Unaware that the Shah meant to take his life
Happy riding an Arab horse, off he sped
What he took for robe of honor was blood-debt
You set out content, a hundred times replete
Borne on toward an evil fate by your own feet

195.   In his mind were riches, power, high status
"Go on, you'll have them," said the angel of death
When he arrived, now a stranger from afar
The physician ushered him to see the Shah
He brought him to the Shahinshah as a tease
So he'd burn in that candle flame at the feast
The Shah received him and showed him great regard
He bestowed on him a treasure house of gold
"O great Sultan," the physician said to him
"Deliver that girl unto this gentleman

200.   So that by union the girl will recover
And the water of union drive off fever
The Shah bestowed that moon-faced girl upon him
Joining those two who had so craved communion
They satisfied their appetites for six months
Until that girl was fully restored to health
Then he concocted a sherbet for the man
So before the girl's eyes he'd grow thin and wan
When illness had left no beauty in his face
His blight on the girl's spirit did not remain

205.   As he grew pale of cheek and became ugly
A coldness came into her heart gradually
The kinds of love that arise for color's sake
Are not love; in the end they are a disgrace

If only he'd been disgrace from start to end
And that evil judgment not been passed on him
Blood ran like a rushing river from his eyes
His face became the enemy of his life
The peacock's fine plumage is its enemy
Many a shah has been slain by his glory

210.   He said, "I am the deer for sake of whose musk
The hunter comes to shed my innocent blood
Oh, I am the fox they ambush in the wood
Skinning off my fur and cutting off my head
Oh, I am the elephant the mahout struck
They shed my blood in order to seize my tusks
He who has slain me for what is less than me
Is unaware that my blood will never sleep
What befalls me now tomorrow will strike him
How should blood of such as I be shed in vain!

215.   Though the shadow cast by a wall may be long
Still that shadow returns to it before long
This world is a mountain and our actions, shouts
Our cries come back to us echoing our shouts."
The earth took him at the moment he said this
The girl was purified of love and sickness
For love of the dead is not everlasting
For those who die never will be returning
Love of the living in vision and spirit
Is fresher than a rosebud with each instant

220.   Choose the love of that living one who abides
Who is serving up spirit-increasing wine
Choose the love of Him of whom the prophets all
Found in love of Him the glory and the power
Do not say: "We're not admitted to that Shah."
Dealings with the gracious are never that hard

The padishah spirit sent envoys to Samarkand. Two loyal and competent envoys went and found the goldsmith. They duped him with praise and promises of money and robes of honor. Deceived by gifts, flattering words, and especially riches, the goldsmith left his family and home and followed the envoys.

He mounted the horse of desire and lust, which appeared to him to be a fine Arab horse. He was so swept away by the words suited to his nature and the gleam of eye-catching jewels that he did not realize what he was being dragged into.

The divine physician brought that man who had come from afar into the presence of the Padishah. The Padishah honored him with gifts and compliments. He even gave his beloved concubine to this goldsmith, again on the orders of his murshid. The two lovers had their desire of each other for six months. This waiting period of six months is for the purpose of seeing whether or not the concubine will become pregnant by the goldsmith. Another reason for it is so that the concubine will see the unpleasant sides and various realities of the personality of the goldsmith she is so taken with and become disillusioned.

And so, six months later the divine physician gave the goldsmith a sherbet which brought all the ugliness within him out into view. When the concubine saw those states of the man she so loved, she began to grow cold toward him.

This deceptive love, actually consisting only of carnal desire, dies out. It is even transformed into a profound hatred. What happens in the end, happened to the goldsmith.

The goldsmith began to weep over what had become of him. He was destroyed like a deer hunted for its musk, a fox slain for its fur, an elephant struck down for its tusks.

The goldsmith was distraught and offended at the treatment deemed worthy of him. He thought that one day the same would be done to those who did this to him, that the good and bad actions of people, like the echoes of a mountain, would one day strike the mountain of truth and justice and come back on them, and in this state of reflection and despair he withdrew, died, and became earth.

The concubine no longer really loved the goldsmith and was completely freed of her suffering for him.

All of these events make one think that the beautiful concubine gave herself over to a completely metaphorical love. That events extinguish the concubine's love shows how fleeting lust and physical love is. On the other hand, those who cannot free themselves from pleasures of the flesh and worldly filth pass away in their mortal, futile loves and become trapped in a prison of earth where they cannot rise to God. For it is the spirits who have matured on His path, not the elements of the mortal body [*vücût*], which ascend to God.

It is spiritual, not material love, that is superior. It is the love of those spirits who have arrived at a state in which they see the great beloved wherever they look which is abiding [*bâkî*]. Because that love raises the spirit to that great being. That love brings the spirit to union and everlastingness [*ebedîlik*] with Him.

But for someone who remains bound to the flesh and pleasures of the flesh, everlastingness is an illusion [*hayâl*]. Such spirits become only nothing, like their bodies and their transitory pleasures.

If you will, drink of the divine love served by the cupbearer of pre-eternity [*ezel*] and post-eternity [*ebed*]. For those who drink that wine do not die. Know that all of the arrived and the prophets drank only of that wine. If you have any intelligence, seek out someone who has drunk of that wine. Don't look down on yourself in despair and say: "How could I ever reach their degree and drink of the wine of divine love they have drunk; how could destiny ever bring one of those greats before me!" God is very great, and will bring a friend to you one day; one day he will show you the light of guidance. Because dealings with the truly gracious are never difficult.

****

EXPLAINING THAT THE SLAYING AND POISONING OF THE GOLDSMITH WAS ACCORDING TO DIVINE SUGGESTION, NOT LUST OF THE SOUL AND VICIOUS INTENT

> The killing of this man by the doctor's hand
> Was not out of hope or fear of any man
> He did not kill seeking favor from the Shah
> But by command and inspiration from God

225. The reason that Khizir cut the young man's throat
Is a mystery not grasped by common folk
When God the Truth answers and inspires someone
The essence of good works is in each thing he's done
If He who grants spirit, slays, it's as should be
His hand is God's hand and he's His deputy
Like Ishmael lay your head before his sword
And give up your life to him in laughing joy
So that your spirit may forever laugh on
Like Ahmed's pure spirit, living with the One

230. Lovers drain the cup of mirth the moment when
The beautiful ones with their own hands slay them
The Shah did not spill that blood for sake of lust
Dismiss thoughts of bad intention and contest
You suppose he committed impurity
When does filter leave alloy in purity?
These abstentions and austerities severe
Are so the forge may extract dross from silver
The purpose of putting good and bad to trial
Is so scum will rise when gold is set to boil

235. If his actions had not been inspired by God
He'd have been not a shah but a sharp-toothed dog
He was unstained by lust and passion and greed
He did good, although a good that evil seemed
Although Khizir scuttled a boat in the sea
Khizir's act was thousandfold fidelity
The mind of Moses, with all his light and skill
—don't you fly without wings—was screened by a veil
It's a red rose, don't see murder in his act
Don't suppose him mad, he's drunk on intellect

240. If it was his wish to shed a Muslim's blood
I'd have been a kafir to bring his name bring up
The throne of God trembles at a villain's praise
A pious man thinks of evil at his praise
He was a shah and he was a heedful shah
He was elect and he was elect of God
When a shah like that does away with someone
He draws him to felicity and fortune
If he had not seen the goodness in his wrath
How could that absolute kindness have sought wrath?

245. The child trembles to see the blood-letter's blade
While the kind mother rejoices at that pain
He takes half a life and gives a hundred lives
He gives more than can ever fit in your mind
You judge him by analogy with yourself
But you fall far, far behind, consider well

Are your still wondering here how the divine physician could have wronged the gold-smith? How he could have given him a sherbet to drink which made his entire being ugly, how he could have killed him?

Remember that here, the beautiful concubine is the soul. The goldsmith signifies the worldly ambitions of the soul, the soul's connection with those showy aspects of the world which seize the eye and heart, and finally with worldly filth. The Padishah is the padishah spirit. That is, the divine spirit detached from the whole [*kül*]; and the divine physician represents the Perfect Human, the arrived individual who shows the ways for spirit to reach God.

Under these conditions, killing the goldsmith meant annihilating the ties to the world and worldly filth in the concubine's heart and freeing her from that filth.

In the end, such an unexpected development in the story showed in particular the reality that although a murshid, meaning a Perfect Human, may at first do something we cannot comprehend, his is a unique action due not to his personal concerns but entirely to divine inspiration. Now we will explain the wisdom of that act.

First, remember the following story:

> One day Messenger Moses promised Khizir that while he was learning what Khizir would teach him in the acquisition of divine knowledge [*ledün ilmi*] he would not interfere with Khizir's work or actions.
>
> But during the training there were three things Khizir did which Moses could not stop himself from objecting to:
>
> 1. Khizir secretly made a hole in a new, sea-worthy boat, causing it to sink.
> 2. Khizir slit a young man's throat, killing him.
> 3. Khizir had a wall repaired In a village where no one would give them any-thing to eat.[11]

In each of these events there was wisdom which Moses could not know or see: The boat belonged to poor men. If it had not sunk, the ruler would have seized it because it was new. The child, whose parents were Muslims and good people, was going to grow up to be a kafir. The damaged wall concealed a treasure belonging to two orphans, and time was needed to bring it to light.

The behavior of those who act upon God's inspiration is acceptable to God.

The messengers and the friends are great ones who have annihilated their selves in God's love and God's being. Their hands are like God the Truth's hands, they carry out His commands. Although the giving and taking of life is proper to God, God has depu-ties on earth who perform every office.

One has to lay down one's head in the path of God like Ishmael. Because it is only the spirit bestowed upon him that, like the spirit of Ahmed, arrives at everlasting life and the secret of everlasting joy.

It is because lovers die to their own being and find life in divine being, whether by following the prophets or with the help of the friends, that they recognize death at the hands of those beloveds as the great felicity.

Neither the padishah spirit nor the arrived physician destroyed the goldsmith for their

---

11. Koran 18:65-82.

own self-interests. Do not doubt the arrived! Try to see the wisdom in what they do.

The arrived are people who are detached from the concerns of soul common to worldly people, and they are purified of all worldly filth. It is fruitless to search their actions and behavior for the intentions characteristic of people who are dominated by the passions. They have arrived at a level where they are instruments of God's commands. They have been freed of every kind of filth of the soul and purified of worldly dross. They bring not only themselves but others to the same level as well.

Reaching God, melting in a crucible surrounded by flames and filtering to the bottom like pure silver or gold freed of the soul's dross, is not the result of a simple experience. The spirit takes on all those grueling hardships in order to be purified like that. Those who reach such a high degree know how to endure, with a tolerant heart, the hardship and hunger necessary to avoid the many deceptive and transient worldly pleasures which seize the eye and heart and drive a person to greed.

Do not forget that the floods, passions and trials of life that come by the hand of events are a refining crucible necessary for the spirit's training and purification from worldly filth. They free the gold of the spirit from dirt and scum and ensure its purity. One must tear apart all the veils between oneself and God and surmount all contrary obstacles in order to destroy everything other than God in the heart and be filled by, and remain with, Him alone.

You should not be misled by how the padishah spirit appears. He has in fact found the right path. Consider that even Moses could not understand why Khizir scuttled the boat. Seek to understand the wisdom in how the Padishah freed the goldsmith of his own soul by killing him.

Do not suppose that what happened was unfair to the goldsmith. If you do, you will be like those who suppose that God's friend Majnun, who was drunk with the universal intellect, that is, passed away from self in love of God, was just crazy [*majnun*].

Here praise of the Padishah who shed blood is not just empty words. It is not praise of a villain, it is praise of an arrived man. That Padishah was someone who grasped the reason why a person comes into the world. He was near to God. His killing of the goldsmith ensured him a high spiritual degree.

People are like children afraid of the blood-letter's blade. But an arrived man is like a mother who surrenders her child to the blood-letter in order to save him from disease.

Give up, let your weak, borrowed spirit go. Know that eternal spirit will take its place. The troubles and torments of the world exist to take away your mortal spirit. You will become immortal [*ebedî*] to the degree that you tolerate them with understanding.

All of the commentaries on the Mesnevi point to the reality that a human has two spirits, one half, one whole. By "half-spirit" [*yarım can*] is meant mortal life, animal spirit [*hayvânî can*]. "Whole-spirit" [*bütün can*] is divine spirit [*ilâhî rûh*], which is merely a guest in the cage of the flesh. That is the eternal spirit. In order to destroy the half-spirit, God may set upon a person one or a thousand of His creatures as instruments of severity and calamity. To tolerate them, especially to tolerate them knowingly, with comprehension, is to arrive at the immortality worth a hundred, a thousand spirits God may give.

This is how it occurs: The gaze of an arrived person touches the body [*vücût*] of someone who believes in him. The love of God, the divine mysteries and lights of self-disclosure in that gaze restrain the half-spirit in a person from the animal behavior he desires. It washes and purifies his soul of worldly filth. The person who tolerates the hardships of such a purification will have been given everlasting life. He senses with profound pleasure that everlasting life is taking the place of the half-spirit in his soul. Then he arrives at the secret of becoming the site of manifestation [*mazhar*] of blessings [*lütuf*] greater than the eye can see, the ear can hear, or the intellect comprehend.

That is why a person must not weigh by his own measure the actions of God the Truth's personal bondsmen [*has kulları*]. He must not compare with his own actions their wisdom, which is not apparent to everyone. Such erroneous comparisons distance a person from those great ones. One must be extremely attentive and use all subtlety of intellect in this regard.

Because there are many who have not been freed of their bodily passions [*vücût ihtiraslarɪ*], yet still suppose they are imitating God's own bondsmen and suppose they are like them, and they bring to mind the wisdom contained in the following story.

****

THE STORY OF THE GROCER AND THE PARROT AND HOW THE PARROT SPILLED OIL IN THE SHOP

> There was a grocer and he had a parrot
> A sweet-voiced, green-colored and talking parrot
> On the counter he would guard over the shop
> And speak smartly with the merchants in the shop
> 250. He would talk when he addressed human beings
> and was versed in the parrot's art of singing
> The shop-keeper one day had gone to his home
> While the parrot in the shop kept watch alone
> Suddenly a cat ran up and leapt inside
> To pursue a mouse, and he feared for his life
> He sprang up from the counter and flew around
> Spilling bottles of oil of rose on the ground
> His master returned from home and took his seat
> At the counter like merchants do when at ease
> 255. He saw oil everywhere, oil got on his robe
> And he smacked the parrot's head and made him bald
> For the next few days the parrot would not speak
> In regret the man began to sigh and weep
> He tore at his beard, "Oh, alas!" he cried out
> "My sun of success has gone behind a cloud
> Would that my hand had been shattered that moment
> When I struck that sweet-tongued bird upon the head."
> He gave gifts to dervishes, many of them
> So that bird of his might start to speak again
> 260. After three days and three nights dazed and distraught
> He was sitting without a hope in his shop
> Yoked to thousand-fold anxiety and grief
> Wondering, "Will this bird ever again speak?"
> He kept showing marvelous things to the bird

So it might happen that he would say a word
When a shaved Javlaqi dervish passed the shop
With a head hairless and smooth as bowl or pot
Instantly the parrot recovered his speech
"Hey, you, fellow!" he yelled at him with a screech
265.   "How did you, Pumpkin Head, come to join the bald?
Or have you too knocked over a jar of oil?"
People laughed at the analogy he struck
For he supposed himself a man of the cloak
Don't think deeds of the pure and yours are the same
Though in Persian "lion" and "milk" look the same
For this reason everyone gets lost, so few
Become aware of God the Truth's substitutes
They suppose themselves the equal of prophets
They imagine that they resemble God's friends
270.   "Behold," they say, "they are creatures as are we
We both are enslaved to hunger and to sleep."
What they do not know in their blindness is this:
There is between them an endless difference
Two species of insect feed on the same things
But one makes honey and the other just stings
Two deer species graze on grass and drink water
One produces dung, the other musk so pure
Two reeds drink from the same bank by a river
One is empty, the other full of sugar
275.   Ponder hundreds of thousands such likenesses
Ponder their seventy years' road differences
This one eats and from him feces is discharged
That one eats and becomes all the light of God
This one eats, envy and greed are his offspring
That one eats, love of the One is his offspring
There the earth's brackish and bad, here it is pure
That angel's a beast, a devil, this one's pure
For two forms to seem alike is prevalent
Both sweet and bitter water are transparent
280.   Who but a man who can taste knows—go find him
The bitter and sweet are distinguished by him
Others have compared miracle with magic
And imagined both are based upon a trick
Hostile magicians in the time of Moses
Raised up staffs in hand like the staff of Moses
From this staff to that staff there's a great divide
From this deed to that deed a journey sublime
The curse of God follows this deed by the nape
The mercy of God repays that in good faith
285.   The kafirs are ape-natured when they contest

Their nature is misery within the breast
Whatever a man does, so does an ape too
Constantly whatever he sees the man do
"I have done as he did," so the ape thinks
How could that pretender know the difference?
This one acts by divine command, that in rage
May dust be poured upon the contentious-faced
That hypocrite prays beside the conformant
Not to pray God but for sake of argument
290.   In prayer and fasting, alms and pilgrimage
The believers play against the hypocrite
In the end believers are vindicated
In the next world hypocrites are checkmated
Although both are contestants in the same game
They're as far apart as men of Marv and Rayy
Each one travels onward toward his own state
Each one's journey is according to his name
If he's called a believer, then he is glad
If you say hypocrite, he is fiery mad
295.   Because of his essence that one's name is loved
Because he brings evils, this one's name is loathed
Meem and *vav* and *meem* and *nun*[12] is not honor
The word "mu'min" [believer] is merely a descriptor
If you call him by the hypocrite's vile name
Like a scorpion's sting, it causes him great pain
If this name has no derivation in Hell
Why is there inside of it the taste of Hell?
Letters are not what gives that vile name its fault
A container does not make sea water salt
300.   Letters are like pots, meaning, water in them
Meaning's sea is *mother of the book with Him*[13]
In this world there is the sweet sea and the salt
And between them a *"barzakh they do not cross"*[14]
Know that both these two flow from one origin
Pass on by them both, go to their origin
In the scales are coin adulterate and gold
Judgment will not let you know without touchstone
When God puts a touchstone in someone's spirit
He knows certainty from doubt by means of it
305.   A piece of trash flies into a creature's mouth
He is at ease only when he gets it out
In a thousand mouthfuls there is one straw stalk
The creature's sense will find it and root it out

---

12. The Arabic letters in the word *mu'min*, "believer."
13. "Mother of the book," Koran 13:39.
14. Koran 55:19.

The worldly sense is a ladder in this realm
Religious sense climbs to the celestial realm
Ask physicians for the health of worldly sense
Pray the Beloved to heal that other sense
Thriving flesh is the well-being of this sense
Ruin of the body is health for that sense

310.   Though the spirit's way brings the body ruin
It makes that ruin a thriving home again
O happy spirit that for love of the One
Spends unstintingly of self, household and home
It wrecks the house for the sake of buried gold
Then builds it better again with that same gold
It cuts off the water, clears the conduit
Then lets good water again flow into it
It slices the skin, takes out the arrowhead
Then fresh skin appears to grow anew again

315.   It razes the fort and drives the kafirs out
Then rears up a thousand towers and ramparts
Who can say the how of He who has no how?
I say only what constraints here will allow
Now it is like this and now the opposite
Religion's work is naught but bewilderment
Not bewildered so one's back is turned on Him
But bewildered and drowned and drunk in the friend
There is one who keeps his face turned toward the friend
And one whose face is none but the face of him

320.   Look into each one's face carefully, keep watch
In service you'll learn to know faces perhaps
Many a satan has the face of a man
So one should not give one's hand to every hand
The fowler makes the sound of a whistling bird
So that the bird-catcher may deceive the bird
That bird hears the whistling call of his own kind
And swoops down to find the knife-point and birdlime
The inferior man steals from dervish talk
So with their words he can enchant simple folk

325.   Real men's work is luminosity and heat
Vile men's work is shamelessness and trickery
They make a lion of wool to go and beg
They call Bu Musaylim by name of Ahmed
"Liar" is still what they're calling Musaylim
Muhammed is still "Man of Understanding"
The seal of that wine of God is purest musk
The seal of the other is torment and funk

The grocer and his sweet-talking parrot spent many a merry hour together and each loved the other sincerely. The parrot was quite ingenious. But one day he got into trouble.

He was alone in the shop when a cat jumped inside pursuing a mouse, and the parrot thought the cat meant to kill him. He sprang up in fear and knocked some bottles of rose oil off a shelf. When the grocer saw this he was very angry and smacked the parrot on the head. He hit him so hard that the parrot become bald and dumb. The grocer's regrets were to no avail.

The reality was that the cat of fear and illusion was chasing the mouse of intellect, and the parrot of speech, frightened and confused thereby, was forced into erroneous and unconscious speech; just at that moment the baton of the shariat came down on his head and he lost the faculty of speech which had distinguished him from the other animals, becoming dumb like they.

In the end the one who brought down the baton suffered, true conscience and justice felt disquiet.

Although the grocer gave gifts to dervishes and made votive offerings, he could not get his parrot to speak. It did no good when he showed his bird things to surprise him either. But three days later a Javlaqi dervish with a completely hairless head[15] passed by the shop and things changed.

What amazed the parrot was that the man was completely hairless. He found his voice again and called out: "Hey Pumpkin Head! Did you spill rose oil and get hit by your master too?" This amusing story showed that the parrot was surprised to see someone like himself. It gave clear proof that in reality such external resemblances have nothing to do with origin and inwardness.

Such is the case with for example, the resemblance between the word for milk and the word for lion, both of which are written *şîr*. A resemblance between two words does not mean that they denote the same thing.

Two people seem alike but one of them is an ordinary person and the other is a Perfect Human. He is a friend of God. So many, simply because the eyes of their hearts did not see, have thought the prophets were like themselves. That is what it is to not recognize the Muhammedan reality [*Hakîkat-i Muhammediye*].

Because in Sufism a friend [*velî*] is a person who frees himself of all duality by making himself The Truth with The Truth, uniting with God in sensing, thinking and behavior.

A prophet [*nebî*] is a Perfect Human who has been given the duty of calling people to God the Truth, showing the way and drawing them away from infidelity [*küfür*] and defiance.

A messenger of God [*resûlullah*] is a person, great among the great, who has united the degrees of prophet-hood and friend-hood in himself and to that degree become annihilated in God. Every state and action issuing forth from his hand, his tongue, and his eye is considered to be in reality a state and action of God the Truth.

And there are the Substitutes [*abdâllar*] who have covered a great distance on the path of reaching God. From one point of view there are forty of them, and from another point of view, seven. They have achieved the miracle of appearing in one place while being in another quite far away, at the same time. They have attained the secret of appearing in another body [*vücût*] substituted for their own, and they have communicated

---

15. In tarikat parlance, Bektashi, Haydari or Qalandari dervishes who shave their hair, eyebrows, moustaches and beards are called Javlaqi, in Turkish, Dazlak.

great meanings with this wisdom of theirs.

They wander from land to land, either themselves or through the more numerous persons who by progressing along their path have become their substitutes, and they work to show people the ways to reach God. They are greats possessed of various degrees and duties at the same time.

In this way there are around us, in their cages of the flesh much resembling ours, so many spirits made of spirituality [*mâneviyattan ibâret rûhlar*] who are charged with varying degrees of duty in the education [*tâlim*] and training [*terbiye*] of humanity.

However, our resemblance to them does not mean that we are them.

In the same way, although bees and wasps drink the sap of the same flowers, only bees make honey. Not every deer produces musk. Not every reed is sugar cane.

Dirt, sweat, and dispositions like stinginess and envy come forth from what evil persons eat. But the power and strength that comes forth from what the friends eat gives rise to goodness, to love of God and God's light.

It is right to draw lessons from the examples of fertile and infertile earth, and sweet and salt water. Liken salt water to kafirs and those who associate others with God, and sweet water to the prophets and friends.

To be sure, viewed from outside, the friends and prophets appear to be like anyone else, and people cannot distinguish them from others. In order to do so one must be dyed with the same dye as the arrived and the prophets.

In short, there is a great difference between the people of form and the people of meaning. Not every person, not every heart, can tell the difference.

Those who are not masters of gnosis cannot tell the difference between magic and miracle. It was because the sorcerer who took up a staff was void of gnosis that he could think he was a Moses.

In the same way, actions leading to God the Truth's mercy or His curse are not the same.

The human soul inclines to the corruptions of which it is fond. Even the way kafirs imitate one another in obstinacy is due to the incurable illness in the darkness of their own breasts.

Many people are reminiscent of apes in the way they are defeated by their own souls. So are those who imitate the prophets and friends. The imitators are unaware of the virtues of those who have a true calling [*vazîfe*]. Just as monkeys do not know the difference between their actions and those of their masters.

Of the person who comes to prayer for the sake of prayer and the person who comes to prayer merely for the sake of imitation, only the former is in God's presence.

To be sure, their external actions in worship are identical. Those who view them from outside will see the true Muslims and the imitators of worship in the same place, side by side in the same row. But in reality they are far, far away from one another.

In conclusion, every person acts according to his own quality [*şan*]. This means that every person has a name [*ad*] written on the preserved Tablet [*levh-i mahfûz*]. In reality, whatever is written on a person's brow, written on that spiritual tablet back in pre-eternity, that is what self-discloses. If a person's name on that tablet is a good name, in this world he does what that name requires. If the name written there is a bad name, the person's worldly actions will be bad also.

In sum, whatever of subjugation [*kahır*] or beauty [*cemâl*] that name leads to, that is where its owner will settle, however roundabout his course. That is why Hazret Ali said: "Everyone fears for his end, but I fear my beginning."

If you call a believer a kafir or a hypocrite, he will become fired up like a child who screams his heart out when he is scolded and beaten although he has done nothing wrong. Because his name and his attribute [*sıfat*] do not tolerate, and are not appropriate or prepared for, such a slur. Even hypocrites are pleased only when they are called good and believing. Because they mistakenly suppose their erring ways and actions are right.

In the time of Hazret Muhammed there was a hypocritical group who pretended to be Muslim while remaining Jewish or kafir, and they believed they were right to do so. However, when the Koranic verse was revealed, "Then seek death, if you speak the truth,"[16] their reaction exposed their hypocrisy.

The names of believers are pleasant to everyone, even loved. Because the virtues of faith are expressed in their names. They are beloved of God too. Even the names of hypocrites are not loved, because their attributes and acts [*hareketleri*] are each expressed in those names. Hypocrisy is the great calamity which makes even the names of hypocrites ugly in language and meaning.

No honor or fault can be attributed to the letters, taken as letters, which spell the words "believer" or "hypocrite." The honor or fault is not in the letters or even the words, but in the persons qualified by them.

At the same time, it is as if there were a feeling hidden in the words. The spirits qualified by those words feel it, even if they do not understand the words. When a believing person is called a hypocrite, the torment his spirit experiences gives him pain and anxiety like the sting of a scorpion or the fire of Hell. The quality attributed to him racks his pure spirit with suspicion, doubt and torment as if it were the expression [*ifade*] of a real bad act [*suç*].

One senses that the word "hypocrite" earned its meaning in Hell and is the expression of an offense of the soul driven from there into our world. This may be the reason that there is a hellish taste and atmosphere in the saying and the meaning of it. The believer can virtually sense that it is possible for so many torments that will be felt in Hell to be tasted as a painful lesson even in our world. That we should be considered deserving of such a lesson, even as a slander, could be due to a hidden bad act of ours which necessitates it.

Good and evil are not properties of forms [*kalıplar*] but of the matter, even the meaning itself, which is put into the forms. Even when sea water is put into the most beautiful container, it will still be salty and brackish. In the same way, when meaning is put into the form and container of letters and words, it will like flowing water take the shape of the container in which it is put, but will not lose it own characteristic.

This means that the commerce between the human body [*beden*] and soul is like that too. The human body [*vücût*] is a container, a form. Good and evil are not properties of this form but of the spirit put inside it.

Even seas can be sweet or salt. Sometimes there is between them a fine veil, a berzakh, which does not allow the water of one to mix with the other. In reality salt and sweet seas are like spiritual and physical forces [*kuvvetler*]. Although so many people, some of them representing light, some darkness, are side by side in the world, even knee to knee, the light of the one cannot illuminate the darkness of the other. Sometimes these

---

16. Koran 2:95.

spiritual and physical elements even self-disclose as good and evil in one single body [*vücût*], yet cannot mingle. They continue to remain in the same cage of flesh, each without obliterating the other.

The sublime feelings and the base feelings in the human body [*beden*] are like sweet and salt seas, and what separates them is the veil of the heart.

To put it another way, the veil of the heart separates the divine light from the evil darkness in a person and does not let them mingle.

Because while God was hidden like a treasure in His own realm of mystery, the elements of goodness, beauty and being in His divine nature were freed from this hiding and turned toward showing themselves in a realm of creation. Such a manifestation and self-disclosure felt the need for a vehicle capable of comprehending that being, that goodness, and especially that beauty.

The human was created with the duty of comprehending that being and that beauty. It was as in the hadith, "God, may He be exalted, created Adam upon the form of The Merciful," and the human, qualified with the value of the names and attributes of his Creator, was wrapped in a mortal body [*vücût*].

But the manifestation and self-disclosure of God the Truth's names and attributes is not the same in every human; it is various and in varying degrees. Moreover, this manifestation and self-disclosure is luminous or dull according to the pre-eternal receptivities [*kabiliyetler*] of spirits.

But not every spirit knows which of these self-disclosures within it is manifest, or which of them is dominant. That is why it is the duty of the arrived, who sense and comprehend that they have attained the reality of the divine self-disclosure and its highest degree, to awaken human spirits to the divine qualities entrusted to them and to free them from the dark realm of their own souls.

Thus the purpose of these two forces which remain separate by virtue of the heart's veil in the body [*vücût*] is in fact to reach the same reality. That they appear to be opposites is not an obstacle to their being partners in function.

Actually, it is right for you to pass beyond both of them and turn toward and reach the goal that these two contrary forces, which in reality show the way to reach the same goal, indicate. You will reach this goal with the measures of comprehension and gnosis in your heart.

It is just such a measure that distinguishes a believing soul from a soul pretending to believe. The measure of gnosis within you will perform the function of a touchstone distinguishing adulterate gold from pure gold.

There are many whose comprehension has died in ignorance while the body [*vücût*] is alive. The right thing is for a person to be alive and vital with knowledge of God. A person who has love and the light of faith in his heart, and the touchstone of gnosis in his conscience, can distinguish between the doubt [*şek*] and certainty [*yakîn*] which comes from God. This means that he can be freed from suspicion and anxiety and know the great reality by way of gnosis.

When a person is eating and a piece of straw gets in his mouth, he cannot rest until he gets it out. Just as a person notices that a piece of straw has gotten into his mouth along with his food, his heart can sense and comprehend what a person awakened with God the Truth's self-disclosure and attraction [*cezbe*] does when bad acts mix in with good behavior. With the one condition that the heart's mirror of such a person is pure enough and bright enough that he can immediately sense any dust placed upon it.

Worldly feeling can only serve the prosperity of this world. But religious feeling does not merely bring worldly prosperity. Like a ladder of light, it carries a person to the skies, that is, to the sublime degrees of conscience and spirituality.

Physicians can cure you with medicines when your health is ruined by worldly affairs. But the only physicians who can cure illnesses of religion and conscience are physicians beloved of God; they are the friends who are successors [*halîfe*] to the Prophet on earth.

If your body [*vücût*] prospers, your world is powerful; if it is ruined, your faith is powerful. Only here is the word "body" [*vücût*] correct in both its meanings. The second meaning of "body" is "soul" [*nefis*]. The soul is that body which is the source of the disease of duality. If your being [*varlık*] is divested of that body [*bu vücûttan harap olursa*], that is, by that soul, the dark powers in your body are defeated and you are prepared for the potential of the powers of light.

The spirit's journey ruins the body [*beden*], but it is after such ruin that the spirit becomes prosperous.

This means that all during a person's life he should expend great effort to make the way of the spirit thrive. In order to free the soul of lust, and the body [*cisim*] from the greed and avarice that brings animality, you should destroy the false prosperity established with these in the body [*vücût*] and the pleasure felt in that prosperity. Then only power of spirit and gnosis will remain in you. If with these two powers, that is, with spirit and gnosis, you make prosperous the ruin of the bodily habitat you have destroyed, as a result your soul will be destroyed, but your spirit will be repaired.

The spirit of a person who spends all he has for love of God the Truth is happy. A person who knocks down the house where he lives in order to obtain the rich treasure buried underneath may later build palaces. You must first empty out a dirty tank before putting clean water into it.

The flesh may appear to have no wounds externally, but a surgeon makes a large wound in order to clean the fatal wound of an arrow inside the body [*vücût*]. A sovereign demolishes an enemy fort polluted with the bodies of kafirs in order to capture it, but after he captures it he makes the fort more prosperous than before.

So, the destruction of the evil dispositions of the soul is for the purpose of allowing the treasure of goodness beneath it to emerge. A brain muddied like a dirty tank by harmful and faithless thoughts must be cleared of all that muddy water so that you can let the pure, clear water of faith flow into it. And so with the other examples. All are for the purpose of convincing you that it is necessary to educate and train your soul, and by decisive means. At the same time, the way of destruction is not the only one by which God shows you the ways of guidance and the way to reach the goal.

We mention this way because we see that it is necessary. In reality it is not possible to put limits on the power and art of God the Truth. When He wishes, he can reward a believing bondsman of his without subjecting him to any punishment. That is, he can take a bondsman of his who is drenched in ignorance and heedlessness and in an instant illuminate him with the most valuable of knowledge and gnosis.

Those who are awed [*hayran*] by God sense His wisdom. Just as it is possible for those who have been kafirs all their lives to reach God the Truth and reality in the instant of death, those who have passed their lives in worship may go to the hereafter as kafirs.

It is not enough to be considered a kafir or a friend, to appear so to people. The desired goal is to be sincere enough in knowing and reaching Him to rise to the degree of the arrived in God the Truth's sight. Have no doubt that the worship performed in order to impress other people [*halk*] will bring God's bondsman not to light but to darkness.

Those who are in reality awed by God the Truth are not those who have their faces turned toward other people and their back to God the Truth. To turn one's face toward other people is the work only of those who are able to see God the Truth in the being and countenance of other people. In fact it is in this way that awe for other people is in reality awe for God. Such arrived persons show the companions they gather around them the path to God the Truth and they become happy on that path.

There is also a group of the arrived who have passed away from themselves drinking the wine of divine love. They are intimate [*hemhal*] only with the Creator, they no longer see the creatures and therefore no longer see other people. Those who are sites of manifestation of this form of self-disclosure are people of attraction who have completely forgotten the world even while they are still in the world. They are the gnostics whom a poet described as follows:

One who knows the world and what is in it is not a gnostic
A gnostic is one who doesn't know the world and what's in it

There is a type of arrived person whose gaze of eye and heart is turned only toward that great Beloved. His spirit is awed only by Him. His attraction is such that in every place he looks, in every being he sees, he sees only Him. However, such arrived persons have not completely passed away from their bodies [*vücûtlar*]. Although they have come close to annihilation [*fenâ*], they are still not freed from the demands of being human.

But there is also a type of arrived person whose gaze is turned toward other people as another appearance of God the Truth. Such arrived persons have drunk of the wine of oneness and reached the degree of subsistence [*bâkîlik*] by way of the degree of annihilation. They are within a oneness complete.

Since oneness means the removal of duality, even when they look at other people and not God the Truth, still they see that great beloved. This state is the state of seeing oneness which is apparent to the eye in the form of multiplicity. In Sufism, it is looking with God and seeing God. This truth is expressed in Yunus Emre's lines:

Yunus is the one who's "I"
Let's take him from in between
He who looks along with You
Sees only You, oh my Lord

Know those friends well! Serve them. The only way to acquire gnosis, that is, to learn the truth, is to know and understand them.

At the same time, it won't do to suppose that every hand extended to you in initiation is the hand of a friend. Beware of tricksters who come to you in the guise of a murshid and whose goal and self-interest is to encourage you on the wrong path!

Just as there are hunters who lure birds by imitating their calls, there are also tricksters who hunt people by imitating the speech of the friends. Simple people are duped by such tricksters just as birds are duped by hunters.

But true friends are known by the truth of their love and the divine light awakening in their countenances.

You have heard of Musaylama al-Kazzāb.[17] He claimed to be a prophet in the years after Hazret Muhammed had passed away. Abu Bakr was forced to do battle with him. In the end he was killed by Wahshī, who had killed Hazret Hamza.

Musaylama died. But his lying has not been forgotten.

Because divine wine is one thing, and ordinary wine is another. Their effects are as different as night and day. (Here Hazret Mevlana compares and contrasts in various ways the travelers on the two different paths and, giving very lively examples, demonstrates the difference between light and darkness.

One group of the people on those two different paths are the truth travelers [hakîkat yolcuları], who have turned their faces toward love of God and are walking toward God in perfect sincerity.

The others are hypocrites who exploit the regard people have for the friends.

Look at the faces of each group! So that you may acquire the art of distinguishing between truth and falsehood. For there are people in the form of Satan. These people dupe both others and themselves. If you happen to make the error of giving them your hand, they will certainly dupe you too.)

****

THE STORY OF THE JEWISH PADISHAH WHO KILLED THE CHRISTIANS OUT OF FANATICISM

There was once a cruel shah among the Jews
Who hated Jesus and oppressed Christians too
330.   It was Jesus' time, the covenant was his
He was Moses' spirit and Moses was his
Those two divine friends were to the cross-eyed shah
Treading different ways along the path of God
A craftsman said to a cross-eyed apprentice
"Come, go and fetch that bottle here from the shed."
The boy said, "Which of the two bottles in there
Shall I go and get for you, do make it clear."
The craftsman said, "There are not two bottles, go
Leave off squinting and do not see less as more."
335.   "O master, don't chide me," the apprentice said
"Smash one of the two," the master craftsman said
When he smashed the one, both vanished from his eye
It's propensities and rage make man squint-eyed
The bottle seemed to his eye two, but was one
When he smashed the bottle, the other was gone
Industry becomes veiled when designs arise
Hundredfold veils rise from the heart to the eye
When a judge lets bribery lodge in his heart
How should he know the wrongdoer from the wronged?
340.   The Shah became so squint-eyed with Jewish spleen
That we cry, "Have mercy, O Lord, have mercy!"
He slew a hundred thousand wronged men of faith

---

17. "al-Kazzāb" is a nickname that was given to the man, meaning "the liar."

Saying, "I'm the last resort of Moses' faith

In the time when the turn of prophethood had come to Hazret Jesus, there was a Jewish ruler who felt extreme enmity toward Christians. This Jewish ruler did not know that the power self-disclosed in Jesus was in reality the spirit of Moses. Moses and Jesus are both God the Truth's prophets. They brought people the same truth. The power manifested in each of them was the same light of prophethood. They drew their light from the same source.

The Jewish ruler was like cross-eyed people who see double, who see one thing as two, and he thought Jesus was separate from Moses.

Just as the cross-eyed apprentice saw the one bottle his master wanted as two bottles, and when he broke one of them there was no other bottle left, those whose eye of the heart is cross-eyed see the single truth prophets bring as two, and they imagine that prophets who bring the same truth are two separate beings [*varlık*] different from each other.

Such people, like those who go wild in a moment of rage and lust, are unable to think of the right; they are unable to see the true, the good, and the right. As one of the friends once said, whether the veil between God the Truth and His bondsman be seventy thousandfold or as thin as the skin of an onion, the result is the same: The bondsman cannot see God the Truth.

Once a judge has decided to take a bribe, there is no difference for him between wrong-doer and wronged. The judge takes his decision according to the value of what he will pocket. That was what the Jewish ruler did. The enmity he felt toward Christians made it impossible to show him the truth. That is why he destroyed hundreds of thousands of Christians who believed in God the Truth and in the truth.

****

THE VIZIER INSTRUCTS THE PADISHAH TO STAGE A DECEPTION

His vizier, a Magi intriguer of plots
Could by trickery make flowing water stop
"The Christians," he said, "are in fear of their lives
They are hiding their religion in disguise
Don't kill so many of them, it does no good
Belief has no scent like musk or aloe wood
345.   The inner life's hid within a hundred sheaths
Like you in outward show, different beneath."
The Shah said, "So, tell me, what then is the plan?
What is the recourse for such scheming and sham?
So not one Christian may remain in the world
Neither manifest in belief nor concealed."
"Oh Shah," he said, "cut off my ear and my hand
Rip my nose apart with a severe command
After that bring me under the hanging tree
And have someone intercede to plead for me
350.   Have this proclaimed by the city crier abroad
On the highway at the junction of four roads
Then drive me to a city far from your sight

50

That I may cast amongst them evil and strife.

****

THE VIZIER'S PLOT AGAINST THE CHRISTIANS

I will tell them, 'I am inwardly Christian
O God who knows secrets, you know who I am
The Shah was informed regarding my belief
And in fanaticism tried to kill me
I tried to keep my religion from the Shah
And profess his religion in outward show
355.   But he caught scent of my innermost secrets
And the things I told the Shah became suspect
He said, "Your speech is like a needle in bread
From my heart to your heart there is a conduit
Through that passageway I can see what you are
I'm not fooled by your words, I see what you are."
Had the spirit of Jesus not saved me then
Like a Jew he would have torn me into shreds
For sake of Jesus I'd give my life, my head
I am a hundred thousand times in his debt
360.   I'd not begrudge Jesus my life, however
In science of his religion I'm well versed
It seemed to me a shame this religion pure
Should be lost to the ignorant forever
Thanks be to the Lord and to Jesus that I
Am become to that true religion a guide
From Jew and Judaism I have escaped
And am able to bind the sash round my waist
O people, the age of Jesus is this age
Let your spirits hear the mysteries of his faith'"
365.   When he explained the plot he planned to the Shah
He removed all anxiety from his heart
The Shah did to the vizier what he'd proposed
The people were stunned to see events unfold
He banished the vizier to a Christian place
Where he then began to call them to the faith

This ruler had a vizier who could bring flowing water to a stop by trickery. The vizier told the ruler that the consciences of men could not be influenced by the death penalty and suggested that they should arrange a deception; the best thing would be for the ruler to make it appear that the vizier was being punished. He said: "Cut off my hands and ears, disfigure my face. Send me to be hanged. Then have an intercessor save me. Do this in public so that the Christians will be convinced, and exile me to a far-off city. I will dupe the Christians there. I will tell them my crime was to be a Christian like them, and this was the punishment the Padishah deemed fit for me. It was the aid of Hazret Jesus that saved me from the hands of the Padishah. For it is thus that Jesus saves from the hands of tyrants those who choose his path."

The Padishah understood the vizier's design. He did what he suggested, and exiled him.

****

THE CHRISTIANS ACCEPT THE VIZIER

> Hundreds of thousands came to him
> Gathering little by little around him
> And he expounded to them in secrecy
> The gospel, the sash and prayer's mysteries
> 370. Outwardly he was a preacher of tenets
> But within he was the decoy and the net
> Muhammed's companions, faced with such deceit
> Begged him to explain the ghoulish soul's deceit
> Asking how hidden motives and self-interest
> Corrupt prayer and sincerity of spirit
> They were not asking about obedience
> They were not asking about outward defect
> They distinguished, hair by hair and mote by mote
> The soul's deceit like celery from a rose
> 375. The teachings of Muhammed on this question
> Astounded even hair-splitting companions

Thus the vizier pretended to be sincere and succeeded in deceiving a great many Christians who gathered around him, convinced by his condition and his words. His trickery and his actions showed that the effect of "hypocrisy" is even more forceful than "tyranny."

In fact in this story, the Jewish Padishah is intended to be Satan, who is himself the enemy of every faith. The vizier is the satanic principle which self-discloses in humans in the form of hypocrisy and misrepresentation. Put in another way, the Padishah is the soul in the human being [*insan varlığında*]. The vizier represents the deception of the soul. Jesus represents the divine spirit perched in the cage of flesh, and the Christians in the story represent all the forces of spirit [*rûhânî kuvvetleri*].

The reality is that humans are susceptible to deception and can even fall into the error of supposing that the many hypocrites on the face of the earth are among the friends.

And just so, what the companions of Hazret Muhammed asked him about most often was what they could arm themselves with against those who would deceive them by appearing to be religious [*dindar*]. They learned the answers from him and were amazed by the explications he gave.

****

THE CHRISTIANS FOLLOW THE VIZIER

> The Christians completely gave their hearts to him
> Such is the force of conformity in men
> They planted the love of him within their breasts
> They believed him the deputy of Jesus

Inwardly he was antichrist with one eye
O God, *best of rescuers*, please hear our cry!
380. Moment by moment we're snared by a new lure
Though each of us be a falcon or Simurgh
Every moment you save us and we once more
Go straight toward the trap, O You without desire
We keep laying by wheat in this storage place
Then we lose again the grain we've put away
We do not use our minds to think that this loss
Is due after all to the guile of a mouse
Since the mouse has chewed a hole in our store-house
And his skill made a ruin of our store-house
385. O spirit, stop the evil of the mouse first
Then return to gathering wheat in earnest
Hear the words of the leader of all leaders:
"*Without presence there can be no ritual prayer.*"
If there is no thieving mouse in our store-house
Where is the wheat of forty years' good works now?
Why is it the truthfulness of every day
Is not little by little there stored away?
From hot iron many stars of fire spew out
Drawn in and accepted by that burning heart
390. But under cover of darkness comes a thief
To lay fingers upon the stars secretly
He puts out the light of the stars one by one
So that no lamp will be kindled in heaven
Though there be a thousand traps set at our feet
When You are there with us there will be no grief
When Your kindly grace is with us constantly
What fear is there of that miserable thief?
As the spirits sleep within the trap of flesh
Each night You free them and wipe clean the tablets
395. The spirits are freed every night from this cage
By judgment and speech and story unrestrained
At night prisoners forget their confinement
At night sultans forget about government
No worry for profit or loss, no sorrow
No concern for such-and-such or so-and-so
The gnostic's state is thus even without sleep
God said you would think them awake *while they sleep*
Don't fear them; day and night asleep to the world
Like pens gripped in transformation by the Lord
400. So that one who does not see the writing hand
Thinks the action is due to that moving pen
The gnostic's state is demonstrated in part
By the sleep of the senses seizing all folk

In the wilderness which has no quality
Both their spirits and their bodies are at peace
With a whistle You draw them back to the trap
To justice and judge You draw all of them back
For when the light of dawn raises up its head
The gold eagle takes wing in the firmament

405.　　Like Seraphiel, "*He who cleaves light from darkness*"[18]
Brings them all back into form from formlessness
He puts the expanded spirits into flesh
And impregnates all their bodies once again
He takes off the saddle of the spirit's steed
That's the meaning of *brother of death is sleep*
But so that the spirit will return by day
He fastens a long tether upon its leg
So He may lead it back from that rich meadow
From its grazing ground to go under the load

410.　　If only like the companions of the cave
Or Noah's ark, He kept this spirit away
So that heart and eye and ear could be rescued
From wakefulness and the conscious mind's deluge
Many companions of the cave right now too
Are in the world next to you, in front of you
The cave is with them, the friend is with them too
But with eye and ear sealed tight, what can you do?

The Christians were deceived by the vizier. However, they were raw souls susceptible to deception. A person whose heart burns with the fire of real love will have a spirit that can truly sense and differentiate between good and evil and adulterate and pure.

To be sure, the vizier practiced every deception necessary to trick them and appeared to be a believer perfect in every way.

Only the light of God's guidance can save us from the trickery of such persons. We are people who have many times laid by wheat in grain cellars but, without our realizing it, mice have carried off the wheat. If a person is to avoid losses in the heart's wheat of faith and purity, he must first of all prepare a heart mice will not enter, and clear the cellar of mice.

This is expressed by Hazret Muhammed's: "Without presence there can be no ritual prayer."

Here the wheat and the cellar, like the mice and the Padishah, the vizier and the Christians, are each elements of parable. The cellar is intended to be the human body [*vücût*], the wheat, work accomplished by the spirit, and the mice, the soul. Just as the Jewish vizier performs a satanic function, deceiving the Christians, in the same way the soul in the human body turns the good actions of the spirit to evil and destroys them.

So, to first of all destroy the mice means to free the body from the deception of the soul and even from the soul itself.

---

18. Koran 6:96. Seraphiel is the angel who blows the horn on Resurrection Day, upon which the spirits of the dead re-enter their bodies.

Those who seek to deprive sight of every kind of light, snuffing out with their hands even the sparks like stars which fly off red-hot iron, are not few.

But a heart sparked by attraction to God the Truth and love of Him should be provisioned against those who would leave him deprived of such light. In reality the red-hot iron is the murshid, the arrived person. The spark flying from that iron into pure hearts is the light of divine love. The evil person who seeks to extinguish that spark in the heart is often not external but within our souls, in the avarice of our souls; it is our soul. Again, it is only God the Truth who can protect us from such evils and evil ends. The person in whose heart there is only His true love will not fall into the traps prepared for him.

It is for the purpose of erasing memories, particularly evil thoughts, from the tablet of the mind [zihin] that God separates the spirit from the body [vücût] every night and gives it the potential to roam. The spirit which separates from the body and goes to the realm of spirits at these times is the divine spirit in a human. The animal spirit in a human still remains in the body and sometimes, with an instinct that comes of long association side by side with the divine spirit in the same body, even sees the dream of the departing spirit and remembers its states.

In fact dreams are seen in the realm of likeness [misal âlemi], which is located in between the realm of spirits and the realm of bodies [vücûtlar yâni cesetler]. An indication of this is found in what Hazret Ali said about how when the body [vücût] is asleep and the spirit leaves it to ascend to the realm of spirits, it leaves behind in the body a bundle of rays [huzme], and it is by means of these rays left behind in the body that the spirit sees a dream.

To sleep is to be unaware of the body's [ceset] many needs and ambitions, unaware of concerns for profit and loss, and even of the body itself. In sleep, neither is the prisoner aware of his prison nor the Padishah aware of his sultanate.

As for the arrived, even when awake they are asleep to everything other than God. It is because the arrived have reached such a spiritual degree that they are complete strangers to the desires and ambitions of the body [vücût], that is, of the soul.

Consider the Companions of the Cave! They were arrived persons who knew God but were asleep to worldly and bodily desires and the wants and avarice of the deceptive and duplicitous world.

Don't misunderstand the apparent wakefulness of all the arrived who, like them, have closed their eyes to the filth of the world. They are awake only like a pen in the hand of someone who is writing. Their every action is on the path and in the manner of what the divine will has drawn. If you possess gnosis, try to look not to the pen but to the hand holding the pen.

Be thankful that you close your eyes to the realm of bodies [cesetler] for at least as long as you are asleep. Recognize your ability to be asleep to the avarice of the body and the deceptions of the soul as a potential bestowed upon you. Know that the purpose of this sleep is to make you accustomed to awakening from desires that are wrong or excessive and from things other than God.

A person is awakened from sleep by a sound reaching his ear. This is a divine breath [nefes]. God illuminates our world in the morning and opens our eyes to the world like the breath of Seraphiel who blows spirit into all the dead with his horn.

As each spirit returns to its body [vücût] it is burdened again by whatever are the encumbrances of its bodily requirements. The baker bakes, the shoemaker makes shoes.

It is the same for the arrived lovers of God. But with the difference that the spirits of the arrived, which roam the realm of spirits while asleep, awaken again to the world in order to work as worldly men awakening their followers [*sâliklerini*] to the mysteries which will raise them up, day or night, to the divine realm.

Thus the steed of the spirit is freed of the saddle of the body [*beden*] at night and takes it back on again in the day. And the animal spirit which remains in the body performs a tethering function for the divine spirit like that of a chain attached to the leg of a horse so that it will not run off and get into trouble.

According to Hazret Ali, spirits remain tied to bodies by means of a ray of light. The ray is a connection whose purpose is to prevent them from leaving their bodies at the wrong time.

In short, in was known to those great arrived persons and mighty spirits that there are persistent and mysterious bundles of rays and beams connecting spirits and bodies.

You will acknowledge how right are those who pray God to preserve our spirits, as he did Noah's ark or the Companions of the Cave, from the deluge of wakefulness to worldly ties and worldly ambitions.

You will consider and awaken to the reality that so many people asleep to the illumination of their gaze by love of God are powerless to see the arrived of God who are right next to them and in front of them, even touching them hand-to-hand.

For that reason so many are unaware of the intimacy the arrived enjoy with the true Beloved, and catch no scent of it from their company and conversation.

In order to be aware of these people of God, hidden like the Companions of the Cave in the cave of non-existence [*yokluk*], the eye must tear apart its veil of heedlessness, awakening to the divine light, and the ear must hear the voice coming to us from the realm of the Unseen [*gayp âlemi*]. As Yunus Emre said, the world is full of God the Truth and God the Truth's friends:

> God the Truth fills up the world, but no one knows God the Truth
> Look for Him in yourself, He is not separate from you

But where are those possessed of quick understanding and comprehension that they might be capable of seeing them with the eyes of inner vision. For they are invisible like spirits which are hidden.

Acquire for yourself an eye and a heart worthy of seeing them. See how the divine light shines in the hearts of those who truly love Him and are loved by Him!

Mevlana tells the following story in order to expound on the bewilderment of the ruler faced with Leyla, and the heedlessness in his bewilderment, unaware of Majnun's love and unable to see the beauty Majnun saw in her.

****

THE STORY OF THE CALIPH WHO SAW LEYLA

> The Caliph asked of Leyla, "Is it then you
> For whose sake Majnun was distraught and seduced?
415.   There are fair ones who are not surpassed by you
> "Be silent!" she said, "For you are not Majnun."
> Whoever is awake, he's the more asleep
> The wakefulness of such is worse than his sleep

As long as our spirit's not awake to God
Wakefulness is like a gate that has been barred
Every day the spirit, kicked about by thoughts
Of profit and fear of decline and of loss
Has left in it nor joy nor grace nor glory
Nor a way to make the heavenly journey

420.   A sleeper is one who with every vain thought
Has new hope and in its discourse gets involved
He thinks a demon a houri in his dream
And with that demon in lust he spills his seed
His descendents' seed spilled on unfertile ground
He comes to himself, no houri to be found
His head in a stupor and his flesh corrupt
Left by an image you see and then you don't
Flying on high through the sky there is a bird
Whose shadow speeds across the ground like a bird

425.   A fool hunts that shadow, off in hot pursuit
Running until all his strength has been consumed
Unaware that flying bird casts the shadow
Unaware what is the source of that shadow
He keeps shooting arrows after that shadow
He empties his quiver searching high and low
His life's quiver empty and his lifetime spent
Overheated from the chase of shadow-hunt
If the shadow of God on earth mothers him
He's delivered from shadows and images

430.   The shadow of God's a bondsman of the Lord
Who's dead to this realm and alive in the Lord
Have no doubt, take hold of his skirt right away
That you may be saved in time for the last day
In the image of "*He made the shadow long*"[19]
God's friends prove the light of the sun of the Lord
Don't enter this valley without evidence
Like God's friend say: "*I do not love those that set*"[20]
Go by the shadow and find yourself a sun
Grab the skirt of Shah Shams of Tabriz, hold firm

435.   If you don't know the way to this wedding feast
Learn it from Ziya al-Haq Husameddin
If on the path your throat be seized by envy
It's Satan who exceeds all bounds in envy
He holds Adam in contempt out of envy
Out of envy he wars with prosperity
There is no harder turn than this on the path
He without envy as companion is glad

---

19. Koran 25:45.
20. Koran 6:76. "God's Friend" (Khalīl Allah) is a title of Abraham. Koran 4:125.

> Know that this body is the house of envy
> The whole household is polluted by envy
> Though the body is envy's house, nonetheless
> God made that body purified and pleasant
> "*Clean My house*"[21] is the clear proof of purity
> Though spellbound by earth, it is light's treasury
> When you envy and dupe one free of envy
> Black spots stain the heart because of that envy
> Be the dust tread by the men of God the Truth
> Cover envy's head with dust just like we do

Those who saw Leyla did not find her beauty to be superior to that of other women. Kays loved her madly, coming to be known as Majnun [madman], because he saw her inner beauty. It was a unique beauty not visible to every eye, clear only to those who could see her through the eyes of Majnun. In order to see it, one had to be asleep to Leyla's external beauty and, correspondingly, awake to the divine beauty alight in her inner world. The Caliph did not see the mysterious beauty in Leyla because he did not, could not, look at her through Majnun's eyes.

What this means is that it would be better for those who are awake to the physicality, not the spirituality of beings—living or not—to stay asleep.

At the same time, there are so many who appear to be asleep but whose eyes of the heart are open to all wisdom [*hikmet*].

Remember the man who saw Satan at the entrance to the mosque and asked him what he was waiting for. It seems Satan, in order to go inside, wanted to seduce someone occupied with prayer there, but was unable to do so. He said: "I can't because one of the friends is asleep in a corner of the mosque. I'm afraid he will see me and expose my deception."

A spirit is close to God the Truth to the degree that it is awake to mysteries and sublimities. Correspondingly, a spirit awake only to the world, swept away by satanic emotions and stuck in the quicksand of worldly filth, will experience only fleeting pleasures and feelings of shame.

It is not possible for such a spirit to ascend to the realm of likeness and view that sublime realm, that is, see the lofty and divine of even the spirits.

Such a spirit is like a person who takes pleasure in sexual intercourse with Satan in a dream, and when he awakes, sees that the image which appeared to be a houri is gone, leaving him in worldly filth with an aching head.

Consider the fool who hunts the shadow of a bird on the ground while the real bird is flying in the air. He exhausts his strength and power and is left out of breath for nothing. The poor thing! He doesn't know that there is a bird in the air. He can't imagine it. He chases the shadow of it on the ground.

The blockhead shoots arrows at the shadow of the bird running on the ground. He uses up all the arrows in his quiver in this vain pursuit, but he can't hit the fleeting shadow. Many are they who exhaust in vain the arrows of time, valuable as gold, in the quiver of their span of life. The fool sunk in worldly heedlessness does not know that the shadow he chases is the reflection of God the Truth's names and attributes. To put

---

21. Koran 2:119.

aside the real and run after the image is to waste one's life and end up empty-handed and broken-hearted.

Again it is God's arrived who save people from being so mistaken and from running after seductive images. In reality, God's arrived are the reflections, the shadows of God on earth.

If you are going to seize anything, seize their skirts, so that they may protect you from spending your life in pursuit of seductive images.

Consider what your spirit has been through in order to be enveloped in your body [*vücût*] and become human in your heart:

> It fell from the sublime heavens. It passed through the realms of meaning and like-ness. It became air, it became fire, it became water, it became earth, vegetable and animal. Thereby it reached you. Staying in you is not its goal. Perhaps its goal is to stay in you without you and return to the heavens to mingle with that divine being [*ilâhî varlık*].

Don't attack it on the way like a bandit, or bar its path like the stone-hearted mountains that block roads.

Consider that your spirit has been separated from the greatest beloved. It is your discovery of the right path which will take it to its divine source.

The ones who will show you the way to that right path are God's arrived, God's friends.

You know the Koranic phrase, "How He extended the shadow." Consider how the power of God and the divine attributes are self-disclosed in the forms of the creatures. If God wished, he could have remained in His own secret realm alone like a hidden treasure. It is out of His goodness and beauty, wishing both to create us and give us great potentialities, that He created His own imagination in that vastness of his called non-existence [*adem*]. Just as He created "shams," that is, the sun, light, and shadow, in order to show to us the world He created, He created Perfect Humans, the friends, and murshids so that we would better know and see His own great reality.

Just as nothing can be seen if there is no light, it is not possible to see the great reality, that is, the greatest being, goodness, and beauty, without the illuminating support [*him-met*] of Perfect Humans.

Messenger Abraham's statement, "I do not love those that set," is also in the Koran (6:75-79). To set means to be extinguished and become invisible, like the setting of the moon, stars, and sun.

One night Messenger Abraham went to look for God, acting on a feeling he had within him, and when he saw the planet Jupiter, he said: "This is my Lord." But when it set and became invisible, he realized he had been mistaken. "I do not love those that set," he said. The next evening he saw the moon rise, and until it set, he thought it was God. Afterwards, when he saw the sun rise, he no longer had any doubt. The sun, larger and more dazzling than the others he'd seen, was God Himself.

It was when the sun set like the others that Abraham understood God was the one who had created heaven and earth, the starts and the sun.

The sun in the sky may bring an understanding person to know God, but if you find a sun like Shams of Tabriz, you will learn the realities from closer up. Bind yourself tightly to his commands and warnings. Shams of Tabriz brings one to union with God the Truth, but if you cannot find him, ask the ray of God [Ziya al-Haq] Husameddin.

But beware of envy! What perverts a person's soul and sets in motion the satan within him is that abominable envy. It was because Satan was jealous of Adam that he did not bow down to him. That is why he was driven away from God the Truth and the realm of light. Do not you then regard with envious eye those who are superior to you, especially the Perfect Humans. It is that envious gaze which makes the universe appear black as black can be. As long as you avoid envy, as long as you do not fall into the trap of the satan of envy, you will see that great light.

Think of the body [*vücût*] as a home in which intellect, comprehension and emotions [*duygular*] take shelter. The function and safety of each of them is shaken when envy intervenes. Envy blackens the pure white of their faces. Just as God makes the hearts of his prophets and friends totally purified of envy, he purifies by means of knowledge and gnosis the hearts of all those who tread the path of His love. It is enough that you intend and decide to acquire that true knowledge, that is, acquire gnosis.

God's saying to Prophet Abraham and Prophet Ishmael, "Clean my house," does not mean that the house to be cleaned is the Kaaba alone. To be sure, God did say they should clean His house because people would circumambulate it and pray inside it.

However, God's true house is the human conscience, the human heart. Every believing person will keep his heart clear of every kind of filth, including the most perilous of all heart-filth, envy.

The heart is darkened especially by envy felt toward those whose hearts are pure. Hazret Mevlana says: "Learn from my example. Before I met Shams of Tabriz I thought I knew so many things. My eye and heart were lit with the light of knowledge. But when I met him and, without feeling the slightest envy, bound myself to his gnosis, his grace, my gnosis was increased many hundredfold. My heart filled with the light of the greatest knowledge."

****

CONCERNING THE VIZIER'S ENVY

> Envy was that little vizier's origin
> In vain he cast his ears and nose to the wind
445.   He was hoping that by means of envy's sting
> His venom might reach the spirits of Christians
> Anyone who in envy cuts off his nose
> Leaves himself without ears and without a nose
> The nose is the organ by which scent's conveyed
> And by scent it's to a given place conveyed
> A person has no nose if he has no scent
> By "scent" here it's the religious scent that's meant
> If he catch a scent and leave thanks for it owed
> It's denial of grace and that eats up his nose
450.   Be thankful and bind yourself to the thankful
> Be dead before them and become eternal
> Don't invest in brigandage like the vizier
> Do not you deter the people from prayer
> That kafir vizier was counselor to the faith

But by guile he put garlic in almond cake

The vizier, so full of envy and corruption that he was willing to give up his nose and ears, was in fact a person incapable of hearing and smelling anyway. Because what use is a nose to someone incapable of catching the scent of the divine fragrance, the scent of faith, and following that beautiful scent in the direction from whence it came. And to catch the scent and not feel grateful for it is equal to not being able to smell it in the first place, or equal to being deprived of the organ of smell.

To catch a scent of faith and not be thankful for it means not to recognize the grace bestowed on you, and to persist in that will end in becoming a kafir.

****

The Sharp-Witted among the Christians Realize the Vizier is Deceitful

Everyone who could taste perceived in his speech
Something bitter coupled by a flavor sweet
He made points in which there were mixed together
Poison poured into sugary rose-water
455.   Outwardly he said, "Be steadfast on the path."
But the effect on the spirit was, "Be lax."
Though silver may appear to be white and new
Yet it blackens one's hands and one's clothing too
Although fire's face be red as sparks fly out
Look at the black work its action brings about
Although lightning appears brilliant to the eye
Yet its nature is to steal sight from the eye
For all but those who could taste and were wary
His words locked round the neck like a pillory
460.   While he was parted from the Shah for six years
Jesus' followers sought help in the vizier
People gave him their hearts and faith completely
Ready to die at his command and decree

Those among the Christians who could distinguish good from evil sensed the vizier's deception. While the vizier spoke sweetly to them, they could taste the bitterness of the poison in his words.

Just as pure white silver stains the hands black, as fire though red in color leaves black ashes behind, and as everything looks black after lightning dazzles the eyes for a moment, the darkness and corruption behind the vizier's attractive and charming words and behavior were quite clear.

The scheming vizier fooled only those whose eyes of the heart and insight [i'zan] were not open. Unfortunately their number was greater than that of the wary. The vizier had fooled common folk and made them believe in him.

****

How the Shah Secretly sent Messages to the Vizier

Messages passed between the Shah and vizier

> The Shah had assurances from the vizier
> The Shah then wrote to him: "Oh my favored one
> Unburden my heart quickly, the time has come."
> He replied, "I am now preparing mischief
> To cast into the religion of Jesus

There were letters written between the Shah and the vizier. This meant the penetration of Satan into the human soul and the inciting of the corruption in his nature which is designed to pervert it and lead it astray. The reply which the Shah received from the vizier announced a victory for sin that would make even Satan glad.

****

CONCERNING THE TWELVE TRIBES OF THE CHRISTIANS

465.   The people of Jesus had in dominion
> Ten and two commanders ruling over them
> Each single faction followed one commander
> In hope of gain each served its own commander
> These ten and two commanders and followers
> Were all bound to that evil-doing vizier
> They all put their trust in everything he said
> And took example from everything he did
> Each commander was prepared to give his life
> At the time and hour the vizier might say die

At that time the people of Jesus consisted of twelve tribes. Each was led by one Christian commander. All of the commanders and their followers had been duped by the vizier and believed in him. They were so deceived by him that they were ready to sacrifice their lives for him.

****

THE VIZIER CONFOUNDS THE TENETS OF THE GOSPEL

470.   In the name of each one he made up a scroll
> Designing a different sect for every scroll
> The tenets of each differed from the other
> From end to end contradicting each other
> In one, fasting and austerity was said
> To be the path of return and repentance
> In one he said, "Austerity profits naught
> Charity is the sole haven on this path."
> In one, "Your fasting and charity," he swore
> "Associates false gods with Him you adore
475.   All but trust in God and complete surrender
> In grief and comfort is trickery and snare."
> In one, "Service is what is necessary
> Without it, trust in God is just calumny."
> In one, "Commands and prohibitions are not

For observance, they show our efforts are naught
So our powerlessness may be clear to us
And the power of God the Truth known to us."
In one, "Don't consider yourself powerless
That is denial of grace and treacherous.

480.   See your own power, for that power is His
Know your power is the grace of Him who is."
In one, "Put aside these, for other than God
Anything held in regard is a false god."
In one, "Do not snuff out this candle of sight
For regard is the assembly's candle light
When you put by sight and imagination
You have snuffed out midnight's candlelight union."
In one, "Put it out and fear not, you will gain
Another hundred thousand sights in exchange

485.   Killing spirit's candle will make it swell higher
Make your Leyla a Majnun with self-denial
All who by renunciation leave the world
The world comes to them and much more than the world."
In one, "That which God has given unto you
He made it by design to be sweet to you
He made it nice and easy for you, take hold
Do not twist yourself with agonizing groans."
In one he said, "Renounce all that is of self
It's wrong to accept the nature of the self.

490.   Many are the easy roads, so various
Each by a people held dear as life itself
If the path were what God made easy to do
Jews and Zoroastrians would know Him too."
In one he said, "What is made easy is this
That the heart's life be the spirit's sustenance
When what our nature enjoys is past and gone
Nothing more comes of it than from brackish soil
The result it yields is nothing but regret
Nothing but loss can come of bartering it

495.   This is not easy when it's viewed from the end
It's name becomes 'difficulty' in the end.[22]
Distinguish the easy from the difficult
Consider which is in the end beautiful."
In another one he said, "Seek a master
You will not find foresight in your ancestors
The end has been seen by every kind of sect
They fell into error as a consequence
Seeing the end is not like the weaver's trade
Else how would there be contention among faiths?"

---

22. See Koran 92:10.

500.   In one he said, "You are the master yourself
        For the one who knows the master is yourself
        Be a man and not a slave to other men
        Go and take your head, don't roam in a head-spin."
        In another scroll he said, "All this is one
        Whoever sees two's a squint-eyed little dunce."
        Then, "How can a hundred things be one?" he asked
        "Whosoever thinks that must surely be mad
        Each doctrine is contrary to the others
        How are they one? Is poison one with sugar?"
505.   Until you go beyond sugar and poison
        How will you catch scent of oneness and the One?"
        That enemy of the faith of Jesus wrote
        Ten and two books of this fashion in this mode

The plotting vizier continued working to spread total depravity among the Christian tribes. On the one hand, he made the commanders so believe in him that they became his slaves. On the other, he prepared twelve scrolls, one for each of them. Each scroll contained religious tenets which contradicted the others. By demonstrating proofs in each of them, strong enough to convince the reader, the vizier broadcast varied ways of thought and belief and varied differences in belief about religion. His goal was to sow dissension among the religious leaders, each of whom would believe only in the scroll he received, and arouse total discord among the Christian tribes that believed in them.

The vizier, such a master of trickery that he could make flowing water stand still, wrote in the scrolls pronouncements of a strength sufficient to confuse those who thought the single truth was the one written in his own scroll. Each commander, supposing the truth was written in his scroll alone, would not believe in the other scrolls and because of the difference in doctrine would fall into total dissension with the other Christian commanders.

In fact, each of the varied statements of belief, thought and doctrine in these scrolls, apparently in contradiction with one another, was in reality an example of one of the varied appearances of God the Truth.

These pronouncements, proscriptions and recommendations, apparently statements of contradiction and division when viewed from outside, were for those possessed of insight [*basîret*] not a way of division but of unification [*tevhit*].

For example, one of the scrolls said: "A person must know that he is powerless before the power of God. Because he who is able to see himself as powerless is capable of comprehending the power of God."

And another: "Don't see yourself as powerless! Because you yourself are a manifestation of God the Truth's power and force. The power and force within you is a gift from God. To deny that is denial of that grace, and to say so is not to speak contrary to divine truth. The human is of a station to have a share, to the measure of his power, in both of these manifestations, and to comprehend both of them to a certain degree."

This was like first saying: "Only a perfect murshid can show you the way to reach God. Friends and prophets have been sent to so many tribes that followed not them but the satans within themselves, and thus strayed from the path. They were left in fire and darkness both in this world and the next."

And then saying: "What good can the friends, murshids, and prophets do for you? You will find the way to the truth yourself. If you cannot tell the difference between good and evil yourself, what can a murshid do for you? Suppose that two people go to a murshid, one intelligent and the other not. Even if one of them receives grace from the murshid according to his capacity, the other will not find the way to truth. Even if while he is with the murshid, he senses the right path for a moment due to the murshid's prompting and influence, even if feelings of goodness and beauty arise in his heart, when he leaves his teacher's presence he will change back to his own color and not hesitate to chase after perverse pleasures. So don't keep seeking a murshid! Reach God the Truth by means of your own will."

In reality the two statements are not contradictory, but rather perhaps, given the actualities of the soul and of the world, complete each other.

Just as the opposing elements which constitute the unity and vitality of a human body [*vücût*] are reconciled and gathered together in a single organism exhibiting the form of a whole, it is clear to every gaze, seeing or unseeing, that the one who created the creatures, seemingly as the opposites of one another, has in the same way brought forth a whole compounded of those countless and various creatures.

The tricky vizier was himself a person trapped in an imitative spirit and in the duality of imitation. He did not, he could not, see the unity formed by the contraries of the universe, or pretended not to, and with pretentiously logical statements exhibited them as "dualities" to the spirits he duped.

In order not to be trapped in the vizier's trap of divisiveness, the hearts of those who confronted him needed a spirit inclined to unity and a harmoniousness of joy and attraction.

The vizier gathered around himself the common folk who were deprived of these dimensions, and while he advised some to practice austerities and fasting, he told others that such practices meant torment for the soul and that the act of avoiding the worldly benefits which God the Truth bestows upon a person was itself an expression of disrespect for God's gifts.

He said to one, "No currency is accepted in the path of God the Truth but generosity and beautiful character traits," while he said to another, "What is the meaning of generosity? It is a claim of partnership with God. What is a human being that he should compete with the one generous God in giving gifts?" Thus he tried to exploit the clash of what he thought were opposites.

He said to one, "Only God has power." And then to another, "No, you represent the divine power on earth. Believe in the power given to you!" This is another example of how he led people astray.

Likewise, it was nothing but a trick designed to enflame the great confusion he believed he was sowing when he said, "Believe neither that you are powerful nor powerless! The best thing is to banish all that from your mind. When that is gone, the duality self-disclosed as you-ness and I-ness will be gone too." But everything he said was a lamp illuminating the way to the truth. These pieces of light were of such value that they could bring forth the great light in whatever heart, whatever mind, they might unite.

On the one hand, the vizier said, "Behold the world! He created it so that He would be shown to you," and on the other, he lined up such bright sentences as: "Extinguish the gaze that sees the world so that the eyes of the inner realm may open. Whoever abandons the world, the world will come to him."

With all of these and similar declarations, apparently contradictory but of such a quality [*mahiyet*] that each completed the other to bring forth the greatest truth, the vizier believed he'd found cause for total disagreement among the Christians.

For those unable to see the realm of manifestation, those whose eyes and hearts are swept up in error and shut to the truth, Hazret Mevlana was showing a different realm by enumerating these varied and contrary manifestations, these truths which apparently cancel out one another. But in the light of the same words, for those able to view creation with the eye of oneness, he was bringing out into the light the single and great oneness of that same realm.

It is not without reason that the number of scrolls in this story is twelve. The twelve scrolls containing twelve different doctrines point to the twelve disciples of Hazret Jesus. Here Hazret Mevlana wished to indicate that the same divine speech [*Tanrı kelâmı*], with differences great or small, can be expressed in twelve separate ways by twelve different apostles.

You will see the great truth unified in their differences and the great unity expressed openly in that truth.

****

Demonstrating that Contradiction is in the Surface Form, not in the Reality of the Way

He had no inkling that Jesus is one-hued
His nature was not with Jesus' dye imbued
From that pure vat a robe dyed a hundred shades
Comes out simple and single-hued like a ray
Singleness of hue does not bring weariness
No, it's as it is with pure water and fish

510.   Though there are a thousand colors in dryness
The fishes are engaged in war with dryness
In this parable, who's the fish, what's the sea?
What alike to the King of might and glory?
Myriads of seas and fish in existence
Bow before that bounty and munificence
Many's the rain of abundance has rained down
So the ocean might with precious pearls abound
Many suns of generosity have blazed
So that cloud and sea might learn to give in grace

515.   The rays of knowledge have struck on clay and dirt
So that seed might be accepted by the earth
Soil is trustworthy and all that you sow there
You reap of the same kind without betrayal
This trust of the soil is derived from that trust
For upon it has shone the sun of justice
Till the springtime brings the sign of God the Truth
The earth will not bring its inner secrets forth

That gracious One who gave inanimate dust
These signs and this precise action and this trust
520.   Though His grace may instruct the inanimate
His severity blinds the intelligent
There's such ferment nor heart nor spirit can bear
Whom shall I tell? In the world there's not one ear
Where there is an ear, He makes an eye to see
Wherever there's a stone, there fine jade will be
He's an alchemist—but what is alchemy?
He bestows miracles—what is sorcery?
This praise is from me abandonment of praise
For proof of my being would be a mistake
525.   [In His being's presence, one can't exist too
In His presence, what is being? Blind and blue
Were it not blind, it would be melted by Him
It would have known the heat of the divine sun
And were it not in mourning indigo blue
How would this region be like ice frozen through?]

It was clear the vizier did not realize that the light which emerges from the prism of the world in seven colors is in reality one color. He was confused by the multiplicity of the varied reports and manifestations of the religion of Jesus and had not comprehended the unity of color they expressed.

In fact that multiplicity of color, and that unity of color in multiplicity, were among the miracles of Hazret Jesus.

Messenger Jesus would put clothes of the same color into a vat. When he took them out, they would be dyed different colors.

On the other hand, when he put a garment dyed one hundred different colors into the vat, it would come out dyed one color.

What is intended by the multi-colored garment here is the garment of the human body [vücût]. The human body is dyed with the colors of human character [beşerî ahlâk]. The various desires, ambitions and worldly wants of the soul existing in it [onda nefis varlığı] appear in the variety of colors.

But this great number and variety of colors were dyed one color in the vat of Hazret Jesus's nature [mizaç]. The ambitions and contradictions of the soul did not remain in the bodies of those who conformed to the truth he showed. Their bodies were illuminated with the light of oneness and wrapped in the purity of the divine illumination [ilâhî aydınlık].

This unicolority is never a matter of monotonous sameness [yeknesaklık]. Just as fish who live underwater in a unicolored world take pleasure in the sea they live in and cannot live outside of it, in the same way there is infinite pleasure in the composition [terkip] of the divine color, which in fact is the expression of oneness, for those who can taste that light and be wrapped in that color.

In a sense, it is because the fish in that sea of oneness—the lovers of God—have tasted the great flavor in the color of oneness that they are engaged in struggle with the spectacular and absolute dryness they see in the realm of form and multiplicity and the multiplicity of color and form.

Like the fish in these parables, the seas too are each an instrument of expression. So many likenesses have been struck in order to express the multiplicity of appearance and the oneness of being. In fact the divine being [*ilâhî vücût*] is a unique being [*özge varlık*] beyond all these likenesses and is worshipped by every being likened to It.

In reality, all the seas taken together are not even one drop of His being [*vücût*]. All the suns are not one mote of His light, and all worldly gifts are not one grain of His store of generosity.

It is He who rains mercy [rain] from the skies and makes bounty rise up from the earth. With the heat of His light the soil is prepared for seed and harvest. Pay attention to how all that is born finds fresh life by His grace! This is merely one self-disclosure of His power, wisdom, and justice.

All vegetation sprouting from the soil, every bud flowering in color on the trees, every molecule [*zerre*] which finds girth and life through seed, is in reality singing hymns of His mysteries in its own language. The news springtime brings to the soil is merely one kind of divine permission for the renewal of life and the bringing forth of mysteries.

While divine power makes Its being felt in inanimate earth, how pathetic is the blindness of apparently animate and intelligent persons who remain unaware of It. But in fact there is wisdom in this too. While so many have sought God in multiplicity with the philosophers, wearing out their minds, producing opinions and splitting hairs, they have not been able to sense Him even as much as sprouting soil and budding flowers do. They are far from comprehending Him, and they are left in darkness without the light of His truth. If that too is not strange and mysterious wisdom of sublime God, what is it?

Where is the ear able to hear divine wisdom? In all the world there is not one ear that can hear those secrets. If there is, it is a rare thing, and because it is rare, almost nonexistent. If an ear able to hear as if seeing those mysteries and divine wisdom is called an eye, is it not fitting? Only the lovers of God approach this mystery, to the measure of their annihilation.

The ear of a person becomes an eye, and he acquires the capacities of taste and unveiling [*keşf*], when his stony heart has been polished like a mirror by the self-disclosure of God the Truth and he has reached the station of substance [*cevheriyet*].

God's true bondsmen [*öz kulları*] are spiritual alchemists of a sort, who melt the mines of denial [*küfür*] and defiance in people and illuminate their hearts with the light of faith. They are the ones who have with the elixir of faith illuminated the copper of denial and defiance in so many people's hearts and transformed it into pure gold. I praise them.

But only if one is able to lose one's own being [*vücût*] is it right to praise God the Truth and His lovers. If we can praise God the Truth not as "we" but in so far as we are annihilated from "we," these words will be the language of truth.

Consider: Faced with the divine being [*varlık*], to what degree is human being [*vücût*] blind and with what blueness is it veiled?

If human and all visible being [*vücût*] were not in reality wrapped in that blue color which is the color of death and mourning, and veiled from seeing the divine being [*vücût*] by the density of that color, how could it be that this world you see does not melt away before the light of His beauty, but rather remains frozen like ice and hard as stone?

In short, that beings [*varlıklar*] have a density which can be touched with the hand, and a form that can be seen with the eye, shows that they are as yet distant from becoming [*olmak*] The Truth with The Truth and blind to seeing Absolute Being [*Vücûd-ı Mutlak*].

So, according to Hazret Mevlana, to really see is to be unable to see any being in the universe but God. And just so, according to the Sufi thinkers [*mutasavvıflar*], it is easier for one of the friends to see the Creator in the beings [*varlıklar*] than to see the created.

****

The Downfall of the Vizier in this Deception

The vizier was a rash ingrate, like his Shah
He was boxing with the necessary cause
With a Lord so powerful that from no-thing
His breath sets a hundred worlds like this spinning
530.   He displays to sight a hundred like this realm
When He gives to your eye vision through Himself
If the world seems to you vast and without end
Know that for the Power it's less than an atom
This world is indeed a jail for your spirits
Hurry, go beyond into the wilderness
This world has limits and that in truth has none
That meaning is held back by image and form
Pharaoh's hundred thousand lances were turned back
By a Moses armed with just a single staff
535.   Galen knew a hundred thousand ways to cure
Jesus and his breath made them all seem absurd
A hundred thousand volumes of poetry
Blushed at one word from a man who could not read
With a Lord so completely invincible
How not die, if one is not despicable
He moves many a heart like a mountain firm
He hangs up by its two feet the cunning bird
Sharpening the mind and wit is not the way
Only those who are broken gain the Shah's grace
540.   So many who've hoarded treasure in a cave
Were turned into cow-beards by that scheming knave
What is a cow that you should be made its beard?
What is dust that you should be weeds growing there?
When a woman paled before her wickedness
God transformed her into heavenly Venus
From woman to star[23] was metamorphosis
What then, O rebel, to become clay and dust?
While spirit conveyed you to the highest sphere
You went for the lowest clay and water here

---

23. In the medieval parlance Mevlana shared, no distinction was made between stars and planets.

545.   You metamorphosed yourself by this descent
       From that being envied by the intellects
       See this metamorphosis for what it is
       Exceeding vile compared with that of Venus
       You urged aspiration's mount on to the stars
       You did not recognize Adam the adored
       But you are sprung from Adam, O reprobate
       How long will you think it noble to be base?
       How long will you say, "I'll conquer all the world
       And by my self I will fill up all the world"?

550.   If snow filled end to end all the world's expanse
       The sun's heat would melt it with a single glance
       With a single spark the Lord transforms to naught
       The vizier's sin and so many more like it
       He makes wisdom of that deceit's entity
       He makes sweet drink of that poison's entity
       He makes certainty out of what raises doubt
       He makes causes of resentment yield forth love
       He kept Abraham safe in the fiery pit
       He changes fear into safety of spirit
       His burning of cause makes me melancholic
       In His realm of specters I'm like a sophist

The heedless vizier did not realize that by abusing the religion of Jesus—a religion of God the Truth—he was warring with God.

God is not only the Creator of the universe, but of hundreds of thousands of universes, and if He so wishes, He can bestow upon you the felicity of seeing Him with His own gaze. If He does, you can reach the degree of knowing and seeing what He has created, how He has created, and what all He has the power to create, not only with the eyes in the head but also with the eye of the heart.

In that sense, the world you are now in is an obstacle, a veil, preventing you from seeing those other worlds. The day your spirit is freed from the thrall of worldly show and you begin to see the reality which the friends and prophets of God have attained, the expanse of your viewing and your felicity will be infinite.

You will call this world, where beings are on the one hand created and on the other decline and degenerate, the realm of generation and corruption. If you are taken by the eye and heart-distracting images of this world of generation and corruption, and suppose that is all there is, you will be wasting time on the path that leads to being able to see the reality of them. Being the sultan of a world is not an accomplishment [*marifet*]; accomplishment is to be a padishah [shah of shahs] with the Padishah of the two worlds.

The force of your heart should be like the staff of Moses, not like the soldiers of Pharaoh. Then you will understand the secret of how one single staff overpowered tens of thousands of soldiers.

And you will see more closely Jesus, who represents the power to do what so many great physicians working over centuries could not do, to raise the dead and bring the blind to see with one breath.

As you know, the poets of the Arabic language had even back in the age of ignorance invented the metrical system *aruz*, which adds the power of music to language, and over the centuries they composed countless numbers of passionate poems. Such poetry, the pleasure of countless hearts, was hung on the walls of the Kaaba and filled books upon books both before the time of Hazret Muhammed and afterwards.

But the day an unlettered man among them brought His revelation in the form of language, everything said before and after became an embarrassment compared with such divine speech. Because from beginning to end the signs [verses] of the Gracious Koran give voice to the most divine of music. With its rhymed prose, musical phrases and divine wisdom, it was and is the great miracle of that great unlettered prophet, and lives and will live in all centuries.

Staff, soul, and speech . . . You will come to know each of the three as a language giving voice to the divine reality. However, not a language of those who speak, but rather the language of the One who causes them to speak—you will know that.

And this:

A miracle by a prophet shines in the branches of science, art and skill which are most developed and widespread in his time. For example, in the time of Messenger Moses, belief in magic and spells was widespread as a kind of piety. Sorcerers were the most respected and feared people of the age. It was in such a time that Moses wielded his staff. He awed and terrified the sorcerers by transforming his staff into a dragon.

In the time of Hazret Jesus, medicine was known as the most excellent of professions and arts, physicians were greatly respected, and the science of medicine was showing real progress. It was in this age that Hazret Jesus stunned all physicians by performing such miracles as making the blind see by caressing their eyes with his hand and blowing upon them, and more importantly, by raising the dead in the same manner.

In the time of Hazret Muhammed, it was eloquence, beauty and artistry with words that was much in demand. Preachers and poets were the most respected people in society. The entire society felt profound awe for masters of the arts of speech. Poets and eloquent speakers were viewed as virtually holy people. It was in such a time that Hazret Muhammed declared the Koran. The masters of eloquence and rhetoric of the time were stunned by the beautiful, sublime, artistic verses recited by God's illiterate in a language whose power to influence was superior to all other forms of speech. For it was God making Hazret Muhammed speak, it was the great Creator speaking through his tongue. That is why for centuries, and still today, it has not been possible to translate the gracious Koran into any tongue with the divinity and beauty of its own melodious language. For the language of the Koran is a language of divine music. Even an ordinary music cannot be and has never been translated into another music, and that is why it is not possible to translate the verses of the Koran, each one a musical phrase, into another language with the same aural and literary power.

Only people who do not use their minds cannot understand the power and force of God. They are even more backward and pathetic than the pure who, although they are not learned, are gnostics and comprehend the greatness of God with the feeling of their hearts and the insight of their spirits. It is the person whose spirit is not backward and degraded who senses that great Being; he hastens to annihilate his own worldly being [*vücût*] as soon as he can, and taste solely the pleasure of being eternal with Him.

Since the beginning of time, fortune's wheel has been raising and throwing down those who think only their own intellect and selfhood [*benlik*] are superior to all and their own strength is indomitable. So many who believe only in their own intelligence have had knowledge apparently firm as a mountain which became their downfall.

They are like swift birds in pursuit of seed who get stuck in birdlime, and their knowledge robs them on the road like bandits. In other words, what is needed before God's grace, His power and sublimity, is not pride and mightiness but a burning heart and a bowed neck. Fantasy and pride have made laughing-stocks of many a pedant, and buried many a sorcerer in the darkness of his own spells. Like Harut and Marut, who forgot their duty to wisdom and justice when confronted by Venus's beautiful face, and who while in the land of the body [*beden*] charged with carrying out justice, were tripped up by lust and fell headlong into the well of soul and nature to remain hanging there upside-down.

So many great thinkers and philosophers have tried to find God by way of intellect and knowledge. To be sure, the efforts of those who devote their minds to finding God and informing others of God's being [*varlık*] and oneness are worthy of gratitude, and many of them have been of benefit to others, not by virtue of the ends they attained, but by the beauty of the trail they blazed. But which thinker, which philosopher, has been able to define the station reached by those who tread the path of the heart and reach Him through suffering, not by way of thought and philosophy?

Those who sense and comprehend God in their own consciences alone and find Him shining in their own hearts are the ones who attain the secret of knowing Him, of finding Him. In the end, what has been understood is that since creation began, the one way to know God, to reach God the Truth and reality, is the way of love, the way of gnosis, in a word, of the heart.

When a cow shakes its head, it shakes its beard along with it. It occurred to people watching cows that they seemed to affirm a truth by nodding their heads. To see the movement of the beard as an affirmation of the movement of the head is pleasing to the eye because it reminds one of the movements of so many bearded men.

So, when people nod their heads in affirmation like cows when others tell them a story, they conform to them like the beard of a cow. In reality, neither does the person talking to them have more brains in his head than an ox, nor does the beard nodding in affirmation have consciousness.

Those who were duped by the words of the vizier supposed they'd been inspired by an intelligent thought and conformed to his hot air like the beard of a cow. In reality, that vizier was a worldly ox. The others became his beard.

The vizier was like uncultivated ground and the others like his weeds, rather than his crop. The star [planet] Venus represents beauty and brightness. People thought that she had been ashamed of a sin she committed, and because she was ashamed, God forgave her and metamorphosed her into the star Venus. The story goes like this: Venus was in fact a very beautiful woman. She did not get along with her husband and went to bring suit against him before the two angels Harut and Marut, who were judges on earth at that time. But both of them fell in love with her beauty. They forgot they were angels, forgot even that they were judges, and invited her to be with them in private.

The woman gave various conditions if she was to agree to their desire. She wanted them to worship the idol she worshipped, to kill her husband, and she offered them wine.

The angels could not worship idols or commit murder. But they saw no harm in accepting the third condition. However, when they drank the wine and got drunk, they fulfilled the woman's other two conditions as well.

The woman went further and got the angels to tell her the Greatest Name, which they used in order to ascend to the sky. She uttered the name and ascended to the sky.

She must have begged pardon of God, for He metamorphosed her form into that of a star and made her the star Venus. As for the sinner angels on earth, he condemned them to be forced to hand upside-down in the Tower of Babel until Resurrection Day.

In reality the angels in this story, Harut and Marut, represent spirit and heart. They were charged with the duty of bringing justice and uprooting superstition. This was the reason and the duty for which they came to the human body. But they came across the mortal, seductive beauty of Venus and fell in love with her. They saw her not as a warning but as an object of lust. They drank the mind-numbing wine she served them. They became addicted to it. Because of that addiction they lost themselves in the wine of heedlessness and became capable of committing every kind of sin. In the end they tumbled down from the highest realm to the lowest and suffered horribly. Spirit is sublime and tends toward the heights, while soul and nature are base and incline toward the vilest of the vile.

While your spirit seeks to take you to the realm of likeness, the realm of meaning, why do you tie such a spirit to the earth with the bonds of the body?

Humans have been created by God in the best of statures [ahsen-i takvîm] envied even by the angels, that is, in the most superior form and composition with the most beautiful proportions upon a divine character [sîret].

That is the human reality [hakîkat] , that is why it is sublime. You bury the human, created for a realm of light, in the darkness of worldly filth and bodily [vücût] passions, transforming the human reality into animal attributes.

While the grace of God transformed a dark sinner woman into Venus, isn't it a shame that you transform a spirit created for light into earth and mud? These are two separate realms, as far from each other as earth and sky. But you are a piece of God [Tanrı parçası] sent to earth in order to rise to the skies.

You are a descendent of Adam. And like Adam you incline toward the world. But think of all Adam lost by this worldly inclination, the heavens he lost. At the same time, it is Adam who opened to you the doors of worldly trial and gave you the opportunity to prepare your spirit for the heavens.

You will learn this by seeking the ways to ascend to the stars through this worldly trial. Since you see that there are Venuses in the skies and you are even educated in astronomy, don't stay on earth, try to rise above the stars.

Your effort and action will raise you to the sublime position of a descendent of Adam. Hold your soul superior to worldly inclination, to worldly fame, dominion [saltanat], lust and other kinds of avarice! Worldly dominion is like snow, it is always condemned to melt before the sun of truth. It is enough for you not to forget that there is a light of mercy and sun of God which is now and will always be melting all evils away.

He has the power to ignite with one spark all evils and evil thoughts and melt them away. It is He who turns doubt to truth, resentment to love, and non-existence to being [varlık].

Abraham was thrown into a mass of fire and saw it as a rose garden, and picked roses in the midst of the fire. He found this virtue by knowing God and burning with love for Him. There is no fire that can burn the spirit accustomed to burn only with love of God and the fire of His attraction.

Being burned in that fire is the only thing that can save you from the fire of every kind of suffering and torment, doubt, fear, and all existing and predestined modes of going astray.

Since you hear and think, seek the ways to free yourself from doubt and sense the profound wisdom of God! In following spirit and spiritual feelings there is sublimity; in being dragged after the lusts of matter and body there is degradation. While God was creating humans, even the angels envied their humanity, awed by it . . . The human is the self-disclosure and manifestation of divine light on the face of the earth. You are a descendent of Adam . . . do not forget it! Do not thrust yourself into the condition of Harut and Marut, who were thrown from the angelic state into the prison of nature. Do not deceive yourself that you are as you have always been, that you do not change. The most pitiable change on earth is not in a person's form, his outward appearance, it is in his way of proceeding being, his state, in his character and behavior.

Focus all of your effort on action and behavior that contributes to the perfection of your soul! Do not hear the voice of the satan within, who constantly takes you by surprise! Think how poisons can bring health, how great beliefs are born from doubts, how love can take the place of resentment! The reason why the raging fire did not burn Abraham was not because it lost its fieriness but because Abraham had attained a state in which he did not burn even in such a fire.

****

THE VIZIER HATCHES ANOTHER PLOT TO LEAD THE TRIBE ASTRAY

That vizier made up another tricky ruse
He stopped preaching and withdrew in solitude
He cast his disciples into ardor's blaze
He stayed in seclusion forty, fifty days
The people went mad with longing for his states
For his conversation and his sense of taste
They kept begging and weeping the while as he
Bent double from practicing austerities
560.   They said, "There is no light for us without you
With no one to lead them, what can the blind do?
For the sake of God and your kindness to us
From now on do never stay apart from us
You are our nursemaid and we are like children
Spread upon us your shadow of protection."
"My spirit is not far from friends," he replied
"But I am not permitted to come outside."
Those commanders came in intercession
Those disciples came in self-abnegation
"O kind sir, this is for us great misfortune
We are orphaned in heart and faith without you

565.   You are making excuses while we in trial
        Heave frozen sighs from the depths of hearts on fire
        We have grown accustomed to your sweet discourse
        We have drunk of the milk of your wise discourse
        Oh God, oh God! Do not treat us cruelly
        Don't make today tomorrow, treat us kindly
        Does your heart permit that these who've lost their hearts
        Should without you end as those who have lost all?
570.   They are all writhing like fishes on dry land
        Let the river water flow over the dam
        There is nobody like you in this whole age
        Oh God, oh God! Hasten to the people's aid!"

By imitating those who withdraw into seclusion in order to be closer to God, that vizier sought to further convince those he had duped.

Now those who believed his deception pined in his absence. The vizier went so far in his ruse that he spent his retreat in a full fast, as if he believed in his own deception. When he came out into the light again and people could see him, his back was bent double, his face was pale and his lips were dried out.

This means that murshids can be phony too. They appear so golden your cannot tell the difference between the pure and the false. Of all disasters that befall people, this is the worst. To be dragged into the worst of errors by a false murshid.

His disciples called out in desperation for their false murshid, they screamed that they couldn't do without him and they believed they could not. They had been so duped by him that they sighed, wept, sent others to intercede for them, and believed every word from him would cool their own dry lips and illuminate their own darkened inner worlds.

****

THE VIZIER PUTS OFF THE DISCIPLES

        He said, "You so taken in by talk, beware
        You who seek counsel by way of tongue and ear
        Stuff wool in the ears of the baser senses
        Free your eyes from the blindfold of those senses
        The ear of the head stuffs up that inward ear
        Until this one becomes deaf, that one can't hear
575.   Be without sense and ear and be without thought
        So that you may hear the call, 'Return!' of God
        While you are awake to idle talk and speech
        How will you catch scent of the discourse of sleep?
        With talk and action we roam externally
        It's beyond the skies we travel inwardly
        Sense was sprung of earth and so dryness it sees
        The Jesus of spirit set foot on the sea
        The dry body's journey takes place on dry earth
        The spirit walks on into the ocean's heart

580.   You have passed your lifetime traveling the land
On the mountains and oceans and hinterland
Where is the water of immortality?
How will you ever cleave the waves of the sea?
Our doubt, thought and grasp are the waves of the earth
Those of the sea are effacement, wine and death
With this wine you remain distant from that wine
While drunk on this here, you are to that cup blind
Outward talk and idle chatter are like dust
Take heed! For a while make habit of silence."

The deceitful vizier took his subterfuge so far that he drove away the disciples who came to intercede with him. He said to them: "Oh you whose skills consist in seeing externals and listening with the ear! Put aside such things . . . Try to see realities with the eye of the heart and listen inwardly! Listen not to my voice, but turn within yourselves to hear the call of God the Truth, and see the vision of God the Truth, not my face. Know that the taste of the inner world will remain blocked for those whose emotions and thoughts are swept up in the external appearances of creatures. As long as a person does not annihilate his own human being [*varlık*] in the way of God the Truth, and become without eyes for worldly show and without ears for the call of the world, it is impossible for him to reach God the Truth."

(Then the vizier spoke in what was virtually the language of sincerity, saying things a true murshid would say to his disciples:)

As long as our seeing is merely worldly, we can see only the realm that is visible to us. But if we attain to the degree where we see the creatures inwardly and set out for the realms rising beyond this one, there is no end to the sublimities we will be able to see. Only then will we roam beyond the heavens, only then will we reach such a realm of felicity that we will be able to see with heart and spirit the realm of sovereignty [*melekût âlemi*], where the sublime spirits and angels are found; the realm of domination [*ceberût âlemi*], where divine power and beauty will be seen from closer-up; and finally, the realm of divinity [*lâhût*] or the Unseen [*gayp âlemi*], where absolute being is found in a state of complete incomparability [*münezzehlik*] and sanctity.

The realm which can be seen and touched is a realm of matter [*madde*]. We may call it the realm of humanity [*nâsût âlemi*] or the realm of form [*sûret âlemi*].

O children of Adam! You have lived on the land, traversed mountains and wildernesses, and you have crossed distances on the waters and oceans. While you spend your lifetimes in these potentialities and environments, let them not be wasted in misguided desires, impossible thoughts and immature fantasies.

Gnosis [*mârifet*] is to ascend to the spiritual realm [*mânâ âlemi*] and be able to drink of the water in that realm which bestows on a person eternal life. Messenger Jesus sensed the divine spirit in the cage of his flesh and put his spirit in the midst of the sea of spirituality and meaning [*mânâ denizi*]. In order for you to take wing to the heaven of the realm of reality [*hakîkat âlemi*] and rise to those levels, you must pass through the waves of the realm of form, that is, you must free yourself of the bonds tying you to the realm of matter.

To free yourself from these waves is to break away from matter [*cism*], appearance and show on the path of approaching God the Truth and to attain to the degree of annihilation, to lose oneself, on the path of God. For that, you must abandon bad habits and acquire the character of divine character alone [*ancak ilâhî ahlâkı ahlâk edinmek*].

It is after transcending these and similar degrees that a person leaves his own borrowed and mortal being [*vücût*] in an absolute annihilation and ascends to the degree of subsistence in God.

The doors to the taste of eternity are closed to a spirit on the day that spirit becomes accustomed to and addicted to worldly flavors. This is the case not only with the material tastes of the world, but even with worship of God; the day that a body [*vücût*] experiences even worship of God as a flavor, that is, becomes overly fond of any pleasure and experiences it as a "high" [*keyif*], even worship will become a poison to it.

Worldly flavors are set up in the path of eternity like obstacles, and those which are veils of light are still veils, just as much as those which are veils of darkness. Gnosis is to be able to pass beyond all the different kinds of these veils.

That is why spiritual drunkenness keeps one distant from God, just as physical drunkenness does.

In short, in the path of divine oneness you will so lose the flavors of your own body [*vücût*], your own duality of spirit and body, that you will not be able to see your body even in the clearest and most highly polished mirrors; you will reach a state of annihilation expressed centuries after Mevlana by Neşati, shaykh of the Edirne Mevlevi cloister:

> We have so removed ourselves beyond becoming, Neşâtî
> We are concealed within the burnished mirror's radiant sheen[24]

This was recalled centuries later by Yahya Kemal:

> The Shaykh of Edirne, Neşati, now at rest, has said: We
> Are concealed within burnished mirrors, we are so unseen

But where is that clear, shiny mirror? The idle chatter of the world, worldly ambitions and filth, leave the mirror of the heart covered with dirt and rust. Like the old mirrors which used to be made of metal, once the mirror of the heart is rusty it no longer shows the reality appearing in it. So don't talk too much. Either say what it is you have to say well and rightly . . . or be silent!

****

THE DISCIPLES REPEAT THEIR REQUEST THAT THE VIZIER BREAK HIS RETREAT

585.   They all said, "O wise one, you seek an excuse
      Do not tell us such things, blandishing and cruel
      Burden a beast only as its strength can bear
      Give the weak no task their power cannot bear
      Each bird's bait is but the measure of that bird
      Figs are not a morsel for just any bird

---

24. Ettik o kadar ref'-i teayyün ki Neşati / Âyine-i pür tâb-ı mücellâda nihânız.

If instead of milk you give a baby bread
Be sure the poor baby will die of that bread
But in time when that baby comes to have teeth
It will by its own self ask for bread to eat
590.   When a baby bird without wings takes to flight
Every sharp-clawed cat finds it a tasty bite
When its wings grow in it will fly by itself
Without effort, without signals true or false
Satan is left silent by your eloquence
Your discourse gives to our ears intelligence
Our ears have awareness when it's you who speak
Our dry land's a river when you are the sea
When we're with you earth, not heaven, is our bliss
You shine on all from The Fishes to the fish
595.   For us dark overcomes heaven without you
What is heaven when compared to you, O moon!
Heaven may have the form of sublimity
But the pure spirit is sublime inwardly
For bodies the sublime is in form retained
Essence is to body as meaning to name."

Fired up by what the vizier had said to them, the disciples began begging him anew. They told him what torment it was for them to be without him and remain without him.

"We," they said, "have tasted what it is to see reality in you, to attain expansiveness of heart with your guidance. Don't burden us with what we cannot bear! You don't give large bits of food to a small bird, or bread to a newborn baby.

"Perfect persons do not set tasks for those within the circle of their training which exceed their preparedness. On the contrary, they hold them for a long while within the shadow of their protection, within the circle of their gaze and their guidance, and raise them to a degree in which their animal feelings are whittled away.

"Your sublime discourse gives us intelligence, it illuminates God the Truth and the way to reality. The light gleaming in your face, in your words, shows us the light of love of God.

"Faced with the power of your words, the head of the satan of our souls is crushed, and his hands and feet are bound.

"We believe from the depths of our spirits that the path you have shown us is for us the way to reach God the Truth. Fellowship with such a friend of God as yourself gives us the sublime feeling that we are in fellowship with God the Truth Himself. Although today our feet are on the ground, we believe that it is better to be on earth with you than to be in the heavens with the angels.

"Although this universe we are in, with its heavens we see, is vast compared to us, it is nothing compared to the universes God has created and has the power to create.

"But although you too, in terms of bodily grandeur [*vücût heybeti*] and considered as a material being [*varlık*], are nothing compared to the universe we see, it is not materially but spiritually that you are great. A friend of God of your degree expresses grandeur and meaning through the greatness in his spirit even if he is small in stature.

"O you who fill the universe with light, from the stars of Pisces in the sky to the fish in the depths of the sea!

"It is difficult for us to find God without you. We are as if left in the dark and cannot see around us. It is not enough for us to merely speak your name. Just as a person may pronounce the word 'sugar' hundreds of times, but not taste it until he puts sugar itself in his mouth, neither can we sense spiritual tastes without you!"

****

THE VIZIER REPLIES THAT HE WILL NOT BREAK HIS RETREAT

"Cut your disputations short now," he replied
Make way in spirit and heart for my advice
I should not be held suspect if I'm trusted
Should I call heaven earth, I should be trusted
600.   If I am perfect, you should not deny me
If I'm not, why do you trouble and scold me?
I will not break my seclusion, soon or late
For I am occupied with my inner states

The vizier told his disciples to be silent, saying things like: "If you believe in me, you must also believe what I say. If I am your murshid, what I am doing now too can guide you. Either you will listen to me and leave this place, or you will withdraw your hearts from me and leave me spiritually as well. As you see, I am in solitude with the mysteries of the heart. How should I abandon such a state."

The answer the vizier gave to those who wanted to draw him out of his retreat was very meaningful. Although this was the inner state of a corrupt vizier, and these words were his words, it still expressed a great truth.

The vizier was saying: "If I am of the degree of the arrived, a man of this degree cannot be accused on account of his actions. He cannot be removed from his actions and his states of joy and attraction. Even if a person who has reached this degree says that white is black and earth is sky, the right thing is to think there must be wisdom in that too and believe in him.

For to be a dervish is to hear and obey [*buyruk dinlemek*]. This is the state of affairs between us and what is required of you."

****

THE DISCIPLES OBJECT TO THE VIZIER'S SECLUSION

They said, "O vizier, we're not denying you
We are not like others when we speak with you
It's out of separation that our tears flow
From the depths of our spirits we sigh and moan
A baby does not debate with its nurse, true
But it weeps knowing neither evil nor good
605.   We are like harps, you strike us with the plectrum
The plaint is not ours, you make lamentation
We are like the flute, our melody is yours
We are like a mountain whose echo is yours

79

We are moved in check and mate like chess pieces
You, O man of qualities, move the pieces
You are spirit of spirit, what can we do?
How could we exist at all when next to you?
We are bits of non-existence, our beings
Are mortal while you are absolute being

610.   We are all lions, but lions on a flag
The wind keeps them constantly on the attack
Their attack is seen and the wind is unseen
May we never be deprived of the Unseen!
Our wind and our being are your donation
Our existence is all by your invention
Not-being found the taste of being in you
You made non-existence fall in love with you
Do not hold back the delight of your bounties
Don't hold back the wine, the wine-cup and the sweets

615.   And if you do, who is there should seek them then?
Can pictures contend with him who painted them?
Do not look at us, do not gaze into us
Gaze upon your own gifts and beneficence
We were not, and we had no claims on you then
But your graciousness heard what was unspoken
The picture before the painter and the brush
Is like a babe in the womb, bound and helpless
People come before omnipotence at court
Helpless as cloth underneath the needle's point

620.   Sometimes He forms a demon, sometimes a man
Sometimes an image of joy, sometimes of pain
There is no one can move a hand in defense
None can speak concerning loss or recompense."
The Koran has explicated this, now you
Read what God said: "*You did not throw when you threw.*"[25]
It's not we who shoot the arrow from the bow
The archer is the Lord and we are the bow
This is not compulsion but domination
For sake of humility it is mentioned

625.   Our humility is proof we are constrained
The proof of our free will is our sense of shame
If there is no free will, what then is this shame?
This regret, this bashfulness and this disgrace?
Why do masters force their pupils to obey?
Why do minds vacillate from the plans they've made?
And if you say free will is just heedlessness
Of compulsion and a cloud that's hiding it
There's a good answer, and if you will listen

---

25. Koran 8:17.

You will quit denial and cleave to religion
630.   Weeping and remorse come at times of illness
Times of illness are times of full wakefulness
Times when you are ill are times when you regret
Asking pardon for trespasses you commit
The ugliness of your offense is made plain
You resolve that you'll return to the right way
You make promises and vows that from now on
Your one choice will be obedience to God
Illness, it becomes completely clear to you
Bestows conscience and wakefulness upon you
635.   Know this principle, then, you who seek the root
If you suffer pain, you catch the scent of truth
Anyone who's more awake is more in pain
Anyone more aware is more pale of face
If you're aware of His force, then where's your pain?
The vision of His all-dominating chain?
When has a person in chains been full of cheer?
When has a person in jail been free of care?
And if you see that your feet in chains are bound
And the Shah's officers keep you under guard
640.   Then don't you act like a guard with helpless folk
For that's not the way and trait of helpless folk
If you don't feel His constraint, don't say you do
And if you do, where is the sign that you do?
When you do something that you're inclined to do
That you act through your own power is clear to you
When you are disinclined and would rather not
You're fatalistic and say that it's from God
In things of this world prophets are fatalists
Kafirs view the afterworld as fatalists
645.   The prophets use free will for the afterworld
The ignorant use their free will for this world
For every bird takes wing off to its own kind
Its spirit leads on while it follows behind
Since kafirs are of the same genus as Hell
The imprisonment of this world suits them well
Since Heaven is the genus of the prophets
They speed toward the heaven of heart and spirit
This discussion has no end, and therefore we
Will go back to tell the rest of the story

All the disciples again made objections to the vizier; they showed how sincere their tears were. They said: "Our body is a harp. It is you who strike it with the plectrum and make us moan with your love. Whatever sound comes from us, and whatever we say, the composer and speaker is you! We are pure bondsmen; and it is you who makes us burn with the fire of love of God. The action and will found in us actually consists in conformity to the divine will self-disclosed in you. We believe that, according to the Koranic verse, 'God is the Creator of all things,' all of our works, words, and actions are the work of the great Creator, whom you have made known to us best of all. It is not possible to say of our being [*vücût*] that it 'is.' We are now covering distance on the path of 'not-being' [*yokluk*]. It is you who have shown us this great path." They likened themselves to chess pieces and said that the hand moving them to victory or defeat was the hand of their great murshid, who represented the divine will in their consciences.

Although in the person of the vizier they were addressing a murshid in whom they believed, it was really God they were addressing. That is why they said: "Just as pictures of lions on a flag appear to move when the wind makes the flag fly, so too is our action; the invisible wind which makes us move comes from you; it is the wind of your pre-eternal [*ezeli*] will."

The hearts of these disciples, enflamed with a true love for God, were now so excited that they addressed God the Truth directly: "It is you who created [*var eden*] us out of not-being! It is you who bring not-being to taste the flavor of being!" [*varlık*].

What is intended here by "not-being" is the immutable entities [*âyân-ı sâbiteler*] of the prophets and friends and lovers of God. God made these immutable entities fall in love with Him in pre-eternity before they'd yet had scent of body [*cisim*] and created existence [*vücût*].

If we now are imprisoned in a cage of flesh in this realm of appearances, it is so that we can feel and sense you and your separation more profoundly. Don't leave us without the flavor of the love we feel for you! Let us taste the wine of your being [*varlık*] and love. Do not leave us without the felicity of being drunk with its intoxication!

If you withhold that spiritual bounty from us, our door of entreaty will be closed as well. For even to be able to seek out your intimacy and the flavor of your love, in short, even the power to desire you, is your gift. Do not withhold from us this greatest gift.

We are images you have made. You are the sublime artist who creates us, our colors, forms, and the material and spiritual beauty reflected from you in us.

How can a picture talk to the painter who has drawn it and given it the light and shade that determines its color and form? How can it object, asking why you have given it a particular color and form? If we, forms of this mortal world, feel longing for you and entreat you, this too is the language of the power you have given us. It is the voicing of your power.

O Lord! Do not look upon us! Gaze upon your own kindness and generosity.

We see that the painter of pre-eternal nature [*ezel tabiatı*] makes for our mortal beings [*varlıklar*] sometimes the picture of a human and sometimes of a satan. We are able to comprehend the pleasure of being human, but we do not have the power to rid ourselves of the torment of being drawn in the form of a satan. O divine one, do not make us suffer the torment of remaining in a satanic form whose cage of flesh we cannot shatter!

In His Koran, God the Truth told His final messenger: "You did not throw when you threw."[26]

No, we are not the ones who shoot the arrow, we serve the function only of the bow in this affair, and the One who shoots from us is certainly God. This means that we have action and speech only by virtue of the power God gives us.

---

26. Koran 8:17.

But it is not correct to interpret this as [divine] compulsion [*cebir*]. To be sure, God is the author of every act. However, God has given us the power to distinguish between the good and evil of what we do and will do. The great proof of this truth is that we are able to entreat God, sometimes blushing in shame, "O my God! Show us the right way!" and ask for the good, the right, and the beautiful from the One who created us.

For if we had no power and no free will, how could we entreat God to bestow upon us the best of acts and actions, how would it even occur to us to do such a thing?

Considering that animals, who have spirits as we do, do not think to be shamed of their actions either before God the Truth or before the creatures, since they do not even know of doing so, how can we be heedless of the partial free will [*cüz'î ihtiyar*] given to us, the power by which we distinguish between good and evil?

We are not content with so many of our actions and behavior, even our own private perceptions and thoughts, and we seek advice from others who know better than we, or whose thinking is better or different than ours, in sum, people who are either more intelligent than us, or whom we believe to be more experienced. Many are the times when our paths have been illuminated by the lightning flash of truth born of the clash of thoughts.

In reality, it is right neither to be headless of divine compulsion nor unaware of our free will.

To suppose that there is no free will is to think that humans are lifeless matter and to misunderstand divine compulsion to such a degree as to pervert understanding.

In reality, one must know the greatness in God's attributes, "the Powerful" and "the All-Subjugating" [*kahhar*], and grasp the vastness of the capacity of the divine power to perform and direct every act [*hareket*]. In this way people may see intimately the wisdom and power of God the Truth in this realm of subsistence and annihilation, and corruption and ceasing of existence.

At the same time, it is not felicity for the human created by God as the essence [*zübde, öz*] of the worlds to be able to remain heedless of his duty to sense and comprehend the powers of will and free will within him.

A human is human to the degree that he is able to be a gnostic [*ârif*] of such power coming to him from God the Truth.

It is only when a person is ill that he awakens to awareness of good health. When you suffer some malaise and are in pain, you begin on the one hand to complain and moan, and on the other, you remember your sins and begin to repent.

Why is it that those sins seem ugly to you in times of illness and helplessness? At another time you took pleasure in committing those same sins; you so bathed in the pleasure of sin that you did not realize you were sinning.

Why have you woken up now, and to what? What is the power of this sound reasoning which has awakened in you, that you have realized the difference between good and evil? You make promises to yourself, telling yourself that if you recover from this illness you will not be bad anymore, you will not neglect your prayers, and will not be defeated by the satan within you.

Are you able, at such times of illness and helplessness, to say, "O my God! I am sinless. Because it is You who have made me commit those sins," and to attribute all of the guilt to the One who created you?

If the answer is no, it means that you have will, a free will. Know the worth of this value [*kıymet*] and wisdom which makes you sense the existence of your free will!

Hazret Muhammed said: "I know God more than any of you and I fear Him more than any of you." This beautiful saying is among the greatest of those which awakened his community to reality. Hazret Muhammed also said: "The heart is between two of the fingers of the All-Merciful; He makes it fluctuate as He desires."

So, first of all you will know the degree of God's greatness and power. Then, you will understand the worth of the value He has given you by bringing you to the human degree.

You are not a captive in the prison of God the Truth's will. You must realize that you have divine freedom, given to you so that you may enjoy peace of heart and mind as free people do.

A person whose feet are bound and who is being watched by officers has reason to think himself defeated and helpless. But it is at the very least impertinent for a person in such a situation not to realize that he is helpless and for him to try to tell others what to do.

Consider the realms through which the human spirit has passed! You set out from a realm of truth. From there you came to the realm of domination. But the angels came to you like officers of the ruler and guardians of the law. "This is not your place," they said. From there you came to the realm of likeness and meaning. They didn't let you stay there either. You continued on. Now you are at last in this realm of subsistence and annihilation. If a feeling within you is telling you, "Don't stay too long in this realm! Return to your land of origin!" know that this is the way of God the Truth and reality. Look to walking this path. But this is the path of true lovers. Those who are able to keep their lips pure of worldly tastes and their skirts pure of worldly filth walk this path.

If when you commit a sin you enjoy, you see yourself as powerful, praising yourself, "I am the one who does this!" and when you have to do something you don't like, tell yourself that it comes from God, it means you believe neither in God nor in yourself.

This is the most erroneous kind of fatalism [*cebirlilik*]. As you know, the work of the afterlife is sweet to prophets, and the tastes of the world are sweet to the ignorant.

Know that every bird flies toward its own kind. The human spirit drags the human body along behind itself. The body follows wherever the spirit leads. The spirit walks in front, the body behind.

Kafirs whose hearts find pleasing the prison of the world do not hear the inner voice calling them to return to their original homeland. They are annihilated only in the pleasures and lusts of their souls.

The prophets and friends, who hear the voice of God the Truth's invitation and comprehend the tastes of the spiritual realm, have turned their hearts not in this direction, but in that.

They have chosen not the prison of the world, but the heights of the realms of luminosity [*nûrâniyet*] and sublimity. That is why they have become established in such realms. But let us return to our story and finish it. Because there is neither limit nor end to what can be said on this subject.

****

THE VIZIER MAKES THE DISCIPLES LOSE HOPE THAT HE WILL ABANDON SECLUSION

650.   That vizier called out from within his retreat
       Saying, "Disciples, let this be known from me

That Jesus has sent me a message and spoke:
'Separate yourself from all friends and kinsfolk
Face the wall and sit alone in seclusion
From your own existence, too, choose seclusion'
I am not permitted to speak from now on
I have nothing to do with speech from now on
Farewell to you, O friends, for now I am dead
I have carried my goods to the fourth heaven

655.   So I'll not burn under the skies' fiery hoop
In corruption and in toil like tinder wood
But sit by the side of Jesus from now on
Way up high on the top of the fourth heaven."

The vizier still would not show himself to the disciples. He called out from inside to say that he was under the command of Hazret Jesus and following his path. He said that Messenger Jesus had told him not to leave his retreat and furthermore, not to speak with anyone. He revealed that Jesus, who resides in the fourth heaven, had called him to his side and that he had passed away from worldly concerns in the felicity of having reached the same degree as Jesus.

The more that the ardor and longing of the disciples increased, the more distant the vizier kept himself from them. He told them he had died to the world.

If these words were spoken in the language of a true murshid, they would mean that that a person must cut off all worldly ties of the soul, even the spirit, in order to ascend to the heavens of truth. This is the only way for a person to escape burning like a piece of wood in the circuit of worldly fire.

****

THE VIZIER SEPARATELY APPOINTS EACH ONE OF THE EMIRS AS HIS SUCCESSOR

Then he summoned the commanders one by one
To converse with each one of them all alone
To each one he said, "You are God's deputy
In the Christian religion and succeed me
And those other commanders will follow you
Jesus has made all of them depend on you

660.   Seize any commander who dares to rebel
And either kill him or keep him locked in jail
But as long as I live tell this to no one
Till I am dead do not seek this dominion
Take this scroll and the Messiah's articles
Read them clearly one by one to his people."
He spoke to each commander separately
Saying, "In God's faith you are sole deputy."

665.   He treated every one of them with honor
What he said to one, he said to the other
He gave to each one of them a different scroll
Each scroll was contrary to the other scroll

> Each of the scrolls was as different from the next
> As the shapes of letters in the alphabet
> The rules of one scroll differed from the other
> We have spoke of these differences before

The vizier summoned only the twelve commanders to his retreat. He met with each of them in private and made them the instruments of the most satanic [*İblisçe*] plot the satan within his soul had devised. He said to each of them separately: "You alone on the face of the earth are and will be my successor, and thus you alone will act for me, the sole deputy of Messenger Jesus.

"The others are required to follow you. If any rebel, certainly you can destroy them. You will do this after I am dead. I am not long for this world.

"Here is a scroll I have prepared for you. All the commands of Hazret Jesus are recorded in this scroll. You will announce them to the people of Jesus!"

That was the vizier's horrendous plot. He told each commander the same thing, as if he were choosing that commander alone as his successor, and each of the scrolls he gave them contained tenets which completely contradicted one another.

We have previously explained the contradictory thoughts in the scrolls, which would create not one division among the Christians, but twelve, and we will not repeat them here.

****

THE VIZIER KILLS HIMSELF IN SECLUSION

> Forty days more he shut the door in retreat
> He killed himself and from his body was freed
> 670.   When the people became aware he had died
> It was Resurrection Day at his graveside
> Such a great multitude gathered at his grave
> Tearing their hair and their garments, wild with pain
> That the Lord only knows what their number was
> There were Arabs and Turks, men of Rum and Kurds
> They threw the earth from his grave upon their heads
> They saw grief for him their recourse in his stead
> Those people kept watch by his tomb for a month
> Shedding tears from their two eyes in streams of blood
> 675.   Crying out in anguish at his absence, all
> Mighty shahs and personages great and small

The vizier completed his scheme by killing himself. His death increased the people's belief in him many times over. Countless people of every ethnicity wept over his grave. They mourned him bitterly. They lay on the earth of his grave, according to the custom of the time. They poured the earth of his grave on their heads. They tore their hair and clothes. Everyone, from padishahs to the humblest of folk, wept for him sincerely.

****

THE PEOPLE OF JESUS—PEACE BE UPON HIM—ASK THE COMMANDERS, "WHICH ONE OF YOU IS THE SUCCESSOR?"

After one month they asked, "O elders esteemed
Which commander has been chosen for his seat?
We want to know who takes his place as imam
And give our hands and our skirts into his hand
Since the sun has gone and marked us with its brand
Is not the recourse instead to find a lamp?
Since the loved one's union is far from the eye
We need someone who'll recall him to our mind
680. Since the rose is gone and the garden in ruin
In rose-water we shall enjoy rose perfume."
Since there is no such thing as sight of the Lord
We have prophets as deputies of the Lord
No, I have spoke wrongly, for if you conclude
Lord and deputy are two, that's vile, not good
No, they are two as long as you worship form
They are one to him who frees himself of form
When you're looking at a form you have two eyes
But you look with one light coming from both eyes
685. A man can't distinguish between each eye's sight
When he concentrates his gaze upon their light

The people began to wonder who would succeed this great friend of God. They asked the twelve commanders. "Since he is no more, who will bring us his scent?" they asked.

They wanted to find a successor for the great man they'd lost and in his being [*varlık*] and his words satisfy the need in their hearts for belief.

For God, who is not visible to the eye, is represented on earth either by the prophets or the friends.

When people surrender themselves to such a friend, it is an expression of their need for belief. For when a rose fades and withers away, that cannot be the end of everything. There is the rosewater made from that rose. The lovely smell of the rose is in the rose-water, and with it one can satisfy one's need for rose scent. The lovely scent in rosewater is in fact none other than the fragrance of the rose.

This means that the prophets are in reality not separate from the One who sends them. People who adhere to appearances [*zâhir ehli*] may suppose that God the Truth is separate from each one of His messengers. In reality His messengers are nothing other than waves of the same sea of unity, stirred by wind blowing from this or that direction.

The sea is the same sea, and when the wind dies down, all of the waves sink into that sea, passing away within it.

****

EXPLAINING "*WE DO NOT DIFFERENTIATE ANY ONE OF HIS MESSENGERS FROM ANOTHER,*"[27] FOR ALL ARE MESSENGERS OF GOD THE TRUTH

> If you have ten lamps in one place together
> Each is different in form from another
> But when you turn to face their light, you cannot
> Tell the difference between them beyond doubt
> Count up apples or quinces by the hundred
> But if you crush them, they're one, not a hundred
> In spirit there are no parts or numbering
> Neither individuals nor dividing

690.
> Unity of the Friend with the friends is sweet
> Form is headstrong, hold on tight to spirit's feet
> Melt rebellious form away by means of grief
> So you'll see oneness like treasure underneath
> And if you don't, divine grace most bounteous
> Will melt it away, O heart whose Lord He is
> He will even show Himself within our hearts
> He stitches up the dervishes' tattered frocks
> We were expansive and of one substance all
> Headless and without feet in that expanse, all

695.
> We were one single substance, just like the sun
> Pure like water, without articulation
> When that faultless light then entered into form
> It was plural like shadows of a notched fort
> Smash the fort's battlement with the mangonel
> That differences between these troops be leveled
> I would have explained this point straightforwardly
> But that even one mind may slip worries me
> The points in it are sharp as a sword of steel
> Turn and flee if you do not possess a shield

700.
> Do not come without shield against this keen blade
> For a sword is not ashamed to slash and maim
> That is why I've put the sword back in its sheath
> So a contrary reader will not misread
> We come to the story's end and now relate
> How the righteous congregation kept the faith
> How after their leader's death they rose to claim
> Their right to have a deputy in his place

Even if the number of lights burning in one place is ten, the brightness striking your face is one. If you get apple juice by squeezing a hundred apples, it is still single as juice.

This means that there can be no duality or multiplicity in the realm of God's oneness. There is no other being [*varlık*] in that realm but the being [*vücût*] of God the Truth. Look carefully at the things of the world which appear in so many colors and varieties to

---

27. Koran 2:285.

your eyes! Try to see the oneness gleaming within their variety.

To see the light of oneness is not easy, however. Many are they who have borne the ordeals of seclusions and austerities and still not been able to see that light. There have been those who could not taste the wine of oneness. But don't let that discourage you. For the wine you will taste is so delicious, and the degree you will attain so sublime, that it is worth burning in the most violent fires of separation.

For that beloved is so sublime in heart that He will show you His light one day. You will tug and tug and tear away the veils that keep you from seeing Him.

Only thus does one wear the cloak of gnosis which He sews, the cloak that is in one sense the garb of the true dervish.

In short, rise above appearances! Turn your gaze in the direction of meaning. Form is headstrong, and it does not display oneness like spirit does.

If you do not think you have the strength to do all this, then leave it to God to ordain [takdîr-i Allah]! He can easily do what you cannot. Let Him fill your heart with Himself, and be illuminated with the light of God the Truth. The love this light creates is the one power that can overcome all others.

In the realm of pre-eternity we were in the state of a single substance [cevher]. God created everything that is visible from this substance. Back when we were in that substance, we were pure as the light of day and clear as water. We consisted of light.

First of all the divine light called "the most sacred effusion" [feyz-i akdes] descended to the level of the immutable entities, and forms and pluralities in great number appeared, like notched battlements and their shadows. Then, at the level of the most sacred effusion, they entered the state of lights and spirits. At this level of spiritual being [vücût], each spirit was differentiated with a separate individuality [şahsiyet] according to its preparedness. That was how spirits came to appear in a cage of flesh called the human body [insan vücûdu] after Adam and Eve were created. Each spirit was clothed in the garment of a mortal body [vücût].

If you want to reach God the Truth and reality, you will catapult stones from a mangonel against the notches of the battlement and destroy the fort! Partitions will cease to exist and being [vücût] will become one.

However, the mystery of the subtle points of oneness in being [varlıkta birlik] is not one every understanding can easily grasp. Its points are hard like keen swords. If you do not come before them with the shield of faith and love, you will be sliced to pieces. Know that a sword is not ashamed to cut. Cutting is its duty. Don't come before that sword until you have arrived at a state in which you cannot be cut!

****

THE COMMANDERS CONTEND FOR THE SUCCESSION

One of those commanders came forward and spoke
Standing up before that righteous-minded folk
705. "I am that man's deputy, behold," he claimed
"I'm the deputy of Jesus in this age
Behold this scroll, it is proof that verily
The succession after him belongs to me."
Then another commander emerged to claim
His contention to succession was the same

He pulled a scroll from underneath his arm too
And between them came the fury of the Jew
One by one the other commanders followed
Drawing swords of tempered steel, and came to blows

710.   Each of them bearing scroll and sword in their hands
Fell upon each other like drunk elephants
Hundreds upon thousands of Christians were killed
Until their severed heads were stacked up in hills
Blood was spilled left and right, streaming in a flood
In the air mountain upon mountain of dust
The seeds of sedition sown by the vizier
Brought disaster crashing down on their heads here
Walnut shells were cracked, and those with nuts inside
Had spirits nimble and pure after they died

715.   The form of the flesh suffers slaughter and death
Like crushing of apples and pomegranates
That which is sweet becomes pomegranate sauce
While what's rotten brings forth only hollow noise
What has reality becomes clear to see
While what's rotten is left in ignominy
Strive for reality, you who worship form
For reality is wing to fleshy form
Be with reality's people so that you
May find favor and become a hero too

720.   Spirit without reality in this flesh
Surely is like sword of wood inside a sheath
While hid inside the sheath it seems to have worth
But when drawn it's only something good to burn
Do not take a wooden sword into the fray
Take a look first, so you will not lose the day
If it's made of wood, go seek another sword
And if of diamond, go then gaily forth
The sword's in the armorer's shop of God's friends
There is alchemy for you in seeing them

725.   All who know have said the same, these very words
That the wise are *divine mercy to the worlds*
Buy a pomegranate when its cleft flesh smiles
So it tells you about its seeds by its smile
O blest is its laughter, showing through its mouth
A heart like a pearl from inside spirit's pouch
But the laughter of that tulip's mouth is not
When it shows inside the black spot on its heart
When pomegranates laugh, so laughs the garden
Fellowship with manly men makes you like them

730.   Though in the wilderness you're stone and marble
You'll be a gem when you reach the heart's people

Plant love of the pure deep within your spirit
Don't give your heart save to hearts that are content
There is hope, don't go the way of hopelessness
There are suns, do not go into the darkness
The heart draws you to where the heart's people stay
Flesh draws you to prison in water and clay
Nourish the heart by the heart's compatriot
Make haste, seek your fortune from the fortunate

The pure-hearted, loyal people needed to believe and asked, "Which of you is his deputy?" The commanders immediately went into action before them.

The first to come forth called out, "I am his deputy! The scroll in my hand is my witness. His commands are written in this scroll!"

But then the second, the third, and finally all of the commanders followed him. They all made the same claim with the same belief and force. They showed their scrolls as witness.

A great argument began. The commanders drew their swords. They set upon one another, sword in one hand, scroll in the other. There was a great battle. There were severed heads everywhere. Blood flowed in a flood. Many heads were separated from their bodies. The seed of dissension and corruption sowed by the vizier had borne fruit, great misfortune had befallen the Christians.

As they were being crushed like walnuts and pomegranates in that battle, it became clear who had the light of faith within and who was rotten inside.

It is more often with death that it becomes understood who is a person of form and who a person of meaning [mânâ]. The virtues of many a human spirit become clear with death, with the breaking of the cage of flesh keeping it. It is then that every spirit rises to the level it can reach. When the spirits freed from the body are those who while still in the body [vücût] were not limited by the body, that is to say the soul, and became people of meaning, people who have reached the sublimity of meaning, they take wing to God the Truth.

But for those bodies [vücûtlar] whose interiors are rotten like the interior of a walnut or a pomegranate, death is death in every sense.

So, there are people of meaning on earth. Strive to find them and please their hearts. Then only your body will be mortal [fânî]. Don't remain empty like a sheath without a sword. Or like a wooden sword in a fancy sheath.

Don't be a wooden sword. Look to becoming a sword of meaning! The best of weapons needed for the exaltation of the spirit are found in the armory of the hearts of the arrived. The arrived, those possessed of gnosis, know the realities [hakîkatler] and are the heralds of the divine realm.

Read attentively the fruit of the pomegranate tree! Its fruit resembles the perfect murshid. It has a special way of blooming, opening the seeds inside it to view. It is as beautiful and meaningful as the laughing of a mouth with pearly teeth. For the hearts of the friends are jewel boxes for the pearls of meaning, the seeds of meaning. The seeds within a pomegranate are like the mysteries within the hearts of the friends. It is only when they smile on you that you will see the mysteries within them and the beauty of those mysteries.

How beautiful it is when that friend who knows the realities, that jewel box of jewel mysteries, opens his mouth like a smiling pomegranate. He shows you pearls of mysteries and oneness.

And pay attention of the laughing of the tulip, the tulip who on the outside is red as a rose, how dark and black is its interior. When tulips laugh, that is, when they bloom, the mourning—or perhaps the evil, who knows—within them comes into view.

The laughing pomegranate is the joy of the garden. Just as the laughter of a friend brightens the garden of the heart, it brings animation and joy. Not only the faces of the friends but their interiors, their hearts, are filled to overflowing with such a divine [*ledün*] joy. If you will taste a sip of that joy, do not miss out on their fellowship. Fellowship with those pure people will purify your heart as well. You too will become a jewel, pure and clean.

Do not lament, doubting that you will ever find those pure-hearted friends of God. Seek them out, open your interior to the fire of love of God. Prepare your heart for their fellowship. In short, desire them. Once you seek them, you will see a day when God will give them to you.

****

HONORING OF THE WORDS IN PRAISE OF MUSTAFA, PEACE BE UPON HIM, MENTIONED IN THE GOSPEL

735.   The Gospel contained the name of Mustafa
    Chief of messengers and ocean pure of flaw
    There was mention of his countenance and form
    How he fasted, how he ate and how made war
    A group of Christians who sought to do good works
    When they reached that name in reading from the book
    Would bestow kisses upon that noble name
    They would rub their cheeks upon that lovely fame
    During this mischief we've mentioned, that group here
    Were safe from the troubles and were safe from fear

740.   From the wrong the commanders and vizier did
    They sought protection in the name of Ahmed
    And their progeny also was multiplied
    They had friend and defender in Ahmed's light
    And among the Christians was another sect
    Who reviled the name of Ahmed in contempt
    They were despised because of the ruined peace
    Through the vizier's evil mind and evil deeds
    Their religion and their law were discomposed
    By the twisted, cross-eyed vision of the scrolls

745.   If Ahmed's name can be such a friend as this
    How much more when his light watches over us
    If the name of Ahmad is a fort secure
    How much more the essence of that spirit sure

It will be appropriate here to mention how a sect of Christians believed that Hazret Muhammed was heralded in certain verses of the Gospels. This faith of theirs protected that sect of Christians from following the confused ideas in the vizier's scrolls.

It was known to those Christians how Hazret Muhammed would emerge, what his beauty and created nature would be, and his missions. Before Muhammed was born they would kiss and rub their faces on the places where his name was mentioned.

Such Christians, even Jews of the same spirit, became dear to God. It was as if the light of Hazret Muhammed struck them first. But there was also a sect of Christians who did not believe in this. They fell into the clutches of the vizier's weighty plot. Their faith and the principles in which they believed became completely confused. They found right the judgments and counsel in the opposing scrolls and fell to fighting with one another.

Whereas what great felicity it is for those who even just mention Hazret Muhammed's name with a loyal heart. He is the one who protects all those who love him, who believe in his intercession, from so many troubles. Have faith in God's beloved! Know that God sent him because He loves all human beings. The great Creator out of His glory opens the doors of this world and the afterlife to those who will taste the pleasure of taking Hazret Muhammed's path.

****

The Story of Another Jewish Padishah who Made Efforts to Destroy the Religion of Jesus

> After that blood-spilling shah had, beyond cure,
> Been ruined by the evil of the vizier
> A shah from the same lineage as that Jew
> Tried to destroy the people of Jesus too
> If you want to know of this other divide
> Read: *"By the heaven of zodiacal signs"*[28]

750.
> The evil way that the first shah brought about
> On that same path this other shah set foot down
> Whoever sets an unworthy practice down
> Is pursued by maledictions every hour
> The righteous move on and their practice remains
> From the vile, oppression and curses remain
> Till Resurrection Day, all like those bad men
> Who come into being, will be facing them
> In separate veins these waters sweet and salt
> Flow inside the creatures till the trumpet call

755.
> Sweet water is inherited by the good
> What inheritance is that? *"We left the book"*[29]
> The prayers of the followers, if you will look
> Are rays shining from the gem of prophethood
> The rays circle round according to their gem
> A ray moves in the direction of its gem
> Window light runs through the house because the sun

---

28. Koran 85:1.
29. Koran 35:32

Walks the zodiacal mansions one by one
If one has an affinity with a star
He will be traveling companion to that star

760.   If Venus is his ascendant, he will then
Love and seek joy in all his inclination
And if it be Mars, he will be blood-thirsty
He will seek war and slander and enmity
There exist beyond the stars other stars too
In which there's no conjunction, no misfortune
They are traveling in other heavens beyond
Other than these seven heavens known to all
They subsist in the beams of the lights of God
Neither connected together nor apart

765.   If one's ascendant is from amongst those stars
His soul burns the kafirs like a shooting star
His anger is not like one who's under Mars
Dominating, dominated, changing form
Safe from lack or dimming is dominant light
There in between the two fingers of God's light
God the Truth scattered that light to the spirits
The fortunate held their skirts out to catch it
Whoever could that light's scattered coin obtain
From all that is other than God turned away

770.   Whoever has not possessed a skirt of love
Has got no share of that scattered coin of love
Parts have faces that are turned toward the whole
Nightingales play the game of love with the rose
The color of a cow is on the outside
Seek a man's red and yellow from the inside
Good colors are from the vat of purity
The ugly from dark water of cruelty
The dye of God is the name of that fine hue
The curse of God is the scent of this gross hue

775.   That which comes from the sea, to the sea it goes
Wherever it came from, that is where it goes
From the tops of mountains rushing streams flow down
And from our flesh the spirit mingled with love

A second Jewish Padishah appeared, a descendent of that first Jewish ruler who wanted to wipe out the religion of Jesus, and he was of the same mind and had the same fanaticism. He too wished to destroy, to wipe out, those who believed in the religion of Jesus. The coming of this second Padishah is written in the Koran.

It was during the first manifestation of Islam and its propagation, when the kafirs of the Kureysh tribe in particular saw fit to torment the first Muslims, that God the Truth sent down the chapter of the Koran, "The Zodiacal Signs," and let it be known that the kafirs had earned the punishment of God, who is the All-Dominating, the All-Subjugating.

It is said there in the Koran: "By the heaven of zodiacal signs / By the day [of Judgment] which has been promised / By the witness and what is witnessed / . . . Those who persecute the men and women believers, and do not turn in repentance, will have the penalty of Hell; they will have the penalty of the burning fire."[30]

It is said that "witness" here refers to Hazret Muhammed, and that what is witnessed is his community.

But the people of realities think that what is intended here by "witness" are the gnostics who see God, the real "essence" [zât]. What is witnessed is God Himself.

Among the children and grandchildren of a person with wickedness in his blood there will be bad ones too. There are bad ones like that in every age. In contrast, the memory of good people stays with others like a beautiful voice. There will be many good people among their children and grandchildren.

In short, neither the good nor the wicked endure in this world. But the good leaves beauty and sweetness behind in the world. Bad and damnable things ensue from the wicked, and so it will be until the Day of Judgment.

The sweet and bitter waters flowing underground flow through veins which do not mix. The sweet water-like good temperament, fairness, knowledge, skills, ideas, loves and enthusiasms of so many people come alive, without being mixed with evil, in the new generations born of them. To the contrary, those of the same ancestral line who swim in sin, arrogance and pride and all the filth of the world, making humanity miserable, are usually the grandchildren of wicked spirits.

The inheritance left to the good people is the inheritance of sweet water. You will find the virtues of that blessed water in the Gracious Koran. The Gracious Koran is a divine inheritance for good people, people who have comprehended the virtues of being human.

If you pay attention you will see the great light in all the travelers of God the Truth, whether they are arrived or on the way. That light is the light of a gem [mücevher] which illuminates all of creation, Hazret Muhammed.

Without a gem, there is no ray of light. What is fundamental is the gem. Pay attention to the light which gleams from it and returns to it and is reflected around that gem constantly! The believers who gather around Hazret Muhammed like a beautiful halo are always taking light from that gem.

In truth the sun does not endure in our sky. It travels from one sign of the zodiac to another, but no matter how long its journey, the light of the sun is never separate from the sun. That great light continues to illuminate our world and the heavenly bodies. If a house has windows on all sides, although the sun moves away from one window, it will come in through another and illuminate that house.

That is what the light of Hazret Muhammed is like.

The zodiacal signs it travels are the Perfect Human beings. The houses with windows which the light comes through are hearts seeking the path to reach God the Truth.

Thus as the great light called the Muhammedan Reality moves from one of the friends to another, it is reflected in their hearts, strikes the heart-windows of the travelers to the Truth, and enters there to illuminate the houses of faith.

You know that every person has an affinity with a star.

Heavenly bodies are as bright and near or dim and distant as the qualities God gives

30. Koran 85:1-3,10.

a person by the measuring-out [*kader*]. A person lives out a lifetime on earth according to the nature of his star.

A person whose lucky star is Venus has a temperament resembling hers. All his desire is for song, love, and desire. Just as those whose star is Mars like bloodshed, war and battle . . .

So, just as sweet and brackish water flows underground in different channels without mixing, above ground good and bad character too flows through separate conduits. The characteristic of every spirit living under these same heavens is separate and does not mix with another.

While everyone supposes he follows his own star, there is another realm of stars beyond this seven-layered heaven. The stars in that realm are the stars of the attributes [*sıfatlar*] of the sublime God. For those heavenly bodies there is no dimming and no darkness. So, if a person's fortune takes light not from the stars visible to us but from the stars of God the Truth's own names, His own attributes, which shine in His own realm of the Unseen, that person will destroy the evils of this mortal world and remain firm in goodness, beauty and being [*varlık*].

Beyond these visible heavens there are very different heavenly bodies unlike those which the sun makes invisible or which orbit around it. They are lit directly by God's light. It is unthinkable that their light could become dark, or that their existence could burn out.

That is why a person is mistaken if he thinks that his star has an independent power and effect. Like the visible stars, the divine stars of the Unseen realm have effect only in His will and His geometry, they are bright or meaningful by His judgment.

According to the Koranic verse "And We made them as stars shooting at satans,"[31] just as shooting stars hit the satans traveling with them, the Perfect Human beings who are divine stars, with their spirits which are sites of manifestation of divine aid, have the power to burn and destroy the infidelity [*küfr*] of kafirs.

So, as there are heavenly bodies burning in the state of God's names and attributes in an Unseen realm, in our world there are stars shining in the state of Perfect Human beings.

Those stars are sites of manifestation of His names and His attributes and they have risen above all deficiencies of waning or setting.

Those who concern themselves with the heavenly bodies and find a connection between the fortunes of human beings and the planets know that Mars is the instigator of many evils, disorders, massacres and great fires. Those whose heavenly body is Mars and who are subject to its rage are considered victims of its bad luck.

It is unthinkable that there could be in the stars of the arrived something apparently bright but exuding ill luck. If severity or violence should appear in the countenance of such a person, it should be known only as the self-manifestation in that countenance of God's names, the All-Subjugating and the All-Dominating.

In short, the rage of the friends is not like the rage of people who are dominated by their own souls. Because those who are dominated by their own souls get puffed up only before the weak among people. But they have been dominated by God's bondsmen [*kullar*] since pre-eternity.

Remember the hadith, "The hearts of the believers are between the two fingers of

---

31. Koran 67:5. See also 15:18.

God, He turns them as He will"! What is intended by the fingers is that the divine light is turned upon the friends. God is all His divine generosity has scattered that light over the spirits, but they have been illuminated according to their preparedness [istîdat]. They are the ones who hold out the skirts of preparedness and fill their skirts with divine light.

The sky of their hearts is illuminated. The light of the essence and divine love has filled their interiors. That is why they can no longer see any being [varlık] but God.

The skirt that gathers up the scattered light is the skirt of love. A person who has not beautified the figure of the spirit with the skirt of love will certainly not hold out that skirt to the light. If the skirts of the rose were not so beautiful, could they have been filled with the cry of the nightingale? The rose and the nightingale are in reality the lover and the beloved. But which is the lover and which the beloved? Who is scattering light, and who gathering it up? Let those who are in a position to see the lover as separate from the beloved consider that.

Parts have been turned toward the whole and the nightingale toward the rose. Love is a piece of light broken off from the divine source which longs to return to that source and pass away in it.

To whom is it granted to drink light from the divine source? Or if you should ask to whom it is not granted, that is not easy to know. Because the motley color of human beings is internal, and the motley color of animals is external.

The Perfect Human being is that vat of clarity which dyes the hearts of lovers the color of its interior. That color is colored with the color of God and that dying is colored with the dye of God. It is only after a person has been dyed with that dye that he understands the secret of the great light. He feels the pleasure of the color which the gaze of a perfect man has dyed him. Those who deny and remain in the darkness without God's light are in a black dye, they can not see the light of reality. The dye of God means the true faith in a person's heart.

My Lord! Let it be our lot [nasîb] to be dyed with that dye! The sea is the lot of the river which flows to the sea. The water of that river came from that sea, and it will go back there again. To be sure, in order to get there it will surmount many mountains, pierce many boulders. It will evaporate, become rain, become floods and rivers, always running to the sea.

The spirits of human beings also travel such pathways. With the goal of reaching the sea of oneness, they seem in a single day to cross several climes, viewing happily the roads, mountains and valleys they pass over, hollowing out beautiful cavities which they leave behind, as they flow without cease in its direction.

****

HOW THE JEWISH PADISHAH MADE A FIRE AND PUT AN IDOL BESIDE IT, SAYING, "WHOEVER PROSTRATES HIMSELF TO THIS IDOL SHALL ESCAPE THE FIRE."

> See what that cur Jew endeavored to contrive
> He set up an idol by a burning fire
> He said, "Whoever bows to this idol god
> "Is saved, and if not, he'll sit in the fire's heart."
> Since he gave this idol soul no punishment
> Another idol was given birth from it
> 780.   The mother of idols is your idol soul

That one's a snake but this one's the dragon soul
Soul is iron and stone, the idol's the spark
And with water one can extinguish that spark
When was stone and iron by water allayed?
How can a man with these two ever be safe?
Stone and iron have the fire inside of them
Water cannot have an effect upon them
River water can quench fire which is outside
How can it touch stone and iron from inside?

785.   Stone and iron are a fount of smoke and fire
From which pours out Christian and Jewish denial
Though water in jug and pitcher may run out
Spring water will flow forever without stop
The idol is foul water in a pitcher
The soul is a spring of that dirty water
The sculpted idol's like a filthy flashflood
The sculptor soul is a fount on the high road
A hundred jugs will break with one piece of stone
While water from a spring instantly spurts forth

790.   Breaking idols is easy, very easy
To think the soul easy is folly, folly
If you would, O son, know the form of the soul
Read the story of Hell with its seven doors
Every moment there's deceit and in each one
Drown a hundred Pharaohs and the Pharaoh's men
Take refuge in Moses and in Moses' Lord
Do not spill the water of faith like Pharaoh
Keep you hand tight on the One [*ahad*] and on Ahmad
O brother, be free of flesh's Abu Jahl[32]

The malicious Padishah said he would throw into the fire anyone who did not worship the idol he set up next to it. In reality, the idol was the material form of the evils of his soul within him. If that lifeless idol was a snake, the soul idol within a human being is a dragon. To kill a snake is easy, but to destroy the soul dragon is difficult. For them to still worship idols, despite the religions of God the Truth, means that they worship the dragons of their souls.

If the soul is flintstone and iron, that false idol is their spark. Even if you extinguish that spark with water, the soul will continue to produce more sparks.

Whenever flintstone and iron touch, they put forth that fire. If flintstone is the soul here, iron is lust. Each is like a fount of fire and smoke. Although an idol goes away like a flashflood, water flows without stop like fountains along roads where idols are set up, fountains whose water is bitter and polluted.

You can take a stone in hand and shatter hundreds of pitchers to be filled from that fountain: But however many pitchers are broken, the water from that spring will still not

---

32. Literally "Father of Ignorance," a nickname by which the prophet Muhammed referred to one of his enemies.

be cut off. So although the idol you can see is easy to break, as long as the satan of soul occupied with creating those idols is not broken, the world will still be filled with idols.

You know the story of Hell with its seven gates. That story also tells of the soul's adventure. There are seven levels in Hell, and sinners burn in those levels according to the degree of their sins.

The soul likewise has seven gates. These are the gates of love of the world, rage, lust, concern only for oneself, pride, envy and hypocrisy.

In short, the soul is like that treacherous and deceitful person whose beguiling and deceitful power influenced so many Pharaoh-natured people who, because they did not believe in Moses and were deceived by their own souls, were drowned, dragging their followers along with them, in the open seas of their own selfhood [*benlik*] and selfishness.

Think of this, and do not run after Pharaoh and his kind! Find a murshid who has the nature of Moses. He will protect you and save you from both worldly floods and your own soul.

Or lay down you heart and will on the path of Hazret Muhammed! Thus you will be freed in the soundest way from the Abu Jahl called the soul.

****

How a Child Raised his Voice in the Midst of the Fire and Urged the People to Come into the Fire

795.   The Jew brought forward a woman and her child
Before that idol beside the blazing fire
He took her child and he threw it in the flames
The woman's heart lost faith she was so afraid
Just when she would bow down to the idol god
The child cried out, "*Verily, I am not dead*
I am happy here, O Mother, come inside
Although in form I am in the midst of fire
The fire binds the eye in order to keep hid
That this is mercy divine raising its head

800.   Come inside, Mother, behold the proof of God
And see the feasting of the elect of God
Come inside and see water that seems like fire
Leave a world seeming water but really fire
Come in, see the mysteries of Abraham
Who found inside the fire cypress and jasmine
I thought it was death when I was born from you
My fear was great when I was parted from you
But in birth I escaped a confining jail
To a world of lovely colors and fresh air

805.   Now I see the world is like a womb to me
For inside this fire I have discovered peace
Inside this fire I have seen a universe
Every bit the life-giving breath of Jesus
A world naught in form existing in essence

While that world has form that has no permanence
Mother, by right of motherhood, come inside
See that there is no fieriness in this fire
Felicity is here, Mother, come inside
Don't let it slip through your fingers, come inside

810. You have seen the power of that Jewish dog
Come and see the power of the grace of God
It's out of compassion I tug at your foot
I'm so joyful that I have no thought for you
Call the others to come too and come inside
For the Shah has lain a table in the fire
O you Muslims, all of you, come on inside
All is torment but the sweetness here inside
Come flying like moths, all of you, come inside
The lot of those here is a hundred springtimes."

815. From amidst the multitude rang out his call
The spirits of the people were filled with awe
Then beside themselves, the people in a trance
Threw themselves into the fire, woman and man
It was for love—no one forced or prodded them—
Of the friend who makes sweet every bitter thing
Until there came such a pass that the Shah's men
Tried to stop them, crying, "It's fire, don't go in."
That Jew's face was black with mortification
He was heartsick and regretted what he'd done

820. For in faith the people grew more passionate
In destruction of the body more constant
Satan's trick got him twisted up, thanks to God
The demon saw himself black-faced, thanks to God
What he tried to rub the Christians' faces in
Ended up on his face, piled up all on him
He who tried so hard to tear the people's robe
They were left unharmed, while his was the torn robe

That malicious Padishah had a woman and her child brought up to the fire. The fire was burning in a terrifying blaze. He had the child thrown into the fire. The woman agreed to worship the idol for love of her child. But the child was not burned. It called out to her from the fire, saying, "Mother, don't worry that flames surround me, I am happy here. Don't be afraid of this fire, you come in too!

"Mother! Come! This fire is nothing but an external appearance. It looks like fire on the outside, but it is a divine light, it is the fire of love. It is the kindness God shows to his most beloved bondsmen.

"This fire is the fire of love, which best purifies everyone of worldly filth. That malicious Padishah lit it in order to kill love of God, but he did not understand what a divine love he had set aflame.

"Mother, God's most beloved bondsmen are now enjoying themselves in this fire.

I am no ordinary child, I am the child of intellect. You are the mother of my creation. Come! See how the table of love's wine has been set in this fire, see who is drinking here, how they are refreshed!

"Mother, the fire that really burns is the fire of that mortal world with arms of fire where all of you are with that malicious Padishah. Whereas in this world where I am, the secrets of Abraham bloom as great roses.

"Mother, I thought I'd seen the largest world there is when I was in your belly. The day I was born from you into the world, I died.

"In fact the world is a place so much bigger and freer than a mother's belly. But now your world seems to me as narrow as a mother's womb. I have really been born into the world of freedom now in this fire.

"Mother! Here I have ascended to the heights. I have nothing to gain here by your coming or not coming. But come, and see here the greatness of God up close. I call you to come here because I have compassion for you. Your spirit child has fallen into the fire of annihilation in God. His duty is to call you and those like you into this festival of fire. In a sense, this is the fire of purification and defense against the filth of the world.

"You too, call all those you love, all humanity, into this fire! In this fire of annihilation from worldly filth, the head is no different from the foot, and the foot no different from the head."

The child's mother could have ignored this invitation even if her child were really on fire. But her motherly spirit immediately sensed the felicity her child was enjoying.

Both child and mother, seeming to whirl in mystic audition [*semâ*] with shouts of joy, called all the people into the fire.

Their voices were so moving that those who heard understood the secret of the burning fire. They lost their will. They threw themselves into the fire, women and men, first one by one and then in droves.

Things went so far that the malicious Padishah now had to forbid the people from approaching the fire.

Thus the Jewish Padishah got himself into the most shameful situation, and the cruelty he'd wrought upon the people brought them felicity. For the people were even more bound to love of God and the fire of divine beauty than they had been before.

The Jewish Padishah himself fell into the well he had dug. That is how it is, if someone breaks the hearts of the people and oppresses them, in the end his lot will be to burn in the fire of their sighs. That is how the Jewish Padishah gave the believers a boon in the fire and prepared hellfire for his own spirit.

The dervish path is to abstain from excessive worldly pleasures and worldly passions. But this is the only path ending in God. In the fire of love, the dervish grasps the secret of being [*varlık*] refreshed by the divine elixir. When he looks back as he drinks in the light of God under green leaves in a rose garden, he sees those he has left behind in worldly passions and indulgences of the soul burning in fire. He invites them to leave the fire of the world and come to the rosegarden of the fire of love because God's attributes of goodness and kindness bloom like giant roses in his dervish spirit.

****

How a Man spoke the Name of Muhammed, Peace be upon him, derisively, and his Mouth remained twisted

He twisted his mouth intending to defame
It stayed twisted when he pronounced Ahmed's name

825.   He came back and said, "Pardon me, Muhammed
You possess subtleties of divine knowledge
In my folly I was ridiculing you
When I was the one worthy of ridicule."
When the Lord wishes to tear a person's veil
He makes him inclined to ridicule the pure
When the Lord wants to conceal a person's fault
That person breathes nothing of another's fault
When the Lord wishes to give us assistance
He makes us incline toward weeping lament

830.   O happy the eye that's weeping for His sake
O lucky the heart that's been seared for His sake
The result of weeping's laughter in the end
Blessed the bondsman who's a man of the end
Blooming green appears wherever water flows
Divine mercy appears wherever tears flow
Like the water wheel be teary-eyed and moan
So in your spirit's courtyard the green will grow
If you want tears, have mercy on those who weep
If you want mercy, have mercy on the weak

When the man ridiculed Hazret Muhammed and his mouth became twisted, he threw himself at the Messenger's feet. He said that what he'd done came out of ignorance and he asked for intercession. Tears flowed from his eyes. He was comprehending the greatness of God. He'd understood the virtue of weeping. He had faith that just as flowing water brings forth greenery, flowers and trees from the earth, tears shed on the path of God the Truth would win a person God's forgiveness.

In short, he'd learned to have faith and take refuge in the light of Islam, compassionate only to the orphans, the helpless, the oppressed, smiling on those who repent their sins, the greatness of Hazret Muhammed, and in the end he learned to taste the pleasure of weeping and being refreshed on the path of goodness.

****

The Jewish Padishah reproaches the Fire

835.   The Shah turned to the fire and said, "O fierce One
Where is your world-consuming disposition?
Where's your special quality, why don't you burn
Or has our luck caused your intention to turn
You don't forgive even those who worship you
How will he be saved who does not worship you?
You have never, O fire, been a patient one

Why do you not burn, can you not, what is wrong?
Is this a spell binding the mind or the eye?
How does fire not burst into flames climbing high?
840. Has someone bewitched you, or worked alchemy?
Is your nature reversed by our destiny?"
The fire said, "I am the same, I am still fire
In order to feel my heat just come inside
My nature has not changed nor my element
I'm the sword of God and cut by His permit
The dogs of Turkmens at the door of the tent
Cringe and fawn submissively before a guest
But if someone with a strange face should come in
He'll see the dogs pounce like lions upon him
845. I am not less than a dog in loyalty
God is not less than a Turk in mastery
If the fire of your nature brings you to mourn
The King of religion ordered it to burn
If the fire of your nature brings happiness
The King of religion put the joy in it
Ask forgiveness when you experience pain
The Creator's command gives effect to pain
If He wishes, that pain becomes gaiety
A hobble is transformed into liberty
850. Wind and earth are bondsmen, and water and fire
With you and me they are dead, with God, alive
Before God the Truth, fire stands ready always
Ever writhing like a lover night and day
Strike iron against stone and it will leap out
It puts forth its foot by the command of God
Don't strike the iron of the soul against whim
For the two propagate like men and women
Stone and iron seem to be the causes, but
O man of good character, look higher up
855. For that cause has brought forward this other cause
When did cause proceed from itself without cause?
And those causes which are to the prophets guide
Compared with these causes, those are more sublime
That cause makes this cause operate in effect
And sometimes makes it without fruit and effect
Intellects may with this cause be intimate
Those causes are with the prophets intimate
What is this cause? Say in Arabic: a *rope*
Into this well artifice lowered this rope
860. The rope moves by turning of the pulley wheel
It's wrong not to see the mover of the wheel
Beware! These ropes of these causes in the world

> Do not think them moved by fortune's giddy whirl
> Lest you stay empty and giddy like fortune
> Lest in brainlessness you burn like tinder wood
> Wind becomes fire by command of God the Truth
> But have got drunk on the wine of God the Truth
> Son, both clemency's water and rage's fire
> You'll see are from God when you open your eyes

865.   If wind's spirit were not cognizant of God
> How could it tell between the people of Ad?"[33]

The Jewish Padishah was bewildered that the fire did not burn anyone. He quarreled with it, trying to vent his rage on the fire. He screamed at the fire: "Hey, you of severe nature! Isn't it your custom to burn things? Why have you changed your ways?

What kind of strange situation is this? How can a fire of such great size not burn anything? Is it you who've changed, or has someone played the witch and put a spell over our eyes? Or is it rather our mind, not our eyes, which has been bewitched, or our fortune reversed? What is wrong, is this worthy of you?"

The fire spoke with the language of its existential state [*hâl diliyle*] in answer to the sovereign thus:

> If you want to know whether I've changed or not, if you dare, come on in! Then you will know very well how and with what force I can still burn! But I am a being [*varlık*] who represents the power of God. I am the sword of his power and I cut only if He wants me to. If He does not will it, I do not cut, and if He does not will it, I cannot burn even those creatures who most easily burn! What a pathetic ignoramus you are, you don't know that beings [*varlıklar*] are in the command only of God's power and will.

> You do not consider the following: Sublime or base, all creatures are slaves to his command. The terrifying ferocious dog who watches the door of a Turkmen tent merely wags its tail and fawns at its master's guest, just as it does at its own master, showing love and loyalty. But if a thief or an enemy approaches the tent, it turns into a lion, tearing and rending.

> To be sure, as a great fire, I am no less than a dog. And certainly God, when He wants to show His power and force, will be more powerful than a Turkmen.

> What can fire do to those who are friends of God and lovers of God? No fire can burn faith. There is no snake whose tooth can poison believers. Just as all the burning, searing, killing powers of nature are helpless before God, they are helpless before the lovers of God.

> Know this, that sorrow and gaiety, infidelity [*küfür*] and faith, are self-disclosures which befall the human heart by God's command. A person is worthy of one of them according to his heart or deed. If you experience sorrow or non-faith, ask forgiveness of God immediately. Burn like me, beg; rub your face on the threshold of God the Truth and beg that God will transform your sorrow to joy and your non-

---

33. For the people of Âd, see Koran 8:65-72, 11:50-60, 26:123-140, 46:21-26 and elsewhere (The wind was a pleasant breeze for those who believed in the Messenger, but a cause of destruction for the people of Ad, 54:18-21).

faith to faith; that knowledge and gnosis will take the place of the ignorance you have today, especially your distance from the Truth and realities.

Earth, water, fire and air appear spirit-less and dead to you and me. But they have an ear which hears only the command of God the Truth.

In the same way, fire is under God's command and constantly at the ready. You know how God's lovers are constantly waiting at the Beloved's door full of longing, wondering how and when divine beauty will appear, in the same way fire waits for God's will, wondering when He will give the command, "Burn!" That is why every fire can not burn everyone, but when it does burn, does not stop until it reduces what it burns to ashes.

You know that when iron strikes stone it produces sparks. Beware that you do not strike the stone of the soul against the iron of the soul. For just as rebellious children are born of the union of many a woman and man, from those two come sparks of infidelity, mayhem and corruption which set everything on fire.

In fact stone and fire are only the apparent causes of the birth of such fires. Pay them no mind and consider the God the Creator, who is the sole cause of all goodness and evil.

Because all exterior causes are under the command of interior [bâtın] causes, every force becomes effective according to its nature if God wishes it so. If God does not so wish, even fire whose nature it is to burn loses that effect it has.

Consider that it is not the first time that I, as fire, do not burn. Once the great fire into which Abraham was thrown by mangonel became a rose garden for him.

From that day to this, no fire has ever burned a person with the created nature [yaratılış] of Abraham.

This is a mystery, and this mystery is unknown to those who have not come to know with God. The heedless [gâfil] are like those who see only a pen writing and do not see the hand holding the pen. But what brings the hand to move too is the spirit in the body and the will in the brain [dimağ].

Thus the prophets and friends are those who see the great will that commands and gives motion to beings. That is why they see nothing but that will, in other words, God the Truth. Because in fact in the whole universe of the created and the uncreated there is no being but God the Truth.

You know the dictionary meaning of the word "cause" [sebep]. Arabic sabab, Farsi [sic] rasan, and Turkish ip all mean "rope." Turkish sebep comes from sabab, which in Arabic denotes the kind of rope used to draw up water from a well.

Now, while you draw up water from a well you see the rope, you see the bucket coming up full or empty, you even see the pulley which moves the rope and winds it on itself like a spool, but if you can't see the one who moves the pulley, you won't understand the meaning of the well, or the bucket, or the water being drawn. Because in reality it is the one who turns the pulley who brings up the water.

Do not suppose that everything that happens under this dome of the sky is the work of giddy fortune's whirling.

With the command of God the Truth, according to its place and turn the cool breeze becomes fire, fire becomes a rose garden . . . because both wind and fire are drunk with love of God the Truth and move by His command. If you have an intellect, know that sweetness and suffering are both from God. If you can open your eyes of insight, if you can tear the veils covering those eyes, then you will see that both benefit and loss are created by God; you will understand that both the goodness and evil of the soul is by the will of God the Truth, even reach the degree in which you will realize the wisdom of this.

****

THE STORY OF THE WIND WHICH DESTROYED THE PEOPLE OF AD DURING THE TIME OF HUD, UPON HIM BE PEACE

All around the believers Hud drew a line
The wind died down when it came up to that line
While it was dashing to pieces in the air
Everyone who was outside of that line there
Just the way Shayban-i Raî[34] used to draw
A circle that circled all around his flock
So when he went Fridays for the time of prayer
Wolves would not come running like Turk raiders there
870.   Not a single wolf would ever go inside
Nor a sheep wander and cross over that line
The wind of the wolf's greed and the sheep's greed too
Was bound by the circle the man of God drew
Just the way the gnostics find the wind of death
As mild and pleasant as the scent of Joseph
Fire did not sink its teeth into Abraham
For he was God's elect, how should it bite him?
By fire of lust the religious are not hurt
It bears all the rest into the depths of earth
875.   The waves of the sea rushing by God's command
Sorted Moses' people from the Egyptians[35]
When the divine command came, the earth dragged down
Qarun into its depths with his gold and throne[36]
Water and clay grazed on the breath of Jesus
And became a bird, spread its wings and flew up[37]
Water and clay breathe out your praises of God
A bird of heaven quickened by sincere heart
The light of Moses brought Mount Sinai to dance
As a perfect Sufi delivered from lack
880.   If a mountain be a great Sufi, what's strange?
The body of Moses also was of clay

---

34. Abu Muhammed Shayban-ı Râî was a Damascene. He was a friend of Sufyân al-Thawrî and famous recluse. He abandoned the world and became a shepherd in the mountains of Lebanon, thus his name Râî.

35. Koran 2:50. When Moses struck the sea with his staff, it parted into twelve paths and Moses' twelve tribes went down the twelve paths. The paths are called *sipt* and those who went down the paths, *Siptî*. When the *Siptî* passed by and it was the turn of Pharaoh's soldiers, the Kiptî, the waters closed in and they were all drowned and destroyed in the sea.

36. Koran 28:76-81.

37. Koran 3:49.

> All these wondrous things the Jewish shah could see
> Yet had nothing but denial and mockery

There was going to be a great storm. The wind went into action by God's command to destroy the Âd tribe, which had strayed from the path of God and run riot. Messenger Hûd gathered those from the tribe who believed in him and in the religion of God the Truth which he had shown them. He drew a circle around them with his staff. The terrifying wind tore to pieces whomever it found outside that circle, but inside the circle blew cool and soft as an eastern breeze.

There was a perfect man called Sheybân-ı Râî who like Messenger Hûd was accepted by God. His real name was Muhammed. He was from Damascus. He had abandoned his ties with the world and withdrawn as a shepherd into the mountains of Lebanon.

When Sheyban-ı Râî went to prayer on Fridays he would draw a line around his flocks, like Hûd had done with his staff, and entrust his flocks to God.

After he had left, neither could the sheep go outside of that line nor could a wolf cross that invisible line and attack the sheep.

The true people of God, like those sheep entrusted to God or the believers protected by the line Hûd drew around them, are safe from the harm caused by wolves of greed and storms of. As long as they stay far from worldly filth and worldly ambitions, no wolf's paw can snatch and no storm can blow away the gem of humanity from within them.

Even the wind of death gives them a new life, like the scent of Joseph which reached Jacob.

Even the fire of lust cannot burn them, just as fire could not burn Abraham. But the same lust does not hesitate to produce wolf's paws and terrifying winds and thrust the kafirs into the depths of the earth.

That is why the same sea let the people of Messenger Moses pass while destroying Pharaoh and his army.

Think of the command which thrust Qarun into the depths of the earth with his throne and his treasure! Just as water and clay were transformed into a bird of paradise when the breath of Jesus touched them, with the breath of God's affection, love and knowledge of reality, the human body made of clay and water escapes its materiality and takes wing to God.

Was not Mount Sinai material, and more, matter as large as a mountain? How is it that the mountain danced upon God's self-disclosure, whirling around?

Don't say a mountain couldn't become a friend of God, think about it. Moses was actually a piece of clay and God gave him life, power, knowledge, gnosis, will, and messengership; if He wishes, he can make every piece of clay as honored as Moses.

But show that Jewish ruler as many miracles as you like, living proofs, great powers like great fires which change their natures with God's command and do not burn those thrown into them. He will still persist in denial. Because his substance [*cevher*] is bad, his leaven is corrupt. And anyway, if those who are bad did not turn into the path of denial and spread their evils of denial over the world, how would those who are good find the path to God the Truth and reality?

****

How the Jewish Padishah engaged in Mockery and Denial and did not take the Counsel of his own Advisors

His counselors said, "Do not go beyond bounds
Do not drive the steed of obstinacy on."
He bound their hands and had them thrown in prison
He conjoined oppression upon oppression
A voice was heard when things had reached to this pass
"Brace yourself, O dog, for now arrives our wrath!"
885.   Then forty cubits high the fire flared anew
It turned into a ring and burned up the Jews
From the first in fire had been their origin
They returned to their origin in the end
They were born of fire, the members of that cult
Unto the whole leads the pathway of the part
They were only a believer-burning fire
They consumed themselves like trash in their own fire
Anyone *whose mother is al-Hawiya*[38]
His abode shall ever be al-Hawiya[39]
890.   Mothers are the seekers of their own children
Derivatives are pursued by origins
If water is imprisoned inside a tank
Wind plucks it up, for it's of the elements
Wind bears it off to its mine in liberty
Little by little, so you don't see it leave
And this breath of ours takes our spirits also
Little by little from the jail of the world
The perfumes of speech ascend on up to Him
Ascending up from us to a place known to Him[40]
895.   *In purity our breaths rise up as a gift*
From us on to the abode of subsistence
Then there comes to us recompense for our speech
Doubled mercy from the God of majesty
For in speech He gives us recourse to the like
That His bondsman may attain again the like
Thus they ascend while it descends constantly
May your ascent and your descent never cease
Let us speak Persian: I mean that attraction
And that flavor come from the same direction
900.   Every people has its eye turned to that place
Where they have formerly satisfied their taste
Each kind surely in its own kind has delight

---

38. The deepest pit in hell.
39. "But he whose balance is lacking will have his home in a pit (*hawiya*) . And what will explain to you what that is? A fire blazing fiercely" (Koran 101:8-11).
40. "Beautiful speech ascends to Him" (Koran 35:11).

The part, observe, has in its own whole delight
Or if it has the capacity of kind
To join and become one with another kind
As water and bread, which are not of our kind
Increase inside us and become of our kind
Though they do not have the form or our kind, yet
Consider them like us with regard to end
905. And if our taste is for something not our kind
It will turn out to be something like our kind
Something which bears a resemblance is a loan
In the end there's no permanence in a loan
In the fowler's whistle the bird takes delight
When it sees it's not its kind, then it takes fright
To a thirsty man a mirage brings delight
When he sees it's not water, then he takes flight
Those who have lost all take delight in base gold
But when taken to the mint it's dishonored
910. Lest you be thrown from the path by gilded things
Lest you be thrown in a well by perverse dreams
From *Kalila and Dimna* now read this tale
And seek to find the moral inside the tale

Several good-spirited people gave the sovereign advice. "Abandon denial and do not whip on the steed of obstinacy so fast," they said. The good people's recompense was that the sovereign had them bound and thrown into prison like criminals.

But at that moment divine justice, which stands against every tyranny that goes beyond bounds, self-disclosed as an overwhelming fire. "Stop!" said a voice from the Unseen. Then the same fire that had failed to burn the believers flared up forty cubits high and spread in a circle. It burned up the Jewish Padishah along with his followers.

For in pre-eternal knowledge [*ezel bilgisinde*] that Padishah and his men were creatures of Hell. Their origin was fire. Their nature was to burn like fire, and according to the principle that all things return to their origin one day, according to the law that parts which have broken off from a whole will one day return to that whole, they submitted to that great power attracting them to fire and to burning in fire and they burned in that huge fire.

Just as every woman with the preparedness to be a mother dreams of having a child in her arms, and every mother wants her child, in the same way all origins seeks those who have broken off from them.

For the same reason the water in a pool feels attracted to the water of the sea. Water trapped in a pool has a herald, unseen like wind. The heralding wind strikes the water and draws it to itself silently. It turns the water into mist and sweeps it off. It drives the many waters it has made into clouds that way off to the horizon of the sea. Then it rains it down like mercy, reuniting the water broken away from the sea back to the sea.

As something is in the objective [*âfâkî*] sense, so it is in the subjective [*enfüsî*] sense.

Like the water in the pool transformed into mist, our souls too follow a hidden wind which extricates us from the prison of the world and gradually brings us to our origin. That is why it is those who do not waste the water of life who win the victory.

It is even the same with words. For when beautiful words, those which are noble and sublime and express faith, reflection and goodness, emerge from our hearts and through our lips, they rise up to God. It is possible to call this the Miraj of speech. Fundamental to the beings which come to be with God's speech, that is, with His saying, is the spirit of speech and the meaning of creation in speech. Thus:

> That God draws toward Himself our beautiful words which ascend to God is also due to the inclination of every thing to its origin. The one who draws the most beautiful words to Himself is God, who Himself is the creator of beautiful words.

On the other hand, that God the Truth rains down mercy upon us in recompense for our beautiful words which reach God and our prayers for mercy shows that speech and prayer are accepted at that sublime court: The divine will has been pleased by that prayer.

A person who finds something beautiful and gives his heart to it should know that this means there is a resemblance of origin and meaning between him and that beautiful thing. Because every genus [*cins*] is pleased by its own kind. It can only feel distress in relation to an opposing genus.

But if another genus has in inclination to and preparedness for a genus higher than itself, it is possible that it will in time enter into that genus and become of that genus. For example, if you graft a pear sapling onto a wild pear sapling it will become a pear tree, or if you graft a peach sapling onto an almond sapling it will become a peach tree.

We are neither bread nor water . . . but the bread we eat and the water we drink becomes human with us, even increases the power of our humanity. Bread and water become in us not only flesh and fat, they become feeling, thought, faith and virtue in us.

Yes, each to his own kind. If someone takes pleasure in something not of his origin but like it, that pleasure is not abiding.

The spirit of a person of knowledge [*âlim insan*] is pleased by another's knowledge, and the virtuous person's spirit is pleased by another's virtue.

If a spirit who is not in origin a friend and virtuous, a common [*avâmdan*] spirit, is pleased by the path to God and the virtue of greatness, it means that it has a constitution favorable for the grafting of virtue.

On the other hand, if a bird is deceived by the call of a hunter who imitates a bird, and it falls into his trap, the pleasure it felt while being deceived changes in an instant into sorrow and mourning.

A mirage is not water but it resembles water. For a person whose lips are dry, a mirage is the most beautiful sight in the world. But this fantasy which grows further away more one tries to approach it does not satisfy, on the contrary, it increases thirst.

False gold is a sweet hope for someone who has lost everything. But at the mint the shame of that gold becomes evident.

Every spirit who supposes the imaginary to be real, the mirage to be water, is a confused person who is fooled by gilding and does not see the falseness of the gold. He is condemned to suffer loss in the well of heedlessness and error, and if he is human, to burn in longing for his origin.

If you want to learn about this, go and read the story of the lion in *Kalila and Dimna*.

****

HOW THE WILD BEASTS TOLD THE LION TO TRUST IN GOD AND ABANDON EFFORT

> In a sweet valley a group of wild beasts lived
> While a lion there kept them in fear and dread
> It kept springing from ambush upon them all
> And made that meadow a hard place for them all
> They plotted against the lion and they said
> "We will provide the means to keep you well-fed
> 915.   Do not now hunt prey beyond your allotment
> Lest this grass be for us a source of regret."

In a beautiful valley there were beasts of prey living in fear for their lives. A terrifying lion would eat one or several of them every day, turning their valley into a prison. In this story Hazret Mevlana likens the lion sometimes to the spirit, and sometimes to the soul.

In a sense, this lion was the lion of spirit. In the valley of life it chased after the beasts of prey likened to the feelings and material ambitions. Or this lion was the lion of soul. It hunted the spiritual faculties wandering its alley in the form of beasts of prey.

The beasts of prey thought they would choose one of their number for the lion each day, rather than live in continual. Thus the lion would not have to tire itself, and they would not live in constant fear for their lives.

****

HOW THE LION ANSWERED THE BEASTS AND SPOKE ABOUT THE BENEFIT OF EFFORT

> "Yes," he said, "If I see good faith and not fraud,
> For from Zayd and Bakr I have seen much of fraud
> I am done to death by sham and fraud of men
> I've been pricked by blow of snake and scorpion
> The man of the soul lain in wait inside me
> Is worse than all men in fraud and trickery
> *'The believer is not stung . . . ,'* is what I've heard
> Heart and spirit I take the messenger's word."

The lion did not agree to this at first. Apart from sacrificing the pleasure of the hunt, he was worried that the animals would not keep their word. And he'd had experience in this vein. The lion spirit had undergone so many things as a spirit broken off from God, taking the various roads on the way to being self-disclosed in the appearance of a human being, what scorpion stings and snake's teeth he had been target of. The lion spirit remembered the hadith of Hazret Muhammed paraphrased as, "A true believer isn't stung twice in the same snake hole," and said that a believing spirit would not go again to a place where it had suffered loss. It asked the animals if they would keep their word, wanting to establish the covenant firmly.

****

HOW THE ANIMALS ASSERTED THE SUPERIORITY OF TRUST IN GOD OVER EFFORT AND AC-QUISITION

920.   "O informed wise one," the beasts all declared then
       "One can't escape destiny by precaution
       In precaution vice and madness are stirred up
       Trust in God is better, go and trust in God
       O ferocious one, don't box with fate lest you
       Find that fate itself has picked a fight with you
       One must be dead before the decree of God
       Lest there fall the blow of the Lord of the dawn."[41]

The animals gave their word again. They told the lion to trust in God. They said that in fact whatever God has written is what will happen. But they were not able to easily convince the lion.

****

HOW THE LION ASSERTED THE SUPERIORITY OF EFFORT AND ACQUISITION OVER TRUST IN GOD AND SUBMISSION

       The lion said, "Yes, but if the guide be trust
       These means also are the Messenger's practice
925.   The Messenger in a strong voice said out loud:
       'Bind the knee of the camel with trust in God.'
       From '*God loves him who works and earns,*' take a hint
       Do not let trust in God make you indolent

The lion said to the animals: "To be sure, trust in God [*tevekkül*] is right, but only after tying the leg of the camel . . . " Because one day a Bedouin came into Hazret Muhammed's presence. He said: "O Messenger of God, shall we take the precaution of protecting the camel by binding its leg? Or shall we trust in God and leave its reins loose?" The answer the Messenger gave him was this: "First tie your camel, then trust in God!"

    Also do not forget Hazret Muhammed's hadith, "He who works and earns is beloved of God." Remember that one day Hazret Omer asked people who were not working, "Who are you?" They said, "We are those who trust in God." Omer said to them: "You are not those who trust in God [*tevekkül edenler*], you are those who eat [*teekkül edenler*]. Those who trust in God are people who first plant seed in the earth and then trust in God."

****

HOW THE ANIMALS ASSERTED THE SUPERIORITY OF TRUST IN GOD OVER STRUGGLE

       They said, "Creatures work because they're weak, you know
       Work's a mouthful of deceit sized to the throat
       Work is not superior to trust in God
       Than submission what is there dearer to God?
       Many flee affliction and find affliction

---

41. ". . . I take refuge in the Lord of the dawn" (Koran 113:1).

Many flee from a snake and find a dragon
930.   A man sets a trap and it's a trap for him
That which he thought life drained the life out of him
He locked the door with the enemy inside
Pharaoh's machination was of this same kind
That spiteful man killed a hundred thousand babes
While in his house was the one he sought to slay
Since there is so much defective in our sight
Go annihilate your sight in the Friend's sight
His sight for ours is wonderful recompense
You'll find in His sight the aim of all intents."[42]
935.   Till a child is able to run and to grasp
He can only mount upon his father's back
When hand and foot grow strong and he becomes vain
Then begins the ordeal of struggle and pain
The spirits of creatures flew from loyalty
Without hand and foot on into purity
When the command "*Get you down*"[43] took hold of them
Rage and greed and contentment imprisoned them
We crave milk, we are Presence's family
He said, "*The creatures are of God's family.*"
He who causes rain to come down from heaven
Is capable in mercy of giving bread

The animals considered belief in work to be a weakness and said that a person cannot properly be said to have faith as long as he does not believe that every benefit is given by God and that God will not leave his believing bondsman without sustenance; those who do not believe this and who earn and work in order to earn are those who dilute their faith with trickery.

Those who flee rain to get caught in hail and those who flee a snake to fall into the lair of a dragon are both afflicted by the same disease of greed [*tamah*]. And so it is to be caught in the paw of the malady of profit and earnings when there is such an easy, sure and harmless way as trust in God. Many are they who have given their lives in the ambition to earn. They fall into the well dug by their own disease of earning.

A person who has an enemy inside his house can shut the house's doors and windows and secure them against the enemy's assault as much as he likes, but to what avail? While there is within the body an enemy like the soul overcome by greed, what external bandits is a person waiting for?

You know the story of Pharaoh: Because the oracles said a child born of the Tribe of Israel would bring disaster upon the pharaohs of Egypt, the ruler of Egypt ordered that all males born among the children of Israel be killed. For that reason perhaps one hundred thousand children were killed. But when the woman who gave birth to Moses put him in a basket and left him in the Nile, and the basket caught in some branches by Pharaoh's Nile villa, Moses was rescued from the water by Pharaoh's wife Aasiyah herself. She

---

42. Hadith: "When I love him, I become his eye, his ear."
43. Koran 2:36,38, 7:24.

loved the child very much and raised him in secret. Thus while a hundred thousand children were lost outside, the one who would bring disaster down on Pharaoh's head and punish him was raised in his own house.

Only when we annihilate our sight in the sight of that great Beloved and see the creatures with His eye are we saved from seeing wrongly, and only then do we see the most beautiful of realities and understand that all of the beauties and all of the riches we want to see and want to reach are in the place we see with His sight.

You know that grown-ups carry children who do not yet know how to walk and talk and ask for what they want. The child is an innocent who surrenders himself to that grown-up and is content with what he is fed. If we too remain innocent like children toward God, submit ourselves to Him and are content with the sustenance He gives us, we will taste the felicity and security of being in the embrace of God the Truth.

If we do not do that and behave in the selfish and arrogant manner of a babe whose hand and foot grow strong as he gets older, and trusting in the strength of his hand and foot, rejects the truth and thinks he can do anything and earn anything through work, then like that child we will meet with various difficulties and trials.

Before we came to this world, that is, to the "hand-and-foot" level, we used to take wing from "loyalty" and with the wings of this spirit fly to "purity." When our spirits reached the level of humankind [*beşeriyet*] we acquired various attributes and continued down our path in this realm.

But in this realm the spirits, having earlier seen God's pre-eternal [*ezelî*] kindness and grace, did not fail to remember the beauties of that pre-eternal world they had separated from to come here and to long for that original homeland.

Why should we be afraid to trust God in this realm? Why should we fear, when we are all that great God's children. The great power carrying us in its embrace, giving us bounty and sustenance, is His kindness, his gift. Just as He lets rain fall from the sky for us, He surely and without difficulty gives us every kind of mercy and gentleness in kindness and bounty.

****

THE LION AGAIN ASSERTS THE SUPERIORITY OF EFFORT OVER TRUST IN GOD

"Yes," the lion said, "but the Lord of bondsmen
Has set down a ladder right in front of them
One has to climb up toward the roof rung by rung
Here fatalism is vain expectation
You have sound feet, why do you pretend to limp?
You have hands, why do you keep concealed your fist
When the master put a spade in the slave's hand
He knew without words what his master had planned

945.   Hand and spade alike are also signs of Him
Thoughts about the end are expressions of Him
If you will take His signs upon your spirit
And in loyalty to them give your spirit
He will give you many signs of mysteries
Take your burden and give you authority
You carry burdens, He will have you carried

You receive commands, He will have you received
You hear His command, it will be you who speak
You seek union and united you shall be
950.   Free will is the work of gratitude for grace
Your fatalism's denial of that grace
Gratitude for free will makes your free will more
Fatalism takes divine grace from your palm
It is like sleeping on the road, do not sleep!
Lest you miss seeing gate and court, do not sleep!
Do not sleep, you thoughtless fatalist, beware!
Except beneath that tree laden with fruit there
So the wind will shake the branches constantly
And pour on the sleeper's head fine things to eat
955.   Fatalism is like sleeping among thieves
How shall a chick that flies too soon find safety?
And if you should turn up your nose at His signs
Thinking you're male, you're female, you'll realize
You will lose the measure of your intellect
A head becomes a tail without intellect
For ingratitude is ominous and vile
It bears ingrates into the depths of the Fire
If you trust in God, trust Him with your working
Sow seed, then count on the All-Dominating."

The lion does not deny the correct aspects of this view. He knew that God is able to give fortune to His bondsmen even if they do not work.

But he believed that great God had placed a ladder under His bondmen's feet. They had to climb this ladder in order to get to a high place. They could go up to the roof rung by rung. Why should a person who could walk make himself lame? For example, God the Truth has given all humans a duty, even a skill. And for example, when a master puts a spade in his slave's hand, it is clear what he wants the slave to do and what the slave will do.

Like the spade, every hand and foot God has given to his creatures, especially humans, is certainly the instrument and sign of a charge to be performed. He gave the intellect to humans as instrument of a sublime charge also. Since that is so, how is it that people can leave all these instruments rusty, or leave them to get rusty?

Be true to what God has given you and show your loyalty to that sign; signs of divine mysteries will be given to you to the degree that you are loyal.

Your duties now are piety [*tâat*] and worship, they are incumbent on you. Now you listen to commands. Tomorrow you can be giving commands and showing the way. Your word can be God's word, your will can be God's will. But if you do not do that and have recourse to perverse fatalism [*cebrîlik*] and the path of compulsion [*cebir*], you will let all these graces escape your grasp!

If you have intelligence, do not fall asleep on the road before seeing the gate of the court of oneness! Don't let your place of refuge be far from the shadow of that fruit tree. Because from the branches of that tree, which is the body [*vücût*] of the Perfect Human, fall the fruits of love and gnosis. Seek him! Let those fruits fall upon you.

Fatalism is to fall asleep among thieves, abandon work and combat and conform to the soul, bending one's neck to its voice. But like the flight of a chick whose wings have not yet grown, that will end in a painful fall.

Do not forget that a head is a head to the extent that it has an intellect and can use that intellect. When a head has lost the ability to use its intellect, how is it different from a tail?

Know that you are charged with the duty of expressing gratitude toward God! So work, struggle, and trust in God! Don't forget that in this way you will have such a protector and forgiver as God!

****

THE ANIMALS AGAIN ASSERT THE SUPERIORITY OF TRUST IN GOD OVER EFFORT

960.   They all shouted out, saying, "Those men of greed
       Those who sowed the seed of trusting in the means
       Hundreds of thousands of women and of men
       How is it they were deprived of fortune then?
       Myriad ages since the world has begun
       Hundreds of dragon-like mouths gaping open
       Those knowing folk have concocted such designs
       They tore mountains from the ground by their designs
       The Lord of majesty has described their plots
       'Though they be such as to shake the mountain tops'[44]
965.   But the share allotted pre-eternally
       Nothing by hunting or work has been received
       They all failed in their designs and industry
       There remains the Maker's acts and His decrees
       Acquisition's but a name, Ye of good name
       O trickster, don't think work more than fancy vain."

Although the dispute was represented as being between animals, this was a debate over intellect, thought, and sound reasoning [*akl-i selîm*] between humans who possess self-knowledge and humans who do not. The lion's position in this debate was reminiscent of something Hatem-i Assam said. One day someone came and asked Hatem-i Assam, "Where does your food come from?" He received the answer, "I eat of God's treasury." Then he asked, "Does God give you bread from the sky?" Hatem said, "If the earth were not His, He would give it from the sky."

But the animals persisted in their view. They raised their voices, trying to convince the lion that he had to believe them.

Throughout history hundreds of thousands of men and women have passed through this world, working and struggling, but they were unable to attain their desires and died in poverty and deprivation.

Furthermore, people who have concocted plots and designs to raise mountains from their foundations in order to escape from destiny [*kazâ ve kader*] have also had to bend their necks to the writing on their brows. To work against that writing on the brow has

---

44. "Such as to shake the hills" (Koran 14:46).

never been more than a vain fancy. In the end, whatever God has willed, that is what has happened.

   Hazret Ali has said as much also. If sustenance had been distributed in the world as the bondsmen wished, no one would have served anyone. But the wishes of Sublime God [Yüce Tanrı] have not self-disclosed in that way, He has given in the degree measure that He wished.

****

How Azrael Glanced at a Man and the Man Fled to the Palace of Solomon, and Exposition of the Superiority of Trust in God over Effort and the Paucity of Benefit in Effort

> In the forenoon there arrived a freeborn man
> At the Palace of Justice of Solomon
> His face pale with pain and both of his lips blue
> Solomon asked, "O Master, what's wrong with you?"
970.   He said, "Azrael just gave me such a glance
> Full of animosity and virulence."
> "Ask whatever you desire," Solomon said
> "Order the wind, O life-protector," he said
> "Off to India to carry me away
> Maybe once there your slave can keep his life safe."
> How people flee the dervish's poverty
> Thus are they gobbled up by vain hope and greed
> Fear of poverty is like that man's terror
> See India as greed and exertion here
975.   Solomon then commanded the wind to speed
> Him to India to an isle on the sea
> The next day at the audience and council
> Solomon then enquired of Azrael
> "Did you look at that Muslim in anger so
> That he would then go and wander far from home?"
> He said, "When have I looked at anyone out of spite
> I passed him on the road and looked in surprise
> For God the Truth had commanded me to take
> Charge of his spirit in India today
980.   Stunned, I thought had he a hundred wings to fly
> India would be too far for him to fly."
> Now you come, consider by analogy
> All the world's affairs, open your eyes and see
> Whom should be flee from? Ourselves? Absurdity!
> Whom shall we steal from? From God? What perfidy!

A simple person ran to Messenger Solomon in fear and dread. He said that he saw Azrael on the road and Azrael gave him a look full of rage and violence. He begged Messenger Solomon, saying, "Command the wind! Let it take me to India. So that Azrael will not see me here and take my spirit!"

The state of this simple person is like that of those who run from dervishood[45] to take refuge in the world, while they could avoid worldly ambitions and mature in the contentment and renunciation of dervishood.

What good can come of fleeing to India to escape what is written on one's brow? What is to be gained by fleeing the virtues of dervishood and drowning in greed? Hazret Ali has said: "People have excessive greed for the pleasures of the world. But worldly pleasure is mixed with sorrow." Many a time it has been understood that a padishah could only be saved from the malaise he suffered by putting on the shirt of a happy man; and many a time it happened that a happy man did not have even a shirt on his back to give such a padishah. And if the grace called daily bread could be gotten by strength and force, hawks would get the food of sparrows.

So, Messenger Solomon commanded the winds. They brought the man fleeing from Azrael to an island at the end of India. The next day Solomon told Azrael about it. "Why did you look at that man so angrily?" he asked. Azrael said, "I didn't look at him angrily, I looked at him in surprise. Because God the Truth had ordered me to take his spirit in India. I thought to myself that if this man had had not two but two hundred wings, he would not be able to be in India at the hour I would take his spirit there."

So, even with the help of Solomon, the result of fleeing the contentment and virtue of dervishood for the pleasures and ambitions of the world is the same. In fleeing from yourself, and worse, from God, you arrive at the most dead-ended of roads, the most perilous of errors.

Compare yourself in Azrael's eyes with the man who fled to India! Consider that you yourself are that man.

****

THE LION AGAIN ASSERTS THE SUPERIORITY OF EFFORT OVER TRUST IN GOD AND EXPOUNDS THE ADVANTAGES OF EFFORT

> Said the lion, "Yes, but you should consider
> The struggles of the prophets and believers
> God the exalted made their struggles succeed
> And the cruel trials they endured in cold and heat
985.   The plots they made were subtle in every way
> *Graceful is everything that is done in grace*
> The celestial bird was snared by traps they set
> Their deficiencies all turned to increment."
> As much as you can, Master, exert yourself
> Following the path of God's friends and prophets
> Struggle's not to engage fate in fisticuffs
> It is what fate itself has imposed on us
> I'm a kafir if there can be injury
> In walking the path of faith and piety[46]
990.   Your head's not cracked, don't bandage it anymore

---

45. *Dervişlik*, the condition of being a dervish.

46. "And never would God make your faith of no effect (Koran 2:143). Also, regarding how God will never allow the rewards of the believers and the virtuous to be lost, see 3:171,195; 7:170; 9:120; 11:115; 12:56,90; 18:30.

Work a day or two and laugh forevermore
He who seeks in the world seeks in the wrong place
He who seeks the afterlife seeks a good state
Cold and lifeless are plots set for worldly things
But inspired those set to renounce worldly things
To dig one's way out of prison—that's a plot
To block up the tunnel—that is a cold plot
This world is a jail and we are prisoners
Dig a hole and be your own deliverer!

995.   What is the world? It's to be heedless of God
It's not merchandise and silver, wives and sons
As for wealth borne for the sake of religion
The Prophet said, *Good are wholesome possessions*
Water inside a boat decimates the boat
Water underneath the boat supports the boat
Since he cast from out his heart wealth and lucre
Solomon referred to himself as "pauper"
A jug with a stopper on a stormy sea
With its heart full of wind will float on the sea

1000.   When you have poverty's wind inside of you
On the water of the world you rest secure
Although the whole world may be your property
Kingdom in the eye of your heart is nothing
So bind the mouth of the heart and seal it up
And from the divine wind chimney fill it up[47]
Pain and remedy are real and so is work
The doubter works in his denial of work

The lion spirit again answered the beasts of prey. Among those who have worked hardest in the world, and made war when necessary, there were also God's messengers and friends. If these messengers of God had only trusted in God, could they have enjoyed victory for their beliefs? They chose both to believe in God and trust in His grace and forgiveness, and to work ceaselessly in order to put forth good works and prepare good possibilities for their peoples. And that was the command and reality which the great Creator announced to those sublime spirits.

So, to work and achieve great material and spiritual rewards is not contrary to trust in God and not a lack of resignation to fate. It is right for us to choose the way of those greatest and most intelligent of humans too. One should consider that the actions, like the words of the messengers and other believers who were created with a great subtlety of spirit and achieved spiritual maturity, are of a subtlety and grace in conformance with themselves.

Consider what God says in His Koran! There is no one who has suffered loss in the way of faith and never can be. Know the truth in the statement, "If anyone has suffered the slightest injury in the way of faith and piety, I am a kafir," and go toward that truth.

Don't choose laziness. Work as much as you are able and increase your strength by

---

47. "We taught him knowledge from Ourselves" (Koran 50:65).

working. Go work and then see! They say a person who weeps in his sleep laughs when he wakes up.

You are like a man who bandages his head although it is not wounded, for although your have the strength for both work and worship, you think yourself to be handicapped, sick, broken and forced, and you are losing the chance to both work and struggle, and to devote yourself to God and train your spirit. In this transient world which passes quickly as a dream you need to cook, mature by being cooked in the fire of love, zeal, and lawful combat and holy war. If you can enter the presence of that greatest padishah in a state of complete spiritual maturity, it will be the greatest happiness you could ever enjoy.

To desire the world is to be unaware of God. Beautiful clothes, honorable earnings, love of wife and son is not the world. The world is everything that distances you from God. When the things I say to you are of such a degree as to separate you from God, they too are the world. As long as wealth, children, women and clothes do not separate you from God the Truth and from worship, they do not injure you.

The example of the water and the boat is like that too. For a boat to move forward, for it to do beneficial work, it of course needs water, that is, the sea. As long as sea water stays outside the boat it is beneficial, it acts as a road. But when the same water gets inside, it sinks the boat. A tightly-stoppered jug will float on the surface of water. If the water of the world does not enter a person's heart and his heart is full of the love of God, he will float out to the ocean like a ship with unfurled sails.

The best recourse in order to rise out of the prison of the world to the sky of eternity and freedom [*âzatlık*] is to take a spade and dig a hole big enough for you to get out. While digging the hole, you must sprout the wings of love and try to destroy the burdens of humankind [*beşeriyet*], that is, worldly bile, which you carry in your body/being [*vücût*].

The only way is for your spirit to find the potential to rise up and take wing to great God's sky of immortality and eternity. Messenger Solomon possessed great worldly fortune and it was only after expelling the love of wealth and property from his heart that he was able to taste the pleasure of dervishood more profoundly. Solomon generally liked to be with poor people who had rich hearts, and eat with them. One day a heedless person said to him: "Why do you sit with paupers and lepers and eat with them?" Solomon answered: "Because I love only those whose hearts are rich."

A tightly-stoppered jug containing only air will float in water, traveling on it without sinking. And consider the person whose interior is filled with the air of love of God while his mouth is shut tight against all the unruliness of the soul and the world. Such a person will certainly move forward over the ocean of the world without sinking, and reach sublime destinations.

A person whose heart is filled with the air of dervishood will move along the surface of the water of the world, that is, will not be distracted by love of the world but travel the realm of spirit. Worldly possessions are not a matter of concern in their sight but a natural development. It is furthermore a pleasure and a duty for them to benefit from worldly wealth and bounties, and to work for their increase and benefit to others.

But there is no love or desire for worldly goods in their heart's eye. All the bounties of the world are as nothing in their heart's eye. If you have understood this wisdom, bind tightly the mouths of your hearts! And seal them! So that the water of love for the world does not leak inside; but do not leave your heart empty. Fill it with knowledge of God and love of God so that it will be easy for that great love to take wing to the skies.

****

HOW THE SUPERIORITY OF EFFORT OVER TRUST IN GOD WAS ESTABLISHED

> Many such proofs were brought forth by the lion
> The fatalists were fed up answering them
> 1005. The hare and the jackal and the deer and fox
> Gave up on fatalism and further talk
> To the fierce lion they swore then covenants
> That in this bargain he'd suffer no expense
> That each day's ration would arrive without pain
> And he would not need to make another claim
> On whomever the lot fell from day to day
> Cheetah-quick to the lion he'd make his way
> That cup went around and when the hare's turn came
> He cried, "How long will this tyranny remain?"

The lion kept bringing forth proofs. He convinced the fatalists. Most of the animals gave up the debate. They were convinced of the virtues of work. In the end the animals gave their word to the fierce lion that an animal would be assigned to him every day, without his having to go to any trouble or being kept waiting for even a moment, and the lion would not be able to find cause for complaint in any of their behavior.

That is what they did. Every day whichever animal was chosen, he would run quickly to the lion and surrender his flesh and spirit.

When it came the hare's turn, he shouted, "How long will this trial continue?"

It has been explained previously that Hazret Mevlana assigned various meanings to the lion in this tale depending on the context. To an exterior view [*zâhir gözüyle*], the animals are lazy people who reject work, and the lion is someone who makes efforts and is hardworking. In the tale's inner meaning [*bâtın manasında*], the animals represent the faculties of the soul and satanic thoughts, and the lion, the intellect of return [*akl-i maâd*] (the intellect which seeks its origin). In these couplets, the lion has been taken as the commanding soul [*nefs-i emmâre*], and the animals as spiritual faculties, and the hare as the intellect of return.

The hare's objection meant that he was not willing to be the prey of the lion of the soul nor for the faculties subordinate to him to be food for the lion, and was beginning to take measures to annihilate the soul.

****

HOW THE ANIMALS OBJECTED TO THE HARE'S DELAY IN GOING TO THE LION

> 1010. They all said to him, "How many times have we
> Sacrificed our lives in troth and fealty
> O Rebel, don't seek to dishonor our name
> Go, be quick, lest the lion become enraged!"

The animals argued with the hare. "We've kept our word all this time, we sacrificed our lives for the word we gave," they said. The animals, who think the lion soul cannot be defeated, or these spiritual faculties who have been defeated by the soul, are unaware of the knowledge and mysteries of the intellect and, unable to think of a plan to deal with the disaster, can't think of any way except to sacrifice themselves as food for the lion. "Hurry! Hurry! Don't offend the lion and don't make him angry!" they said.

****

THE HARE'S ANSWER TO THE ANIMALS

"O friends," he replied, "grant a respite to me
By my ruse you may escape calamity
By my ruse it may be that your lives are saved
A legacy to your children to remain
Every messenger in his community
Has bid them come thus to a place of safety
1015.   Though he seemed small like the pupil of the eye
He'd seen the Creator, not the earth and sky
They thought him small like the pupil of the eye
None reached the might of the pupil of the eye."

The hare thought differently, and he represented the intellect of return; he'd found a way to be free of the lion soul. "Give me time and opportunity, and I will free you of that calamity," he said.

The hare was speaking like a friend or prophet of God, reminding them that the friends and prophets had freed their followers or communities from so much filth of the world and so many dragons of soul. To be sure, most of their peoples had at first thought the prophets were small men and did not believe in the truths they brought and the paths they showed.

And so it happened this time.

****

THE ANIMALS OBJECT TO WHAT THE HARE SAID

The animals said, "You ass! Listen to us!
Don't forget you are a hare, keep to your place
What is this nonsense, that never has occurred
To the minds of others who are your betters
You are prideful, or fate must have us in view
If not, when could this speech suit the likes of you?

The animals told the hare to mind his place. "You be a hare, not an ass," they said. Clearly these faculties of body and soul looked down on the intellect. Many an animal much more powerful than the hare had sacrificed himself to the lion without complaint. How could a little rabbit stand against that mighty force?

The brainless soul dragon was unaware of the beneficial existence of intellect and its power to overcome difficulties.

****

THE HARE ANSWERS THE ANIMALS

1020.   "O friends," he said, "God the Truth inspired me
       Strength of mind was given to a mere weakling
       That which was taught to the bees by God the Truth
       Is not for the lion and the wild ass too
       The bee constructs hives full of fresh, juicy sweet
       God opened that door of knowledge to the bees
       That which God the Truth has taught to the silkworm
       Is that skill something an elephant could learn?
       Adam, made of earth, learned from God such wisdom
       That it shone through up to the seventh heaven
1025.   He shattered the angels' name and good repute
       Blind is he who is in doubt of God the Truth
       Iblis, the so many thousand years' zahid
       Was made to muzzle the mouth of that young steed
       So Adam would not roam that lofty mansion
       And drink the milk of knowledge of religion
       Devotees of the sensory sciences
       Muzzled by them, get no milk from that knowledge
       Into the drop of the heart there fell a gem
       Which God did not give to the skies and oceans
1030.   O form-worshipper, how long this love of form?
       Has your meaningless life not got free of form?
       If form were the thing that made a man humane
       Ahmad and Abu Jahl both would be the same
       A painting on a wall's like a man in form
       Take a look and see what's lacking in that form
       It's spirit that picture lacks, for all its glow
       Seek that rare gem so difficult to find, go!
       The head of every lion in the world bowed
       When God gave a hand to the Companions' dog[48]
1035.   What harm to the dog from its abhorred form
       When its spirit is plunged deep in light's ocean?
       It's not in pens to set form's qualities down
       In letters we write are 'just' and 'learned' found
       'Learned' and 'just' are all meaning, say no more
       You won't find them anyplace, behind or fore
       The sun of spirit does not fit in heaven
       From not-place it strikes in body's direction."

The hare, that is to say, the intellect, spoke again. He said to the animals: The inspiration I receive is from God. That is how great and mighty thoughts have been granted to a weakling. Don't be preoccupied with how small or large a form may be. Can a lion make honey like a bee, or an elephant weave a cocoon like a silkworm? Isn't the same

---

48. Koran 18:9.

true of humans? That humans, created of earth, have illuminated the seven heaves with the intellect and knowledge learned from God the Truth is the work not of the human body but the intellect and gnosis humans have.

God gave humans such intellect and virtue that the angels comprehended the power in humans and learned that they themselves were deficient compared to them. You know that Satan had worshipped God for hundreds of thousands of years. In the end, he abandoned the right road because his thinking was envious and greedy and he did not use his intellect and fell into the greatest of errors.

Just as a strap is tied around the muzzle of a calf in order to prevent it from drinking its mother's milk, the mouth of Satan's intellect was bound too. Because of his pride and arrogance, Satan was deprived of God's greatest bounty and great God presented the knowledge of His own sublime realm to the hearts of Adam and the progeny of Adam.

That is why to think material knowledge enough and remain unaware of the knowledge of truth brought to you by the prophets and friends of God, not learning the knowledge of God, is to be like a calf who cannot drink its mother's milk because its muzzle is bound with a strap.

Neither the spirit mind [*can dimağı*] nor heart's lip of persons who act according to their own intellects in matters of the world and the afterlife, and remain uninformed about the mysteries of the friends and the prophets, are wetted by divine knowledge or the taste of love of God.

Only those who have been able to turn the faces of their hearts toward the arrived [*ermiş insanlara*] rise up from the pleasures of this material world and grasp the secrets of the delights of the heart. The like of that gem which falls into the heart exists neither in the seas nor the skies. Inside the heart there is a drop of blood the size of a pearl, but soft like a drop of April rain and so beautiful, and that is the gem in which life [*hayât*] and spirit are found like buried treasure. This tiny spot is the center [*merkez*] of spirit and life, and it is called the heart's black speck [*süveyda-yı kalb*].

But neither angels nor oceans have the strength to carry the sacred [*mukaddes*] spirit carried by this tiny speck [*noktacık*] in the heart. For the breadth of the skies and the oceans is not enough to contain the spiritual greatness in this tiniest of specks. And O you whose heart's eye is closed! There are all around you so many sublime meanings[49] in forms so small as to be invisible to the eye, and all of the divine mysteries are within them. Only those who look at them with the eye of the heart can comprehend the divine mysteries in these tiny atoms [*zerre*].

In any case, it is one thing to see meaning, and another to see form.[50] The gnostic is someone who can see not form in form, but meaning in form. Both Hazret Muhammed and Abu Jahl had the form of a man, but where is Hazret Muhammed and what is Abu Jahl's nature?

Look at the pictures of humans made on the surface of stone, and the sculptures carved out of stone. It is only because the gem of life [*can*] is lacking in these forms, which are in appearance no different than humans, that they do not have the spirit and heat of live bodies.

---

49. Note that "meaning," *mânâ*, is often synonymous with "spirit." The idea is that the interior reality of something is its meaning.

50. Note that "meaning," *mânâ*, is often contrasted with form and synonymous with "spirit." The idea is that the interior reality of something is its meaning.

You know that the only animal to receive the good news it would go to Heaven was Qitmir, the dog belonging to the Companions of the Cave, whereas the king of the animals and the most awesome of them, the most sublime in both form and power, is the lion. But to what avail, since no lion has had the interiority [*mânâ*] that was found in an apparently contemptible and despicable dog.

In letters we write, pens cannot relate the forms and pictures of what we write but only their spiritual values [*mânevî değerler*], such as knowledge and rectitude. Because knowledge and rectitude are meanings, not forms. For that reason it is not possible for them to be contained in drawings and pictures. And thus there is no spiritual virtue we can tie to a form and located in place or time.

One must know that all of these qualities invisible to the eye strike the material world from the world of not-place. So how could the spirit sun [*can güneşi*], which is not contained by the skies of that realm of not-place, be limited by the forms and shapes of the material world.

****

ABOUT THE HARE'S KNOWLEDGE AND THE VIRTUE AND ADVANTAGE OF KNOWLEDGE

This discussion has no end, now lend an ear
Pay mind to the story of the long-eared hare
1040.   Sell your ass ear and purchase another ear
For this discourse can't be heard by an ass ear
Go and see the foxy tricks played by the hare
See the lion-catching trap laid by the hare
Knowledge seals the dominion of Solomon
Knowledge is spirit and the whole world is form
It's because of this art that before humans
Helpless are creatures of sea, plain and mountains
Before him panther and lion shake like mice
Before him crocodiles pale and jump in flight
1045.   Fairy and demon make haste for the coastline
Each one finds another secret place to hide
Man has many enemies hid in secret
A cautious man is a man of intellect
There are hidden creatures, evil and goodly
Who strike blows upon the heart's door constantly
If you enter into a river to bathe
And a thorn in the water causes you pain
Though the thorn beneath the water's not in view
You know it is there because it's pricking you
1050.   Pricks of inspiration, also temptation
Come from thousands of beings, not just from one
Wait until your senses have become transformed
Till you'll see them and the question is resolved
Till you see whose speech it is you have denied
And who it is you have taken as your guide

125

This discussion has no end. Now give ear to the hare's story. Abandon your ass ear, which hears only the sounds of externality, and achieve an education of the ear whereby you can hear only the sounds of the heart. Perhaps a Perfect Human may give you that ear.

Only with such an ear can you hear how a tiny little hare got a great big lion to fall down a well and understand it not merely as an event but in its meaning [*mânâ*].

Messenger Solomon commanded the birds, the wolves, the jinn and the ants by virtue of his seal. That seal was actually the seal of knowledge, the charm [*tılsım*] of knowing the truth.

The power which makes human beings able to rule those in the mountains, seas and skies resides in their knowledge and gnosis. Knowledge is also the virtue which makes the human, who is made of water and earth, that is, clay, human. Only those who possess knowledge and gnosis know by their knowledge the right road to take.

It is the gnosis in a person which leaves savage beasts like lions and tigers in the position of a mouse facing a human, and the single power which makes demons and fairies flee and hide in the shadows in fear of humans.

But it is also for this reason that humans have countless enemies hiding in the shadows. They make humans anxious, discontented and fearful. So that that the human heart is a realm wherein mix the whisperings of satans and the sublime inspirations of angels. People who have good spirits in which real gnosis and love of God reside are far from these dangers.

These many enemies of humans, psychic [*mânevî*] enemies like anxieties and material enemies like creatures that crawl and sting, are actually powers [*kuvvetler*] of God, some of light and some of fire. Those of light are close to people whose leaven is of light, and those of fire to people who have Hell in their destiny [*kader*].

You go into a river to bathe. A thorn on the river bottom pierces your foot. You only notice this hidden enemy when it pricks your foot. But you do not notice many a thorn of evil piercing the foot of your heart. Love of the world and various kind of greed are such unanticipated thorns which pierce the human heart.

You'll say there is no such thing as jinn or angels. If you doubt their existence, wait a bit. When death comes, you will have the secret of seeing them with the eye of certainty [*yakîn gözü*].

If you have not given your heart on the path of God's friends and prophets and attained the realm of ardor they have attained and shown the way to; if you have instead been duped by the corruption of duplicitous beings, internal and external, who show you an evil path, you will understand the meaning of the path you have taken on earth that day too.

Whose good path have you taken, which evil path have satans led you down? The day and the place you will know this intimately is there.

****

THE ANIMALS ASK THE HARE THE SECRET OF WHAT HE IS THINKING

> Then they said to him, "O hare who are most fleet
> Set forth that which is in your mind openly
> O you who have with the lion been entwined
> Speak out the opinion you have in your mind

1055.   Counsel gives comprehension and awareness
        Other intellects are friend to intellect
        'Seek counsel, Counselor,' the Messenger said
        For *the counselor deserves to be trusted*

The animals said to the hare, "Reveal your secret. What are thinking and what are your intentions?

"Speak, and let us say what we think too. The illumination of the lightning bolt of truth is born of the clash of thoughts. Seeking counsel increases thought and intellect. This motion outstrips ignorance. Hear the hadith of Hazret Muhammed. That great messenger said, 'O Counselor! Take counsel with someone you trust!'"

****

How the Hare withheld the Secret from them

        He said, "Every secret can't be spoke out loud
        Sometimes odd is even, sometimes even odd
        If you speak with a mirror of purity
        It soon gets fogged over and is hard to see
        Do not budge your lip to expound these three things:
        Your convictions, your money, and your beliefs
1060.   For those three have many enemies and foes
        Who will wait hidden in ambush once they know
        And if you say farewell to just one or two
        Every secret is known that goes beyond two
        If you keep two or three birds together bound
        They remain imprisoned in grief on the ground
        They have counsel which they take pains to secrete
        In allusions mixed with things meant to mislead
        The Messenger had counsel he kept covert
        Some remained unaware as they gave answers
1065.   He would use analogy to hide his thought
        So the enemy would not know head from foot
        He would get the answer he sought out of him
        While the other had no scent of the question."

The hare said, "It is not right to tell every secret." It is a mistake to think every person a friend and expect every plan to succeed. Do not forget that Hazret Ali said: "Do not tell your secret to anyone else." It is not enough that the person you tell is pure and faultless.

If we come close to the clearest, brightest mirror and tell it how pure it is, the mirror will fog up with our breath and show us to ourselves no more.

Know well that a person's sole intimate and secret-sharer is himself, his own heart.

Don't tell anyone of your convictions, your money, or your beliefs. For these are the values which bring a person the most enemies. If your enemies know about these things, they will lie in wait to ambush you. It is impossible not to suffer injury if you tell your secret to someone thinking them a friend.

Once a secret passes between the lips, it has spread throughout the world. If your are going to tell your secret to someone, bid that secret farewell, for it will certainly spread throughout the world. Once a secret goes beyond two people, it is no longer a secret. If you absolutely have to tell, tell it covertly. Let your state, not your tongue, tell the secret. Or have recourse to the Perfect Human who is truly qualified and intimate with you. He will keep your secret hidden even from himself.

You can take example from the language of state [*hâl dili*] used by birds. When birds which have been caught with birdlime and tied together realize that they cannot fly, they keep perfectly still and silent. You think that they can no longer fly, and you untie them, and then you see them suddenly fly away. The secret which frees the birds is their keeping their secrets from everyone and knowing the virtue of absolute silence and stillness.

Hazret Muhammed would speak carefully when seeking counsel from others. He would not reveal his real intent, but gather ideas to support it. Traitors and enemies would not understand our Messenger's intent and would not be able to prevent its realization.

He would definitely communicate his thoughts by means of analogies, but not reveal the spirit of the matter he discussed, leaving no opportunity for others to understand. For those who did not know and understand the religion of Muhammed, his discussion would be a riddle, and only the Companions understood his questions and answers.."

****

THE STORY OF THE HARE'S STRATAGEM

The hare delayed going inside for a while
Then he went and stood before the savage lion
And because he had been late in coming in
The lion was tearing the ground and roaring
"I said promises from those weaklings," he said
Would be raw, raw and feeble and never kept
1070. I'm thrown from my ass by their carryings-on
How long will this world bamboozle me, how long!"
The commander with a feeble beard is pressed
When he sees nor fore nor rear from foolishness
The path is smooth though beneath pitfalls remain
There's dearth of meaning within the midst of names
A pitfall is what a word or name is like
Sweet talk is sand for the water of our life
That kind of sand from which water gushes out
Is exceedingly rare, go and seek it out
1075. That sand, O son, is the man of God himself
He who connects with God separates from self
From him religion's sweet water gushes forth
Which to seekers is life and flourishing growth
Know others than men of God dry sand to be
They drink the water of your life constantly
Be a seeker of wisdom from a wise man
So that you come to see and know through that man

128

He who seeks for wisdom becomes wisdom's spring
He no longer needs to acquire anything
1080.   The preserving tablet becomes the preserved
His intellect becomes by spirit favored
When a man's teacher has been his intellect
Later his intellect becomes his student
Intellect says, like Gabriel to Ahmed
"It will burn me up if I take one more step.[51]
You go on, leave me and henceforth advance on
This is my limit here, O Spirit's Sultan."
A laggard without gratitude or patience
Knows only how to be dragged along by force
1085.   Whoso pleads necessity, he feigns illness
Till he is brought to the grave by that illness
The Messenger said that illness faked in jest
Brings such illness that one's lamp goes out in death
What's necessity—to bind something shattered
Or to tie up a vein that has been severed
If on this path you have not broken your foot
Whom do you mock? Why do you bandage your foot?
As for him who wore out his feet striving on
Buraq came for him and he got mounted on
1090.   He carried religion and it carried him
The command he accepted, accepted him
Until now he'd received commands from the shah
But he'd give commands to soldiers from now on
Until now the stars had had effect on him
But now he would be commander over them
If this brings you a difficulty of view
Then you have doubt that *the moon was split in two*
Refresh your faith not by movement of the tongue
O you who renew your desire in secret
1095.   As long as desire is fresh, then faith is not
For this desire upon that gate is the lock
You make anagogy of the virgin word
Make anagogy of yourself, not the Book
You interpret the Koran as you desire
You degrade and twist the meaning most sublime
Your state resembles that strange fly's condition
It liked to think of itself as a person
Drunk without need for wine's intoxication
It supposed its tiny body was the sun
1100.   It had often heard tell of the falcon's praise
And thought itself the Anqa bird of the age

---

51. Koran 53:8-10, 13-15.

The hare was late in going to the lion. The lion had long since gotten angry and was roaring. He believed that he had not performed his duty as Padishah well and that by doing what the animals wanted, by showing them too much favor, he had violated the rules of wise government. He was suffering from having fallen into the trap lain by those worldly animals. He condemned himself for being naive and stupid. A ruler definitely must think of the long term and take sound precautions. If not, he would be reduced to powerlessness and become the laughing-stock of hares. "Their carryings-on have lost me my donkey, how much longer will the world deceive me?" the lion moaned, thinking dejected thoughts while having an intuition of unity which made him aware of the filth of the world.

Many roads which are apparently smooth and in good condition may have holes and pitfalls beneath the surface. And just so, not everyone's name is like its owner. So many persons named "Just" have been tyrants, so many named "Believer" have had no faith.

Words and names are like pitfalls in the road which have been covered over. If you are fooled by people's names and the meaning of their names and suppose they are, like their names, good, virtuous, beautiful, clean or brave, you will be duped. You will fall into the trap of these names and be desolate.

It is the same with being duped by bright words. People are awed by beautiful speech and those who speak well. To be sure, to know the value and mightiness of speech, to recognize great and wise speech, is a virtue. But there is also the speech which is internally as empty, meaningless and even predatory on the heart as it is on the outside bright and attractive to the eye and heart. Such words are like water flowing into sand. Just as sand soaks up water so that the water disappears in the sand, the brightness and attractiveness of such words, even their meanings and effects, are transient also. They do not even leave any moisture where they flow. If you do not want to lose the water of your life in the sand of such shiny words, give ear not to the shininess of words, but to God the Truth and the one who speaks the truth!

But there is speech which is a spring of knowledge and gnosis, even in the form of one word; speech which is spoken while stringing pearls of knowledge and gnosis on the string of words; know that such words are beneficial and mighty like waters bubbling up from sand and scattering blessings everywhere, and enrich your pouch of knowledge and gnosis with such words.

The sand from whose breast water gushes forth is the man of God. Son, that sand is like the friends of God. He is a perfect murshid who has become distant from himself and near to God. He has abandoned duality, annihilated the human ego [*benlik*] in himself, reached self-disclosure and arrived at the secrets of being eternal with God the Truth.

The river of the sweet water of faith gushes forth in the breast of that friend of God and flows into the hearts of those who know him as murshid, and it bestows eternal life on the hearts it flows into like the water of eternal life.

Know that those other than the friends of God do not bestow water, they are a dry desert which soaks up water and annihilates it! Seek out the one who makes you human, who gives you to taste the pleasure and pride of being human; from those people of wisdom ask for God the Truth and the truth, ask for knowledge and gnosis from that master of gnosis who is the source of thought, so that you may become like him.

The person who seeks wisdom and who is able to digest the wisdom that is given him becomes a source of wisdom one day, he becomes someone who takes wisdom, mystery and gnosis from the greatest source. He will no longer have need of acquisition and the means of perfection. While a person's heart gathers various kinds of knowledge for a while, when he embarks on training by that man of God, with the true knowledge he acquires from the Spirit of Muhammed he becomes someone who takes grace directly, without intermediary. Because earlier it was teacher of intellect to him and conducted his training by way of intellect. But when the knowledge of God the Truth [Hak ilmi] covers his being [varlık], intellect becomes student to him, and this person whose heart has been occupied by love of God accomplishes the spiritual Miraj.

To transcend the limit of intellect is to go beyond the point where Gabriel stopped. While Gabriel was ascending to God with Hazret Muhammed on the Miraj, they came to a point where he said, "O Muhammed! If I take one step higher, the light of self-disclosure will burn me, destroy me, this is my limit," and he remained behind while Hazret Muhammed continued on the path to reach God.

It is the same with the intellect. When one reaches the point where intellect must be transcended, intellect speaks with the heart as Gabriel did.

And it says, "O Sultan of Spirit! You too, abandon me at this place! This is my limit. Mount now on the Rafraf of love!" And, "O great rider! Drive your mount on to the heights of the path of reaching God!"

There are some people who do not know patience and gratitude. The reason is laziness and aging. They do not thank God, they have no patience for and cannot bear God's commands and the worship He has commanded. The aged spirit, like all laggards, finds a reason for this also. It says: "If God wanted me to worship, He would have given me ardor and desire for worship, He would have shown me the way." In saying this, it conforms to the command not of the spirit but of the soul. It takes not God's path but the path of the world.

Such people are compelled in the exact sense of the term [tam bir cebir içinde]; they are people without will, bound by the chain of compulsion [cebir]: A person who exhibits disobedience on the path of piety and supposes himself to be powerless and too ill to worship, who conforms to his soul out of sloth, using the excuse of a fictitious illness, will one day become really ill. He will either die or, tired of life, weary and fed up, be buried in the grave of baseless fears [vehimler].

Those who supposed themselves crippled on the path of God's commands, and flee from the work which is God's command, are those who abuse the power given to them, which will one day leave them really powerless.

That is why Hazret Muhammed said: "Illness in jest brings on real illness and extinguishes a person like a candle."

The dictionary meaning of the word "compulsion" [cebir] is the bandaging and re-setting of a broken or dislocated bone. To bind up a broken bone, or re-connect a severed vein, is "compulsion."

"Compulsion" is aiding, repairing.

If you have not tired yourself out on the path of worship and pious obedience, not broken your foot on that path, why are you now bandaging your foot? You flee your own potentialities, your swiftness, your health, and bind your foot with the bandage of compulsion. You do not obey God's commands and, saying that you are powerless, ill, you stay behind on the path of death while alive.

If you are going to be, be like the one who tires out his feet on the path of worship, so that Buraq may come to your aid on the path of God the Truth; let it be a reality for you to mount that Buraq of faith and spirituality and roam the realms of the heart.

The story one needs to know here is the following: The one who wears out his feet on the path of God, on the path of worship, represents Hazret Muhammed. For that Messenger of God the Truth performed namaz so much that his knees swelled up. His wife Hazret Aisha reproached him: "O Messenger of God, God the Truth has forgiven all of your past and future sins. Since that is the case, why do you torment your body to this degree?" Hazret Muhammed said: "O Aisha! Should I not be a thankful bondsman to God?"

Then the chapter "Tâ-hâ" of the Koran came down. God said to His messenger: We have not sent down the Koran in order to trouble you. O My beloved, do not subject your soul to hardship, for We have guided you since pre-eternity. We sent down the Koran so that you might give news of Our essence and Our attributes to the believers. So that you might relate the mysteries of faith and bondsmanship to Our believing bondsmen. May they hear from you of the wisdom of gnosis and the sublimity of God and become gnostics.[52]

For so long Hazret Muhammed, who was the greatest of the messengers, carried from the divine source to the human world the commands of religion and the responsibilities humans should perform on the path of goodness, beauty and eternity.

He performed his duties with that greatness of spirit and one day he was carried by Buraq to the presence of God the Truth, as if he was consisted of a spirit rather than a body, although he was still alive.

For years commands were sent to him from God the Truth. In the end he became someone who gave commands.

He performed the office of messenger of God not only to one people but within such a limitless breadth as messenger to all humanity and jinn.

Until he became a messenger, he tread the path of the star which held out light to him. Until that time he lived according to the writing on his own brow, but when the duty of messengerhood arrived and he became a messenger and became the truth with the Truth, he was the ruler and commander of not only his own star and his own destiny, but of all stars. Because now he drew his power not from nature, from food and drink, but directly from God.

When people asked Hazret Muhammed for a miracle and he showed them the moon in the sky, it split in two and came back together again. There is an indication of this in the first gracious verse of the chapter Qamar in the Gracious Koran. Can you respond to this with doubt?—for such doubt is no different from non-faith. But the meaning of the splitting of the moon does not end there. In the commentary on the Koran by Qashani, the splitting of the moon was cited as evidence that the Day of Resurrection was near. And the moon has two faces. One is its visible, light-filled face, which represents the spirit. The other is its invisible face, which is dark and represents the soul. In short, the moon is the heart, and the heart is what gathers in itself two opposing realms, one, the spirit, the other, the soul.

So refresh your faith with your heart, not with your tongue . . . . Because the tongue

---

52. Here Rifai paraphrases the Koran very freely, as he does elsewhere with Mevlana's work and other texts.

speaks, but if the tongue which means the heart is silent and does not affirm it, that faith cannot be faith.

If you are after newer and newer desires in the command of the soul, your faith is not fresh. If the human heart is not clean like a clear mirror, the spirit cannot find the road to its true home, the land of God.

Don't take the way of making the Koran and hadith suit you, make yourself suit the Koran and hadith! If you try to understand letters and words according to the wishes of your soul, you will be mistaken. You should put your soul under the command of what is intended in the holy word, that is the right way.

Try to hear and understand the Koran! Because it shows the path that never bends.

Your condition is like that of the fly which thought it was a man. The fly, like those who become drunk without drinking, thought that its nothing of a body was the sun and that its powers of comprehension, which brought no understanding and shed light on nothing, were like the light of the sun.

It had heard the praises of the falcon, and thought itself not even a falcon but the Anqa.

****

THE FALSENESS OF THE FLY'S SHALLOW ANAGOGY

That fly sailing on a straw in donkey pee
Held its head up like a ship's captain at sea
It said, "I've read of the sea and about ships
I've been pondering a long while over this
Behold, here is the sea, and here is the ship
I'm a captain and a seaman well-equipped."
On the surface of that sea he drove his raft
The amount of liquid seemed to him so vast
1105.   Compared to him that urine was limitless
Where was the gaze that could see the truth of it?
His world extended as far as he could see
As much sight as he had, he had that much sea
Like the fly, he whose anagogy is false
Has pee for thought and his fancy is a straw
If it left anagogy by thought aside
Fortune would make a Huma out of that fly
He who grasps this example is not a fly
His spirit is not by form measured for size

A stalk of straw was floating on some donkey urine. The fly lighted on the straw and supposed itself the captain of a great ship. It held its head high in pride. It thought it understood seamanship, it believed it had read books on the subject. It thought that it knew the map of the world and had crossed many seas and seen many countries and shores.

The fly was not completely wrong. The liquid it was sailing on appeared to be a sea in its eyes; the straw it rode upon had gained the importance of a raft. It thought the world consisted of what it saw with the eye of a fly.

Such are those who suppose reality consists of what they can see with their own eyes and know with their own intellects.

If the fly could have got free of the error it made with its fly intellect, free of erroneous vision and erroneous understanding, destiny would have made it not a fly but a Huma bird.

In fact, the spirit which succeeds in knowing reality, succeeds in viewing events with the eye of meaningful example [*ibret gözüyle*], will not self-disclose in the form of a fly. Such a spirit will become human, and a human with great spirit.

****

HOW THE LION ROARED AT THE LATE ARRIVAL OF THE HARE

1010.   Like that hare who challenged the lion to fight
       When was his spirit in measure of his height?
       In a fit of rage said the hotheaded lion,
       "By means of my ears the foe has bound my eyes
       The tricks of the fatalists have got me trapped
       By their wooden sword my body has been racked
       I'll not listen to their palaver again
       It is all the ravings of ghouls and demons
       Hurry, O my heart, and tear them limb from limb
       Rip their skin off, for they are nothing but skin."

1015.   What is skin?—It is speech that is fraudulent
       Like water ripples that are not permanent
       Know these words as the skin and meaning, the pith
       These words are as form and meaning is spirit
       Skin may serve to cover up a rotten core
       The rivalry of God keeps hid a good core
       When the book is water and wind is the pen
       Whatever you write will soon become nothing
       It's form on water, and if you seek therein
       Constancy, you'll wring your hands when you return

1020.   The wind inside of man is whim and desire
       His message remains when you put whim aside
       Lovely are the messages which God has sent
       For they are from head to foot all permanent
       The prayers for shahs change and their champions except
       The champions and prayers recited for prophets
       The pomp of a padishah is vanity
       The command of the prophets is majesty
       Thus they remove names of padishahs from coins
       While they mint the name of Ahmed evermore

1125.   Ahmed's name is the name of all the prophets
       Ninety's still with us when we reach one hundred

And just so, the hare's spirit was of a measure to combat a lion, a spirit greater than the spirit of a hare.

At this point the lion was grumbling, roaring with the rage and torment of believing he had been duped by the beasts of prey. The perfidious beasts had wounded his pride with their wooden sword and he had virtually become ill.

O heart! Don't wait! You've been fooled enough! Run and rip off their skin! For they are nothing but skin anyway. They are mere appearance. Merely flesh and skin. They are worthy of destruction in the paws of God's wrath, the lion, those perfidious beasts.

Skin and hide are a bunch of pretty words. They are like empty bubbles on the surface of the water: Although they appear to reflect the seven colors with the light that they get from outside, the slightest movement makes them break up, burst and die out.

They are like meaningless speech. If speech is a picture, an icon, meaning is in the position of its spirit. A meaningless word is like a spiritless body. It makes listeners bored instead of giving them pleasure.

Skin conceals all the faults of a useless body. It is the shell which conceals a rotten walnut or a bitter almond.

So skin and shell conceal the faults of the rotten or bitter, of that which has a bad core. That which has a good core, that which is sound and sweet, also has skin and shell. But in reality, the wisdom of God conceals the spiritual sublimity of the good-spirited. God has concealed His friends, who have within them beauty, perfection and gnosis, from those who will not understand them, by giving them the skin and appearance of all other people.

But God's friends have a light-filled beauty projected outward from within themselves which only eyes able to see that beauty can see. If your pen is made of wind and your notebook of water, your work will no more endure than forms written on water by the wind. Meaningless speech is like forms written on water. It gives only the torment of regret to those who expect faithfulness from it. Here the wind means people's whims. It means a weakness for worldly pleasures and worldly ambitions. If you can get free of such desire, if you can give up passing whims and greed, then your spirit will reach a level at which it can receive messages [*haber*] from sublime God.

God's messages are beautiful, eternal. They give you the pleasure of reaching limitlessness. But in order to receive messages from God the Truth, one needs a heart worthy of His inspirations and an intellect with that preparedness. Seek the way to obtain these!

As you know, the *khutba* part of the Friday prayer sermon is devoted to mention of the names of padishahs. One prays that a padishah's reign will never end. But with the passage of time, neither the padishah nor his rule remains. But the *khutba*s recited in the names of prophets are not like that: The rule of the friends and prophets of God endures.

For the reigns of padishahs are worldly sultanates. That is why they break down and pass away. But the messengers are mighty spirits who give us news of the sublimity of God the Truth's sultanate and bring us to God the Truth. Just as it is inconceivable that God, who is pre-eternal [*ezeli*] and post-eternal [*ebedi*], should decay, neither can those who bring us news of His reality decay.

You know that the names of padishahs are removed from coins. But wherever the name of Hazret Muhammed is found, it is eternal. Do not write in your heart the names of padishahs and the worldly sultanates of padishahs. If you are going to write, write the blessed name of that sultan of eternity, so that your heart will not lose value one day like a false coin.

The names of all the messengers are gathered together in the blessed name of Hazret Muhammed. Because the shariats brought by each of God's messengers found perfection in his shariat, reached their sublime expression in the Koran. The truth he brought is the greatest truth that can be related to humans. His religion gathers together all realities in itself. It shows all spirits the path to be attained, the Koran which was revealed to him is a garden of gnosis which is the only garden from whose branches all creatures breath in the scent of enormous roses.

When you mention his name, you have mentioned the names of all the prophets and all the friends. Just as the numeral 100 contains within it all the numerals up to 100.

****

ALSO IN EXPOSITION OF THE HARE'S STRATAGEM

The hare made a great delay of going in
While he rehearsed to himself his stratagems
After long delay he set out to whisper
One or two secrets into the lion's ear
What realms there are in the core of intellect!
How very wide is this sea of intellect!
Our forms run on this ocean of sweet water
Like cups floating on the surface of water

1130. As long as they're not full, they float like basins
When the basin becomes full, it sinks down in
Intellect is hid, and a world manifest
Our forms are the waves, or spray, of intellect
Whatever means that may be devised by form
By that means intellect's sea tosses off form
If the heart does not see who gives its secret
If the arrow does not see who's shooting it
One thinks one's own horse is lost, while stubbornly
One drives one's own horse down the road with all speed

1135. That hero thinks that his horse is lost to him
And his horse is carrying him like the wind
That silly fool looks everywhere, lamenting
Going from door to door, searching and asking
"Who is it who stole my horse and where is he?"
O Master, what is that there between your knees?
"Yes, this is the horse, but the horse, where is it?"
O horse-seeking horseman, gather up your wits
Spirit's lost because it's evident and near
Your belly's full, lips dry like a water jar

1140. How will you see red and green and russet hues
Unless before these three you have seen light too?
But when your consciousness is lost in colors
A veil against light is made of those colors
When those colors are covered up by the night

136

Then you know that seeing them depends on light
One sees no colors without external light
Even those of imagination's insight
From the sun and Suha comes external light
And internal from reflected sublime lights
1145.   The light of the heart is light of the eye's light
The light of the eye is reaped from the heart's light
And the light of the heart's light is God's own light
Which is pure of intellect and sense's light
At night there's no light and you see no color
So, it's manifest to you by light's other
Seeing light then is the seeing of color
And you know this right away from light's other
That is why God created pain and sorrow
So that joy might by these opposites be known
1150.   Hidden things are manifest by opposites
God is hid because He has no opposite
The gaze falls on light and after on color
Like Greeks and Blacks, opposite shows its other
So, you know light by knowing its opposite
As things come forth, opposite shows opposite
God's light has in existence no opposite
That He might be revealed by His opposite
Consequently our eyes do not perceive Him
He perceives, know this by Moses and mountain
1155.   Forms come from meaning like lions from forests
Or like speech and voice from the thoughts they express
This speech and this sound of voice have sprung from thought
You do not know where is the ocean of thought
But you've seen the subtlety of waves of speech
So know that they must come from a noble sea
When the waves of thought speed on from His knowledge
He fashions forms out of words and sounds for them
Form is born of speech and then it dies again
The wave takes itself into the sea again
1160.   Form comes out of formlessness and then returns
For *Verily unto Him is the return*
Thus you have death and return every instant
This world is only an hour, Mustafa said
The entire world is extinguished each instant
At the same time it appears to be constant
The world's being comes and goes with every breath
None is from this stripping and dressing exempt
Our thought is an arrow He shot in the air
It goes back to God—how should it stay out there?
   1165.   Every instant the world is renewed and we

> Don't see the new within perpetuity
> Life arrives ever new like a flowing stream
> Though in matter it seems to have constancy
> Its form seems constant because it moves swiftly
> Like a spark you whirl round with your hand swiftly
> If you quickly whirl around a branch on fire
> It seems to be one very long line of fire
> This apparent length of duration in time
> Comes from swiftness of the artistry divine
> 1170. If the seeker of this secret is book-wise
> Here's Husameddin, he is a book sublime

The hare first planned out in his mind the kind of trick he would play on the lion. He practiced what he would say to the lion by talking to himself. Then he set out down the road in order to whisper a great secret into the lion's ear. The hare here represented the intellect of return. That is why he was behaving in a prudent and thoughtful manner.

Prudence and thoughtfulness are self-disclosures of intellect. The intellect, which is God's great wisdom [*Allah'ın büyük hikmeti*], is such an ocean that the human form is like a basin floating on this ocean. If a basin floating in water gets filled with water, it sinks. In this way, when the basin of the body begins to take in the waters of the sea of intellect and be filled with mysteries and meanings, it passes over this visible realm of color and form and, understanding that they consist only of appearance, dives into the sea of wisdom. It fills with intellect and understanding and begins to see the oneness in being [*varlık'taki birliği*]. Its spirit fills with as much of this profound pleasure as it can carry.

The intellect here is the universal intellect [*akl-i kül*]. Universal Intellect is perfect and absolute intellect; it is the self-disclosure of the creative power in the state of action.

So, God created the universal intellect, and this universal intellect, in order to be known and to display its power, brought the realms called universal soul [*nefs-i kül*] into being. It is due to the insufficiency of universal soul in relation to intellect that intellect, by way of perfecting itself, set universal soul into action and the nine heavens and four elements—fire, air, water and earth—came into being through this act. The vegetal, animal, and human self-disclosures, which ensure that spirit matures in a body, are also the result of this act [*hareket*]. The goal of all these acts is for spirit to be re-united with God once more, and for it to be able to pass through stations to reach God, especially for it to be the site of manifestation [*mazhar*] for the Perfect Human's self-disclosure.

That is why the sea of intellect is hidden. What is visible is this world of form, which self-discloses as a realm ensuring that intellect be known.

Whatever means may be used in order to bring body and form closer to intellect, it will on the contrary separate them further. What will bring a person to the sea of intellect is the divine light hidden within his mortal being [*geçici varlık*] like a secret. What will light the way for you is this light, which is a drop or spray of moisture from the sea of intellect.

On the other hand, the arrow which does not know the one who shot it, or the heart that does not see that pre-eternal beloved who gave it a secret, the heart which does not, in short, sense and comprehend that the one relating mysteries and understanding them is located in itself, is like the heedless rider who searches for the horse he himself is mounted on.

In order to reach God, a person has mounted such a horse that runs like the wind, has been mounted upon such a horse. Heedlessness is not to be aware of the horse one is riding.

The horse here represents the intellect and spirit of a person who is heedless of God the Truth. To be heedless of the intellect and spirit one has been mounted upon is to run this horse around aimlessly and to seek the horse elsewhere while one is running it, to seek it violently and heedlessly; a person can be heedless of this spirit and intellect to such an extent that he is like the rider who runs his horse this way and that and everywhere shouts, "Who stole my horse?"

The gnostic asks that rider: "You are on top of your horse, what are you searching for?" But the rider still will not understand. He will even ask: "Yes, this is the horse, but where is this horse?" What answer can be given to that but: "O rider, come to yourself!"?

A person has found his way when he wants to find not the realm of spirits [*rûhlar âlemi*] in his own spirit, but the realm of universal intellect in his own intellect and the realm of divinity [*lâhût alemi*] in himself.

In reality, spirit is not hidden. It is possible for those who know it [*erbabı*] to see it. It is not apparent because it is too close to you. In this respect a human is like a mysterious jug containing sacred water that bestows eternal life. From outside, this jar seems to be empty and dry.

So, like a person who does not see the water of life in the jar, a person whose eye of the heart is not open will not succeed in seeing the spirit in a human being and the divine beauty in that spirit.

Because his sight does not have in it the light to see and indicate that beauty.

If there is no light in a place, how can one perceive colors? The first thing which appears and displays other things is light. Just as the sun or moon ensures that we see the colors and forms of the exterior world, the light of a person's heart ensures that he can see the great beauty and limitless reality.

To see colors and forms and not see that which shows them is to be heedless of such light. For such people colors are veils preventing the seeing of divine light. You will surely not be able to see it if you remain behind the veils of color and form.

An arrived person, a perfect murshid, is someone who first sees the divine light, that is, who comprehends God, and then finds the secret of the beings illuminated by His light.

This is the station of seeing first the artist and then his artistry. The light which illuminates the realities of the Koran, the light of gnosis, the light which self-discloses outside and inside of humans, is for all that is illuminated by those lights the single light of God.

Intellect, speech, writing, feeling and thought are all the self-disclosures of that great light in a person worthy of it.

Just as the colors and forms of beings cannot be seen in dark of night, the spiritual beings in the heart are condemned to remain colorless and hidden as long as the light of God the Truth does not self-disclose.

The light of a person's eye is in reality the light of his heart. Because in reality the light of the eye comes into being out of the light of the heart.

Great God has brought into being pains and sorrows so that the heart should taste that suffering and see the light of pleasure and joy.

Without illness a person cannot know the value of health; without hunger, of satiation; without trouble, of ease; without evil, or good; without ugliness, of beauty; and finally, without non-being [*yokluk*], of being [*varlık*].

Furthermore, all hidden powers and hidden bounties become evident through their opposites. Only God has no opposite. His sublime attributes of being, beauty and goodness have opposites. They are non-being, ugliness and evil. But there exists [*mevcut*] no opposite of God Himself. That is why sublime God, who has no partner in being and no opposite in God-ness, will always remain hidden.

The limitlessness of God's concealment lies in the perfection [kemâl] of the attributes which self-disclose Him to us. For in contrast to His infinite concealment, every color and every light and every form in this realm of the created is, for the eye that sees and the heart that loves, nothing but the self-disclosure of divine being in a limitless mirror.

And so we know light [*nur*] by darkness, the opposite of brightness [*aydınlık*]. In other words, everything becomes known by its own opposite. But it is in this world of the created [*yaratılmışlar*] that things are known by their opposites. That is why no opposite can be conceived of for God the Truth's being [*varlık*]. Because there is in created existence [*vücûtta*] no opposite to God the Truth's light. That is why it is not possible to know God, who has no partner and no likeness, by means of His opposites. Our eyes cannot comprehend God. Because He is beyond [*münezzih*] encompassing [*ihâta*]. And comprehension is only possible by encompassing. In order to better understand this truth, you should consider the story of Moses and Mount Sinai.

When God's light was reflected onto Mount Sinai, the mountain was shattered. And Moses swooned at the moment of that light's self-disclosure.

A lion grows up in the forest, and later returns to the forest. Know the realm of meaning to be such a forest. This visible world has roared from a forest of meaning, come into manifestation from there, and in the end will return there.

You feel and you think. But neither your feeling nor your thought is visible. They are known only when your feelings are excited and your thoughts multiply, and you speak or cry out. Your voice acquires a tone which expresses your feelings and thoughts. We hear words and sound. But we cannot see the realm of feeling and thought which brings them into manifestation.

If the feeling and thought in a person's being [*varlık*] are so hidden and invisible to him, consider the realm of feeling and thought of the divine being [*ilâhî varlığı*]. Try to comprehend that sublime meaning. Perhaps in that way you will understand the wisdom, and the grandeur, in His being hidden and invisible.

Before the time when God thought to create the universe [*kâinât*] as a realm of forms, it was just a divine thought. Then came letters, sound, and finally speech: the divine thought began to enter the state of speech with God's first word, the command, "Be."

In short, this world of form came into manifestation from a sea of meaning, and it returns there also.

Forms are born from speech; words, sentences and meanings become manifest. But these forms pass away with time. New ones take their place. Forms come into manifestation in the realm of formlessness and later return whence they came. That is why in this world there is every instant death, quickening [*dirim*], coming and going.

The self-disclosure of forms is the work of the universal intellect. Every form and every act is for the expression of the meanings of the divine names. These divine names are the expression of God the Truth's infinite attributes with words, the meanings in the words, and finally the things and events [*eşyâ ve hâdiseler*] which these meanings bring into existence [*vücût*].

Each instant the entire world becomes nothing and each instant it manifests. That gives us the sense of continuity. Our existence, the world and everything in it, dies and quickens with every breath; but because we see it as continuing, we cannot realize that it is dying and quickening.

People's thoughts and anxieties are like an arrow. This arrow is the arrow of meaning which the divine inspiration of the divine thought shoots into the human heart. But just as an arrow does not stop still in the air, and rushes to its target, that arrow of thought and meaning too will arrive at its final target, God.

The span of a human life is like a flowing stream. The waters which come and go, each following the other, appear constant in rivers. What gives water continuousness is that ceaseless flow.

This is like waving a firebrand swiftly. If you wave it in a straight line, the fire will appear to be a line, and if you twirl it, it will appear to be a circle. That is because of the swiftness and plurality of motion. The eye cannot comprehend that what appears to be a line or circle of fire really consists of one point.

In the same way it is not easy to see a point of oneness in the plurality of forms of being and continuity of the visible world.

In reality it is the swiftness of the divine artistry that makes a span of life, which is a single point, appear to a person like a line.

It is when a person pays attention to all of these truths that he can be considered to have taken a step toward comprehending the importance, and the degree, of the difference between the divine realm and the realm of form.

A person who puts his thumb in front of his eye will not be able to see the sun or anything else. Whereas the world he cannot see is so much bigger than the finger preventing him from seeing it.

So, great mysteries cannot be known by means of small thinking. And in order to know them it is not enough to be learned in books. Find Husameddin Chelebi, who is a sublime book, and the perfect man who in every age is the heir of such great ones; thus acquire the knowledge of God you need and become a gnostic of God the Truth.

****

THE HARE CAME TO THE LION AND THE LION WAS ANGRY WITH HIM

> The lion, full of fire, enmity and wrath
> Saw that the hare was arriving from far off
> He was running unafraid, audaciously
> Rash and sharp and stern, he came on angrily
> For it would be suspicious to seem ashamed
> And insolence would remove all cause for blame

When he came up to the shoe-rack by the door
"Hey, you wicked prodigal," the lion roared
1175.   "I who have torn oxen apart limb from limb
I who've pulled the ears of ferocious lions
Who then might a half-wit hare pretend to be
That he throws aside my command so rudely?"
Leave off the sleep and heedlessness of a hare
O you ass, give ear to this lion's fierce roar!

As the lion was frothing with rage, he saw the hare coming from far off. The hare was approaching with a fearless manner. He had the self-confident air of the blameless. As for the Padishah of the Animals, he was in a rage, unable to stomach being neglected by a tiny hare. Those looking from outside could have sensed an insolence in the hare's manner, and in the identity [şahsiyet] of the lion, the meaning of a lion of death with the power to grasp every living thing in its paws.

It was obvious that there was no place for insolence in confrontation with such a great and invincible force. To sleep the sleep of a hare, that is, to sleep with one's eyes open like a hare, before a power which had turned the most powerful Khans, Pharaohs and Nimrods into dust in its paws, was the most extreme sort of heedlessness.

****

THE HARE APOLOGIZES

The hare said, "Mercy, I will relate to you
If your Lordship's pardon permit, an excuse."
"What excuse, failure among fools!" said the lion
You dare come before a shah at any time
1180.   A cock that crows out of time should lose its head
One should never hear fools' unworthy pretexts
The excuse of a fool is worse than his sin
An ingrate's excuse is bane that kills wisdom
Your excuse is lacking in wisdom, O Hare
Am I a hare, that you'd put it in my ear?"
The hare said, "O Shah, count worthless me worthy
Hear a plea from one who's suffered tyranny
As alms for purification of your throne
Don't drive one who is lost away from his road
1185.   The sea feeds water into each riverbed
With pieces of straw upon its face and head
This generosity does not make it less
Generosity makes it nor more nor less."
The lion said, "I give unto each its right
I cut the robe according to a man's height."
"Hear me," the hare cried, "If I am not worthy
I submit to the dragon of cruelty
I set out at breakfast-time upon the way
With my companion to see the shah today

1190. The beasts had assigned for you another hare
      To companion me so we would make a pair
      On the road a lion attacked me, your slave
      He attacked us both as we were on our way
      I told him, 'We are slaves of the Shah of Shahs
      We are lowly slaves of the court of the Shah.'
      He said, 'For shame! The Shah of Shahs? Who is he?
      Do not speak of every nobody to me!
      I will tear both you and your shah end from end
      If you turn away from my door with your friend.'
1195. I said to him, 'Let me go so that I may
      Tell the shah of you and once more see his face.'
      He said, 'Leave your companion as surety
      If not, your life will be sacrifice for me.'
      We entreated him greatly but to no end
      He left me go alone and kept my friend
      My friend was so fat he was like three of me
      Both in size and goodness and delicacy
      From now on that lion will keep the road closed
      This is how it is with us, you have been told
1200. Give up hope of the allotment in future
      I am speaking truth, and the truth is bitter
      If you must have the allotment, clear the road
      Come, advance, and drive away that impure foe."

The hare was going to apologize to the lion, but the Shah of the Beasts was not in the mood to hear excuses.

He was determined to cut off the head of a cock crowing out of time, and not hear stupid excuses. The pretexts of such fools were greater than their crimes. But this hare was a different kind of hare. He was determined and able to make the lion listen to him.

He knew what to say in order to flatter the lion's pride. There are vast oceans before whose rising waves every being is helpless. But even when these awesome seas are most violent, they cannot thrust pieces of straw underneath them, they still carry rubbish on their heads.

That could not be counted a flaw in the grandeur of such seas of greatness, the sea could not be shamed because of it.

Hearing these things, the lion agreed to talk. True, he did say: "My generosity is for those worthy of generosity, and just as it is not right for those who are impious and worship-less to take refuge even in the generosity of most gracious God, it is not fitting to show a hare who has not done his duty the generosity of a lion." But the lion had, willing or no, begun to talk with the hare.

The hare was saying, "Beat me, but listen. I wasn't coming to you alone. I was coming along with a hare more well-fed, more to your taste than I. But another lion, a rival of yours, cut us off on the road. He took my friend. We definitely wanted to come to you our shah and give you our lives. I insisted that I at least see your face. He took my friend and kept him as a hostage, and worst of all, he maligned you. He said that he did not recognize your sultanate and that there could be no other lion but he on the face of the earth. I begged and pleaded, but he would not relent. He would not let go my beautiful, fat brother hare, who is three times as big as I.

Perhaps this is not important, but what will happen from now on? That raiding lion will now no longer let through any of the animals coming from us to you, who are dying to come to you. I have come to inform you of this. That is why I was delayed. Now let my life be your sacrifice. But you devise a plan for that lion who is setting up rule in your domain."

Here it was not the hare who was speaking, but intellect. The lion represented the soul. The other hare, whom the hare called his companion, who was invisible and known only by his attributes, represents divine aid.

At the beginning the soul was on the way to satisfying all its desires. If the animals, which are the form of his desires, are a little late in coming, he flew into a blind rage of greed, and he would cut down, eat and rip apart the animals who bowed to his desires in a timely fashion.

But the hidden spiritual forces inside the same soul were trying to control his greed.

And that is why here the hare represented the intellect of return, that is, the intellect which comprehends spiritual values.

And that is why the hare went into action to save the lion from becoming a slave to the soul.

The hare would thus bring the lion to the right road through trickery, and at the end of that road the soul would be destroyed, that is, the body would die to its own animal attributes and greed.

****

The Lion answers the Hare and sets off with Him

"In the name of God, let's go," the lion said
"To see him, if you speak truth, go on ahead
I'll give him and hundreds more what they deserve
Or if you lie, I'll give you what you deserve."
Taking the lead like a guide, the hare set out
So he could ensnare the lion in his plot
1205. Toward the pitfall which he had marked with a sign
The deep well he'd made to trap the lion's life
So they went till they came to the well at last
Behold a hare like water underneath grass
Water bears a blade of straw down to the plain
When, I wonder, will it bear off a mountain?
His guile's snare became a noose for the lion
Wonderful hare, who could bear off a lion
A Moses kills Pharaoh by the river Nile
With Pharaoh's army and multitudes entire
1210. A single gnat with no more than half a wing
Without a fear cleaves Nimrod's skull through a seam
See the end of one who heard his enemy

See the punishment of the friend of envy
The end of a Pharaoh who heard Haman out
The end of a Nimrod who heard Satan out
If your enemy speaks to you like a friend
Know that it's a snare, although he talks of grain
If he gives you sugar, know that it's poison
If he's kind to your body, it's subjection

1215.   When destiny arrives, you see but the skin
You cannot distinguish enemies from friends
Since that's so, begin supplication of God
Lament, do the fast, and count the names of God
Cry out loud, say, "O You who know the Unseen
Do not crush us with the stone of evil schemes
Creator of the lion, if we're currish
Do not set the lion on us from ambush
Do not give the form of fire to sweet water
Do not put fire in the form of sweet water

1220.   When on the wine of Your wrath you make us drunk
You give form of existence to what is not
What is drunkenness—blindfolding of the sight
So that wool seems jasper and stones, jewels bright
What is drunkenness—the senses are confused
So that tamarisk seems to be sandalwood."

The lion could not abide any partner in his rule: What he heard from the hare made him leap violently into action. He ordered the hare to show him that enemy who blocked off the road. If the hare was lying, he would be in deep trouble, and if he were telling the truth, the lion soul was going to punish the other lion.

The hare went along in front of the lion. He had marked a well he'd seen before and took the lion there. He went straight for his destination like water flowing invisibly underneath straw.

It is true that water can carry away a blade of straw. But how can it carry away a giant mountain? But behold the power of God the Truth, for now a small stream was carrying away a giant mountain, a tiny hare was carrying away a great big lion.

Yes, in the hands of the greed of the lion soul, before his power, a person can be as feeble as a blade of straw. Those looking on would anxiously suppose that the helpless blade of straw would never escape that lion's clutches. But there is God's help, and if intellect goes into action, everything can change with the speed of a miracle. In that case, a blade of straw can obliterate a mountain-like body.

Messenger Moses appeared very small to Pharaoh, his family, and his entire people. But Moses parted the sea with his staff and passed through it easily. Pharaoh, while taking the same way, was drowned as the waters came over him.

That's how it is, a mosquito with half a wing can painlessly enter into a great Nimrod's ear and make him dash his head against the ground and crack open his skull.

Read these verses of Yunus Emre with that in mind:

> A mosquito shook an eagle and made him hit the ground
> This is no lie, it is the truth, I saw his face also

Beware the words of an enemy, listen to the stories of those who befriended jealous, envious persons.

Pharaoh listened to Haman. Haman was an enemy to Pharaoh but pretended to be his friend. Whenever Pharaoh, at the prompting of his wife Aasiya, began to follow the path of faith, he would see Haman and seek his advice. Thus Haman would deprive Pharaoh of his faith.

In the same way, Nimrod did what Satan told him to. Satan would take on human form, appear before Nimrod, flatter him and deprive him of God the Truth by saying, "How could there be another God? If there is one God, it is you! Don't believe Abraham."

Do not be duped by the friendly behavior of the enemy! If he gives you sugar, know that it is poison. If he does good, assume that he is doing so in preparation for oppression. Remember the hadith, "When destiny arrives, the eye is blinded." If you meet such a fate, neither the eye of your heart or intellect will see the truth. You won't be able to distinguish goof from evil or friend from foe.

At such times surrender yourself to God the Truth! Begin supplication! Perform the prayers, perform the fast!

Say: "O my God who knows all hidden things! Do not crush us under the weight of the stone of evil thoughts!

"O my Lord who created the lion! If we have behaved like dogs, do not set the lion soul upon us from ambush!

"Do not make a bridge of fire of the path leading to worship as beautiful as pure and cool water, and to You in such beauty. In sum, show us the roads that lead to You!

"My God, You who give the raiment of form to those who are in reality naught and have become in You naught, who give them love of the world, who send them far away from their homeland. They fall into such a condition by drinking the wine of Your wrath, they become drunk on love of the world.

"Whatever they look at seems beautiful to them. They think common stones are jewels. They swim on the drunkenness of jewels, colors and worldly pleasures, they just cannot come to themselves and see the great truth. Their eyes are blindfolded to the truth.

"This is the condition of those drunk on the wine of God's wrath. It is a condition in which one sees everything that is empty, useless and vain as beautiful and valuable. But my Lord, one day You will awaken those same worldly travelers, tear the veil from their eyes and show them the great light, that is, the sun of truth. Make us one of those who see it, and do not blindfold our eyes as in the story of the hoopoe and Solomon!"

****

THE STORY OF THE HOOPOE AND SOLOMON, DEMONSTRATING THAT WHEN DESTINY ARRIVES, CLEAR EYES ARE SEALED

> When they had set up the tent for Solomon
> The birds offering him their service would come
> They found him a confidant who spoke their tongue

They sped to him fast as they could one by one
1225.   All the birds abandoned their chirping twitter
And spoke *more clearly than* you *with your brother*
It's close affinity to speak the same tongue
With non-intimates a man is in prison
Many share a tongue although Hindu and Turk
While many do not, although they be two Turks
The tongue of intimacy's a thing apart
Better than shared tongue is to be one in heart
From the heart spring myriad interpreters
Which are not speech, not signs and not registers
1230.   All of the birds, each of them singly revealed
Their secrets and arts and knowledge and their skills
One by one to Solomon in praise of self
So to offer a petition for itself
Not out of self-conceit or pride in the self
But so that he would admit them to himself
When a captive seeks to be slave to a lord
He makes summary of the arts he offers
When he thinks the purchaser will bring him shame
He pretends he is sick, palsied, deaf and lame
1235.   The Hoopoe's turn came to offer flattery
And expound upon his thought and artistry
He said, "O Shah, it is better to be brief
I will mention just one art, one of the least."
"Go on, what art might that be?" Solomon said
"When I fly to the zenith," the hoopoe said,
"With the eye of certainty I gaze around
I can see water in the depths of the ground
So I know depth, color and location
And whether it's rock or clay which it springs from
1240.   O Solomon, take this wise one on campaign
To choose sites where your army may camp and stay."
Solomon said, "O companion excellent
In the waterless wastes of the wilderness!"

Messenger Solomon's tent was set up in a wilderness with the aim of administering justice to all creatures, human or not. When the birds heard about it, they came in haste to serve him.

    A conversation commenced between Solomon and the birds. They seemed to speak in the clearest terms with the greatest, most heartfelt sincerity. To speak the same language is friendship, it is intimacy. The magic charm that brings people close to one another and makes profound love and understanding possible is unity of language. Many are the magical functions performed by a language which is known, spoken with knowledge and loved more the more it is spoken, and which both increases love and serves as a means to its finding expression.

If there is between people no such unity of language which serves as a tie and increases love, and if, for example, a person goes to a foreign country where he does not know the language, if fortune sends him to such a clime where people are deaf to his heart and tongue, there he will become as despairing and sorrowful as if he were in prison. The melancholy of infinite loneliness will sink into him.

This is like when the arrived who see God with the eye of certainty [*Hak yakîni*] are in lands deprived of gnostics where people do not understand divine reality. There is a great truth, and a person to relate it, but if there is no one to who understands the language of the mystery, that community, that congregation of ingrates, will for the gnostic be a community of pain and suffering.

Many are the Turks and Hindus on earth. They do not speak the same language, but they can understand one another with the language of existential state, the language of the heart. At the same time, two Turks speaking the same language may come together at a certain time and place; supposedly they speak the same language, but they cannot understand one another. They persist in not understanding one another. Because their spirits have been contrary to one another since the gathering in pre-eternity, and that contrariness has continued on earth.

So, to speak the same language is not always to use the same words, but to confide in one another with the same language of the heart, in short, to speak with the language of existential state. Once the human spirit has become aware of the oneness of God and the mysteries of the sea of oneness, it makes no difference if people are Turkish or Hindu, Arab or Persian, they will understand one another.

Just as the language of the eye is sometimes more eloquent than the language of words, for people of heart and state the language of the heart speaks more clearly, more profoundly and more beautifully. But in order to understand that language one has to be a person of states, one has to reach a state of spiritual superiority capable of sharing in divine mysteries.

And so, all of the birds gathered around Solomon's tent of right and justice were dying to win his heart so they could be his eye of certainty and serve him.

Just as a slave wants to be the slave of a good master, and so that the master will like him and to prove he is worthy of serving him shows every skill, service and likableness he has. At the same time, when the same slave realizes he will be sold to a bad master, he tries to pretend to be sick, deaf, and crippled. So the birds, wanting to be slaves of the best, the most just master of all, whirled around Solomon like moths.

When it came the hoopoe's turn to display willingness to serve, loyalty and skill to Solomon, the bird said: "O great Messenger, I will be brief. My skill is that I fly to great heights and when I look down I see the waters that flow beneath the ground. Those waters which people on the ground cannot see, and because they cannot, think the pace is a desert. Army upon army of people without water, people dizzy with thirst, whose lips have cracked and whose insides are scorched, pass over deep, gushing waters.

"O great Solomon! Keep me by your side so that when you go anywhere with your army, I can tell you where they should camp. I know where such waters spring from and flow, and where they emerge from the ground, or will emerge. I will serve you well in this regard."

Solomon greeted the hoopoe's offer with joy. He said to him: "O good friend, be with us in these endless, waterless deserts! Find us water in the deserts! Don't leave without water and with no recourse!"

Solomon assigned each kind of work to those who did it best, an instance of his foresight which has served as an example throughout the ages. Because if a job is not given to the person who knows best how to do it, loss and regret are inevitable.

And just so, the subjective [*enfûsî*] meaning of this tale is given in Ismail Ankaravi's commentary thus: "Each person is the padishah of the country of his own body [*vücût*]. And so with Solomon. That is, in reality Solomon represents the spirit. When the spirit takes the throne of the heart in order to govern the exterior and interior faculties, it is as if these material and spiritual faculties are ranged before it. They offer to serve it. Each one tries to display its own art, skill and knowledge."

Here the hoopoe is intellect. And so it comes into conflict with the crow which will become involved in events later in the tale. The crow represents the faculty of fantasy [*kuvve-i vâhime*], which rejects the knowledge and gnosis of intellect. It is jealous of intellect and begins denigrating it.

The hoopoe as intellect says to Solomon spirit: "O ruler of the body, flying at great heights makes me wander above the veil called human-ness. From the skies of intellect I gaze below with the eye of certainty, and see the origin of each thing and its secret. I know where the water of knowledge and gnosis spring from and which underground riverbeds they flow through. Wherever you go with the army of the senses and creaturely faculties, I can with the water of knowledge, wisdom and love of God quench the thirst and love for the world which may destroy them, I can protect the spirit from the danger of being destroyed on paths of drought.

"Therefore, whether in war or peace, do not let me, that is, intellect, leave your side!"

Solomon spirit listens to this skill and wisdom of intellect, and answers:

> O beautiful friend! Never leave me! Do not leave me alone, and aid me truly in my beautiful and good path!

****

THE CROW IMPUGNS THE HOOPOE'S CLAIM

> When the crow heard this, he came full of envy
> And told Solomon, "The hoopoe spoke falsely
> Right conduct is not to speak before the shah
> Lying and absurd self-praises least of all
> 1245. If he's always had such sight, how is it then
> That a handful of earth hid a trap from him?
> How did he come to be caught inside the snare?
> How was he forced to go into the cage there?"
> "O Hoopoe, is it fit," Solomon said then
> "That in the first cup from you there be these dregs?
> You have been fed on yogurt with fragrant herbs
> Now you brag like a drunk, speaking lying words?"

But the crow was envious when he heard the hoopoe's speech. He vilified the hoopoe. "He is lying," he said. "If this bird could see underneath the ground, he would have seen the trap set for him under a handful of earth and would not have fallen prey to it.

How can it be that a bird who flies at such heights, and talks so big, falls into a trap and remains helpless in a cage?"

Here the hoopoe represented a master of insight [*basîret ehli*] who knows mysteries and is able to see into the realm of the Unseen, and the crow those evil-spirited persons who reject their virtue and gnosis. And this to such an extent that the evil and corruption of his spirit made even Solomon reconsider.

Solomon turned to the hoopoe and said: "He is right. Why have such dregs poured from the cup of your mouth instead of intoxicating wine? Why did you choose to lie in my presence and pretend to a skill your do not possess? Is that worthy of you?"

****

THE HOOPOE RESPONDS TO THE CROW'S ATTACK

He said, "O Shah, for the sake of God, don't heed
The enemy's words against bare beggar me
1250.   If this what I have claimed can be falsified
I lay down my head, sever this neck of mine
Since the crow denies decree of destiny
With thousands of intellects, kafir he'd be
While one 'k' of kafir still in you resides
You're stench and lust, like the 'k' cleft of the thigh[53]
I see the trap from the air, if destiny
Does not shut the eye of intellect for me
Knowledge slumbers when divine destiny comes
The moon grows dark and eclipse blots out the sun
1255.   When was such behavior rare from destiny?
It's by destiny he denies destiny

The hoopoe responded to Solomon. He spoke the language of intellect. He said to Solomon: "O great Messenger! Pay no heed to the words of crows and those with the disposition of crows, they deny the authority of destiny. They do not understand the great truth. There is no intellect in a crow's head. Even if there were, it would be a negative intellect surrounded by darkness and infidelity.

"What I told you is true. If I have lied, or lie in future, you will punish me. But in you there should not be any part of the word 'kafir,' nor belief in a kafir's words. If there were, you who are most beautiful and most clean would descend to the ugliest and dirtiest of positions. You cannot be complicit in a spiritual murder or secret evil. Because you have been bathed in the water of unity and purified with the scent of gnosis.

"However, what the crow said does not lack an insidious truth. When I am flying the heights I see traps set for me under the ground. But you know that there is God's destiny [*kazâ*] and measuring-out [*kader*]. If God the Truth's destiny suddenly comes to pass, and my capture in a trap is predestined [*mukadder*], then my eyes will be veiled as if in sleep. I will not be able to see at all, let alone see over long distances. That moment is such that the bright moon turns dark and suns are eclipsed. What I want to say is that just as the moon and sun may be eclipsed when God's measuring-out turns into destiny, my

---

53. "The infidels are filth . . . " (Koran 9:28).

seeing eyes become blind. My flying wings do not fly.

"God's destiny cannot be avoided. There is no trickery, no recourse against that command. Know that if someone tries to deny God's destiny, that denial is nothing but the coming to pass in destiny of an evil measuring-out."

One sees that in this tale the function of Solomon, representing the divine spirit, is to express wisdom. The divine spirit has ranged the material and spiritual faculties in the human being against each other; he has engaged the human faculties of feeling, knowledge, insight and logic in this conflict.

On the surface, this conflict appears to be a war of words in which each side says things were are right. This is so to such an extent that Solomon goes so far as to find the crow, who represents material power and material logic, in the right and be fooled by that logic.

At the same time, the hoopoe, who represents the view of the heart, speaks again as intellect and reminds him that divine destiny can delude even the eye of the heart. He gives frank account of times when the heart is misled and wins the argument with these frank words.

So the hoopoe, who has the power when flying at the highest heights to see the deepest waters running under the ground, cannot see anything at all if divine destiny veils his eyes and is easily caught in any trap set for him.

In the same way, when the spirit of an arrived person who is God's beloved is charged with a duty, he will perform that spiritual duty with all of his power. Even if that spiritual duty surpasses his strength, he will still succeed in it. But beyond that, such spirits have human states, such as when the bodies of messengers bow to death like all mortal creatures, and it is natural that it be so.

****

THE STORY OF ADAM, PEACE BE UPON HIM, AND HOW DESTINY BOUND HIS SIGHT FROM OBSERVING THE CLEAR MEANING OF THE PROHIBITION AND REFRAINING FROM ANAGOGY

> Mankind's father is Bey of "*He taught the names*"[54]
> With myriads of sciences in each vein
> The name of each thing came unto his spirit
> As it is and will be till the end of it[55]
> Whatever he called a thing, that hasn't changed
> That which he called 'quick' has not to 'slow' been changed
> He saw from the start who'd be a believer
> It was clear to him who'd end up a kafir
>
> 1260. Hear the name of every thing from the gnostic
> Hear *He taught the names* as its symbol's secret
> For us each thing's name is its exterior
> For God each thing's name is its interior
> In Moses' eyes, 'staff' was the name of his rod
> But 'serpent' was the name that it had to God[56]
> Here Umar had the name of 'idolater'

---

54. "God taught Adam the names . . . " (Koran 2:31).
55. Koran 2:31-33.
56. "Then he threw his rod, and it was clearly a serpent" (Koran 7:107).

But at *Alast* his name was 'true believer'[57]
That semen which for us had the name of seed
Was for God you who now stand in front of me

1265.   That semen was a form in non-existence
Present before God, no more than that, nor less
What in reality is our name, in sum
Was in the presence of the Lord our outcome
It's on a man's end that He bestows a name
Not on that state which He gives a borrowed name
Since the eye of Adam had seen by pure light
He had the names' spirit and secret in sight
Since the angels found the lights of God in him
They fell in prostration and rushed to serve him

1270.   The praises of Adam whose name I mention
I'm short if I count them till Resurrection
He knew all of this, and when destiny came
In knowledge of one prohibition was shamed[58]
Wondering if it meant that the thing was outlawed
Or an anagogy and a cause for thought
When his heart came to prefer anagogy
His bewildered nature went straight for the wheat
When the thorn got stuck inside the gardener's foot
The thief saw his chance and carried off the goods

1275.   When his shock had passed he came back to the road
And saw a thief had taken wares from the store
'Alas!' he cried, and '*O Lord, we have done wrong*'[59]
Meaning the road is lost and darkness has come
This destiny is a cloud across the sun
It makes mice of the lion and the dragon
If I miss the snare at the time of decree
It's not just I ignorant of destiny.'
O happy he who has taken up good works
Who takes to supplication and gives up force

1280.   Though destiny shroud you like the night in black
It will also take you by the hand at last
Though it may a hundred times threaten your life
Destiny also heals you and gives you life
If a hundred times it takes all that you've got
It will pitch your tent way up on heaven's top
Know God frightens you in generosity

---

57. "... 'Am I not your Lord?' They said, 'Yes, we testify.'" (Koran 7:172). The gathering where the spirits were called to testify, referred to in the Koranic verse, is called the gathering of *Alast* ("Am I not" in Arabic).
58. Koran 2:35-36, 7:19-22.
59. "O Lord! We have wronged our own souls" (Koran 7:23).

To bring you to the land of security[60]
It is late and this subject goes on and on
Listen to the tale of the hare and lion

Which tree in Paradise was it that Hazret Adam ate from, although he was told, "Do not eat from it!"? There have been those who thought it was an olive tree, a fig tree, or an apple tree. There are those who believe wheat was the forbidden food that was eaten, and those who suppose it was grapes in bunches hanging from vines.

There have also been those who said that the fruit could have been a completely spiritual fruit, and the tree, for example, a tree of knowledge. We are of the opinion that it was "the tree of love," that this tree was adorned with God's sacred lights, clothed in the raiment of lights, and that a self-disclosure occurred at this tree. That was the force which attracted both Adam and Eve to the forbidden fruit, the force sufficient to make them so wretched that they would forget it had been forbidden by God.

We know that when the desire to see divine light, to taste it like a flavor, set Moses' heart aflame centuries later, God said to His messenger, "You cannot see Me!" But when Moses persisted in his plea, God, by self-disclosing His light on a mountain, led Moses to experience the disappointment of exceeding the limit in love. Moses swooned before he could have full sight of even the light of God reflected on the mountain, let alone of God Himself. We may say that this too is the story of an untimely desire to taste the same forbidden fruit.

When Messenger Adam came to the level of love from the level of intellect, he began to see the beauty of God in all beings [*varlıklar*]. His veins filled with wisdom. He saw a self-disclosure of God in each being and he saw its name. Adam had a power of comprehension which even the angels did not have. That is why Adam's knowledge was superior to that of the angels. Adam knew each thing's truth, and that is why it is said that *He taught the names*. Messenger Adam knew all the names and all the knowledge which God presented to his comprehension.

That is why whatever name he called a thing, that name did not change. For example, if he called a being quick and swift, it never became grave and slow. Names are according to the forms in which we are able to see beings.

We know things in the form in which they are visible. In reality, beings have mysteries not evident to us. Reality is in those mysteries.

Messenger Moses knew the rod in his hand only as a "staff." He only learned that in God's reality it was a serpent when he got permission from God to perform a miracle with it.

The kafirs knew Hazret Umar as an idolater. Hadiths showed that he had been a Muslim even at the gathering of Alast.

In our eyes the function of the human seed is only the propagation of generations. But for God it is bearer of the sublime wisdom in the wish to be known of the divine being who by creating the human sees Its own image, Its own form, once again and more powerfully in the pupil of the eye in the mirror. So that in the human seed is the mirror displaying all creation [*kâinât*], or all creation itself.

Our original name and our true meaning is the name given, found, and known in the presence of God. Whatever form or garb we appear to take on in this world, tomorrow

---

60. Koran 10:62-64.

we will still come before God with the identity we had in His presence. Because it is He who knows us, who created and sculpted us according to His own knowledge.

So, whatever name or nickname other people may give us because they see us that way, for God we are the meaning of the name he gave us.

Sometimes it happens that a person who is known as a pure Muslim reaches the afterlife as a kafir. And another person whom people think is a kafir is met there with the attribute of a representative of pure faith.

Only to Messenger Adam were evident the meanings of all names and the mysteries of all beings, and that because he saw what he saw in the light [ışık] of God's light [nûr].

And so the angels, who found God's light in Adam, prostrated themselves to him and ran to serve him. His duty on earth was great, his meaning, vast. The virtue self-disclosed in him was the essence [zât] which was evident in him, and it was really that which the angels worshipped and prostrated to.

That same Messenger Adam whom pen and speech may be incapable of praising could not escape the clutches of destiny although he knew almost all mysteries; and along with Eve he suddenly approached the tree God forbade, saying, "Do not approach that tree, you will become one of the oppressors." He ate of the fruit on the tree. And as he walked toward the tree and its fruit, Adam took the way of anagogy. "I wonder," he thought. "Is this a forbidding [tahrim] prohibition, or a purifying [tenzih] prohibition?" For in Islamic belief there are two types of prohibition, which has the meaning of God says, "do not do it."

The first is the forbidding prohibition. The person who violates it deserves punishment and hellfire; the action ends in hellfire and punishment.

The second is the purifying prohibition. The person who violates it is definitely not punished. However, a person must definitely purify himself, must be purified, of such an act.

For example, the hadith saying that a person who has eaten onion and garlic should not approach a mosque does not prohibit a Muslim from performing namaz by himself. After the odor of the person's mouth is gone, he again has the right to go to the mosque.

For Messenger Adam, swayed by a desire coming from within himself, to consider a loophole is nothing other than for the measuring-out [kader] to become destiny. He and Eve bowed to that destiny and ate that forbidden fruit with relish.

And like the gardener who was distracted by a thorn stuck in his foot, they did not drive away the thief stealing from the garden, or even see him. When they were free of the bewilderment and shock which was the command of destiny, the fruits of the garden they were guarding had been stolen.

Messenger Adam realized immediately that he had committed a great sin. "My God! We have wronged our souls, the sin is ours!" he moaned. Everything had grown dark and the right path was obscured. For the divine destiny was like a dark, thick cloud blocking out even the sun. The divine destiny was that great power before which lions and dragons were like mice.

The hoopoe, who had been recounting all of this, addressed Solomon again:

"Now, O Solomon," he said, "I am not the only one to be so heedless as to not see the trap when divine destiny arrives. Even prophets and friends of God have not escaped such states.

"If God's destiny fills you with the dark of night and your soul remains in darkness, of course you will not be able to tell good from evil.

"The only way to be free of destiny is to believe in His power and fear Him. Happy is he who at the moment when destiny arrives does not forget the wishes of God the Truth and is able to conform only to His commands and think only of that!"

At the same time, one should understand the saying that there is no choice but to be reconciled with destiny thus: Although divine destiny might almost take your life a hundred times, it is destiny which gives you life. If you feel fear of destiny, know it is God's favor. Because that fear will carry you to the land of security. That land of security is the level at which one sees divine beauty.

This tale from the *Spiritual Couplets* opens another of the Koran's treasuries of meaning. It displays to us gems of truth:

God created Adam. He blew His own light into him. He put him in His paradise. He created Eve as a companion for him.

But suddenly they both saw the tree of love before them, which they were forbidden to approach. The tree of love and its delicious fruits robbed Adam of his will.

And Adam was a gnostic of God. It had been clear to him since pre-eternity what the bounties and evils of the world were. He knew the true nature of things. He was a gnostic of great truths, a great personage filled with God's light. Yet divine destiny blindfolded his eyes also. So, there is no escaping divine destiny. Or, the only way to be free of it is to understand it, to accept it, and reach the land of the heart under its protection.

****

THE HARE DRAWS BACK FROM THE LION AS HE APPROACHES THE WELL

1285.   As the lion came near the well, he noticed
That the hare was lagging and held back from it
"You are holding back, why's that?" the lion said
"Do not drag your feet, come on and go forward!"
"What feet? I've nor hand nor foot left," the hare said
"My spirit is trembling and my heart has fled
The color of my face is gold, don't you see?
My color tells you about what's inside me
The court crier, God said, is the countenance
So gnostics keep an eye on the countenance[61]
1290.   Color and perfume, like camel bells, inform
A horse's neigh makes one aware of the horse
You learn about each thing by the sound it makes

---

61. "You shall know them by their countenances" (Koran 2:273); "On the Heights there are men who know everyone by his countenance" (7:46); "Men on the Heights will call to certain men whom they know by their countenances" (7:48); "You would have known them by their countenances" (47:30); "On their faces are their marks, the traces of prostration" (48:29); "The sinners are known by their countenances" (55:41).

You know an ass's bray from a creaking gate
On discerning kinds of men, the Prophet said
When his tongue is folded up, a man is hid
In color of the face there's sign of the heart
Have mercy, plant love of me within your heart
A ruddy face has the sound of thankfulness
A yellow face, of patience and endurance

1295.   Hand and foot are seized by what's come over me
Countenance and color and power are seized
It shatters every thing it finds into bits
It tears up every tree it finds from the roots
It checkmates, this thing which has come upon me
Vegetable, inanimate, and man and beast
These are merely parts, totalities also
Are corrupted in scent and become yellow
So that the world is now thankful, now patient
The garden now bare and now clothed in raiment

1300.   As the sun rises it's the color of fire
But it will sink headlong at another hour
The stars shining brightly in the firmament
Can't escape burning out moment by moment
The moon exceeds the stars in beauty of face
But becomes a phantom as it wanes and wastes
This earth, still and seemly in its demeanor
In earthquakes is seized by feverish tremors
Many mountains have been transformed in the world
To bits and sand by this pulverizing scourge

1305.   This air which bears a resemblance to spirit
Is made by destiny foul and hideous
The sweet water that was sister to spirit
In a ditch turns yellow, bitter and turbid
The fire twirling its moustache, so conceited
Just one gust is enough to pronounce it dead
From the sea's commotion and effervescence
Plumb the alterations in its consciousness
In the ceaseless seeking of whirling heaven
Its condition is like that of its children

1310.   Its hosts of stars unlucky and fortunate
Now at the nadir, midway, and the zenith
From yourself, O Part linked with totalities
Apprehend the state of the most simple things
If totalities can have trouble and pain
How should particulars not be yellow-faced?
Especially one assembling opposites
Assembling water and earth and fire and wind
It's no wonder if the sheep flees from the wolf

The wonder is it gave its heart to the wolf
1315.   Living is the concord between opposites
What arouses discord between them is death
The grace of God has bestowed intimacy
On lion and wild ass—distant contraries
Since the world is a sick prisoner in pain
What surprise if one who's sick should pass away?"
The hare gave the lion counsel in this vein
Saying, "I have lagged behind due to these chains."

Let us return to our story. For it is another treasury of wisdom and it has large gems too.

As the hare got close to the well, he stopped taking the lead. He lagged behind the lion.

The lion noticed this. When he asked the reason, he learned from the hare that he had no strength to approach the well. The hare was so afraid of the lion inside the well that his hands and feet had gone limp, there was no courage left in his heart and his face had gone pale. The hare: "I have no hands or feet . . . If you want to know how I am, look at my color and my face, this color and this countenance will tell you all. Because colors are uncanny. Because faces tell many a secret. That is why gnostics read secrets in faces. Many a person's face tells of what is inside of him. Colors and scents are like sounds. It is not possible to know what is behind a wall unless one climbs over it. But if a mare begins to neigh behind the wall, you understand that there is a horse there, and perhaps a stable.

"This is also true of speech. Hazret Muhammed's saying, 'a person is hidden under his speech,' expresses this truth. With every feeling and thought people express by means of language, in their choice of words and the way they pronounce them, they make themselves known to those who understand their language. They sometimes tell all by means of the sounds they give to words. They even express the words they do not want to say, the thoughts and feelings they are anxious to hide.

"The color of a person's face tells us about the state of his heart.

"A pink complexion expresses its owner's gratitude, especially his gratitude to God the Truth whose bounty he has enjoyed. A pale complexion expresses its owner's trouble and suffering.

"The complexion of a person who is not comfortable and does not experience enjoyment cannot be ruddy. Nor will the face of someone who has no trouble, no fear, grow pale."

That is how the hare spoke to the lion. The hare intellect now knew that the time was approaching when he must escape from the clutches of the lion soul. But he was full of doubt and fear.

The hare intellect, pale and trembling, said to the lion soul: "Something has come over me. My hands and feet have gone limp. My spirit quails as if I were face-to-face with death. I am overwhelmed by the power which obliterates all living creatures and plants, and even inanimates."

In fact these three obliterated classes of things, which are called the three kingdoms of nature [*mevâlid-i selâse*], are nothing other than particulars [*cüz'iyât*]. But along with the three kingdoms of nature—animal, vegetable, and mineral—there are greater, more formidable beings among the universals [*külliyât*], and they too will be broken when faced by the same force and taste the flavor of obliteration.

For example, the heavens and stars are among the universals, and they will deteriorate. In short, death encompasses everyone and everything.

For this world, this universe [*kâinat*], and all created things are inside a realm of generation and corruption [*âlem-i kevn ü fesâd*]. This means that every thing is subject to an unchangeable law by which it is created on the one hand and deteriorates, decays, on the other. This law is not only for humans, not only for the other living things and plants, but the law for what we call inanimates [*cemâdât*], for all beings, far and near, which we suppose dead, lifeless and unmoving.

Fuzuli muses in one of his prayer-poems [*münacát*]:

Now Your wisdom secrets within the earth a thousand moon-faced youths
Now Your artistry fabricates from earth a thousand moon-faced youths

Thus is the world. Sometimes it looks upon us with the face of severity, sometimes the face of grace; sometimes it fills us with patience, sometimes with feelings of gratitude. The same earth at times smiles with trees sprouting green leaves and beautiful fruits. Then autumn comes and, as if calling to mind God's attributes of severity and majesty, nor fruits nor leaves remain on those trees. All of this gives us the opportunity to ponder being and nothingness. It brings us winds of being and nothingness.

Thus is even the sun, which illuminates the worlds. It rises, ascends to the heavens, then begins to wane, falls headlong and sinks.

And the stars . . . These beings which adorn the night skies one day come to close to one another, collide and burn out. And so with the moon, more beautiful to us than the sun, which wanes with time like a consumptive and later becomes only a phantom.

So, everything in nature [*kâinat*] declines and bows to obliteration.

The quiet earth may become unrecognizable with an earthquake, many a mountain may dissolve into dust in time, the air which gives us breath and life may one day fill with poisonous gas and become deadly, and water, the source of life, become turbid and smelly and dirty by remaining still in the same container, pool or lake for a long time; terrifying fire may glow and be put out by a gust of wind and, for example, a candle proud to illuminate its surroundings may be put out with one breath—all of these things are examples which come to mind of the same concepts of being and nothingness.

Philosophers [*hikmet ehli*] have said that a sea has consciousness. What that means is that there is an intellect which owns and directs it, and that is the active intellect [*akl-i faal*]. The state of the sea's consciousness [*denizin hâli*] is understood from its agitation and effervescence. Sometimes it is disorderly, combative, terrifying and deadly, like a person tearing out his hair, overwhelmed by suffering. That is the reflection of this vast consciousness. If you see a human who bears the self-disclosure of the same consciousness [*şuur*], frenzied, disorderly and suffering, you know that this state comes from his intellect.

What truth does this whirling dome of the sky seek as it whirls without cease? What is the great truth sought by the stars in its bosom and all the animate and inanimate beings in the bosom of the stars, all of them altogether in constant motion? What difference is there between their state and that of the dervish lovers of God who wander from land to land seeking God the Truth?

As those who study astronomy know, stars are sometimes at the zenith and sometimes at the nadir. So, even in the realm of the stars and the heavens, sometimes there is felicity and sometimes, bad luck.

O you who have come from a father to a mother and from a mother's womb into the world, going either from joy to joy or sorrow to sorrow, or from joy to sorrow! You are a mote in the universe. You are an itsy-bitsy part subject to the great whole. Now, many are the tiny beings like you subject to that law. When all of the parts, having passed through state after state, subject to that law, are gathered together, they form the great whole.

A totality each of whose parts passes from one state to another. This means that not only the parts, which pass from one state to another and keep going in order to reach the final state, but also the totality they form when they all come together, is subject to the same law.

If a person has a wound in his smallest member, his entire body feels pain because of it. A small affliction burns the entire body with fever.

If on the contrary the entire body suffers a general affliction, a person's every member, every cell of his body, takes it on and under its influence becomes jaundiced, pale and listless.

It is the same with the totality of this world, made of such opposing elements as fire, air, water and earth.

For this world is compounded of four elements which challenge one another as much as possible.

Don't wonder at how the wolf eats the sheep, and the sheep fears and flees it. Wonder at how the sheep gives its heart to the wolf! For the sheep to give its heart to the wolf is the same as for a person in the world to incline to the world. To give one's heart to the world, which uses up the creatures in it, and especially humans, as a wolf tears apart a sheep, is a very strange thing.

Since this world has been founded of such opposing elements, these opposites will anyway separate from one another, and every being, animate, inanimate, will die. You now regard those four members, how they appear to be united, to have given their hearts to one another in the world, and take warning.

For life and health is with the concord of these four elements. And death is the emergence of the opposition between them, and the falling of the four into conflict and war with one another.

Know that fire and water, earth and air unite and remain in concord within the human body by God's grace, and think: If the world itself is this way, sick, feverish and dark, is it any wonder that one or several hundred people in it become sick?

So, the hare intellect spoke to the lion soul in that way. He said: "Now do you understand why I have lagged behind?"

****

THE LION AGAIN ASKS THE HARE WHY HE HAS LAGGED BEHIND

> "Of the reasons why you're sick," the lion said
> "Tell me the real one, for that is my interest."
> 1320. The hare said, "That lion lives here in this pit

He is secure from harm within this fortress."
Rational men choose the bottom of a well
For in solitude the heart's purity dwells
The dark there is better than that of people
He'll not save his head who keeps pace with people
The lion said, "Come, my blows will bring him low
Go see if that lion is in the well now."
The hare said, "I have been burned once in that fire
But if you would keep me safe drawn to your side
1325. So that I, O mine of generosity
May with open eyes look in the well and see."

The lion was saying he understood. He knew that this world was diseased, that it was changing constantly and moving towards extinction. But he wanted the hare to explain: "Why are you afraid to go near this well, why do you want to stay away from it?"

The rabbit answered the lion, saying, "Because the lion who took my friend lives in this well. He has made this castle a secure fortress for himself."

In other words, a lion is going to find divine guidance in this well. In the well the lion will understand the secret of avoiding worldly filth and worldly greed, in short, his own material existence [*vücût*]. The intelligent man is he who chooses the bottom of a well. Because in the solitude of that well there is purity of heart.

Know that the darkness of living in this world with greedy people is more terrifying than the darkness in that well. Let me explain this mystery in a different way: A person who seeks help from other people cannot save himself from the trial of this world. In contrast, a person who seeks help from God has found the way which will save him from every kind of darkness.

Those who remain far from the path to God the Truth, heedless of the fellowship company of such people, let their hearts be captured by worldly ties and they become kneaded together with those swimming in people's greed.

In contrast, the sole beautiful path is the path of intimacy with friends and dervish lovers of God the Truth.

"If that's the case, don't fear, go ahead," the lion cried. "I know how to give the lion in that well what he deserves. But you take a look and see if that lion is in the well at the moment."

The hare did not agree. He claimed to be very frightened. "But if you take me into your embrace as if you were hiding me in your bosom to protect me, I will approach the well with you. If not, I cannot put myself in such danger," he said.

****

THE LION LOOKS INTO THE WELL AND SEES THE REFLECTION OF HIMSELF TOGETHER WITH THE HARE

When the lion held him within his embrace
Under his protection the hare went forth in haste
When they looked in the well into the water
A ray from them projected on the water
The lion saw his reflection shining there

The form of a lion hugging a plump hare
Having seen his enemy in the water
He dropped the hare and sprang into the water
1330.   He had dug a well and he fell into it
Because his oppression came back on his head
The tyrant's tyranny becomes a dug pit
That is what all the men of knowledge have said
The more cruel one is, the more frightening his pit
Justice decrees for evil the like of it[62]
O You digging with iniquity a pit
You are setting a trap for yourself with it
Do not like a silkworm weave around yourself
Measure, since you're digging a pit for yourself
1335.   Do not think the weak are without a champion
Recite the verse, "*When the help of God shall come*"[63]
Though you're an elephant and your foe flees you
The *ebabil birds* arrive to punish you[64]
When a weak man on earth cries out for mercy
A tumult breaks out within Heaven's armies
If you bite him with your teeth and make him bleed
What will you do when the pain seizes your teeth?
The lion saw himself in the well and he
Did not know his own self from his enemy
1340.   He thought his reflection was his enemy
He drew the sword on himself consequently
Oh, many the evil you see in others
Is your own nature projected on others
Your own existence is shining forth in them
Your hypocrisy, cruelty, dissolution
You are that, and you are striking at yourself
The one you curse at that moment is yourself
You do not see that bad in yourself clearly
Or you would be your own mortal enemy
1345.   O simpleton, you are charging at yourself
Like the lion who went charging at himself
When you reach the bottom of your own nature
Then you'll know that meanness was your own nature
At the bottom it was clear to the lion
That what seemed someone else was his reflection
Whoever tears out a poor weak wretch's teeth
Does the work of that lion who saw wrongly
In your uncle you see evil's reflection
You see on your uncle's face an ugly mole

62. "The recompense for an evil is an evil like it" (Koran 42:40).
63. Koran 110:1.
64. Koran 105:3.

It's not his, it's the reflection of your mole
The evil's you, don't flee yourself, it's not him

1350.   The believers are mirrors to each other
They relate that saying from the Messenger
Before your eye you hold up a glass of blue
That's the reason why the world seems blue to you[65]
If you're not blind, know that blue is from yourself
Speak ill of yourself, not of anyone else
If believers did not *see by light of God*
How would the Unseen be shown to them unclothed?
But since you were seeing *by the fire of God*
You did not discern between evil and good

1355.   Little by little throw water on the fire
O man of woe, that light may come of your fire
O our Lord, do throw that water purified
So the fire of this world may be wholly light
The water of the seas is in Your command
O Lord, water and fire are yours to command
Fire becomes sweet water if You wish it so
And even water turns to fire if You don't
This request of ours, too, You brought to exist
Freedom from injustice, O Lord, is Your gift

1360.   You gave us this request without our request
You've given gifts numberless and limitless

The lion picked up the hare and went forward, and inside the well he saw the image of a lion like himself holding a hare.

He thought that his image in the water was the other lion, his rival. He had no mercy for that dreadful rival who so dared to stretch out his hand to take possession of the sultanate of the world. He announced his rage and ferocity with roar that filled the emptiness of the well. Then, dropping the hare at the head of the well, he threw himself into that well which, in a sense, he had dug with his own paws.

The lion himself had prepared this end for himself, which would never show him the light of day again, in a dark well. Because he had been tyrannizing the beasts of prey. The reality was that those who commit iniquity in this world would fall into a well as terrifying and dark as the iniquity they wrought. This truth is expressed by the saying, "An hour of justice is better than sixty years of worship." The idea that "God may forgive infidelity, but He never forgives cruelty," is true for the same reason.

O you who oppress the people for the sake of status and power; this means that you will fall into the well you have dug, like the lion in the forest. What a pity that the darkness of cruelty, that is, the thickest darkness of all, prevents your eyes from seeing and your ears from hearing. Do you suppose that you harm others with this violence and compulsion you display, that you rule over the helpless? No, the person you really oppress is yourself, and what you rule over is your soul, prisoner of worldly filth.

Seek the way to make yourself forgiven. This way is the way of repentance and

---

65. In those days, to see the world through a blue glass meant to see the world as dark.

seeking the forgiveness of God. Don't suppose that the people you now see as weak and powerless have no one to protect them! Consider that their protector and helper is God. If you want proof of this, read the Koranic verse, "When the help of God shall come"! Consider that the Muslims, however small their strength and however much they may have been in the minority, with the help of God exhausted all those powerful enemies.

Even if you are as awesome and powerful as an elephant, punishment will reach you by means of the *ebabil* birds.[66]

If one weak person pleads sincerely to God for help, all the heavenly armies go into action.

God does not give temporary opportunities to rebels and oppressors because He has forgotten to punish them but because He has left them behind. Giving them time is also a delay which means that divine justice gives the opportunity to repent and ask forgiveness. But if oppression continues, the oppressors, along with those like them and those who support them, will be forced to bow to God's true justice.

All of God's severe and subjugating names go into action in this way. Punishment is in divine measure and horrifying.

A ferocious oppressor who bites a victim has his teeth broken in the end. That lion saw himself in the well, not his enemy. But he was such an animal and so wild-eyes with animal fury, he could not tell that the image in the well was his own. God's justice made that lion destroy himself with his own power.

O you who are like a lion attacking yourself, you think you have made others do what you say and that you are oppressing them. But with your own sword of oppression you are preparing the way for your own blood to flow. Clean and purify the mirror of your heart with mention [*zikir*] of God and look into the well of nature. There you will see the animal attributes of your soul clearly. If you attack them, you will destroy them.

The image every person sees in the mirror is not only his own face but the face of his own attributes. It is enough that the mirror he looks in is clear.

O you who see an ugly mole on your uncle's face! Beware, do not be disgusted by your uncle. The ugliness you see may be projected from within you.

Why do they say that the believer is the mirror of the believer? Because when a believing person looks at another believing person, he sees his own inner nature in that clear mirror, whatever his outward appearance. Sometimes he can faint when confronted by the beauties of his own believing spirit.

If a person who puts a blue glass in front of his eye sees the world all blue, it is not because the world is blue, but because of the color of the glass. If you too are seeing the world from behind a glass, everything you see, the apparently beautiful as much as the ugly, the apparently perfect as much as the flawed and shameful, takes its character from the glass you are looking through. That is, you are looking at everything through the glass of you soul.

In short, while you are preoccupied with other people's flaws you fail to see your own, and while you wear out your tongue gossiping about other people's evils, you unfortunately don't say anything good to those around you.

A believer looks at the world differently. Consider the verse of a dervish poet:

---

66. "Do you not see how God dealt with the Companions of the Elephant? Did He not make their treacherous plan go astray? And He sent against them ebabil birds, which struck them with stones of baked clay. He made them like a field of devoured chaff (Koran 105:1-5).

Let me look along with You, so I may see You, my Lord

Look at this world not with your own eye, but with the eye of the Creator who made you, and try to see the Creator who made you, for that is the one and only absolute beauty you will ever see.

Look around with God's light [*nûr*], not with His fire [*nâr*]! It is those who look at beings with God's fire who will always remain distant from Him, and cannot tell good from evil. In order to transform God's majesty into His beauty, that is, to distance yourself from His burning fire and see His beauty, look around you with the gaze He wishes you to.

O Lord! Give to us of that pure water of love and friendship, so that our fire of the world will go out and your light take its place. You can plunge us in fire or light, whichever You choose. Choose light for us. Let us burn with the light of Your beauty, not the fire of Your punishment!

Both water and fire are soldiers You created who offer their power according to Your decree. If You wish, You put the most violent fire into the state of cool water, or make of it a rose garden. But when You wish, Your turn water to fire and destroy and burn those who remain in darkness heedless of You, those who see fit to oppress the innocent.

Take us into Your presence. Take us far from ourselves and bring us close to You. Fill our hearts with Your own secret, the most beautiful secret of all. Erase the images of this very colorful world from our eyes so that we may see only You.

****

THE HARE BRINGS THE ANIMALS THE GOOD NEWS THAT THE LION HAS FALLEN INTO THE WELL

> The hare, overjoyed at being free again
> Went running to the animals in the plain
> The lion was dead in the well miserably
> The hare hopped now to grazing grass happily
> He'd escaped the hand of death and clapped his hands
> Fresh and dancing in the air like leaf and branch
> Leaf and bough are set free from the jail of clay
> They lift their heads to join the wind in play
> 1365.   When the branches are burst by the blooming leaves
> The leaves go rushing to the tops of the trees
> Each and every single leaf and every fruit
> Sings the praise of God[67] in the tongue of *its shoot*:
> "Our root was nourished by the Lord of Bounty
> Till *it grew thick and stood upright* as a tree."[68]
> The spirits imprisoned in water and earth
> Glad in heart when they escape water and earth

---

67. "There is no thing which does not praise His glory; but you do not understand their praise"(Koran 17:44).

68. The Companions of the Prophet are " . . . like a seed which sends forth its shoot, then it strengthens, then thickens, then stands on its own stem, and the farmers marvel at it" (Koran 48:29).

Dance in the air of the love of God the Truth
Flawless like the perfect disk of the full moon
1370.   Their bodies dance, their spirits—don't ask of them!
And those who are all spirit—don't ask of them!
The lion was put in prison by the hare
Shame on the lion so outdone by a hare!
The wonder of it is that despite his shame
He asked to be called "Religion's Pride" by name
O you lion at the forsaken well's foot
Your rabbit-like soul has shed and drunk your blood
Your hare soul is feeding on grass in the wild
While you are deep in this well of how and why
1375.   That lion-catcher ran to the animals
Saying, "*Rejoice, O people, I bring good news*
Good news, O you pleasure-seekers, listen well
That dog of hell has now left again for Hell
Good news, good news, that our mortal enemy
--the Creator's wrath has rooted out his teeth
He who struck off so many heads with his paws
Death's broom has swept him too away just like straw

When the hare saw the lion destroyed in the well, he began to dance in joy of life and freedom like leaves and branches on the trees. The leaves and branches which, once trapped in water and earth, become free and joyous like the spirit escaping the bounds tying it to matter, and sing with gaiety at having approached the goal.

The spirits thus freed from the bounds of the body [*vücût*] are the pure spirits [*hâlis canlar*], and have reached the level of pure spirit; our tongues cannot describe their beauty.

One should also consider those who pass themselves off as lions yet fall into a trap set by a hare. They are people imprisoned by greed and love of the world who become imprisoned in the well of their own material existence, remaining distant from real and eternal happiness.

Many are they like the lion of the forest who despite all their sins want to be called religion's pride [*fahrüddin*]. They want people to know them that way and applaud and praise them, and even if they are plunged in filth both spiritually and bodily, they think there is no harm in that.

One should say to them: O you who are slave to your body and desires! You are in reality a helpless person who has fallen into that well of material existence [*vücût*]. It is of no benefit if you appear like a lion to those who see you from outside. The hare of your soul is now grazing in pasture. Why and how is it that you, heedless of this, are in the bottom of a well? Consider these things.

The hare ran to the beasts of prey. He gave them the good news that a lion had been hunted down. He tasted the pleasure and enjoyed the good deed of giving them good news and making their suffocated hearts joyful. He told them the lion soul had been destroyed. The beasts of prey represented the spiritual faculties. The hare intellect cheered them with the good news that they were freed of the soul.

****

THE ANIMALS GATHER ROUND THE HARE AND SPEAK IN PRAISE OF HIM

     Then all of the wild beasts gathered around him
     Laughing with pleasure and joy in excitement
1380. He like a candle, they circled around him
     All the beasts of the wild prostrated to him
     "Are you a fairy, or angel of heaven?
     No, you are the Azrael of fierce lions
     Our lives belong to you, whatever you are
     You have gained the upper hand, long live your arm!
     God diverted into your stream this water
     Blessings be upon your hand and your power!
     Tell us how you deceived him by means of guile
     How you crushed that cruel tyrant by means of guile
1385. Tell us, so that story may become our cure
     Tell us the story, so that we may be soothed
     For we suffer a hundred wounds in spirit
     Caused by the oppression of that cruel tyrant."
     "Great ones," he said, "it was by aid of the Lord
     For otherwise, what is a hare in this world?
     He gave strength to me and filled my heart with light
     My hand and foot drew power from my heart's light
     Pre-eminence comes to us from God the Truth
     Change in fortune also comes from God the Truth
1390. God shows this aid in every time and in turn
     To the friends and those who see with sight certain

The beasts of prey gathered like moths around the hare, who stood among them like a shining light. They told him how awed they were by him, they congratulated him. They praised him with beautiful feeling. Then they told him to tell them what he had done, and how, that he had destroyed that lion in the well. They asked him to tell them about the way he found and the plan he made, so that they could know how a lion soul can be defeated.

It was obvious what these representations of pure spirits who have been victorious over their bodies [*vücûtları*] wanted to say: What did travelers on the path of God the Truth, travelers who turned to blunting and annihilating their souls, do and how did they do it, so that they could defeat the lion soul in their bodies? For that reason they were asking the way from a Perfect Human who had succeeded in killing his own lion soul with divine love, asking a being who represented such a Perfect Human.

That is why the hare intellect told them the truth:

Friends, he said, can a hare say anything about such great matters? It was not I who did this, it was the One who made me do it. If God's inspiration, aid and mercy had not been with me, I surely could not with this incapable being of mine have succeeded at such a great task. My victory is due only to the greatness and soundness of my faith in Him. In short, those who have control over their souls and defeat them are those who have love of God in their hearts.

Those who set out on the path with love of God succeed in defeating the greatest forces and overcoming the most insurmountable obstacles. For the power that overcomes all difficulties is that divine power which is filled with pleasure at helping those who have taken the way of knowing Him.

It is important to know that God displays this power at every opportunity to presumed friends [zan ehli[69]] and those who see with the eye of certainty [yakîn erbabı]. The presumed friends and those who see with certain sight are sometimes given great functions, they perform miracles. But as they do so, they know very well that it is God who does their great work and creates the miracles they perform. They are seeing the recompense for having given their egos [benlikleri] to God on this path.

****

THE HARE ADVISES THE BEASTS OF PREY TO NOT BE OVERJOYED AT THIS

> Don't rejoice in kingdom that changes, take heed!
> O captive of change, don't act like you are free
> For those whom kingdom's beyond turn of the hour
> They drum the shah's hour beyond the seven stars
> Those beyond change are the everlasting kings
> Spirits circling constantly with the Saqi
> If for a day or two you renounce this wine
> You will dip your lips in the eternal wine."

The hare intellect here felt the need to address the creatures who were so pleased to think the turn of worldly kingdom was theirs. He spoke to them and said: "Do not become drunk, thinking the world is now yours to rule! One should feel distress at this, not content. For to have prosperity and position really means to be enslaved to them. Worldly kingdom is definitely transient, it reaches annihilation. Gnosis is to abide [bâkî] in the universe [âlem sahîfesinde]. And that is only possible through freedom from the soul's desires.

If you are pleased that the turn for worldly bounty has come to you, know that you are taking pleasure in your own bad fortune. True fortune is to not be bound to this turn, to be able to remain above it. If you are so heedless as to think they are playing the drums for your turn, playing the drums of your sultanate, that the sound of these drums filling space is declaring your good fortune, know that God's friends and prophets whose sultanate is everlasting attained to that eternal sultanate by avoiding the worldly turn of which you are enamored.

Their spirits tasted the pleasure of drinking the wine of oneness from the hand of the Saqi of truth. They became companions of the one and eternal perpetual sultan of the universe. Those spirits plunged into the self-disclosure of God's essence and attributes. They attained the mystery and good fortune never seeing anything but God.

O good spirit, renounce the wine of the world that one day you may wet your lips

---

69. By zan ehli is meant a person whose status as friend of God [velîlik] is presumed [maznun, zannedilen].

with the wine of Paradise and drink that wine from the hand of the Saqi of truth. Touch the lips of your spirit to the cup held out by the Saqi of truth and never seek others than He.

****

EXPLICATION OF "*WE HAVE COME FROM THE LESSER JIHAD TO RETURN TO THE GREATER JIHAD*"

1395.   O shahs, we've slain the external enemy
      But within there remains one much worse than he
      He cannot be killed by intellect and mind
      Hares can't compel that interior lion
Hell's a fiery dragon, and the soul is Hell
      Which oceans can neither extinguish or quell
      It consumes, and should it drink the Seven Seas
      Its burning of creation would not decrease
      Stones and stony-hearted kafirs enter it
      Weeping miserably and ashamed in it
1400.   But with so much food it still is not subdued
      Until there arrives this call from God the Truth:
      "Are you satiated?" "Not yet," it replies
      And God says, "Here is heat, here burning, here fire!"
      It swallows a whole world while its belly roars
      After such a mouthful, "*Is there any more?*"[70]
      From out of not-place God sets His foot on it
      Saying, "*Be and it was,*" and that quiets it
      Because this soul of ours is a part of Hell
      And every part has the nature of the whole
1405.   That foot which kills it belongs only to God
      Who can draw back that bowstring other than God?
      They string only straight arrows upon a bow
      But the arrows are crooked upon this bow
      Be straight as an arrow and fly from this bow
      For straight arrows will surely spring from this bow[71]
      When I came back from the war exterior
      I turned to confront the war interior
      For "*We have returned from the lesser jihad*"
      With the Prophet we fight the greater jihad
1410.   I ask God strength, help, and right to boast from Him
      So I may uproot this Mount Qaf with a pin
      He who breaks the foe is not much of a lion
      A man who can break himself—now that's a lion

Sultans! We have destroyed a foe who was external to us and who appeared from outside to be very strong. But the enemy within and the satan within us is really much worse than

---

70. Koran 50:30.

71. This verse is inspired by Koran 11:112: "Be firm in the direction you are commanded . . . "

he, stronger than he. That enemy is our soul.

There is a lion inside of us called the soul. The hare is merely the intellect used in the effort to kill that lion. But this soul is Hell, it is a seven-headed dragon. Oceans many times over will not extinguish that Hell, not every hunter can kill that dragon. That dragon will drink the seven seas and its thirst will still not be quenched, its fire will still be just as strong.

God created Hell in the form of the soul, and the soul with the character of Hell. Each gate of Hell is one of the seven attributes of the soul. These are the gates of pride, greed, lust, envy, rage, miserliness, and hatred.

Those stony-hearted kafirs are dragged through these gates of Hell in the most shameful condition, commensurate with how they looked down on people in the world. And into Hell which knows no filling, those stone-hearts are thrown as fuel every moment.

Hell swallows the whole world and all the worlds, but is never full. In order for it to be full, it must receive a command from God and hear a divine voice say, "Stop burning!"

So that is the Hell of which the human soul is a piece. Pieces always conform to the whole. That is why we, having the nature of Hell, take more pleasure in the ways of Hell.

In short, we enter this world called Hell, which holds a person back from every kind of humanity, making him really Hellbound, on the path of hatred, through the gate of lust, through greed for position, addiction to reputation, and the gates of envy, rage and pride.

If we know that our soul is a part of Hell, and try to rescue it from the ways of Hell, there will be salvation in the end. If we do the opposite, and drive our souls on to Hell, there will be no way out.

Only the foot of God can kill the dragon soul. Only the hand of God the Truth can draw the bow of the soul. If the arrow set on this bow is a straight arrow, it will hit its mark. Try to be straight as an arrow on the bow of God! If you are an arrow which has not been bent or shot astray, then the training and support of a perfect murshid will be beneficial to you. If you are an arrow that will not agree to rectitude, what can a murshid do with you?

Have I explained this sufficiently? May the story of the lion soul be an example to you. Now let us leave the external enemy and set a trap for the lion within us. When returning from a battle, Hazret Muhammed would alert his companions with this saying. He would say to them: "To do battle with the enemy and defeat him is our minor war; but to do battle with our souls and defeat them is our great jihad."

So, to defeat the soul is harder than to overcome the enemy in battle. To defeat the soul is as difficult as to break off a boulder from Mount Qaf with a needle. To be victorious over the soul and rule this difficult country is possible only with the help of God the Truth and by following the path shown by the friends of God the Truth. Defeating the soul does not require steel weapons and long lances. It is made possible by the illumination and filling of the human heart with the light of divine love.

Remember the saying of Hazret Ali on this same subject: "To abandon one single attribute of the soul is truly more difficult than to conquer the fortress of Khaybar.

The lion who scatters the ranks of the opposing army is not important. The true lion is he who wins the war he wages on his own soul. He defeats his own soul in battle and annihilates it.

****

HOW THE AMBASSADOR OF RUM CAME TO THE COMMANDER OF THE FAITHFUL UMAR, MAY
GOD BE PLEASED WITH HIM, AND SAW THE MIRACLES OF UMAR, MAY GOD BE PLEASED
WITH HIM

> In explication of this hear a story
> And take from what I relate the mystery
> Caesar sent an ambassador to Umar
> In Medina 'cross the desert wide and far
> "People, where is the Caliph's palace," he asked
> "That I may take there my horse and my baggage?"

1415.   "He has no palace," the people said to him
> "Umar's palace is the bright spirit within
> Although he has great fame as a commander
> He lives in a hut like a dervish pauper
> O Brother, how will you see his palace there
> When the eye of your heart's overgrown with hair?
> Clear from you heart's eye all hair and malady
> And then you may expect his palace to see
> Whosoever has a heart cleared of desire
> Soon beholds the Presence and threshold on high

1420.   Since Muhammed of this fire and smoke was pure
> He saw *the face of God* wherever he turned
> If you make malicious whisperings your mate
> How can you comprehend *"There will be God's face?"*[72]
> When the gate is opened in a person's breast
> He sees a sun in each particle of dust
> 'Midst the others God the Truth is manifest
> As the moon amidst the stars is manifest
> Upon your two eyes place your two fingertips
> You see nothing of the world, do you?—be just

1425.   Though you don't see it, it has not been wiped out
> The finger of your vile soul is what's at fault
> Lift the finger from your eye, do, come and see
> You can then view every thing you wish to see
> Noah's people asked him, "Where's the recompense?"
> He said, "Beyond *they cover with their garments.*"[73]
> You have wound your robes around your face and head
> Consequently you have eyes but are blinded

---

72. Koran 2:115. According to the explication and the meaning of this gracious verse, because
God the Truth is manifested everywhere, it is possible to see Him everywhere. As Mısrî Niyazi
said: "To the gnostic the names of God are apparent in the things; the named is apparent in all the
names."

73. "And every time I have called to them, they have thrust their fingers into their ears and covered themselves up with their garments . . . " (Koran 71:7).

The remainder is but skin, man is all eye
The beloved is the sight seen by that eye
1430.   Better to be blind than not see that vision
If not everlasting, best without a friend."
When the ambassador of Rum had took in
These fresh words, he was filled with greater longing
He then set his eye to seeking out Umar
He let his horse and his baggage stray afar
He went searching everywhere for that great man
While he asked all about him like a madman
Saying, "Can there be such a man in the world
That like spirit he remains hid from the world?"
1435.   He sought for him that he might become his slave
From a seeker one day is a finder made
An Arab woman saw he was not from there
And said, "Look, Umar is under that palm there.
There he is under that date-palm all alone
The Shadow of God asleep in its shadow."

An ambassador from the Caesar of Rum traveled long through deserts to come to Hazret Umar, and sought out Umar's palace. They told him that Umar did not have a palace. For Umar gave value not to worldly show but to the construction of the house of spirit and conscience.

He has a small house, but a vast palace of the heart, they said. But you will not be able to see that palace or its beauty. In order to see it, you have to be purified of the world.

Hazret Muhammed was an example to his community in this regard. He attained the talisman of freedom from the fire of rage and lust and the smoke of human opacity, and becoming pure spirit free of the dross of body.

Hazret Muhammed was such a superior leader that his spirit was the Noah of the ship of meaning and his light, the light of the path of truth. He was such a sun that the rays of his brightness shone in the hearts of lovers.

In short, he came to show the great light to creation, and he showed such a light only to those whose heart's eye was open or whose heart's eye had the preparedness to open. Umar heart, like that of The Gracious Messenger, was freed of bounds, and was filled with the light of Muhammed and the Muhammeden mystery. Wherever he looked, he too saw his Lord.

God is apparent amongst what in reality it other than He as the moon appears bright amongst the stars. But only those whose heart's eye is open can see Him.

Just as a person who covers his eyes with his hands cannot see the world, although this does not mean that there is no world—that is, the world does not cease to exist because we have closed our eyes, or our eyes are closed—in the same way, a person who has the curtain of material existence, the curtain of soul, before his eyes will not be able to see the realm of truth [hakîkat alemi].

Only those who can lift the fingers of the soul from off their eyes find the secret of being able to see the great truth [büyük hakîkat], because the curtain preventing them from seeing has been lifted.

At the same time, those whose eyes and bodies are wrapped tightly in the coverings of I-ness [*benlik*] and soul are very far from seeing that light, as when the sun is covered in thick clouds and dark night falls upon God's day.

If you do not see, and will never see, God wherever you look, what good are your eyes to you?

When the Roman ambassador heard these words from Hazret Umar's people, he felt a brightness within him. He had the desire to meet such a great murshid and be illuminated by the light of his heart. He had a more profound longing to see Umar.

The mystery of why the ambassador sought out Hazret Umar and came to feel that to see him was a kind of felicity, and to long to see him, was obvious. That was how a true seeker should search for the murshid who would show him the truth. Only if he seeks in this way, sees the murshid with such love and fire and binds himself to him, is it possible to see God the Truth with the support of that murshid, or stride along the path whose end is God.

An Arab woman saved the Roman ambassador from further searching. She pointed out Umar asleep under a date-palm tree. "Here is the one you seek," she said. The woman pointed to a palm tree, but the tree was a symbol [*timsâl*]. That date-palm tree was in reality the fruit-laden tree of Islam. Umar sat at the trunk of such a tree, the legacy of Hazret Muhammed, and found peace there.

****

THE AMBASSADOR OF RUM FINDS UMAR, MAY GOD BE PLEASED WITH HIM, SLEEPING UNDER THE PALM-TREE

> He went over and stood looking from afar
> He began to tremble when he saw Umar
> Awe for the sleeping man then came over him
> His spirit felt a sweet state come over him
1440. Love and awe are opposites of each other
> Yet he saw them mingled in his own liver[74]
> He said to himself: "I have seen many shahs
> I have been great and preferred before sultans
> I've felt nor awe nor fear of shahs before this
> But awe of this man has robbed me of my wits
> I've gone in the leopard's and the lion's den
> But my color did not change because of them
> I have often been in ranks in battle fire
> Like a lion when the position was dire
1445. Many were the heavy blows I took and dealt
> I have been stouter than all others in heart
> This unarmed man lies asleep upon the ground
> I am trembling in my seven limbs—what's wrong?
> This is awe of God, not of created folk
> Not awe of this man who wears a dervish cloak."
> Whoever fears God and chooses fear of Him

---

74. The liver was considered to be the seat of emotions.

Is feared by men and jinn and all who see him
In respect he folded his hands, deep in thought
And in one hour Umar awoke and sprang up

When the Roman ambassador saw Hazret Umar and the beauty of the light of Umar's spirit reflected in Umar's body, he felt the light of a sun awaken within him. His body trembled at the grandeur of the view he beheld.

This state is the state which awakens within a traveler on the path of God the Truth when he attains the good fortune of seeing a great murshid.

What was this trembling, this excitement which penetrated throughout the entire self [*benlik*] of the Roman ambassador, who had seen many a sultan, many a padishah, had been accepted at many a palace by awesome rulers with great pomp and ceremony, and was so accustomed to seeing such worldly rule?

The ambassador was questioning himself about this mystery. "I have been in forest lairs of lions and tigers, in battles with armies attacking like lions and so many other awesome and terrifying situations of turmoil. But I never had a feeling like this. What is this awe inspired in me by that commander of Islam sleeping unarmed, without show, silently and without pomp under a date-palm tree?"

Such states would come over people who were seeking God the Truth and found a murshid along the way. In the forests of their own material existence [*vücût*], that is, their souls, they would see such awesome, such terrifying monsters; they would brave such hardships in order to grapple with them and overcome them and walk the straight path. But no difficulty and no fear would overtake them like that which they felt when confronted by a great murshid, nothing else could make them feel what they felt then. Because that awe was awe of God the Truth. Because what the dervish saw in the murshid is nothing but the self-disclosure of God the Truth.

For the Roman ambassador, Hazret Umar was as awesome as a lion sitting on a lambskin, but he was a sight not displayed by any being, let alone a lion, or even an imagined being. In this apparition there was no contention, no self, but there was light, humility, in short, a greatness reflected from God.

Such inspirations and feelings filled the ambassador of the Caesar of Rum. And feeling a fear of God which could almost be called love of God, he experienced state upon state confronted by the awesomeness of Umar's humility.

Before his beauty in sleep, the ambassador folded his hands in respect and humility and waited. A short time passed in this way.

****

THE AMBASSADOR OF RUM GREETS THE COMMANDER OF THE FAITHFUL, MAY GOD BE PLEASED WITH HIM

1450.   He paid homage to Umar and gave salam
The Messenger said, "Talk after the salam."
Umar returned the salam and bid him come
He reassured him and sat him before him
Do not fear is the gift given those who fear
That is hospitality for those who fear
If someone is afraid, they make him secure

They give soothing comfort to a heart in fear
Why say, "Fear not," if he has no fear in him?
Why give lessons if he has no need of them?

1455.   He made glad at heart him whose heart was in pain
He made his ruined mind a flourishing thing
Then he addressed to him an eloquent speech
On God's pure attributes—a good friend is He—
And how God gives the Substitutes loving aid
So that he should learn of station and of state
The state like unveiling of that lovely bride
And the station like seclusion with that bride
The disclosure seen by others and the shah
The seclusion for none but the mighty shah

1460.   She unveils for commoners and elite both
But only with the shah is the bride alone
Sufis who enjoy the states are quite common
Rare among them are those who enjoy stations
He recalled to him the stages of spirit
And the journeys undertaken by spirit
And spoke of a time which always is timeless
And the sacred station of magnificence
And the air in which the Simurgh of spirit
Used to soar in expansive flights before this

1465.   Greater than the horizons its every flight
And the ardent lover's hope and appetite
Umar found him a friend who stranger had seemed
He found that his spirit sought out mysteries
A perfect shaykh and an eager disciple
The mount was ready[75] and the rider agile
The murshid saw the disciple was worthy
And he planted in that pure ground the pure seed

Umar finally awoke and got up. The Roman ambassador and Hazret Umar exchanged salams. Umar showed the ambassador his smile. He distanced him from fear. To fear God is a virtue. God Himself gives peace of heart to those who fear God, he eases them with the good news that they should not fear and should not be sad. He pities those without belief who do not fear God, and He wishes them to know the great truth of His bondsmen. A true fear of God is in reality a great love of God. That fear means the believer is anxious that he is not able to love God, who is so beloved in his heart, with a love worthy of Him, not able to know intimately His infinite greatness and be a bondsman worthy of Him. God the Truth will surely be merciful and kind to those burning with such anxiety, and make their hearts feel the pleasure of certainty and safety.

Hazret Umar understood the Roman ambassador's condition and brought his heart to

---

75. Nicholson explicates the word *dargahî* [ready] thus: A horse, saddled and bridled, was kept, day and night, at the gate of the palace in readiness. The custom is said to have originated with the Caliph Mansur.

expand with the knowledge he gave him of divine mysteries and beautiful feelings.

He spoke to him of God the Truth's Substitutes and friends, of how alive with love of God they were, how happy the mysteries of intimacy with God made them, he informed him about what states and stations on the path to God were and talked about the realities and beauties of these things.

State [*hâl*] was such a feeling filling a person's heart that those who felt this feeling even just once would taste a beauty and sublimity whose divine pleasure made a person lose consciousness. But the attributes of the soul could cause that state to flicker like the color of twilight, or appear and disappear like the smile of a beautiful bride, that is, could block its continuity. In short, those who arrive at the mystery of possessing state can only taste that profound pleasure from time to time.

But to possess station [*makâm*] is a much superior virtue. To possess station is to reach the station where one is able to see or to know the self-disclosure of God the Truth without ever being separated from it.

State is such a spiritual beloved that during it all travelers on the path to God, the commoners [*avâm*] and the elite [*havâss*], all of them, see her face and are included in her circle of converse and fellowship; but the felicity of raising that beloved's veil, attaining her secrets and enjoying union with her continuously has been given to those who possess station.

For Hazret Umar to tell the Roman ambassador about the stages of spirit [*cân*] and the travels of spirit [*rûh*] meant that he spoke to him of the way-stations through which the spirit passes or sojourns from the time it falls from the realm of spirits [*ervâh âlemi*] until it comes to the realm of material existence [*vücût âlemi*], and of the ways it takes in order to return to its origin, that is, to God the Truth. If the spirits which break away from God and descend to our realm of transience have comprehended the level of state, they could proceed from the pleasure and joy of such possession of state and rise to the degree of possession of station, which meant that pleasure and joy would never be extinguished. Umar was telling the Roman ambassador how one began this great journey, where one sojourned, and how it ended.

Finally he told of that time in which there is no time. No morning, no evening, no time, no place. There spirit unites with God, melts in the oneness of His being, becoming either annihilated or subsistent with His being.

And he spoke to the ambassador of such an atmosphere, such a space without limit or bound, where the bird called spirit flew before descending to alight in our world of today.

Every flight of that bird of sacred spirit transcended the horizons. For the horizons were limitless, and the divine realm [*lâhut alemi*] was limitless and without end. The spirit which knows no bounds flew in that limitless realm. But what is meant by spirit is the spirit of those who are perfect. The spirit of the common does not have the power to go beyond the horizons.

Umar spoke openly to the Roman ambassador, telling him sublime mysteries. For Umar had seen that ambassador's inner face, not his external face, and found there a virtue of preparedness for taking on such mysteries.

Umar was an arrived person and had reached the great goal. The Roman ambassador was among those who are travelers on that path from birth, who are seekers of that felicity. In short, a guide to the path had found a seeker of the path, and was showing his wings spiritual horizons. The rider was a royal horseman, and the horse prepared to transcend the horizons, waiting bridled and saddled.

Umar had found soil favorable for the planting of sublime seeds. He constantly adorned that soil with seeds of mystery.

****

THE ROMAN AMBASSADOR QUESTIONS THE COMMANDER OF THE FAITHFUL, MAY GOD BE PLEASED WITH HIM

"O Commander of the Faithful," he asked him
"How did the spirit come to earth from Heaven?
1470. How came into this cage that measureless bird?"
"God read spells over the spirit," he answered
"Non-existences which have nor eye nor ear
When he reads over them, they begin to stir
Due to His spells, speedily non-existence
Dances gaily to bodily existence
When over the existent He reads again
It rides post-haste to non-existence again
He spoke in the rose's ear and made it smile
Spoke to stone and made it agate in the mine
1475. Gave matter a sign and it became spirit
Spoke to the sun and it became radiant
He breathes again in its ear something fearsome
And a hundred eclipses fall on the sun
What did that Speaker say into the cloud's ear
That like a waterskin its eye squeezed out tears
What did God the Truth say into the earth's ear
That it has remained a silent watch-keeper
Whoever is perplexed in hesitation
God the Truth has whispered a riddle to him
1480. So he would be trapped between two conjectures
'Shall I do what He told me, or the reverse?'
Also God makes him prefer one of the two
And on that basis it's that side he will choose
If you don't want spirit's mind to be unsure
Do not stuff cotton wool into spirit's ear
So you may understand those riddles of His
So you may grasp what is clear and what hinted
Then spirit's ear is site of inspiration
What's that? Speech hid from sensory perception
1485. Spirit's ear and eye are other than that sense
Intellect and sense's ears are insolvent
Mention of compulsion made me leap for love
Compulsion is jailed by men who do not love
This is not compulsion but union with God
This is the moon's self-disclosure, not a cloud

And if it's compulsion, not the vulgar kind
The commanding soul's self-interested kind
Only those whose insight in the heart, O son
Has been opened up by God know compulsion
1490.   The Unseen future is manifest to them
Recall of the past is as nothing to them
Their freewill and compulsion is something else
In oyster shells drops of water become pearls
What outside is a water-drop, large or small
Inside the shell becomes a pearl, large or small
That people's nature is like a stag's belly
On the inside musk, while blood is what you see[76]
Don't say, 'this substance which outside looks like blood
How does it inside the navel become musk?'
1495.   Do not say, 'This base metal which is copper
How is it gold when mixed with the elixir?'
Freewill and compulsion, in you illusion
Become the light of majesty inside them
Bread on the dining cloth is inanimate
In the flesh of men it becomes glad spirit
It will not, left on the dining cloth, alter
Spirit transmutes it with Salsabil water
O true reader, thus the power of spirit
What power then in that spirit of spirit?
1500.   With spirit and intellect, the hand of man
Makes water channels and mines in a mountain
The strength of mountain-cleaving spirit splits stone
The strength of spirit of spirit *splits the moon*
If my heart opens the flap of secret's purse
Spirit will then rush the Throne fast as a Turk."

The Roman ambassador said to Hazret Umar: "O padishah of the believers! I want to ask you about the spirit. Why and how did spirit, having attained the secret of being in the colorless, space-less realm, descend from the heights? What happened and how did it happen that spirit, flying through a realm without limit or bound, measureless and beyond measure, longed to squeeze into this narrow box we call the cage of flesh?"

Umar said to him: "Because God gave spirit love of bodily existence. He gave it a profound desire to be in a body. He made it excited to enter a form. In this excitement, spirit set out to stroll through creation. It knew that God the Truth would support it with all of His protecting strength; it knew that on this long tour God would not be separate from it. It set out on the road with that command. I tasted the pleasure of taking on color and form, of flourishing in a body, and finally of owning a body. And it became accustomed to the mercies of serving a body.

---

76. The umbilical cord of the male musk-deer is dried and used for its scent. The musk extracted from the stag's body is bloody. The true character of God's friends is veiled by outward appearance (as musk is veiled by blood).

Let God not once give spirit in the bodiless realm the pleasure of a body. Let it not be enchanted by that taste. Of course spirit would fulfill that command in the most beautiful way; of course it would fall under the spell of body. And so it was in conformity with divine will that the spirits in the bodiless realm ran to bodies as if celebrating a feast day.

*

The realm of non-existence is a realm there is no eye to see and no ear to hear. Or it is far from needing to be seen and heard. Let God only loose his sublime and enchanting attribute upon that world, and at that instant all non-existences will begin to dance in an infinite exaltation and run to material existence [*vücût*] and body [*cisim*].

That realm of non-existence has the function of God's mirror. When God self-discloses in the mirror, when God's light strikes that mirror, that sublime realm comes alive with an order and arrangement and God's names and attributes are clothed in countless forms, meanings, colors and life. Then every power [*kudret*] and beauty in these boundless and limitless colors, forms, patterns, bodies and animate beings self-discloses in a more centralized way in the descendents of Adam. This manifestation of God's names and divine attributes again in humans means their self-disclosure in the material and spiritual human architecture.

This is such a self-disclosure that when a human looks in a mirror, he sees both himself, and if he knows how to look, the One who created him.

And if having completed that descent from the heavens to earth, a person finds a tarikat and way of purification [*ihlas yolu*], and then achieves the rank of ascension from earth to the heavens, the entire adventure is reversed and forms, colors and patterns remain in the mortal world. Created existence [*vücût*] attains the level of invisibility. Spirit returns the way it came and ascends to the realm of oneness and joins the sea of oneness, and abides [*bâkî*] there and in it. All of this is by God's will and command.

God whispers a secret in the rose's ear and beautifies it with a reign of color and fragrance. He tells a secret to stone and makes it agate in the mine. In other words, self-disclosing with His self-disclosure of delicacy, He beautifies the rose and gives value to stone.

He tells the human body a secret, a sign, and raises it to the firmament. That is why bodies [*vücûtlar*] which hear a voice from the divine realm put their matter [*cisimler*] in the state of spirit [*cân hâline koyarlar*] at that instant and attain the felicity of salvation from matter [*cisim*].

When God tells a secret to the sun, His name of light self-discloses and makes the sun illuminate the worlds.

The fact that the sun, whose function is to illuminate the worlds, is eclipsed and gives no light; that tears flow from clouds as if emptied out glass by glass; that in spring the soil speaks in the language of flowers, leaves, branches and fruits, and when the time comes does not speak in any language at all; all of this occurs because a divine word, a divine command, coming from the self-disclosure of the names "Contractor" [*kâbız*], "Preventer" [*mâni*] and "Repeller" [*dâfî*] reaches the ear of every particle making up the whole of creation.

Whatever may be the external causes of these natural events, the power which makes them occur in an order and arrangement says many things to them and by way of the languages of their states, to humans.

In the same way there are those in whose ears God speaks very mysterious secrets and they are bewildered in confrontation with truths they do not understand. This is so to such an extent that they do not know whether to take the path of merciful God or of Satan.

They take the path which has been written on their brows. Only the mercy of God the Truth can save them from evil paths.

If you want to understand divine secrets and walk the path God wishes, you must lift the veil from your eyes in order to see the path of God the Truth, which is actually very clear, very obvious. In order to hear the words of God the Truth you must take the cotton wool out of your ears.

Then you will learn the secret of hearing with the ear of your heart and seeing with the eye of your spirit. The two will show you the most beautiful path. Not every heart knows the excitement of being filled with God the Truth. Not every eye sees God and not every eye hears the voice of God. In order for those things to happen one must know love, feel love.

I have mentioned compulsion [*cebir*] to you before. I discussed the varieties of compulsion. I will discuss the term again here. But this compulsion signifies love. This compulsion is the approved kind of compulsion. A person who has devoted his being to love-compulsion understands the secret here. There are the phrases: I am locked by you [*meftûnunum*], I am struck by you [*sana vurgunum*], and, I am forced by you [*mecbûrunum*].[77] Now I will tell you about forced compulsion:

> Majnun, who used to say "Lā ilāha illā"
> When they urged him to gather his wits, would say "lā"[78]
> He was compelled by Leyla to such a degree
> That when he should have said "God," he would say "Leyla"

It is those who know the compulsion of being forced as in the quatrain—meaning to be struck with love—who comprehend that pleasure fully with their eyes and their ears and their hearts.

So here, compulsion is union with the greatest beloved.

Mevlana in these verses was expounding the degrees and meanings of two different kinds of compulsion. This means that there is a group called fatalists who do away with the partial will [*cüz'î irâde*] and consider God's bondsman to be at the level of inanimates. They violate every kind of religious system, they consider a person who breaks the established rules of good character excused. For according to them humans, like other animate and inanimate beings, have no responsibility at all. That is the thinking of those who reject the great bounty given to humans, the free [*ihtiyârî*] and partial will. The compulsion of such people is a commoner's compulsion swept up in the self-interests of the soul. But that compulsion is not what is discussed here. Here is discussed the compulsion of people whose heart's eye God with great grace has opened. They are those who know the divine secret. The Leyla they are forced by is that secret itself.

Let it be known that the pearls in oyster shells become pearls by means of raindrops.

---

77. The three phrases all mean, "I am in love with you," but I translate literally because the author is making a distinction between them.

78. Arabic *Lā ilāha illāllāh* is the Muslim profession of faith, "There is no god but God." Majnun is saying, "There is no god but . . . " The *lā* at the end of the second line can be taken as completing the phrase, but it is also the case that *lā* written independently means "no."

So of course there will be small pearls and large pearls inside shells. Because some raindrops are small and others, like drops of April rain, are huge drops which bring forth shah pearls.

Know the hearts of the arrived as shells which bring forth giant pearls from April rain. And consider the pearls which appear in those shells to be the unique beauty by which those hearts are forced.

The heart-shells of arrived persons know how to make giant pearls of every beauty which falls into their hearts. And they have no difficulty making divine love of out of the soul's defeat in what we have called commoner's compulsion. Nor do they fail to make pearl shells of the hearts of many a raw person who shows the purity of approaching them. It is enough that you know how to be a raindrop hiding in that shell.

There is in the nature of the arrived a power which makes musk and musk scent from the foul blood of a deer. To transform filthy blood into beautiful scent is a mystery of the sac in that deer's belly. When you learn that mystery you will understand the virtue of the transmutation of a foul drop of blood into the beauty of the color and scent of a loved one's hair.

The elixir which makes gold from copper is also in the same hearts. They are such hearts that the blood which in you is fondness of the soul, greed, and avarice becomes in their hearts divine light.

So it is with the bread which sits on the dining cloth like a mere thing, which like water that gives all beings life, becomes inside the body a source of goodness, beauty, health and faith. In a body fond of the soul, the same precious bread becomes despicable, vile and foul like a corpse. But in the body of an arrived person, bread is the food of greatness, beauty and goodness.

You see that I have spoken to you of the material and spiritual food of the spirit in humans, and of the power and strength the spirit takes from this food. To be sure, the power taken from this food by the ordinary spirit is one thing, and the power produced in the spirits of the friends who are the spirit of spirits will be another.

This is true to such an extent that if even unapproved substances come into the hands of, become the share of, the friends who are the spirit of spirits, they are purified of all their faults and become clean, sweet and beautiful.

Let us say that the hero Farhad, legendary lover of Shirin, ate meat and bread and drank water. What was the greatest benefit he could display with the power these bounties produced in his body? Was it not merely the splitting of a steep mountain?

But the day that the same food became spirit and power in the body of the spirit of spirits, he split the moon.

One man splits stone on earth and the other splits the moon in the sky. This is only one of the differences between them.

What is meant by the spirit of spirits is the Prophet and the friends who are his heirs. Those friends in whose mirror of the heart shines the light of Muhammed are the owners of the spiritual heavens. They too split their heart-moons, of which one side belongs to soul and the other to spirit.

At this point let us choose to be silent. If once I have started to talk, I open the pouch of secrets a bit more and my heart reveals a bit more of this mystery, spirits not suitable for the knowing and seeing of great mysteries to this degree may not be able to stand the weight of the burden of mystery. It is right to always keep hidden those secrets so great as to make the spirits of such people fly from their bodies.

****

HOW ADAM ATTRIBUTED THAT FAULT TO HIMSELF, SAYING, "O LORD, WE HAVE DONE WRONG,"[79] AND IBLIS ATTRIBUTED HIS OWN SIN TO GOD, SAYING, "BECAUSE YOU HAVE LED ME ASTRAY."

> Look at both the acts of God and at our acts
> It is obvious that indeed we do act
> If there is no such thing as the creature's act
> Do not ask anyone, "Why did you do that?"

1505.
> Our acts come to exist by God's creation
> Our acts are the effects of God's creation
> A speaker sees the letter or the intent
> He can't grasp two accidents in one instant
> If he goes for meaning, the letter is missed
> No glance sees fore and behind in one instant
> At the time when you're looking in front of you
> How can you also see in back of you too?
> Since spirit can't grasp meaning and letter both
> How should spirit be creator of them both?

1510.
> God does comprehend both of the two, O son
> His one act does not hinder the other one
> "*Because You have led me astray*," said Satan
> The vile Devil tried to keep his act hidden
> Adam said, "*Unto ourselves we have done wrong*"
> He was not, like us, heedless of God's action[80]
> From respect he concealed God's act in the sin
> He enjoyed the fruits by taking on the sin
> After he repented, God said, "O Adam
> Did not I create that trial and that sin?

1515.
> Was it not My measuring and destiny?
> Why did you conceal that in apology?"
> "I observed right conduct out of fear," he said
> "I have also observed that for you," God said
> Whoever shows respect also gets respect
> Whoever brings sugar will eat almond cake
> For whom are *the good women*? For *the good men*
> Bear your friend well; hurt him and see what happens[81]
> To demonstrate, O heart, tell a parable
> That you may discern compulsion from free will

1520.
> There's a hand which due to tremor has the shakes
> And a hand which you yourself move from its place

---

79. "O Lord, we have wronged our own souls . . . " (Koran 7:23); "Because you have led me astray . . . " (Koran 7:16,15:39).
80. Koran 7:23,15:39.
81. Koran 24:26.

Know God is of both movements the creator
But they're not analogous to each other
When you make the man's hand move, you beg pardon
But the man with tremor does not beg pardon
This is intellect's topic. Whose? That trickster's!
So that a weakling may take the road to there
Intellect may fine as pearl and coral be
But spirit is something else entirely

1525.   Spirit's discussed at a station different
The temper of spirit's wine is different
Intellect's discussions were appropriate
When Umar and Bul Hikam were intimate
But when Umar left intellect for spirit
Bul Hikam became Bu Jahl on that subject
Perfect in sense-perception and intellect
But with respect to spirit, he's ignorant
Know sense and intellect as effect or cause
Spirit's topic is awe or father of awe

1530.   No more, O light-seeker, when spirit's ray comes
Of binding, negation, premise, conclusion[82]
For the seer upon whom divine light dawns
No longer needs proof which resembles a rod

God of course performs actions appropriate to His Glory. Know that humans also perform acts appropriate to them and by their own will. Consider what God the Truth does, and what His bondsman does! See the difference.

If you know all of what the creatures do to be the work of God the Truth, than what right do you have to chide a person for doing something bad? Why do you try to punish or reward God's bondsmen for what God has done?

To be sure, God knows of our actions and God is even the creator of our actions. But we have a share in our acts [*fillerimiz*] and actions [*hareketlerimiz*] which we call our partial free will [*cüz'î ihtiyar*] or partial will [*cüz'î irâde*], and it is right to know this intimately and see it profoundly. For most of the time what we do, for well or ill, we do ourselves.

When we talk, we no longer think about the letters which make up the sentences we speak. If we try to think about that and keep track of it, the intent which is called the meaning of our words will weaken, even cease to exist. In short, we speak the meaning. The letters and words for us to express the meaning come to us of themselves.

This is like a person's not being able to see in front and in back of himself at the same time. Since a person cannot grasp at the same moment and with the same force both the meaning of his words and which letters and how many letters make up what he says, how can the spirit be the actor in both of these actions?

God confronted Both Satan and Adam because of the sins they committed.

Satan said to God: "You led me astray, You even seduced me." He attributed the guilt for all of his actions to God. True, the creator of the acts and actions was God. But

---

82. Terms used by logicians.

He left humans the freedom to choose which of them to do and which of them not to do. That is why Messenger Adam though differently, and said: "My God, I and Eve let ourselves be fooled by Satan. We could have performed the good act, but we performed the bad act. Thus we wronged ourselves. If You forgive us, we will be saved. If You do not, we will suffer the punishment and be among the deprived."

Although the creator of the acts was God, Adam observed right conduct [edep] and did not try to regard what he had done as coming from God. Although he knew that every act which is performed is tied to the pre-eternal will, he considered the role of his own partial will or lack of will in his act and took recourse to repentance.

Then God said: "Without doubt, your acts and the disasters that befell you occurred by My destiny, my will and my measuring. You know that well. So why, when you begged my pardon, did you put forth this point?" The answer He received was worthy of Messenger Adam:

I was afraid of You and I did not abandon right conduct.

That statement was acceptable to God. He told Adam: I saw that in you and I protected you. Your right conduct and the delicacy you showed is My help and My gift to you. Because of that act of yours, I protected you and will protect you.

Is that not how it is in the world as well? If a person wants to be respected by someone, first he shows that someone respect. A person only eats halva in a place where he brings sugar. How can you ask someone to love you if you do not love him with all your heart? And it is the same way with divine truth. Surely God will give His heart to those who love Him the most.

Good things are for good people, pure things are for pure people. Love is for those who love. The wine of divine love is for those who can drink it.

As you know, there are two ways for a hand to move. Either a hand gets a tremor through illness or old age, or you make it move for some reason, make it shake or appear to shake.

If you knock someone's hand on purpose, and it breaks something or spills a drink, you are at fault. Because your will made it move. But how can you blame someone whose hand shakes in itself for such things? You should have known his hand shakes and not made him do whatever it was, you should have done it yourself. If your sin is doubled in this way, it is due both to your intent and your thoughtlessness.

All of these things I've said are connected to topics belonging to intellect. If you ask what intellect that is, let us say that it is not the intellect you have. For the partial intellect [cüz'î akıl] is not considered to be true intellect. True intellect is the universal intellect [küllî akıl] that shines in the prophets and friends of God.

But you should not look down on those whose intellect comes only in hindsight. To be sure, a head without an intellect will knock against this stone and that stone. Sometimes it will attribute the guilt for its actions to God, and sometimes it will rise to the right conduct and maturity of being able to take on the guilt itself.

At the same time, there is a power higher than the topic of intellect, that is, higher than intellect. Its name is spirit.

The discussion of spirit is elsewhere, its station is different. So that the wine of intellect is one thing and the wine of spirit is another. The wine of spirit has a temper such that when a person arrives at the level of drinking that wine, a level beyond the highest levels of intellect, he will have difficulty understanding through intellect how high he has reached.

Learn that from the story of Hazret Umar and Abu Jahl! There were two Umars among the Arabs. One became a Muslim and the Caliph Umar. The other Umar was his close friend and confidant, at first more highly thought of, and who because of the attention he drew among the Arabs with his knowledge and thought, was known as Bul Hikam, "Father of Wisdom."

But when Islam shone like a light among the Arabs, Bul Hikam did not become Muslim. That is, his intellect did not reach Islam. His great knowledge was not enough for him to understand that great religion. That is why they then called him Bu Jahl, "Father of Ignorance."

But when Umar chose Islam, telling the difference between good and evil more by means of the spirit than by way of intellect and knowledge, he was called Umar al-Fâruq [Umar the Discriminator].

So, let the light of spirit shine. Once the light of the spirit has shown, all the proofs and terms of knowledge and intellect and left in the shade.

This means the shining of the sun of love within the heart. When that happens, the stars of knowledge and intellect fall into invisibility.

For Hazret Umar to go from intellect to spirit meant for him to come from non-faith into Islam. For spirit is the light which has no need of even the most valuable of guides, of intellect and knowledge. It is the light which finds love.

Take the rod from the hand of a blind man who can only find his way with a walking stick, who can only see the edge of the sidewalk with his rod. The poor thing will not be able to walk. But what should a person do with a stick when the eye of his heart is open with the light of spirit and illuminated with the power of love? The stick showing the way is for those whose heart's eye does not see. Those who are shown the way by love walk on top of all ways and all knowledge. That is why Fuzuli wrote:

> Whatever is in the world is love
> Learning, so it seems, was idle talk

****

EXPLICATION OF "AND HE IS WITH YOU WHEREVER YOU MAY BE."[83]

> Once again we have returned to the story
> But have we ever really left that story?
> If we come to ignorance, His jail is there
> If we come to knowledge, His palace is there
> And if we come to sleep, we are drunk on Him
> If to wakefulness, we're an epic of Him
1535.   And if we weep, we're clouds full of His bounty
> And if we laugh, then we become His lightning
> If to rage and war, His reflected fury
> And His love, if it's to peace and to pleading
> In this twisting and turning world, who are we?
> We who like alif have nothing else but He

---

83. Koran 57:4.

God is with you everywhere and in every circumstance. But the human intellect is incapable of understanding this happy togetherness. In a sense, this is to be heedless of the greatest possible felicity. Since God is not visible, many a heedless person is heedless of the virtue of being together with Him.

And many a happy spirit comprehends the wisdom of the invisibility of God, who is in the hearts of believers. They know He is everywhere and in every thing. And they are entranced by His manifestation and self-disclosure in beings.

But let us return to our story. Or let us remember that we really are inside of a pre-eternal and post-eternal story, and even if we wanted to get outside of it, we do not have the power to do so.

We should know that to be with Him is to be inside that story. To be heedless of God, ignorant of His truths, is to be in His prison. Just as the guilty rot in prison, so are those ignorant of God despised in the prison of soul and body. Because not to pass away in the oneness of God and to stray to what is other than God is to remain in the prison of nature and be obliterated there.

To the contrary, to know Him, to try to know Him, will make us happy with the truest of loves.

To slumber in such a love of God and knowledge of God is to be entranced by His attraction. That sleep rushes us to be annihilated in His being. And to awake from such a drunkenness is to rise to the level of intellect in His being. When we reach that level, we see and understand that our whole adventure is in truth the story of that greatest Beloved. All that we say is really His adventure.

Our weeping is His rain of mercy, and our laughing is like His lightning flashes which illuminate terrifying darkness. Our wars are a manner of the power in His all-subjugating attribute, and our peace is an expression of His infinite love and friendship.

In short, in this topsy-turvy world, we do not exist, He does. Each thing we make or destroy is a flash of His various self-disclosures. We are each a particle of His extremely varied appearances in a mirror without limit or bound, and the many, varicolored, very bright, very active manifestations occurring every instant in the universe are the reflections of His wisdom in that unique mirror.

****

HOW THE ROMAN AMBASSADOR ASKED UMAR, MAY GOD BE PLEASED WITH HIM, ABOUT THE CAUSE OF THE TRIALS OF THE SPIRITS IN THESE BODIES OF WATER AND CLAY

> When the ambassador heard that from Umar
> An illumination appeared in his heart
> For him there was no more question or answer
> He was delivered from recompense and error
1540. He had found the root and put aside the branch
> He began to ask about divine science:
> "What's the wisdom and mystery, O Umar
> In imprisoning the pure in this dirt here?
> Why has pure water been hidden inside clay?
> Why is pure spirit in body shut away?"
> Umar said, "You're making a rare inquiry

You are binding the letter to the meaning."
You've imprisoned meaning free and singular
You've shackled the wind by means of a letter
1545.   You have done this to obtain a benefit
You who are indeed veiled from that benefit
How should He from whom all benefit is sprung
Not see that which is already seen by us?
There are myriads of benefits and each
Myriad is few compared to that blessing
The breath of your speech, part of a part, is good
So why should the whole of the whole not be good?
You are a part, and your act beneficial
Why do you raise your hand to reproach the whole?
1550.   Do not speak, if there's no benefit in it
If there is, show gratitude and don't object
It is a binding duty to give God thanks
Wrangling and making sour faces is not thanks
If all required to give thanks were looking sour
There would be no thanksgiving like vinegar
If vinegar needs a way to the liver
Tell it to become oxymel with sugar
Meaning in poetry is just blundering
It is not under control, it's like a sling

The Roman ambassador had listened with great attention to what Hazret Umar said. He learned of the level of unity [*vahdet mertebesi*] and the story of the spirit which descends from the sublime realm to this earth.

The ambassador's heart was cheered. He found within himself the great love which must be felt toward God. He attained a profound illumination.

Question and answer, concepts of right and wrong, were no longer for him. He was on the path to oneness and had covered a great distance in little time.

But it was still necessary to ask. It was right to request that more truths be brought out into the open, in order to illuminate other travelers on the same path and clear up their difficulties. It was with this thought that the Roman ambassador said to Hazret Umar:

> O Umar, what is the mystery which makes that pure spirit, so far from every kind of body [*cisim*] and the ties of body, run toward this material world and enter this cage of flesh? Why did the pure spirit, the sublime spirit, fall from the heights to this miserable world? Why was spirit, suffering a fate like water which is originally pure but gets mixed with earth and is dirtied in the mud, forced to sojourn in this worldly clay? What is the mystery of this, what is its wisdom?

Hazret Umar gave the ambassador this answer:

> Ambassador, you have touched on a profound topic. Hazret Muhammed did not agree to reveal the mysteries and wisdom of the spirit's adventure here. A major reason is that it is akin to the wisdom of God's invisibility. Not every spirit can bear

to comprehend that wisdom. There are mysteries which not even people's spirits can bear, let alone their bodies or their understanding. This is like God's saying to Messenger Moses, "You cannot see Me." As you know, Mount Sinai could not bear the reflection of His divine light for an instant.

You want totally free "meaning" to be imprisoned in words and letters. The reason for that is the groundless fear that one cannot communicate meaning without putting it into the form of words and letters. It is not absolutely necessary for every meaning in a person's treasury of thought to be brought out. It is appropriate for such meanings to not be explained but made felt as feelings and sounds.

Since people imprison free meaning in letters and words, they have grown so accustomed to that one way that they want even the highest mysteries, those least amenable to form, to appear in such forms. They suppose there is a benefit in this, and have reason to believe it because they see many meanings in such forms and understand them in that way.

God, who is in reality the creator both of meaning and of our ability to put meaning into words, of course knows the benefit of meanings being put into the form of words. God is the creator of that benefit also.

Certainly there is wisdom in God's not having put that greatest of meanings into words. Now, you want that mystery explained. While wishing for this, you are thinking that the result you obtain will have great benefits, that is what you suppose.

But you are veiled from knowing the benefit of the spirit's being in a body. Just as you need a means of hearing in order to hear sounds and words, it is necessary for the ear of your spirit to be open in order for you to understand the great meaning of the spirit's being in a body. If you had that vehicle of understanding, or it were open, you would have long since found the meaning without limit or bound written on the tablet of comprehension of your intellect.

However, we can still think over with you some of the benefits of the pure spirit's being bound to this dense body.

The first of these is doubtless that divine love and divine mysteries thereby find a means of self-disclosure and manifestation of in this realm of images, forms and matter.

One of those mysteries is that the most beautiful and sublime Beloved seeks eyes to see His beauty and hearts to love His beauty, that is, He gives to certain eyes and hearts the good fortune and the potential of experiencing all of the flavors of such a love. But in order to understand that benefit, one must comprehend the greatness of that love and the vastness of the divine light filling the heart which feels that love. A spirit which has tasted the pain of being separated from that must be able to burn with the joy of union of being reunited with it again.

Consider the fact that you are a part, even part of a part. Although that is the case, you find great benefit in putting into the form of words, or seeing in the form of words, the feelings born in your heart and the thoughts awakening in your mind.

Now consider the whole. Try to imagine how meaning which is the whole of the whole may be a meaning beyond words, forms and patterns. Then you will not spend time trying to understand that great meaning by asking, but rather my means of insight [sezgi], and only then will you grasp that pleasure.

If you did not take on a form, if you did not suffer separation, how could you know the virtue of the realm of formlessness and the pleasure of the realm of union, how could you conceive of it?

Consider that while the spirit which has come to the realm of bodies and forms was in God's realm of formlessness and immateriality, it scattered the seed of many a secret it possessed onto this ground. It was witness to the creation by that sublime seed of countless forms and beauties whose every manifestation would draw the love of thousands of hearts. The love and longing spirit felt for body comes from the profound mystery of its taking on such form in material existence [*vücût*].

That is also the meaning of the line in the *Spiritual Couplets*, "Since they cut my stalk away from the reed bed." The reed bed is the realm of spirits, and by thus falling into the prison of nature, the spirit separated from the divine realm begins to comprehend the value of the realm it has left. In the ream of material existence it dreams of the beauty of that realm. It feels the pain of exile from it, actually tastes the pain of exile.

In short, by leaving that realm, it is possible to know its value.

The coming of the spirit from the level of the immutable entities [*âyân-ı sâbite*] to the realm of humanity [*nâsût âlemi*] means the self-disclosure in this realm of the values within it. That is the mystery expressed by God the Truth's sacred hadith, "I was a hidden treasure and I loved to be known."

While in the realm of spirits, the spirit knew God only according to its own preparedness [*istîdadı*], and knew God only in His essence [*cevher*]. The reflection of light from that essence in seven colors, that is, the apparition of the essence in countless colors, forms and events, is possible in this world. In short, it is in this world that the spirit knows God rightly [*hakkıyla*], that it tastes the infinite pleasure of descent into thought and love in order to find Him and reach Him again.

You who say there is no benefit in the spirit's taking on a body! If there is no use in words, don't speak. Understand, leave off objecting and give thanks.

Consider the pleasure and virtue that comes of feeling, thought and meaning being put in a series of letters, in short, in a word. Then set your mind to the incomparably great event of spirit's taking on a body and the virtue in the pleasure, joy, form and meaning gained there! Pay attention to the infinite delicacy of spirit's unique self-disclosure in each body, and ask no more! Give yourself over to the pleasure of prostrations of gratitude.

Give thanks [*şükret*] to God. Be pleased that he gave you the potential to know Him and love Him! Giving thanks is the greatest worship performed by people of conscience [*vicdan sâhipleri*]. Gratitude [*şükür*] is a duty, a debt of conscience. To wrinkle your nose and screw up your face, in short, to remain in the yoke of doubt, is not gratitude. Gratitude is a virtue which can put a smile on a person's face even when he is afflicted with suffering and trial.

Do not give thanks like vinegar, whose face is always sour. If you really want to have vinegar in your body, mix it with sugar to make a drink of oxymel. That means to make vinegar become a delicious flavor deep in your body.

Sour things are only beneficial if they can go into the body as a sweet drink, without complaining and making a sour face. Give people health in that way.

If after all of this the meaning is still not clear, seek it in the profundity of the fact that meaning can not always be put in the form desired! There has been many an artist poet who attained the secret of writing poetry in meter and rhyme and genre form, while what he wrote was one thing, and what he wanted to write was another.

The poet has often wanted to put the meaning which arises in his spirit into verses, but either that meaning did not come out precisely as he intended or another meaning resulted. Poetry is in that way like a stone placed in a sling. You take aim at a certain point and draw the sling. The stone flies out and hits a different point.

If poetry is that way, how can a precise expression be found for the profound meaning of the coming of the spirit into the body and the self-disclosures which take place in creation. Such things are not known only through words and speech. The conscience must be ready for it, or be prepared for it by the fellowship of a perfect murshid. .

****

On the Secret of "Let him who desires to sit with God sit with the Sufis."

1555.   The ambassador, with these one or two cups
        Forgot himself, forgot mission and message
        He became distraught at the power of God
        That ambassador arrived and was a shah
        A stream comes to the sea and becomes ocean
        A seed reaches a corn field and becomes corn
        When bread is connected with animate being
        Dead bread gains awareness as a living thing
        When wax and tinder are to fire sacrificed
        Their dark essences become all filled with light
1560.   When the fine stone dust of kohl has lined the eyes
        It becomes a scout as it turns into sight
        O happy the man who has from self been freed
        Who has been united with a living being
        Alas for that live one who sits with the dead
        Life speeds away from him and he becomes dead
        When you've fled to the Koran of God the Truth
        You are mingled with the prophets' spirits too
        The Koran is the prophets' experience
        The fish of the sea of pure magnificence
1565.   If you read but do not take the Koran in
        What avail should you see God's prophets and friends?
        If you do accept the stories of their lives
The cage round the bird of your soul will grow tight
        If a bird in a cage does not try to flee
        It's because of ignorant simplicity
        Those spirits who from their cages have escaped
        Are the worthy prophets who show you the way
        Their voices come from religion's land, outside
        Saying, "This is the way out for you to fly
1570.   This is how we escaped from that narrow cage
        It is the only way to escape that cage
        Seem to be ill, raise a great lamentation
        And be freed from the cage of reputation

> Worldly reputation is a rigid chain
> For travelers no less than an iron chain."

Sufism is for God to make you dead to yourself, obliterating the materiality in you, and give you life from His own limitlessness, making you eternal in His own being.

Sufism is to acquire the divine character [*ilâhî ahlâkla ahlâklanmak*]. That character brings the spirit to immortal life, or the life of the Single Immortal. And just so, the Roman ambassador drank exquisite sips from the wine of divine love and truth which took on the form of words in the speech of Hazret Umar. He so passed away from his self under the effects of that wine of eternity that he reached the state described by Fuzuli:

> I am so drunk that I can not comprehend what the world is
> Who I am, which one the Saki, and what white and red wine is

His mission and the message he'd brought from Rum to the Arabs were gone from his mind.

The ambassador had now heard about God's power and greatness from Hazret Umar, a man who had reached God the Truth while still alive. His heart was filled with God's light, faith and truth. While even a day earlier he had been ambassador and slave of the Roman Caesar, he now donned the crown of the greatest secret and was released from slavery, so much so that he became the sultan of the spiritual levels he had reached.

If you ask what it is for a person to rise from slavery to become a sultan, consider that many flowing waters on the face of the earth have rushed forward in frothing rivers to reach the open sea; streams have become seas. The Roman ambassador moved forward like a stream to join with the sea of Hazret Umar's mysteries and arrive at the secret of the truths of that sea. Isn't that also how a seed which finds a well-watered field becomes fruitful?

You know that bread in itself has nor feeling, nor comprehension nor thought. But after bread has been eaten by humans, it becomes feeling, comprehension and thought. Although even just yesterday it was but matter which knows nothing, in feeling and thinking humans is becomes conscience and learns of the greatest reality, God the Truth.

It mixes with light the way wax and tinder wood do. Wax and tinder are in themselves bodies dark as night in the dark of night. But once they are touched by flame and set alight, they not only burn, they illuminate their surroundings.

Humans are also like that: Once they are free of the darkness of body and burn with the fire of love, they melt away from their own being, becoming the ashes of their own bodies, and are transformed into a divine light.

Antinomy stone, from which kohl is made, is also like that: When this dark, black stone is crushed into dust and applied to the eyes, it improves the sight, making it more full of light.

It is like when an aspirant whose heart is full of darkness meets a perfect murshid and, illuminated by the murshid's guidance, is transformed into a state brighter than that of the sun. Because a great murshid is someone who illuminates the darkness within. That is why any God's bondsman is so very fortunate to meet one of God's friends who has become free of the soul, of greed and its shame and worldly filth, and been resurrected with God!

At the same time, there are so many people to whom God has given the preparedness for life but who plunge into desires of the soul for the world which is truly dead, even non-existent, and kill themselves on the way to eternity. A person who is not alive to the knowledge of God's truth, that is, gnosis, is a dead person.

In order to become someone who does not die, one must take refuge in the illumination in God's Koran. This means to become familiar with the spirits of the great prophets and bring one's spirit up to the level of theirs. For the Koran informs us about the spiritual states of the great prophets. It shows a person how to acquire their states. The prophets are the ones who know the secrets of the sea of divine truth. The Koran brought by the greatest of the prophets is the book which brings to light all the secrets beyond the dome of the sky. To read the Koran means to see the reality behind the curtains it opens wide. A person who does not illuminate his spirit in the light of the Koran can gain nothing from the fellowship of the prophets and friends. Because the great mystery is the speech of the Gracious Koran offered to the spirit by means of the friends and prophets. A person who reads the Gracious Koran and yet does not reach its heights, does not enter into its climate of truth, cannot be considered to have read the Koran. That is why Hazret Muhammed said, "There are many who read the Koran whom the Koran curses." Here to be cursed means to remain far from God's acceptance.

To hear the Koran, to take it as one's own to such an extent that one's being is melted in its speech, is virtually to become the Koran with the Koran. A person who attains that condition acquires a sweet spiritual state. His spirit leaves its cage of flesh and roams the vastness of not-time and not-space. This is the sweetest, most sublime state the spirit can reach.

An ignorant, cowardly, weak bird does not want to leave its cage. The spirits of the prophets and friends are the ones who escape their cages and fearlessly flap their wings is the sky of truth.

They are not the puny voices which come from inside the cages and call us to be confined there, they call to us from outside the cages and offer us the pleasure of faith. In their melodies are hidden saving truths which will rescue us too from our cages. Those melodies takes us away from the converse of dead hearts, and shout the virtue of taking refuge in the Koran.

Thanks to the light they shed, we have been freed from that cage of flesh which seems so strong but is in reality rotten. We illuminated our hearts with the torches held by those prophets and friends.

If you too want to make headway on this path, look to getting free of those people who promise you good reputation, who gather around you because they think you are strong and sound in the ways of the world. Do not show yourself to them as a strong person worthy of every kind of renown and position, so that they will not take you away from the right path into the sea of passion for position and rank, not applaud you and make you lose your way. For people are pleased by those whose world and worldliness is strong.

To be renowned in this way is such a binding, unbreakable chain that once it is around you, you cannot get free of it. You will finally be the property only of this world. For you there will no longer be the transcending of veils, nor nearness to God the Truth, nor illumination with the light of the Koran. The doors of the material world will have opened for you and, as pretty and bright as it is, the paths of spirituality will be closed to you in that measure.

If you want to understand this truth more clearly, listen to the story of the parrot. That is what it did. It broke out of the cage of flesh and found the way to fly in the skies of meaning.

****

THE STORY OF THE MERCHANT WHO WENT TO INDIA AND THE PARROT THAT GAVE HIM A MESSAGE FOR THE PARROTS OF INDIA

There was once a merchant who had a parrot
Which he kept in a cage, a pretty parrot
When the merchant, whose travel preparations
For departure to India had begun
1575. Asked his male and female slaves generously,
"What shall I bring back for you, tell me quickly,"
Each of them made of him one desired request
And that good man gave to each one his promise
To the parrot, "What gift would you like," he said
"Me to bring you from India's continent?"
The parrot said, "When you see the parrots there
Tell them of my condition and how I fare
Tell them, 'So-and-so parrot, who longs for you
Is imprisoned in my cage by Heaven's rule
1580. He sends you his greetings and asks for justice
And inquires the means and way to reach guidance.'
He says, "Is it fit that I in longing here
Should give up my life and die all alone here?
Is this right, that I remain in slavery
While you live amidst the trees and greenery?
Is this how fidelity of friends should be
I in prison, you in gardens roaming free?
Call to mind, O noble ones, this weeping bird
With morning wine drunk in meadows filled with birds
1585. To be remembered by friends is good fortune
If your friend is Leyla and you are Majnun
O you who are near to the one you hold dear
Shall I drink down goblets of my own blood here?
Enjoy a goblet in memory of me
If indeed you wish to do justice by me
Or in memory of me as I sift dust
When you're drinking, spill a drop into the dust.""""
O where, I wonder, is that promise, that vow
The oaths sworn by that candy-lipped beauty now
1590. If you exile your slave because he is bad
How do you differ, repaying bad with bad?
O you whose worst done in anger and conflict
Is gayer than whirling dance and harp music
Your cruelty's better than fortune's delight

And your revenge is more beloved than life
This is your fire; what then must your light be like?
This is mourning; what will your feast day be like?
The sweetness that there is in your cruelty
None can plumb your depths, and the delicacy
1595.   I wail and fear my beloved will believe
And generously lessen that cruelty
I'm in love with that wrath and that gentleness
It's·a wonder that I love two opposites
By God, if I do go from thorn to garden
I'll wail like a nightingale for that reason
What a strange nightingale, opening its mouth
To devour the thorn along with the rose flower
What nightingale?—it's a fiery crocodile
In his love, pleasing to him are all things vile
1600.   He's a lover of the whole, and whole himself
He's in love with himself, seeking love of self

A merchant had a beautiful, colorful parrot. The bird was fed in a cage. One day it became necessary for the merchant to go to India. He bade farewell to his household. He
asked his family what they wanted him to bring them from India. He told them he would
do what they asked.

Then it was time to bid farewell to the parrot. The merchant asked his bird the same
question. The parrot told his master:

> You are going to my country. There you will see many parrots. But they are not in
> cages like I am. They perch on green bushes in gardens and on trees. Bring them my
> greetings, my love and tell them of my longing.
>
> Tell them: "My parrot longs for you. By divine decree he is now in my country
> imprisoned in a cage. All he wants is that you here be free; that you be near the ones
> you love; that the sun of love may rise on the horizon here and that while all spirits
> are enlightened by the sun which illuminates the dawn of your horizon, you may all
> plunge into contemplation of the greatest Beloved together, drink of the wine of love
> He offers, and lose consciousness; and that he, far, far away, should both be sepa-
> rated from you and imprisoned in a cage.'
>
> "And so my request of you is that you do not forget me when you are with the
> beloved, and if possible, that you drink a sip of wine for me too.
>
> "What blessed fortune it is for friend to remember friend. Especially if the one
> remembering is Leyla and the one longing is Majnun."

****

From what the parrot says we understand that here he is speaking the language of the
spirit imprisoned in a cage of flesh, far from the realm of spirits. Here the merchant is
meant to be the spirit who has arrived at the secret of how to flow to that realm. Just
as India is meant to be the realm of spirits, the parrots there are meant to be the mighty
spirits of the friends and prophets who have achieved their desire and intent.

But it is possible that those great spirits, or people who have drunk the love of God like glasses full of wine taken from an arrived person and thus become happy, do not forget those still in the world trapped in the cage of flesh, and if they now and then request help for those hearts in exile or intercede for them, they will one day receive news from that realm.

Their spirits will be enlivened by a breeze coming from that realm. Their interiors will be cleansed with water flowing from there. The brains of their spirits will faint at a beautiful scent reaching them from there, and they will set out on the path to that realm.

****

The parrot was speaking that language and Mevlana, who thus far had spoken in the person of the parrot, was addressing the arrived who will awaken the spirits bound by the desires of the soul and its ties to the earth like a bird in a cage from their misfortune.

Then he went a step further and gave his address the language of supplication [*münâcât*], that is, he raised his voice directly to the greatest beloved, the greatest beloved who is the Creator.

This is a special characteristic of Mevlana's style.

So, addressing God in that manner, Mevlana said:

O my Lord! What kind of unexpected thing is this? Those promises, those vows, where are they? What those beautiful lips of Yours like sugar promised, where is it now?

And what he meant was: What about the spirit's covenant at the gathering of Alast? When the spirit was commanded to enter the cage of flesh and be bound by the limitations of nature, it was told: Drink the wine of separation so that in the exile of distance from Me it will be possible for you to understand the taste of reunion with Me and being with Me.

Go into the cage of flesh now so that you may attain the felicity of seeing the reflection of eternal beauty in the bright mirror of your heart.

If on your way you fear the trickery of the soul, if you have difficulties or are in danger, know that My divine aid will protect you.

My God! That is what You said to us. You sent us far from Yourself so that we would love You, long for You, and return to You again. The good news you gave us was great. Although it is true that in order for us to return to You, we would have to fulfill our vow and not break our promise.

Many of us forgot our vow. We plunged into the pleasures of the mortal world. We remained veiled from You.

But my Lord, that is no reason for our sin not to be forgiven. Our forgetfulness, our wrongs, in short, our sins, belong not to God but to His bondsmen. If you do to us as we have done, if you recompense our wrongs with wrong—may my mouth dry up—what difference would there be between You and us?

There is also the fact that we are happy with the suffering You have given us, have seen fit to give us. As Fuzuli said in entreaty:

Torment and pain are what I'm used to, what would I be without them
May Your torment have no limit and Your pain never end, O Lord!

Those who faint with the joy of You and give themselves over to the thrill of the flute and harp and the whirling dance know the felicity in want and longing for You. Fuzuli described the love and torment felt for You in the following lines also:

The pain my lover gives me is all loyalty, not pain
It is disloyal to say that my lover brings me pain

My spirit, my world, my cure for every ill, O my sense, my thought, my everything! To feel the torment you cause is better than happiness, to die in your path is sweeter than life.

If Your severity is so beautiful, how beautiful is Your kindness, I wonder? When exile from You is so sweet, what would be the taste of reunion with You? What feast would that feast be which is granted to the bondsman worthy of You?

Only those separated from You know Your beauty. But since none but You can really know You, who knows how inadequate that knowledge is compared with Your beauty.

Again, as Fuzuli said in entreaty:

Do not lessen the grace you display to the men of pain
I mean to say, do subject me to more calamities

Do not begrudge us Your cruelty, it is the greatest kindness You can offer us. What You give us is pain whose poison is health and whose taste is profoundly pleasurable.

We know that all of this is the law of love, it is what love necessitates. The pain of love comes neither from the faithlessness of the beloved nor from great cruelty. The pain of love is its natural law. Because for those who love, the beloved's cruelty is as beloved as loyalty. We love both the beloved's loyalty and cruelty. Although the two seem to be contraries, they are one and the same. This apparently bizarre truth loses all its strangeness only in the law of love.

If I avoid the thorns of calamity and suffering and rush to smell the roses of comfort, I will fall from the cliff of separation from suffering and thorns. I will wail in separation from them.

I am that lover nightingale who transforms thorns into rose gardens with the wails of my love and the fire of my sighs. The fiery-colored thorns there seem to me like red roses. This means that I am a spirit who finds pleasure in calamity and cruelty. The real calamity is to be heedless of the One who brings calamity.

The nightingale of whom I speak is not a nightingale but perhaps a crocodile of fire. For that crocodile, pleasure and unpleasure are the same.

The true lover loves not roses but coals.

Here the word "coal" expresses that great Being, with all its names and attributes. To be a lover of coal is to love not only God's beautiful, good and forgiving attributes, but His all-dominating and all-subjugating self-disclosures as well. In short, in whatever form that great Beloved self-discloses, forgiving or compassionate, subjugating or avenging, the heart that loves Him loves those self-disclosures also and feels pleasure in His cruelty as much as in His felicity. And with that sublimity of feeling and those states of love, he approaches so near to Him that he melts within that coal. He dies in that coal. In the end the love he felt becomes a love felt for himself. To feel that love is to attain the station of annihilation [fenâ].

So, there is in the crucible of love a power uniting opposites. That is why the true lover loves severity and suffering as much as he loves goodness, beauty and bounty. A Perfect Human who has reached that level is freed from duality, as if he had collected all of the divine names and attributes within himself. Such people have risen to stations beyond the degrees of annihilation and attained the mysteries and good fortune of abiding [*bâkî*] in God.

****

THE ATTRIBUTES OF THE WINGS OF THE BIRDS OF DIVINE INTELLECTS

> Thus the story of the parrot of spirit
> Where is he who can be the birds' confidant?
> Where is that bird who though weak and innocent
> Has Solomon and his soldiers within it?
> When without thanks or complaint he weeps and shouts
> Inside the seven heavens riot breaks out
> Each instant a hundred notes from God arrive
> He says, "O Lord!" and God, "*I'm here*" sixty times
> 1605. For God his faults are better than piety
> Faith threadbare beside his infidelity
> God gives him a constant Miraj of his own
> Upon his crown a hundred crowns of his own
> His spirit is in Not-place, his form on land
> A Not-place beyond dreams of men of the path
> Not a Not-place you could ever understand
> Or produce new fancies about each instant
> Place and Not-place are both under his control
> Like those in Heaven the four rivers control
> 1610. Turn your face away, cut short comment on this
> Do not breathe a word, for God knows what is best
> Let us return from this discussion, O friends
> To the parrot, India and the merchant

Just as a parrot imprisoned in a cage desires to escape from there and fly, so the parrot of the soul in the cage of flesh feels the same desire. It wants to flap its wings and fly in space to the realm of Not-place.

Solomon, who knew the language of birds and ants, told of that desire of the birds especially. He understood that secret of theirs.

But the Solomon of all truths is God. God knows all the torments of the spirit struggling with the helplessness of a weak bird in the bodies of the arrived. This weak and innocent bird imprisoned in the human form is filled with the love and attraction of God. It is the mirror for the self-disclosure of that love and attraction. But the heart of an arrived person is so vast that all the names and attributes of God the Truth can fit into the space of such a heart.

That is why Hazret Ali said of people who are unaware of that endless breadth of their own reality: "O people, you think you are a tiny body. But the macrocosm is contained within you."

From the heart's wound of a person annihilated in the love of God such a wail and a sigh rises up that it is neither gratitude nor complaint. It is an involuntary moan and that sort of cry. It is as if they have melted gratitude and complaint, two contrary emotions, in a magical crucible, and abandoned their existences and attributes. All that remains is a cry, and since creation earth and sky have been moaning with this cry which arises from the changeability and impatience of divine love, its sound reverberating throughout all the worlds.

Messages come to one who wails for love of God in this way. Countless states of joy and attraction come to him. He wails in love for You, "O my Lord," and You answer countless times, "I am here!" You give him the good news that You accept his every request.

They are the lovers whose flaws God prefers to the worship of others. The faith of so many is worthless compared with their non-faith. For their non-faith is their rejection of their selves. They leave their own souls in darkness and rush to the divine light. As many a great arrived person has said, Heaven is the first station of those who die in such non-faith will reach.

And such lovers have a Miraj, an ascension to God, every instant. They have the wings of the lights to which they ascend and the pleasure of divine witness in the realm of spirits. Crowns of light are placed upon their heads by the hand of divine power.

Those lovers appear to be in human bodies in the world. But I tell you that their spirits are in the realm of divinity [*lâhût*]. They are in the universe of Not-place. The realm of Not-place is a realm beyond all that those who enter the path to it can imagine.

In that realm there is no intellect, no understanding, no color, no quiddity. There is only joy, pleasure and reverence.

Just as the four rivers of Paradise are under the control of the inhabitants of Paradise and at their disposal, the spirits in that realm, in short, those who reach that realm, have control of place and placeless-ness.

It is proper to cut short here the story of those intellect birds who fly to the divine realm. We have our story of the parrot, the merchant, and India.

Now let us return to it. For even the story of these three is in reality the story of the spirits who ascend to the heavens.

****

THE MERCHANT SEES THE PARROTS OF INDIA IN THE WILDERNESS AND GIVES THEM THE MESSAGE OF THAT PARROT

> The merchant now agreed to bring this message
> He'd bring the parrot's congeners the message
> When he reached India's far and distant land
> He saw many parrots in the hinterland
> He brought his mount to a halt and then spoke up
> He conveyed the greeting and fulfilled the trust
> 1615.   One of the parrots began to tremble then
> He fell down dead and his breath came to an end
> The merchant was sorry for what he had said
> "I have been cause of the creature's death," he said
> "This bird must be kin to my little parrot
> It seems they were two bodies but one spirit
> Why did I do that, why did I give the news?
> By my raw speech the poor creature's been consumed."

The tongue is both like a stone and like hellfire
That which springs forth from the tongue is like a fire
1620.　Strike not iron against stone without forethought
Just to tell a tale or to make idle talk
It is dark, and there is cotton wool all 'round
What happens with sparks where cotton wool is found?
Cruel is that people who sew their eyes shut tight
While with words they set an entire world alight
One word can leave a whole universe in ruins
And transform dead foxes into mighty lions
In their origin spirits are Jesus-breath
But here one breath strikes while one's a healing breath
1625.　If the curtain were removed from each spirit
Messiah-like speech would flow from each spirit
If you want your own speech to be sugar-sweet
Restrain your greed, do not eat that halva sweet
Patience is what the intelligent long for
Halva candy is the thing children long for
Whoever is patient strides upon the sky
Whoever eats halva will be left behind

Our merchant arrived at the farthest reaches of India. He saw many a parrot in the hinterlands of India. He greeted them. He told them of his own parrot's sense of exile. One of the Indian parrots trembled when he heard the news and fainted away, falling to the ground.

The merchant thought the parrot had died and regretted having conveyed the message to him so suddenly. "For shame," he said. "Clearly the two parrots are relatives, their bodies separate but their spirits one."

It is true that the speech which emerges from between two lips sometimes burns like fire. If the steel of the tongue strikes the flint of the brain, the sparks of speech which thus emerge can set many a place alight and cause many fires.

Consider your words before you speak. For you cannot know, it may be that you are in a dark place surrounded by cotton wool. Consider that just as fire burns wool, a wrong or malicious word can also burn and give rise to corruption where none exists.

They call that person cruel whose ears do not hear what his mouth says, who sets the world afire with an inappropriate, thoughtless, bitter word.

What-all is there that such words cannot do, what dead foxes can they not transform into lions. How evil are such words, which awaken corruption and evil dozing as if dead like sleeping snakes, and spew poison out into the world. Thank God all speech is not like that.

In contrast to those who speak such evil and spew forth the fire of corruption, there are those who make people happy with their words and help them with their troubles and soothe their wounds.

In reality all spirits have a share in the breath of Jesus. Each spirit is adorned with such beautiful and enlivening qualities while in the realm of spirits. As they descended into this world and became limited by the cage of the flesh, the body [*vücût*] made them lose their purity and sublimity. If the judgments of the soul rule in a person, and the veils of greed surround the spirit, its innocence and purity will be hidden.

It is only at the end of the merciless struggle with the soul that the spirituality in mankind is victorious over the realm of bodies and matter. The attributes of the soul go into motion and become actions and words. It is the speech which arises from such pure spirits that bestows life like the breath of Jesus. So, the speech of the soul kills, and the speech of the spirit gives life.

If you have the ambition to become one of those who are brought to life like that, do not be swept away by the deceitful goadings of the soul. Work to break and tear down the soul obstacles which have surrounded your spirit like iron curtains. Put aside the tastes of the soul and look to acquiring a taste for patience. The latter is superior to all other tastes.

Consider that it is children who love the material taste, sugar and halva. It is as people mature that they acquire a taste for spirituality. It is those who attain to the degree of taking pleasure in patience and with that weapon of patience tear down the fortresses of the soul whose souls are freed from being condemned to and trapped in nature and reach the sublime realms.

That is why Hazret Ali said: "What the head is to the body, patience is to faith." Patience is the power that reunites the spirit with its origin and the divine beloved.

****

EXPLICATION OF THE SAYING OF FARIDUDDIN ATTAR, GOD SANCTIFY HIS SPIRIT, "YOU ARE A MAN OF SOUL, O HEEDLESS ONE, DRINK BLOOD IN THE DUST; FOR IF THE MAN OF HEART DRINK POISON, IT WILL BE HONEY

There is no harm to the man of heart if he
Even drinks down deadly poison openly
1630. He has health and is from abstinence set free
Though the poor seeker suffers feverishly
The Messenger said: "O boon-seeker, do not
Struggle against anyone who is the sought"
There's a Nimrod in you, don't enter the fire
First be Abraham and then enter the fire
If you cannot swim and you're not a sailor
Don't vainly throw yourself into the water
Swimmers bring up pearls from the ocean's deep pit
Out of losses they can discover profit
1635. In a Perfect Human's hand, dust becomes gold
An imperfect one makes ashes out of gold
Since the righteous man is accepted by God
His hand at work in things is the hand of God
Satan and demon are the hands of the flawed
They are in the trap of vain effort and fraud
Before him knowledge comes out of ignorance
But knowledge in the flawed becomes ignorance
A sick man makes sickness of all things he takes
Perfect humans transform non-faith into faith

1640.   You try to contend with horsemen while on foot
         You'll not save your head, at least now stay your foot

It is natural that poison should not harm a person of heart. Because his spiritual health is perfect, he has risen above all material pains.

But a person who is still at the level of seeking suffers diseases of the soul, which are like being inside a burning fire. It is appropriate for him to abstain from worldly desires and to achieve a humanity by means of that abstinence.

That is why Hazret Muhammed said: "Beware of struggling against Perfect Humans who have attained the degree of the desired and the sought."

If a person is still a Nimrod, that is, if his body [*vücût*] is a substance of lust and soul fit to burn in any fire, he should not think himself an Abraham and go near fire. In order to plunge into raging fires, a person must first become an Abraham. Only for those who are Abraham is it possible to find health in poison and gather roses inside a fire.

Manias like greed, avarice and gluttony resemble burning fires. They can burn you up just as fire burned Nimrod. In order to escape burning in the fire of all these worldly desires, you have to find within them the good, the right, and God the Truth, as Abraham did.

On the other hand, these lusts and manias of the soul are like oceans. For those who don't know how to swim or float, to plunge in is to drown. Those who understand the states of these oceans are arrived persons, sublime spirits who are informed, forewarned, and armed against the dangers of the soul.

They know how to bring pearls up from the bottom of such oceans. The pearls they bring up are extremely valuable gems of spirit and truth.

There is a reason why the arrived person turns dust into gold. For he is a person who has reached God. His hand means the hand of the great Creator who has power over all things. The arrived person is an intermediary instrument. The power which turns dust into gold is the power of God.

A person who is not a traveler on the path of God the Truth uses the hand of Satan in his work without realizing it. To be sure, such a hand urges a person to evil and to bad and ugly deeds.

Since one of them is the hand of God the Truth, and the other the hand of Satan, you can expect goodness, truth and justice from the former. You will find that those who possess the hand of God the Truth remain distant and secure from every kind of worldly filth, evil and calamity. Know them and earn their affection. Do what they say and be as they advise you to be. For they are God's people and the heirs of the Messenger.

While there are such people to be found, do not err and be drawn into the false pretences of evil and materialistic people. They will lead you to disease and non-faith, and in particular, lead you away from the path of God the Truth. In short, leave such infantrymen aside and take the hands of cavalrymen. They will bring you to goodness and truth.

But if you are going to try to contend with horsemen while you are on foot, realize your foolishness now and desist.

****

How the Magicians honored Moses, Peace be upon him, saying: "What is your Command? Shall you cast down your Rod first, or shall we?"

The magicians in accursed Pharaoh's age
Though they contended with Moses in bad faith
Still they granted to Moses the precedence
They displayed to Moses honor and respect
To the extent that they said, "The choice is yours
If you wish, you may first cast that rod of yours."
"No," he said, "first you cast yours, O magicians
Bring those deceits of yours into the open[84]

1645. This much of respect purchased them religion
Which cut off hand and foot of their contention
Because the magicians acknowledged his right
Their hands and feet were in that sin sacrificed
All food and speech is lawful for the perfect
Do not eat, be mute, for you are not perfect
He's a tongue, not of your kind, you are an ear
Listen was what God commanded to the ears[85]
When a milk-fed babe is born, it is all ear
For a time it does not speak but only hears

1650. For a long while it has to keep its lips sewn up
And not speak, so that it may learn how to talk
If not, if it keeps chirping gurgling non-words
It makes itself the dumbest dunce in the world
One who is really dumb has no ear at first
Can never speak, how should he burst into words?
For to speak, one must first be able to hear
Approach speech first of all by way of the ear
"*Enter into houses by way of their doors*"[86]
And *Seek after the sought by way of its cause*

1655. Independent on the ear there is no speech
But the speech of the Creator without need
He follows no master, He originates
He is the base of all things, He has no base
All the rest, whether in speech or artistry
Follow masters and of a model have need
If you are no stranger to this kind of talk
Weep in a ruin and take on dervish frock
For Adam escaped reproof by means of tears
The speech of the penitent is his wet tears

1660. Adam came down to earth so that he might weep
So he might be sorrowful and wail and weep

---

84. Koran 7:115-116;
85. "When the Koran is recited, hearken and listen silently" (Koran 7:204).
86. Koran 2:189.

Cast from the seven heavens and Paradise
He went to the corner to apologize
If you are from Adam's loins and progeny
Be a seeker too amongst his company
Prepare candy from heart's fire and tear perfume
It's from sun and clouds the garden comes to bloom
What do you know about the flavor of tears?
You are a lover of bread, like blind beggars
1665.   If you empty the bread out of this wallet
You will cause glorious jewels to fill it
From devil's milk wean the babe of your spirit
Then make an angel's companion out of it
As long as you are stirred up, weary and dark
Know you feed on the accursed Devil's milk
That morsel perfect which gives increase of light
Is obtained through gain which is lawful and right
That oil which works so as to put out our lamp
Call it water which extinguishes a lamp
1670.   The lawful morsel spawns knowledge and wisdom
The lawful morsel spawns love and compassion
When you see envy and guile from a morsel
Ignorance, heedlessness, know it's unlawful
Has barley been reaped from wheat that you have sown?
Have you seen a mare give birth to an ass colt?
The morsel is the seed and its fruit is thought
The morsel is the sea and its pearl is thought
The lawful morsel in the mouth will give birth
To service and resolve for the other world

It was to the benefit of the magicians that they showed profound respect to Hazret Musa, that they recognized him to be great and precious and treated him well.

For Moses also looked favorably upon them and requested that they demonstrate their magic first. Thus they lost the contention they had entered into with Moses; they were left powerless; but this loss made them acquainted with the true greatness of Moses, and with God, who had given Moses his superiority. The magicians came to believe, and for that reason they emerged having gained.

Leave subtleties in the discussion of unity and divine mysteries to those who know the meaning and depth of what they say and find the words to express that meaning. Subtlety [*nükte*] is the kind of beautiful speech so fine and meaningful that not everyone can understand it. The most beautiful of speech is that uttered in the path of God and for the sake of God. The arrive know how to speak subtleties like that.

Because every food they eat becomes the light of the Lord, or speech which while clearly display the Lord.

If what there is inside the cage of the soul and the flesh is a person bound to the world, whatever he eats is in vain. Because in such bodies all foods become darkness instead of light, heedlessness instead of knowledge and lust and greed instead of goodness, they all nourish those branches of aberration.

If you are still the soul's prisoner, do not try to speak subtleties, choose to be silent. For your speech may express darkness instead of light, and non-faith instead of truth. Before you begin to speak, perform service for the arrived. Learn their path and manner, find the ways to attain their degree, and then talk. Then you too will speak subtleties.

Consider, you are still an ear. You are in the position of the listener. One day you will become a lip and you will speak. That is why God told those who are still at the degree of the ear to "Be silent and listen." In order to begin to speak, it is right to wait for the command of God the Truth.

There are many phases in material development, not to mention spiritual perfection. It takes time for humans to speak.

A child does not talk as soon as it is born. First it uses its ear, it listens and learns and then it speaks. So the right path is to listen first, to learn, and then to speak.

On condition that you are not born deaf. For those who are can not earn to speak because they do not hear. This means that since they cannot listen and understand the subtleties of arrived persons, they have not been given the right to speak to them. It is not possible for them to speak, not possible for the lock on their tongues to be opened.

You know that it says in the second chapter of the Gracious Koran: "Enter houses by their doors." Just as there are houses in the structure of a city, there are houses in the structure of the tongue, that is to say, there are words. Ears are the doors of word-houses. One enters the houses of subtlety and gnosis through the ears. The perfection of this point is Hazret Muhammed's saying: "I am the city of knowledge and Ali is its gate." Since you cannot find Ali, if you want to go into the city of knowledge and truth, rush to the door of an arrived murshid who has the quality of Ali. So, arrived persons are the doors to the palace of knowledge of God. One enters into knowledge of God the Truth and reality through those doors. You should do likewise. Enter the houses of gnosis by their doors.

If you wonder whether there is no other door but the ear, no other instrument but hearing, by which one may sense a voice, hear a meaning, understand a subtlety, know that there is. However, only God Himself can make you sense such a voice. For to speak silently without letters or words, that is, to make you hear speech without need of any instrument, is the artistry solely of that greatest Artisan of all.

That great Creator continually creates the most unattainable things without need of learning from others or of seeing from others how it is done. Although everything that exists [bütün varlıklar] and all the creatures depend on Him, trust in Him and learn from Him, He depends on no thing and no one can be His teacher.

Now, if you really have an ear and you are strong enough to hear these words and understand, give up running after the material kingdom of the world and the world's material pleasures. Shed tears in perfect humility, for the beginning of your reaching Him is in the size and heat of those tears.

The humility being proposed to you here does not mean that you should abandon the conditions of your life and the rules of society and life and really be content with a morsel and a sweater and seek annihilation in a hut.

Because real withdrawal from the world, that is, the state of being completely alone with God, is not something having to do with matter and form, it is a work of the heart. It is a condition of choosing by way of the heart to distance oneself from fondness for the world. With your heart you distance yourself from the plurality which makes a person forget the sublimity in divine union, yet on the other hand you fulfill all the human and social functions, that is, you give yourself to God as if you were going to die tomorrow, and you also work for humanity and civilization as if you were never going to die.

Your annihilation here is annihilation in the being [*varlık*] of God under all these conditions, and you will understand the felicity of it only when you have taken that path.

You know the story of Messenger Adam. Hazret Adam could be saved from the reproach directed at him only by weeping tears of regret. There is a language special to the tears of those who take a wrong step on the path of God the Truth. Such tears express the heart's fire and the truth of that inner burning more powerfully than any words.

The world is for Messenger Adam a place of seclusion chosen for him, a kind of dunce's corner [*pay-ı mâcân*] where he may feel contrition, weep, and taste the torment of exile from God.

The dunce's corner was a place where shoes were left by the door. A dervish who committed any sin was sent to there to look after the shoes as punishment. The dervish would stay there until his punishment was over.

That was what the world was for Messenger Adam, a place where he looked after the shoes. Adam fulfilled his initiation here. If you are the progeny of Messenger Adam, do the same! Burn as he did in the fire of penitence! Like him, or like the reed flute which symbolizes him and all humanity, burn within and transform the sounds of your heart from flames to voices.

Just as gardens become gay with sun and rain, that is, with fire and water, make the garden of your heart gay with the fire of love and the rain of tears of repentance. Taste the profound pleasure of such sincere tears!

For lovers of bread and the world do not know the pleasure of flowing tears, lovers of God the Truth do.

Fill your body with gems of truth and gnosis instead of wheat and bread. Nourish yourself as the angels do with the food of the spirit and the heart!

As long as you remain far from divine illumination, trapped in the well of nature and body and fogged by the smoke of the soul, you can be counted only a brother of Satan. For all of these are the tastes of that accursed being.

While in the world, eat only lawful morsels! Unlawful morsels feed heedlessness and perversion in the body. Lawful morsels feed love of God in the heart. The light of faith shines. Spiritual pleasures develop.

The lamp oil that does not illuminate the lamp of the heart when it burns is not oil but water. In the same way, the morsel which does not illuminate the lamp of the heart is unlawful.

The lawful morsel feeds wisdom, knowledge and gnosis in the body; love of God, joy in God and affection for Him, arises in the heart.

Just as barley does not grow where you have sown wheat and corn does not grow where you have sown barley, and as a horse never gives birth to a donkey, if the material or spiritual food entering your body is not lawful food which gives you the power to power to recognize God, you will derive no benefit from it.

Love of God is the fruit of such lawful morsels. Sublime wisdom and thought are found only in the form of big pearls of gnosis within the sea of lawful morsels.

It is said that God declared in a sacred saying: "I am ashamed to call to account My bondsman who avoids the unlawful."

So, you must choose the lawful among all the fruits in the valleys through which you pass in the corridor of this world. Only the voices which come from within you and the lawful of foods will bring you to walk the best path, give you divine emotions and make you think wisdom, and give you the strength that will one day take you from the prison of the world and bring you to God's light.

****

THE MERCHANT TELLS THE PARROT ABOUT WHAT HE OBSERVED OF THE PARROTS OF INDIA

1675.   The merchant then finished up with his business
      And returned to his home glad and pleased with it
      He had brought a gift for every male slave
      He bestowed a share upon each female slave
      "Where's the gift for me, your slave," the parrot said
      "Report on what you have seen and what you said."
      "But no," the merchant said, "I repent of that
      I bite upon my fingers and gnaw my hand
      Why did I in foolishness and ignorance
      Rashly deliver such a loutish message?"
1680.   "O Master, why this remorse?" the parrot said
      What is the cause of this sorrow and regret?"
      He said, "I told those complaints you told me to
      To a group of parrots who were just like you
      One of those parrots who caught scent of your pain
      Burst his gall bladder and perished trembling
      I was sorry, what was it that I had said?
      But what was the use, it was already said."
      That which leaps suddenly from the tongue, you know
      Is like an arrow which speeds off from a bow
1685.   It does not, O Son, turn round to come back in
      One must stem a torrent from whence it begins
      Once it leaves its source it overwhelms a world
      It's no wonder that it lays waste to the world
      In the unseen effects arise from action
      Creatures can not control what is born therefrom
      Without partner all's the creation of God
      Though the results be attributed to us
      Zayd let fly an arrow which sped toward Amr
      Like a leopard his arrow grabbed hold of Amr
1690.   For the space of a year pain arose therefrom
      It is God the Truth who creates pain, not man
      If the archer Zayd had right then died of fear
      Until Amr's time of death pain would arise there
      If he died from the results of that complaint
      You should say the murderer was archer Zayd
      Consider him to be the perpetrator

Though it all was the work of the Creator
So with sowing, speaking, sex and trickery
Their effects are all in God's capacity

1695. It is from God that the friends derive their force
They turn back a speeding arrow from its course
By that hand of God, the friends when they repent
Close down against causes the doors of effect
They make what's said unsaid, opening the door
So that neither spit nor meat is burnt therefore
They erase it from the hearts of those who heard
Making naught and imperceptible that word
O sir, if you need proof and demonstration
Recite: "*We cancel none nor make forgotten*"[87]

1700. Recite: "*It made you forget mention of me*"[88]
They can make you forgetful, know that surely
Since they cause remembrance and oblivion
They can subjugate the hearts of creation
They make you forget and block your way of view
You can not act although you may know how to
Do you think those lofty ones can be jeered at?
Read the Prophet, up to "*It made you forget*"
A landowner is the body's padishah
A master of heart is the shah of your hearts

1705. Without doubt, action is derived from vision
So there is no man but the eye's little man[89]
I may not reveal in speech the whole of this
Masters of the center are forbidding it
Remembrance and forgetting belong to him
And he answers cries for help from creation
So each night that good one empties from the hearts
A hundred thousand goodly and evil thoughts
In the daytime he fills the hearts up with them
He fills up with pearls those oyster shells of men

1710. All preoccupations of the day before
Are guided by God to recognize their souls
Your business and your skill return unto you
So they'll raise the gate of ways and means to you
The ironsmith did not get the goldsmith's craft
Good temperament did not go to the bad

---

87. "None of Our revelations do we abrogate or cause to be forgotten but We substitute something better or similar" (Koran 2:106).

88. "There was a group of My bondsmen who used to say: 'Our Lord! We believe! So forgive us and have mercy upon us, for You are the best of those who show mercy.' But you treated them with ridicule, and it even made you forget the mention of me while you were laughing at them" (Koran 23: 109-111).

89. The pupil of the eye.

Like one's property, craft and disposition
Return on Resurrection Day to their kin
After sleep, also, craft and disposition
Hurry quickly to return to their own kin
1715.   When the dawn leaves, craft and preoccupation
Go where that beauty and ugliness had been
Like carrier pigeons from distant cities
They bring news beneficial to their cities

The merchant brought gifts from India to all the people of the house. He related the news he brought to his parrot from his relatives in India with profound regret. He still felt torn up inside as he told of how an Indian parrot had fallen dead because of his parrot. He repented in vain, wishing he'd been struck dumb and not told them everything so recklessly.

He was right:

Because a word that emerges from a person's mouth is like an arrow that flies from a bow. It could not be turned back. If water was going to flow in a flood, it was right to dam it at the very source. Once raging water began to flow, it would destroy, rip away, or carry off whatever got in its way.

Words that come out of a person's mouth may often do the damage of a raging flood. Wisdom [*mârifet*] is to be able to hold back such words in the heart or between the lips. Once words that will let loose mischief [*fitne*] upon the world have got out through the lips, once should not be surprised if they burn many a heart and destroy many a home.

Things we have done may have come by way of our own hand, our own head or our own mouth. We are the agent of these actions. We may have committed these actions by the command of destiny [*kader*], or protected ourselves from committing bad acts by using our partial will [*cüz'i irâde*].

But whatever we do, good or bad, once we have done it we no longer have control over the consequences born of it. Action proceeds from us, it begins with us, but its consequences are outside of our will. God the Truth determines [*tayin*] those consequences. God is the true author [*yaratıcısı*] of the works [*eserler*] which we consider our own creation [*îcâd*].

Once an arrow shot by Zeyd hits Amr, Amr's pains and cries, his fever, even his death, are not the work of Zeyd, they are beyond his control. And if Amr recovers from that wound and gets well, it is not of Zeyd's doing.

Let us think of it this way: If the pain Amr felt from his wound were the work of Zeyd, and he happened to shoot the arrow by accident [*tesâdüfen*] or died after shooting it, then Amr would not feel pain. Because the one who wounded him would be dead.

If on the other hand the arrow killed Amr immediately, Zeyd would be his murderer. If it does not kill him immediately, if it causes him to feel pain and burns him with fever, then Zeyd is merely the cause. It is God who gives or does not give the torment which is felt.

This is not only so in the case of the arrow. The acts people perform in sowing, speaking, setting traps for others and even in copulation are their own. But the products of sowing, the good or bad effects of speech, the trapping of prey and the having of children all depend upon God's will.

To turn an arrow back or redirect it toward a harmless target once it has left the bow, to transform the bad effects of words to good or remove their effects so that it is if they have never been said—such great powers are miraculous. Only the friends can perform such miracles.

It has been said before that if the friends deem it necessary, by their request and desire fire, whose function is to burn, may not burn. Water, whose function is to cause drowning, may not drown. Poison, whose one effect is to kill, far from being lethal may bring health like the water of life. They have the power to make something which has been said forgotten, or to silence something in a dervish's heart which wants to be said but is better unsaid.

For arrived persons are the representatives of divine power on earth. Their powers are no longer their own but God's, with whom they have united themselves.

If you wish to verify this for yourself, hear the proof not from me but from the gracious Koran! Recite and memorize the gracious Koranic verse: "None of Our revelations do we abrogate or cause to be forgotten but We substitute something better or similar" (Koran 2:106) . . . ." If you have forgotten it, read it again and again. Read and understand!

To be sure, God also gave to His friends the power He has to set aside a judgment or make it forgotten. God the Truth says in another verse: "There was a group of My bondsmen who used to say: 'Our Lord! We believe! So forgive us and have mercy upon us, for You are the best of those who show mercy.' But you treated them with ridicule, and it even made you forget the mention of me while you were laughing at them."

This means that it is dangerous to look down on the arrived and the gnostics and ridicule them. Because they have powers from God's essence and His qualities. They can put forgetfulness in your hearts and leave you in shadow and darkness deprived of your in reality very weak light of faith.

For the friends of God are allowed disposition of the hearts of mankind. If they wish, they put beautiful emotions in people's hearts, releasing faith and conscience into them. And if they wish, they can erase many emotions from people's hearts, many lies and false beliefs and dark feelings.

However skilled a person may think he is, and however much he may trust in his accomplishments, if a friend of God binds up his experience and thought, he can no longer display any skill.

Fear and avoid offending the arrived, whose hearts are filled with knowledge of the truth, with gnosis and love of God, who have been joined in God's oneness while still in the world; fear and avoid placing material or spiritual difficulties in their way, and ridiculing them. To offend their hearts is the same as to offend the heart of God. As the illustrious verse "it made you forget" asserts, they were granted powers derived from His will. Not wanting to remain any longer in your narrow, dark hearts, God may make Himself forgotten by means of his friends. The friends can make you forget the thought and mention of God. Consider that if a heart is without God and has forgotten God the Truth, it fills with darkness and unites with denial. Yes, it unites with denial, therefore read once again and with your whole heart the Gracious Koran as far as the gracious verse "it made you forget."

Know that a padishah who owns cities, villages and countries is the owner only of the material wealth of those countries. But the friends are sultans of spirituality, not materiality; of hearts, not bodies.

In short, the friends know many a secret of the two worlds. By supposing them to be of flesh, blood and skin, you will make the greatest error of your life. There can be no doubt that the things we plan and do are the results of what we see and think. So, a person sees colors and forms only with his eyes, and cannot see without them. What the pupil of the eye is to the body, so are the friends created with the attribute of pupil of the eye to the two worlds. That is why they are owners of the two worlds, the material and the spiritual.

At the same time, one must not say more about the qualities of the friends, for the prophets are sending news from the center, saying they do not find it right to give more information or tell secrets about the degree of the arrived. Give thanks that I have said this much and strive to intuit more with your own heart, your own spirit and your own conscience.

And since it has also been given to the friend of God to remind and inform you as well as make you forget, he will rush to your rescue if a cry rises from your heart, and he will not refuse to become your murshid.

That murshid is God's caliph, and every night he can draw hundreds of thousands of good and bad memories out of the hearts of humankind, and every day he fills many a heart with peals of faith. He pours pearls of feeling, thought and mystery into the heart shells.

If you are on the gallows, he will rescue you. If you are joyful, he knows you are joyful, and you will even see him giving you joy and increasing your gaiety.

While you sleep, the many beautiful feelings, many true thoughts which leave you know the heart where they were formerly hid well enough to come all together to you when you awake.

And so human life after death is like wakefulness, and death, like sleep. In order for beautiful dispositions and illuminated thoughts and goodness and gnosis to come to you, they must remember and recognize you when you wake up.

Know that when every bondsman of God's awakens from the sleep of death, the things that belong to his own heart will come to him, his skills, his goodness, knowledge and worship will return to him.

The acts of humans are like carrier pigeons. They fly from you, and when you awake they return to you as your birds of feeling, thought, conscience and faith.

Then it is said to you: "Read your own book, for today your own self is sufficient to call you to account"(Koran 17:14)

If you have intelligence, speak with the tongue of Sinan Pasha, both here and there. Supplicate God and say:

My God, acceptance is yours, rejection is yours, well-being is yours, suffering is yours. Whomever you accept, you make precious, however mean he may be, and whomever you reject, you make despised, however excellent he may be.

My God, whatsoever you made into a rose garden, so did I; I took hold of whatever you put into my hand.

My God, whatever you burn in the fire of my heart, that is what smokes; whatever you plant in the garden of my body, that is what grows.

(I know that) non-existence is required on the path of the friend. One has to be humble before the friend, with the robe of the flesh rent, the house of the heart pure.

****

THE PARROT HEARS WHAT THOSE PARROTS DID AND DIES IN THE CAGE, AND THE MERCHANT LAMENTS FOR HIM

When that bird heard what the parrot there had done
He began to tremble, went cold, and fell down
When the merchant saw him fallen on the ground
He leapt up and dashed his cap upon the ground
When he saw him in this state and so upset
He jumped up and tore his garment at the neck
1720. He said, "O good parrot, with your wailing song
Why have you been affected so, what is wrong?
O sweet warbling bird of mine, O alas
O companion and confidant, O alas
O alas, my bird who sings melodies sweet
Wine of my spirit, my garden, basil sweet
If Solomon had possessed one like this bird
How should he have minded any other bird
O alas, I obtained my bird so cheaply
And I turned away from him so easily
1725. O my tongue, much loss have you incurred for me
What can I say, since you are the one to speak
O my tongue, you're both the haystack and the fire
How long will you keep setting this stack on fire?
Deep inside me my spirit complains of you
Though it does everything you tell it to
O my tongue, you are both treasure without end
And a sickness no cure can bring to an end
You're the decoy and the whistle luring game
And an intimate friend in exile's dread shame
1730. Won't you have mercy on me, merciless one
You who seek vengeance on me with your bow drawn
You've made my bird fly away, look what you've done!
Do not graze in the pasture of oppression
Either give me my answer or my redress
Or instruct me in the means of happiness
O alas my dawn that burns the dark away
O alas my light that illumines the day
O alas my bird who so sweetly takes wing
And has flown from my end to my beginning."
1735. The ingrate forever loves trouble and care

Rise and read until *and trouble* from *I swear*[90]
With your countenance I was from trouble freed
I was pure of churning foam inside your stream
These sighs are due to the vision of my dreams
And to separation from my own being
It was God's rivalry, there's no cure for God
Where's the heart not shattered by the love of God
Rivalry is this: there's no rival to Him
He is beyond any words or expression

1740. "O alas, that I could weep a sea of tears
And scatter on that beauty a wealth of tears
My ingenious-minded bird, my dear parrot
Interpreter of my secrets and my thought
!!!Whatever has come to me of wrong or right
He spoke it first that it came into my mind."
A parrot whose voice comes of inspiration
Prior to the beginning of creation
Deep within you that parrot is secreted
You have seen him in this and that reflected

1745. He takes joy away, and you have joy by him
You accept tyranny as justice from him
O you who burn spirit for sake of body
You burned spirit, and illumined the body
I am burning, if anyone wants a light
That they might by me set sticks and straws alight
Seeing that tinder is easy to set fire
Take tinder from me so it may catch on fire
O alas and O alas O woe is me
That such a moon should by cloud concealed be

1750. How should I speak, my heart's fire burns too fiercely
The lion of loss is wild and bloodthirsty
One who when sober is violent and mad
How will it be when he takes wine-cup in hand?
The fierce lion no adjective can contain
Will not fit in the expansive grassy plain
I think of rhymes while my beloved says to me
"Do not think except of the vision of Me.[91]
O my rhyme-seeker, sit down and be at ease
In My presence you're rhymed with felicity

1755. What are words that you should give them any thought?
What are words—thorns in the vines of garden walls

90. "I swear by this city that you will enter this city victoriously. I swear by your ancestors Abraham and Adam and yourself, their sole progeny, that We created man to be subjected to toil and trouble" (Koran 90:1-4) [paraphrase is Rifai's].
91. Vision [*didâr*; rhyming with *dildâr*, "beloved"]: the divine beauty which God the Truth has promised to show to human beings in Paradise.

       I will smash together word and sound and speech
       That I may converse with you without these three
       That word I kept from Adam in secrecy
       I'll tell you, you who are the world's mysteries
       That word I did not pronounce to Abraham
       And that pain which is not in Gabriel's ken
       That word the Messiah never did speak of
       Nor without *mā*[92] in His rivalry did God

1760.   What is *mā*? It can affirm and can negate
       I do not affirm, essenceless, I negate
       I have found personhood in personlessness
       I wove my personhood in personlessness
       All shahs are enslaved by those enslaved to them
       All people die for the one who dies for them
       All shahs bow before those who bow down to them
       People are drunk on those who are drunk on them
       The hunter of birds becomes hunted by them

1765.   Girls lose their hearts to boys who've lost hearts to them
       All beloveds are prey to those who love them
       All who seem lovers, know them beloved to be
       For they are both this and that relatively
       Though the thirsty seek for water in the world
       Water too seeks out the thirsty in the world
       Since he is the lover, be silent and hear
       Since he's pulling your ear, make yourself an ear
       Dam the torrent when it's running in a flood
       Or it will work shame and ruin if you don't

1770.   What is it to me if all goes to ruin
       There is sultan's treasure beneath a ruin
       He who's drowned in God wants to be drowned the more
       While his life's tossed like a wave over and over
       Is it better above or under the sea?
       Is His arrow or the shield more enticing?
       O my heart, you'll be shred by the Whisperer
       If you think joy different from disaster
       Though the object of your desire may taste sweet
       Is desirelessness not what the loved one seeks?

1775.   His each star's worth a hundred crescent moons' blood
       It is lawful if he sheds the whole world's blood
       We have obtained both the price and the blood-price
       We have hastened to gamble away our life
       Oh, the source of life for lovers is in death
       You'll not find the heart except by losing it
       I sought his heart with a hundred coquetries

---

92. See next verse. In Persian, *mā* means "we"; in Arabic, it can be a negative particle—"not"—or a relative or interrogative pronoun.

And he finally became weary of me
"My mind and spirit are drowned in you," I said
"Go on, do not tell such tales to me," he said
1780.   "Is it not so that your thoughts are known to me?
You see two, how could the friend be what you see?
O gross spirit, you've held me in slight esteem
For the reason that you bought me on the cheap
What one obtains cheaply will be cheaply spent
A child may give a pearl for a loaf of bread
The love I am drowned in has drowned inside it
The loves of men of today and the ancients
I've not explained it, this is an epitome
Or consumed would be understanding and tongue
1785.   When I say "lip," it is the lip of the sea
And when I say "not," "none but" is what I mean
I sit with a sour face out of sweetness
Out of the fullness of words I am silent
So that from view of the two worlds our sweetness
May be hid behind a veil of sourness
So this discourse is not heard by everyone
Of a hundred divine secrets I tell one

When the parrot learned of the suffering of its congeners in India, and that one of them had died of longing for him, he was seized by a profound sense of mourning; he fell down and died.

For the merchant who had not been able to hold his tongue while in India now rattled on in the same way with his own parrot. The merchant felt sincere regret that by not holding his tongue he had been cause of the poor bird's death, yet he now gave similarly disturbing news to his own bird and had to mourn his death.

The merchant was frantic with sorrow over his parrot's death, bewailing the terrible loss of his sweet-voiced bird, his bosom confidant and secret-sharer.

From all of this it was understood that one of the parrots the merchant saw in India was the murshid of the merchant's own parrot. By dying himself, the parrot in India had demonstrated the way for spirit to escape from the cage of flesh. It was because the merchant's parrot received this message about death and salvation, and understood it as an example, that he followed the path of his murshid and put an end to the life of his spirit in exile far from its true homeland; and so by dying as his murshid did, he freed his spirit from the cage of flesh.

It was understood that without the guidance of a murshid, it would not be possible to be annihilated in divine being [*ilâhî varlıkta fânî olmak*] and thus by means of a death like bliss to be freed of the limitation of flesh.

This was the sort of parrot whose loss the merchant suffered; for that reason he complained bitterly of his own tongue, or of not being able to hold his tongue:

O tongue, why can you not be silent? Although when you speak well, you create a harvest of beauty, then you set forth a string of words that burn like fire and burn up your own harvest with your own words. If the good of what you say is worship and the witness of divine unity, the bad is non-faith, mischief and degradation.

You are the golden key which opens the treasuries of knowledge, bright thought and discovery. You are both the salve and the wound that takes no salve. You are the illness which responds to no cure.

The sin of your mouth is tiny. But your work of making and destroying is great as mountains. The best thing is for you to be silent. That is why the truest of sayings is, "Speech is silver, but silence is golden."

You are the whistle luring poor innocent birds into the lime. By imitating the voice of truth, goodness and reality you speak lies, tricks and violence.

On the one hand, you make the spirit parrots who have fallen far from God forget the pain of separation. You make them say good, beautiful and sincere things, you teach them love of God with the most beautiful words. On the other hand, you try to drive them into the wilderness of separation and solitude to moan there.

Words which fly from the most beautiful mouths like arrows make such profound wounds in so many bodies, so many breasts and hearts. Since you have such power, use your power well. Do not be cruel, do not shed blood! Teach me wisdom, how shall I get free of the harm you cause?

Since you have destroyed my beautiful bird, now end your cruelty, make me happy, teach me the secrets of goodness. Make me say the words that will fill me with love, let me know His love and sing the refrain of nearness to God the Truth.

You have taken such a bird from me, that spirit bird who flew from my beginning to my end. Still the wings that will carry me from my end to my beginning are with that spirit bird.

The words "beginning" and "end" in these verses describe the experience of the spirit along the arcs of descent and ascent [*nüzul ve uruç kavisleri*] in Sufi belief. They call to mind the journey of the spirit broken away from God along difficult and varied paths to return to God's being [*varlık*] again and be annihilated in His oneness.

According to this doctrine, the last stop [*intihâ*] is the degree of human nature [*beşeriyet*] and entification [*taayun*]. The spirit that reaches this station, or comes upon it, will by virtue of its nature and origin wish to immediately rise to its own starting point, the degree of oneness [*ahadiyet*], to reach God.

In the story, the parrot who falls dead after having received news from his own homeland and origin represents this truth, that is, represents the spirit which has received the good news that it will return to its beginning.

Thus the spirit of this story is the continuous, profound attraction and joy of flight which the spirit parrot, who is in a continuous state of journeying between beginning and end, feels for his origin from whence he comes.

To the extent that the gnostic is a traveler of spiritual heights, the ignorant person is to that extent a lover of worldly troubles, pains and pleasures. If you want to understand this beyond any doubt, read attentively and understand the four verses of the Gracious Koran from "I swear . . ." to "We created man in toil and trouble." It says there: "I swear by this city, and you are living in this city. And I swear by father and son that We created man to be subjected to toil and trouble."

Only by the self-disclosure of divine beauty is man freed from the helplessness of pain, sorrow and ignorance of the truth. He will not waste his life by giving his heart to others than God.

Albeit the spirit has its sighs and cries in this case as well. But these are tears of joy; due to imagining the beauty of the great beloved and to the profound pleasure of loosing oneself in achieving the mystery of seeing the varied self-disclosures of that beauty. This loosing of oneself is the state of being cut off from one's own material being, and seeing His being, becoming and remaining all pleasure and feeling.

To experience apparently profound pain at the death of the bodily and material parrot [*vücut ve madde tutisini*], to be frantic with grief at it, is in reality the self-disclosure of a joy felt in pain, a union felt in separation. For the death of the bodily parrot means the flight of the spirit parrot to the greatest and truest beloved. The cry of the lover of God the Truth is not due to separation from worldly delights and the pleasures, manias and torments of things other than God the Truth.

In reality, the force which takes the bird's life, and takes the spirit parrot away from the bodily parrot, is God's rivalry [*gayret*]. Rivalry means jealousy [*kıskanma*]. If you seek an explanation of that, consider this: both self and God cannot coincide within the lover of God the Truth who has become the site of manifestation [*mazhar*] of God's self-disclosure, who feels the presence of God the Truth in his own selfhood [*benlik*], who has reached a state in which he finds Him, sees Him and feels Him in himself. God's jealousy does not want anything but His essence to remain in such a place of self-disclosure. When that is the case, when a heart is filled with love of God, worldly rivalries cannot enter it. Such hearts spontaneously discharge every kind of worldly filth.

When God's rivalry self-discloses in a human heart with His name The Rival, He destroys everything other than Himself there. He fills that heart which loves Him with the light of His own attraction, and leaves it to the pleasure of burning in the fire of that light.

Tears are shed for the apparition of such beauty and the tasting of such delight. And the heart says: "If only I had oceans of tears, so that I could shed all of them, all of them in weeping over separation and union with that endless beauty."

My beautiful bird! My parrot who gives voice to my love and my secrets! He was such a bird that he came to me whether I fed him or not. There has been friendship between that spirit parrot and me since pre-eternity, since the moment the question was asked, "Am I not your Lord?" Considering that the coming into being of the spirit was much prior to the coming into being of the body [*vücût*], my beautiful bird's melodies were prior to the manifestation of body.

In reality, the spirit parrot is hidden within you. It is he who illuminates beings, like a light whose source is invisible. You see that things are lit up, but you cannot see the one who illuminates them. And for that reason you are in the dark about the existence [*varlık*] of the spirit.

If the spirit parrot leaves you, it will only break up the conviviality and harmony of your body and soul. But you will still be joyful and bright. When the spirit leaves the body, so does the body's heat, organization, consistency, color and harmony. The body is in fact the forum where the spirit roams and rules. Death destroys the outward organization, but because the spirit, which once gave the body color, harmony, life and locomotion, is eternal, its organization is not harmed. On the contrary, it flies in delight at being near its goal and free from the cage of flesh. That is why the *Spiritual Couplets* says, "He takes joy away, and you have joy by him / You accept tyranny as justice from him."

And the person the *Spiritual Couplets* seeks to awaken by addressing him, "O you who burn spirit for sake of body," is the worldly person who takes the opposite path. If needed, the address could be expended thus:

You who have sacrificed the progress of the eternal spirit toward divine union for these transient bodily pleasures. You have hobbled the spirit on the most beautiful path with worldly desires and ambitions. For the sake of the wishes and worldly ambitions of this transient body, you have counted as naught the delight and peace of the spirit. Thus you have both harmed yourself and not done your duty; and your spirit has lost its path.

March on now, if you have intelligence! Burn up the physical desires and ambitions accumulated around the body and observe the deeds of the owners of knowledge and gnosis who illuminate their spirits in that fire.

This is how they call out to the spirits gathered in circles around them: I am a spirit burned and illuminated in the fire of love of God! Let all who want to burn in the same fire of love come, let them light the tinder of their own hearts in the hearth of my heart and hasten to awake in this fire, and burn in this fire.

Let them not forget that their own hearts in fact have the preparedness [*istidât*] to hasten to the good and the beautiful. Every heart is tinder wood capable of catching fire. Every heart is a wing on the path of God.

The terrible waste is that such a moon should be invisible behind clouds. Such a spirit sun is left behind the haze and darkness of things other than God and worldly filth.

How shall I explain that I catch fire as I speak. Flames are burning up my insides. The pain of loss claws at my heart. The lion of exile roars within me. Its mane stands on end in violence and savagery. It is not longer possible to quench such a fire, or to resist such a bloodthirsty lion. When the lion of loss is this excited it is like a person drunk even when sober. And if you then serve such a person glass after glass, what will he become?

Imagine what will become of those lovers of God whose heads spin and faint even when sober if you make them drunk and dazed with the wine of divine love!

I am like a roaring lion who thrills when it comes upon a vast meadow and leaps with joy, throwing itself at the horizons. I have followed the path of love and fallen upon the wilderness of reality. He is before me in all His beauty, in all his reality. That most beloved friend is conversing with me. I talk with Him. I think one speaks with Him in the language of poetry and the voice of rhyme, and my Beloved tell me to leave off rhyming to think of nothing but the beauty He has promised to display in Paradise. O my rhyme-chasing lover, beware! In my eyes you are the rhyme of felicity and the couplet of good fortune. The harmony of My fortune and felicity is completed by you.

What are words, what use is rhyme, that you should be concerned with them? Forget them, the truth is beyond them.

Do you not know that I in fact speak silently, without letters or words? I speak mysteries, and thus my discourse is mysterious as well. O beloved who is the single mystery of the world and creation! Let me tell you a secret I kept even from Messenger Adam:

Let me now tell you the secret I did not tell My friend Abraham, the state of which I did not inform Gabriel, the truth of which even Jesus did not breath a word:

Know that God the Truth did not self-disclose without the human being. For His self-disclosure is with the human, with the human state of feeling Him in his own self [*kendi benliğinde*]. If you know how to look, if you know how to see, look upon all I have created, and within all that I have created, look at the secret and the cause of creation—the human being! In each human you will find a different self-disclosure of my qualities and states. I gave to a drop a power not possessed by a sea; I gave to a mote a power not seen in the sun.

Think of the word "not." "Not" exists as a word, but not as a thing or idea.

In the same way the human being who has been annihilated in love and divine being is "not." Even the smallest I-ness will not fit inside such persons, they are the fortunate who have grasped the perfect delight and perfect meaning of being "not" in God. They have grasped that in reality the one who is speaking is also the one who is listening. The one who loves, is the one who is loved, the one longing, the same as the one who is prized.

Therefore, if you want to abide in God the Truth, forget the body and everything concerning the body! Abandon the soul and the desires of the soul. For the goal is to become "not" in the greatest being.

Do you not know that in reality all padishahs are servants of their people? However much they may appear to be sultans living in pomp and wealth and ease, in reality their duty is to serve their people, their own servants. If their justice, their taxes, their way of life does not please their people and make them happy, if they do not strive to bring this about, they will be overthrown by their own servants.

So it is with hunters. Just as in order to hunt birds a hunter hides himself, spends a great deal of time doing so, in short, is under the command of the birds he hunts, God too longs for those who long for Him.

That is why the love God feels for us, the good he wants for us, the blessings he creates in order to bestow them upon us, are endless to a degree we cannot know or imagine.

****

Like birds of prey, beautiful young people hasten to those who lay heart's birdlime for them, they are captured heart and spirit in traps of love. If someone loves truly, it ensures he will be loved with the same profound love by the one he loves. The wing of every beauty becomes a moth in order to touch the flame burning with its love.

Who in fact is the lover and who the beloved? It is not easy to tell them apart. You suppose that love begins with one of them. That is how it appears, but what you see is merely outward appearance. In fact love begins in the hearts of both Leyla and Majnun at the same moment, with the wine drunk at the table of pre-eternity. Every person you see as a lover is spiritually a beloved. So, since each person who loves is beloved, lover-ness and beloved-ness exist on both sides simultaneously. In fact both loving and being loved are from God. Both lover and beloved are God the Truth. That is why love is so divine for all spirits who lose their hearts to Him.

This recalls the passion between water and the thirsty person. Just as the afflicted person searches desperately for water, water, which is God's precious boon, longs for an afflicted person whose thirst it can quench. As is the case with all beings in nature, there is as if a heart hidden in water too. It is as if water feels that its value is only known in the bosom of the thirsty. It knows that if there were no one thirsty on the face of the earth, water would have no purpose and no delight.

At the same time, we have spoken a bit too openly about the subject of lover and beloved. It behooves us to be silent at this point. Since the greatest beloved has given you secrets from His heart, given you voice from Its own lips, now it behooves you to be silent and listen. Listen to that greatest beloved, for He is the one who says all these things and causes them to be said.

It is best to dam a torrent which may froth up and overflow. If you don't raise a dam and build it strong, it may overflow with such an overflowing that it will destroy the world and bring it to disgrace.

This means that a person must not go too far in giving away the secrets of oneness. He must sense that he is going too far and wake himself out of his excitement and withdraw within the measures and frame of intellect. In short, as one transcends degrees in the skies of oneness and love, one must stop now and then and rein oneself in. For once a torrent, especially a torrent of love and drunkenness, has rushed forth and overflowed, it is no longer possible to stop it.

And once a wave has risen too high, what can come of it?

Once a person dives into the sea of love, once the ship of the body has been buried in the waters of the sea, what follows is involuntary.

Yet love of God has made a ruin of me, burned me and destroyed me, and so what? Aren't the treasures of padishahs buried under many a ruined palace?

To be sure, a person who sinks in the sea of love of God wants to dive into the endlessness of that sea. Who am I anyway; what wine is this wine I drink; who is it that serves me this wine—am I not on the way to being unable to know these things? Is this not the path I've sought and the goal I desire?

Is the bottom of the sea better, or its surface? What need is there to know this? I have achieved the delight of diving into this sea called the sea of oneness, without hands or feet. I am freed from thoughts whether the sun rises or sets in east or west, or thoughts of any direction.

Is the arrow the beloved shoots better, or the shield shot at by that arrow? Is the wound made in the heart by the arrow of a glance sweeter, or the heedlessness which holds up a shield and prevents the wound? If they ask me, I don't know these things. For in order to know them, there must be a body which can be the target of an arrow. I am freed of that body. There is no bitter or sweet for the fish of the sea of love, just as there is no torment or peace.

The truth is that if the heart is able to tell the difference between pleasure and suffering, it is still in the clime of the world and the body. The proof that one has dived into the sea of love is that one is unaware of such contrary effects.

The true lover is someone who sacrifices his object of desire to the beloved's object of desire. Whatever the beloved's object of desire may be, he makes it his own. Because for the traveler in love, an object of desire is a sign of being. For those not on this path, the object of desire, striving to reach it and reaching it, constitute a felicity whose pleasures one cannot get enough of. In reality there is a greater felicity than this, which is to renounce one's object of desire for the beloved's, and remain without an object of desire. To be annihilated in the beloved's desire is to be annihilated in God, it is that beautiful.

Every mote of that great beloved's self-disclosure shines bright as a star. Each star in this self-disclosure is worth a hundred blood-shedding new moons. For this is not just any shedding of blood, it is a murder which adds spirit to spirit; which brings eternal life, in short. The lovers of God die in the path of divine love and in return for their shed blood they see the greatest recompense, divine beauty.

We have taken the path of this recompense for our blood. Although we gambled our lives and sacrificed our spirits, we saw that beauty.

If you do not give Him your spirit, you cannot live; if you do not give your heart, you cannot achieve the pleasure of being a person of heart.

And just so, three hundred years after Mevlana, with these verses Fuzuli expressed this truth and this state of true lovers:

The lover makes his spirit sacrifice to his beloved
He who will not sacrifice should not approach the beloved

The claim of love's malady will countenance no remedy
They call the approved cure for this ill giving up the spirit

I asked for His heart. He feigned reluctance and treated me with disrespect. I said He was my desire and my object in this world and the next, and he did not believe me, he told me to go and not tell Him such tales.

I was helpless and drowning. He spoke up, saying, "Don't I know what you think, especially how mistaken your thinking is? You still say and think things like, 'I asked for His heart,' and 'I told Him he was my object," believing that you and I are two separate beings, you can't get away from that duality, you are still under the illusion that you have your own existence, you haven't got free of such a dreadful duality, how can you ask for My heart, how cam you wish for the vision of Me, how will you lose yourself and achieve the end of being annihilated in Me?"

O coarse-spirited man. You are far from sacrificing head and spirit in the way of love. That would be to think you could get your beloved very cheaply. If one gets something cheaply, one doesn't know its value.

A child may easily trade a jewel for a cookie. You are like a rooster who finds a pearl on the road and wishes for a grain of seed instead, or like a good-for-nothing who inherits a book from his father and rushes to sell it for money!

Know that those aware of flesh and body cannot achieve the secret of becoming bodiless [*bedensiz*] for the sake of love.

But someone buried in the sea of true love has gathered into the sea of his soul all the loves prior to him and those to come after, and he has sunk in that sea.

Love is this, and more than this must not be said on the subject of love. Neither intellect nor tongue can bear to tell more openly of the mysteries of love and creation. Let us speak of them in veiled language. Know this much that even if you see true lovers as human [*beşer*], their hearts are drawned in the sea of oneness. And when I say "lip," for example, I mean the edge of the of the sea of oneness.

And when I say I am nothing, or I am not, don't suppose I am there before you! For what I mean when I say "naught" is to say that there is only God the Truth. Since there is in fact nothing but God in the universe, how can I exist?

My face can be sour when my insides are full of sweets. Confronted with endless beauty, munificence and greatness, I may do the right thing and choose to be silent. Don't be fooled! These things are because spirit approaches that eternal source its lip touches that delight.

The heart has touched such a delight, but you cannot betray what it has tasted. Because strangers will not understand what it says. In short, I can only tell one in a hundred of the things in divine knowledge and divine mysteries, and I know that for those whose hearts incline in that direction, to that felicity and that source, what I say will be more than enough.

****

EXPLICATION OF THE SAYING OF HAKIM SANAI: "WHAT DOES IT MATTER WHETHER A WORD THAT KEEPS YOU FROM THE PATH BE OF NON-FAITH OR FAITH; WHAT DOES IT MATTER IF A FORM THAT KEEPS YOU FAR FROM THE FRIEND BE UGLY OR BEAUTIFUL?" AND ON THE MEANING OF THE SAYING OF HIM UPON WHOM BE PEACE, *"VERILY, SAAD IS JEALOUS, AND I AM MORE JEALOUS THAN SAAD, AND GOD IS MORE JEALOUS THAN I; AND OUT OF HIS RIVALRY HE HAS FORBIDDEN FOUL ACTS, BOTH MANIFEST AND INTERIOR."*

God the Truth took precedence in rivalry
For that reason all the world's in rivalry
1790.   The world is like the body and He, spirit
Body receives the good and bad from spirit
He who has turned his prayer-niche to the source
Know it shameful should he go to faith once more
He who is Master of the Robe for the Shah
And goes back to trade suffers loss by the Shah
He who has become the Sultan's companion
To wait at the door is shame and fraud for him
When permission to kiss the Shah's hand arrives
To prefer to kiss his foot becomes a crime
1795.   Though to lay one's head on his foot is service
It is fault and sin compared with that service
To have seen the Shah's face and prefer his scent
Will bring upon a man the Shah's resentment
While wheat is the likeness of God's rivalry
A stalk of straw is like human rivalry
Know the root of all rivalries is from God
Those of mankind, without doubt, all stem from God
I'll leave explication of this and lament
Of the way that fickle beauty works torment
1800.   I cry out because cries are pleasing to Him
Cries and pain are what the two worlds must give him
How should I not groan at His tales bitterly
I'm not in the circle of His devotees
How should I not mourn like night without His day
Without seeing His face which lights up the day
His unseemliness is seemly within me
For my cruel friend let my life sacrificed be

I'm in love with my own pain and malady
So that my own singular Shah may be pleased
1805. I'll make a salve out of grief's dust for my eyes
So that pearls may fill the two seas of my eyes
The tears people rain down for his sake are pearls
And yet people imagine they are just tears
Do I complain of the spirit of spirit?
I do not complain, I relate tales of Him
My heart keeps on saying, "He has injured me"
And I keep laughing at its hypocrisy
O glory of the righteous, do right by me
I'm the threshold of your gate, you are the seat
1810. In truth, where's the threshold and where is the seat?
If our friend is there, how can be "I" and "we"?
O You whose spirit is free from "I" and "we"
In woman and man You're spirit's subtlety
When woman and man are one, that one is You
When the ones have been wiped out, behold, that's You
You have brought about this "I" and "we" so then
You might with Yourself play worship backgammon
So the "you"s and "I"s might all be one spirit
In the end drowned in the spirit of spirits
1815. There's all that. You come, O You who command, "Be!"
O You who transcend all coming and all speech
Body can only see You physically
It imagines You in pain and smilingly
A heart that is bound by laughter and by gloom
—Do not say it's worthy of vision of You
That which is bound up by laughter and by gloom
Is alive by these two borrowed attributes
The garden of love, unbounded and verdant
Has many fruits beyond joy and discontent
1820. The lover is greater than both of these two
Without spring or autumn he is fresh and new
Pay the fair-face tax, O fair of countenance
Interpret the spirit that's been torn to shreds
For that beautiful spy with one side-long glance
Has burned into my heart another new brand
I absolved Him although He did shed my blood
I was saying, "I absolve you," when He fled
Since You flee from the moans of those in the dirt
Why do you pour out pain on those pained at heart?
1825. O You whom every dawn gleaming from the east
Found bubbling like the spring gleaming from the east
How did You evade those frenzied with Your love
Your lips' sugar is valued all else above

For the worn-out world You are a new spirit
Hear the flesh groan bereft of heart and spirit
For God's sake give up explicating the rose
Tell of the nightingale parted from the rose
Our emotion does not come by joy or care
Our awareness is not by fancy or fear
1830.   There is a different state, and a rare thing
Do not deny God, for He can do all things
Do not judge it by the human condition
Do not dwell between kindness and oppression
Good and ill, grief and joy are ephemeral
Worldly events die, and God inherits all[93]
Dawn is here, O safekeeper of the morning!
Ask pardon from my master Husameddin
And universal intellect and spirit
You, coral's luster and spirit of spirits
1835.   The light of dawn shines and taking in Your light
We drink your Mansur's wine for our morning wine
While what You bestow keeps me in such a state
While I am kept thus by what You give me here
What is wine that it should bring me any cheer?
Wine in ferment begs us for our high spirits
Whirling heaven begs us for our awareness
Wine is drunk on us, we are not drunk on it
Form exists by us, we don't exist by it
We are like the bee, and form like honeycomb
We have made form, cell by cell, like honeycomb

The story goes like this: Saad was very jealous of his wife when she was around those outside of the family circle, and one day she complained to Hazret Muhammed, saying, "Saad is jealous, O Messenger of God!" This served as the occasion for Hazret Muhammed to pronounce the noble hadith, "Verily, Saad is jealous, and I am more jealous than Saad, and God is more jealous than I; and out of His Rivalry he has forbidden foul Acts, both Manifest and Interior."

As for Mevlana, he believed it necessary to keep the mysteries of oneness from strangers, to be jealous of these mysteries around strangers, and for that reason he mentioned this profound hadith.

To be sure, people jealously guard from others those they love, those to whom they give great value and importance. This jealous and protective feeling is among the most rooted of human emotions. For jealousy is something human beings share with Hazret Muhammed and with God. Just as the Messenger's is a jealousy according to his own capacity and rank, so that of God's is the highest of highest, a godly jealousy.

In fact the human being takes his susceptibility to jealousy from that divine source. Jealousy is present in the dough of creation. Each spirit is sublime to the degree that it can jealously guard its goodness, virtues and beauty.

---

93. Koran 3:180, 15:23, 21:89, 28:58, 57:10.

For what feels jealous within man is God. Those who can see things in essence [esâsen] know that there is nothing in the human being but He who created him. This is so much the case that when an arrived person stands in prayer before the one and true being, he transcends even the degree of faith. Confronted by God's works and the manifestations of these works, they [those who have faith] believe there is One who created them. But the arrived are those who reach the degree of seeing the great Creator not in His works but in His own true being and beauty. For them, faith in the unseen is a degree they have left behind.

After a person has become Master of the Robe to a Padishah, can he leave the palace in order to go back to his old trade, making clothes for others and selling cloth? If he does, it will be both a reduction in status for himself and a loss for the Padishah. For while he was once in the presence of the Shah night and day, he is now distant from Him and lost to Him.

While one can be near the Padishah, would one hasten to leave him and wait by the palace gate? Like trying to kiss the Sultan's foot when he extends his hand, this would be an action contrary to good manners.

For those who kiss the skirts of padishahs are not the same as those who kiss their hands. For a person who has reached the degree of kissing the hand to the then again kiss skirt and foot shows a lack of self-knowledge.

For someone who has seen the beauty of the Sultan to leave the Sultan himself and look as his picture instead is an error. The Sultan will not accept this. He will be jealous.

God's rivalry is the root. As in the case of wheat, where the grain is the essence and the stalk the plurality, in rivalry God the Truth's rivalry is the root and man's is the branch. But since the root is the rivalry found in God, there is infinite value hidden in this branch. Just as it is Saad's rivalry to keep his wife from the eyes of strangers, the rivalry of the arrived is to keep the beauties of divine mysteries from those who are not capable of seeing them or will look upon them askance.

The rivalry of the arrived in the most sublime kind. For although God is the God of all creatures, He does not show the beauty of divine mysteries to those of His bondsmen whose heart's eye is veiled, or remains veiled. He continually seeks the eye to see that beauty and the heart to love it as it should be loved.

Thus within the plurality of beings the mysteries of oneness are known only to those worthy of them. Shaykh Ekber [Ibn Arabi] has said: "God the Truth is the mirror of all things. But He conceals this reality with varied appearances. The concealment is due to His jealous guarding of the sublime reality."

This means that God, who comes into the realm of manifestation in our being, is veiled in our being as well. Those who can transcend this veil and see God are those who reach such a degree that God the Truth does not jealously guard divine mysteries from them and they achieve the secret of being God the Truth with God the Truth.

Now let us put aside the mystery of oneness and the explication of rivalry and complain of the torment of that fickle beloved; let us moan in pain.

"The fickle beloved" is God, who shows us varied self-disclosures. His "torment" is the love He present to our hearts. With that love we go from state to state, maturing from matter to spirituality, until we know no goal but the attainment of that great beloved.

Although I say I shall burn with His pain and speak of His torment, do not think this is a cry of complaint!

For my burning is not only disease, it is also the cure. What I suffer is not only the pain of separation, it is also the joy of reunion. In short, this is such a state of torment that its cure is in its disease and it's union in its separation. Love makes one complain of these states just as it makes one weep tears of joy and happiness.

I moan like the ney flute because He enjoys my wailing. He knows that this wailing is for Him. He knows very well that this wailing is a remembrance of Him coming from deep within heart and spirit.

And he knows very well that those who wail are not yet within the circle of His devotees. But it is because they moan in separation from Him that they will sooner or later enter that circle.

The appearance of His beauty is brighter than day and the night of His separation is darker than night. Daylight is the color of His union, and night the color of His loss. And the lover is the more beautiful as he loves, while the beloved is more beautiful in disdain. Wisdom is to know the meaning of that disdain and not stop giving Him your heart. Do not lose patience in seeking to reach Him. In short, this saying expresses my state:

> I am high with pain of love, don't reach for medicine, doctor
> Do not cure me, for my destruction is in your cure's poison

For the value of tears shed for His sake is higher than that of real pearls. Only a pearl expert knows the value of such a pearl. For this pearl is a pearl of the heart. It is the jewel-state of the love felt for the greatest beloved.

If I am a ney and the voce that comes out of me is burning, in reality I am not a ney, nor is my voice what is burning. For He is the one who burns me and dries me out in fire like a ney, and the one who makes my wailing burn so. This means that my voice is in reality His voice. My ney-like being is really His being.

You can pay attention to the complaints of my heart or not! The heart is always saying that it is hurt by the beloved. I laugh at this knowing heart of mine. I know that it is high on the pain of love, but still complains about it. It seems to me that this complaint is a self-veiling against happiness for those who cannot stand, who cannot understand, the heart's union with the beloved.

Don't you part from the right path! For the truth Hazret Muhammed brought is the path you have chosen and you walk on. Show me that path too. You are the Sultan of creation and the leader on the path. I am the threshold on the door you have passed through. But where is the seat of honor, where the threshold, and what is the door? Don't ask me! This is like the question, "Who am I, who is the Saki, and what is wine?" and its answer. We are in fact people who have held a mirror to each other's beauty and in it seen ourselves.

O Perfect Human, you who are the mirror to the Muhammeden Reality [*Hakîkat-i Muhammediyye*]! O you who have been freed of the bonds of "I" and "we"! O spirit's subtlety [*latîfe-i ruh*], woman or man! Listen!

What I mean by spirit's subtlety is not a meaning so beautiful, fine and profound that even the most subtle and beautiful speech cannot express it. My spirit's subtlety is a special kind of spirit just as impossible to express. This is a spirit which is the expression of a spirit in a sense even more interior than the one Yunus Emre descried when he said: "I love you more inwardly than spirit." This subtlety of spirit, this different spirit, is the most sacred being in us.

You know best that there is no one in creation but You, You have strung giant pearls around the neck of creation. You know that in reality these pearls are images reflected from You in the mirror You have created. In reality You are the greatest judge and it is Your greatest wisdom that in order to set up this most difficult equation, You have made it seem that what we call "I" and "we" exist. Shaykh Ekber asks: "Is man the created or the Creator?" I believe Your most profound wisdom is concealed in the asking and the answer to this question. For the one who made Shaykh Ekber ask the question is none other than You.

Thus we know that when You come into manifestation the states called "I" and "we" become naught, as great stars do the moment the sun appears.

Come, O You who bring all that is visible out of the unseen with the command, "Be!" But it is wrong of me to tell you, "Come." For you cannot be addressed by means of sounds, letters and words. There is no need to address you in secret or openly. You are the one who is above all concerns for address, announcement and explanation.

And we are those who cannot get free of the habits and necessities of having or being a body.

In reality the heart of a true gnostic thinks neither of suffering nor joy. For an arrived person is someone who has so been freed of such bonds that he is not able to see suffering or joy, and has achieved the mystery of seeing the true being.

Know that suffering and joy are unstable and transient states which appear and fade away like froth on the surface of the ocean. They are borrowed states in humans. A person who has not freed himself from their bonds cannot help but be the slave now of suffering, and now of joy. Such people live to the degree that they are tied to these limitations. The only thing in humans which is not borrowed is the love of God.

Love of God has its sorrow and its infinite gaiety and joy. But the fruits of the garden of divine love do not consist in this. What fruits there are there, fruits whose delight not every spirit tastes! There is neither spring nor autumn in the garden of love. It is forever green, every season bears fruit. The flowers of joy and ardor are always fresh there, colored with varied kind of beauty every instant.

O fair-faced beloved! O most superior of all values, beauty too has its pious tithe [zekât]. Give the tithe of the greatest wealth of all to us! Tell the tale of spirit to those whose hearts are distraught with the pain of losing You.

That is how I begged. From that most generous of all those who give, I wanted, as the tithe of beauty, to learn the truth of spirit and its true story. He said that if I wanted the tithe of His beauty, I should take it, and He looked at me with the most beautiful of looks and the most affecting to glances that would the heart.

In short, arduous to see His beauty, to know His truth, I experienced His grace which cannot be told in words. Although I want to relate by means of metaphors what was the delight that made me lose myself at that moment, to say what delight it was, I don't think I have been able to.

Has my heart been wounded, my blood been shed? Whatever happened, I absolved Him of it all. Although I begged Him even to kill me with the sword of love, He fled from doing so.

I said: "Since You flee the cries of spirits you have bound to earth, why do you give them pain? Can it be known to everyone that this pain is not pain but a cure?" While I am saying this the sun has risen again in the East. I understand that in the self-disclosure of that beauty there is no change, certainly no decrease. Like a river of light that flows without cease, He is always ebullient with grace and goodness.

Let us look to ourselves. We are bound by the limitations of the realm of plurality. Only when we annihilate all but You within our hearts, when only the sun of Your love shines there, illuminating our entire being, we realize that it sends us only beams of goodness and love, and with them we taste the most divine of felicities.

O You who give the greatest delight to hearts! Since You are the one who divinely bestows goodness and beauty, why do You not give those who wish to dies in the path of Your love what they desire, why do You delay your great grace? Why do you use varied pretexts to prevent them from reaching You?

My God! Whatever the case may be for those still bound by earth and plurality, I come to You with a heart free of all these things, and more, I come sacrificing heart and spirit. Here the cry that rises from such a spirit!

And for the sake of Your infinite being, leave off the story of the rose! Listen to the nightingale who has given its heart to that rose, whom You have filled with creation, beauty and its beautiful story! Listen, for this nightingale is struck with love not for the roses of the gardens of the world but those of the gardens of love. Its cry is not for illusory, imaginary roses, but arises from the pain of separation from the rose of truth.

You are the rose of truth, O my great God, for the state of Your lovers is beyond intellect and comprehension. This love is not body, not material, not sexual; it is the state created by loving You, who are beyond and above all these. That is why this state is superior to sorrow and joy. For sorrow and joy are events belonging to the world. These events pass; sorrow and joy are wordly phenomena. They are creatures of a spiritual nature. These phenomena change, these creatures die. But God who has never been created is infinite, and in the end only He remains. For he is the sole inheritor of all creatures, physical and spiritual.

But dawn has come again while we have been composing the *Spiritual Couplets*. Chelebi Husameddin is sleepy again, having written and written. O my God who creates all mornings! Please ask Husameddin the necessary pardon for his service!

(Hazret Mevlana often composed the *Spiritual Couplets* at night, and dawn would break while he improvised verses and Chelebi Husameddin wrote them down, but the raging overflow of that sea of gnosis and wisdom could not be stopped. On the morning of yet another such night, Hazret Mevlana, again fired up with such ecstasy and passion, requested the honor, respect and reparation he showed his great murid from God the Truth and thus declared to all the world the value of his great murid.)

What Mevlana meant to say here is: My God, I don't have the strength to thank Husameddin for such service, to ask his pardon. Just as You forgive the flaws in worship of You and take Your believing bondsmen into the sea of Your mercy, take on the request of pardon for this too.

The dawn light is glowing. And we are illuminated by Your light. We have drunk the morning draught. We are now drinking the wine of love and oneness, my Lord, in order to shout that there is nothing in the universe but God the Truth, drinking with such a drunkeness, with Mansur who said "I am the Truth."

We know no wine but the wine of Your love. Worldly wine, or the wine of love for others than You, does not make us lose ourselves; it does not make us joyful or gay. Is there any place for mention of wine beside our ardor and abandon? Although these heavenly domes whirl as if unaware of themselves, they are beggars for our intellect.

It is the nine heavens which rule and have disposal over the three kingdoms of nature, that is, the mineral, vegetable, and animal, and the four elements, that is, water, air, fire and earth. Intellect is what has disposal over the heavens, and what has disposal over intellects is none other than universal intellect [*akl-i kül*].

Universal intellect is a reality expressed differently in the language of every people. But although expression may differ, the beauty of the beloved is single.

Wine is merely an impotent simile for the love which makes us lose ourselves. And we are they who lost ourselves with the wine of love of God before wine was created. Of us it can be said:

> Do not suppose that grape wine is what intoxicates us
> We are tavern folk, Alast is what intoxicates us

Just as we were spirit and later entered form, we existed before form and are not made of it.

On the path we came by, and will again take to reach our origin, spirit is prior, and body [*beden*], after.

Our bodies [*vücût*] are full of holes like hives. Like bees that fill hives with honey, our spirits fill the hives or our bodies according to their capacity with knowledge and gnosis.

Spirit thus settles into the hive of the body like honey, and what is in reality universal intellect becomes partial in the body. In a sense, universal intellect is the spirit of Hazret Muhammed, and all created things, all beings, have been created so that spirit may be seen.

The spirit of Hazret Muhammed is the purest of spirits and of beauties which are the self-disclosures of divine beauty in countless mirrors.

At the same time, you cannot see the spirit in Hazret Muhammed or the friends who bear his reality in their own mortal bodies. Because spirit is "He" reflected in those bodies. He is unseen.

All His wisdom, all His mystery, is in His not being seen and known only to those able to see with the eye of the heart.

RETURN TO THE STORY OF THE MERCHANT

1840. This topic is quite long, tell of the merchant
       The story of what happened to that good man
       The merchant, in fiery longing and pain
       Uttered a hundred scattered cries of the same
       Now pleading, now haughty, inconsistently
       Now burning for truth, now for its simile
       A drowning man suffers throes of agony
       He takes hold of every straw that he sees
       In fear for his life he flails with foot and hand
       So in his distress someone may take his hand
1845. The Friend has love for this wild agitation
       Struggle in vain is better than submission

He who is the Shah of all is not idle
Though for Him to cry'd be strange, He's not unwell
For that reason the Merciful said, O son
"Each day He's engaged in an affair,"[94] O son
So scrape and scratch, in this way exert yourself
Do not sigh in relief until your last breath
So that your last breath is drawn is such a way
That your secret-sharer is the divine grace
1850.   When the spirit in a man or woman strives
Spirit's Shah is at the window, ear and eye[95]

This topic is long, so long it has no limit. It is not easy to speak directly about the realities of Hazret Muhammed and the subtleties of the human spirit. So listen again now to the story of the merchant and the parrot.

Listen and try to extract the moral of the story. And it may be that you will find many of those realities and subtleties in this story.

Burning in pain, the merchant raved. Sometimes he said contradictory things, sometimes he was haughty, sometimes he begged. Clearly the merchant was in love, and abject because he was in love.

The merchant was like a person who falls into the sea. Just as a person who falls into water may in fear for his life clutch at a straw floating on the surface; just as he may wave and kick his arms and legs hoping someone may see him, thus was the merchant bewildered and wretched.

Only the great Friend was pleased with this state of his. For to struggle like that was better than to stay completely still. And because this struggling was in reality for Him. It was because of a wretchedness caused by Him.

Him, the Shah of the worlds. He is always in motion and loves those who are always in motion.

On the other hand, it is natural for someone who suffers, who has a wound in his heart, to cry out. And there is nothing surprising about crying out in the greatest pain of love in the heart. The surprising thing is for someone to cry out when he is not sick or wounded.

Here do not ask why someone should cry out when has in his heart the love, the torment of that greatest beloved? Do not say it would be fitting if such a person were happy, rather than sorrowful, for he is fortunate to have found the beloved's way and laid down his head on that path; someone whose path leads to God in the end should be filled not with torment but with joy and ardor, and run along leaping like a gazelle.

No, do not say that. For someone who has found the path of God and made progress on it suffers as well, because there is no end to the degrees of approach to God. Someone who has reached a degree on this path suffers because he has not been able to reach the next degree of nearness.

For those who know and are able to feel it, this pain is certainly greater than the suffering of those whose breasts are pierced with worldly wounds.

---

94. All that is in the heavens and on earth seeks from Him, every day He is engaged in an affair (Koran 55:29).
95. Koran 4:58, 134; 17:1; 22:61, 75; 23:20,57; 26:11; 31:28; 58:1; 76:2.

Isn't that why, O son, merciful and compassionate God says in the Koran: "All that is in the heavens and on earth seeks from Him, every day He is engaged in an affair."

Some he raises up, some he brings low. He gives each of His bondsmen another share, another boon or difficulty.

One must move forward on His path without stopping, transcend obstacles, overcome the passions of the soul and struggle until one's last breath. He will show you the right way to the degree that you struggle in this aim.

Do thus until death. Taste the delight of being on the path of God the Truth until you die. If in all the years you work, struggle and worship, God's help does not clearly fall to your lot, know that you will receive it at the last moment, maybe when you take your last breath, and you will be freed from the darkness of the world and dive into His realm of light.

For His gaze is never off you. That greatest One has not sent you into this world alone. He is with you at the moment when you of course mistakenly feel you have no one in all the earth and are most wretched and hopeless. He is your greatest friend, beloved and protector.

And because He is, He continually seeks you, sees you, and knows everything you do.

That is why God says in the tenth chapter of the Koran (10:62-64):

Know that the friends of God have no fear, nor do they grieve.
Those who believe and guard against evil.
For them there are glad tidings in the life of the world and the hereafter.

****

HOW THE MERCHANT TOSSED THE PARROT OUT OF THE CAGE AND THE DEAD PARROT FLEW AWAY

> Then the merchant took the little parrot out
> From the cage and he flew up to a high bough
> The dead parrot had took flight in such a way
> Fast as a Turk, like the eastern sun of day
> The merchant was stunned by the flight of the bird
> Suddenly he saw the secrets of the bird
> "O nightingale," he said, lifting up his face
> "Share with us the explication of your state
1855. What is it that he did there which you have learned
> And devised a stratagem to leave us burned?"
> "He advised me by his act," the parrot said
> "To abandon my sweet song and my friendship
> For my voice had made a prisoner of me
> He played dead so to give this advice to me:
> 'O you who entertain all folk with your song
> Die like me so that you may find salvation
> If you are a grain, the birds will peck you up
> If you are a bud, children will pluck you up
1860. Hide the kernel and become wholly a snare

229

Become like grass on the roof, hide the bud there
He who offers up his beauty at auction
A hundred dread fates go in his direction
Plots and enmities and jealousies for him
Pour upon his head like water poured from skins
His enemies tear him apart out of spite
Even friends carry off the days of his life
He that's heedless of planting and the springtime
What does he know of the value of this life?

1865.   You must flee for refuge in God the Truth's grace
Who poured out for the spirits thousandfold grace
When you find that haven, you'll be safe from harm
Water and fire will become your men at arms
Was the sea not friend to Noah and Moses?
Did it not subjugate their foes with vengeance?
Did not fire become for Abraham a fort
To make smoke rise up from out of Nimrod's heart
Did not the mountain call out and summon John
And drive off his pursuers with falling stones

1870.   It said, "O John, flee and take refuge in me
That from sharp swords you may find safety in me."

The merchant sadly took his parrot out of the cage. But the parrot, who had seemed dead in the cage, came alive when it was free of it; it took flight and perched on the high branch of a tree. It flew so quickly, it seemed to reach the sun with one flap of its wings. The merchant was astonished and sensed the parrot's mysteries in this flight.

He said to his beloved bird: "O my nightingale! What is this? Give me a share of the degree you have reached. Tell me the secret, inform me of the realities. What sort of truth did that parrot murshid of yours in India teach you that you have played such a trick on me, what is the meaning of your actions?

The parrot said to his master: "My murshid in India taught me a great lesson by means of the actions and behavior you related to me. He taught me that the only way to escape the cage was to die. My means of his actions he told me, 'O you who sing for the great and the small, who intoxicate both the learned and the ignorant with your song, give up this song of yours. Die like me so that you make escape your cage.'"

Be neither grain nor flower bud, so that neither will birds eat you nor children pluck you. If you are grain, the bird of time will feed on the grain of your life. If you are a bud, events chasing one upon the other like children will pluck you from your branch and you will see your delicate leaves scattered and faded on the ground.

Don't be a grain, be a snare for grains. Don't be a flower bud, be like grass growing on a rooftop. In short, avoid being known, being seen. Be humble and hidden. Thus will escape both the evil eye of envy and excessive self-regard.

A person who offers his beauty for sale exposes himself to disaster. He draws upon himself all envious regard. Enemies will work to destroy him in one way, and friends in another. The one will envy him, and the other flatter him, wasting the days of his life. What does a person who does not plant in the planting season know of time and the value of time?

So, when you have escaped the filth of the world and taken refuge in God, catastrophe will bow before you, not you before it. Why did the flood not harm Noah? Why did the raging fire not burn Abraham? Why did the mountain landslide protect John the Baptist and crush his pursuers?

All of these stories being told to you carry morals which provide answers to these questions. So, the spirit parrot trapped in the cage of flesh seeks ways to escape this cage, to break these bonds. He sends his news and greetings to his fellow-traveler spirits in India. He asks the arrived parrots there for a way to escape the cage of flesh.

In order for the spirit to be freed from the bonds of soul and body on the path to God, one must ask for intercession only from the friends of God the Truth, the fellow-traveler of pre- and post-eternity.

And so, when the parrot in India, who is designated in this story as one such friend, receives the greetings of that prisoner of the cage of flesh, he falls dead. With this action he was saying: "You die too! That is, before natural death comes, get free of your own soul, die voluntarily to your soul-being [*nefsâni vücût*], and come alive to spiritual life, take wing to the spiritual heavens." For the life of those who are unaware of their own origin and reality is nothing but the throes of the spirit struggling inside a cage of flesh. Real life begins with dying to the soul. For this death is life itself. Life only yields to the dead who are freed of their souls.

It was no coincidence that fire did not burn Abraham, that the flood did not harm Noah, and the boulders sliding down the mountain spared only John. Those who escaped these disasters were in fact spirits who had achieved the secret of escaping their own souls.

So, O parrot! Be silent! Abandon your beautiful voice and your displays of fine talk. Because all of these are the strongest bonds tying you to your cage.

****

HOW THE PARROT BADE FAREWELL TO THE MERCHANT AND FLEW AWAY

> The parrot gave a little more keen counsel
> And then turned to give a last parting farewell
> The merchant said, "Go, in all divine safety
> You have now pointed out a new way to me."
> The merchant thought, "This counsel is the right way
> I will take his way, for it's the shining way
> When did I have less spirit than a parrot?
> One must take the good path, such must be spirit."

Thus the parrot gave the merchant counsel full of profound meaning and spiritual delight. He revealed mysteries and then bade the merchant farewell: "The time has come for us to part. Don't keep me from my path . . . I am flying to the heaven I told you of.

"My good-spirited master, I am journeying to my homeland. Actually it is the homeland of all pure spirits. Come there yourself someday. Be well, my master, I pity you. You have indeed been instrumental in my finding my way to salvation. You saved me from worldly ties and from the darkness of all that is other than God. Thank you."

The merchant understood his parrot. He said to him: "Go now, may God protect you. I am content with you. For you showed me the way to reality." Then he thought to himself: "This bird has taught me love and the way to God.

"He showed me how to remove what is other than God from my heart, how to be free of the body and become spirit. He taught me the meaning of being free from the cage of flesh and taking flight to eternal being.

"Now I have work to do. Should my spirit be less than the spirit of this little bird? I must look to how I may be free of the flesh and free so many others trapped like me in the cage of flesh."

****

THE HARM IN BEING PROMINENT AND HONORED BY PEOPLE

1875. Flesh is like a cage, it's a thorn in spirit
With the lies of those who enter and exit
One says to him: "I'll be your secret-sharer."
And another says, "No, I am your partner."
One says, "There is none like you in existence
For beauty, generosity, excellence."
One says, "Both of the two worlds belong to you
All of our spirits feed off your spirit too."
When he sees that people have become entranced
He loses self-control out of arrogance

1880. He does not know that the Devil has thrown in
The waters of rivers thousands just like him
The world's flattery and fraud's a sweet morsel
Eat less of it, for it's a fiery morsel
Its fire is hidden, its delight manifest
Don't say: "How should I swallow that flattery?
I'm on to him, he just wants something from me."
If he then satirizes you in public
Your heart will burn for days from the sting of it

1885. Though you know he said it out of resentment
When he did not obtain from you his intent
The effect of what he said remains with you
You experience the same with praise of you
That effect too will for days in you reside
Leaven of spiritual deceit and pride
But since praise is sweet, it does not show itself
Since satire is bitter, evil shows itself
It is like boiled medicine and pills you take
For a long time you feel discomfort and ache

1890. But the taste of sweets is but momentary
The effect's not like that other, enduring
Is it not? It endures imperceptibly
Know every thing by its own contrary
Sugar's effect continues on in secret
It brings on a boil that calls for the lancet

232

Abundance of praise turned it into Pharaoh
Be mild, not domineering, curtail the soul
Be slave, not sultan, as much as you're able
Don't be the stick, take blows like a polo ball
1895.   If not, when your grace and beauty has left you
Those companions will become weary of you
That set of people who were deceiving you
Will call you a devil when they next see you
When they see you at the door, they all will say
A dead man has risen his head from the grave
Like the beardless youth they call "Lord" for his name
So that by deceit they may ruin his name
When he has grown a beard disgracing his name
To seek him out makes the Devil blush with shame
1900.   The Devil seeks out a man to work evil
He won't seek you if you're worse than a devil
So long as you were a man, he pursued you
Offering you wine and running after you
When you've become absolutely devilish
The Devil runs away from you, worthless wretch[96]
They used to hang on your skirts in former days
But when you became like that, they ran away

For spirit, the body [*vücût*] is in reality a cage. Not one but many, many birds enter and exit this cage. The birds that go in are forces of the soul, desires of the body and satanic anxieties. Those that come out are sycophants, people who for sake of their own self-interest flatter others.

All those who enter and exit the body in this way say all sorts of things. One says he is your true friend. Another calls out saying, "No, only I am your companion and friend."

Another flatters you, saying you are beautiful, generous, good and forgiving. Another, that both of the two worlds were created for you, and the rest of humanity is just there to serve you.

Spirits in love with the cage of flesh, those who are unintelligent and immature, are fooled by such things. They think they are something important, they even think they are everything.

The poor things do not know that there is many a satan within them; the satans have planted many such a bomb in their bodies.

To be sure, for those who fall for it, worldly flattery is a tasty morsel. Don't you eat that morsel! For it is in fact a morsel of fire, satanic food.

First there is the delight of that morsel, then comes its fire and smoke. Most of the time that smoke is only evident on the Day of Judgment. Beware, do not trust yourself in this regard! Don't say they can flatter you as much as they want, but what harm can there be, since you will not believe them, you will not fall for it! Don't puff out your chest,

---

96. "Like Satan, when he says to a person, 'Deny God!' but when the person denies God, he says, 'I have nothing to do with you, I fear God, Lord of the worlds'" (Koran 59:16).

thinking you won't become arrogant due to such words! You will. And without realizing it, you will fall prey to those who deceived you, sick with pride and self-importance. If you want to understand this better, consider its contrary!

Consider how grieved you will be if they speak against you instead of praising you, if they tell all and sundry that you are evil and have done evil things when you aren't and have not, how you will pass days suffering in anxiety.

In just this way the traces of praise remain in a person, as do the effects of ridicule and calumny. Once the impression of praise in left in the depths of your heart, once your spirit has grown accustomed to the food of praise, once your spirit begins to attract such words, you have been corrupted and cannot get free.

Criticism and satire are like bitter medicine. When it's effect mixes into the blood, it continues for days. You taste the bitterness on your tongue, in your mouth, for days. Praise is sweet at first, like eating halva. Then that taste passes away. But it will make you miserable just like indigestion does people who eat too much halva.

Although the taste of sugar passes quickly, illnesses which come of eating too much of it bring forth boils on the body which can only be lanced with a scalpel, and so it is with praise. The wounds and torments caused by praise emerge later.

Remember these words of Hazret Ali: "Two things destroy a person. One is to conform to the desires of the soul, and the other is to love being praised and lauded."

God the Truth says: "We have allotted the happiness of the next world to those who do not wish for worldly position, grandeur, magnificence and wealth, who do not work corruption in the world and whose hearts surge with love of God."

The sole recourse for salvation of the soul made pharaoh-like by praise is humility; humility is to save the soul from the illnesses of conceit, pride and position.

For if you someday lose all of this power, authority and position, you will see that those who vied to flatter you will suddenly become your enemies. They will think you ugly. They will be sick of you, even flee from you as if they'd seen a satan or a ghost.

They are like the degenerates who run after a handsome youth and idolize him. One day the boy gets older, he grows a beard, and everyone, even Satan himself, no longer sees his beauty and never thinks of him. They scatter and flee from him.

Now put yourself in the place of that innocent boy. If when you were young and beautiful, you were duped by those who said they worshipped you and you lost your chastity to them, woe is you. For when you get older you will see all those who worshipped you scatter and flee. You will thrash about in the greatest of torments. You will be spiritually degraded. You will be a bad person. Satan will flee from you because you have become what he wanted you to be—fooled by praise and laud, beautiful words, alas, he will have led you too astray and made you satanic.

****

EXPLICATION OF "WHATEVER GOD WILLS COMES TO PASS"

> We have said all this, but however ready
> If not for God's grace, we are nothing, nothing
> 1905.   Without the favors of God and God's elect
> Though a man be an angel, his page is black
> O God, O You whose bounty fulfills all need
> Mention of any with You is not worthy

You have bestowed so much guidance upon us
That all this time our flaws have been covered up
Make the knowledge-drop You have bestowed on me
Be conjoined and mingled in with Your own seas
1910.   There is one drop of knowledge in my spirit
From lust and the dust of flesh liberate it
Before this earth's dusty clay swallows it up
Before these winds tear it down and sweep it up
To be sure, if they do carry it away
You have the power to redeem and reclaim
Has a drop that dries up or spills on the ground
Ever evaded the storehouse of Your power?
Should it fade into not-being hundredfold
It will make a foot of its head when You call
1915.   Myriad contraries kill their contraries
And are conveyed back again by Your decree
There are caravans and caravans of being
Constantly arriving, O Lord, from not-being
And each night all judgments and anxieties
Become naught as they're plunged into the deep sea
At the hour of dawn those divine ones again
Raise their heads up like fishes in the ocean
In autumn those hundred thousand boughs and leaves
Go off into the sea of death in defeat
1920.   The crow like a mourner all wrapped up in black
Laments in the garden over withered grass
Again comes the order from the village head
For not-being to give up what it has et
"All that you have devoured, O black Death, give back
Of plants, beneficial herbs and leaves and grass!"
O brother, collect your wits for one moment
There's autumn and spring within you each moment
See the garden of the heart, green, moist and fresh
Teeming with rosebuds and jasmine and cypress
1925.   The leaves so numerous they hide the branches
Roses covering deserts and palaces
These words from the universal intellect
Are all rose and cypress and hyacinth scent
Have you caught the scent of rose where there is none?
Have you felt the joy of wine where there is none?
Scent conducts you on your way and is your guide
It will take you to Kawsar and Paradise
Scent is medicine for eyes, it bestows light
It was a scent that regained Jacob his sight[97]
1930.   A foul scent can cause darkness to fill the eye

---

97. Koran 12:84-96.

The scent of Joseph is a friend to the eye
Be a Jacob, since you are not a Joseph
Spend your time like him weeping in wild distress
From Hakim of Ghazna hear admonition
That you may feel new in that old flesh again
"For disdain you need a face like a rosebud
Don't be ill-tempered, since you do not have one
Disdain ill-suits a face that's not beautiful
Pain in a blind eye is insufferable"

1935.   When you're with Joseph do not play the beauty
Offer nothing but Jacob's sighs and pleading
Dying for the parrot meant he was pleading
Make yourself dead in poverty and pleading
That the breath of Jesus may bring you alive
That you may also be beautiful and thrive
Has the spring ever made a rock green and fresh?
Be earth, that you may sprout colorful roses
For years as a rock you have filled hearts with dread
For just once why not try being earth instead

We have said so many things about the way to reach God, given so much advice and drawn so many analogies. In so far as we have been able, we have adorned our words with the jewels of gnosis. But in order for all these wishes of ours to be realized, we need God's help above all. For as it says in the noble hadith, "Whatever God wills comes to pass, and what He does not, does not." Without God's will and help, everything is empty.

Even if a person be an angel, if he does not meet with divine aid, his book turns out black. One needs the help of God the Truth and the intercession of the Perfect Humans who are His personal bondsmen, and even of the angels.

My God! You greatness and power are without end. It is not possible to relate or number. You know everything, hidden and open, everything.

My God! All wishes depend on Your beneficence and grace. You cause whishes to be wished, and You give those who wish what they desire. It is not fitting to mention anyone with You.

It is You who show Your bondsmen the straight path. It is You who bestow upon them intellect and thought. And it is You who conceal their many flaws.

You gave us a drop of knowledge at the gathering of Alast. Bring this drop to the endless ocean it burns to reach.

I am someone who carries in my spirit a drop from Your sea of knowledge. Liberate this drop of knowledge, this truth, from the desires of the soul and the earth of the body, make it reach the sea it wants to reach!

This dust wants to drink that drop, these winds want to turn it into steam, mix it with the lust of bodily desires and deplete it. Before they move to act, before they have the chance, bring it to Your sea of being.

To be sure, even if the winds of desire and lust do desiccate that drop, You have the power to take Your own drop from the hands of the winds. Where in fact can such a drop, evaporating in the air or draining off and disappearing into the earth, go but to the treasuries of Your power?

Even if it disappears into nothingness a hundred times, You can bring it into being again if You wish. Once You have wished it so, that tiny drop can dry up hundreds of times and seep into the earth hundreds of times, and it will hasten to rub its face on Your threshold like a tear appearing in eyes gone dry.

So many contrary beings set on destroying each other, like fire and cotton, or water and fire, or water and earth, can try whatever they can; they can burn, quench, dry out; but if You wish, You can bring all these which have become naught back again into the realm of life and motion, bring them forth with Your own qualities again.

Is not that why caravan upon caravan journeys from the realm of not-being to the worlds of being each moment? Caravan upon caravan of beings appear as humans, animals, and plants.

It is like the nights and days of our world. Night buries all thought, all wakefulness in a sea of mystery and makes it naught. But once the dawn breaks and morning comes, all the thoughts and feelings You have bestowed on us rise with Your light from the horizons of mystery. They wake from nothingness to being, from invisibility to visibility, from darkness to light.

And so the seasons. Every fall countless leaves and branches leave life and wake to death.

In rose gardens rise the laments of crows dressed in black who take the place of nightingales. Certainly You see this falling and scattering, You hear this wailing. For in reality it all happens by Your will.

See Your bondsmen the lovers of God who die and come back to life each instant, in love with Your beauty. When they approach You they sing like nightingales. But when their paths and inner states are straitened, and the whirlwind of exile surrounds their hearts, like crows screeching in gardens of fallen leaves they too wail and mourn.

Just as when spring comes again, the voice of the master of the world of life and being says to the world of not-being, "Give back what you have taken," and there comes a breath bringing everything to life, O my Lord, turn those who have given You their hearts back from the realm of exile to happiness and to You!

God orders the world of nothingness, "O Death! Whatever you have stolen, whatever you have taken from the trees, from the flowers, from the roots of trees which give life to life, now give it back!" For only Your call can being them back to life.

O brother! Consider that you too are a world like the world whose night and day, whose spring and fall you have seen. In your being too there are times of spring and fall every season, even every moment.

This means that you are a human being, floundering between the attractions of spirit and soul. The soul draws you to autumn and not-being; the spirit to become eternal in God.

There comes a time when your heart sheds its leaves, buffeted by the rage and violence of a soul cyclone; it dries up, becomes impoverished and ceases to be. And there comes a time when your spirit, in ardor for some divine beauty, takes back all it has lost and becomes enriched, adorned with flowers like spring.

Keep the garden of your heart in springtime with joy of the love of God! Work to make the boughs of wisdom green and the buds of gnosis bloom there! Let the cypresses of justice and rectitude grow tall. Let the fragrance of the jasmine of sincerity be scented there. Let a beautiful road lined on each side with the flowers of the tarikat [*tarîkat çiçekleri*] there take you to God the Truth.

The leaves of wisdom and thought have grown so thick they hide the bough of the heart. The roses of beauty and the hyacinths of gnosis have bloomed, giving so many flowers that intellect is concealed by them. You are in fact in such a flower garden. Let your spirit expand in this garden, let your heart fill with the ardor of divine love. In that same garden you will see nightingales of gnosis who sing hymns and relate the greatest of secrets like epic songs. They are friends of God who have made progress on the path. Listen to them! Let your spirit fill with beautiful voices and words and speech.

These points, I've made, these beautiful words, are in fact not ours, they do not come from our intellect. They are from the universal intellect, and you will understand by their fragrance which garden's roses they are, and by their curls which meadow of gnosis's hyacinths they are. The cypress stature of their straight, beautiful growth will show them what direction they came from.

Did it ever happen that you smelled roses where there were none? There may be no scent of roses in a place filled with them. But wherever the air is filled with rose scent, there must be roses there, or that fragrance must have come from beautifully scented roses.

Likewise wherever there are hearts thrilled by wine, wine must have been drunk there, or there must be wine there which has not been finished off.

Since that is the case, look, where is the scent of speech filled with rose-scented words and sentence coming from? Which divine garden's roses does this beautiful scent come from? Or pay attention, from what wine comes the ardor of those who have fainted with love of God, with the wine of divine love? For roses are known by their scent, and those struck with divine love by their burning.

Don't say it's just a smell! Scent makes manifest many a trace, many a mystery. Every beauty, every wisdom, even every path to God, has a scent. Scent is something that makes the distant near, that gives news of what is lost. When Jacob's back had bent from torment and old age, and his eyes gone blind with weeping, didn't Joseph's scent on his shirt make Jacob recover his sight?

But scents too are good or bad. A bad scent veils the sight. The eye does not want to see a bad-smelling thing. In the same way the smell of evil veils the eye of the heart. The smell given off by bad-spirited, degenerate people makes hearts unable to see God the Truth. Only the scent of godly and true Josephs liberate you from darkness and open the eye of your heart.

Since you are not Joseph, be Jacob. Plead with god like Jacob. For Joseph is the beloved and Jacob the lover. Joseph was that arrived of God in whose beauty shone the light of God. As long as you have not reached that degree, do as Jacob did, burn with love of God and wait for the beautiful scent from the greatest beloved which will bring back the eyes you have lost.

If you want to understand this better, listen to this advice from Hakim of Gazna! If you understand this, it will give new life to your worn-out body and bring you to live a new springtime:

In order to one to be disdainful, one must have a face like a rose; since you do not have a face like that, abandon ill-temper and contrariness. For disdain makes an ugly and colorless face uglier still. Shall an eye both be blind and hurt? One can't put up with that.

Hazret Muhammed said: "By knowing the degree of his own state, a person prevents its advance and grows near to God." It is because this is so that for an ugly person to claim to be beautiful is like a blind person's claim to see well. Both distance a person from God the Truth.

In the presence of a beauty like Joseph one should not show off and pretend to loveliness. On the contrary, the right things to do is to view Joseph's beauty and believe in the power of God, and to feel the exile of being separated from Him and beg to be closer to Him.

This way of understanding will bring someone who really and sincerely pleads from the heart closer to Joseph. Even in the countenances of such spirits there is a spiritual sweetness and freshness. Look carefully at the light-filled faces of elderly people who grow more beautiful rather than ugly as they grow older. In their faces you will see reflections of the beauty in their spirits.

You heard the story of the parrot. That bird died to soul and body because he pleaded and sought. In that case, you too give yourself over to supplication and look to dying to your soul.

So that a person with the breath of Jesus may bring you alive with his breath that gives life to life. Let him make you fortunate and beautiful like himself.

But if you ask what need there is for you to struggle to achieve this pleading, this seeking, and this dying to self; let the friends of God the Truth, if they are able, bring us to life as we are, let them make us dead to ourselves and eternal in God, consider this:

In springtime it is only living trees that sprout leaves, only moist earth that sprouts grass. Dried-up trees never have leaves, and rocks do not sprout greenery. Become earth, so that colored roses may sprout in your body.

If you want to receive a divine gaze or share from murshids whose breath is like the breath of spring and whose hands are like the hands of spring, be like trees which have not dried up and like wet earth. Be low and humble like earth so that the sun may serve you and you may bloom with roses of meaning and hyacinths of wisdom.

All you have done by being hard stone for so many is years is break hearts.

That means you have been a person who grieves the hearts of others with a harshness like hard stone; a person who wounds others.

You have gained nothing but evil from these states of yours. Now try being earth!

Understand the meaning of Yunus Emre's saying:

Dervish Yunus, do not be proud with the arrived, be like earth!
Be the earth of the rose garden and grow roses from the earth!

Become earth so that the sun of the arrived of God the Truth will strike you and awaken green sprouts in you.

Let giant roses and varied flowers bloom in the garden of your body.

****

THE STORY OF THE OLD MINSTREL WHO IN THE TIME OF UMAR, MAY GOD BE PLEASED WITH HIM, WAS STARVING ONE DAY AND PLAYED THE HARP FOR GOD'S SAKE

1940.   Have you heard about the splendid musician
Famed for his harp playing during Umar's reign
Nightingales would swoon at the sound of his voice
Joy was multiplied hundredfold by his voice
His breath graced assembly and congregation
And at his song commenced the Resurrection
Like Israfil, whose art of voice will again
Bring the souls back to the bodies of the dead
Or for Israfil he'd be accompanist
Listening to him gave wings to elephants

1945.   One day Israfil will make a mighty sound
And give life to those rotting years in the ground
Prophets also have internal melodies
Which give life invaluable to those who seek
The sensual ear won't hear those melodies
For that ear has been defiled by tyrannies
Man does not hear the songs sung by the faeries
For he does not know the faeries' mysteries
Though the faeries' song also is this-worldly
The heart's range is higher than man's and faerie's

1950.   For they both are in prison, faerie and man
Both of them are captives in this ignorance
Read: *O community of jinn and of man*
Understand: *If you are able to pass, pass!*[98]
The friends harbor deep within them certain tones
Which say at the first, "O particles of *no*
Lift your heads from the negating *no*,[99] take heed
Lift your heads from this illusion and fancy
Rotten in generation and corruption
Your eternal spirits sprout not nor are born

1955.   If I relate just a little of those songs
Spirits will lift up their heads from out the tombs
Bring your ear close, that song is not far from you
But I have no leave to convey it to you
Heed! The Israfil of our time is the friends
From them come life and growth for those who are dead
The spirits of the dead in the tomb of flesh
Start up inside their shrouds hearing those voices
They say, "This voice is different from the rest

---

98. "O assembly of jinn and mankind! If it be that you can pass beyond the zones of the heavens and the earth, pass! (Koran 55:33).
99. This is the "no" of "There is *no* god but God," the Muslim profession of faith.

It's the work of God's voice to quicken the dead
1960.   We had died and we were completely destroyed
We all rose up when there came the call of God."
The call of God, be it veiled or manifest[100]
Gives man[101] that which God gave Mary[102] from His breast
O you rotten with death underneath the skin
Turn back from not-being with voice of the friend
Certainly that voice is coming from the Shah
Though it issue from throat of bondsman of God
To him, "I am your tongue and eye," God has said
"I am your senses, your fury and assent
1965.   Go, for you are 'He hears and he sees by Me . . . '
You're the secret, why say you guard mystery?
Distraught, you've become *'He who exists through God . . . '*
Therefore I am yours, for *'To him belongs God.'*
Sometimes I say 'you,' and sometimes, 'me,' I say
I am the shining sun whatever I say
Wherever I shine from the niche of a word
Resolved there are the conundrums of a world
1970.   When there's darkness the sun can't carry away
Through Our breath that darkness becomes like bright day."
To one man He revealed the names in person
To the others He revealed them through Adam
Either from Adam or from Him take His light
Either from the jar or the gourd take the wine
For this gourd is steadfastly linked with the jar
The blest gourd is not happy the way you are
"Happy he who has seen me," Mustafa said
"And who sees him who has seen my countenance."
1975.   When a lamp derives its light from a candle
All who see the lamp surely see the candle
If a hundred lamps take light from the candle
See the last and you see the original
Take into your spirit from the last of them
It's the same as light from the candelabrum
See His light in the lamps of those who've come last
Or the candle of those who came in the past

In the time of Hazret Umar there was a harp player famed for his beautiful music and beautiful voice. His voice was so beautiful that it made nightingales swoon. The joy of those who listened to his voice was increased hundredfold.

This voice was beautiful enough to raise the dead. All who loved and were loved would think of one another as they listened to his songs, long for one another, and those

---

100. Koran 42:51, 52.
101. Koran 46:13-14.
102. Koran 4:171; 66:12; 21:91.

who suffered and were far from those they loved would sigh at this voice and weep together.

This was a musical art brought life into dead bodies like Israfil's horn; it renewed forgotten heartaches.

This was such a beautiful voice that even if the spirits who heard it had bodies as huge and heavy as elephants, they would feel as if they took wing to the skies like the lightest of birds.

In truth one day Israfil will blow his horn and the sound rising from his divine instrument will be heard by all who have died. Bodies rotting for centuries and centuries will tingle with that voice and come alive with its joy. The horn Israfil will blow will be the most enlivening of such instruments and the one that bestows true life. But Israfil is not alone in making such enlivening sounds. The words of the prophets and friends do too. Understand well these words and the meaning of these words. The prophets are those who bestow eternal life upon those who hear, understand and believe their words, and who rejoice in those words. Only those who believe in them and in God's friends, who take wing with their words and speeches, will attain eternal life and be raised after the real death, and after dying to their souls. Remember the Psalms [*mezâmir*] of Messenger David, who was one of those who sang in that way! While singing his hymns he blew into his flute called the *mizmar* with such heat that the memory of its *davûdî* [103] sound lives in the spirits and ears of mankind as the most divine of sounds.

These voices which come out of the hearts of the prophets, whether heard for centuries like the voice of David, or like Jesus raising those who have just died, are in fact more spiritual than material. It is only the ears of the heart prepared for them which will hear that invaluable voice and attain eternal life. These voices address more the heart and conscience than the external ear. In fact the world is always filled end to end with these hymns and enlivening sounds like the horn of Israfil, the breath of Jesus, and David's voice. But not only people, instruments and external and inner nature have their own sounds and voices, even the invisible faeries do.

Yet the melodies of the faeries are not sounds of the divine realm, the eternal realm, but like the voices of mankind still under domination of the body and soul, are rather sounds of this world.

To be sure, human beings are unable to penetrate the mysteries of the faeries and so cannot hear their voices.

But know that in reality both faeries and humans are in prison. They are prisoners of the jail of ignorance. Like people who are ignorant and heedless, faeries in the prison of the world are unaware of the great felicity and their ears are stopped up against the sounds which bestow life.

Read from the Koran: "O assembly of jinn and mankind! If it be that you can pass beyond the zones of the heavens and the earth, and have the power to escape death, pass! But you will not be able to pass without authority from God." So, like mankind imprisoned in the jail of the body, the community of jinn and faeries, busy with worldly goals, is also ignorant of the great reality. They are unaware of the heavens where the spirits of the prophets and friends of God roam, and unaware of the knowledge belonging to those heavens.

The melodic tones overflowing from the hearts of the friends address the ears of the

---

103. The lowest-pitched Turkish ney reed flute is called a Davudi.

hearts of those who are not deaf, making a deep impression. They say, "O representatives of not-being on earth! O particles of that which will disperse into not being in the end! Wake up!" and they continue:

> Do not keep on saying "No." If you will say it, say "There is *no* god but God," say "There is *no* god but God!"

Say that! In order to be able to say it, rid yourself of desires for all that is other than God! For every desire felt for other than God distances a person that much more from God.

O you who live in the world of those who are created and made to live, and who rot away and are destroyed! If you do not hear the voice rising from the hearts of the friend, if you do not see the various self-disclosures of divine being around you, know that there is no eternal and subsisting spirit in your body. That spirit was not born with you. Or the ear of your spirit has not opened, the eyes of your heart have remained unseeing.

In truth if there were anyone in the worldly realm to hear the holy tones in the hearts of those friends, not only the living but even the spirits of those dead for centuries and buried in the ground would raise their heads from their graves.

Hold the ear of the spirit close to those who speak to you with the language of meaning! In every age, every place in the world, unceasingly, there are those who will articulate that beautiful voice for you. But often they are not permitted to transmit that divine music [*ledün musikisi*] in words and meaning to you.

If you bring the ear of the heart near you will hear the voice within them. For the friends of God are the Israfil of the time and place in which they live. Many a dead spirit lying in the grace of the body and the cage of flesh hears the voice of the friends and awakens from the sleep of death, comes to life, tears its shroud and gets up on its feet.

They listen to the voice they hear in a swoon, they feel that divine music bringing them to take wing to the heavens, and they say, "The voice of the friends is a music completely different from that of other creatures. These voices point to the voice of God. These are the voices of God the Truth. We were spirits buried and lost in the tomb of the body and the graveyard of not-being. The voices of God the Truth have come to us by means of God's friends. It is because the ear of our spirit has heard that voice that we have been brought to life, we have risen up and found life with that voice."

The command of God, whether manifest or veiled, is the powerful command which, if He wishes, sends spirit to Mary by way of Gabriel and with that spirit blown into her body, a prophet such as Jesus is born of Mary.

The same great God calls out to those who have annihilated their souls and material being in His path. This call tells the spirit, whether like revelation in the form of inspiration or by means of a friend or prophet:

> O My friends who on My path pass away from metaphorical existence and walk on the shah's road of My truth. You are my intimates. Hear this voice of the Friend.
>
> You have while still within the human body and under the veil of human nature [*beşeriyet*] become this close to Me, and I have brought you to eternity. Since you have passed away from your selves, subsist in Me and return, and awaken my other bondsmen who come to you, who approach you. Show them the way to reach Me and be reunited with Me.

Although such words are often heard spoken by one of God's bondsmen or several of them, in fact it is God who causes them to speak.

God says to such friends of His: "Your tongue, your sight, your senses, your assent, your fury, are Mine."

He says, "You are my personal bondsmen, you hear by Me, you see by me." As in Yunus Emre's cry, "Let me look and see through You, and let me see You, my Lord!" He says, "You are he who sees with Me and sees Me." And He adds: "There are many who say that you possess great mysteries, that you know God, and they see you that way and because they do, they know you as a sublime person. In reality you do not possess mysteries, you are mystery itself.

"Since you have arrived at the secret of "He who exists through God . . . " and become one of those who annihilates himself in God, I am for you and will be for you.

"And furthermore, my arrived bondsman, although I always address you as 'you,' in reality you are not separate from me and I am none but you. When I address you with this 'you,' your gnosis will certainly understand it to mean 'I'; when I say 'you,' the ear of your heart will hear 'I.'

"For whatever I say, in reality I am a you-less and I-less sun of unity illuminating this entire world apparently filled with you and I.

"Wherever a light shines from me, there all the difficulties of the world are resolved. This means that wherever there is one of my friends in the world, one of my arrived bondsmen, and he brings news of me, there are all the difficulties in the world overcome; the bondsman will have no difficulty remaining.

"If the darkness of heedlessness, ignorance and non-faith falls over a region and even the sun does not penetrate and illuminate it, when our breath and word touches it, that place is a bright as the noonday sun. The being of one of our friends liberates that place and the people of that place from every kind of darkness."

You know that God showed His names and attributes, with all their power and meaning, to Messenger Adam. He made His names and attributes known to those who came after Adam either by means of the guidance of Adam or the friends and prophets who are his progeny.

Whether you take light from man, who is a mirror of God, or from the Lord Himself, it is the same. Learn the science of the truth and the mysteries of creation from a friend or a prophet, or through direct divine inspiration, there is no difference.

Likewise, drink an old wine, a wine of divine love, either from the jug or from the cup. The intention and the goal is to be filled with such a light and be able to pass away from self with such an elixir.

For the deputy's cup of being is connected to the jug of unity belonging to the one who sent that deputy. For the deputy's inner life is filled with divine wine.

When thinking about the connection between the cup and the jug, know also that when the cup was being filled with that wine it transcended the pleasure you feel. It no longer feels the delights of the soul. For it not only drank the wine, it assimilated it so that it has become the wine itself.

There are many people who have become the Truth with God the Truth and appear to be like everyone else. In reality they have no truck with anything but God. The pleasure and joy in their being is not due to intoxication with worldly wine but to the friendship and intimacy that fills them from the jug of oneness.

That is why Hazret Muhammed said: "Happy is he who has seen me and happy is he who sees him who has seen my countenance."

For that means not only that a person who takes the truth and light of Hazret Muhammed directly from the Prophet takes the same light from an arrived person who has seen that light, but that if one takes it from a friend who comes along centuries later, since the light is that same light, he has taken it from Hazret Muhammed himself.

This is like when one or a thousand candles are lit from the flame of a single candle. The flame lighting the candles, and by means of them illuminating the world, is the same flame.

If you see even the last of the candles lit in this way, know that the light you see and are illuminated by was lit by that first light and is showing you its light.

Take that light from the last of the friends to come along, or from the prophet who first brought it. Since what you receive is the same divine light illuminating creation, what difference is there?

Thus Hazret Mevlana indicates here that all who have taken the light of oneness from God the Truth and offered it to the people have always been guides and models of the same truth. With these words he liberates mankind from so many different kinds of despair and loss. He gives news of the reality that with so many friends of God who have come since Hazret Muhammed the same light of Muhammed will be carried to those in the world today and the people of ages to come, and that those who will illuminate humanity with it are the friends of God who carry the same light, who have arrived at the same llevel of oneness and mystery of oneness.

To be the murid of any friend who bears that light and is the inheritor of that light is the same as to receive grace and aid form the light of Hazret Muhammed. Beware, do not look at the variety and plurality of matter and suppose that meaning too can change.

In light shining in the bodily vault of all is always that single, sublime and true light.

In short, in whatever sign of the zodiac the sun rises, it is the same sun.

****

EXPLICATION OF THE HADITH, "*VERILY, THERE ARE FRAGRANT BREATHS OF YOUR LORD IN THE DAYS OF OUR TIME; BE ATTENTIVE TO THEM.*"

> The Messenger said, "In the days of our time
> Fragrances of God the Truth outstrip the time
> 1980. Keep ear and consciousness fixed on these moments
> Seize upon the exhalations of such scents
> One of them came, saw you, and it went away
> It gave life to whom it pleased and went away
> Take heed now, another fragrance has arrived
> Beware scholar, don't you again lag behind
> The fiery spirit found what puts out fire there
> The dead spirit found the stirring of life there
> The spirit of fire was extinguished by it
> Those clothed in death found the robe of subsistence
> 1985. This is the fresh stirring of the Tuba Tree
> Not like the motions of animality
> If it fell upon the earth and firmament

Their guts would run like water in an instant
Terrified by this endless exhalation
Read, "They would not carry it," from the Koran[104]
If not, why would they have been *"afraid of it"*
If the mountain's heart did not bleed fearing it?
Last night it held out its hand another way
I ate a few mouthfuls and that blocked the way

1990.   For a mouthful's sake Luqman was held in pawn
It's the time of Luqman, O mouthful, begone!
For the sake of a mouthful, so many thorns!
From the sole of Luqman's foot pluck out the thorn
There's no thorn nor shadow of one in his feet
Though you can't tell the difference in your greed
Know the thorn to be what you think a sweet date
Because you are so blind and such an ingrate
Luqman's spirit is the rose garden of God
Why should his spirit's foot be hurt by a thorn?

1995.   This thorn-eating body is like a camel
Those born of Mustafa ride on that camel
O camel, you carry a bale of roses
A hundred rose gardens grow from its fragrance
Your preference is for sand and great big thorns
What roses will you gather from worthless thorns?
How long will you cry, "Where is that rose garden?"
In this search you have wandered hither and yon
Until you extricate the thorn from your foot
Your eyes will be blind, how will you move about?

2000.   The human being can't squeeze inside the world
Yet he is concealed on the head of a thorn
Mustafa arrived to fashion harmony
He would say, *"Speak to me, O Humayra, speak!"*[105]
O Humayra, put the horseshoe in the fire
That this mountain become ruby by its fire
This word "Humayra" is a feminine noun
The Arabs call "spirit" a feminine noun
But there's no harm if spirit is feminine
It has nothing to do with man or woman

2005.   It is beyond masculine and feminine
It is not where dryness and moisture come in
This spirit is not increased by eating bread
It is not sometimes like this, sometimes like that
It sweetens, is sweet, it's the essence of sweet

---

104. "We offered the Trust to the heavens and the earth and the mountains, but they refused to carry it and were afraid of it. And the human being carried it. Surely he is exceedingly ignorant, a great wrong-doer" (Koran 33:72).

105. "Humayra," meaning "red," was a nickname the Prophet gave to his wife Aisha.

Without sweetness, O bribe-taker, there's no sweet
When sugar is the thing that has sweetened you
That sugar may in time be absent from you
When you are sweetened by much fidelity
Then when can sugar from sugar absent be?
2010. When a lover is nourished by wine within
Mind is lost there and bereft of companion
Partial intellect is a love-denier
Though it pretends to be a secret-sharer
It is clever and knowing, but is not naught
The angel is Ahriman until it's naught
Though it may be our friend in word and in deed
When it comes to inner states, it is nothing
Nothing for it's not come to naught from being
Many are naught by force, since they're not willing
2015. Spirit is perfect, and perfect is its call
Mustafa would say, *"Refresh us, O Bilal!*
O Bilal, raise your voice and let it flow out
Drawn from that breath I exhaled into your heart
From that breath by which Adam was struck senseless
And the wits of the heavenly host witless
At that fine voice Mustafa swooned with delight
He missed prayer like travelers who halt at night
He did not awaken from that blessed state
Till the dawn prayer-time had become the bright day
2020. That night halting in the presence of the bride
His pure spirit had kissed the hand of the bride
Love and spirit are, both of them, veiled and hid
If I've called Him the bride, don't find fault in it
Fearing to vex the Friend, I'd have been silent
If He granted me respite for one instant
But He keeps saying, "Speak! There's no fault in it
The destiny of the Unseen requires it
The fault is in him who sees nothing but fault
Does spirit flowing to the Unseen see fault?"
2025. Fault's in relation to ignorant creatures
Not in relation to the Lord of favor
For the Creator, too, infidelity
Is wisdom, but for us is calamity
And in a hundred virtues one single shame
Is like one wood stalk among the sugarcane
Both are put in the scales and weighed together
For the two are sweet like spirit and matter
Therefore have the great ones said, in knowledge sure
Clear as spirit are the bodies of the pure
2030. Their speech and their souls and their forms all alike

Have become absolute spirit without sign
Merely body is the spirit that hates them
Like a struck backgammon piece, there but in name
This went into earth and wholly earth became
That went into salt and wholly pure became
—The salt by which Muhammed is the most sweet—
He's more eloquent than that salty hadith
This salt has survived in his inheritance
His heirs are among you, go seek and find them
2035.   He is sitting before you, but where's "before"?
He's there, but where's the spirit that thinks "before"?
If you fancy there's a front and back of you
You're body-bound and deprived of spirit too
"Over," "under," "front" and "back" describe the flesh
There's no direction to bright spirit's essence
Open up your vision with the Shah's pure light
So you don't opine like those who're short of sight
That you are just this one who feels joy and lack
O non-existence, where is your front and back?
2040.   It's a day for rain, journey into nightfall
Not this rain here, but that raining of the Lord

Hazret Muhammed said that the beautiful fragrances of God waft on the wind in our days. God has beautiful breaths of scent and these divine fragrances are sent to us in all ages as a kindness, a mercy of God.

At such times turn the ear of your mind to the quarter from which the scents come. His scents are in the sounds you will hear. Do not miss those sounds and scents. All times and places are full of them.

His beautiful fragrances bring you eternal life, spirit and faith; but if they find you heedless, if they see that you are asleep to divine truths and callous, they will give the eternal life they bring to those who wish for it, who wait for it and are awake to it, and then they go away.

In fact the world that God created and the air you breathe in this world is every instant full of the Lord's fragrance and voice.

But are you in any state to take in this scent and hear this music? If not, awaken to these sounds and scents! Don't waste time, let the lights and exhalations of the friends who have come into this world to awaken you reach your spirit.

In fact, while the spirit allied with fire, which is filled with satanic rather than merciful emotions, swims in heedlessness and ignorance, thanks to that scent it is liberated from the disaster of being fiery-natured and having fiery desires. Even a dead spirit which is spiritually extinct, achieves life and motion with the help of the arrived person who senses the divine light and the divine music and the fragrance of God which fills the universe and makes you sense it too.

With his help the burning nature of the spirit allied with fire is put out, and with his breath the spirit that has bowed to death is quickened again and finds eternal life.

He brings to earth not the fire of lust but the fire of love. He disperses spiritual light and divine fragrance. In his freshness and aliveness there is the wisdom of the sacred Tuba Tree, and this freshness and aliveness is not like that of worldly life.

That arrived person takes those who want to partake of the scent he brings, those who awaken to the eternal life he brings, under his green wings like the giant leaves of the Tuba Tree. With that light he awakens those in the heedlessness of human nature and the darkness of the soul, and shows them the way leading to the eternal world.

Consider that not every being is suitable for the breathing of divine fragrance; if that scent falls on the earth or disperses in the skies, the guts of earth and sky would run like water because of its power.

Is that not why the earth, the mountains and the heavens declined to take on that divine power. If you wish to better understand this mystery, read the gracious Koranic verse, "They refused to carry it." In that verse it says. "We offered the Trust to the heavens and the earth and the mountains, but they refused to carry it and were afraid of it. And the human being carried it."

To be sure, if it were not so difficult to carry that Trust, if it had not seemed too heavy to the mountains, skies and stars, would it say in the Gracious Koran that "they were afraid of it"?

One can see that as it says in the verse "We offered the Trust," God the Truth offered the divine exhalation and divine love to the heavens, the earth and the mountains in turn, but earth and sky were afraid to bear that grave responsibility. It is only the human being who was not afraid of the oppression his soul would suffer by accepting it.

Yes, thus it says in the Gracious Koran and the intention is that none but the human being had the preparedness and capacity to bear the divine spirit and the divine fragrance, but because only the human being is so capable of oppressing his soul that he sees no harm in accepting that immense Trust and is so bold that he throws himself into the greatest fires, as a result the share of breathing in the divine fragrance falls to the human being.

This divine fragrance came to us last night with a different kind of inspiration. But whatever happened, however it happened, I ate a few mouthfuls and that road of self-disclosure closed.

Thus the Luqman-natured spirit was deprived of the great pleasure because of a mouthful of food.

That is how it is, spiritual and Lordly ascents are always hobbled by these little mouthfuls, mouthfuls of lust and food for the soul.

But O mouthful! Get out of the way! Now is the time of mystery, the age of wisdom and truth. The time, in short, is the time of Luqman; go, don't hobble us on the divine path, don't deprive us of reaching the divine heights!

Since you are suffering because of a mouthful, make an effort and pluck the thorn stuck in Luqman's foot. So that the non-spiritual lust of the soul needling Luqman's heart, and the torments born of them, may begone.

In fact there is no thorn in Luqman's hand or foot. But you who have lost the ability to tell the difference between good and evil due to varied kinds of greed, you cannot see the matchless purity in Luqman's heart. O empty stomachs that see thorns as dates! In reality it is when you have begun to see the dates of worldly lust and greed as thorns that your spirit, unconquered by the soul, will taste the felicity more delicious than the most delightful dates.

Luqman's spirit is the source of God's rose gardens. Why should the foot of such a soul be wounded by a thorn? Is it fitting to keep such a spirit from walking and even running on the path of God?

Don't you see that a descendant of Mustafa has mounted the thorn-eating camel? The light and reality of Hazret Muhammed self-discloses most of all in human beings. That is why it is right to call "born of Mustafa" the spirit who is of his community and shines with his grace.

Such a spirit thinks of the body it has as a camel and goes down the roads of life on that camel. And the roads it travels are graced with the light of its self-disclosure.

Although that is the case, the camel is usually unaware of the rose garden it carries on its back. The camel is unaware that because of the rose scent it carries, many a rose garden sprouts up on the roads it travels, and many a rose of gnosis blooms in these gardens. Because its eye is always on the thorns and sandpits of the world. Every soul looks out for the food and worldly goods it desires. But let us see how long he will believe that a rose will bloom from a giant thorn, how long will he live with the goal of picking roses from desert thorn bushes.

If the thorns of soul-mouthfuls stick in the eye of one's spirit, one is probably deprived of the capacity to see and the light of the eye. How will such people see the God's rosebeds of gnosis; how can they stroll those gardens? This is such a strange self-disclosure that sometimes a person cannot fit in all the world. Then you see that he is wandering around on the head of a thorn.

Hazret Muhammed came into this world to create a harmony within people's consciences. But he carried the spirit of the heavens, not the world, and the light of God. That is why he often had moments when he was overcome by the self-disclosure of oneness and sloughed off the requirements of human nature completely. At such times he would feel the need to return to the conditions of time and place, and would address his wife Aisha, saying, "Speak to me, Humayra!" The meaning of this cry was: "O Aisha, talk with me, make me feel I am in the world," even, "Draw me back to the world!"

O Humayra! Put the horseshoe in the fire so that this mountain of body will turn to rubies.

"Put the horseshoe in the fire" is an expression in Persian literature, a love charm. Sorcerers would write the name of the person to be bewitched on a horseshoe, and the horseshoe would be put in the fire. It was believed that when the iron became white-hot a coal would fall into the heart of the person whose name was written on the horseshoe, and his or her feelings would be aroused toward the person who put the horseshoe in the fire. It was said that even slaves who ran away from their masters and their masters' oppression and became lost would usually return with such a spell.

What Hazret Muhammed wanted from Hazret Aisha was for her to draw back his spirit, which had been roaming the realm of divinity and swooning in the realm of oneness, and ensure his return to his unfinished duties in the world.

On the other hand, when he was overly preoccupied with his worldly duties and felt the need to withdraw from the noise and materiality of the world and take refuge in the spiritual realm and rest there, he would call out to Bilal Habashi, "Refresh us, O Bilal!" For spirituality delights in the beautiful human voice. The human voice raises a person to the realm of spirits. Bilal Habeshi's voice was beautiful, deep and spiritual. Hazret Muhammed would drift into the world of meaning with the joy that rose from that voice, and repose at a point midway between this world and the next.

The word "humayra" is feminine. (Arabic words are either masculine or feminine.) And the word "spirit" [*rûh*] is considered a feminine word in Arabic too. But the spirit has nothing to fear from this femininity. Spirit is beyond being male and female, it is pure and far from the requirements of masculinity and femininity. But this spirit is a divine spirit existing in the human being as a trust. It is not the human spirit, that is, the animal spirit [*hayvanî can*], which is affected by cold, heat, dryness and wetness, which eats and drinks and gains strength from food and drink or becomes weak without them. This spirit is a light which has no need of any of those things and which liberates with its being only the human body from human nature and directs it toward the heavens and divine oneness.

This spirit gives a person sweetness, because it is itself the source of sweetness, goodness and beauty. In a word, it is eternal being itself. Sweetness cannot come to a person from something that is not essentially sweet.

You eat sugar and say that sugar has sweetened your mouth. Then you look and see that there is no taste of sugar left in your mouth, and often there is a bitter taste instead.

But if you are faithful, loyal, generous and reach perfection on the path of God, you yourself will become sweet and will be delight and sugar itself. If you become pure sugar, how shall that taste leave you? For a person who comes to sense divine light and divine delight in his own body and achieves such self-disclosure, the lights of the worlds are no longer necessary. The woman who gave birth to Mustafa said:

> They offered to me a cupful of sherbet
> I drank and my body was plunged into light
> I could not distinguish myself from the light

Just as at that moment she became light itself, a person whose spirit fills with love of God and reaches self-disclosure too becomes light like that and no longer has need of mortal daylight.

O friend! A lover of God who finds within himself and take joy in the wine of divine love that delights the spirit, such a lover no longer has need of intellect. Essentially, such a lover no longer has an intellect. Since the partial intellect cannot attain this lover's mystery, it swoons. If intellect remains in such a person, it will try to deny love.

For pure love is a joy surpassing intellect. If intellect has not melted away in the one called lover, this will harm love. Because intellect does not understand the mystery of the joy of love, it will want to know it but cannot know it. Unfortunately man hates what he does not know. When he cannot comprehend the power and sublimity of love, he becomes its enemy.

Those who possess the partial intellect sometimes suppose that they also possess mysteries and resent this state. They ask, "Does our intellect have no understanding?" One should tell them that although the partial intellect is smart and knowing, it has never experienced becoming naught. Even an angel is no different from a satan as long as it has not become naught.

Just as Satan, who was created from fire, claimed to be superior to the human being created of clay and refused to bow down to Adam, nourished a claim to selfhood and for that reason was driven out of God's heaven, even an angel made of light would be the same as Satan if he refused to bow down because he was made of light.

The partial intellect appears near to us in word and deed and can be our friend. But when it is a matter of states, it cannot go on.

Like Gabriel, who on the night of the Miraj accompanied Hazret Muhammed to the final station but said that if he took another step forward he would catch fire and burn up, the partial intellect cannot go beyond its own limit.

For the partial intellect is still the property of mortal body. It has not yet transcended that illusory being, it has not yet arrived at the mystery of being annihilated in oneness. But spirit is in fact perfection itself. What makes it flawed is the dominance of the animal spirit and bodily desires. Only if it is liberated from the limitations of those animal and bodily bonds and finds its origin and perfection, then its word and voice and behavior will be perfection itself. That is why Hazret Muhammed would call out to Bilal Habeshi and ask him to serve him, saying, "Refresh us, O Bilal!"

"O Bilal! Give us the call to prayer. Raise up your voice! Repeat the name of great God! First of all make lovely melodies out of the grace I have given to your heart! Translate the truths I told you, the mysteries I gave you, into sounds."

Sing compositions made of the divine exhalations, the divine tones which made even Hazret Adam faint, intoxicated and bewildered. Sing the enchanted sound that dumb-founded the heavenly host.

Saying that, Hazret Muhammed fainted with the sound of Bilal's voice and missed the prayer, like a Bedouin who travels all night and stops to rest in the morning. This signifies Hazret Muhammed's having reached the station of complete annihilation and, conforming to the right conduct [*âdâb*] of that station, being subsistent with God [*Allah'la bâkî olması*].

That night was a night of union [*vuslat gecesi*] for Hazret Muhammed. That night was the night pure spirits attained the felicity of the kissing of the hand in the presence of that bride-like Beloved.

What, did I call that great Beloved a bride? If I said that, do not be shocked by it and do not blame me. Consider that in my tongue words like love, spirit and beloved are in reality metaphorical ways of speaking.

When I say "love," I mean love of God; if I say "spirit," I mean the light separated off from God, and if I say "bride" or "beloved" I mean only that greatest Beloved.

These ways of speaking of mine are out of love for Him. If that greatest Friend were to be even the slightest bit annoyed by what I say, I would not say it. And if He kept me away from such love for an instant, I would not have the power to say these things. At the same time, this means that there are still moments when I am awoken from the world of ecstasy and rapture [*vecit ve istiğrak*] I have been lost in; how else can I explain my being aware of what I say while I am unconscious in ecstasy and rapture? But such moments are so few, so short, that still I am always drunk with excitement and love for Him. In fact if that great Beloved had cut off the self-disclosure of love in me for even a moment, I would have spoken prudently like everyone does who is in his right mind. I would not bring up the subject of the boundless pleasure of the night of union, or at least I would not have said what I did.

But He does not make such agreements with me. He says to me: "Whatever those who love Me say to Me, and in whatever way they say it, it is acceptable to Me. Speak, there's no disgrace in it, speak, for what you say is due to a love that takes you from yourself. You string such pearls from the pure shell of your heart in the lines of words because the love you feel for Me leaves you without a will. Like that shell, those words have come out of the billowing waves of being in the realm of manifestation." It is the behavior of those who see nothing but disgrace in such a realm that is a disgrace. Can the spirit which takes wing by command of the empowering and destiny of the realm of the unseen and ascends to that realm see any disgrace in its surroundings?

An ignorant person puts the stamp of disgrace on so many of the exaltations of love. But for God, who even accepts repentance for sins and forgives sins, can exaltations arising in His own path be a disgrace?

In the regard of sublime God, even non-faith [*küfür*] is not a disgrace, let alone the exaltations of love. Because there is no creature in the universe that was not created by God. Therefore the creator of non-faith is also God, and God's creation of non-faith is also one of His great judgments. Considering that God would not create something bad, in the creation of non-faith too there is a reason, a meaning, and therefore wisdom.

Here one should remember the connotation of "darkness" associated with the word non-faith [*küfür*], and that a kafir is someone who is in darkness bereft of divine light.

To be sure, God, who created the beautiful, the ugly, angels and satans, would have created darkness in order to make known the value of light. Even if every intellect does not see the wisdom in this world of opposites, the friends whose hearts are illuminated with the light of God certainly see these mysteries.

Besides, considering that a person has many virtues, life, and efficacy, if along with these there is also disgrace, what is there in that?

Such disgrace is a natural flaw, like the core of a pear or the seed of a grape.

And so those who sell such fruits sell them without removing the cores and seeds, for every fruit and vegetable is a whole with its seeds. It is like the body and spirit of a person. Does the body not suffer in order to support that eternal spirit which comes from God and wishes to return to God, suffer to bring it into existence and carry it to its desire? Does it not burn in the sun?

That is why so many of the arrived have said: "The bodies of the sublime spirits are clear and pure like their spirits."

Like their words, their souls and bodies [*vücutları*], in short all of their states and their matter [*cisimleri*] have become limitless and boundless spirit.

The bodies of those who do not understand the friends, the pure-hearted and arrived of God, and who look upon them with malicious intent, are mere matter. For if there were in the material beings of such people a spark of a ray of light, a tiny piece of spirit's lightning bolt, they would see and understand in the light of their own spirits the realities of the arrived. The closeness like feels for like necessitates that spirit feel intimacy with spirit. There is of course no trace of spirit in those who cannot sense the spirit in the arrived.

Like an undefended checker in the game of backgammon, such people are condemned to be hit and carried off the board at a suitable throw of the opponent's dice.

When those who look upon the arrived with malicious intent go into the ground they will turn to earth and remain there. The bodies transformed to pure spirit, whom they malign, will not remain the ground but become pure in every particle like bodies buried in salt beds.

This is the salt of divine purity and beauty. Hazret Muhammed passed through this salt bed and became the most pure, the most beautiful, and the most eloquent of all creatures. The beauty in his being is a beauty superior to his own hadiths, each of which is a masterpiece of every art of words and meaning.

If you seek the same delight of divine love and the same beauty in your own time, you will not search in vain. For in every instant of time and in every place of every location the friends of God are the inheritors of the truths and beauties of Hazret Muhammed.

They are living around you. But where is "around you"? Where is "in front of you" and "beside you"? They are in front of you, but where is "in front"? Where is "in back"? In order to see these things and know these things a person must have spirit.

If you are constantly worried about "in front" and "behind," tied to the six directions, know that you are still body. You are tied to body and remain within the environment of its inflexible geometry. You are as yet distant from human nature and from the achievement of spiritual degrees.

All directions are for the flesh, they are material appearances with which the body is confronted and is sometimes forced to turn in, one way or another. But there is no direction for spirit. The divine light can have no right or left, no front or back. It is found every moment and everywhere.

Open the eye of your heart to the light spreading from a friend of God. Only such a light will show you the truth. If you remain within defeating and degrading doubts and suppositions you will be lost.

You who are not yet liberated from the requirements of body, you still suppose that what passes through your head and inner life while you are inside of the world's joy and sorrow is true sorrow and true joy, you are living unaware of joy of spirit or the longing the spirit feels for God. This means that you are in non-existence [*adem*]. If you die one day and disappear into nothingness, will that nothingness have a front and back? If this limitation of direction is keeping you from God, look to getting free of it before you die.

God's mercy is raining upon the universe. Look to taking a share of that mercy, look to filling the pot of your heart, while the light of day is still illuminating your surroundings.

Know well that the mercy raining upon the universe is the fellowship and guidance of the arrived of God. Gnosis is to be able to see the divine light burning in their words, their eyes and their hearts. What is being recommended to you is that you not remain in darkness deprived of that light.

****

THE STORY OF HOW AISHA, MAY GOD BE PLEASED WITH HER, ASKED MUHAMMED, ON WHOM BE PEACE, "SINCE IT RAINED TODAY AND YOU WENT TO THE GRAVEYARD, HOW IS IT THAT YOUR CLOTHES ARE NOT WET?"

> One day Mustafa went to bury a friend
> To the cemetery bearing the coffin
> He filled up the grave and covered it with earth
> He made that seed of his live under the earth
> These trees are like people who have been interred
> They have raised up their hands from out of the earth
> They make a hundred gestures to people here
> They speak plainly to those who have ears to hear

2045. With their long arms and their tongues of greenery
From the mind of the earth they speak mystery
Like geese with their heads plunged into the water
They're like peacocks though like crows in the winter
If in wintertime the Lord imprisons them
He makes peacocks out of those crows in the spring
Though in winter it was death He gave to them
He brings them alive and gives them leaves in spring
The deniers say, "It's been that way of old
Why should we connect it with the gracious Lord?"

2050. God the Truth does cause to grow, in spite of them,
Plots of flowers and gardens within the friends
Every rose within that is sweet in fragrance
That rose tells of the Universal's secrets
Their scent, beating the deniers on the nose
Tearing veils apart, round and round the world roams
The deniers shrink from the scent of that rose
Like beetles,[106] or nervous brains at a drum's noise
They pretend to be busy and occupied
And from the lightning bolt draw away their eyes

2055. They withdraw their eyes, yet there's no eye to see
The eye is that which sees a place of safety[107]
When the Messenger from the graveyard returned
He went to Siddiqa[108] and he talked with her
When Siddiqa's eye fell on his countenance
She came forward and she touched him with her hands
On his face and on his hair and his turban
On his collar and his chest and on his arm
"What are you looking for?" the Messenger said
"Today rain fell from the clouds," Siddiqa said,

2060. "I am searching your garments to find moisture
But they are not wet with rain, how wonderful!"
He said, "What veil have you thrown over your head?"
"I used that cloak of yours as a veil," she said
"That is why God revealed," he said, "O chaste girl,
The rain of the Unseen to your eyes so pure
That rain you saw is not falling from these clouds
There's another sky and there are other clouds."

One day Hazret Muhammed went to the funeral of a friend. With the felicity of his prayer and intercession he left that great Muslim lying in divine light in his grave. He

---

106. The dung beetle [*jâl*] is a black beetle disgusted by the scent of the rose who turns away and faints. In order to revive it one must place it in feces.
107. "Many are the jinn and human beings We have made for Hell. They have hearts with which they do not understand, and ears with which they do not see . . . " (Koran 7:179).
108. A name of the Prophet's wife Aisha.

threw earth into the grave. He bestowed the potential for renewed life upon the seed of spirituality hidden under the earth. For there are divine secrets hidden in trees. Every thrust of life in their branches is news of that great mystery. For those who can see, the branches of trees are the arms and hands of people under the ground opened in prayer.

These arms and hands, in short, these branches, send greetings to people from the next world. To those who can see their movements and those who can hear their voices, they sing the story of spirit separated from body.

As if interpreting a dream, they tell varieties of truth with the language of colors melding into one another and branches conversing with one another.

Each of their branches is a hand stretching out. Every leaf is a green tongue. Speaking with these hands, these branches, these tongues, they tell of how after the seed of the body is thrown into the grave, a spiritual tree sprouts, shooting off roots and stalks, and prepares a completely new springtime. And they say that on the Day of Resurrection the tree of the body will here be decked with the flowers of the deeds, the good and bad actions every person has done on earth. White, red, even black flowers which by means of their colors tell varied mysteries to those who can see.

Trees in winter are like crows clothed in black. They are buried in the earth like geese that plunge their heads into the water and with time, in spring they deck eye and heart like peacocks spreading their colorful feathers.

The trees relate with their stories how by a change of season the divine power can turn crows into magnificent peacocks. They tell of how the life-spans of human beings, the life which passes away in winter and comes to a stop, will stir in spring, shake itself off, get up and rise again decked with flowers and leaves.

Those who do not believe are in a darkness that comes of not being able to know and not being able to hear that world of likenesses [*timsal âlemi*] and all that metaphorical, even real speech of nature, and they think differently.

They say: What is a metaphor, what is a likeness? What are you saying? These are simply natural events, the result of the moon, the sun, the turning of the earth.

Why should one think God does all of these things? This world will live its own life from pre-eternity to post-eternity, and will do what it does according to the requirements of its own nature.

Those who say that are unfortunates who cannot see the universe with the eye that takes lessons from things [*ibret gözüyle*], who cannot hear with the ear of the heart the sounds rising up from creation, who cannot understand its language of inner states nor smell the divine fragrance wafting from it.

Thanks be to God that the friends, who conquer with the divine light in their hearts all this blindness, deafness, unknowing of language and inability to smell, have brought to us hymns, lights, sounds and scents from the realities of God and his gardens of gnosis.

That is why every beautifully-scented rose in the human heart conveys to us, above all, mysteries from the great Universal; and makes us taste the felicity of being able to catch the scent of God in the fragrance of roses in spring, as Hazret Yunus said:

> Branches of the Tuba swaying
> Its leaves the Koran reciting
> The roses of Heaven blooming
> Fragrant, saying O God, O God

Despite all the materialist judgments of the unbelievers, the scent rising from those roses and those varied flowers tears the veils of so many doubts and so much disbelief they stretch out with their hands, and leaves the spirits of believers in profound and fragrant delight. A morning breeze takes up those scents and travels around the world spreading them over creation, whose every color, every shape, every action says, "God." Wherever it goes it distributes fragrance from the divine realm to those spirits prepared to smell it. Whatever their religion, their color, wherever they may be, the instant that people take in that scent they become followers of the faith of Islam.

As for the unbelievers, they are like the *câl* beetle which is disgusted by rose scent and cannot bear its color or its fragrance, and so turns away and faints whenever it smells rose scent.

And there are such people, whose brains cannot bear sounds, they cannot even stand to hear the sound of drums of joy and victory. For such people even the smallest, softest noise disturbs their brains, let alone the sound of drums.

But what the prophets and friends bring fro the realm of mystery is rose scent. The words they speak are the sounds arising from various instruments. Unbelievers are people who do not smell those scents or hear those sounds.

They are those who, preoccupied in the opacity of human nature, do not lift up their heads from their worldly affairs and whose spirits are deprived of the windows opening out onto the realm of meaning. That is why they pay no heed to the advice and the calls of those who wish to refresh them and invite them to God the Truth, to reality and the realms of meaning, and stuff up their ears to their music and close their eyes to their light.

They are the ones described in the seventh chapter of the Gracious Koran. In the gracious verse 179 of that chapter, God says: "Many are the jinn and human beings We have made for Hell. They have hearts with which they do not understand, and ears with which they do not see. They are like cattle—no, more misguided, for they pay no heed."

But this story is long. Let us put those heedless one aside and return to the conversation between Hazret Muhammed and Hazret Aisha:

> The conversation began when Hazret Muhammed returned from the graveyard and went to Hazret Aisha. When Hazret Aisha saw the Messenger of God she was amazed. She ran to him and searched him with her hands, looked him in the face, surprised, and caressed his beard, turban, collar and chest.
>
> Hazret Muhammed asked her: "O Aisha, what are you searching me for so anxiously? What are you worried about?" Hazret Aisha answered: "O Muhammed! Today the sky was covered with great clouds and it rained. That is why I am searching your clothes, but how strange, you are not wet."
>
> Hazret Muhammed then asked. "O Aisha, what were you wearing on your head when you saw clouds and rain in the sky?"
>
> Aisha said: "I used your cloak as a veil." Then the Messenger of God said: "O pure-hearted Aisha! What you saw was not the rain of the worldly skies, it was the

mercy of the Unseen. (Give thanks for your pure gaze, be glad, give thanks and praise that] God showed you His own essential rain."

That is how it is, many are the eyes that do not see the mercy raining upon the world where they are and were they live. And many a pure gaze illuminated by divine light sees the rain falling in the realm of mystery with God's love for the sake of breasts that are burning and thirsty.

****

EXPLICATION OF THE VERSES BY HAKIM SANA'I:

> THERE ARE SKIES IN THE REGION OF SPIRIT
> RULING OVER THE WORLDLY FIRMAMENT
> IN THE SPIRIT'S WAY THERE ARE LOWS AND HIGHS
> THERE ARE OCEANS AND THERE ARE MOUNTAINS HIGH

> In the Unseen clouds and water aren't the same
> The firmament and the sun are not the same
2065. Only for the elect is that manifest
> There's *doubt about new creation*[109] for the rest
> There is rain for the purpose of nurturing
> There is rain for the purpose of withering
> Wonderful is the benefit of spring rain
> Gardens become feverish with autumn rain
> That spring rainfall nurtures it delicately
> This autumn rain makes it yellow and sickly
> In the same way know that cold and sun and wind
> Are to varied purpose—find the thread therein
2070. These are various also in the Unseen
> In loss and gain and in profit and deceit
> This breath of the Substitutes is from that spring
> It makes heart and spirit produce gardens green
> The effect produced on trees by springtime rain
> Their breath brings about within fortunate men
> If there is a dried-up tree in any place
> Don't impute to the life-giving wind the blame
> The wind did its duty, it blew and increased
> He that had a spirit, for it chose that breeze

As Hakim Sana'i of Ghazna said in one of his verses, there are skies in the land of spirit which rule the skies of this world, dominate them and tell them what to do. On the road leading to that land there are hills, steep inclines, high mountains and vast oceans.

What is intended by the skies of the land of spirit are the spiritual degrees achieved by the spirit. But the spirit reaches these spiritual degrees by ascending through the realm of likeness, the realm of spirits, and the realm of domination, each of which is limitless beyond any comparison with our universe. The highest and most limitless of

---

109. "Were We then wearied by the first creation, that they should be in doubt about a new creation?" (Koran 50:15).

these realms is the dazzling realm of divinity, which is the realm of the essence of God who is absolute being.

These realms, unknown to people of the world, make up a realm of the Unseen where divine secrets reside, which is evident to those these divine secrets reach. The clouds of the Unseen ream are different, its waters are different, its rain is different.

The skies of that realm are different, and its sun is different from the sun we know, because there rain falls not on the ground but on hearts, and the sun is not the sun we know but the self-disclosure of divine being in the sky of spirit. There the varied appearances of divine beauty cause flowers of gnosis and truth to bloom in the heart, as spring rain makes flowers bloom on the ground.

In short, the conditions of the Unseen realm are evident to God's elect bondsmen. It is those who are liberated from the skies of the body and the bonds of the soul, and ascend to the heavens of the Unseen realm who there attain the mystery and felicity of seeing the divine self-disclosures. Those who are not heedless of the declaration of "a new creation" in "The Letter Q" chapter of the Koran [chapter 50] attain that mystery. In that chapter there is the good news of re-creation.

As Muhyiddin Arabi said, for those whose heart's eye is open the births and deaths, beings and not-beings of this world in which we reside are all a likeness of Resurrection. Gnostics viewing all these events see occurrences of the new creation [*min khalqin jadīd*] announced in the Koran, they are witnesses to re-creation and they view the Creator in a different self-disclosure every instant.

There is rain which is life-giving, like the rains of spring. Nature is quickened by that rain, and people feel more alive, they feel more joy in life, in the natural world enlivened by that rain.

And there is rain that rots things in the world, trees and leaves. And in this rot of the natural world people feel the sadness of autumn and its meaning. Spring rain falls on gardens like mercy, and autumn rains fall like malaria. One makes things green and full of color, and serves as a likeness of the self-disclosure of God's creation out of nothing. The other withers, yellows and kills, and tells of the great power in God's annihilation of all things which appear to be.

One sees that autumn is the obvious contrary of spring. But the contraries in the universe do not consist merely of these two. Night and day, cold and heat, white and black, shadow and light, and life and death are only a few of those countless opposites.

These thoughts should awaken us. They should give us a clue to the great mystery. Like the sun which rises again after its light has been blocked out, like the trees which are once again decked with leaves and flowers after their leaves fall and they become like skeletons, the coming of a Day of Resurrection, when all the human beings who have been dead for centuries will be raised up again, is a reality announced by the Gracious Koran.

If you attain a level where you begin to sense spring and fall, darkness and light, material and spirit in your own body and grasp the profound meaning in these, your spiritual gain will be limitless, whatever your material loss may be.

A likeness of these events occurring in our world, these springs and autumns, occurs in the Unseen realm as well, in the measure of its own greatness and vastness. The springtime of the Unseen realm sends its powerful winds of life blowing into our world. The hearts of the arrived in our world sense the scent of spring coming from the spiritual world. A profound spiritual delight sprouts within them like an eternal springtime. Their spirit horizons and spirit valleys fill all at once with greenery, leaves and flowers.

Every act of worshipping God in all sincerity of spirit and heart, for example every prayer, every fast, is a breeze blowing from the eternal realm. On the other hand, every act of evil, pride, envy, greed and lust that conquers the human soul in the world causes profound damage, torment and death to the spirit like an autumn storm rushing out of the Unseen realm.

But the words and exhalations of the friends of God, and of God's Substitutes who roam the earth from land to land, are life-giving spring breezes blowing from the realm of divinity. With their words and exhalations the heart becomes as green and beautiful as a garden in Paradise.

But if the winds of springtime blowing on earth come upon a dried-up tree, they do it no good. Why has that tree dried up? Was it due to its own fault, or was it dried up by others? Whatever the reason, springtime has no effect upon a dried-up tree.

In the same way the exhalations of arrived persons, and even the rain of their tears, do good only to mortals with life in their spirits, who have the power to take in wind and rain. If a spirit resists awakening to eternal life despite all the exhalations of a murshid, it is not due to any flaw in the murshid but to the impurity of the murid's spirit.

Once spring breezes blow and have the necessary effect on the branches, once spring rains have fallen and water has run down the branches of trees, then see the green sprouts and blooming flowers.

Once the mercy raining down with the winds blowing from the Unseen realm has begun to nourish a spirit, then view the profound self-disclosure arising in that spirit.

So, the winds blowing from the Unseen realm and the rain falling from that realm's skies are for those in this world who have a window open to that life; for those whose spirits thirst for that realm, not for dried-up hearts.

****

ON THE MEANING OF THE HADITH, "*SEIZE UPON THE COOLNESS OF SPRING . . .*"

2075.   "Do not cover your flesh," the Messenger said
      "Against the cool air of spring, take heed, O friends
      It does for your spirits the very same thing
      That is done for trees by the season of spring
      However, flee from the cold air of autumn
      For it does what it does to vine and garden."
      Transmitters took this hadith in outward form
      And have been content with that external form
      Members of that group were heedless of spirit
      They saw the mountain, but not the mine in it
2080.   To the Lord that autumn is desire and soul
      Intellect and spirit are spring eternal
      Hidden in you is a partial intellect
      Search the world for one perfect in intellect
      Your part becomes universal through his whole
      Through its whole the partial becomes manifest
      As date wine intoxicates the intellect

The universal intellect yokes the soul
So the anagogy is that like springtime
Pure exhalations are life of leaf and vine
2085.   What the friends say, whether it be soft or harsh
Supports your religion, do not shield your flesh
Tolerate it, whether he speak hot or cold
And you'll escape hell-fire and all heat and cold
His "hot" and his "cold" are life's season of spring
Leaven of truthfulness, service, certainty
The garden of spirits is alive through him
And with those pearls he fills up the heart's ocean
The man of intellect has griefs by thousands
If one sliver's missing from his heart's garden

Hazret Muhammed said: Friends, expose your bodies to the coolness of spring. (Take broad advantage of the spring air.) For whatever effect spring has on trees, it has that same effect on your bodies, it gives you life and vitality.

On the contrary, beware of the damp and cold of autumn. For its effect is the same as that which can be observed in trees. Look at what autumn does to gardens and vines and take care that you do not become like that too.

For those who look at the outward form of this hadith it may appear to be merely about the life of nature. In reality it was an inward meaning and that is the meaning which must in fact be known.

In short, the autumn in that beautiful saying is the soul, the souls desires and ambitions. Spring represents the intellect and spirit. It tells of the eternity of the spirit and how in the path of God it finds a new and immortal life each instant.

One should consider that human beings have an intellect, however partial. This intellect works to obtain and ensure what the body needs in order to live. But one cannot know with this intellect the great mysteries which place creation in an order having a beginning and end, this intellect is not enough for the attainment of the great and eternal realities beyond the veils.

The duty which falls to a person here is to seek out an arrived person in the world and act according to the requirements of the intellect perfected in him. The universal intellects [külli akılları] of the arrived cause the partial intellect in you to mature. They bring it to perfection. They do not leave it adrift. They ensure that it not go to waste. That is their duty. The intellects of the arrived certainly perform this great duty, which is to tie human hearts to God and bring their spirits to God, with infinite joy and enthusiasm.

Just as the juice of dates becomes wine and makes the intellect lose its wits, so do people who possess partial intellects drink the wine of divine love which those who possess universal intellects serve with neither cup nor lip, and thus pass away from their souls.

So, like the winds of spring, the pure exhalations of God's friends bring life, and as the winds of spring bring water and leaves to thirsty and naked trees, so do they refresh and beautify the spirit.

The method of God the Truth's arrived is like that of spring. Like spring, whose winds sometimes blow harshly, whose waters sometimes rise up and rush in floods, they sometimes rage as well.

With their sometimes soft and caressing, sometimes harsh and branch-breaking behavior, they show you the horizons of eternity.

You must put up with this. A person who tolerates the thorns of roses will certainly pass over the thorn fences of the rose gardens of eternity and enter in.

Just as the value of spring is not known without autumn, if it were not for the harshness of the arrived, which withers the leaves of soul in a person's body and causes then to fall, the gates of the countries of eternity's spring would remain closed to that person.

The breezes that blow through the gardens of spirit have the effects of the breath of Jesus. The heart is full of giant pearls of gnosis and spirituality. Guard like your life those magnificent pearls in the treasury of the heart. For every pearl lost from the heart takes away a kind of joy. Hearts that lose their pearls are embraced only by a profound sorrow.

****

How Siddiqa, may God be Pleased with her, asked Mustafa, God bless him and give him Peace, "What was the Mystery of Today's Rain?"

2090. Siddiqa said, "O kernel of all being,
        The rain that fell today, what was its meaning?
        Was it one of the rains that falls in mercy
        Or a warning of justice and majesty?
        Was this one of those sweet graces of the spring
        Or one of those catastrophes autumn brings?"
        He answered, "This rain was to allay that grief
        Which comes to Adam's seed in adversity
        If mankind were to keep suffering that heat
        It would fall into much ruin and decrease
2095.   This whole world would all at once be desolate
        Selfish desires within mankind would come out
        O dear spirit, heedlessness holds up this world
        Intelligence is disaster for this world
        Intelligence belongs to that other world
        And when it prevails it overthrows this world
        Greed is ice and intelligence is the sun
        Intelligence is water and the world is scum
        Intelligence trickles from that yonder world
        So that greed and envy don't roar in this world
3000.   If the trickle should increase from the Unseen
        Nor virtue nor vice would in this world remain
        There's no limit to this, go back to the start
        To the story of the man who played the harp

Hazret Aisha asked the Prophet: "O essence of created beings! What is the hidden cause of the rain that fell today? What season's rain was it? Was it spring's rain of mercy, or autumn's disaster?

"Was what appeared to me as rain a self-disclosure of divine beauty, or was it a manifestation of divine majesty [*celâl*] and violence?

Hazret Muhammed said that the rain had been a kindness and mercy driving away grief and bringing quietude to the spirit.

If people remained in the fire of torment for a long time and divine mercy did not cool them down, this world would be a ruin. If people devoted themselves only to God and cleansed themselves of all greed and ambition, the world would collapse and neither would there ever be any repair, nor would people be able to have goals and hope. People would contemplate the transiency of the universe and withdraw from worldly affairs, and they would have no descendents.

It is people's ambitions and delusions that keep this world going. The worst catastrophe for the world would be for everyone in it to have their wits about them. Consider: "If it weren't for fools, the world would be destroyed." Those fools, devoted only to the world, are so spellbound they cannot see anything but the world. For in fact they are people who have only a material intellect. The world can only prosper in the hands of such people who have that kind of ambition and intellect.

Intellect is a sun and greed is ice. Just as the sun melts ice, so does intellect destroy greed.

Because intelligent people give no importance to the world and their eyes are open only to the spiritual world, they can leave the world in ruins. Because they will world only for spiritual life, the material life of the world atrophies in the hands of the intelligent.

As Hazret Muhammed says in another hadith, people on earth are beneficial to the world to the degree that they live for the world as if they were never going to die, and work for the afterworld as if they were about to die. This means that people are satisfactory only to the degree that they have the consciousness to create harmony and balance between these two.

That is why intellect only trickles drop by drop from the other world to this realm, so that greed and envy do not roar and spread over the world.

If the rain coming from the Unseen realm were greater and faster, that is, if more intellect rained into this world, this world would be left in the hands of people without any ambition or desire, people with no art or skill, and would no longer be this world.

And so, when at a difficult moment Hazret Aisha's heart was full of grief at the tribulations of the world, and she wanted to leave the house and put the Hazret Prophet's cloak over her head, God's wisdom self-disclosed in the form of rain.

But what was falling was not rain, it was a spiritual mystery trickling from the skies. This mystery opened the eye of Aisha's heart to the spiritual realm and showed her a realm others can not see. It distanced her from the world for a moment. Thus the worldly grief oppressing her heart was quieted.

But there is no limit to these kinds of divine knowledge and sublime mysteries. So let us return to our story of the old minstrel.

****

THE REST OF THE STORY OF THE OLD MINSTREL AND EXPLICATION OF ITS MORAL

> That minstrel who filled the world with gaiety
> From whose voice there sprang wonderful fantasies
> Whose song made the bird of the heart take to flight

And whose melodies bewildered spirit's mind
When the days passed by and he was an old man
The weak falcon of his spirit catching gnats
2105. His back curved like the bottom of a wine-vat
The eyebrows looped over like a crupper-strap
His fine voice that made the spirit grow became
Ugly and no one thought it worth anything
That voice which Venus herself had once envied
Now became like the bray of an old donkey
What fair thing is there that does not become foul
Or what rooftop that will not carpet the ground
Save for voices in the hearts of the great ones
Echoed by the trumpet of Resurrection
2110. A heart that makes all hearts intoxicated
Not-being by which our existence exists
Amber magnetizing voices and ideas
The taste of what's secret, inspired or revealed
The minstrel, older and debilitated
Could no longer earn and was hostage to bread
He said, "You've given me a long life's respite
O God, You've bestowed favors on a poor wretch
For seventy years I've worked iniquity
Yet You've not withheld one day's bounty from me
2115. I've no earnings and I am Your guest today
I am Yours and for You my harp I will play."
He took up his harp and went in search of God
Toward the graveyard of Yathrib,[110] crying, "Ah!
I ask God the price of silk harp strings," he said
"For he will accept bad coin in His goodness."
He played harp a long while, then lay down and wept
Falling on a grave, harp pillow for his head
Sleep took him, his spirit's bird escaped the cage
It let harp and harpist go and sprang away
2120. It was freed of flesh and the pain of this world
It the wilderness of spirit, the pure world
His spirit singing of what had taken place
Saying, "If they'd only permit me to stay
My spirit happy in this garden and spring
Drunk on this vast flower-field of the Unseen
I would travel without head and without foot
Eating sugar without lip and without tooth
Memory and thought freed from anguish of mind
I'd play with the inhabitants of the sky
2125. With my eyes shut tight I would see a whole world

---

110. The former name of the city which in the time of the Prophet came to be known as Medina.

Without hands I'd gather roses and basil."
The water-bird plunged in a sea of honey
The wellspring of Job for *drinking and washing*[111]
Whereby Job was purified from crown to feet
From all affliction like the light of the east
If the *Spiritual Couplets* were in extent
Like the sky, not half of this would fit in it
For earth and sky, though exceeding abundant
Are so narrow they have rent my heart to shreds
2130.   And the world opened up to me in that dream
Its expansion spread wide my pinions and wings
Were that world and the way to it evident
Few are they who would stay here for an instant
The command came, "No, don't be so covetous
Since the thorn is out of your foot now, be off."
His spirit was lingering there, wonderingly
In the expanse of His mercy and bounty

Those who listened to the sound rising from this old harpist's instrument would be lost in dreams and varied states. The bird of the spirit would take wing to the sky with his voice and fly in vast expanses ending in love. Whatever was in a person's heart, he would be awed by those melodies.

But time aged that harpist and left him helpless and poor, his back bent. He had developed a hump, his eyebrows were askew and fell down to veil his eyes like hair.

His voice had gone bad, he had lost his fame. There had been a time when even Venus, the beautiful woman of myth, had envied that voice and now it reminded one of a donkey's braying.

As the Sultanu'l-Ulema Bahaeddin Veled said, if a person who admires you praises your brows, your eyes, your face and the beauty of your body, these will rot away and become dust. If he admires the beautiful things you say, one day that tongue of yours will fall silent. If the person who admires you praises the sacred spirit which illuminates your countenance and makes your speech beautiful, and if he does this knowingly, he is right, for it means that gnosis makes him say that, gnosis makes him find the true beauty. For the spirit is pre-eternal and post-eternal. The spirit is the beauty of beauties and does not die.

Is there anything of beauty that has not become ugly in the end? What roof has not collapsed eventually?

Only the voices rising from the breasts of God the Truth's arrived blow life into the dead like the trumpet of Israfil.

They serve up the love of God to us, cup by cup. They themselves are drunk on that wine. They have passed away from self to the point of not-being and it is the not-being of these arrived which makes us know the taste and meaning of being.

They are the amber of all beautiful voices and thoughts, and like magnets they draw

---

111. "Remember our servant Job. He cried to his Lord, "The Evil One has afflicted me with distress and suffering!" "Strike with your foot. In this you may wash, cool and refreshing, and drink" (Koran 38:41-42).

sounds and thoughts to the gems of their hearts. Beauty collects there. The delight of divine mystery is distributed to other thirsty spirits from this source.

When the harpist had become too old to work and was in need of a piece of bread, he begged God:

> My God, You have given me a long life and many opportunities. For seventy years I have committed many a sin and yet You have not withheld Your bounty from me. People's hearts have been delighted by my playing, so many of Your servants, young and old, woman and man, have had beautiful fantasies and sweet dreams listening to its sound.
>
> But now I am helpless. No one seeks me out anymore, no one looks after me or asks after me. Now I am Your guest alone. Now, with my shaking hands and broken voice, I will play for You alone. Will You hear my voice?

He tuned his lute. He went to the graveyard of Medina, sighing from the heart. He turned himself over to God's greatness, mercy and compassion. He wept for a long time and played his lute as if wanting to make its voice rise to the heavens. Then he was exhausted. He fell asleep on the ground in the graveyard and his spirit, freed from the cage of flesh, went to wander the realm of likeness. You know the realm of likeness, it is a barzakh realm located between the realms of spirits and bodies where the spirit of a sleeper sees images and dreams appropriate to its preparedness [*istîdâdına münasıp*]. Sometimes it rises from this degree to the realm of sovereignty and is included in the gathering [*meclis*] of those in that realm.

The old minstrel's spirit dove into that spiritual realm. He was so free of worldly sorrows, and so aware of his escape, that from the depths of his spirit and heart he tasted the delight of spiritual peace and loss of self in a spiritual realm, and wished for this delight to continue, saying, "Ah, if only they would let me stay here always, if only I could always fly here without hands and feet, without pinions and wings, always strolling these gardens of meaning, drinking tulip cupfuls of the wine of divine love in this realm of the Unseen, if only my spirit could always stay lost to self and never recover . . . "

The old minstrel's spirit so much liked that realm of meaning and likeness stretching between the realm of spirits and the realm of bodies that he wished he could always close his eyes and see it. He longed to gather the roses and basil of that realm and be drunk and happy with their fragrance.

For even a person who reaches that likeness realm in a dream and experiences a state of gnosis there can tell that whatever he sees in this world, whatever he learns here, is empty. If he can, from what he sees and learns in this world, obtain a result pertaining to the divine world, that is useful.

In order to see in the realm of wakefulness what they saw in their dream, those who reach the likeness realm and have such an insight take refuge with lovers of God who will raise them up to that realm, and they arrive at the great truth in the illumination of the path to God they indicate.

The spirit of the old minstrel dove like a water fowl into a sea of endless delight. That sea was like the springs Messenger Job washed in and drank from, becoming cleansed of all external and internal ills.

That water was cure for every pain and wound, like the springs mentioned in the Gracious Koran, of which God the Truth said to Messenger Job: "Strike with your foot. In this you may wash, cool and refreshing, and drink" (Koran 38:41-42).

That was such a realm and such a sea that were these *Spiritual Couplets* I have composed as wide as these heavens and earth we see, not even half the mysteries under the dome of the sky would fit into it.

If the skies and earth we see as so very wide were to be compared with the realm of likeness and meaning, they would be so narrow that they could not contain the meanings and mysteries of that realm, and would shatter to pieces if they tried. So much so that when the firmament of my heart began to be filled with the lights of that realm, the mysteries and meanings of the Unseen realm did not fit in the world of my emotion. My heart is now and for that reason shattered in pieces.

That beautiful world appeared to me in my sleep and gave me profound delight, it made me take wing to its skies. My wings of intellect and spirit were bound to this world by the ties of body, and the Unseen realm I saw freed me from those ties.

That was what the old minstrel was saying to himself. In fact, if that realm of likeness were apparent to every eye and heart, and especially if there were a visible way leading from this world to that, there would be no one remaining in this world, no one would wait for even one instant, they would fly to that realm.

But we still have a job to do in this world. The divine [*ilâhî*] command and inspiration [*ilhâm*] is that it is not yet the time to fly without restraint in the Unseen realm and pass away from self in those skies of divinity [*lâhûtî*].

So, the thorn is out of our foot. Now the right thing for us to do is walk. It is our duty to awaken others of this world. Let us continue to walk this world so that we may also take the thorn of all that is other than God from the feet of many a traveler of the Lord [*Hudâ yolcuları*] who follows us. Let us be the means for this to happen, let us serve. Thus let us light the way, as much as we are able for many a happy servant of God to see the divine beauty.

Thus was the old minstrel thinking, feeling, and saying. But his spirit was still in that realm. He called out to that limitless space of God's mercy and bounty, "Leave me here, let me stay!"

****

HOW A VOICE FROM THE UNSEEN SPOKE TO UMAR, MAY GOD BE PLEASED WITH HIM, IN A DREAM, SAYING, "GIVE SUCH-AND-SUCH AMOUNT OF GOLD FROM THE PUBLIC TREASURY TO THAT MAN WHO IS SLEEPING IN THE GRAVEYARD."

> Just then God had overwhelmed Umar with sleep
> He could not keep himself from falling asleep
2135.   Surprised, he thought, "This is no familiar thing,
> It comes not without purpose from the Unseen."
> He put down his head and slept and had a dream
> And a call came to him from God in his dream
> His spirit heard the root of all cries and sounds
> That is the real call,[112] the rest are only sounds
> Turk and Kurd, Arab and Farsi-speaking man
> Can without lip or ear that call understand
> Why speak of Turk, Tajik, or Black man at all?

112. Koran 7:172.

Even wood and stone have understood that call
2140. *"Am I not your Lord?"* comes from Him each instant
And there comes to be substance and accident
If there does not come from them the answer, *"Yes!"*
Their arrival from non-existence is *"Yes!"*
Attend to a tale expounding what I've said
Of the familiarity of stone and wood
Hear without delay a story to address
The awareness I said wood and stone possess

Right then the Caliph Umar felt very sleepy. God the Truth put Umar into such a state that he dozed off. As he was falling asleep he thought to himself: "It is not my habit to doze off like this, it must be a command coming to me from the Unseen, I must obey it." Thus he surrendered himself to sleep.

He fell asleep immediately, and as soon as he did, he had a dream. A call reached his ear. He heard that voice with all his spirit.

Every spirit, even while the body is asleep, hears this call at least once in its lifetime. That call is the voice of God, it is what He makes heard. That call is the root of all voices and musical compositions. All other sounds are born of that first outcry. Whatever human beings speak, whatever they say or sing, even the sounds they make with instruments, originates from that voice. That voice is the voice which said at the pre-eternal gathering, "Am I not your Lord?" All other sounds and speech born of and echoed from it are the return call, the sound of the spirits answering, "Yes!" All other sounds may be voices but they are not that call nor are they a call like it.

Nations speak various languages, Turkish, Persian and other languages, and usually do not understand each other's languages. But when that call comes, every spirit knows that language, and understand what it says without feeling need for ear or lip.

Not only the Turk, the Kurd, the Persian and the Black man, but even trees and stones understand that call. There are divine commands in that call, God's invitations and God the Truth's awakenings are given voice. That is why all beings which appear senseless or inanimate awaken with that voice, and even sometimes stir and dance and whirl; that is why the ground itself moves and creation is filled with limitless sky-fulls of sounds, cries and buzzing. Because beings hear that voice of divinity.

The call, "Am I not your Lord?" was not only made at the Alast gathering, at that ancient gathering where the spirits called out, "Yes!" from the depth of their hearts. God the Truth asks His servants the same question almost every moment; sometimes this questioning is a hidden voice rising from beings [*varlıklar*], a music of nature, and sometimes it is the call of an Unseen voice [*hâtif*] which comes out of the depths of the skies. Sometimes that call is a voice, and sometimes, for those hearts that can hear, a word, a speech which communicates the most divine realities in the most eloquent language.

That voice is the voice which creates beings. It cries out to them, "Be!" The origins [*asılları*] and the parts [*cüz'üleri*] of beings have all come into being from that voice. To be sure, it is not easy for those who remain on the surface of things to hear the "Yes!" which arises from beings. For the firmament of beings is seen with the eye of the heart; the call of beings is heard with the ear of spirit.

So, the creation of beings out of nothing and their coming into the Realm of Being [*vücût âlemi*] and their taking on visible forms is nothing but the sound of their saying "yes" with the language of their state.

Consider what is said in the seventh chapter of the Gracious Koran: "When your Lord took their offspring from the loins of the children of Adam and made them bear witness concerning themselves—'Am I not your Lord?'—they said, 'Yes, we bear witness!' Lest you say on the Day of Resurrection, 'We were heedless of this.'"

And consider that the spirit coming away from that gathering does not, can not forget that testimony. So, for the spirit the pre-eternal gathering is both an inconceivably ancient past, and something always and everywhere before us. In the divine realm and from God's perspective, there is no yesterday or today, just as there is neither night nor day.

In that realm night is the same as day, and the end is side-by-side with the beginning.

Everyone who is born comes from that beginning, and everyone who leaves the world returns to the reality of having said "yes" to God the Truth. And in reality, the One who at that gathering asks, "Am I not your Lord?" and the One who answers "yes" to His own question is He.

That is why my saying that trees and stones hear the call of God is also based on wisdom, on a story. If you want to understand that wisdom a bit more clearly, listen with the ear of your heart! Learn from this tale that the inanimate night and day call out, "God!" and that the vegetal kingdom is possessed of awareness.

****

HOW THE HANNANA PILLAR MOANED WHEN THEY MADE A PULPIT FOR THE PROPHET, PEACE BE UPON HIM, BECAUSE THE COMMUNITY HAD BECOME GREAT AND THEY SAID, "WE DO NOT SEE YOUR BLESSED FACE WHEN YOU PREACH TO US," AND HOW THE MESSENGER AND HIS COMPANIONS HEARD THAT MOANING, AND MUSTAFA CONVERSED WITH THE PILLAR PLAINLY

The Hannana pillar, missing the Prophet
Moaned like a creature possessed of intellect
2145.   At the gathering for the Friday sermon
So that young and old became aware of him
The companions of the Prophet were surprised
That a pillar could moan like that, far and wide
"O pillar, what do you want?" the Prophet said
"Without you my spirit is bleeding," it said
"You have left me, though you once leaned upon me
In the pulpit you've another place to lean."
"Would you rather be a date palm tree," he asked
"So they'll come to take your fruit from East and West?"
2150.   Or become in that other world a cypress
So you may remain forever moist and fresh?"
"I want that which is everlasting," it said
Hear, be not less than wood, you who are heedless!
He buried that pillar so it would be raised
Like mankind will be upon Religion's Day
So you may know that all whom the Lord has called

Remain disengaged from all things of the world
Whoever has from God his burden and work
Leaves his burden there and leaves off worldly work

2155.   How should he who has no gift of mysteries
Verify cries of inanimate beings?
He says, "Yes," not from his heart, but to agree
So they won't accuse him of hypocrisy
If no one were aware of the command, "Be!"
None would accept that inanimates can speak
Myriads conform or base their faith on proof
And are cast in the abyss by one reproof
Their conformity and argumentation
Is all—wings and pinions—based on opinion

2160.   That vile Satan raises a doubt in their minds
And they fall in head first, all these who are blind
The leg of those who rely on proof is wood
Very unsteady is a leg made of wood
But the Axis of the Age, who has vision
His stability makes the mountain's head spin
The leg of a blind man is a staff, a staff
So he won't fall headlong on the stones and chaff
That horseman who led the troops to win the fight
Is for the believers who?—men of insight

2165.   If with aid of staff the blind have seen the way
With help of people their sight is clear as day
If there were no shahs and were no seeing men
All those in the world who are blind would be dead
From the blind comes neither sowing nor harvest
Neither cultivation nor trade and profit
If He did not give you mercy and virtue
The wood of your deductions would break in two
What is that staff? Your proofs and analogies
Who gave them that staff? The seeing Almighty

2170.   Since the staff is the tool of war and combat
Shatter that staff into pieces, O blind man
So you might approach Him, He gave you a staff
You struck in rage even at Him with that staff
O circle of the blind, what are you doing?
Bring a lookout who can mediate between
Take hold of His skirt who gave the staff to you
Think of what defiance made Adam go through
The miracles done by Moses and Ahmed
The snake from a staff, the pillar with knowledge

2175.   The pillar moaned and the staff became a snake
They are beating the five watches of the faith
If this taste were not non-intelligible

Why would there be need for all these miracles?
Intellect eats what is intelligible
Without contention and without miracle
Deem this virgin path unintelligible
Deem it accepted by the acceptable
Just as demon and beast wary of humans
Fled in terror or envy to the islands

2180.   So in fear of the miracles of prophets
Skeptics hide in the grass keeping down their heads,
So they may live with the good name of Muslim
Without you knowing the real truth about them
Like counterfeiters who take coin that's debased
And disguise it with silver and the shah's name
Outwardly their words are law and unity
Inwardly like bread made out of darnel weed
The philosopher does not dare breathe a word
The true faith will tangle him up in his words

2185.   His hand and his foot are things inanimate
Whatever his spirit says, they're ruled by it
Although with their tongues they propound suspicion
Their hands and feet give evidence against them[113]

When Hazret Muhammed preached to the companions, while he talked he used to lean on one of the mosque pillars made from the trunk of a date palm. The pillar would sense the Prophet leaning on him and be pleased with the attention.

The day came when the companions listening to the sermon in the mosque became so numerous that many of them could not see the Prophet's face through the crowd.

"We cannot see your face!" they complained, and rightly so. They asked for a pulpit to be built in the mosque, and for the Prophet to climb up and speak from it so that his beautiful face would be visible to every Muslim.

The pulpit was built and the Sultan of Prophets began to climb up that pulpit to talk, but just then something unexpected happened: the pillar he used to lean against began to moan and sigh, crying out like a human being in exile and longing.

Like the profound, burning sound of the ney reed flute, this was such an earnest outcry that everyone at the gathering, all the Muslims young and old heard that wailing. The cry was beyond sound, virtually a kind of speech, a language.

Those gathered were amazed and terrified to find a tree trunk giving voice to its longing and suffering in such clarion language.

Hazret Muhammed climbed down from the minaret and came up to the pillar. He addressed it like person, saying, "O pillar! What do you want?" with profound sympathy.

The pillar spoke in the language of its own state, as if weeping, and said:

O Muhammed! I am filled with longing and loss. I am bleeding inwardly. I was the happy pillar you used to lean against while giving the sermon. Now you have aban-

---

113. "On that day We shall set a seal on their mouths. But their hands shall speak to us and their feet bear witness to all that they did" (Koran 36:65).

271

doned me and climbed up a pulpit. Now that pulpit is your support. Acknowledge that I am in the right, what being in the world could bear such a loss?

Hazret Muhammed understood the pillar's pain. He said to it: "O date palm trunk! Since your cry is out of the pain of loss, tell me what it is you wish for. I will beg God if you wish. Shall He make you a tree producing fruit for all people of East and West?

"Or shall He make you a tree in Heaven, a cypress tree in Heaven, so that you remain forever young and pretty like the most beautiful and fresh of bodies?"

The pillar, with the great gnosis of a being whom God causes to speak, answered Hazret Muhammed: "O Muhammed! The best of these two is for you to destroy me and free me from this mortal body of mine. For a tree, however fresh and beautiful, takes its nourishment from sun and water. But my life has been nourished by the light of your beauty. It has tasted the delight of being your support and being warmed by your heat. I can no longer be without these. Destroy me, so that I may be annihilated [*fânî*] in you and your God, and become eternal in that unique light."

Thus spoke a tree. O human being, upon whom is bestowed the highest values, intellect and comprehension, bestowed neither on trees not water nor birds! Hear this truth from a tree and take example from it! Do not chain yourself to the desires of the body and the world. Know that true happiness and the highest of stations is beyond all bodies! For the most righteous path is to wish for nothing but God.

And so Hazret Muhammed buried that pillar in the earth. So that on the Day of Resurrection it might be raised up like a human being who is the site of manifestation of divine forgiveness and reach his goal . . .

We see that a date palm can be the site of manifestation of the Prophet's intercession. Because it does not want this transient world but wishes to reach the degree of the Perfect Human, its prayer is accepted. While yet an inanimate body, it reaches a spiritual degree many a creature possessed of life has not attained.

Can one not learn a lesson from this? So many created in the human form, given the felicity of humanity, remain less sensitive than rocks and less favored than trees, unable to understand the realities of their humanity.

Here it is obvious that every being which God invites to Himself knows this world to be a passageway to be passed through consciously and with honor. It is not swayed by the deceptive delights of the world, by the passions which degrade as they exalt. It takes the most infallible pathway to its goal.

For those whose hearts are on God, the various ins and outs of the world, its chatter, are things which are in reality not seen, not heard. The Perfect Human is beyond these things and above them.

It is only those whose heart's eyes and heart's ears are not open to divine mysteries who cannot believe, cannot conceive that a tree should talk and be able to speak such great truths.

Even if such people appear outwardly to affirm such profoundly meaningful and spiritual events, the satan within them deceives them and tells them, "Do not believe!" In fact they do not believe, but they appear to.

They think it dangerous to their own world to appear not to believe, to deny, in the midst of so many who do believe so strongly. They appear to believe not because they fear God but because they fear other people.

If inanimate beings had not heard and comprehended God's command "Be!", the meaning of this event could not be understood. But since the command be was given to all beings, animate and inanimate, it means that not only humans but inanimate beings too hear divine commands.

Those beset by opinion and doubt cannot understand that truth. The eye to see spiritual realities and such training [terbiye] have not been given to them. They seek evidence they can touch with their hands in order to believe. They do not see the evidence which can be seen with the eye of the heart and they do not hear the voices that can be heard with the ear of the heart.

Treacherous Satan puts a doubt in their hearts so icy that they cannot melt it with their own heat. That doubt freezes all their conscience and perspicacity [iz'an]. Although their eyes see forms, they cannot see their meanings. Thus does the satan within them throw them headlong over a foreordained [mukadder] cliff.

Such people have legs of wood. Tree-footed people cannot feel the pulse of the stones and earth they step upon. No heat or current of comprehension flows from their own world of feeling and warmth to those stones and earth either.

In short, matter that does not conduct current cuts off the pathways between the spirit and the body, even between the spirit and the universe and the spirit and God, and drives a person into a state of severe incomprehension.

All of the travelers of the path of inference and deduction are people with no share of intellect or comprehension. But that gnostic who has attained the mystery of seeing not only the outward appearances of beings and events but their spirits, their inner worlds, he is the Perfect Human who is the axis of the age and is never swayed by the disease of disputation. The vision, knowledge and steadfastness of such people awes even mountains and rocks.

It is those whose heart's eyes cannot see who are forced to use the path of disputation as a blind man uses a cane. Although that cane may prevent them from running into boulders and falling down, their condition cannot be compared with the security, certainty and clearness of goal of people who are able to see where they are going.

It is the Perfect Humans, meaning the pupil of the eye of divine being—as when a person sees another image of himself in the image of the pupil of his eye when he looks in the mirror—and created in that value, who show the way to God to the masses of people who are no different from a caravan of the blind. They are the Shah's horsemen; they lead the armies of gnosis and truth, they guide humanity down the most difficult path reach true victory.

You know the blind. They cannot sow, nor can they reap, they cannot thresh nor harvest. It is possible neither for them to cultivate the world nor advance their people with understanding of trade and economics.

They cannot even use their canes properly without the help of God the Truth and those who love God the Truth.

You understand that here when I say "the blind" I mean those whose heart's eye is closed. They are the ones who take the path of disputation and seek material evidence in order to see God the Truth . . .

In any case, those who do not know God do not know Him because they cannot see Him. The most sublime wisdom of divine Being is that It shows itself not to those whose blue eye sees but whose heart's eye sees.

And the blind, who wander miserably among us seeing where they are going not with their eyes but with a cane, are for us likenesses of divine wisdom.

If you ask what is this blind man's staff, which has been discussed so much here, it is an analogy, it is a proof. It is the seeking of proof regarding God's existence and sublimity proceeding by means of opinion and doubt. If you ask who gave them that staff, of course it was God. But this gift was not so that they should vainly argue, debate and proceed in the dark, but rather, perhaps, so that they should find and see the God who gave them the staff.

O blind man! Whenever the staff in your hand shows its capacity as an instrument of combat and assault, break that staff and do not use it.

While God is before the eyes of the heart, do not expend your time trying to find evidence for seeking or proving God. Know that when you are freed of such a staff, you will find on the ground what you sought in the sky, right in front of the eyes of your heart.

Do not seek to strike the one who gave you the staff in your hand. For to torment the friends of God is to torment the Prophet, and to torment him is to rebuke God Himself.

Remember the story of Hazret Adam. Was not that first of the prophets swayed by Satan's temptations and prey to his whispering? Was it not by means of such thinking that he picked the fruit God had forbidden and ate it?

Did not Prophet Adam, wondering to himself if the command, "Do not eat it!" meant it was absolutely necessary to abstain [*tahrîmî*] from that fruit or that to abstain from would be worthy of reward but to eat it would not entail punishment [*tenzîhî*], use reason and analogy to interpret the divine command clearly given to him as being other than what it was? And you know what end that interpretation led to. It was such opinion and indecision which caused Adam to be driven out of Heaven.

If Prophet Adam had not relied on such a stick of disputation, certainly the staff would not have broken, and he would not have tumbled out of the skies of Heaven into the abyss of the world.

Consider the miracles of Prophet Moses and Hazret Muhammed with the same heart. How the staff of one of them became a serpent. How the pillar Hazret Muhammed leaned against spoke with the language of its state, how it moaned and sighed and in the end attained a degree of gnosis and truth which many a traveler on the path of God the Truth has not been able to reach.

Perhaps you will persist in stubbornness and blindness of heart and say that the staff of Moses did not turn into a serpent, or that the dry date palm trunk never moaned. In that case look at look at the pillars made of stone called minarets. From there five times a day rises up God's name and the voice of faith. Think of the Padishah of padishahs, around whose court the watch is played five times a day. Until the Day of Resurrection the sound rising up from those narrow pillars made of stone will be the outcry of minarets to God.

If every difficulty could be solved by means of the intellect, there would have been no need for miracles. If the intellect of every person were suited for comprehending divine mysteries and the mystery of God Himself, there would be no need for even judges on earth, let alone for prophets and friends of God. To be sure, not every intellect can attain every mystery. It is not possible for intellect and rationalism to sense the delight in spiritual truths which are seen with the heart's eye and felt with the heart's comprehension. It is completely impossible for intellect to reach the mysteries attained by the heart.

It is futile to try to understand by means of intellect what inanimate beings say, to comprehend by means of discernment [*ferâset*] the voices glorifying God which rise from the branches of trees. Only spiritual faculties sense such mysteries by way of the heart. Like the sixth sense of humans and animals, that insight [*seziş*] is always beyond intellect and the intelligible.

Just as Satan and all savage animals, envying the humans on earth or wary of them, have fled in fear to take refuge on steep mountains, in caves and dens, so have all deniers and all those whose eyes are harmed by brightness and light fled in fear of the miracles of the prophets; like animals seeking a place to hide in fear of the hunter, they have fled and hidden behind material and spiritual veils.

So it is when such people hide behind the veil of Islam. They falsely appear to believe and to be Muslims so that you will not see their inner faces, realize that they are hypocrites and harm them, and cut them off from the material and spiritual largess you bestow on all good people.

They are counterfeiters who apply silvering to copper coin and stamp it with the Padishah's seal. They even pretend to be God's messengers and officers of the divine law.

Although their outward appearance may seem bright with the light of Muhammed, their hearts are dark.

Those who wish to reach divine realities by way of philosophy diverge into denial because of their fear of those who believe. For faith defeats their sophistry.

It is as if there were in their bodies only the animal spirit [*hayvânî can*]. If that spirit says, "Walk!" they walk, and if it says, "Stop!" they stop. The same spirit makes their tongues, which are pieces of meat, speak many blasphemies. But when that same spirit departs from their bodies one day and goes away, their hands will not grasp, their feet will not walk, and their tongues will not speak.

Because they are deprived of the divine spirit [*ilâhî can*], or do not know the value of such a spirit, they will not be able to speak even as trees do; they will not be able to glorify the name of God even as tree branches do.

While they are alive they do not believe inanimates can speak, they deny this. But their own hands and feet make their lies evident.

They say, "O mindless one, even though we are inanimate beings, the divine power has given us motion and skill. It has made us perform actions no other animate beings can. While your mouth and tongue were inanimate bodies, did not God make them speak all kinds of speech? In that case, O you who lack swift understanding, why should the Lord not, when He wishes, make a date palm tree recite a poem of longing, loss and passion?

****

THE MANIFESTATION OF THE MIRACLE OF THE PROPHET, PEACE BE UPON HIM, IN THE PEBBLE IN THE HAND OF ABU JAHL, MAY HE BE CURSED, AND THE TESTIFYING OF THE PEBBLE TO THE TRUTH OF MUHAMMED, BLESSINGS AND PEACE UPON HIM

> Abu Jahl was holding pebbles in his fist
> He said, "O Ahmed, quick, tell me what this is
> Hid in my palm, if you are God's Messenger

And of Heaven's mysteries you are aware."
He said, "Do you want me to say what this is
Or for this to say I am true and honest?"
2190.   Abu Jahl said, "The second is rarer still."
Muhammed said, "God is yet more powerful"
From inside Jahl's fist every piece of stone
Bore witness without delay that God is one
"There is no god," they said, *"but God,"* and they thread
The pearl: *"The messenger of God is Ahmed"*
When Abu Jahl heard the pebbles saying this
He threw them down upon the ground in a fit

One day Abu Jahl wanted to try to outwit Hazret Muhammed. He took some small stones into his hand. He came up to the Prophet and said, "Since you say you are the Messenger of God, you must know everything. O Muhammed, let's see if you can tell what is in my hand, come, tell us quickly.

"If you are really the Messenger of God, if you really know the mysteries beyond the veil of the sky, then you must know things as nearby as this," he insisted.

Hazret Muhammed said to Abu Jahl: "Shall I tell you what you have inside your palm? Or shall the things you have inside your palm speak and bear witness that I am God's messenger?"

Abu Jahl was going to say: "That second thing is impossible. It is enough for me that you yourself know," but Hazret Muhammed said, "No. Great God has much more power than it takes to make what you have in your hand speak. If He wishes, all inanimate things can become animate, all inanimates can speak like humans. In fact they are animate beings who speak of many a mystery around God's being and oneness, and even rise up in the whirling dance with love for Him. But of course you cannot understand their language and their dance."

As Hazret Muhammed was saying that, the pebbles inside Abu Jahl's palm began to speak one by one. Each of them recited the profession of fatih, saying more eloquently and affectingly than well-spoken humans, "I bear witness that there is no god but God and I bear witness that Muhammed is the Messenger of God."

When Abu Jahl heard the pebbles speak he was afraid, he flew into a rage and threw them on the ground, crying:

It's a lie, it's a lie! This is no miracle, it is sorcery, and there is no sorcerer on earth to compete with you, you are the master of sorcerers!

Because he said that, he became the most cursed of kafirs. He was distanced from the mercy of sublime God forever, the most grievous of punishments.

Just as when Satan looked at Hazret Adam, he was only able to see a pile of earth in the shape of a man and not a man created of earth, and because he saw Adam as dirt he did not bow down to him, and for that reason rebelled against God and was driven out of the heavens and earth, in the same way Abu Jahl could not see the divine self-disclosure in Hazret Muhammed. His eyes were shut behind a thick veil of heedlessness, violence and denial, and stayed that way.

******

THE REST OF THE STORY OF THE MINSTREL AND HOW THE COMMANDER OF THE FAITHFUL UMAR, MAY GOD BE PLEASED WITH HIM, CONVEYED TO HIM THE MESSAGE SPOKEN BY THE VOICE FROM THE UNSEEN

Come back and give ear to the minstrel's sad state
He'd been waiting so long he was desperate
Umar heard a voice cry out, saying to him,
"Umar! Our servant is in need, redeem him!
We have a special servant We have honored
Make the effort to walk out to the graveyard
Rise up and take into your hand, O Umar
From public funds full seven hundred dinars

2200.   Saying, 'We have chosen you,' give them to him
Say, 'Take this much now and excuse the small sum
For the harp strings made of silk spend this amount
Then come back here again when it has been spent.'"
Umar leapt up at the grandeur of that voice
To perform this service he girded his loins
Umar set his countenance toward the graveyard
Running to search for him, purse under his arm
He searched the graveyard a long while round and round
There was no one but that old man to be found

2205.   "It's not him," he thought, and circled round again
He exhausted himself but found none but him
"God told me, 'We have a bondsman,'" Umar said
"'Who is pure and who is deserving and blessed.'
How should an old minstrel be chosen by God?
How great are the hidden mysteries of God!"
He circled around the graveyard once again
Like that lion hunting for prey on the plain
Sure none but the old man was there, he remarked,
"Many a luminous heart dwells in the dark."

2210.   He came and sat with a hundred courtesies
The old man jumped when Umar happened to sneeze
Seeing Umar there he stood still much amazed
He resolved to go but he began to shake
He thought to himself, "O my God, rescue me!
The Inspector has now come to torment me!"
When Umar cast his gaze on the old man's face
He saw that he had turned pale and was ashamed
Umar said, "Do not fear, do not flee from me
From God I bring you news of felicity

2215.   God has often given your temperament praise
Thus He made Umar a lover of your face
Sit before me and do not attempt to leave
That you may hear secrets of favor from me

God sends greetings of peace and asks how you fare
Suffering in your distress and boundless care
I've brought gold pieces to buy silk strings, look here
Spend it and then afterward return back here."
The old man heard this and trembled through and through
He bit his fingers and rent his cloak in two

2220.   He shouted and said, "O God who has no peer!"
For melting in shame he became like water
After he'd wept long, his grief gone beyond bound
He smashed his harp into bits upon the ground
He said, "You've been a screen for me against God
You have kept me from the highway of the Shah
For seventy years you've been drinking my blood
Blackened my face fore the perfection of God
O bounteous and faithful God, have mercy
Upon a life that's passed in iniquity

2225.   God gives a life whose each day has a value
That is known to no one except God the Truth
I have expended my own life breath by breath
I have exhaled all the breaths, treble and bass
Ah! My mind on the notes of Iraq maqam
I forgot the bitter note of loss to come
With the minor Zirafgand, alas, so fresh
My heart's fruit dried up and now my heart is dead
These twenty and four maqams were what I played
While the caravan passed and the day got late

2230.   O God, I cry out against this crying self
I seek justice from this justice-seeking self
My justice will come from none other than He
Who is closer to myself than I can be
This I-ness comes from Him continuously
Thus I see Him when it becomes lost to me
When you are with someone counting out gold, then
You forget yourself and fix your gaze on him."
In this way wailing aloud and all in tears
He counted out the sins of his many years

Let us return again to the story of the minstrel. We have said many things to awaken those with understanding, we have offered knowledge regarding many things. But we forgot the minstrel in the graveyard. The poor old man has been at his wits' end waiting in the Medina Graveyard for the conclusion of this matter.

A voice came to Hazret Umar from the Unseen and he heard a divine cry. God the Truth was saying, "O Umar, get up! Leave off this deep sleep! Rescue a sincere servant of ours from the poverty and desperation that has befallen him! Move! Go to the Medina Graveyard!" and it continued:

Before you leave take seven hundred gold pieces from the Public Fund; bring them to that saintly person and give them to him. Know that the money you bring will not cure all his ills. Comfort him and say: This money will not be enough for you, I know. But with this you will obtain the things you most need. Spend it all and when it is gone, come to us. God has given you this much and will certainly not leave you in dire straits.

Hazret Umar heard the divine voice giving him this command. The grandeur of the voice made him leap up from sleep. He did what he was told immediately. He put seven hundred dinars in a purse. He arrived at the graveyard and began searching for that pure servant of God's. He looked everywhere. In the whole graveyard he could find no one but that old minstrel. This pitiful minstrel could not be the person commended to him by the voice from the Unseen. Hazret Umar continued to search for the person entrusted to him, but but there was not one single other person in that huge graveyard that day but the minstrel.

Hazret Umar began thinking to himself: "Could this old minstrel be that sincere servant, that pure and clean person God commended to me? Is this possible? O realm of mystery, what unknown and unimaginable wisdom is there yet in you to plunge a person from awe to awe, from terror to amazement?"

But he did not let the old man go. Hazret Umar wandered around that graveyard from end to end like a lion hunting prey. Finally he felt it within him that this minstrel was the person his Lord had commended to him. Then he was amazed that it had not occurred to him. Should it not be possible for God the Truth to bring make friends of the most unhoped-for people in the most un-hoped for places? He thought to himself: How could you be fooled by appearances, O Umar, who knows how broken a heart this old minstrel has, and how burning his pleas to God, that he achieved such great favor.

Umar approached the old minstrel feeling great respect. He sat down beside him feeling the same respect. But the wisdom of God made him sneeze at that very moment. The sound shook the old minstrel from his sleep and he leapt up.

The old minstrel saw Hazret Umar beside him in all his glory. At first he was struck with terror. He began to tremble. He did not know who the Caliph was or what intention he had in coming there. He thought it was another case of the torments and unfairness he had suffered up until that moment and called to God within himself: "My God, hear this hidden cry of mine, for now the Inspector has come to plague Your poor minstrel."

When Umar saw this old man shaking and ashamed and pale with fear, he tried to comfort him. He addressed him in as kind and gentle a voice as possible:

Do not fear me, old man, for I have brought you glad tidings from God," he said. "God described the beauty of your inner world in such a way that Umar fell in love with you before he saw you and your face.

Sit by me. Do not stay so far away, so I can give you glad tidings and tell you secrets from the realms of mystery and felicity. I have brought you God's greetings and bounty. This money is for the things you need most immediately. Spend it and come back to me! God knows what a state the torments you've suffered have brought you to, and knows what degree of what feeling you are now experiencing.

These words completely astonished the exhausted old man. He felt infinitely ashamed before God. How could God's grace and mercy be shown to a pathetic and unruly old man who had committed sin all throughout his lifetime, swimming in iniquity, and in the end been abandoned by all? The old minstrel was so moved that he cried in sorrow, bit his fingers and began tearing at his clothes, and cried:

O my great God! The greatness of Your mercy and grace makes me wish the earth would swallow me up. I melt before the absolute good [*hayr-ı mutlak*] of Your beneficence. I am naught, and I better understand how powerless I am!" he wailed aloud. Then he grabbed his instrument laying there next to him and dashed it on the ground, smashing it to pieces. "O my harp, you have led me astray all these years! You have drunk my blood. I spent my whole life on you, playing and giving voice to you, entertaining people with you. You are my shame! You decoy, you will shame me in the presence of God for all eternity! May the earth swallow you up! Be silent from here on, be naught!

Clearly, in addressing his instrument the old minstrel was addressing his soul, which distanced his spirit from God. For the stiffest curtain drawn between the bondsman and God is the soul. The soul is a stranger to spiritual delights and distracts a person with material and bodily delights, and with all its material filth and seductions it becomes an obstacle to a person's self-purification and turning toward God.

The minstrel passed away from himself and turned again toward God. He addressed His sublime being:

O my Lord who with His mercy and compassion to His bondsmen is the most sublime of sublimities! A bondsman of Yours who has passed his life in torment and sin is now turning to You in perfect repentance and begging You with all his heart. Take pity on my empty life of loss. Make me one of Your bondsmen who lives only for You, even if just for a short while.

You have given me such a life that none but You can know the value of its days, even its moments. I did not know the value of life. I was not able to attain the sublime pleasure of living every instant to be lived on the face of the earth for You and taking every breath to be taken for You. I took my breaths in order to blow into my instrument and passed my life tuning the thick and thin strings of my instrument and finding accord for its notes.

This life went from the deserts of the Hijaz to Iran [Acem Irak] and sometimes passed by reaching the first from the second. In music I conformed to either the Arabian or Iranian [Acem] style. I exhausted my breath finding the Iraq maqam and playing compositions in that maqam. While thinking about Iraq maqam I forgot the time when the spirit separates from the body. I did not think of the regret to be felt when the time to leave the body arrives, and the final regret making a person beat his head against the wall.

The playfulness, beauty and freshness of Zirafgand maqam stole my heart. And because of it my harvest dried up. The field of my heart was left unwatered; I have become someone whose heart is dead.

In short, the caravan of my life marched to the tunes of the twenty-four maqams. I have wandered aimlessly in the desert without reaching the Kaaba of union, without even thinking of reaching it.

Life is over. The daytime of my life has reached the night of death. Searching for the road to Hijaz, the road to Iraq, I remained unaware of the one road to be traveled, the road leading to God. If I had been able to put those melodies aside and listen to those of God's friends, and find an arrived person and grasp his skirt, I would not have been defeated by my soul and I would have transcended this obstacle.

In any case, what happened. My God! Now I seek help from You. My complaint is against my own soul. It is my soul that has done me all the evil, and I seek refuge in Your justice.

You are closer to me than I myself. You are more beloved than life. I expect neither help nor grace from any but You.

True being [*hakîkî varlık*] will reach my better-naught existence [*yok olası vücûdum*] only from Your absolute being [*mutlak vücûdun*]. May my illusory existence [*mevhum vücûdum*] burn with the fire and light of love, may it be destroyed, may Your light strike the mirror of my heart; may my heart become such a pure and bright mirror that there, O Friend, only Your beauty appears.

I want to view my heart with You and see You there. For when someone is counting out gold for a person, he looks only at the face of that person and nowhere else, my God! And You give to the bondsmen You create a heart purer and more golden than gold.

And receiving such a heart from You, I am in awe of You and wish to look only at You and see You.

The old minstrel said many more things and kept counting his sins of so many years. He repented hundreds of times and preyed God.

****

HOW UMAR, MAY GOD BE PLEASED WITH HIM, MADE HIM TURN HIS GAZE FROM THE STATION OF WEEPING, WHICH IS EXISTENCE, TO THE STATION OF ABSORPTION IN GOD, WHICH IS NON-EXISTENCE

2235.   Then Umar said to him, "Your grief and distress
Is also a sign of your self-awareness.
Annihilation's way is a different road
For awareness is another kind of fault
It increases knowledge of what's gone before
Your past and future divide you from the Lord
Set the both of them afire; how long will you
Be knotted like a reed because of these two?
While filled with knots, a reed flute won't share secrets
It will not join with the player's voice and lip

2240.   You circle apostasy while circling self
When you arrive home you are still with yourself
He gives knowledge, you know without knowing Him
Your repentance is a thing worse than your sin
You repent of the way you were in the past
Tell me, when will you repent this repentance?
Now you take the bass notes as your prayer-niche

Now you make weeping and cries your prayer-niche."
As Faruq mirrored the mysteries divine
The old man's spirit awoke from deep within
2245.   Like spirit, he neither laughed nor did he cry
His spirit left and another came alive
He was filled with such amazement deep inside
That he went beyond the earth, beyond the sky
A searching and seeking beyond search and quest
I do not know, you tell me, if you know best
Speech and state beyond all other state and speech
Plunged in the beauty of divine majesty
Drowned not so there would be salvation for him
Nor that any but the ocean should know him
2250.   Partial intellect would not tell of the whole
If not for prompting after prompting for more
Because prompting after prompting does arrive
The surging of that ocean does here arrive
Since the story of the old man's state led here
The old man and his state slipped behind the veil
The old man shook his skirt free of talk and words
Half the tale has been left in our mouth unheard
It is fit for sake of this pleasure in life
We gamble away a hundred thousand lives
2255.   Hunting through spirit's forest be a falcon
Gamble away your spirit like the world's sun
The exalted sun on high sheds forth spirit
It empties out and is filled up each instant
Shine out the light of life, O Sun of meaning
Show this old world a display of novelty
Life and spirit reach bodies of human beings
Like flowing water that comes from the Unseen
Newly coming from the Unseen constantly
The cry: Come out, leave the realm of the body!

If people think constantly of their past mistakes and feel crushed under the weight of their former sins, it means that they have not yet got free of the body [*vücût*].

To mourn over the past, or think on future material or spiritual accounts, is to lose time on the path leading to God. Travelers on the path of unity are those who have dedicated themselves to God without any doubt whatsoever. They have risen so far above taking account of past and future that they repent even of repentance.

That is why Hazret Umar felt it necessary to give the old minstrel advice. He said: "This weeping of yours shows that you are still awake to anxieties of the world and the body [*vücût*] and that you are not freed from its calculations and anxieties.

"For those who attain the spiritual degree of annihilation there is no longer any past or future, fear or mourning." Umar continued:

The path you have taken is not the infallible path to annihilation.

On that path one must be free of worldly and bodily attractions and even concern for sin. As our Prophet said, "The body [*vücût*] is such a sin that no other sin can be compared with it."

In short, it takes awareness to remember the past. Past and future are a veil separating the bondsman from God. In fact the arrived couldn't care less about the past and future, they care only for God.

Set both past and future afire, let them burn to ashes. What use is there is being knotted with the past and future like a reed? If the flute made of reed has knots stopping it up, it can't share a lip's secrets. It won't produce a sound when it is blown. These knots are veils inside the reed. If you think of the human body [*insan vücûdu*] as a flute, the veils inside it are anxieties about the past and future and the ties binding it to time and space, in short worldly desires and connections. As long as the body is veiled like a reed, the spirit can not find the way to get free of these veils and take wing to divine mysteries.

If you continually think about your own body, virtually circumambulating it, how will you circumambulate God? The person struggling on the path of seeking God will abandon everything but that goal, especially his own self. For a spirit that has earned the human degree, that is the one condition for being annihilated in God.

As long as a person is bound by the limitations of the soul, as long as he thinks constantly of his own being, his own works, his pleasures and even good deeds, and does not get free of selfhood [benlik] and duality, he is like a person preoccupied with thinking about the insufficiences of his own house while circumambulating the Kaaba.

How can a person think of other things while circumambulating the Kaaba, and not pass away from himself in ecstasy?

Those who circumambulate the Kaaba remove their usual clothes and put on the plain white ihram. In the same way, lovers must remove the clothes of body and soul and wear the ihram of annihilation in God so that their circumambulation of divine beauty and divine being may be acceptable.

O you who spends time continually repenting of past sins! What you should really repent of is this repentance.

I see that sometimes you pay attention to the melodies of the most inconsequential words, continually turning toward them as to a prayer-niche. Sometimes you touch your lips to your own wailing, your own moans, and kiss them alone.

****

Hazret Umar was distinguished with the name and quality of Umar Faruk, who did not comprehend truth, yet he came before the old minstrel like a mirror of divine mysteries, and as he illuminated many a truth the minstrel's spirit awoke from its profound sleep; he was freed of claims to "I" and "we" and his will awoke out of the grip of worries for past and future.

It was the spirit which is a piece of divine light in the cage of flesh that awoke, not the spirit which keeps the material body [*maddî vücût*] on its feet. He was amazed in the true sense of the word. He became a seeker in a realm of heart and spirit beyond all seeking. He became such a man of spiritual states [*hâl adamı*] that I cannot tell his state in words.

It is not a mystery to be known and told by those living in a body.

This is a state beyond all words and states. In short, the old minstrel plunged into the ocean of divine beauty. None but the ocean he plunged into can know that plunge, and if they did, they could not speak of it. The old minstrel was swimming in the ocean none can leave once they have plunged into it. He himself no longer existed [*mevcut değildi*], he was naught, and what did that nothingness mean? Only the ocean into which he plunged could know.

But while the partial intellect wishes to comprehend all these things, to attain such mysteries, it is obliged to think that there is a power in the Unseen which causes him to move along this path. In fact if it were not for the urging, even coercion, of the Unseen in awaking the partial intellect, how would this intellect know the universal intellect, how would it find it, why would it struggle to understand the universal intellect's mysteries?

The reason is obvious. Just as the waves of the sea push against one another, conveying a body floating upon them to the shore, the waves of the ocean of truth push against one another to convey the great truth they carry to this realm; they present it to our partial intellects in the state of a brightness of meaning and truth.

That is why great truths take on the state of light in the human conscience and become sentences and verses in human languages.

That was the old minstrel's state. The lonely old man has now attained the end of spiritual experience, seen what he would see, learned what he would learn. Thus he was freed of the mortal body and had begun to see beyond the veil, and he even transcend the veil of annihilation and attained the degree of subsistence in God.

He had now gone beyond all talk. He had nothing left to say and nothing unknown to hear. Only on our tongue has his story remained thus half-finished.

Does this story also have an ending? Let me put it this way. If only you could sacrifice not one but thousands of lives in order to taste the delights of the realm of unity he reached and drink of the wine of unity and love, if only you could awaken to what Fuzuli said:

Were there in broken-hearted me a thousand lives
So that with each one I could be your sacrifice

A person must sacrifice like that in order to enjoy the pleasure of the spiritual realm. He must be like a falcon on the hunt for meaning in the forest of spirit. In order to capture his prey he must drive his spirit on without regard for gain or loss. In short, like the old minstrel, he will gain meaning and give his body, even his life. He will gamble with life like the sun which illuminates the world.

Like the sun strews forth light and life upon the world, and each instant as the universe is emptied of light refills it with light, O spiritual sun, strew forth life, bestow spirit! Show something new to this old world!

Sacrifice your spirit for that spirit of spirits, so that this time you may find the true spirit. For there is a river of spirit flowing constantly from the realm of the Unseen. It conveys intellect and spirit to this realm and the human beings in this realm.

And whatever you give to God, God always has the power to give the greater, more beautiful and eternal.

Listen to the sound of spirit coming from the Unseen realm . . . If you can hear it, the one thing it says to you is: Leave that world of body and be free!

****

COMMENTARY ON THE PRAYER OF THOSE TWO ANGELS WHO PROCLAIMED IN EVERY MARKET EVERY DAY: *"O GOD, GIVE ALL WHO SPEND FREELY THE LIKE OF WHAT THEY SPEND! O GOD, BRING ALL MISERS TO RUIN!"* AND EXPLANATION THAT HE WHO SPENDS FREELY IS STRIVING ON THE PATH OF GOD[114] AND NOT A PRODIGAL ON THE PATH OF VAIN DESIRE

2260. "There are a pair of angels," the Prophet said
  "Who are always crying in admonishment
  'O God, recompense those who spend without stint
  Hundred-thousandfold for each dirhem they've spent!
  As for the niggardly of this world, O God
  Give to them naught other than loss upon loss!'"
  O, to withhold can be better than to spend
  Do not give what is God's lest by God's command
  So that you may acquire infinite treasure
  And may not be numbered among the kafirs
2265. Who sacrificed camels hoping that their swords
  Might take victory from Mustafa in war
  From one united with God seek God's command
  Not every heart can find out God's command
  The Koran contains warning to the heedless
  That all they spend will bring them only distress[115]
  Chiefs of Mecca at war with the Messenger
  Offered sacrifice hoping to gain favor
  Like a rebel slave who thinks it just to waste
  The Shah's property by giving it to knaves
2270. For the Shah what does the justice of this slave
  Increase but estrangement from him and disgrace
  That is why believers always say in fear
  "Show us the straight path,"[116] when performing the prayer
  For the generous to spend dirhems is right
  The generous lover surrenders his life
  You'll receive bread if you give bread for God's sake
  You'll receive life if you give life for God's sake[117]
  If the leaves of this plane-tree fall, it receives
  From the Creator provision without leaves
2275. If through liberality your wealth be lost
  How should God's abundance let you be downtrod?
  A man's storehouse empties when he plants his field
  But the harvest will reap goodness from the field
  If he keeps the seed inside and stores it up
  Weevils, mice and misfortune will eat it up

114. Koran 2:262.
115. Koran 8:36.
116. Koran 1:5.
117. Koran 6:160.

> This world is the no, seek in the affirming
> Your form is a nothing, seek in your meaning
> Let the sword take the brackish, bitter spirit
> Purchase instead the sweet ocean-like spirit
> 2280.   If you can't be one of those who take this gate
> At least give ear to this story I'll relate

These verses are in the nature of a commentary on a noble hadith elaborating upon the Gracious Koran's understanding of what it is to strive in the way of God and spend freely. They delineate the difference between the prodigal and the generous person, who is considered to strive in the way of God because he helps the poor and gives charity to the needy. The generous person is one who gives charity and spends his wealth in good deeds in the way of God. Prodigals expend their property on the pleasures of their souls; they are deprived of real fortune and condemned to pass away like their bodies [*vücûtları*] do.

The hadith on this subject is: There is no day upon which the morning comes for bondsmen of God without them. Two angels come down. One says: My God! Give property and wealth in abundance to every generous person who distributes charity. The other says: My Lord! Cause every miserly and stingy person to suffer loss, so that the property they guard jealously may be exhausted and they may suffer loss upon loss.

Charity and expenditures are approved when they are made in the right way. Excessive and gratuitous generosity is extravagance. You should expend the bounties of God where God commands and in the degree commanded. Since every bounty and fortune is given by God and belongs to God, we must know where it will be properly spent. Expenditure upon unworthy persons in inappropriate places is wasteful. And this is not true only of wealth and bounty; you must give knowledge and gnosis to those who are worthy of it as well.

Learn God's command from those who have reached God . . . If you are going to make expenditures, make them according to their wishes in their path. Win their hearts by enquiring from them and spending in the ways they indicate. For not every heart knows and understands the command of God the Truth.

As you know, the kafirs sacrificed camels in hopes that their swords would seize victory from Hazret Muhammed.

But their sacrifices were not in the path of God, not for the sake of aid and grace, but for their own souls and ambitions. Thus they wasted their property. They met with God's anger.

And just so, there are judgments pronounced in the Gracious Koran about such heedless people. Remember verse thirty-seven from the eighth chapter: "The kafirs spend their wealth to hinder [people] from the path of God, and so will they continue to spend, but in the end they will have regrets and sighs, they will be overcome, and the kafirs will be gathered up in Hell."

That is also what the leaders of Mecca did. They thought the sacrifices they offered for their war against the Messenger of God would be acceptable. They could not have known that it was God's property they expended against God's Messenger, and they did so in loss.

Their actions were like those of the heedless slave who distributed the Padishah's wealth to bandits thinking it just and merciful. What result could the action of that treacherous slave bring but loss of the Padishah's esteem and loss of face?

Is there any error graver than to distribute God's bounty to those who deny God?

That is why all believers, when they stand in prayer in the presence of God, beseech Him: "Guide us to the straight path." In the light of this beautiful verse, they taste the profound delight of fear of God.

To be sure, to distribute wealth in the way of God is something only generous persons who possess wealth can do. Dervishes and lovers may not have such wealth. But the dervish has a greater treasure to give to his God: To sacrifice his soul and give his life to God. As Fuzuli said, the true lover has this sublime wealth to give to God:

> The lover gives his spirit to the Spirit of all spirit
> He who'd not sacrifice his spirit should not seek the Spirit

The reward for the sacrificed spirit is "eternal life" in place of bread.

Great plane trees drop their leaves to the ground and the earth is nourished with the food of leaves. But their great generosity is never left uncompensated. Sublime God provides the plane trees with the nourishment necessary for the months without leaves. And there comes a day when the plane trees, having remained dry throughout the winter, are dressed in the robe of spring and find new life.

God never leaves in dire straits those who help His bondsmen. He gives them wealth in the world and eternal bounty in the hereafter.

Observe the farmer who fills his skirt with seed and walks the ploughed field! How many times over the seeds he scatters from his skirt be multiplied at harvest-time? How many storehouse-fulls of provisions will he harvest in return for the one storehouse he emptied?

If he had kept his seeds in the storehouse, what would he have gained? Nothing. What would he have lost? Maybe the entire storehouse of seed . . . Because mice would eat it and insects devour it.

You are not a body [*bir vücût*], not a piece of matter [*bir cism*], you are a meaning [*bir mânâ*]. Your soul and your body, which consist of form, are anyway not abiding. Work so that you may live in meaning [*mânân*]. So that the spiritual value [*mânevî kıymet*] in you may not pass away.

I have said that there are two separate spirits [*iki ayrı can*] in you. One is bitter and salty, and is the life [*can*] blood coursing through your veins. Know that this spirit which seems sweet to you is bitter and salty, and abandon this sprit, let swords tear it to shreds. For when this indulgence in soul [*nefis düşkünlüğü*) leaves you, spiritual life [*mânevi can*] will come to you and that spirit will not die.

In short, you will destroy your animal spirit [*hayvânî can*] with the sword of love and, thus freed from mortal things and mortality [*fânîlik*], you will attain the truth which never dies.

If you do not know how to enter through this door and cannot manage to find this truth, become an ear and hear this story from me:

****

Story of the Caliph who in his own time surpassed Hatim Tayyi[118] in Generosity and had no Peer

> There was a caliph who in the olden days
> With generosity made Hatim his slave
> He raised the banner of hospitality
> He removed from the world want and poverty
> He was a sea of pearls, pure munificence
> From end to end of Qaf Range stretched his largesse
> In this world of dust he was cloud and water
> He manifested the gifts of the Giver

2285.
> Mine and ocean trembled at the gifts he'd grant
> Toward his generosity hastened caravans
> The prayer-niche of need was his door and gate
> Throughout the world his munificence was famed
> Persian and Greek, Turk and Arab were amazed
> At the liberality of what he gave
> Sea of grace and water of immortal life
> Through him both Arabs and strangers found new life

There once was a generous caliph name Hatim. He seemed to have come to earth to take the indigent by the hand and feed the needy.

He was so rich, and just as generous, that in his time the concepts of poverty and need had disappeared from the world.

Because he existed, because of the security and trust he spread through the world, all the desperate, all the poor, were happy and rich. Just as April clouds scatter magnificent pearls upon the earth they pass over and rain down God's mercy, so was the Caliph, wherever he passed, whomever he came near, whomever he felt was lost, he would run and offer them the mercy of God.

Caravan upon caravan of people from the four corners of the earth would run toward the treasury of his generosity to find a cure for what ailed them and put an end to their poverty. However glad he who opens and distributes a treasury, all who took a share of that generosity and goodness were that glad.

Whether Arab or Persian or Turk, all the community of Muhammed were in awe of this Caliph. Every tribe, every people, took their share from him and added life to life with the water of life he scattered.

Of course you understand that this Caliph was a Perfect Human come to give news of divine self-disclosure on earth. Those who attained the felicity of taking a share from them were his murids and dervishes who were nourished with the bounty coming from the divine source, and with the power they derived from that bounty they moved, in limitless joy and awe, further toward the divine source.

****

---

118. Hatim was of the Tay tribe and the son of Abdullah Ibn Sa'd. He was renowned for his generosity and his heroism was outstanding. He would have fires lit on surrounding hillsides so that people who had lost their way would come to him and be his guest. He died in 604, seventeen years before the Prophet's flight from Mecca to Medina.

STORY OF THE POOR BEDOUIN AND WHAT PASSED BETWEEN HIM AND HIS WIFE DUES TO THEIR PENURY AND POVERTY

> An Arabi woman pressed her mate one night
> Carrying what she said beyond what was right:
2290.   "We suffer all this hardship and poverty
> All the world is happy and we unhappy
> We have no bread, pain and envy are our meat
> We have no jug, our eye's tears are what we drink
> By day we have only the sun's rays for clothes
> By night we have moonbeams for bed and bedclothes
> We imagine the round moon a round a bread
> And lift our hands up toward the firmament
> The poor are ashamed to see our poverty
> Night and day daily bread our anxiety
2295.   All flee from us, both strangers and our own kin
> In like fashion as Samiri[119] fled from men
> If I ask someone for a handful of beans
> 'Shut up, you're a plague and death,' he says to me
> Arabs take pride in giving gifts and raiding
> Among Arabs you're like a fault in writing
> We're killed without a fight, what raids can we launch?
> We are reeling about from the sword of naught
> What gifts can we give, we twist in beggary
> We slit the throats of flies in the air for meat
2300.   As sure as I stand here, should a guest arrive
> I'll go for his cloak when he's asleep at night.

Arabs who live in the desert are called Arabi. One night a woman of those Arabs complained to her husband, nagging him.

In reality this was a night of heedlessness [*gaflet*]. It represents the condition of being in the dark with regard to divine truth. The woman represents the soul on such nights of heedlessness, and she rebukes her husband as the fruit of intellect, driving him to depart from the reality of spirit into the anxieties of the body, the soul and the future.

The woman said to her husband:

> Only we suffer hardship and poverty. Others are happy and enjoying their pleasures, almost everyone in the world does so. But we have deprivation for bread, and for meat we have pain, anxiety and coveting of what others have. We don't even have a water jug. All we have to drink is the tears that flow from our eyes. By day we wear the light and heat of the sun, we take refuge in them. At night the earth is our bed and our comforter is the light of the moon.
>
> We think the disk of the moon is a slice of bread, we are so hungry we think the moon is bread. We lift our hands to the sky not to pray but to grab hold of the bread

---

119. While Hazret Musa was on Mount Sinai, Samiri [the Samaritan] induced the Israelites to worship the golden calf, and was cursed and condemned to be an outcast, and all fled from him (Koran 20: 85-97).

in the sky.

The poor are ashamed of the limitlessness of our poverty, and the extremity of our hunger turns our days to dark night."

You know that when Hazret Moses was on Mount Sinai, a man called Samiri led the Israelites away from God to worship a golden calf. For that reason he was cursed by Hazret Musa and could no longer live among men and had to take refuge alone in the mountains and deserts. For when anyone approached him or, especially, touched him, both he and Samiri would suddenly be seized with fever and trembling. So everyone ran away from him. And whenever he saw anyone he would fear they might approach him and he would shout, "Don't touch me!" and flee like a wild animal.

The woman said:

We have become like Samiri. Even if we don't run away, everyone is afraid of us, both strangers and our own kin. It is so bad that if I ask someone for a handful of beans, he drives me away and insults me, saying, 'Get out of here! You spread death and plague!' Now, O husband! What kind of Arab are you? The pride of Arabs is raiding and gift-giving. Arabs fight and give gifts. But you are like a mistake in Arabic writing. Just as a letter drawn incorrectly alters the meaning, you are among the Arabs someone who alters the nature of Arab-ness, you darken the face of the Arab. This cannot go on. You must find a solution.

What raids? We are dead, killed, our heads are already severed by the sword of poverty without going out on raids.

Never mind gifts, we weave webs around poverty, like spiders hoping a fly in the air will fall into our web and we can suck on the blood in its veins. Thus we stoop to the most vile things. Just see what will happen should a guest visit us. If I don't rob him in his sleep, let them not call me a woman of the Arabi.

****

HOW NEEDY MURIDS ARE DELUDED BY LYING IMPOSTERS AND SUPPOSE THEM TO BE SHAYKHS VENERABLE AND ARRIVED AND DO NOT KNOW THE DIFFERENCE BETWEEN THE FALSE AND THE TRUE AND WHAT CANNOT GROW AND WHAT CAN

> For this reason have said men knowledgeable:
> 'Be the guest of those who do what's beautiful.'
> You are murid and guest of that person who
> Is so vile he'll steal all that you have from you
> He is not strong, how should he give strength to you?
> He makes you dark, he'll not shed light upon you
> How should others, since there is no light in him
> Derive light from association with him?
>
> 2305. He is like a half-blind man doctoring eyes
> How can he put aught but jasper in your eyes?
> Such is our state in poverty and distress
> May no guest ever be deluded by us!
> If you've not seen ten-year famine's shape and form
> Open your eyes and behold it in our form

The imposter has inside what we show plain
His heart's dark while his splendid talk leads astray
He has no trace and no scent of God in him
But he pretends to more than Seth and Adam

2310.   The Devil shows him not even his portrait
Yet he's a Substitute and more, so he says
He has often robbed the dervishes of words
So that he might be thought a person of worth
In his speech he condescends to Bayazid
Although he himself would put to shame Yazid
He's bereft of the bread and meat of Heaven
God has never thrown a single bone to him
'I'm the one who laid the table,' he cries out
'I'm a Caliph's son, the deputy of God

2315.   Welcome ye of simple heart, twisting in want
Eat your fill from my ample table of naught.'
For years in the promise of a tomorrow
That never comes, people linger at that door
It needs a long time for man's inner secret
To become, more or less, something evident
Underneath the body's wall there is treasure
Or snakes and ants and dragons make their home there
When the seeker finds that he was nothing, then
His life is gone, knowledge has no use for him

It seems the Arabi woman not only gives voice to the soul and the lusts of the soul, but at the same time tries to awaken the partial intellect and rouse to action her husband, who represents the partial intellect.

She meant to say that in order for us to be freed from our heedlessness and poverty of gnosis, we should fall upon the skirts of a great murshid, as the poor of the world fall upon the skirts of a rich man or padishah. Let us find a true gnostic of God and be freed as the old minstrel was of every kind of poverty when he fell upon the skirts of a great murshid. Let us take hold of his skirt. Let him bring our spirits, now in darkness, to our God.

That is why the intelligent have said we should be guests not of those who are needy but of those who give gifts in honor and courtesy. But you are the murid and guest of such a stingy man that he will try to take whatever you have, never mind doing the beautiful thing.

How can someone who has no strength in him give you strength? How can someone who has no light in him give you light? How can a doctor who is himself blind heal someone else's eye disease?

So, for training in love of God and reaching God, a murid must find a truly perfect murshid, not a charlatan pretending to be a murshid.

Such charlatans put out that pure light already within a heart, never mind lighting the lamp of affection in one.

It is ridiculous for someone whose soul is in need of training to occupy himself training the souls of others. While he has not defeated his own lusts and not overcome his own unruly soul, how can he reform your soul? A person whose eye's heart does not see, in whom the light of self-disclosure does not burn, who has not arrived at divine truth, how can he open the heart's eyes of others and draw the curtain aside and destroy it? While the goal is to see plurality in the state of oneness and display it, such imposter mushids do the reverse, they make people cross-eyed so that they see one as two.

That is what the Arabi woman intended to say. She was saying: We are so befuddled and poor that no one would be fool enough to visit us, no one asks after us.

What is the state of people in a country where famine has reigned for many years? If you want to see what that is, open your eyes and look at us.

What condition are we in? We are helpless and needy. Our lives are pitch black, like the hearts of imposters who claim to be prophets. Such hearts never know God, they have no fear of God. Their clams are so obviously false, they even pretend to be superior to the true prophets.

Although their spirits are so base even Satan wouldn't show them his face, they consider themselves superior to God's friends and more advanced than the Substitutes.

Although their actions would shame even Yazid, they want to have the effect on hearts that Bayazid has. Even God has turned away from them. He has left them deprived of all grace, but they pretend to be God's deputies on earth. And without considering how they are deprived of all grace, they summon simple, foolish people to their graceless tables. "Come, hurry, only we can give you every grace," they say.

They beguile those who hasten to their table and wish to eat, telling them to come the following day, but the tomorrow they speak of never comes and never will.

Making promises for tomorrow, those false friends of God have gathered around themselves many a ruined murid. Because the bounty they promise is not supposed to be material but spiritual, not visible but invisible, many a simple-hearted person gathers around them and waits, with profound purity of heart, for that great tomorrow and that spiritual bounty.

For the wall of the body is not made of stone. It is difficult to tell if there is a treasure buried inside it or under it. So that by the time the falsity and emptiness of such a false friend comes out, often the lives of the seekers gathered around him will have run out.

But because the aspirant seeks God even in the being of that charlatan, if he has wholly devoted himself in perfect purity of heart, God will certainly not leave him completely bereft. But still the unlucky traveler will have lost a great deal of time.

****

In Exposition of how it may rarely happen that a Murid binds himself to a False Imposter in sincere Belief that he is someone and in this Belief arrives at a Station never dreamed of by his Shaykh, and Fire and Water do not harm him although they harm his Shaykh, but this is rare

2320. But there is the rare seeker who shines so bright
      That he can derive benefit from that lie
      Because of his good intention he arrives
      Though the Shaykh was body and he thought him life
      He mistook the prayer-niche in the heart of night
      There's no niche, but his prayer is still alright

The imposter lacks spirit internally
But we have a lack of bread externally
Why should we conceal ourselves the way he does
And give up our lives for false reputation

A pure murid who flits about a shaykh like a moth is in reality circumambulating God. But for him to be duped by such a shaykh means that he loses time for progress on the path of God and suffers the misfortune of not being able to follow the way shown by a real man of faith.

Because his heart is pure and his intention good, his God will give him what his heart desires. He may attain the goal while his false shaykh is still swimming in the filth of the world and the body.

The situation is like that of a Muslim trying to find the direction of prayer in the darkness of a cloudy night. Because his wish is to be in the presence of God, and perform the prayer in that presence, his prayer is valid whatever direction he turns. For God is not in one place, He is present and facing you everywhere. The prayer of the Muslim who mistakes the direction of Mecca is not made toward the world's Kaaba, but it is a circumambulation of the spirit's Kaaba. Where else can those who have the fire of love in their hearts better find their Beloved than in their own hearts?

To be sure, the unfortunate murid thinks the false friend he revolves around is a true spirit, but the shaykh, far from being spirit, is a completely spiritless body. But what does that body, or even that spirit, matter to the murid? Is not the murid in reality under the influence of the attraction of the greatest Mushid?

The false shaykh is impoverished in spirit, but his poverty is a secret, it is not externally evident to all. But everyone can know if we suffer from a dearth of bread, because it is a material, external dearth. Our poverty is out in the open.

Let the false shaykh conceal his lack of spirit, but why should we keep our visible poverty hidden, or try to conceal it? Why should we be ashamed of our poverty and try to pretend we are not poor? What good is there in that? Is this honorable shame?

If this is what shames us, if this is where we think our honor resides, it will be the death of us. No, let us not be that way. To die is not our right. It is not up to us to determine our time of death. Let us strive to live and tell generous persons, those who have wealth, of our condition.

In one sense, this is what the soul, in the guise of the Arabi woman, was saying. In another sense she was speaking as if with the voice of divine inspiration, directing the active intellect [*faal aklı*] represented by her husband to seek out the spiritual wealth one must acquire on the path to God, and to find for this purpose a perfect and arrived human being rich in spirit and heart and obtain a share from him; in short, she was awakening the partial intellect [*cüz'î aklı*] to illumination.

****

HOW THE BEDOUIN BADE HIS WIFE TO HAVE PATIENCE AND TOLD HER OF THE EXCELLENCE OF PATIENCE AND POVERTY

2325.   Her husband said, "How long will you seek profit?
Most of our life has passed by, what's left of it?
Reason does not focus upon loss or gain

For both pass by like floods in torrential rain
If life be a brackish flood or calm and clear
Do not speak of it, since it does not endure
Thousands of beasts live in this world happily
Ups and downs do not cause them anxiety
The dove gives thanks to God perching on a tree
Though her evening repast is not yet ready

2230.   The nightingale is singing the Lord's praises
"You who hear all, I trust You for daily bread."
In the Shah's hand is reward for the falcon
Who has given up hope of all carrion
They are God's family, gnat to elephant
He *is the best in providing nourishment*
All the pain in our breasts comes of dust and steam
Blown by the wind of our desires and our being
Like scythes these griefs are digging away at us
It's this or that—Satan's whispering to us

2235.   Know that every pain is a parcel of death
If you find recourse, expel that piece of death
When you cannot escape from a part of death
Know the whole of it will pour down on your head
If a part of death has become sweet to you
Know that God will make the whole of it sweet too
Suffering comes from death as a messenger
O fool, don't turn away from its messenger
All those who live sweetly die in bitterness
He who serves the body won't save his spirit

2340.   They drive herds of sheep out of the plains and fields
The fatter the sheep, the sooner they are killed
The night is gone and morning's here, O my soul
How many times will you tell the tale of gold?
You were once young and you were then more at ease
You were gold yourself and now it's gold you seek
Now worthless, you were once a fruit-bearing vine
You have rotted when you should be growing ripe
Your fruit should grow sweeter and fuller in time
Not move back like a rope-maker weaving twine

2345.   We're a married couple, mates must be alike
In order that their affairs may turn out right
Each mate must be the other's similitude
Consider a pair of shoes or pair of boots
If one of the shoes is too tight for the foot
You'll have no use for either of the two shoes
Have you seen one small and one large double door?
Or a lion mate with a wolf in the forest?
Loads don't balance on the back of a camel

If one's of short weight and the other is full
I am moving stout-hearted to contentment
Why are you heading toward what's repugnant?"
2350.   In fond sincerity the contented man
Talked with his wife in this wise til break of dawn

The Arabi man said to his wife:

You are mistaken in your request. It is not wise to continually expect profit, blessings and wealth in this world. How much longer do we have to live? It would be
unsuitable for us to start begging for bread at the doors of rich men now.

The wise do not go to excess in concern for food and drink. They are content
with what the Lord gives them. Whether a person possesses much or little in this
world, poverty and wealth will be swept up in the same flood which carries off this
fleeting life.

Since we too are caught up in that flood, of what importance is whether the water
that carries us along is clear or muddy? Let us say that our lives are as bright, comfortable and bounteous as clear water. Or as stained with sorrow and anxiety and as
a muddy flood. Since both pass away, what use is it to long for one over the other?
Why even speak of these transient values?

Do you not know that there are countless others living in this world we live in?
Whether in scarcity or in excess, God has surely given each of them his daily bread.

The turtle dove on the tree branch and the nightingale on the rosebush both
warble thanks and prayer. Do such birds obtain their daily portion day and night?
Are there provisions stored up for them in some warehouse? Of course not. But they
still give thanks and pray. Can we not take example even from these birds?

You know the story: A falcon accustomed to receiving his daily portion from the
hand of the Padishah is too proud to chase after the rotting, filthy corpses fate has
strewn here and there.

In the same way, it is unimaginable that falcon-like lovers intimate with the
perfect friends who are the padishahs of the spiritual world would feed any longer
upon the desires of body and soul, which are like filthy, rotting corpses. Every living
creature, from the most helpless mosquito to those giant as elephants, is a member of
that great Creator's family. What do they have to fear who have a pater familias as
fond of his children as God? The God who has said:

Those who love their families are beloved of God.

How could He leave hungry the vast but helpless family He established with His own
divinity? Can you believe He would?

It is our greed and covetousness that makes us anxious and sorrowful about what
we will eat and drink.

Our sorrows and anxieties cut away the fruits of our lives like a farmer harvest-
ing his crop. The wise do not worry over the world, over the sustenance and bounty
of the world, they do not cut down the tree of the body with the ax of anxiety, making
it wither away before its time.

Every sorrow is a sickness, and every sickness a part of death. True, it is not within our ability to escape death. But if these sorrows and pains which are harbingers of death begin to seem attractive to you, that is different. Death treats more fairly those who accept illness, pain and sorrow, it treats them more gently, it knows how to show itself to be a sweet turning point rather than a horrifying end.

To be sure, painful and disgraceful is the end of someone who derives his vitality from the pleasures of the body and the desires of the soul. There is no spiritual salvation for someone who expends his effort and aspiration upon the pleasures of the body alone.

Even in the case of sheep, when they are brought from the countryside and the plains to the slaughterhouse, it is the fatter ones who get their throats cut first.

A lifetime has passed and the morning of death is near. Put aside the tale of gold. You have set yourself more upon the world the more you have aged. You have wasted the gold called youth, now you seek gold itself.

In your youth you were a branch heavy with fruit. Just when you were about to give up your fruits, a worm got into you and rotted and ruined you.

O woman, keep your heart bright like a polished mirror, don't let it gather dust. Hazret Ali says the greedy rich person is a pauper. O woman, you are my mate. Mate must be alike to mate. One of a pair of shoes cannot be larger than the other. The wings of double doors are alike. One can't load a camel with a heavy burden on one side and an empty sack on the other. The animal will lose its balance.

O woman, do not overload one end of the scale. Be contented as I am! Know that contentment is virtue, and here your virtue is to conform to me."

****

HOW THE WOMAN COUNSELED HER HUSBAND, SAYING, "DO NOT SPEAK ABOVE YOUR RANK AND STATION—*WHY DO YOU SAY WHAT YOU DO NOT DO?*[120]—FOR ALTHOUGH WHAT YOU SAY IS RIGHT, YOU DO NOT HAVE THAT DEGREE OF TRUST IN GOD, AND TO SPEAK ABOVE ONE'S STATION AND PRACTICE IS HARMFUL AND WILL BE *EXCEEDINGLY HATEFUL TO GOD*[121]

The woman cried, "It's reputation you seek!
I'll not swallow any more of your deceit
Don't talk vainly in pretense and pretension
Don't speak out of pride and arrogance, be gone!
How many more grand words and self-seeking claims?
Look at your own state and actions and have shame
2355.   Pride is ugly, in beggars even more gross
The day's cold, there's snow, and more, you have wet clothes
How much more wind from your mustache and bluster?
For a house you have the home of a spider[122]
When have you lit your spirit with contentment?
All you have learned is the name of contentment
The Prophet said: 'What is contentment? Treasure.'
But you can't distinguish travail from treasure

---

120. "O you who believe, why do you say what you do not do?" (Koran 61:2).

121. "It is exceedingly hateful to God that you say what you do not do" (Koran 61:3).

122. "Those who take protectors other than God are like the spider, who builds itself a house. But the spider's house is the flimsiest of houses, if they but knew" (Koran 29:41).

That contentment is treasure of the spirit
Do not boast, you are travail of the spirit
2360. Don't call me mate, rejoice less at my distress
I'm not a mate to fraud, I'm mate to justice
How do you keep step with bey and with emir
When you slit the veins of locusts for your fare?
You make war with dogs for the sake of a bone
Like an empty-bellied reed flute you wail on
Do not look down on me in contempt that way
Lest I tell others what's running in your veins
You think your intellect is greater than mine
But when have you seen me, with my tiny mind
2365. Do not spring like a heedless wolf upon me
Rather than have your small mind I'd mindless be
Since your mind is a bind fettering mankind
It is a snake and scorpion, not a mind
May God hate your tyranny and trickery
May your mind's trickery remain far from me
How wonderful—you are both charmer and snake!
Disgrace to Arabs—both snake-catcher and snake!
If the crow were aware of its ugliness
It would melt like snow from sorrow and distress
2370. The charmer chants spells, enemy of the snake
The snake is charming him while he charms the snake
If the trap he set were not to charm the snake
How would he be prey to the charm of the snake?
While he's greedy for acquisition and trade
He is not aware of the charm of the snake
'O charmer,' the snake says, 'attend carefully!
You see your own spell, now see my sorcery!
In the name of God the Truth you beguile me
To expose me to ridicule and shame me
2375. It was God's name that enthralled me, not your ruse
You made a trap of God's name, O shame on you
God's name will take vengeance upon you for me
To God's name I commit spirit and body
As I strike, He'll sever your life's vein through me
Or imprison you as you've imprisoned me.'"
The woman recited to her youthful mate
Volume upon volume in such harsh tirade

The woman spoke out against her husband harshly, saying:

You who merely pronounce the name of honor, who make a faith of reputation and
have nothing else! You will not bewitch me any longer. For I will not be fooled by
your charmed words. You have made contentment a matter of honor. But this is

pride, it is arrogance, your are only bewitching both me and yourself.

Don't boast to me any longer, give up your arrogance. How long will you spout bombast rather than obtain food and find peace of mind? Reflect upon your own misery, don't seek to feel superior to others in your misery! How long will your puff yourself up only to explode like a frog in the end?

God has said in the Koran, "The spider's house is the flimsiest of houses." O pretentious man, your heart is like a spider's house. How can you swagger like this when the house of your heart is so flimsy?

What have you to do with contentment? Is your spirit like a spirit illuminated by contentment? You suppose this word to be an empty shell. Hazret Muhammed has said contentment is an inexhaustible treasury. In Persian they call youth a treasure, and trouble and torment travail. You are unable to distinguish treasure from travail.

Contentment is a spiritual treasure, it is spiritual richness. But you subject the spirit to misery and torment. How can you speak of contentment when you are like this?

Don't compliment me in vain saying I am your mate. I am the mate of justice and just people, not of tricksters like you.

On the one hand, like a spider you spin webs in the air to trap flies and try to extract fat from flies, you condescend to the most despicable of foods. On the other, you speak dazzling words to me and try to pass yourself off as a man of contentment. You run in pursuit of a bone like a dog and then cry like an empty whistle.

Don't look at me angrily like that, I know what you are made of and if you make me angry, I will let all the world know of your shame and disgrace you. You think your intellect is superior to mine. And according to you, I am a person of little intellect, common as dirt.

But it is better to have no intellect at all than a shameful one like yours. You do not realize that your intellect hobbles you. You try to fool yourself and me by spouting empty talk and dazzling words. If that isn't conformity to the soul, like a toy in the hands of its passions, what is it? You are a toy in the hands of the corrupting soul, yet you try to give guidance to those defeated by their souls. Don't you see what an ugly and disgusting state you're in, talking like this?

If a crow was intelligent enough to realize how ugly it was, it would melt like snow with sorrow.

O snake-charmer! You know how when an Arab wants to catch a live snake, he recites incantations over the snake hole. The snake is bewitched by these incantations, come out of its hole and is caught. But is this skill the snake-charmer's alone? In truth has not the snake who is caught also enchanted its hunter? If not, would the hunter neglect other work and go to hunt the snake? Would he wish to learn incantations for this purpose?

What snake charmed has realized this, understood that in truth he is the prey of snakes and comprehended that he has sacrificed his whole life to the charm of a snake?

Now, O snake! You have sat yourself down to try to bewitch me with the name of God. Know that if there is something that binds me, it is the name of God, not your trickiness deception. But my being bound like this is a disaster for you. For by your actions you have encouraged me to take refuge in God. I have surrendered my spirit and my body to God, in His great name. I pray God will punish you for what you do to me. He surely sees how you have wounded me. I pray that this wound will sever the vein of your spirit. May God's punishment thus be upon you, and may He let you rot as I do in the prison of the world.

And she said much more in this stringent vein.

****

HOW THE MAN COUNSELED HIS WIFE, SAYING, "DO NOT LOOK UPON THE POOR WITH CONTEMPT, BUT REGARD THE WORK OF GOD AS PERFECT, AND DO NOT REVILE POVERTY AND THE POOR IN YOUR FANTASTICAL OPINION OF YOUR OWN INDIGENCE

"Are you woman or a sire of grief, O wife?
Do not abuse me, poverty is my pride
2380. Wealth and gold are like a cap worn on the head
The bald man needs a cap to hide his bald head
He who has thick and curly beautiful hair
Will be happier when his cap is not there
The man of God is a likeness of insight
It is better to have unveiled than veiled sight
When a slave-dealer presents slaves at market
He takes off the clothes which may conceal defect
And if they had defects, would he strip them bare?
No, with clothing he'd deceive customers there
2385. He says, 'This one's shy of evil and good too
If I strip him, he will run away from you.'
The merchant is plunged up to his ears in vice
But he has wealth, and his wealth conceals his vice
The greedy don't see his vice, due to their greed
Hearts are bound together by feelings of greed
And a beggar's words, although like gold most pure
His wares won't find a place in the merchant's store
The work of poverty is beyond your ken
Do not look upon poverty with contempt
2390. Dervishes are above wealth and property
Their daily bread's from the Lord of majesty
God Most High is just, and how should the just be
Cruel to hearts that are sick with melancholy
Or bestow bounty and wealth on one person
And put another into the fire to burn
He who thinks the creator of the two worlds
Is like that, it is him whom the fire hurts
Is 'Poverty's my pride' metaphor and vain?
No, it is thousandfold glory and disdain
2395. Out of anger you have called me many names
A traitor to friends and a catcher of snakes
I take out its fangs if I do catch a snake

So it won't get its head crushed, I keep it safe
For those fangs are the enemy of its life
I make friend of foe by means of this device
Never for sake of greed do I seek to charm
I have turned this thing you call greed upside down
God forbid! I've no greed for created things
In my heart is a world that contentment brings

2400.   On top of the pear tree you see things that way
Come down and that illusion will go away
When you get dizzy from turning round and round
You think the house spins, but you are turning round

The Arabi said to his wife:

O woman! Are you a woman or a mother of miseries, a father of sorrows? Do not continually beat me over the head with my poverty. Even Hazret Muhammed said, 'Poverty is my pride.' There is no dishonor in me that I should hide under kaftans of wealth. Property and gold are like a beautiful hat worn on a bald head. Their function is to hide the head's defect.

Why should beauties whose heads are adorned with gilded hair wear a crown? They do not need to wear hats. Such heads should stay bare, so that their amber-scented hair may be seen.

A person whose heart is rich with God is the like the eye in a face. If you cover the eye, what can it see? And how will its beauty be seen?

Have you not seen slave-dealers? When they offer slaves to customers they unclothe them, selling them naked to show that there is not flaw in their bodies. It is as when clouds obscuring the beauty of the moon on nights when it is full disperse, or when the darkness of night passes and the sun appears, and all veils hiding its light and beauty are gone.

There are certain slave-dealers who display their slaves dressed in dazzling clothing in order to cover the flaws of their bodies. As an excuse they say: 'How shall I say it, this one has never been seen naked, and is embarrassed to be seen naked, and will hate anyone who strips him or makes anyone strip him.'

Hazret Muhammed has said: "Knowledge and property are veils covering all flaws. Ignorance and poverty make all flaws evident." Many a rich merchant conceals his sins with his wealth, property and money seem flawless to those who love them. Their every word is taken as wisdom, and every thought as wealth.

On the other hand, when a person who is poor speaks, no one listens or takes notice even if his words are pure gold.

If you speak the speech of gnostics to a greedy person whose insides are filled with dazzling worldly desires of the world, do his ears hear? How should such people understand the heat's wealth in poverty? How should a merchant clothed in furs and silks know the pleasure a dervish takes in being deprived of worldly riches, the felicity he feels at being purified of the soul, the body, and all adornment of the body?

The heart of a dervish is beyond property and wealth. Whatever of worldly good you give to the heart of a dervish, it does not please him, he is not enriched by it. But a dervish whose heart is filled with God fills every place he goes with riches.

God gives silk to some of his bondsmen and heart to others. In the paradise of the world He distracts the bondsman whose heart is in Hell, and He burns in the fires of worldly poverty those whose hearts are filled with spiritual riches. This burning is like the burning of green reeds in the fire of the sun so that they may become reed flutes singing of God, or the maturing of fruits in that same fire.

God is just and His justice self-discloses in these ways. God has made our world a place of trial. In this world and the hereafter each body finds what it has done, and every heart what it deserves.

Hazret Muhammed's saying, "Poverty is my pride," is not just a random statement, it is great wisdom. It prefers worldly poverty for sake of the wealth of the light of the heart, and commands contentment. What you need to do is to comprehend the distinction of being chosen among the paupers on the face of the earth.

You are angry with me, you called me a snake-charmer. But I am no snake-charmer, I am a man with a rich heart who charms true human beings, I charm friends. And if I do catch a snake, I do it in order to extract its teeth, to save it from the shame of poisoning others. I don't know, do you understand? Within the human being there is a dragon called the soul snake. A person must catch this snake, which sheds poison into him, extract its teeth and save his spirit from being poisoned with the poisons of the world. Once you have done that, the soul snake will no longer be your enemy, it will be your friend.

You have slandered me, saying lusts and desires lurk within me. In truth there is something hidden within me, even a secret realm. This realm not visible to every eye is the realm of infinity, which will never cease to be. Can anything else come into the treasure vault of a person's heart when the Greatest of great ones and the Beloved of beloveds is there? Is there room for anything else?

Don't sit up in a pear tree looking down on me. For however you see me, I am as I am.

You know the story of the pear tree and the coquette. The woman told her lover that she would make love to him right in front of her husband. In order to prove it, she told him to hide near the pear tree in an appointed place and wait for them. Then she and her husband came to picnic under the tree. She told her husband she wanted to pick her a pear and climbed the tree. She yelled up to him husband: "You shameless fellow! While I'm up in the tree you're making love to another woman down there, aren't you?" Her husband said there was no woman with him, but she would not listen. She came down in a fury and then said she was sorry: "You were right, there is no woman with you, it appeared that way while I was looking down from the tree, the tree must be bewitched. You go up and see if the same thing happens to you."

The poor husband climbed the tree, and the woman called her lover from where he was hiding. They began making love out in the open. The husband saw this and called down from above: "You are right, my dear wife. The tree is charmed, I too see you making love with another man."

The pear tree is meant to be the tree of doubt. Come down from the tree of doubt to the pasture of truth so that you may be freed of the worms gnawing at your insides. You are like a person whose head spins while dancing. If you whirl around wildly where you stand, you see trees, doors and houses turning around you. But what is turning is your own head. So, in order for you to be able to see the inner riches of dervishes whose hearts are full of gnosis and God, your head full of worldly desires must come to a stop and your gazes must be purified. The treasure you will see then will be so rich that your heart, not your head, will rise to whirl in mystic audition [semâ].

****

EXPOSITION OF HOW THE ACTION OF A PERSON PROCEEDS FROM THE PLACE WHERE HE IS, AND HE SEES EVERYONE FROM THE CIRCLE OF HIS OWN EXISTENCE. BLUE GLASS SHOWS THE SUN AS BLUE, RED GLASS AS RED. WHEN A GLASS TRANSCENDS COLOR IT BECOMES WHITE AND MORE TRUTHFUL THAN OTHERS AND THE LEADER OF THEM ALL

When Abu Jahl saw Ahmed, he said of him
'An ugly form sprung from the sons of Hashim!'
'You are right,' Ahmed said to him, 'it is true
'Although you go too far, you have spoken true
When Siddiq saw him, he said, 'O shining sun
You are of neither East nor West,[123] do shine on!'

2405. "You speak truly, O dearest friend,' Ahmed said
'You have escaped from this world of nothingness.'
Those who were present asked, 'O Shah, why did you,
'Though they contradict, say both had spoken true?'
'I'm a mirror,' he replied, 'polished by hand
In me they see themselves, Turk and Indian.'[124]
O wife, if it is greed that you see in me
Rise above absorption in things womanly
This seems to be greed, but really is mercy
How can there be greed where there is that bounty?

2410. For a day or two make trial of poverty
You will see twice the riches in poverty
Leave weariness, have patience with poverty
There lies the light of the Lord of majesty
Do not be sour, and see thousandfold spirit
Drowned in a sea of honey from contentment
A hundred thousand spirits in bitter woe
That have been steeped in rose-sugar like the rose
Oh alas, if you'd capacity to see
My spirit show forth my heart in clarity

2415. In the breast of spirit these words are the milk
They do not flow well without someone to suck

123. "God is the light of the heavens and earth. The likeness of His light is a niche within which is a lamp, the lamp enclosed in glass, the glass like a brilliant star, lit from a blessed tree, an olive neither of East nor West, whose oil is well-nigh luminous, though fire has scarcely touched it. Light upon light! God guides whom He will to His light, God sets forth parables for men, and God is all-knowing" (Koran 24:35).
124. Here "Turk and Indian" mean "beautiful or ugly."

When the hearer's thirsty and a supplicant
The preacher will speak, even though he be dead
When the hearer's fresh and suffers no fatigue
Mute and dumb will find a hundred tongues to speak
When a man not of the family arrives
The women of the house veil themselves inside
If it's a harmless man of the family
The veiled women lift up their face-coverings

2420.   Everything made beautiful, fair and lovely
Is made so for the eye of him that can see
How should strains of melodies, treble and bass
Be made for the deaf ear of one who's senseless?
God did not make musk sweet-smelling in vain, no
He made it for sense, not for the stuffy nose
God has made the earth and He has made the sky
And between them He kindled much light and fire
The face of earth for those who are made of clay
For those who dwell on heavenly spheres, the sky

2425.   The inferior man hates what's high in state
It becomes clear who seeks to purchase each place
Did you ever rouse yourself, O chaste woman
To get dressed up for the sake of a blind man?
If I filled the world with pearls of great value
Since they're not your daily bread, what would I do?
O wife, say you'll quit warfare and banditry
And if you will not, then take your leave of me
What have I to do with fighting good or bad?
For my heart recoils even from peaceful acts

2430.   If you will, be silent—and if you say no
I will at this moment leave my house and home."

Those who are dyed in the red color of the soul's lusts really do suppose that the arrived of God, who are God's gnostics, are dyed in the soul's colors of greed and avarice like themselves. But the gnostics of God have no color. They are so free of soul, body and color that they can not be seen in even the most highly polished mirror. They do not see existents, events, forms and faces as others do; they see them in their own true meanings, wrapped in a light of oneness. They see great truths and great mysteries illuminated to the degree of their station on the path of God and their nearness to God.

****

And just so, because when Abu Jahl saw Hazret Muhammed, he saw him with the bad eye and black raiment of his own station, he said: "An ugly face has appeared among the sons of Hashim." Hazret Muhammed's answer to him was: "Although you go too far, you have spoken truly."

When Abu Bakr saw the same Hazret Muhammed, the seeing and the appearance were completely different. "O Sun," Abu Bakr called out to the Prophet, "You have risen from neither East nor West. But you shine with the most beautiful light of all. You beauty illuminates the earth and sky. Shine on, O great light! Shine and bright the spirits and hearts in darkness with your great light!"

Hazret Muhammed said the same thing to him: "O you who are known as Siddiq! Your words are true and veracious, as so is your name. You are among those who have escaped the materiality of this worthless and transient world. You are among those who have wearied of duality and plurality and plunged into the ocean of oneness."

Then those who were present there said, "O Muhammed! O greatest, noblest of all humans! How can it be that you told both of them that they were right? What each of them said contradicted the other. One said that you are ugly, and the other that you are beautiful."

Hazret Muhammed said to them: "O my companions! I am a mirror polished by the creative hand of God. For that reason those who look upon me see within my frame their own faces, even their own hearts. Those who are beautiful and bright like Turks, see their beauty in me; those who are black and dark like Indians see their own faces too."

The Arabi man told this story to his wife. "What a person sees in others is often his own face and flaws," he said. "O woman, if you see me as greedy and avaricious, get free of this womanly view and rise up! Be manly and depart from fear as the manly do, know the truth and see it," he cried.

"What you liken to avarice, what you call avarice, is in reality mercy itself. Wherever you see spiritual bounties and wealth of the heart, there is no greed, no avarice left there.

"Try for a few days to experience such poverty, such patience. Then you will see the beauty in the treasuries of contentment and chastity of the heart's wealth.

"God's grace and mercy faces toward poverty. Do not make a sour face at what has been apportioned to you. Know that countless contented pauper spirits have reached oceans of pleasure and delight in this way.

"You know that rose sweets are made by crushing rose petals with honey and lemon. Just as the rose acquires taste from the sweetness of honey and the sourness of lemon and is blended with them, the heart also must accustom itself to poverty, contentment and asceticism like so many hundreds of thousands who suffer hunger.

"What a pity it is that I cannot make you feel the treasures hidden in the heart and the delights of the heart. For in this regard both the listener and the speaker must be gnostics.

"Such words are like the milk in the breasts of spirit. If there is no one to suck and take delight in what he sucks, it will not flow and its taste will not be known. If listeners have the temper to take knowledge and taste from the tongue of the speaker, he will come alive even should he be dead, and he will become a sharer of secrets. It is the pleasure and desire of those listening which makes those who know speak, and speak the better the more they speak.

"If the listeners do not let their minds wander, and listen with all their spirit and heart, even if the listener be dumb, face with such desire he will speak enthralled as if he had hundreds of tongues and be the matchless nightingale of knowledge, wisdom, and mystery.

"But just as when a man not of the family appears at the door of the harem, all the beautiful women within scatter and seek a place to hide, so it is with the nightingale of the tongue, it feels it is its right to hide when confronted by those who don't understand its speech.

"On the other hand, just as when a long-lost family member comes to the same harem, the beautiful women with their bodies of rose and light inside want to be seen by him, just as they take delight in this, so it is with words and wisdom, they too show all their beauty to those who understand them.

"Beauty seeks an eye to see it, a heart to love it. Beautiful words also have need of ears and even hearts to hear them. Beauty is not offered to eyes that do not see, and melody not offered to ears that cannot hear.

"What melodies are there for the deaf, what are rose or musk fragrances for those whose noses cannot detect scent?

"God created heaven and earth, and upon the earth and between earth and sky He lit many a fire, raised many a torch. The fires are without doubt for kafirs and those who set up partners to God. And the torches are the prophets, friends and believers who with their light fill the universe and the hearts of humans, each as vast as creation.

"This means that God has calculated that spirits may become degraded, and on the other hand not be degraded but remain sublime, and prepared the earth as a home for those who would stay on the earth, and the sky for those who will rise to the heavens. That is why those whose spirits are dirtied hate the heavens. Their assigned portion is to stay on earth and not rise up. Their works and emotions are all one with the ground, degraded. That is why they think ill of the people of the sky and do evil to them.

"In contrast, those who will rise to the heavens are those who prepare in this world for the sublime station they will one day attain. They purify themselves of bodily filth, adorning themselves with the beauties and purities of spirit, and discipline themselves according to the etiquette of the sublime spirits at the gathering of pre- and post-eternity.

"Consider, O woman, for you love to adorn yourself and be beautiful, wearing what flatters you. Have you ever thought, while adorning and beautifying yourself, to show yourself to the blind and adorn yourself for them? You take pains to be beautiful only for those who can see you and appreciate that beauty.

"Such are the mysteries of the heavens and the wisdom of God. They are manifest to those who can see their beauty and understand them.

"If a spirit is blind and deaf to all this beauty, what shall I show to it, what hymn can it hear?

"If that is how you are, if you are blind and deaf to these things, then I have nothing to say to you.

"O woman, either put aside useless quarreling or depart from me. Consider that I feel like avoiding even that which is lawful. How should I love what is unlawful? My station is such that I withdraw even from peace. How should I spend time in warfare? Consider that beauty, like renunciation and faith, is nothing if it is not perfect. Maturity is to reach perfection in these.

"If you are not pleased by these and by the way I am, I will not keep you. I will set you free from my house and wedlock if you wish.

"Remain here and share with me, or leave! The choice is yours."

****

How the Wife attended to her Husband and repented for what she had said

When the woman saw him angry and severe

She began to weep—a woman's snare is tears
"When have I imagined such from you," she said
From you I had hoped for something different."
The woman took the road of humility
She said, "I'm dust at your feet, not your lady
Body and soul all I am belongs to you
All dominion and command belong to you

2435. If my heart flees patience due to poverty
It does so in concern for you, not for me
In times of trouble you have been my recourse
I am unwilling to see you at a loss
By my spirit and conscience, it's not for me
It is for you, this wailing and lamenting
I swear by God that before you, my own self
Wishes each moment to die for your own self
Would that your spirit—may mine be sacrifice
Could know the inmost thoughts of this spirit mine

2440. But considering you have such thoughts of me
I am weary of both spirit and body
Since you feel this way, O comfort of my soul
I have poured dust upon both silver and gold
You dwell in my spirit and the heart of me
Will you for so little take your leave of me?
You have the power to, so abandon me
But my soul pleads that you won't abandon me
Remember the time when I was beautiful
You were like a shaman serving an idol

2445. Your slave sets her heart alight for you to serve
If you say a thing is cooked, she calls it burned
I am your spinach, cook anything with me
Whether it be sour or sweet, you are worthy
I've returned to faith although I did blaspheme
I submit my head and life to your decree
I had not come to know your magnificence
I came to you on horseback in arrogance
Since I have made a lamp of your forgiveness
I repent and cast aside contrariness

2450. I lay down my sword and my shroud before you
Strike the blow! I lay my neck down before you
You speak of bitter separation from me
Do whatever you wish, but do not leave me
Your inner self is pleading with you for me
If I don't, it intercedes with you for me
What pleads for me is your nature deep within
My heart relies on that when it acts in sin
Unbeknownst to yourself have mercy on me

Your nature is better than pots of honey."
2455.   In this way she spoke gracefully, frank and dear
Until there came upon her a fit of tears
When her tears and sobbing were unbearable
—She who without tears is irresistible—
In that rain a single bolt of lightning flashed
And a spark struck the heart of the lonely man
She whose beautiful face makes of all men slaves
How will it be when she plays the humble slave?
She whose arrogance leaves your heart trembling
How will you feel when she's before you weeping?
2460.   She whose disdain makes your heart and spirit bleed
How will it be when she comes to you in need?
She who snares us with her ruthless tyranny
What plea is left to us when she comes to plead?
What is *adorned for men*[125] is adorned by God
How can men escape what is set down by God?
So he might dwell with her[126] God created Eve
How should Adam be separated from Eve?
Though greater than Hamza or Zal's son, Rostam[127]
He's his old woman's thrall, under her command
2465.   The world may be enslaved to the Prophet's speech
But he'd cry out, "O Humayra, speak to me!"
Water dominates fire with its rushing flood
But fire boils water when it's put in a pot
O Shah, when a cauldron comes in between there
It makes water disappear into the air
If like water you seem to control your wife
Inwardly you are controlled and seek your wife
This is special to man and to no other
Animals lack love because they are lesser
2470.   "Women prevail over intelligent men
Firmly, and men of heart," the Messenger said
And the ignorant prevail over women
For the fierceness of the beast is kept in them
They lack tenderness, kindness and affection
For in their nature animality wins
Love and tenderness are human qualities
Anger and lust are animal qualities

---

125. "Adorned for men is love of what they desire; of women and sons, hoards of gold and silver in stores, horses bearing brands, and cattle and well-tilled land. Such are the objects of this worldly life, but in nearness to God is the most beautiful of goals" (Koran 3:14).

126. "It is He who created you from a single soul, and made its mate from it so that he might dwell with her" (Koran 7:189).

127. Rostam son of Zal is a hero of Iranian legend, and Hamza was an uncle of Hazret Muhammed.

She is the ray of God, not your beloved
Virtually Creator, not created

Hearing these words, the woman began to cry. Her most powerful weapon is her tears. "I expected other things from you," she said. "But I understand that I have not been a woman worthy of you. I should have been our slave. I will no longer be contrary, I believe in you.

"If poverty has worn out my patience, it is not only own account, but yours. For you have treated me so well that my heart could not accept for you to be poor and miserable.

"I am prepared to sacrifice my life for you. If only your spirit could know mine and realize that there is no evil in it.

"Forgive me, for although you give me dust instead of gold and silver, you transform to gold and silver the dust I grasp in my hand. But I no longer need gold or silver, I need you.

"Don't abandon me. For I cannot live without you. Remember that there was a time when I was beautiful as an idol. And you loved me and worshipped me as an idol-worshipper loves an idol.

"You are the one who overcame the idol in me, my soul. Once you were under the power of this soul. Whatever the soul, that is to say I, commanded, you performed without hesitation. But now you, O spirit, have matured and reached perfection. Now I am under your command. But seeing that I still call myself I, this soul has not yet been completely conquered, it has not tasted the delight of being totally naught. Know this and continue to work upon me. I who have only just become your slave will one day be completely naught.

"My heart is one and the same as your command. It is illuminated because it burns for you. You have just to ask. Whatever you want, sweet or salt, I will cook it for you. You are worthy of every delight you wish.

"I blasphemed while quarreling with you. Now I have come to faith. Cover my sin with the skirts of your absolving spirit and blot it out. I was insolent with you. Because of that I was left in the dark. But the lamp of your forgiveness has illuminated me. I have surrendered to you. I am turning myself over to you, do what you will, just do not leave me.

"Within you there actually is something secret asking forgiveness in my name. That intercessor is constantly bringing you to forgive me. If you ask what this secret thing is, it is the kindness and generosity of you male nature. It is that which will forgive me for my fault. Your rage is as beautiful as your kindness! Forgive me!"

Thus the woman spoke and began to cry again, and like every beautiful woman she became more beautiful for her tears. Clouds emerged from the rain of her tears, lightning struck and set her husband's spirit aflame. The man had been suffering in his misunderstood solitude, and was pleased. A deep love for his wife awoke within him.

If a beautiful woman makes herself the slave of a man, if she shows love and intimacy rather than pride and arrogance, if a woman usually cruel and hurtful turns to beg forgiveness sweetly and ardently, what can a man do?

As God has said in the Koran, "Adorned for men is love of what they desire; of women and sons, hoards of gold and silver in stores, horses bearing brands, and cattle and well-tilled land" (3:14).

Certainly it is meaningful that this verse begins by mentioning women. It is a sign that the love of women and the mischief of women are stronger than the others.

And just so, when the Arabi of the desert saw his woman flirting and being intimate with him in this way, he lost al his resolve. Never mind forgiving her, he was violently bound to her. His love and desire were renewed.

The Arabi had good reason. Since God has adorned the love of women, how should his creatures be expected to escape it? Unless God guide them anew. In His verse God indicates woman and lust; children and animal nature; gold and silver and the greed for wealth and adornment; pure-bred horses and camels and the ambition for advancement and position on the part of those who ride them, and crops tilled and ripened, and greed for dominion and leadership, and self-conceit and pride. How can a bondsman get free of all these lusts without the help of God the Truth?

The Prophet Adam was a site of manifestation [*mazhar*] for divine self-disclosure, and when he could no longer bear the lights of self-disclosure, the light of the realms of domination and sovereignty [*ceberût ve melekût âlemleri*] descended upon him also. Eve was created of such a light. So that by growing accustomed to Eve, Adam might not fear the thrusts of self-disclosure.

That is why when Hazret Muhammed dove into the spiritual realm and was terrified before the vastness of the divine realms, he used to call out to his wife Aisha, "Speak to me, O Humayra!" Sometimes he did it because he needed to be drawn into the world.

Even if a man be Rostam son of Zal, the great hero of the Iranian epic, or as great a hero as Hazret Muhammed's uncle Hamza, he is still weak before the woman he loves. You know the effects of water and fire. Water has the power to quench a being as mighty as fire. But if that same water is put into a pot, fire can boil it until every drop becomes steam and evaporates into the air. Fire can make pots and pots of water disappear.

Thus are man and woman like water and fire. Although the man appears to be like water, dominating the woman, the inner truth of the matter is otherwise. The love and attraction of woman, like the heat of fire, has the power to bring the man to boil and exhaust him.

And in the human being the spirit is pure and transparent like water. By contrast, the soul can cause burning and boiling as fire does. Is that not why the fire of soul boils the water of spirit, dispersing its spiritual subtlety within the density of the body, and makes the spirit subordinate to the soul? That is why it boils the spirit like water in a pot. A that is why in the world, man desires woman and appears to dominate her but in reality is defeated and dominated by both woman and his feminine soul. For as long as a man lives he will not be without woman and cannot be.

In fact it is only humans who have these qualities. For intellect and love are special to humans alone. Animals do not possess intellect, and do not exactly love. They are lacking in several ways. It is due to their lack of intellect and love and most animals are not overcome by their female mates.

That is why Hazret Muhammed said that women rule over men who are possessed of intellect and heart. And this is the reality. An intelligent and fine-spirited male is always understanding and generous with women, he avoids treating them harshly and does not wish to offend or harm them. By contrast, it is ignorant and unintelligent males who oppress women, behaving harshly and crudely toward them. For animality dominates their natures.

Love and fineness of spirit are qualities special to humans. Harshness and lust are animal qualities.

This means that the love and attraction a person feels for the woman he loves is not in vain. For woman is a light reflecting the beauty of God on earth, she is not just a beloved; it can be said that virtually, she is not created, she is the Creator [Hâlik].

****

It is after reaching this truth that Hazret Muhammed's hadith, "woman is man's half," is more clearly understood. The mystery in the fact that even the most powerful men are weak before women is brought out.

It is understood here that for man to be overcome by woman is a matter of level and gnosis. A man's being weak before women is a measure of his perfection and gnosis.

The importance given to women in Islam is fixed by the witness the Gracious Koran bears to it. When the Muslims are address in the Gracious Koran, it is almost always as men and women, equal value given to both. The Gracious Koran does not consider believing women separately from believing men, and does not think of them separately.

The value God has given to woman, as in the fact that women posses qualities of His own creative power and perform a great office in the continuation of life, is due to her role as a mighty pillar in divinely appointed destiny.

As is indicated here, "Love for women comes from the ability to witness God the Truth Himself in the mirror of their bodies [vücûtları]."

Ibn Farid has said, "The beauty of every beautiful person is a reflected piece of God's beauty." So the love of man for woman means in one respect that he wishes to reach divine beauty by means of her. And for this to happen, t is natural for woman to be triumphant over man.

But such an idea is correct only for men who have attained a certain level of gnosis and covered distance within the spiritual realms.

****

HOW THE MAN MADE HIMSELF AMENABLE TO THE WOMAN'S ENTREATY THAT HE SEEK MEANS OF LIVELIHOOD, AND TOOK HER OPPOSITION TO HIM AS A SIGN FROM GOD

2475. The man was as sorry for what he had said
   As a cruel officer at the hour of death
   "How could I quarrel with my life's life," he said
   "How could I rain kicks down on my spirit's head?"
   Destiny cuts off one's sight when it descends
   So the mind cannot distinguish foot from head
   Later the mind devours itself in distress
   Distraught and disgraced and tearing at its vest
   "O wife, I'm filled with regret," the man began
   Though I was a kafir, now I am Muslim
2480. I have sinned against you, have mercy on me
   Do not rip up my roots out from under me
   If an old kafir regrets and begs pardon
   Because he does so he becomes a Muslim
   God is the Merciful and the Generous

> Both existence loves Him and non-existence
> Faith and non-faith are in love with majesty
> Copper and silver bow to that alchemy

The gnostics of God recognize that God alone is the agent in all events. They consider His creatures to be intermediary means. Even if they are harmed or offended by one of them, they take it kindly. They think to themselves that there must be some wisdom in it; they believe God is trying them by means of such offending bondsmen. They meet every torment with dignified calm [*vekar*], bowing to what befalls them in the consignment and management of God's creation.

This is what the Arabi man was thinking. He regretted rebuking his wife. Just as when the hour of death approaches, a cruel man remembers with regret the cruelty he has committed and becomes distraught in final, futile regret, so did the Arabi man feel remorse for what he had said to his wife.

He asked himself why he had said such things to the person he loved as he loved his own life, thinking that he had behaved like a person who purifies himself of all evil habits and then, when confronted by his purified soul, is unable to see that purity and continues on tyrannizing his soul.

When the destiny ordained by God arrives, a person's eyes are veiled and he cannot see what is right. His intellect gets into such a state that it cannot tell head from foot, top from bottom, in short, right from wrong.

When it is all over and he gathers his wits, he becomes mad with remorse and violently regrets what he has done. And just so, the Arabi man felt such regret toward his wife and apologized:

O woman, I spoke harshly to you. It was fated to be so, and thus it happened. I strayed into blasphemy. Now I have returned to faith.

I have sinned against you mightily. Forgive me, so that I may not be completely ruined.

O my soul, I have been trying to purify you of worldly filth, trying to annihilate you. I was making such efforts to get you out of the defile into which you had fallen, and had grown so used to doing this, that I did not realize you had become purified of all filth and sublime, that you had risen up to the heavens. You have now reached your station. You are freed from your former evil state. You have shed materiality and become all spirit and meaning. Duality no longer remains, you have attained oneness.

Just as an old kafir asks forgiveness of God with his last breath and becomes a Muslim, and his sins are forgiven, O woman, now forgive me.

You know that great God is generous and kind. He forgives errors made in efforts on His path. He knows that among His lovers there are not only those sparkling with light, but those left in darkness. It is not only those He has created from naught who are in love with Him, but those He leaves in nothingness also. Among those who believe and those who deny, there is none who is not, according to the degree of his consciousness, mad with love for Him.

In short everyone, whether Muslim or kafir, is a work [*eser*] of God, who is reality itself. These works, whether they know reality or do not grasp it, possess in their hearts a profound and constant desire for Him. Whether hard as rock, transparent as water, or subtle and imperceptible as the air we breath, all enjoy the delight and felicity of being His work; knowingly or unknowingly, they are on His path, only His path.

****

EXPOSITION OF HOW BOTH MOSES AND PHARAOH ARE SUBJECT TO DIVINE WILL, AS ARE ANTIDOTE AND POISON AND DARKNESS AND LIGHT, AND HOW PHARAOH BESEECHED GOD IN PRIVATE NOT TO DESTROY HIS GOOD REPUTATION

Moses and Pharaoh worshipped reality
One kept to the road, one did not, outwardly

2485. By day Moses wailed before God in his plight
While Pharaoh came weeping to Him at midnight
"O God, why is my neck shackled by this chain?
Who would say 'I am I' if not for this chain?
By that whereby You made Moses enlightened
You also rendered me turbid and darkened
You gave Moses a countenance like the moon
By that whereby You blackened my spirit's moon
My star is not superior to a moon
Now that I have been eclipsed, what shall I do?

2490. If they beat drums for me as lord and sultan
It's beating on pots when the eclipsed moon's gone
They beat those pots and raise a hullabaloo
With their blows they bring disgrace upon the moon
I who am Pharaoh, piteous is my lot
'My Supreme Lord'[128] is just blows upon a pot
Moses and I are both Your fellow-servants
But Your axe cuts new branches in the forest
Then it grafts one branch upon another tree
And leaves another branch to lie idly

2495. A branch cannot lift a hand against an axe
No branch ever escapes the hand of the axe
I plead by right of the power in Your axe
Out of Your grace, rectify my perverse acts."
Then Pharaoh thought to himself: "Ah, wonderful!
Do I not spend each night crying, 'O our Lord'?
In private I grow more humble and balanced
How will I be when I come to meet Moses?
Though the color of pure gold be ten coats' paint
In the presence of fire it too turns black-faced

2500. Don't my heart and form change by His decision?
Now He makes of me the kernel, now the skin
When he bids me be a sown field, I am green
I turn yellow when he bids me be ugly
Now he makes a moon of me, then turns me black."

---

128. [Pharaoh] "Saying, 'I am your Lord'" (Koran 79:24).

How could it be otherwise when it's God's act?
Before the polo bats of *"Be! And it was."*
We roll within place and not-place by His law
Since color became slave of colorlessness
One Moses has warred with another Moses

2505.   When the colorlessness you once had is reached
Moses and Pharaoh come together in peace
If the question occurs to you about this:
"How could color be void of contrariness?"
The wonder is color from colorlessness
How did color come to fight what's colorless?
Oil derives from water and is formed from it
So how can oil ever be at war with it?
If God created oil from water, then how
Have oil and water become contraries now?

2510.   Since rose is of thorn and thorn is of the rose
Why are the two at war and each other's foe?
Or is this not war, is it divine purpose?
Like ass-traders arguing, an artifice?
Or if it is not this or that, is it awe?
This is the ruin, the treasure must be sought
That which you imagine to be a treasure
—Through that illusion you are losing treasure
Know fancy and thought to be like sowing fields
Treasure is not found in cultivated fields

2515.   In habitation there is strife and being
Not-being blushes at all existent things
Being does not seek help against not-being
No, it's non-existence that sends back being
Do not say: "It's not-being that I flee from."
Enough! No, it's you that it is fleeing from
It seems to beckon you to it, but within
It repels you with the rod of rejection
It's a tale of switched horseshoes, use your good sense
Know Pharaoh's rebellion derived from Moses

God's name "He who Guides" ruled over Moses, while Pharaoh was ruled by His name "He who leads Astray."

With the knowledge and gnosis of his spirit and partial intellect, a person would choose between the right and wrong path. If spirits were of the quality to be able to see reality between the blinking flashes of the lightning strokes born of the clash between God's contrary attributes, of course they would find the right path. If they were asleep to this quality, certainly they would choose error.

A light from the beauty of God reaches the spirits of humans between the lightening strokes of these contraries, and sometimes beams of subjugation and violence. Each spirit has the power to understand the meaning and know the value of both lights which reach it. But some spirits will be aware of the goodness and beauty of the light reaching it, and others embrace the qualities of subjugation and violence in the light which reaches them.

Thus is the story of Messenger Moses and Pharaoh, who appeared to be his exact opposite.

Messenger Moses would come into God's presence night and day, and especially during the day would beg for help and forgiveness from Him, paying no mind to anyone else.

Pharaoh believed in the existence and oneness of God, and also comprehended the messengerhood of Moses, but because of his stubbornness and his inability to renounce his dreams of worldly dominion, he would withdraw into solitude at night and pray to God when he was sure that no one could see him doing so.

He would say:

My Lord, I believe in You, and I know that Moses is Your envoy. But I once was so heedless as to tell the Copts that I was their Lord. Now I cannot go back on my word. Understand me and forgive me! If the chain of error around my neck did not drag me toward the world, toward worldly dominion, in short toward the claim to being and selfhood, how could I make such a claim to selfhood?

The truth is that You illuminate Moses with Your light while leaving me in darkness. The light of Moses' heart shines in his bright face while my face reflects the blackness within me. Even the moon in the heavens sometimes appears, shines and waxes full; sometimes it is eclipsed and stays in darkness. How can the moon of my poor heart escape the eclipse that You have fated for it?

Although I am Sultan to the people and those under my command beat the drums for me, saying I am their Lord and Sultan, and express and sing their servanthood and slavehood with the instruments in their hands and at their lips. The magnificent sounds they make rise up to the heavens.

But it seems to me that the sounds from their instruments are the sounds of the heedless who in their heedlessness bang on pots during a lunar eclipse, believing they are rescuing or have rescued the moon from the darkness which has eclipsed it. It is as if they are trying to rescue the eclipsed moon of my heart and spirit within me. Alas, this beating on pots, this noise and clapping, is not enough to rescue the crescent moon of heedlessness and error within me. In reality the moon of my heart is disgraced just as this folk custom disgraces the moon.

The fervor of the people, their exhibitions of emotion, anxiety and delusion, in particular their supposition that I am God and their efforts insistent enough to convince me that I am God, are all reminiscent of the commotion around a lunar eclipse; for I know well what I am and alas, know my infinite helplessness before Your greatness, and I know that the applause is destroying me a little more with each passing moment.

My Lord, it hurts me most of all that the people make me address them and say, 'I am your Lord Most High!' [129] Are not Moses and I both bondsmen of the same Master? My God, we are in the forest of the beings You have created, but only Your

---

129. The Lord said to Moses: "Go to Pharaoh, for he has indeed transgressed all bounds, and say to him, 'Would you be purified? Would you have me guide you to your Lord, so that you might fear Him?' Then he did show him the great sign. But he rejected it and disobeyed. Furthermore,

axe cuts in this forest and only Your knowledge is in force. Your axe cuts off the unnecessary or unwholesome branches, allowing others to grow and develop. Only You know which branch will be cut, and which branch will grow and bear fruit. The branches you prune dry up and are thrown into the fire.

What branch has speech to challenge the axe of fate? What branch can say, "Don't cut me, I too want to grow and bear the fruit You wish.?"

As long as there is no way to escape the hand of fate, and acceptance of destiny is an unavoidable necessity, my Lord, I too have a request of You: For the sake of the power and justice in that divine axe of Yours, take pity on me! Take pity on all those who are confused as I am and straighten our crooked path! Illuminate our insides with the light of the shariat and the light of the path which leads to You! Let the branch of our bodies too bear the fruit You wish.

Pharaoh fainted away while thus in prayer and after a while woke up. He shook himself and said:

Amazing! I pass the whole night with God. I pray to Him and entreat. When I am like this, I am no different than Moses. In my solitary retreat I promise myself that I will follow Moses, accept his religion, give up pretension to divinity and become a bondsman, but I cannot do it. And as long as I cannot, it is as if I have woken from a beautiful dream and am plunged into a nightmare.

Just as when false gold is held to a fire, the gilt on it melts off and the black of the iron or copper beneath is visible, the spiritual gilt of my time in retreat disappears when I go before the people and confront Moses in the sunlight. The darkness within me spreads over my whole being.

Are not both my heart and my form under God's command? Can He not, if He so wishes, in one instant make me an unwavering friend of His sublime being? And does He not do so anyway? Sometimes I am His friend. And sometimes I am no more than an empty skin. At His command I am a fruitful crop, and at His command I wither and become dry straw.

Is it not the Lord who sometimes brightens us like the moon and sometimes makes us utterly black?

We are tiny balls sent this way and that by the bat of His will in the realm of "Be! And it was."

Thus we keep running this way and that in the realms of place and not-place. For before God self-disclosed in this realm of manifestation, showing His being and beauty by means of these transient beings, he was like a hidden treasure in the Unseen realm. That Unseen realm of His was a realm of not-place, of placelessness. Then by means of His sublime will He created this realm where we are also. This realm came to be with His command, "Be! And is was." It came into manifestation and self-disclosed as a realm of place. It is the bat of God's power and will which sends up this way and that like tiny balls in this realm of place.

Thus does colorlessness become captive to color. God conceals His oneness and brings plurality, its contrary, into manifestation. God's names, which are in fact the name

---

he turned his back, striving hard. Then he gathered his men and made a proclamation, saying, 'I am your Lord Most High!'" (Koran 79: 17-24).

of one single Being, take on varied qualities in this realm of manifestation and appear to be in conflict with one another. That is why Moses comes into conflict with his own self.

For example, when Messenger Moses came together with Khizir in order to learn knowledge of the divine [*ledün ilmi*], he promised not to object to mysteries Khizir would reveal, but when Khizir manifested mysteries not in accord with worldly realities, Moses did object. Differences ensued between them.

It is understood here that the rays of the sun may remain one in color only if they do not strike differing bodies in this realm of created things. It is our differing bodies, separate in color, which paint even the monochrome light of the sun in varied hues.

This means that in order for Moses and Pharaoh to make peace with each other, get along and become united, having not even the slightest difference between them, both of them must rise to the degree of colorlessness.

For these varied beings of contrary color are apparent only in this realm of plurality. In that realm of unity called the realm of not-place there is no contradiction or separation. In that realm spirits no longer have contradictory qualities. It was only when they heard the command "Be!" and came into this world of appearances that they took on the colors of soul and nature and entered into varied forms. They became the representatives of differing qualities. That is how the contraries we see in this world came to be.

In this worldly realm it is possible to become free of color only by learning the secret of that world of oneness. In order to do that we must attain a maturity transcending every kind of plurality, duality and contrariety. For people who have been able to arrive at that degree, life in our world is without contrariety, as in that realm of oneness, and appears in the state of a totality.

If you do not understand this talk of oneness and ask us about the war between Moses and Moses—how can color be freed of itself, how can these contrary colors be gone, and no argument remain?—consider that what we have said—that colorlessness is born of the unification of contrary colors—is not for this world of plurality of ours but for that realm of oneness whose path we tread.

The point to be emphasized here is: Since this realm of color came into manifestation from a realm of colorlessness, how can it be that it now wars against colorlessness?

The answer is that each thing is known by its contrary. If not for plurality, the value and significance of oneness would not be known, and the same it true of color and colorlessness, evil and goodness, ugliness and beauty and especially death—which is to say nothingness, and existence. And that is also the reason why there are kafirs and people who are unrighteous, lustful, without character and without faith, along with prophets, friends, believers and people with pure hearts and spirits loyal to the Creator.

The true reality of spirit [*gerçek mânâ*] has no color. It transcends all color and form. Colors and forms are beautiful and meaningful only to the extent that they are spiritual.

This means that color came into manifestation from colorlessness, and form from spirit. Although each came from the other, it is natural that they should appear to be contraries, and in fact be contraries.

Water trickles down to a dry olive tree, and it bears fruit. Olive oil is pressed from olives. But although it is derived from water, oil will not mix with water and appears to be its opposite. Although those on the face of the earth attached to light and those attached to darkness derive from the same source, they differ from one another as water does from olive oil.

Just as the rose blooms on a thorny stalk and the thorn grows on a stalk from which the rose blooms, and more importantly, as the rose comes from the thorn and the thorn from the rose, many a prophet on the face of the earth is the child of kafirs who in their time knew nothing of God.

So it is no empty matter that spirit is the opposite of soul, and the spiritual the opposite of the soul-inclined. All these things are mysteries arranged by the divine Being, and the expression of those mysteries in this realm of contraries. The disagreements and conflicts between the spiritual and the soul-inclined are in fact a ruse which keeps these mysteries from becoming known.

You may think of it as the pretense to disagreement between donkey-traders which they use to spark the interest of customers.

But this is neither mystery nor ruse, it is amazement in amazement. For all these colors, actions, forms and mysteries and play are due to the skills of the puppet Master behind the screen. The art is to know the Master behind the screen, to love Him and hasten to be with Him. When the curtain falls and all the actors in the visible play disappear, only the reality which never dies will remain.

Be one of the treasure-hunters in this ruin. But don't be fooled into thinking you have found a treasure. The illusion that one has found the treasure of oneness fools many spirits and leaves them far from that treasure, which may be found only through love.

Illusions and suppositions are like cultivated fields. Treasures are not buried in cultivated places. Neither the degree of annihilation nor the treasure of oneness is found by supposing one knows or has found them. The sole way to this grace is through annihilation in God.

In inhabited places one sees colors, forms, and the vain squabbles of life lived among them.

There are no such limitations in the realm of colorlessness. Only those who have come to be ashamed of being and so have attained annihilation are found there.

The world in which we find ourselves is one of metaphorical being. We are in this world and within a bodily form. Those who are annihilated in God are in that vastness of not-being [*yokluk*] which is a spiritual realm. But we came to this world not because we fled from not-being, but because we were sent here. That is why we do not complain of not-being and may even be longing for it. If there had not been One who sent us out of not-being into this metaphorical being, would we ever have left that spiritual realm?

The friends on the face of the earth are in fact members of the realm of not-being. They have long since reached colorlessness while within our world of colors and forms.

Those defeated by their souls scatter before these friends. And they suppose it is they themselves who flee the friends; in reality it is the friends who flee from them. Because the friends have been called to God's path they know who will find the way and who will not. Even if the people of guidance appear to invite others to the path, they expel the erring bodies among them.

It is like the story about the people who nailed their horses' shoes on backwards to fool those who were chasing them.

O simple man! Do you suppose that Pharaoh felt hatred for Moses of his own accord?

Don't be fooled! Would Pharaoh have hated Moses, or even had the strength to hate him, against the wishes of Moses?

This means that Pharaoh fled from Moses because, in reality, Moses was pushing Pharaoh away.

****

THE REASON WHY THE WRETCHED ARE DISAPPOINTED IN BOTH WORLDS: "*HE HAS LOST THE WORLD AND THE LIFE TO COME.*"

2520.   Since the little philosopher is convinced
      The earth is yolk of an egg-like firmament
      When someone asked how this earth remains constant
      In the middle of the sky encircling it
      Hanging like a lamp suspended in the air
      Neither moving to the bottom or top there
      That philosopher said, "It stays in the sky
      Because of the pull exerted from six sides
      The sky is like a dome molded of magnet
      The earth like iron suspended inside it."

2525.   "How should the clear firmament," said someone else
      Work to draw the opaque earth unto itself?
      No, it repels the earth from six directions
      The earth stands amidst forceful inclinations."
      And because the Perfect exert repulsion
      The spirits of Pharaohs stay in perdition
      So, being rejected by this world and that
      Those lost ones are left without both this and that
      If you turn from the Lord of Majesty's slaves
      Know they view your existence as a malaise

2530.   They have the amber, and when they take it out
      They make the straw of your existence distraught
      Instantly, when they put their amber away
      They turn your submission into brutish rage
      Your state is like that of animality
      Which is slave and subject to humanity
      Know humanity is subject to the friends
      O master, as the animals are to men
      Ahmed called all the world's people his servants
      Rightly guiding them; read: "*Say: O my servants.*"[130]

2535.   Your mind is like a camel-driver, and you
      The camel it drives under its bitter rule
      The friends are the intellect of intellects
      The intellects are like camels they direct
      Come now, look upon the friends with due esteem
      For a hundred thousand souls there's one to lead

---

130. "Say: O my servants who have transgressed against their own selves! Do not despair of the mercy of God. For God forgives all sins; He is the Forgiving, the Compassionate" (Koran 39:53).

What camel-driver? What guide? Get you an eye
So that you may behold the sun with that eye
See a world that's been left nailed fast in the night
The day suspended, awaiting the sun's light
2540.   Here in a speck of dust is concealed a sun
In the fleece of a tame lamb, a fierce lion
Here's an ocean hid under a blade of grass
Don't step hesitantly on that piece of grass!
To feel hesitant and to have inner doubt
About the guide is a mercy come from God
Each prophet has come into the world alone
A hundred worlds hid within and yet alone
Enchanting the macrocosm by his force
Folding himself up inside a tiny form
2545.   Foolish people see him as alone and weak
When could the Shah's companion ever be weak?
The fools say he's just a man and nothing more
Woe to those who think not on the hereafter

A poor philosopher who believed in nature rather than in God was likening our world in the center of the domes of the sky to the yolk of an egg. The heavenly spheres were the like white of the egg, and the earth its yolk.

Someone was curious and said, "Alright, but how does the earth stay in the center of these spheres? Does it hang in the air like a lamp which does not rise up or come down? Why is that?"

The philosopher answered: "It stays where it hangs in the air because the sky draws it in six directions at once. Think of a sphere made of lodestone. Our world is like a piece of iron put in the center, that is why it does not move from its place."

Another philosopher said just the opposite: "This pure firmament, this subtle dome, cannot attract dark, dense earth to itself. Far from attracting it from six sides, the dome of the sky repels it in six directions, not allowing it to approach, and thus does the world remain hanging in place amidst strong winds."

Both philosophers spoke of their own imaginings. The truth is certainly not like that. Only the second philosopher's description resembles ours. The friends who have come to our world as sublime spirits and attained the degree of colorlessness, like invisible winds, repel from their center the souls of Pharaohs and keep them at a distance. That is why the unfortunate spirits of the Pharaohs, despite their occasional efforts to understand the truth, remain in darkness and error.

They are acceptable neither in this world nor the next. Neither world is their friend.

If you do not want to be one of the deprived, seek and find the friends of God and be among those close to them. If you are not trying to find them, if you are not seeking them out, it means that those pure spirits are the ones keeping you far from them.

Rejection or acceptance, both are theirs to command. If you are uncertain whether you are one of the rejected or one of the accepted, turn within yourself and listen to your own spirit. If there is in your heart a profound love and inclination toward them, be glad for your good fortune. For your state is a sign of your acceptance by them.

The word *kehribar*, meaning "amber," is made up of the word *keh*, meaning "straw," and the suffix *rübâ*, meaning "-attracting." In the hearts of God's friends there is a spiritual amber which shines with the love of God. When they bring out this heart-amber, they attract the straw of your transient existence to their path; they make you fall madly in love with them and with the One who is in reality the greatest Beloved of all beings.

But if they hide that heart-amber from you, you will approach neither them nor God. It will be your fate to be guided by no light and have no portion of any spirituality.

You know that after spirits break away from God they go through various stages in this world. One of these stages is the mineral, another the vegetal, another the animal, and another the human stage. Every spirit in the animal stage is dominated by mankind.

O Master, know well that those who have attained the level of the friends dominate mankind to the same degree. As much as humans possess and command animals, a friend of God has that much power to dispose of a spirit whose level is still that of humanity [*beşer*].

And so when Hazret Muhammed showed his community the way, he addressed all the creatures of the world, "Say, O my servants." This is a verse of the Gracious Koran: "O Muhammed! Say in My name: O my servants who have transgressed against their own selves! Do not despair of the mercy of God. For God forgives all sins; He is the Forgiving, the Compassionate."

Although when Hazret Muhammed used the form of address "My servants!" he did so in God's name, the one speaking in the language of divine revelation is Muahmmed. Just as the people of a padishah or vizier are considered his servants, God's servants are also considered the servants of His caliph on earth, Muhammed.

Consider that it is your intellect which shows your body the way and leads it to function. Your intellect is like the camel-driver and you are like the camel. No body can act contrary to the command of intellect.

God's friends are the intellect of intellects. This means that other intellects conform to their intellect as the body conforms to the human intellect; other intellects are like bodily parts. Like camels in an infinite caravan, humans all conform to this intellect of intellects, these friends of God. All the creatures in the universe, human, animal, vegetable and mineral, are traces [*eser*] of the universal intellect which embodies them in the realm of appearance, and thus their conformity to it.

So pay close attention to the friends of God! With them get free of body and form, become spirit! You will see that in reality one of them leads a hundred thousand spirits, showing the way like a torch for a caravan making the pilgrimage to Mecca.

You will see that all spirits are at the disposal and under the command of that mighty spirit who is the Axis of the Age [*zamanın kutbu*].

When I call him a leader or a camel-driver, I am speaking metaphorically. I portray those friends of God in forms and bodies. But this is an error. In reality they are not bodies, not forms visible to the eye, but the eyes which see the great Reality. Each of them is a gaze which sees the sun of Reality wherever it looks. This gaze is like the sight of God gazing into the vast nothingness and emptiness of not-being and seeing His own being, His own beauty, as if in a mirror. If you have intelligence, know and find that friend of God, that seer of truth, who gazes thus at whatever he gazes at and sees thus whatever he sees, so that you may distinguish the baseless from the true.

Although this world [*cihân*] remains nailed to the emptiness of night and the darkness of night, all its hope is in the sun and the daylight. It knows that for every night there is a day. Darkness is the darkness of ignorance, heedlessness, infidelity and riot, while the sun of guidance must rise in order for deeds and acts to emerge.

But the world also knows that there is a sun concealed in every mote and many a male lion lies concealed in a sheep's skin. One day those motes will become suns and the lion under the sheepskin will roar.

There is a hidden ocean underneath this straw you see spread over the ground. The bodies, the flesh and the souls of this earth are the straw on top of the sea, and the mysteries of the world and its truths full of wisdom are the sea underneath. If you step contemptuously upon the straw, you will find yourself in a sea that will drown you. But if you give your heart to the divine wisdom here, the same sea will drench you in light.

But it may also be that you will not look for the sun in the mote or the lion under the sheepskin, that in short, you will not be able to seek a murshid. In that case, look upon the person before you as a human being. Love him or her as a person and regard every person you see as God's beloved. No one has ever lost anything by looking favorably upon others, it is unfavorable regard which does not show to us the sun in the mote and the lion under the sheepskin. But when you have once seen the sun, you can no longer say it is not there. As for the doubts and indecision you feel in the search that will bring you to such a light, there is God's mercy inside each one.

Every one of the prophets is an individual indistinguishable from others, like the motes in which suns wander.

You know the expression "macrocosm." The macrocosm is in reality the heart of a perfect human. That a perfect human carries the greatest of realms within a plain, unremarkable body like anyone else's is without doubt the power and wisdom of God.

The art is to become aware of this power and wisdom. For so many people deprived of intellect have said, "How can this man be a prophet? He is no different than you or I." They did not consider that if a padishah takes the weakest, puniest of men as a friend, that man suddenly becomes much more powerful than other men.

If a spirit is chosen by God and made his confidant and companion, how powerful will he be? It is this that the heedless do not consider.

Why and to what degree is a prophet or a messenger or friend of God, though apparently weak and unremarkable, in reality more powerful than others, or why is he like the most powerful of the powerful? If you want to know this, listen now to the story I will tell of Messenger Salih and his camel.

****

How the Eyes of External Sense saw Salih and his She-Camel to be of low Account and without Kin, for when God wishes to destroy an Army He makes them appear in the Sight of their Adversaries to be of low Account and few in Number although the Adversary be Superior, and *"He made you seem few in their eyes so that God might bring to pass a thing that was to be done."*

Salih's she-camel was a camel in form
That cruel tribe in their ignorance did her harm
Since they hated her because she drank water
They became ingrates blind to bread and water

God's she-camel drank water from stream and cloud
It was God's water that they withheld from God

2550. His camel, like the bodies of righteous men
Was an ambush to destroy villainous men

To show what *"Let God's she-camel drink!"*[131] wrought then
On that people through decree of death and pain

The representative of God's wrath prescribed
A entire city as the camel's blood-price

His spirit is Salih, the camel, his flesh
The spirit arrives, the flesh is in distress

The Salih-spirit's not touched by accidents
Blows fall on the camel, not on the essence

2555. The Salih-spirit cannot feel any ill
The light of God's not subject to kafirs' will

Spirit attached the body of dust to it
So they might be tried for the harm they do it

Not knowing that to hurt it is to hurt Him
The jug's water is connected to the stream

God made it attached a bodily form
So it would keep the entire world from harm

Over their hearts there is no one who prevails
Damage is done not to pearls but to their shells

2560. To the camel of the body of the friend
Be a slave, to be the Salih-spirit's friend

"Since you're envious," Salih told the Thamud
"In three days punishment will arrive from God

After three days more, He who takes away life
Will send a calamity that has three signs

All your faces will be altered in color
They will appear to be varied in color

On the first day your faces will be saffron
On the second, red like the *argawan*[132]

2565. On the third day all your faces will be black
God's subjugation will arrive after that

If you seek from me sign of this punishment
The she-camel's foal has to the mountain fled

There is recourse if you can capture it there
Else the bird of hope has now escaped the snare."

No one was able to overtake the foal
Gone in the mountains, he was invisible

Like the pure spirit that from the tight body

---

131. "But God's Messenger said to them: 'It is a she-camel of God, let her have her drink!' Then they rejected him and they hamstrung her. So their Lord obliterated their traces on account of their crime and leveled them" (Koran 91:13-14).

132. A flowering tree whose pink to red blooms appear in spring and soon fall to carpet the ground.

Takes flight to be with the Lord of all bounty
2570. "See, that destiny can't be escaped," he said
It has deprived your hope's phantom of its head."
What is the she-camel's foal? It's Salih's heart
Which you may regain by good deeds on your part
If you do regain his heart, then you are saved
Otherwise despair and bite your arms in shame
When they heard the punishment that was promised
They cast down their eyes and waited there for it
They saw their faces turn yellow on day one
They heaved cold sighs in dread anticipation
2575. On the second day their faces all turned red
The time had been lost for hope and repentance
Their faces all became black on the third day
Salih's prediction came true without delay
When they all were cast adrift despairingly
Like crouching birds they fell down on their two knees
Trusted Gabriel, to explain this kneeling
Conveyed to the Prophet the word *jāthimīn*[133]
Kneel down in this way when they are teaching you
And they make you fear such a dread kneeling too
2580. They were awaiting the wrathful blow of God
It came and leveled the city all to naught
Salih was alone and went toward the city
He saw that it was wrapped up in smoke and heat
He heard a wailing rise up from their limbs there
There was wailing, but the wailers were nowhere
The wails that he heard were coming from their bones
Tears of blood flowed from their spirits like hailstones
Salih heard that and began to weep himself
He began to wail for those who wailed themselves
2585. "O you people who have lived in vain," He said
"On account of you before God I have wept
'Be patient with their iniquity,' God said
'Give them counsel, they do not have much time left.'
I said, 'Counsel is dammed up by cruelty
Counsel's milk flows forth from love and purity
They have heaped upon me so much cruel bane
The milk of counsel has curdled in my veins.'
God said to me, 'I will give to you a boon
I will lay a healing salve upon those wounds.'
2590. God made my heart as clear and pure as the sky
All your cruel tyranny went out of my mind
I was giving admonition once again

---

133. "So the earthquake took them unawares, and in the morning they crouched kneeling in their houses" (Koran 7:78).

Parables and phrases like sugar again
From the sugar I was producing fresh milk
And with my words I mixed in honey and milk
Inside you these phrases became like poison
Because you were poison root and foundation
Now that grief is overthrown, why should I grieve?
O obstinate people, you were grief to me
2595.   Does anyone lament when sorrow is dead?
Who tears his hair when a sore heals on his head?"
Then he turned to himself, "O mourner," he said
They are not worthy of mourning for the dead."
Don't mind my misquoting, correctly recite:
"Say: How shall I mourn a tyrannical tribe?"[134]
Yet he still found his heart and eye were weeping
Mercy shone in him involuntarily
He was bewildered that his tears kept raining
Drops without cause from the ocean of bounty
2600.   "Why these tears?"—his intellect was questioning
"Are such mockers worthy of so much weeping?
Tell me what you weep for, their evil pretense?
For the soldiers of their ill-shod resentments?
For their dark hearts encrusted over with rust?
For their tongues like vipers, vile and venomous?
For their teeth like those of *sagsār*[135] and their breath
For their mouths and for their eyes like scorpions' nests?
For their sneering mockery and contention?
Give thanks to God that He put a stop to them
2605.   Their hands are perverse, their feet, their eyes perverse
Their love is perverse, their peace, their rage perverse
To conform and raise the flag of tradition
They stepped on the face of the sage of reason
Not seeking a sage, they became old donkeys
Mimicking each other's nods as do donkeys
Out of Paradise God conveyed His bondsmen
To show those nourished by Hellfire unto them."

The story of Salih, God's peace be upon him, is told in the Koran in 7:73-79, 11:61-68 and 25:38. This warning example was repeated again and again.

Messenger Salih's camel seemed no different from any other camel. That cruel tribe, because of their ignorance, did not know the wisdom and truth of this camel. They killed it because it drank from a spring low on water and they thought it was preventing their own camels from drinking more.

They withheld from one of God's camels the water He had destined for it. Its water

---

134. ". . . How shall I mourn a tribe of kafirs?" (Koran 7:93).
135. The *sagsar* is a terrifying imaginary creature with the head of a dog, the beard of a goat, and the ears of an elephant.

came from rivers and clouds. One day humans drank from this water, another, camels cooled themselves with it. The water kept flowing to the same degree. God left no creature without water.

The tribe condemned only Salih's camel to be deprived of this right and of life. For that they met with the punishment of God. They were killed. Their bodies quenched the thirst of grave ditches. They became food for graves.

Messenger Salih's camel represents the righteous [*salih*], the friends and the prophets. Thus it is very dangerous to do evil to those who have earned intimacy with God, it can be cause of disappointment in both worlds. God protects His righteous ones, even creating means to punish violently those who do them evil.

Messenger Salih told the Thumud Tribe that the camel God created should drink its share of water, wanting to warn them against evil. This is described in the ninety-first chapter of the Gracious Koran: "When the most wicked man of the Thamud nation rose in rebellion, they disavowed the messenger sent to them. God's messenger showed them his camel and said, 'Do not touch this camel of God's or her share of water.'

"But they thought him a liar and they killed his camel. And because of their crimes God destroyed them and leveled them with the ground."

None of the kafirs, great or small, escaped. There was a horrific earthquake. The she-camel cost the kafirs dearly. The entire city with all its living creatures was razed to the ground.

Why is that these ignorant peoples in every place and time never listen to the righteous who are intimate with God?

Why are they ungrateful and evil to those who recommend goodness to them and show them the right and beautiful way?

Do they not know that no one should offend the spirits of God's friends. For their spirits are like Messenger Salih. And they are in a continuous state of union with God. The body is like the camel. It has many needs.

This means that a righteous spirit who has arrived at union with God has no energy left to feel blows to the body. Such spirits are joyful in that great union, they do not feel material pains. Whatever torment may be applied to their bodies, such spirits are not harmed by it.

Once a spirit has arrived at the degree of coming alive in God, not even bodily death, let alone torment, can overshadow even for an instant the pleasure and joy it feels. For the spirit in the body is like a pearl in a shell. At the worst, blows struck by evil hurt their shells, not the pearl within.

Salih's spirit without a doubt represents the spirits of the friends and prophets. Or the pure and limpid spirits of believers who have conformed to the prophets and succeeded in overcoming their souls. It is the spirit on the path of God, and such spirits are never really defeated by external threats and harm.

For the water of spirit hidden in the jug of the body of a friend has in fact truck with that divine river and is nourished by it. In that sense the light seen in the face of a friend is reflected from that luminous river. That is why God says in a sacred hadith, "Whoever treats ill a friend of Mine has in truth declared war upon Me." A hadith of the Prophet says, "He who offends me offends God."

The answer to the question of what the friends and prophets, whose spirits have truck with God, seek on the face of the earth is that people who wish to reach God may see the light of God self-disclosed in the friends, and be illuminated by it and take it as a guide and example to themselves and be purified of worldly filth and attain to faith, the light of truth, in a word, God.

This, then, is why no blow struck by tyrants or kafirs can reach the spirits of the friends. At most it can harm their bodies.

If you have an intellect, be slave and servant to the camel of the bodies of the friends, so that you may be companion to Messenger Salih! Like his, let your spirit flow into the divine river.

Messenger Salih said to the Tribe of Thamud:

You have followed your own envy and killed an innocent camel. God will ask you to account for this, and in three days will deliver unto you His great punishment. On the first day signs of the punishment will appear and all of your faces will change color. You will see each other's faces in different colors. First your faces will become yellow like saffron, then on the second day red like the flowers of the argawan tree, and on the third day black as ebony.

Yes, all of these things will happen and you will see them. If any of you want to avoid these disasters, the only way is for you to find the camel's foal which has just now fled to the mountains.

If you go and find that foal and take tender care of it, your punishment may be withdrawn."

Those among the Thamud who heard this and feared the punishment went running after the foal.

But the foal represents the pure spirit. It had escaped from its cage among bodily filth and filthy bodies and took the path to that One who owns the worlds that disperse grace and bounty. The Thamud tribesmen who went in search for the camel foal in the mountains could not find it.

Messenger Salih said to them: "You have lost your last chance to change your fate. Once the fate God has assigned becomes destiny, no power can overcome it."

To have offended to the very heart a person whose closeness to God is evident can sometimes make all efforts to mollify him ineffective. The art is never to offend such hearts in the first place and so not be left without recourse in the end. For this one must transcend the veils of ignorance, and in order to reach the lights of truth, one must be wakeful. Repentance made out of fear alone is of no use, one must be sincere.

But there was nothing left for the Thamud tribe to do. They waited in profound fear for the signs of the first day and indeed on that day they saw each other's faces turn yellow like saffron.

On the second day the color was red.

On the third day the faces of the people of the Thamud tribe were now black. They no longer appeared human and their behavior was not human. Then they came to their knees.

And as it says in the seventh chapter of the Koran, Gabriel the Trusted brought this verse to Hazret Muhammed: "So the earthquake took them unawares, and in the morning they crouched kneeling in their houses."

O you who only fear when disaster has become manifest and only then see the power of God's wrath and kneel, and only at such times pray God and take refuge in Him! You have heard the story.

Kneel on the ground before it is too late! See in time the friends of God giving counsel and showing the way; hear their beautiful voices in time, so that when the moment of fear and destiny descends, your knees will not strike upon hard stone.

But for the Thamud tribe there was nothing left to be done. They waited for God's wrath and final self-disclosure. This punishment came right on time and an earthquake brought the underside of the earth to the surface. Black-faced, on their knees, all creatures were buried under the earth in an instant. Wails were heard coming from their broken bodies, or from the parts of their bodies. Their bones wailed, the eyes of their souls shed tears onto the black earth.

Messenger Salih could not bear this state of affairs. He wept as well. He began wailing for those wailing in the earth.

Salih called out a last time to these people, whose bodies like their faces were buried in the black ground: "O you who have chosen the wrong path, I wept like this for you when you were alive, and I complained to God. I suffered much from your cruelty. Now your bodies are no longer alive. But your spirits have begun to confront the truth."

This is like what Hazret Muhammed said to his dying enemies at the Battle of Badr: "We have found what our God promised to us, have you found what your lord promised you?"

Hazret Umar asked him, "O Muhammed, why are you addressing bodies which no longer have souls?" The Prophet answered: "O Umar! They hear what I say better than you do."

****

Messenger Salih continued to reflect upon the dead of the Thamud tribe:

> God told me to bear with cruelty and continue advising them, for their time of death was near. I begged God, saying, "My Lord! They treat me very cruelly, and I can no longer feel love for them and advise them. You know that one must love in order to advise." God told me that He would do me a kindness and heal my wounds.
>
> Thus my Lord made my heart as pure as the heavens. He erased all painful memories from within me and I spoke sweetly to the Thamud tribe, saying, "I will advise you again."
>
> But my words still had a poisonous effect on you. For even sugar does no good to beings created of poison.
>
> What has died along with you today is my sufferings. But still I am unhappy. Who on earth has shed tears for the death of his sufferings? O wailing man, they have gone beneath the earth, they are not worthy of your tears!

In the Koran God spoke in the language of Messenger Shuayb: "O my people! I vow that I have told you the words of my Lord. I gave you advice. Why should I feel sorry for a denying people?" (7:93).

This is what Messenger Salih felt at that moment as well. But still the pain in his heart was not lessened. Tears flowed from his eyes. He himself wondered at his tears. God's sea of generosity overflowed and it was as if the vastness of forgiveness was gathered up in his eyes in the form of tears.

He kept asking himself why he was weeping. What was he weeping for? For the ugly faces and ugly actions of the dead? For the black darkness of their hearts? For their tongues spewing poison, for their dog-like teeth, for the scorpion's nest of their eyes and mouths?

Should you not give thanks that your Lord has covered over all of these evils with the mighty earth, hiding all their ugliness and evil with veils of earth?

Why do you regret the loss of such a tribe, whose hands, feet, eyes, hearts and every state is perverse and ugly? What is the mystery hidden in this heartfelt emotion for the loss of those who did nothing all their loves but follow Satan?

They who closed their eyes to all truth, taking only the path to imitation. While they could have been freed from their souls, they were donkeys instead. God sent them a prophet to guide and illuminate them. So that the spirits worthy of Hell and their hellish ways should be evident, and those heading for Hell should see the path to Paradise.

But alas, between the two is a veil which although not apparent to the eye keeps the deniers separate from God's pure bondsmen, like the barzakh which keeps the two seas apart, one salt, one sweet.

****

ON THE MEANING OF *"HE LET THE TWO SEAS GO TO MEET; BETWEEN THEM IS A DIVISION THEY DO NOT SEEK TO CROSS."*[136]

Those of Fire and Paradise are in one shop
Yet between them *is a space they do not cross*

2610. Those for the Fire are with those for Light mixed in
He has raised the Mountain of Qaf between them
Like earth and gold in a mine, divided by
A hundred deserts and caravanserais
Like white pearls and beads of jet in a necklace
Mixing for only a single night like guests
The sea has one half which is like sugar sweet
Bright in color as the full moon, in taste sweet
The other half is like snake's venom bitter
Dark as pitch in color, and in taste bitter

2615. Wave on wave, both halves dash against each other
From beneath and from above like seawater
They seem to collide, for material form
Is narrow; spirits are mixed in peace and war
The waves of peace dash against one another
From the breasts of mankind digging up rancor
The waves of war in another form confound
Tossing affairs of love up and upside-down
The bitter ones are drawn to the sweet by love
Righteousness is the foundation of all love

2620. Wrath carries away the sweet to bitterness
How should the bitter be suited to sweetness?
Bitter and sweet are not apparent to sight
They can be seen through the window of hindsight
The eye that sees the hereafter sees rightly

---

136. Koran 55:19-20.

The animal eye is proud and sees wrongly
Oh many are they who are sweet as sugar
But there is poison concealed in the sugar
Clever men will know the smell from a distance
Others when it gets as far as teeth and lips
2625. Their lips will prevent it from reaching the throat
Though the Devil be shouting, "Swallow it up!"
In another's throat it will declare itself
And in another's body unmask itself
In another it will burn as excrement
It will teach of its entry by its exit
Another will know it after months and days
Another only in the depths of the grave
And if he be given respite in the grave
It will become known on Resurrection Day
2630. All sweetmeats and sugar candies in the world
Have a respite and time for them to mature
Years are needed for the ruby in sunshine
To achieve tint and luster and brilliant shine
In the space of two months vegetables mature
The red rose reaches perfection in a year
For this reason almighty, glorious God
Spoke of the appointed term in the Koran[137]
You've heard this discourse; let all your hairs be ears
It's the Water of Life; if you've drunk, good cheer!
2635. Don't call it discourse, call it Water of Life
Behold in the old letter's body new life
O my friend, to another point now give ear
Like the spirit, subtle and completely clear
This poison and snake, at a certain station
Is digestible through God's dispensation
In one place it's poison, in another, cure
There it is blasphemy, here it is lawful
Although it is harmful to the spirit there
It becomes medicine when it reaches here
2640. The juice is sour in the young and unripe grape
But sweet and good is the fully ripened grape
As wine it's bitter and unlawful again
But as vinegar excellent seasoning

The meaning of the Koranic verse, "He let the two seas go . . . " is that there is a barrier between the two seas which prevents the water of the salt sea from mixing with that of the sweet. One continues to be salt, while the other continues to be sweet.

Yet compared with the vastness of the seas, how narrow and delicate is the division

137. "It is He who created you from clay and then decreed an appointed term; and another appointed term with Him"(Koran 6:2).

between them! It is only because the veil is God's veil that it can bear the weight of the two seas without effort. Although those of Paradise and those of Hell appear to sit side by side in the same shop, they are as distant from one another as stars in the sky. An invisible veil prevents those who wil go to Paradise from mixing with those who will fall into Hell.

The people of light and the people of fire seem to be mixed together. But in reality they are as far from each other as if the Qaf Mountains had been placed between them.

It is as it is with gold and earth, which are found together. Although they have been breast-to-breast for untold ages, still earth remains earth and gold never becomes earth.

If you string true and false pearls together side by side, a pearl does not become a bead and a bead does not become a pearl. Even if they all appear to be pearls when worn around the neck of a beautiful woman at night, when the day dawns they are fated to return to their own stations.

Even when there is no barrier, the water of the same sea can be half sweet, half salt, half pure and clear, the other half dark and dense as pitch.

To be sure, it is not only waters and minerals that do not mix, but spirits as well. The spirits of God's friends and prophets and the pure bondsmen who conform to them remain pure and sublime like gold, or clear, shining water among many an evil spirit that has lost its way, blackened in intellect and heart.

As the ocean moves in waves from below and above as if trying to mix these two waters of separate natures, but does not succeed in doing so, the various events of life and fate throw different-spirited people together but bandit spirits and sincere spirits still do not blend into one another.

There are in the tiny human body opposing waves of movement also. The soul and spirit, the material and spiritual, collide and these conflicts sometimes arouse desires for war and destructive feelings in humans, and sometimes feelings of peace, goodness and quiet. These opposing feelings which arise within one body are without doubt reflections of God's attributes of domination and kindness self-disclosing in humans.

Sometimes people quarrel and the desires in their hearts for conflict with others become an irresistible passion. Cities are destroyed, blood is shed, heads roll.

Sometimes this self-disclosure of subjugation comes to a stop, God's self-disclosures of kindness begin and the world takes on the appearance of a sparkling realm of quietude under a sun of peace and calm.

People begin to love one another. A sweetness embraces the bitter feelings in spirits.

In all this turmoil the good and beautiful spirits continue to long for the good and the beautiful. The evil spirits try ceaselessly to increase the pleasure they derive from evil. As a result, the good are reunited with good and the evil with evil.

Kafirs try to draw believers into infidelity while believers try both to preserve their faith and to rescue kafirs from the path of error they have taken. Love urges people to goodness and rage drives them to evil.

Love is like sweetness and evil like bitterness. Love has the power to make even bitterness sweet. Domination and wrath tries to draw sweetness to bitterness. Thus is the human spirit is tested by instances of kindness and wrath. If a person is among those who see and consider the hereafter [ahir], that is to say, the future, he will see what is right.

But if what he has in view is the barn [ahır]—animal pleasures and passions—surely he will see wrongly. His eyes will be veiled in pride and error.

The effect upon the human spirit of these two opposing self-disclosures, of love and wrath, beauty and majesty [*cemâl ve celâl*], is light that of light coming through two different windows.

There are things which appear to be sweet and subtle and which worldly people suppose to be God's kindness and bounty. But wrath and poison is hidden inside what appears to be sugar. That is why our Messenger Efendi has said: "Paradise is encircled by difficulties and things not pleasing to the soul, while Hell is encircled by delights, lusts, entertainments and pleasures."

That is why the venom of snakes is concealed in many things sweet as sugar. As Hazret Ali said:

That the mercy and forgiveness of God the Truth is concealed within difficulty, and His wrath and violence within bounties and delights—there is certainly great wisdom, concealed or obvious, in all of this.

But again it is those who have reached perfection on the path of God who seem to know the taste of hidden poison by its scent.

Those who remain distant and separate from a share in this path notice the poison in the sweet only when it reaches their teeth, even touches upon their hearts, and when it is without doubt too late.

It is the lip of foresight of those who have set down the path or arrived which, although Satan may invite them with the sweetest voice, saying, "While you eat some of this?" does not take the sweet with poison concealed in its delight into its mouth.

This discernment of delight and poison has degrees and degrees, like the degrees of those who have sent down God's path.

Some sense the poison when it is on their lips, some before it touches their lips. Some try to spit out the poison after they have taken it into their mouths. Some swallow it with great gusto.

Emotions like poison move through the hearts of this last group, and poisonous blood through their veins. They are the souls who do not accept spiritual support, for the cloud of their natures prevents them from seeing the light of the sun.

In many cases the effect of taking poison is delayed by a divine judgment. Some become aware of the poison they have eaten as delicious food only when they pass it as feces. Some sense the pain of it in the grave, when their bodies are covered with earth. Let us call this the torment of the grave. But there are people who do not even sense the poison when in their graves. They can be saved from the torment of the grave by the prayer of a friend of God. Thus they learn of the bitterness they tasted only at the Resurrection.

Many instructions for annihilating the soul have been given. Many ways have been indicated. But the soundest recourse for killing the soul and being able to taste the delights of both God's eternal and spiritual bounties is the maturity of the spirit.

Not only spirits which reach the human degree but even plants, for example, a sugar cane, mature over time. As much as the being of any plant or fruit is obliged to pass through a stage of maturation, so too the cultivation and perfection of the human spirit takes time, according to the requirements of its preparedness and the degree to which it is permitted.

Just as the ruby must be cultivated by the burning sun, and it must so that it may acquire that color of lips, that beauty and shine. This requires uncountable years.

Green plants mature in two months, but a red rose in a year. Every being in this world, be it human, animal or plant, or even mineral, has been given an appointed time of death. God stipulates this in the Koran (7:2):

> It is He who created you from clay and then assigned you an appointed time of death.

Only sublime God knows when that time will come, only He knows the duration of your life on earth and when the Resurrection will come for all creatures.

If you wonder what clay the human was created from, hear this from God as well! For He told Messenger David a secret in this regard, saying, "I created the hearts of those who love and long for Me out of My light. I nourished them with My own beauty. The clay of My friends is the clay of Abraham, Jesus, Moses and Muhammed."

Now, it is not only with your ears, or even your hearts that you should hear all these mysteries and judgments. Hear them with every particle of your being. Let every hair or your body be an ear to hear and a heart to feel. For what I have said is the water of immortal life for those able to sense it. If you have drunk of it, well done. What I call here the water of life is the wisdom within the words. For a spirit to be cultivated and reach maturity, it must go through a period of time required by its preparedness. In what I have said I have lined up old letters in a new order, and given a new life to the letters which the ages have worn away.

Now I will make a new point with the same letters. You know this. It is like the spirit, evident to gnostics. But for those who do not understand such points, it is something which has never been said.

There is a place where the venom of a snake is as sweet and delicious as the water of life, because God has commanded it so. This place is the station of subsistence [*bekâ makamı*].

In this station snake's venom becomes the cure for every ill, and there what is elsewhere infidelity becomes faith. The worldly bounties and bodily delights which are externally delicious but internally bitter are harmful to those who tread the path of God. But this harmfulness is not absolute. For those more advanced on the same path, those who have arrived at perfection, God's empowering [*takdîr*] makes that which is bitter sweet. For those who have reached the degree of annihilation or subsistence, the divine judgment of bounties changes. If you wish for a parable of this, I will tell you about Pharaoh and Solomon, and remind you about Nimrod and Joseph. For Pharaoh and Nimrod worldly dominion and sovereignty was infidelity and error, while for Solomon and Joseph they were faith and good works. Because human delights and the requirements of life are poison to those not yet in command and master of their own souls. For someone who has become a friend of God or a prophet, someone who has risen to the degree of becoming the Truth with the Truth, the same poison performs the function of a healing cure. Thus worldly poisons are for the arrived like trash thrown into the sea. They melt away in the taste of divine love and the waves of the sea of unity and become the same as the sea.

For those who have become slaves to their souls and the pleasures of living, the self-disclosure is the opposite of that.

If they take on spiritual states due to a coincidence, and taste spiritual delights, all these states and delights are lost in the swamp of worldly filth and lust in which they are plunged. If it is a light, it goes out. If it is a flower, it looses its petals and rots, and if a lovely scent, it is overwhelmed by the corruption of the swamp.

So, to rise from evil to goodness, from bitterness to sweetness and from poison to cure depends on the cooking and maturing of the spirit over time in the winds of events and the sun of love.

When grapes are yet unripe there is a bitterness in their juice. But when they ripen and mature, the same juice becomes sweet, tasty and fragrant. Yet if the same juice is poured into a jar and ferments and turns into wine, it becomes bitter again and unlawful. In order for it to become lawful again, it must turn into vinegar.

This means that the purest of God's bounties may lose their purity and taste in the jar of the interiors of those nourished on them. The same grape juice which becomes within immature people lust and madness instead of delight, sheds its sinfulness like vinegar within a mature person. It becomes nourishment and power for the love of God and attraction felt by that person. While it once was matter, it now becomes spirit, love, and faith.

****

ON WHAT IT MEANS THAT THE MURID SHOULD NOT PRESUME TO DO AS THE FRIEND DOES, THAT HALVA DOES NO HARM TO THE PHYSICIAN BUT IS HARMFUL TO THE SICK, AND THAT FROST AND SNOW DO NO HARM TO THE RIPE GRAPE BUT HARM THE YOUNG FRUIT WHICH IS ON THE WAY, FOR HE HAS NOT YET BECOME: *"THAT GOD MAY FORGIVE YOU THE WRONGS YOU HAVE COMMITTED AND THOSE TO FOLLOW."*[138]

If a friend drinks poison it becomes a cure
But if a seeker does, he mind grows darker
From Solomon came: *"O Lord, give me,"* meaning:
"Give none this kingdom and power after me,[139]
Bestow this grace and bounty on none but me."
This was not envy although it seemed to be
2645.   Study the point, *"it suits none,"* with your spirit
Do not think, *"after me,"* is his stinginess
No, he saw in kingdom hundredfold danger
It's always been fear for one's head, hair by hair
Fear for life, fear for soul, fear for religion
There is no other trial for us like this one
One needs a Solomon's spiritual strength
To get through these myriad colors and scents
Even with all the strength that he did possess
The tumult of kingdom still stifled his breath
2650.   Since the dust of this sorrow lay upon him
For all of the world's shahs he felt compassion
He interceded for them and said, "Give them
The perfection You gave me, and this kingdom

---

138. Koran 48:2.
139. Koran 38:35.

> To whomever You give it, and that bounty
> He is Solomon and I also am he
> He is not *'after me,'* no, he is *with me*
> But I have no claimant, so what is *'with me'?"*
> Exposition of this is required, but I
> Will return to tell of the man and his wife

If a friend of God eats poison, he derives from it the delight and power he would have had he eaten honey. But if a murid eats the same poison, the world grows dark before his eyes and he loses his mind and faints away. Here poison represents worldly delights, which cannot overshadow a friend's love of God. But the same worldly delights have such a bad effect on those just beginning on the path, or those who have not even begun, as to make them forget God and His path; such a person loses the light which could take him to God.

It is known that Messenger Solomon asked God for worldly dominion. This is stated in the Koran, 38:35-38: "He said, 'O my Lord, forgive me and grant me a kingdom which will suit none after me, for You are the One who grants bounties.' Then We subjected the wind to his power, to flow gently at his command wherever he willed, and the evil ones, every kind of builder and diver, and others bound together in fetters."

"There were brought before him at eventide coursers of the highest breeding and swift of foot. And he said, 'Truly do I love the love of good in remembrance of my Lord.'"[140] He watched from behind a curtain until the beautiful horses disappeared from view, and then asked for them to be brought back to him and when they arrived he caressed them for a long time as one caresses a lover.

Messenger Solomon's request from God for infinite dominion was not without cause. Solomon wanted dominion only for someone worthy of Him, someone not prideful of dominion, who knew dominion to be a service and a duty for the good of the people. That someone was himself.

This request, which at first glance seems an envious passion for worldly bounty, expresses the idea that peace of mind, goodness and felicity can come to people when dominion is in the hands of those worthy of it, and was a statement of such a faith.

It was not easy to possess worldly dominion. It was filled with many, many dangers. Among these first of all was fear for one's head. But above all there was fear for one's religion, one's conscience.

Dominion had to be in the hands of a person who did not give his heart to worldly delights and worldly governance. They should take it on for the sake of the good and the benefit of the masses, of all humanity, as Solomon did. That is why Messenger Solomon said: "O my Lord, do not give this dominion you have given to me to anyone who cannot bear it, who will be crushed by it, who will lose their way and so harm Your bondsmen." Thus he wished to save his beloved humanity from danger.

But in spite of all his self-confidence and strength and power, worldly dominion still caught him in its prison. He knew that there is no greater test for humans than worldly dominion and delight, and that it is permitted to those who comprehend that this dominion and its beauty are just the appearance of God's divine art and greatness.

That is why, as it says in the thirty-eighth chapter of the Gracious Koran, "One

---

140. Koran 38:31-32.

afternoon he was shown race horses, desired and renowned, which stood on three feet with one hoof raised." While Solomon drifted off in thought gazing at them, he forgot to remember God and did not even notice the sun had set.

And that is why Solomon begged God to give only to the perfect the dominion He'd given to him. "To whomever You are gracious and give such dominion, Solomon is He, and in reality that person is I."

The point here is that persons who occupy the central power driving and directing the masses cannot lose themselves in the being and vitality of the world, that is, worldly dominion and the pleasures of dominion, and lose sight of the true and spiritual goal; they must behave toward the people with justice and goodness. If those to whom dominion is granted act out of this kind of vision and sincerity in governance, they are the Solomons of their time. The dominion and justice which was the portion only of Solomon will find new life in them.

The same parable is doubtless true for all people who are in command of their own souls in the land of their own bodies, performing their function of establishing a stable and balanced spiritual order.

That is why Messenger Solomon said that person was he, that it could be no one but he. Solomon meant that such a person, whether he be a bondsman or a sultan, however far in the future he might be, was in fact the same as he, together with him, and even none but him.

He was saying something on this point which needs explication, even requires it, but let us return to the story of the man and wife, which we left half-finished.

****

THE SUM OF THE STORY OF THE ARAB AND HIS MATE

2655.   A sincere man's heart is now seeking a sum
        Of what passed between the woman and the man
        I've told of what passed between man and woman
        Know they're a likeness of your soul and reason
        This man and woman, who are reason and soul
        Are much needed for telling good from evil
        This necessary pair inside this house of dust
        Spend all the night and day in strife and unrest
        The woman seeks things for the life of the home
        Bread and meat, social rank and reputation
2660.   The soul, like a wife, in order to find means
        Now seeks domination, now humility
        Reason really is not conscious of these thoughts
        All that occupies it is the love of God
        Though this bait and trap's the secret of the tale
        Now hear the entire outward form of the tale
        If spirituality could just be said
        The universe would not have been created
        If love consisted all of meaning and thought
        The form of your fasting and prayer would be naught
2665.   The gifts that friends give to each other in love

Are nothing but forms when compared to their love
So that the gifts may offer testimony
To feelings of love concealed in secrecy
For acts of kindness bear witness outwardly
O wise man, to the love that's felt inwardly
Your witness is sometimes false and sometimes true
Now intoxicated with wine, now yogurt
The man who takes yogurt pretends to be high
He pretends his head is heavy, shouts and cries

2670.   The hypocrite fasts and prays so much so that
People will think he is drunk on love of God
In short, actions are different outwardly
To signify what is conceived inwardly
O Lord, grant us the discernment we request
To know the true indications from the rest
How is discernment acquired by the senses?
When the light of God illumines the senses
And if there's no effect, cause too manifests
Just as when kinship announces love's presence

2675.   When a person's imam is the light of God
He is no longer slave to effect or cause
Love tosses a spark into his inner life
And he's freed from effects as it waxes high
He no longer has need for love's outward signs
For love has shot its own light across the sky
Further details would make this discourse complete
But this is enough for now, you go and seek
And if that meaning within this form is clear
Forms are at once distant from meaning and near

2680.   In showing the way, they are like sap and tree
But quite distant with regard to quiddity
Take leave of quiddities and natures innate
And expound upon that moon-faced couple's state

The heart of a sincere man—Chelebi Husameddin—is wondering about the end of the story. Although this story is thought of as a tale about a man and wife, in reality it tells of the vicissitudes of the intellect and the soul. In the story the intellect is the man and the soul is the woman. In the house of the human body these two are at war, quarreling day and night, asking each other difficult questions of why and wherefore.

At the same time, in order to distinguish good from evil a person must know them, both the intellect and the soul, and all their mysteries and reasons.

Is it not true that woman, that is, the soul, continually speaks of the needs of the home and wants them fulfilled? Food, drink, clothing, pleasure, delight, romance, honor and regard, peace of mind and security—she wants all these things.

She employs various means to obtain them. Sometimes she bows at the man's feet, sometimes she is disdainful and haughty.

All the desires of woman are unknown to the intellect, that is, man. There is nothing in his own being but the love of God the Truth, and so he is far from comprehending these material needs.

The inner side of the story is this tale of taunt and snare, and now you will learn its inner side, its outward side, in short, the whole of it. Consider, if spiritual delights alone were enough, they would fill the world with worship and supplication. The world would lose its worldliness, people would not function, they would not work, they would not do anything, human inventions would not develop and the world could not be improved by the hands of God's bondsmen. Along with the ugly and evil things they do, people would not perform beautiful acts and put forth beautiful works.

The love of God would consist merely of thought and meaning, and people would not rise up with that great love and put forth works singing hymns to rocks and earth. If love of God consisted of meaning alone there could not even be acts of worship in which the body participates, like prayer and fasting.

The gifts people give to those they love do not consist of love and respect alone. Their love and connectedness leads people to give one another material gifts as well.

If love between two persons goes like this, what could be more natural than for a bondsman in love with the greatest Beloved to give his God gifts pertaining to form? Just as to make beautiful works of art out of the variety of materials God has sent into the world, mosques, minarets, prayer-niches, houses, harems, to illuminate texts and write beautiful calligraphy, to build roads and bridges and bring ease to God's bondsmen is to give material gifts to God, in the same way, leading the human body to prayer, fasting, pilgrimage and charity and working lines of form into worship—all of these are heartfelt gifts.

All that is needed is for a perfect love and sincerity, higher than that between two lovers, worthy of the love of God, to be established in a human heart.

Let the love kept in the heart take on forms in the external world, becoming acts and works which prove that love.

For the externalization of love, its function in forms and works, shows first of all its existence, its constructive and creative power.

Form bears witness to meaning. But these witnesses lie as well as tell the truth, in the same way that many people have sometimes become drunk on wine, and sometimes on yogurt drink.

This means that in the world worship pertaining to form can be sincere or false. Actions done for show, with the appearance of religiosity for the sake of material or spiritual self-interest, may appear in the forms of worship, goodness and charity but yet be no different than false witness.

The delight felt in true sincerity, in true love of God, is felt neither in the origins or ends of such acts. It is like the difference between drinking yogurt drink and supposing oneself intoxicated and the loss of self-consciousness brought on by drinking the wine of divine love and approaching God.

The falsity in the behavior of such people of course does not go unnoticed by those who know. Because the yogurt-drinkers imbibe an arrogance, pride, egotism and hypocrisy like sour yogurt, they make a ruckus and behave in an unbalanced manner in order to appear drunk.

Those whose worship is hypocritical behave in the same way. Although they appear to fast and pray and give alms, they are not sincere in what they do.

The rosary in their hand is not counting the names of God, nor is the cloak on their back a true dervish cloak. The sole food for love of God and worship is purity of heart, heartfelt fidelity to God.

That is why we say: My God, give us the ability to distinguish the path leading to You, the pure in worship from the false! Make us drunk with the true wine of love, so that our hearts may be bound to you in perfect love! Serve us the wine of Your divine love. Strike us with the arrows of Your love!

Do you know how and by means of what emotions, wine and yogurt, love of God and love of other than God may be distinguished from one another?

If emotions can look with the light of God and see in His illumination, they have arrived at the degree of distinguishing the sublime from the base. In that case the eye of feeling has been polished with the light of vision [*basiret*], thus it has become possible to distinguish the straight from the crooked.

If you ask if the definite expression of love absolutely must be either material or spiritual gifts, or if the love present in the heart absolutely must express itself with external appearance, of course there are also loves having no need of witness or trace. The love felt between close relatives—mother, father, children, brothers and sisters—has no need of expression by various means. Expression in external forms is also usually unnecessary for people who swear fealty to a friend of God, who establish a union of heart in the path of divine love with a perfect human. For those two hearts already understand one another without intervention of any language or material means, as the poet said:

On spiritual journeys transcending intellect's parts
Gnosis is the sole light showing the way from heart to heart

If God's light shows a person the way, that is, if a perfect human, who is the light of God on earth, extends a hand to a murid, he no longer has any need to display his state with material proofs.

The light of divine love catches fire in the heart, it glows and grows until the heart is joyful in a state of ecstasy. A person whose heart is filled with God in this way no longer feels any need to declare his love. For he is already one and the same with the Beloved in the sea of oneness.

That person has escaped the limitations of humanity and so there is no longer any screen or shadow to be the site of manifestation of God's light. For such spirits the body is no longer an obstacle to divine light and love. Such spirits are embraced by a light of love which is spread over the whole of creation.

Much more explanation and detail would be required to complete this discussion. But I do not fine that necessary right now. Seek the details in your own heart! Ask them from your own ecstatic states. If you want to learn more about this topic, learn it from within your own self.

To be sure, the meaning you seek appears in a form. But the form you see is in one sense very near the meaning, and in another, far from it. Meaning and form are like, let us say, water and a tree. Water and trees are certainly separate things, and they do not resemble each other. But neither can there be a tree without water, nor will a tree bear fruit as long as water does not enter into it. So, the tree is the form and water is the meaning. Whatever tree water enters into, that tree will flourish and bear fruit.

Just as fruit is the manifestation of water in the tree, the manifestation of meaning in the body is life, power, knowledge and gnosis, and a person reaches the great truth by way of that gnosis.

Once again words have strayed far from the story. Much can be said on the topic of the qualities and properties of meaning and form. But leave aside quality and property. I have told you that one of those moon-faced people is a woman and the other is a man. The man represents intellect, meaning, and the woman represents soul. In that case what need is there for long discussion. Look to the reality those two moon-faced ones represent with their words, their lives and their actions. Hear about their lives and the mystery of their lives, and you will learn all.

****

HOW THE ARAB SET HIS HEART ON HIS BELOVED'S REQUEST AND SWORE, "IN THIS MY SUBMISSION I HAVE NO INTENT OF TRICKERY OR TRIAL."

> The man said, "I'll no longer be contrary
> The power is yours, draw the sword from the sheath
> Whatever you say will now be my command
> I will not consider the good or the bad
> I will become naught within your existence
> For I'm a lover, and love is blind and deaf."
>
> 2685. "I wonder are you really my friend," she said
> "Or tricking me to discover my secret."
> "No, by God who knows the secret most obscure
> Who out of the dust created Adam pure
> Who in the form given him of three cubits
> Displayed all in the tablets and the spirits
> And through *'He taught the names,'* from the very first
> Taught the angels all that ever would occur,[141]
> The angels lost consciousness in his lessons
> And gained a new sanctity from his lessons
>
> 2690. In all the vast firmament they had not found
> That expansion that came to them from him now
> Compared with the expanse of his pure spirit
> The seven heavens seemed to be limited
> God has said, as the Messenger has made known
> 'I don't fit into the jar of "up" and "down."
> I am contained, O friend, know this for certain
> Neither by the Throne, nor by earth nor heaven
> I am contained by the true believer's heart
> If you would seek Me, seek Me within those hearts.'
>
> 2695. God said, 'Enter among my servants and meet
> A paradise made of the vision of Me.'[142]
> When the Throne, with all its far-extending light

---

141. "And He taught Adam the names of all things . . . He said: O Adam, tell them [the angels] their [the things'] names . . . " (Koran 2:31-33).
142. Koran 89:27-30.

Saw the spirit of Adam, it took to flight
True indeed, rare is the greatness of the Throne
But when reality is here, what is form?
'In the past,' the Angels said then to Adam
'On the dust of the earth we knew you as friend
We planted the seed of service in the ground
We marveled at the connection we had found

2700. Wondering how there could be a connection
When our nature had always been of Heaven
Why should we who are lights be friend to darkness?
How can light abide together with darkness?
O Adam, we felt near to the scent of you
For your body the earth was as warp and woof
Your body of earth was woven from this place
We encountered your pure light within this place
That which came from your spirit to us of life
Used to shine forth from the earth in former times

2705. We were in the earth and heedless of the earth
Heedless of the treasure buried in the earth
When He ordered us to journey from that place[143]
The change left us with a very bitter taste
We kept on presenting arguments against
Saying, "O Lord, who will then come in our place?
Will You sell the light of magnification
For the sake of mere worthless repetition?"
The decree of God spread the carpet for us.'
"Speak candidly, with boldness," He said to us

2710. "Say all that comes to your tongue, fear no danger
Like beloved children telling their father
If these words should be unseemly, what of that?
'My mercy takes precedence over My wrath.'[144]
Angel, to manifest this priority
I incite you to doubt and perplexity
So that you may speak and I not take offense
So he may not speak who denies I'm clement
A hundred mothers and fathers' clemency
Live and die each instant in My clemency

2715. Theirs is the spray on my sea of clemency
It comes and goes, but the sea will always be."'
Compared with that pearl, this shell—what can I say
Is the spray of the spray of the spray of spray
By the truth of that spray, by that pure sea's truth
These words are not vain and not meant to try you
It's love, purity, humility they bear

---

143. Yunus Emre: Since the command came from God . . .
144. A sacred hadith.

By the One to whom I will return, I swear
If this desire seems to you to be a trial
For one moment put that trial to a trial
2720.   Don't hide your secret, let mine be revealed too
Command of me all I am able to do
Do not hide your heart, let mine be revealed too
That I may accept what I am able to
What is there in my power? What shall I do?
See the state I'm in! What good am I to you?"

The Arabi man said to his wife:

> I renounce all quarrel and opposition to you, yours is the command. Withdraw the sword of your tongue from its sheath, speak, command, I will do what you request and what you say.
>
> Whatever you say I will do. I will not consider the benefit or cost. My goal is not a good or bad result, but merely to conform to your wishes.
>
> I want to annihilate myself in your being, I want to become naught in you. Because I love you. I know that love is as great as its eye is blind and its ear is deaf.

The Arabi man's heart filled with emotions of love and harmony here because he sensed the good and pure feelings arising in the Arabi woman's spirit. Although the soul is in fact bodily, material and materialistic, it can distance itself from materiality through the nurturing of love and faith until it acquires a degree allowing it to become a site of manifestation of God's empowerment. The Arabi man now sensed such a state in his wife, who in reality represents the soul. The beauty he saw in her being was not just an external beauty but this inner beauty. That is why he felt a renewed and profound bond to his wife, like someone falling in love for the first time with a beautiful woman. It was because the corruption, the envy and evil in her melted away and she was instead filled with goodness and beauty.

The woman was astounded, even frightened. She showed her doubts by saying, "Do you have evil intentions toward me, are you trying to test me? Is it your aim to learn secrets you suppose are hidden in me? For I still have many colors. I have not yet reached satisfaction in testing myself, that my wishes should be good and beneficial for you."

The Arabi man insisted. He said to his wife: "I swear that what I feel and say is true by the name of God who knows all hidden secrets and created a pure body like Messenger Adam out of the dark earth."

You know that God made Messenger Adam only three cubits tall. He made his bodily form no bigger than that. But he gave to him powers not found in the stockiest and most giant of creatures. He taught him the mysteries of destiny and the measuring-out, and told him the reasons for creation. He made plain to him all the secrets in the material and spiritual world. Most importantly, he gave Adam's children and their descendants the capacities necessary to attain to such mysteries. He made them worthy and put them in charge of the most sublime and rich treasures, like spirit and intellect. Hazret Ali expressed this truth in his statement: "O child of humanity, you imagine your tiny body is all you are. In reality the greatest realm is within you, hidden in your selfhood [*benlik*]."

Hazret Adam is the one who knew all the names of God. That is, he is "He taught the names": For this first human and first messenger of God is the one who taught the wisdom he learned from God to God's angels. Adam learned from God everything that has happened and will happen in the universe, from pre-eternity to post-eternity.

Adam knew that God, who created all that had happened and would happen, had given each of His creations another one of His names and brought it into manifestation with another one of his qualities, and Adam knew all of these qualities and names of God's. He told the angels these beautiful and sublime names and the qualities taking wing in the meanings of these names.

God the Truth had taught Adam the name of each thing He created. That is why He said in the second chapter of the Gracious Koran: "God taught Adam the name of all things. Then He showed them to the angels and said: 'If you are sincere in what you say, tell me the names of these.' They replied: 'You are sublime and great, we know nothing but what You have taught us. It is You who have created each thing for a reason.'

God said to Hazret Adam: 'O Adam, tell them the names of these!' And Adam stated their names."

It is also stated in the second chapter of the Gracious Koran that God commanded the angels to bow to the ground before Adam. Although all the angels obeyed this command immediately, Satan resisted and, asserting that he was created of fire and Adam of earth, said he could not bow down before a bondsman created of earth. In fact it was because of this that Satan was of the utterly damned.

In contrast, the angels quickly understood the virtues in Adam. They recognized the superiority in his manner of praising God. Confronted by the greatness and sanctity of Adam, who knew the divine names he taught them and according to his own measure possessed and commanded almost all the meaning and qualities of them, they understood the truth and were completely in awe of him. For the angels could possess only one of these divine names. The self-disclosure in them could not be in its entirety; they could only be made the site of manifestation of partial self-disclosure.

That is how it happened, divine wisdom self-disclosed in angel and man in this way. But the angels felt a profound ecstasy in learning from Adam the state of greatness of God in a bondsman, and the infinite and countless powers which made up that greatness. They were bound to Adam by feelings of gratitude.

They understood that despite their heavenly nature and all their intimacy with divine being, they were not sites of manifestation in the way that Adam was. The spirit sparkling in Adam was such that even the seven heavens were too narrow to contain that spirit.

Hazret Muhammed, who said God was not a being who could be contained within the most sublime of the sublime, the most profound of the profound, learned that wisdom from God's saying: "I do not fit within the highest or the lowest."

But is it not astonishing that God, who does not fit in the heavens or even the Divine Throne, has said: "I fit only in the hearts of believers."

God's manifestation in believing hearts is by way of self-disclosure and, as you know, self-disclosure means for God to be sensed in a person's heart.

And God has said in the eighty-ninth chapter of the Gracious Koran:

O spirit resting in satisfaction! Return to your God!
Return to your Lord, pleased and pleasing to Him!
Enter among My bondsmen!
Enter My Paradise!"

If you wish the meaning of these verses, I tell you it is this:

> God's appearance and self-disclosure in the heart, condition of entrance to Paradise, is first to win the love of God's special bondsmen, that is, the love of a perfect human. In this way a person makes his soul-bound being reach the nothingness of bondage to God the Truth. In this way he becomes mature and begins to sea and taste the life of Paradise while still in this world.

Consider this:

> The Divine Throne, whose greatness is infinite, begins to feel its own smallness and nothingness when confronted by the greatness of the heart of a gnostic of God. For the human heart which has known God is the sea of the essence [zât] of God who is and is one. And every concept, be it the Throne, the Footstool, the Tablet or the Pen, becomes invisible in the infinite vastness of such a heart.

Yes, the greatness of the Throne is obvious. But what is the measure of this visible greatness next to the invisible greatness which is the sublimity of meaning? It is with this comprehension that you will understand the limitless greatness and divine power of meaning. And this comprehension will tell you of the value and wisdom of that perfect human who has filled your heart with that sublime meaning.

It was when Messenger Adam taught the angles the divine names that they understood the mystery of their own function.

Each of the angels told Adam:

> We now understand that our association with you began long ago.
>
> We knew ourselves as beings belonging to Heaven. Since that was the case, why did we descend to earth and prepare the ground for your creation before you were created—this we are learning only now.
>
> Although we are of Heaven, we were planting the seeds of service, worship and piety on earth. At that time we asked ourselves: "What business do we have in the darkness on earth, when we are lights belonging to the realms of divine light?"
>
> Now we understand, O Adam! By descending to earth we were weaving the threads of your cloth; we were preparing the consistency of your earthly body so that it would be a jewel box for divine light.
>
> We were on earth before you, but without you the earth told us no secrets, as if it were hiding a buried treasure.
>
> Before your were created, a command came to us from God the Truth, telling us to travel on. It was a command to change our place and station. At first we felt a stabbing pain in our spirits. It was as if we did not want to leave the earth from which you would be created. "O my Lord!" we wailed, "Whom will You send to this realm in our place? Here we have been recalling Your divine name and exalting You and singing Your praises. Will You now bring Adam, who will spread corruption in the earth, in our place?'"

God responded to our objections with His divine compassion. He allowed us to say even more. He said,

> My angels! Tell all of your complaints, do not shy away from Me and conceal anything. Just as beloved, valued children tell their mothers and fathers their every wish and whatever they say seems sweet to their parents, who always show them kindness, compassion and ease, speak in that way also and do not think that what you say will cause severity and anger in Us.
>
> Even if what you say is inappropriate to Our station and not something to be said about Us, say it. For you know that Our mercy vanquishes Our wrath.
>
> My angels! I let doubt and indecision enter your hearts so that you should see once again the mercy of your God and that this mercy spreads through every self-disclosure.
>
> So that you should speak and I should not be angry. Thus you will better understand the beauty in My kindness and compassion, and how that beauty unburdens the heart and bestows peace of mind.
>
> Our gentleness, the love We bear those We have created, is of such a degree that the compassion of hundreds of parents glows and fades away in every breath of Our compassion. Just as countless waves rise and fall in the sea during storms, in every breath of Our mercy profound feelings of compassion arise in the spirits of parents and return to Us, plunging into the sea of Our mercy.
>
> The trembling of the hearts of parents and all those who love sincerely is like one drop, one bubble, of the froth of the waves of the sea of Our love, mercy and compassion. The wind blows, the waves die down, the froth disappears, but Our love and mercy is never exhausted. It longs each moment for opportunities to rise in waves again and adorn the sea of Our compassion with white froth. And it finds them. For to the degree that wives and froth are transient, the sea is to that same degree immortal [*bâkî*].

The Arabi man, his heart full of love for his wife, brought all these things to mind and spoke of them sincerely, saying: "Now, for the sake of that divine froth, that pure bright sea, believe that what I say is not just talk, nor said with the intent to test you.

"For the sake of God to whom we will return tomorrow, I say that what I have said is sincere, it is said out of the fidelity of love.

"Believe this. If you believe that I said what I did in order to test you, then test that test. Conceal nothing from me, speak in all purity of heart and mind. Tell me what I can do for you, so that I can do it.

"I am helpless. Give me strength, support me, and then tell me. Only then will I have the strength to do all." The Arabi man spoke so sincerely, in such heated and divine words, that the woman wept. She said that her husband was walking the path of God. She decided to help him and find ways to make him happy.

****

HOW THE WOMAN CHOSE THE MEANS FOR HER HUSBAND TO EARN A LIVELIHOOD, AND HOW HE ACCEPTED

"A sun has shone forth," the woman said to him
"An entire world has found illumination

344

The Merciful's vicegerent and deputy
Muhammed keeps Baghdad flourishing like spring

2725. If you unite with that shah, a shah you'll be
How long will you sojourn toward disloyalty?
The arrived act upon us like alchemy
Indeed, compared with their gaze, what's alchemy?
Ahmed's gaze struck Abu Bakr, who would become
A Siddiq with just one verification [*tasdīq*]."
"How should I go to meet the shah?" the man said
"How can I do that when I have no pretext?
I must have some stratagem or connection
Without means can any craft be rightly done?

2730. It is as when Majnun cried, hearing illness
Had overtaken Leyla, though just a bit,
'How shall I go when I've no pretext to go?
Yet when she is unwell how can I not go?
Were I a physician skillful and astute
I'd be the first to go to Leyla on foot.'
As a sign to us, God said to us, *'Say: Come,'*[145]
So we might know how shame can be overcome
If bats had the right means, and possessed sight, they
Would happily go around flying by day."

2735. She said, "When the gracious shah comes to be seen
Each lack of means becomes in essence a means
For a means is pretension and existence
The work is lack of means and non-existence."
He said: "How should I traffic without the means
If I do not show that I do not have means?
Thus I must attest to my insolvency
That the shah may pity my insolvency
Beyond words and show offer testimony
So the shah of beauty may display mercy

2740. For this testimony of mere words and show
Before that Judge of judges is overthrown
To the inner state He requires witness true
So that without words the poor man's light shines through."

The woman said to her husband:

The world has been illuminated with the grace of the light of a perfect human.

This sun is a vicegerent of the Merciful on earth; this sun expresses that God is merciful and compassionate; by grace of this sun spring has come to the city of Baghdad.

If you go into the presence of that padishah and are well-accepted by him, you will attain the felicity you seek. If you continue to do the opposite, your road will

---

145. Koran 3:64, 6:151.

end at a precipice. This is what I know. This murshid, your soul united with light, is reminding you, your being which represents intellect; I tell you to run to him.

You know that the nearness of the friends of God is like alchemy, like an elixir. The hearts of those who approach them approach the sun of their divine love and friendship. The shifting flames of that sun transform the hearts they touch and wash with the elixir of love into gold as does alchemy which touches copper. The human heart which had until that time been slave to the attributes of matter and soul is from that moment on transformed into spiritual gold. The heart becomes so rich that it can no longer love any worldly wealth or sultan; it has drunk that divine wine and passed away from self in the divine Paradise.

You know the story of Hazret Muhammed and Abu Bakr: When the messenger of God told Abu Bakr about his mission, without the slightest hesitation Abu Bakr said, "I verify [*tasdîk*] what you have said," and that is why he took on the title "Siddiq."

Then Hazret Muhammed said to Abu Bakr, "You have not seen me perform even one miracle, so how can you be sure what I say is true?" Abu Bakr looked at our Messenger and said: "This face would not lie."

So, when that alchemy, that elixir of Hazret Muhammed's gaze touched Abu Bakr, his heart was washed with that water of gold; the divine love in his spirit rose up in excitement, he fell in love with Muhammed with all his heart and felt deep within himself the reality and greatness of Muhammed's divinely inspired mission.

The Arabi man said to his wife:

How shall I go into the presence of such a shah? How should I be accepted by him? Even if he would accept a pauper like me, how shall I dare to go to him? I have neither an art nor a skill, nor a gift.

You know the story of how Majnun heard that Leyla was ill. Majnun was burning to be by Leyla's side and give her the most heartfelt compassionate care in her illness. But he had no pretext for going to see her. "Ah!" he said, "If only I were a skilled physician, it would be my right more than anyone's to look after her, to make her well and be by her bedside."

God addressed His messenger in the third chapter of the Koran: "O Muhammed! Say to them, 'Come!'"

O woman! There are two ways to approach the great, even the greatest of the great. One is to have a skill or gift worthy to bring them; the other is to be called by them.

I have neither gaze, ecstasy, heart, nor value that would cause me to be called by him. With what shall I go? How shall I go, so that the earth does not swallow me up in my shame?

What you have said makes me think of bats. If bats could see in the light of day, would they wander around by night? They would fly by day like other birds, they would be able to see the colors and forms of the beauties of the world by light of day.

How am I now, before that padishah of light, any different from a bat? What do I have to show that friend of God and with what capacity may I display his light?

The woman heard him out. The soul had chosen the right path and felt the virtue and tasted the pleasure of treading that path. She said to her husband, who represented the intellect: "God has need of no pretext to be generous and merciful to those of His bonds-men who wish to approach Him. Go into the presence of that friend of God padishah, view his beauty and light. Let his rays fil you, that is enough for you.

"It is an error and a sin to seek means and cause for approaching God, to think, 'What shall I do, I have nothing to offer.' That sublime God wants nothing from you but sound-ness of heart and purity of spirit. It is wrong to seek being and gifts in the path of God. For in the path of God only not-being is beautiful, that is, it is right to be not."

The Arabi man found his wife in the right, but did not believe he possessed that degree of pretextlessness and nothingness, and he felt profoundly tormented at the idea of pretending to a degree he had not attained. He said to his wife:

> You must find a way for me to be graced by the kindness of that padishah and a witness, a proof of my matchless poverty, so that I may go into the presence of that personage feeling the courage of such proof.
>
> For a witness consisting only of words and show is like false witness. I need a proof and a witness that can never be false and considered false. Find me that wit-ness, and let my witness make that padishah feel the honesty within me, the sincerity of my heart, without my having to speak."

****

HOW THE ARAB CARRIED A JUG OF RAINWATER OUT OF THE DESERT TO BAGHDAD AS A GIFT TO THE COMMANDER OF THE FAITHFUL, BELIEVING THAT WATER WAS SCARCE THERE TOO

She said, "When people rise up entirely
Purged of existence—that is veracity
We have rainwater in the jug, that is means
It is capital and it's your property
Take this rainwater jug of ours and depart
Take it as a gift before the Shah of shahs
2745. Say: 'The only means that we possess is this
Water is the best the desert has to give.'
Though jewels and gold fill his treasury there
He does not have water like this, it is rare."
What's the jug?—our body, which is circumscribed
The salt water of the senses is inside
O God, accept this jar and this jug of mine
By grace of *God purchased*[146] lives for Paradise
The five senses are the five spouts of this jug
Keep the water that's inside pure of all smut
2750. So that from this jug a way leads to the sea
So my jug may have the nature of the sea
So that when you present it to the Sultan
He will find it pure and wish to take it on
The water inside will then be infinite

---

146. "God has purchased from the believers their selves and goods; for theirs is the Garden . . . " (Koran 9:111).

A hundred worlds will draw and be filled from it
Stop up its spouts and keep it filled from the jar
The Lord has said: *"Close your eyes to vain desire."* [147]
The man's beard puffed up: "Who has a gift like this?
Truly worthy of such a shah as he is."
2755.   The woman did not know that the Jayhun there
Flowed sweet as sugar beside the thoroughfare
That it flowed like a sea through the city's midst
With boats sailing on it full of fishing nets
Behold that pomp and state, to the Sultan go!
See the sense faculties *'neath which rivers flow* [148]
Such sense and comprehension that we have got
Beside those rivers is no more than a drop

The woman repeated that true veracity is to tread the path of God filled with love of God and keeping far from other concerns. "Since you do not want to go empty-handed to that caliph who is padishah of all Muslims, there is the rainwater caught in our jug. It is water you have saved. That water is your only property, your pure and clear fortune. Take that water to the padishah and say to him: 'We have no property other than this, and there is no more beautiful water than this.' Although it is true that in the treasury of the padishah whom you will visit there are countless valuable things, pearls and jewels, there is no water as sweet as it is.'"

The woman, who represents soul, and the man, who represents intellect, did not know that the real value and divine delight lies in the water of gnosis within the jug of the body.

The jug represents our bodily form. It contains the salt water of our senses, of sight, hearing, touch, smell and taste.

My God! For the sake of the gracious verse, "God has purchased of the believers their persons and their goods; for theirs is the Garden: they fight in His cause, and slay and are slain: a promise binding on Him in truth, through the Torah, the Gospel and the Koran," [149] accept our jug, accept our jar! The water of spirit and sincerity in our jug is Yours.

Surely the worship and piety and the struggles of those who declare war on the evils of their souls is no easier and no less sacred than the struggles of those who war against the enemies of religion and faith and are martyred. You are surely God who rewards with goodness and beauty those who attain victory in their determination to annihilate the evils of their souls.

We have first of all a body like a jug with five spouts, the five senses for hearing You, tasting You, seeing You and smelling you. Keep the water flowing from the spouts of this jug pure and far from all filth, my God!

So that the water flowing from the jug of the body may taste the delight in reaching the sea of Your being. May it find the way to union, and pour into the sea of love of God like a jug filled with Your oneness and the wine of love.

---

147. "Tell the believing males to lower their gaze . . ." (Koran 24:30).
148. Koran 2:25: ". . . for them are gardens beneath which rivers flow."
149. Koran 9:111.

So, bring this jug to that great Padishah. When the Shah sees the purity of the water in the jug, He will surely be its suitor.

If that Padishah claims this water, it means you have attained your desire. For then the water in the jug will know no cease and thus fill a hundred worlds with its pure water.

Stop up the spouts and fill the jug from the jar. Don't forget that God has said to close your eyes to lust and vain desire.

So, if a human succeeds in keeping the jug of his own body pure of the filth of the world of nature and humanity, it is possible to say of the jug which finds the way to reach the sea of mercy that the sea it reaches is in a sense itself.

When the Arabi man heard these words his beard puffed up with the wind of pride; he said that the gift really was worthy of shahs—what shah ever had a gift like this from a bondsman?

Neither the woman nor her husband, far from Baghdad, knew that in the land of the Caliph there was a river Tigris flowing with water sweet as sugar.

Upon this water flowing through the city of Baghdad there were ships and fish nets.

This means that a person must not be prideful of the jug of water he presents to God. This gift of yours is not even a drop in the ea of God's knowledge and gnosis. It would not be right for you to suppose the water in your jug to be the sweetest of waters, and forget the bitterness in it. What you should do is work to open a path from the jug of your body to His sublime sea, not boast of the water in your jug.

Go to the palace of the Sultan and drift off in awed contemplation of His greatness. Remember the gracious verse, "But give glad tidings to those who believe and work righteousness that their portion is gardens beneath which rivers flow."[150] Do not forget that these rivers flow in the gardens of love and gnosis, and that the spiritual support of the friends, like rivers flowing in Paradise, rains the mercy of truth upon those dirtied by worldly passions and purifies them!

Do not stay away from their service and support! For the water of truth you need on the path of knowledge and gnosis is in the jugs of their bodies, pure and clear. Bring your parched lips to those jugs! Taste the true water of Paradise.

Know that all our knowledge is not a drop in the flow of that pure river. The sweet and copious water to be drunk to satiation is in their jugs.

****

HOW THE WIFE OF THE ARAB SEWED THE JUG OF RAINWATER INSIDE FELT CLOTH AND SEALED IT, DUE TO THE ARAB'S EXTREME CONVICTION THAT IT WAS PRECIOUS

The man said, "Bring the jug and stop its mouth up
Take care, for this gift will bring profit to us
2760. Inside of a cloth of felt sew this jug fast
That the Shah may use the gift to break his fast
For there is in the whole world nothing like this
There is no water that is so pure as this."
So he said, because those like him are half-blind
And sick from drinking salt water full of brine
The bird that makes its home upon salt water

150. Koran 2:25.

How should it know where to find clear, sweet water?
You who live in a salt spring, what can you know
Of how Shatt and Tigris and Euphrates flow?
2765.   Can you know, in this hostel of transiency
Of extinction, expansion and ecstasy?
And if you do, it's repetition you've heard
From your forefathers, like letters in a word
How clear to all children is the alphabet
Yet the real meaning is extremely distant
Then the Arab, jug in hand, went on his way
Carrying it with him all the night and day
Fearing fortune's mischief he took greatest care
And conveyed the jug to the city from there
2770.   The wife laid out her mat in supplication
Her litany in prayer, *"Lord, salvation!"*
Crying, "Keep our water safe from banditry
O Lord, bring that pearl all the way to that sea
Though my husband is resourceful and wary
The pearl still has yet thousands of enemies
What is the pearl? It's water of Kawsar spring
The pearl's origin is a drop from that spring."
Through the woman's prayers and lamentation
And the man's pains under his heavy burden
2775.   Unhurt by bandits and stones, without delay
He bore it to the seat of the Caliphate
He saw a court overflowing with bounty
Where nets were spread by those suffering in need
Everywhere, constantly, petitioners
Obtained from that court grants and robes of honor
For believer and kafir, ugly and fair
It was like sun and rain, no, Paradise, there
He saw a group favored by the Caliph's gaze
And another standing anxiously in wait
2780.   Commoner, elect, from Solomon to ant
Resurrected like the world at trumpet's blast
Devotees of form were woven with pearl strings
Men of meaning found the ocean of meaning
Those who'd not aspired now found aspiration
Those who had—O, how blest did they now become!

The Arabi man said to his wife:

Wrap the jug in felt cloth and stop up its spout, it will make a beautiful gift. Let me take it to the Caliph so that he may break his fast with lovely, fresh water.

You could not find sweeter or more healthful water if you roamed the face of the earth from horizon to horizon. This is pure water and the essence and source of all pleasures.

One can say that this is the water of gnosis collected in the body, containing droplets from the clouds of worship and piety.

This water is the wine of love which makes those who do not know of it pass away from self when they drink it.

It is because they have not drunk of such water that those among the creatures who do not see the Creator really are as if blind; give me the water so that I may bring it to them and the eyes of their hearts may open. They have always drunk bitter and salty water, let them taste the delight of the water of life in this jug.

Think of a bird that can see only bitter and salty water from the skies where he flies. When he comes down, he can only drink of that water. How should such a bird know of the sweet and clear water beyond the horizons?

O bird of the spirit who has chosen the cage of the body as its home! Your place is at the head of a salt water spring. How should you know of the water of the Shatt al-Arab and the Tigris and Euphrates rivers, when your lips have not touched the source of oneness?

O you who can not free yourself of this world and the pleasures of this world! How can you know the vast delight of nothingness and what it is to be pure spirit? You are among those tied to the body and bodily forms, who see themselves in deceptive mirrors and are pleased. How can you feel the excellence of the invisibility degree tasted by the friends of God?

It is useless for you to say you will attain that degree through knowledge. Can one speak of knowledge where there is love? Knowledge is the easy way taken by lazy spirits. If you have the strength, and your intellect can reach it, learn love and feel gnosis!

You can teach the alphabet and children will learn it. But children do not know the profound meaning hidden in every letter. Every bondsman who is unaware of the water of eternal life in divine pleasures supposes that every salty water with which he quenches his thirst is the source of all pleasures. There is many a caravan of people drinking of this bitter water, worldly people who never go beyond knowledge of how the external form of the alphabet is read and understood. But in order for them to learn the meaning of the alphabet, the birds of their hearts must go beyond the material horizons. If you have an intellect, learn the meaning of the alphabet from a friend of God and find the water of eternal life which flows only under the shadow of the wings of the spirit free of bodily concerns.

The Arabi man set off down the road believing that the water in his jug was the most beautiful of all water. He carried the jug to the city, taking a thousand and one precautions to keep it from breaking or coming to any harm.

Back at home the Arabi woman bowed on her carpet in prayer. She counted on her rosary,

O my Lord, protect the jug. Protect our pure water from disasters that might break the jug and from the stones of evil, carry our one drop of essence to that great sea!

It is true that my husband is clever and knows the value of the pure water he carries. But the enemies of the jewel of faith inside the jug are many.

You know, my God, that the pearls within his jug are drops from the water of Kawsar. Those drops which pour from Your heavens into the oceans and become pearls when they are kept inside shells."

The jug, protected by all these prayers and precautions, reached Baghdad in the Arabi man's hand without harm from the stone of reproach.

There the Arabi man saw the Caliph's sublime court. He found himself at a sublime gate of need like that described by the poet:

> There everyone attains the object of his desire because
> His court is the asylum of the adepts of hope

Each bondsman took his share from this gate according to his preparedness; every heart found here the way to reach its desire.

Whether kafir or believer, beautiful or ugly, here was a door of generosity open to all. It was as if the light filtering through the dome of this court was the sun itself, illuminating all. The gate was great and the gate was beautiful, but it was unlike the gate of Paradise. For this gate was open not only to those destined for Paradise but to all, without discrimination.

Part of the crowd had been accepted in the Caliph's sight. Another part were waiting for this good acceptance. From Solomon to the ant, commoners and elect, every bondsman and every being seemed to have found life as if at the sound of Israfil's horn. Here the people of form were covered in pearls and jewels and the people of meaning were plunged in the sea of meaning. The vastness of the delight they had attained seemed to embrace the horizons.

Those who take example saw at the gate of this court and in its dome everything material and spiritual and every condition of created things, and unraveled many a mystery.

****

IN EXPOSITION OF HOW THE BOUNTIFUL GIVER IS IN LOVE WITH THE BEGGAR, JUST AS THE BEGGAR IS IN LOVE WITH BOUNTY AND IN LOVE WITH THE BOUNTIFUL GIVER; IF THE BEGGAR IS MORE PATIENT, THE BOUNTIFUL GIVER WILL COME TO HIS DOOR, AND IF THE BOUNTIFUL GIVER IS MORE PATIENT, THE BEGGAR WILL COME TO HIS DOOR; BUT THE BEGGAR'S PATIENCE IS PERFECTION IN THE BEGGAR, WHILE THE PATIENCE OF THE BOUNTIFUL GIVER IS IN HIM A LACK

> A loud call was issuing forth, "Come, suitor!
> Bounty needs beggars, it is like a beggar
> Generosity seeks beggars and the poor
> Like a beautiful face seeks a pure mirror
2785.   A mirror makes fair faces more beautiful
> A beggar makes beneficence visible
> So on this account in the Koran God said:
> "Do not shout at the beggar, O Muhammed!"[151]
> The beggar is generosity's mirror
> Take care! Breath obscures the face of the mirror
> The beggar is brought to be by one bounty
> While another bestows on him much increase

---

151. Koran 93:10.

> Beggars, then, mirror God's generosity
> And those who are with God, absolute bounty
> 2790. Except for these two, men are but dead men all
> Not at this door, just an image on a veil

A voice said, "Come, O you who seek the way! For just as a pauper is in need of generosity, so thus generosity and bounty feel need of him. Like beautiful people who rush to view their beauty in clear mirrors, and never leave them, gazing at themselves in the mirror, so are pure, spotless paupers the mirrors of the wealthy and generous. There they see the reflections of the richness of their own hearts.

That is why God said in the Koran, "O Muhammed! Surely your Lord will give to you and you will be pleased. Did not He find you as an orphan and give you shelter? Did not He find you wandering and gave you guidance? Did He not find you in need and make you independent? So do not treat the orphan harshly nor repulse the petitioner, but rehearse and proclaim the bounty of the Lord!" (93:10).

For God has said that all the believers are His orphan bondsmen, and their questions are His secrets.

Is it not so that paupers and orphans are the mirrors of generosity and largess? Know that breath clouds the face of a mirror. And know that God's self-disclosure of generosity is of two kinds. One is that he sets free large quantities of paupers and orphans upon the earth. Once these needy folk begin to seek the things they need and other bounties, God shows the second kind of his generosity, joining them to the bounties in measure with their preparedness and their quests, and with Himself.

So the paupers you have seen, whether they be paupers in terms of bounty or in terms of divine unity, are mirrors of the divine self-disclosure. The divine self-disclosure appears in the form of generosity and drowns them in bounties, or appears in the form of oneness and draws them to itself.

It is not that there are no people on earth other than these two kinds of paupers. But if you see them alive and think they are living, you are mistaken. Their is no love of God in them, or ability to see themselves in the divine mirror; they are not only deprived of divine bounties but of humanity itself. Know that they are like the pictures on door-tapestries. Whether they are there or not makes no real difference.

****

THE DIFFERENCE BETWEEN A PERSON WHO IS POOR IN GOD AND THIRSTING FOR HIM AND ONE WHO IS POOR WITHOUT GOD AND THIRSTING FOR WHAT IS OTHER THAN HE

> Not worthy of bread, he's just a dervish form
> It's a picture of a dog, don't throw a bone!
> He's not poor in God, he's poor in nourishment
> Do not lay dishes before a form that's dead
> The dervish who wants for bread is a land-fish
> He flees the sea, though in the form of a fish
> He's not the Simurgh, he's a bird in a keep
> He's not nourished by God, he devours sweets
> 2795. He loves God only for sake of sustenance
> His spirit does not love beauty and goodness

He is in love with the essence, he presumes
Essence is not supposed names and attributes
Fancy's from attributes and limits begot
But no one gave birth to God, *He's not begot* [152]
Should one who loves his descriptions and fancies
Be a lover of *the Lord of all bounty*?
But if a lover of conjecture be true
Metaphor will draw him as far as the true

2800.   To expound on this requires commentary
But I fear those feeble in mentality
People short of sight and decrepit in thought
Bring a hundred evil fancies into thought
Not all can master the art of right hearing
Figs are not food for every little birdie
A bird that's dead and rotten especially
Filled with fantasies and lacking eyes to see
What is land or sea to a fish's picture?
Neither soap nor ink change a Hindu's color

2805.   You can make a portrait on paper look sad
But it learns naught from looking happy or sad
Its form is sorrowful, but it's free of that
Its form is smiling, but there's no trace of that
Drawn upon the heart, the sorrow and joy here
Are but forms compared with sorrow and joy there
The picture's sorrowful face is for our sake
So that we may remember the righteous way
The smiling face of the picture is for you
That from form, meaning may be fixed in you

2810.   The pictures hanging inside these bathhouse rooms
Are like clothes worn outside the undressing room
As long as you are outside, you see just clothes
Enter in, O kindred soul, put off your clothes
Because there's no way inside when wearing clothes
Body knows spirit no more than garments know

Where do those who do not take the path of God go? Can you consider those who are unable to see the vast emptiness opening out before them to be living beings? Although people who take that contrary path seem to be alive, in reality they are devoid of divine spirit. They are no different from bodies turned to stone. God's bounty does not come to them. For one must be alive in order to be nourished. Such people are like black boulders which divert the rain falling upon them to a different direction, they cannot absorb it themselves. What should God do with them? Why and what should He give to them?

Don't be fooled by such people. They are not the people in need of God, they are images of such people. If you have a bone, don't give it to the picture of a dog, give it to the real dog.

---

152. Koran 112:3.

They are paupers of food and drink, not paupers of God. Upon their plates accumulate the material pleasures for which the soul hungers. There is no room on their plates for spiritual delights. They would not know how to taste such things if you gave them to them, so while there are people truly alive, why put nourishment before the mere picture of a human being?

If you see a creature moving over dry land that appears to you as a fish, don't be fooled and throw it into the sea. Those are land-fish. Regardless of their fish-like shape, they will drown if you throw them into the sea of divine spiritual bounties.

Don't suppose that geese, ducks and chickens are birds of the heavens. Although they have the form of a bird, they cannot take wing into the expanse of the skies. Shut up in coops, they care only for stuffing themselves with seeds and the material foods their owners throw at them, and are nourished with these. They cannot, like the spiritual birds who rise to the realms of the angels, drink the wine of divine love and eat the seeds of real love.

Creatures such as these, even if they take, say, human form, and even appear to be treading the path of God, they only love God because He can give them bounty, food, drink, wealth, delight and position. This love is love of the stomach and ribs. Don't suppose that such creatures are the same as those whose hearts are in love with divine beauty and nourished only by God's beauty. Their material pleasures and material foods are limited. But spiritual pleasures and spiritual foods are without end. If you are going to request something from God, don't ask for spiritual, not material delights, ascend to the level achieved by those whose hearts fill with divine delights. In that realm you will see how and how beautifully are resolved the quandaries you cannot get yourself out of.

Conjecture [*vehim*] is a trick of the soul in a person, not the spirit. Those duped in that way cannot bind themselves to a God they cannot see with their worldly eyes. They think God is what they see, that God is appearances, they give their heart not to God Himself but to phantoms in a mirror. But those who see with the eyes of their hearts do not do that, they are not fooled by worldly delights and worldly show, they bind themselves directly to meaning and truth.

Conjecture does not exist in God but in the creature, and is itself created. There is not the tiniest thing that can be imputed to God, "He does not beget, nor is He begotten." For to create is very different than to procreate.

A person in love with depictions, pictures, statues, and phenomena which can be seen which he thinks beautiful and attractive of course cannot feel love for God who is possessed of bounty and generosity. Only if these beautiful things to which he has given his heart serve as a beginning on the path of transformation into love of God and real love, a bridge and bridgehead, if their gratification is delayed [*vusûlleri gecikse*], can their love one day be considered real. Such people should not be afraid of metaphorical love, because the metaphorical will pull them to the real.

If you ask how metaphors and metaphorical love can become real, can become true love, I too think this requires explanation. For a fear wronging those who will not understand. I fear that they, having been instructed that metaphorical love is desirable too, will fall into wayward loves and, thinking these are God, become completely divorced from reality. Thus they will give evil fantasies beautiful dress and suppose that evil is beautiful.

It is not given to every mortal to find the truth and feel the truth. Although small birds may peck at figs, they should not try to swallow them. Divine mysteries do not open the door to every mind and spirit. If a bird is dead and rotten, how can it see a seed, how can it take food into its beak?

A picture of a fish does not know the difference between land or sea. Put soap on the face of an Indian, or black paint ... it's all the same. What matters is that a person's heart not be black and his spirit among the dead.

If the picture you draw on a piece of paper if of a smiling person, do you suppose the paper is smiling? Or if there is a picture of a weeping person on it, do you expect sobs to rise up from the paper? Know that both the sorrow and joy you seek is in your spirit. The paper is aware of neither.

A painter paints his own soul on his canvas. In his painting there is the image of a person suffering. Both he himself and others see the person's suffering as drawn by hand and a creature that can be touched. But the picture is aware neither of this pain nor the suffer felt by those who view it.

In the same way the picture of a laughing beauty can cheer both the person who draws it and those who view it, and convey both the pleasure and meaning of joy. But the picture itself neither knows that joy nor takes pleasure in it.

Thus do the so-called Sufis who have no knowledge or gnosis in their hearts but, because their appearance makes people suppose they have achieved the degree of God's friends, resemble pictures which give others a pleasure they themselves are unaware of.

The joy or sorrow in the faces of such picture-like people, who have not the slightest stirring in their hearts, can serve only to awaken you. It can keep your spirit and heart awake to joy or sorrow. It ensures that you sense and understand both.

You know how there are clothes hung up behind the glass of windows in bathhouses. Although they make people looking in think of the people inside, they themselves are lifeless forms.

The people who go into the bath leave those clothes hanging there. Thus although the real live people are inside the bath, naked and revealing their true appearance, those looking in from outside see in their clothes not them but their apparel.

In the same way there are so many spirits dressed in human forms which are like lifeless articles of clothing. People looking at their external appearance suppose that these sublime spirits in human form are no more than clothing.

O beloved, one does not enter a bathhouse clothed. What good is it for you to go into the bathhouse wrapped in the clothing of flesh and the varied limitations of soul? Until you throw them off and strip yourself of all limitations of soul, you will not be able to bathe and be cleansed in this bathhouse of spirituality.

****

HOW THE ANNOUNCERS AND GATEKEEPERS CAME FORWARD TO HONOR THE BEDOUIN AND ACCEPT HIS GIFT

> The Bedouin from the desert far away
> Came to the Caliph's abode and reached the gate
> The announcers came to meet the Bedouin
> Sprinkling rosewater of grace on his bosom
> 2815.   Before he spoke they had understood his need
> To give before being asked was their duty

They said, "Chief of Arabs, where do you come from?
How are you after a journey so tiresome?"
He said, "I'm a chief if you show countenance
But I will lose face if you should turn your backs
You whose faces bear the marks of dominion
Glowing with more luster than Jafari coin[153]
One sight of you is worth many other sights
Pieces of gold are scattered round at the sight

2820. You who are all seeing by the light of God
Who for sake of munificence come from God
So you may cast that alchemy of your gaze
On the copper of the bodies God creates
I have come from the desert, I'm a stranger
I have come hoping for the Sultan's favor
The deserts were seized by the scent of his grace
Spirit came to inhabit the sandy grains
For the sake of gold I came all the way here
I am drunk with vision now that I am here

2825. Someone ran to the baker in search of bread
The baker's beauty made him slay his own self
A man went to a garden to find good cheer
But it was the gardener who gave him cheer
Like the Arab drawing well-water, who then
In Joseph's face found water of life instead[154]
Moses went to fetch fire, and beheld such fire
Never again did he need to search for fire[155]
Jesus sprang up to escape from wicked men
That leap carried him up to the fourth heaven[156]

2830. The trap set for Adam was an ear of wheat
And his body became mankind's ear of wheat
The falcon approaches the snare for the food
It finds the Shah's forearm, glory and fortune
The child goes to school for art's acquisition
In hopes father will buy a sweet bird for him
Then he becomes chief of students at the school
Once he paid monthly fees, now he's a full moon
Abbas had come to make war in resentment
For claim to religion and to smite Ahmad

2835. As caliphs, his sons until Resurrection

---

153. Pure gold. At a time when gold was being debased with other metals, Caliph Jafar had pure coins struck which are known as "*ja'farî*." R. A. Nicholson says they acquired this name due to Ja'far al-Safiq's renown as an alchemist.

154. "Then there came a caravan of travelers who sent their water-carrier and he let down his bucket. He said, 'Ah, good news! Here is a young man!" (Koran 12:19).

155. Koran 28:29-31.

156. Koran 3:55.

> Became the face and support of religion
> Seeking worldly things I came unto this court
> When I entered, I became seat of honor
> I brought water as a gift for sake of bread
> I reached Paradise led by the scent of bread
> Bread was what drove Adam out of Paradise
> Bread led me to mix with those of Paradise
> I am freed like angels from water and bread
> I revolve here like the spheres, without intent
> 2840.   Nothing moves without an object in the world
> But the bodies and the spirits of lovers."

The Arabi man traveled through faraway, vast deserts and reached the city which was the center of the Caliph's government and justice. The Caliph's men greeted him and sprinkled goodness and generosity upon him like rosewater.

They knew what the Arabi man was thinking before he spoke, they sensed his wishes. Because the intimates of the Caliph were men of spirit whose way was to sense the unsaid and give without being asked.

They said to the Arabi man: "O mighty and pure Arab! From where and by what road have you come? What land do you belong to? How are you after your long travels?"

It was immediately evident that these men of the Caliph were friends who had made progress in the path of God. That was why they could tell what the Arabi man was thinking and knew that he had walked the paths they had already taken themselves. This knowledge was the miracle they performed.

The poor Arabi was moved by such a reception. With a beautiful, lively manner reflected into his heart by the friends, he said to them:

> What you say is true, if you look at my face I am a pure Arab, I am good, I am noble, but if you contemn me, turn your back on me, turn your face away from me, I will have neither nobility, honor, nor meaning.
>
> O you who read the greatness of spirits in their faces! Your brightness and glory is purer than Jafari gold. Your faces appear more pure than those gold pieces. Without any doubt, you are they who approach the fruition of the road I have set my myself upon.
>
> Those who look into your faces once have the brightness of having seen a hundred faces! Seeing you even just once, reaching you even just once, is worth all the riches in the world.
>
> You who gaze with divine light at what you see, you who know what from country the strange comes and what path the pauper has followed to rub his face in the dust where the Padishah has stepped. Although it is the greatest country which I long for, although I am a stranger to the greatest Padishah, I have come to give my heart to his Caliph and receive his grace.
>
> The fragrance of the roses of grace and bounty of the Caliph of God filled the deserts through which I traveled. By the grace of that great one's kindnesses, as infinite as grains of sand, I saw spirit and life even in the sand I walked upon.
>
> Although I came from beyond the deserts for the sake of obtaining the dinars he

generously offers, the more I walked and the closer I got, I sensed that I was in love not with dinars but the beloved darling.

I fainted away with the sight of his divine beauty. That is why I have forgotten my former desires and knowledge. I need neither prayer mat nor rosary . . . I am one who puts aside the mosque to pray in the winehouse. Give to me of the wine of his love.

In Heaven God showed Adam a tree and said, "You can eat the fruit of every tree, but do not approach this one; you must not taste its fruit." God had decked out this tree in light and decorated it with a heart-ravishing, irresistible beauty.

It was as if God were self-disclosed in this tree. He displayed in this tree in Heaven the self-disclosure he showed to Moses on Mount Sinai. It was such that neither Adam nor his dear wife Eve could resist it. They approached it and ate of its forbidden fruit. For that reason they were expelled from Heaven and sent to earth.

Adam had eaten wheat in Heaven and donned the shirt of heedlessness. But this event had to be considered not a punishment of Hazret Adam by the divine wisdom, but perhaps a kindness.

For Adam was expelled from Heaven for this fault, but because of this event the grape vine of humanity produced cluster after cluster, and spirit entered into the human being, the most divine of creatures, through the gate of his posterity.

The tree Adam and Eve approached, which was really the tree of the measuring-out and destiny [*kader ve kazâ*], served to fulfill the desire of divine beauty to be seen. Among the clusters and clusters of Adam and Eve's progeny God created eyes to see Himself and hearts to love Himself.

It was like it had been with Messenger Moses, who set out to find fire for his pregnant wife, and seeing a fire burning in the distance, walked in that direction, and when he reached the fire he heard a voice saying, "O Moses! I am your Lord!"

Thus Moses, seeking material fire, found the light of God self-disclosed in the form of fire. Matter escaped the fire of soul and creaturehood. True, Moses swooned before that voice rising from fire with divine fire. But this swoon was precisely intoxication with wine of divine love. Moses's spirit found the level of meaning of which he was worthy in such a moment of searching.

The story of Hazret Jesus is no different. When Messenger Jesus was betrayed by the Jews, despite the miracles he performed and the divine signs full of compassion and mercy he brought, God spoke thus to him:

O Jesus! I will raise you up to Myself. I will take you, perfectly pure, out of the hands of kafirs.

And Hazret Jesus rose up, escaping the hands of the Jews, and entered a house, and there Gabriel came to him and raised Jesus up to the fourth heavenly sphere. This meant that Hazret Jesus was freed from all creaturely attributes and bodily ties and rose up to the sacred precinct of the divine realm.

You know the story: Someone went to the baker to buy bread. He was going to pay money and get bread. But the baker seemed so beautiful to him that he fell in love and was ready to give his life instead. Another man went to a rosegarden to enjoy himself. But he found the beauty of the gardener more heart-ravishing than the beauty of the roses. He put aside roses and gazed at the man who tended them.

Like the Arabi man who pulled up Joseph, the most beautiful man in the world, from the well where he went to draw water.

For when Messenger Joseph was thrown into the well by his brothers God did not destroy him there. A traveler dying of thirst threw a bucket down the well, thinking there was water in it. When Joseph grabbed onto the rope and came up the traveler forgot his thirst. He saw before him a beauty who stopped the mind and he stood amazed.

The moral of these stories is that people seeking a variety of goals on worldly paths filled with a variety of pitfalls and difficulties can one day be enveloped in the light of love and joy, and be freed of creatuely passions and desires; they can give their hearts over to spiritual and luminary delights.

Many are the Josephs of spirit have fallen into the wells of soul and nature, but when a divine joy and spiritual delight lights up in their hearts, they take hold of the rope of patience and are saved from the wells their souls have trapped them in.

And it is probably no accident, but a sublime self-disclosure, that when the man who threw his bucket down the well hoping to find water saw the beauty of Joseph he forgot both water and well and fell in love with divine beauty alone.

The reality of divine love has not only light but fire. The spirit who does not burn in that fire, and even taste the pleasure of burning in that fire, cannot experience that light either. As long as he does not suffer the trials and torments of love, surely he will not attain the light he loves.

Thus the Arabi man took on the various trials in order to attain the secret of unity, crossed the deserts carrying the jug of rainwater in his hand and reached the gate of the Caliph of the Padishah of the two worlds.

What he carried in his hand was the jug of worship and combat with the soul. He had surrendered this jug at the gate of the palace. But this jug to be emptied into the Tigris was filled not with drops of water but unique spiritual value as if pearls and jewels.

If you have not had enough, I will give other examples in this vein:

For the sake of seeds, for the sake of a bit of nourishment, a falcon will rush into the trap set for him. He is caught but not killed. He is fed and trained so that he will serve to hunt other birds and one day, carried on the arm or shoulder of a padishah, he is used in the hunt. He becomes a bird of state who never leaves the side of the ruler.

In the same way, a child goes to school and, believing his father when he says, "If you study, I will buy you a bird," goes to school not to study but in order to have a bird of his own. There he acquires reading and writing, knowledge and art.

While he once paid monthly fees to the school and teacher who taught him knowledge, once he has finished his education and become a full moon in the skies of knowledge he makes donations to schools for the advancement of knowledge and no longer thinks of birds or other toys. He knows that one goes to school not to have birds but to acquire knowledge.

But higher than schools one attends in order to acquire knowledge, there are gates which teach people the final knowledge, the final reality, that is, gnosis; and the art is to be able to ascend from the foundation that is knowledge to reach those gates of gnosis.

Hazret Abbas, the uncle of Hazret Muhammed, was an ardent idolater before the advent of Islam. As a champion of idolatry he created many difficulties for both Hazret Muhammed and the Muslims, and even warred against the Muslims at the Battle of

Badr.

Abbas fell prisoner to the Muslims during that battle. As a prisoner he had the opportunity to observe and understand Islam first hand. In this way he himself and his descendents, all of the Abbasi, continuously served Islam as caliphs of Islam.

Thus, however the road leading to the great gate or the attraction of the great gate pulls a spirit to itself, the fundamental thing is to reach that gate and the sublime meaning of that gate.

The Arabi man was amazed at the kindness, generosity and bounty he received from the Caliph and said:

I came to this gate in order to make a request. But as soon as I stepped inside, I was put in the seat of honor.

I brought water from far away, hoping I might find bread. My humble gift was merely a jog of water. Now I see that the scent of the bread I hoped for has brought me to Highest Heaven.

The wheat which made Hazret Adam cast out of Heaven brought me near to heavenly things.

I have understood that by the same cause great God sends some far from Himself and brings some close, and it is clear that once a person is His, once a person is with Him, there is in this realm of limitless distances neither far nor near.

The result is that when I arrived at this gate I became like the angels. I have the struggle for neither bread and water in me. I am freed of worldly ties and feel light as a winged creature. I have become a being of spirit who revolves dancing around a gate of sublime love like the heavenly spheres revolve around the earth.

And I have understood that nothing but the attraction and fire in the spirits of true lovers is without goal and self-interest. It is only the travelers of divine love who burn with the fire of love and forsake their bodies and lives. The goal of all but those who tread that path is only worldly delights and worldly filth. I am a bondsman who has attained the good fortune of reaching the threshold of a gate that leads to light and arriving at the end of a road of none other than light, let alone delights in which creaturely filth resides.

****

IN EXPLICATION OF HOW A PERSON IN LOVE WITH THE WORLD IS LIKE A PERSON IN LOVE WITH A WALL STRUCK BY SUNBEAMS, WHO MAKES NO EFFORT OR EXERTION TO UNDERSTAND THAT RADIANCE AND SPLENDOR PROCEED NOT FROM THE WALL BUT FROM THE DISK OF THE SUN IN THE FOURTH HEAVEN; CONSEQUENTLY HE SETS HIS WHOLE HEART UPON THE WALL, AND WHEN THE SUNBEAMS RETURN TO THE SUN HE IS LEFT FOREVER IN DESPAIR: *"AND A BARRIER IS PLACED BETWEEN THEM AND WHAT THEY DESIRE"* [157]

Lovers of the whole are not lovers of parts
He fails to reach the whole who longs for the part
When a part falls in love with another part
Its beloved soon to its whole will depart
That lover is the fool of another's slave
Drowning, he reaches for one too weak to save

---

157. Koran 34:54.

        Shall his beloved care for him, with no power?
        Shall he serve his own master or his lover?
2845.   Thus they say, "Fornicate with a free woman,"
        And, "If you steal, steal pearls," for the same reason
        Slave goes to master, the lover's left in woe
        He gets the thorn, rose-scent returns to the rose
        He's left far from his desire, his toil in vain
        His foot wounded, and only loss for his pain
        Like a hunter who apprehends a shadow
        How should wealth come to him from a mere shadow?
        The man grasps the bird's shadow and holds it fast
        While the bird perches amazed upon a branch
2850.   Wondering, "What's that cracked-brained fool laughing at?
        Here's folly for you, no good will come of that!"
        If you say the part's connected with the whole
        Then eat thorns, they are connected with the rose
        Part is linked to the whole only in one view
        Prophecy would be in vain were that not true
        The prophets are for connecting part to whole
        How should that be if they are already whole?
        This discourse continues without end, O slave
        Bring the tale to conclusion, the day is late

For those in love with the whole cannot be lovers of parts, and in the same way those who have given their hearts to the parts are deprived of the whole. Know that in knowledge and gnosis this whole is called "the universal" [*kül*], and the part is called "the particular" [*cüz*]. For this means that those who give their hearts to the world are unaware of the Lord. The lovers of God have eyes neither for the world nor what is in it.

In fact, since every particular is part of the universal, it is in a state tending toward and attracted to the universal. For this reason, the moment the particular grasps the particular, it has lost it. But because it has a fondness for it, because it has given its heart to it, it suffers from being deprived of it. That is why those who have a fondness for and feel affection for the particulars of the world and the transient delights born of them are disappointed.

It is those in love with these particulars who becomes servants of others and their buffoons. If a person who falls into the rolling waves of events reaches out not for those who know how to swim but those who are drowning, if he hopes for help from them, of course his end will be drowning.

The person he expects to help him does not have the power protect and save himself let along be of use to someone weaker than himself.

You know the Arab proverb: "If you are going to commit adultery, do it with a free woman . . . not a slave . . . " Another proverb: "If you are going to steal, steal a pearl!"

To be sure, it would be wrong to do what these proverbs say, but their meaning is correct. The meaning is: "O you who are seeking the path or have lost your way! If you are going to run, run after an arrived person! IF you are going to hold on to something, hold on to the skirt of a perfect friend! If you will love, love a beauty created with care by divine art, who will lead you to God, so that all this may be of use to you, so your heart beating with good and superior emotions will not be used in vain."

For he who finds the road leading to his Lord attains a rose, while he who mistakes that road is left only with thorns.

What is gained by the person who obtains a thorn instead of a rose? The springtime of his life is wasted. The time of the rose of union will be past, and he will be both deprived of the felicity of smelling the rose of union, and he will be left, feet wounded by thorns, in utter disappointment, as the poet of the hymn said:

> The roses of Heaven's garden
> Are fragrant, saying God, O God

Those who thus hunt only the shadow of their prey are inexperienced hunters. Like the idiot who tried to pounce on the shadow on the ground of a bird sitting in a tree—even the bird was amazed at what he did and said: "Who is this blockhead? Why did he pounce on my shadow? Now what is he happy about?" Such action, which amuses even a bird, is "vanity" itself.

If you object to this and say the part is bound to the whole and cannot be separated from it, and think this is the meaning of what I have said, I'll tell you to smell the fragrance of this thorn and eat it. For neither can the thorn be separated from the rose.

What I have called shadow is the external appearance of created things, their forms. What I have called a bird is God's beautiful names, God's sublime essence which finds expression in these names. If you put aside the real and bind yourself to appearances, you will either make the path longer or lose it entirely.

Consider that if the connection of the part with the whole, that is, the part's being the whole, was perfect in every respect, there would have been no reason for the Lord to send messengers into the world. The job of the messengers is to tie parts to the whole in every respect that they should be tied to the whole. For example, which events are merciful [rahmânî], and which satanic [şeytanî]? Which bonds bring a person to God, and which leave him lost in heedlessness? Who are the friends, and how and in what manner do they guide the parts?

So, the problem is the struggle to reach a level where one can comprehend how the part is connected in every respect, in every single respect, with the whole.

Since the job of a messenger is to make bondsmen reach God, what need is there of him if a bondsman, who is a part of Him, has achieved consciousness that he is bound to God in every respect? Whom will the messenger take hold of, and to whom will he bring him?

In that case the messenger's job is to awaken not those who have become one being [vücût] with God but those who have not. Think of one who walks at night on a great, a very great road, holding a torch before a caravan of pilgrims to Mecca. The messenger's job is bring not the masters of heart, but those who slip and fall in this darkness of night and lose the path, back to that great road, as the poet said:

> Like the caravan guide's torch on the road to the Hajj
> You're shining among the masters of love, O my heart

But this discourse has no end, O son. Come, let us finish the story of the Arabi man.

****

HOW THE ARAB DELIVERED THE GIFT, THAT IS, THE JUG, TO THE SLAVES OF THE CALIPH

2855.   He presented the jug in that high presence
He was sowing there the seed of his service
"Carry this gift to that Sultan," he then said
"Redeem the Shah's suitor from his indigence
Sweet water in a jug with new enamel
Rainwater that was caught within the canal."
The announcers almost laughed at what he said
But they accepted the jug like dear spirit
For the grace of the Shah, good and well-informed
Had left an impression on his courtiers

2860.   A shah's character settles in his subjects
It's heaven's blue-green wheel makes the earth verdant
Know the shah is like a reservoir whose pipes
Feed the same water everywhere through the pipes
When the water is from a pure reservoir
Every pipe gives pleasant-tasting, sweet water
If the reservoir has brackish, foul water
Each pipe produces that same brackish water
For all are connected with the reservoir
Dive, dive deep into the meaning of these words

2865.   Ponder the royal grace of homeless spirit
How in the entire body it works effects
The grace of good-natured, noble born reason
How to the whole body it brings discipline
Vivacious love, changeable and without rest
How it drives the entire body to madness
The Kawsar-like ocean's water is so pure
That all of its pebbles are like gems and pearls
For whatever art the master may be famed
His pupils' spirits are endowed with the same

2870.   Before the master of the methods of proof
Quick, hardworking pupils read methods of proof
The master jurist teaches jurisprudence
Not the methods of proof to jurist students
And the master who is a grammarian
His pupil's spirit is grammar-like through him
And the master who is in the path effaced
His pupil's spirit is in the Shah effaced
Of all kinds of knowledge, on the day of death
Poverty is for the road best equipment

The desert Arab held out his jug of water. He offered it to the Caliph's men. He declared his service to the Caliph and his court:

Present this humble gift to that great Sultan and save the one begging the Padishah

364

for fulfillment of his need from the poverty making him wretched.

I've brought him sweet water in an enameled jug. The water in it is real water of mercy which I collected in a ditch. In short, I present him with the jug of my body, in which the water of gnosis has been collected by the mercy of God.

The Caliph's men could not keep themselves from smiling at the Arabi man's gift, but they accepted this sincere gift with love and delicacy. For the courtesy of the Caliph had been an example to his courtiers and adorned them also with grace, beneficence and courtesy. If a caliph or a padishah is a great man, especially a man with a great heart, his men and his people will also be great in the same manner. The people benefit from the greatness of the Shah.

Padishahs serve as examples. Their virtue influences the mood and heart of the people. The greenery on the earth is the bounty of the skies. That is why people say, "The earth has turned sky" [göğermiş yer]. Every blade of grass you see on earth is a prayer of mercy that rains down from the sky.

Know that the Padishah is like a fountain reservoir and his courtiers like the pipes which dispense water from it. The water flowing through the pipes makes lakes and pools.

If the water flowing through these pipes is from a perfectly clean reservoir, sweet, healthy water will come through every pipe; if not, if the water is dirty, the water coming out of the pipes will be turbid and bitter.

Padishahs are like the heart, countries are like bodies, and the Padishah's men are like veins. The body is nourished by the clean blood coming through those veins. The hearts of the arrived are completely filled with knowledge of the divine [ledün bilgisi] and love of God, and they offer what is in their hearts to their murids.

It is the mercy coming from these hearts which reaches the minds of spirits who tread the path of God. In short, only what is in a container can seep out of it. Now you dive into the pool of the meaning of these words, cool off and think deeply. If you pay attention you will see that the beauty and varied attributes of the spirit padishah, who has no visible country, are reflected in various ways upon the body of the servant.

A well-bred, pure and beautiful intellect brings about goodness and beauty in the body. Modesty, faith, the feelings of a pure character, are only possible with intellect. That is why all the good and beautiful things people do are works of intellect.

The love the spirit feels for all beautiful things and beautiful people spreads throughout the entirety of a person's being [varlık]. As Hakim Sanai said, "Love is not myth nor enchantment. Love is not the art of every base person. All who claim to love cannot be lovers. All who speak of love cannot be faithful. Not everyone can be a man of love, and not every heart can feel the pain of love."

Love is an alchemy that can only be found in the mine of spirit. And love is an essence whose only source is God. Look at a transparent lake or a calm sea. Through the clear water the stones at the bottom appear to be as beautiful as pearls, rubies, emeralds and other valuable jewels.

A goldsmith's apprentices become goldsmiths too. A student learns whatever you teach him. One does not learn grammar at a school of jurisprudence, or jurisprudence at a school of grammar.

So it is with sown fields. You reap what you sow. If a master is a traveler on the path of God and a gnostic of that path, his students and murids learn truth from their master. From a mushid who knows how to die in the path of love, his student learns mortality.

Consider that of all the knowledge that can be taught to people, the only great knowledge that will be beneficial to us on the day we die is this knowledge of not-being.

****

THE STORY OF WHAT PASSED BETWEEN THE GRAMMARIAN AND THE BOATMAN

2875.   A grammarian embarked upon a boat
        Conceited, he asked the helmsman of the boat:
        "Have you ever studied grammar?" "No," he said
        "Then half of your life has gone to naught," he said.
        Broken-hearted, the boatman suffered torment
        But held back from answering at that moment
        The boat was thrown in a whirlpool by the wind
        And the boatman called to the grammarian:
        "Have you ever learned to swim?" he asked, "Tell me."
        "No, my good man, fair of face and repartee."
2880.   "Then your whole life's gone to naught, grammarian
        For the boat is plunging into the ocean
        Self-effacement, not grammar, is needed here
        If you are dead to self, plunge in without fear."
        The dead are lifted on the head of the sea
        How should he who is alive escape the sea?
        When to creaturely attributes you are dead
        The sea of secrets will keep you on its head
        You treat everyone as if he were an ass
        Now it's you who're stuck on the ice like an ass
2885.   Though most learned man of the time in the world
        Now you see the end of the time and the world
        We've stitched in the tale of the grammarian
        To teach you grammar of annihilation
        Law of law, grammar of grammar and of sense
        You will find, O valued friend, in being less
        That jug of water is all of our knowledge
        The Caliph is the Tigris of God's knowledge
        We are carrying full jugs to the Tigris
        We may not know it, but we are the asses
2890.   Say the Bedouin may be excused from this
        He new nothing of rivers or of Tigris
        Were he aware of the Tigris, as we are
        He'd not have carried that water jug so far
        No, if he had been aware of the Tigris
        He would have shattered that water jug to bits

A grammarian boarded a boat. He was of the opinion that the sole condition for life on earth was grammar. Thinking thus, he turned to the boatman and asked proudly, "Do you know grammar?"

The boatman said, "No."

The linguist, intending to display the superiority of his own knowledge, said condescendingly, "Then half your life has been spent in vain. You have wasted your life in ignorance."

These words affected the boatman deeply. He was heartbroken. But he said nothing. He found it best to be silent.

Soon afterwards a gale blew up and drove the boat into a whirlpool. The storm had grown violent and the grammarian was pale. The boatman saw this and called out to the master grammarian so proud of his worldly knowledge, "Master! Do you know how to swim?"

Still pale, the master answered faint-heartedly, "No, O handsome, witty boatman! I don't know how to swim."

Then the boatman said simply, "Then all of your life has been wasted. O Grammarian! For our boat is going down in this whirlpool."

****

The pathetically arrogant grammarian did not know that the sole knowledge to make a person happy in both worlds is not knowledge of grammar [*nahiv*], but knowledge of annihilation [*mahiv*]. And the boatman was saying: "Master! What is needed here is not grammar, but annihilation. If you are not only a grammarian but an annihilationist, that is, if you know the nothingness and not-being of your own being and have worked to attain the secret of annihilation in God and mastered it, fear not! Let yourself fall into the water's embrace. It will take you where you wish to go."

That's how the water of the ocean is. When a person is dead, it carries him on its surface. You can see the corpse floating on the water, it does not sink.

But while a person is alive, he cannot stay long in the water. He either comes out onto the land and leaves the sea behind, or sinks to the bottom.

O Grammarian! If you are free of pride, arrogance, lust and passion, in sum, if you have died to the limitations of the body and worldly filth, the sea of gnosis and truth, the sea of God's unity and sublime wisdom, will carry you too on its head.

But O Grammarian enslaved to pride and selfhood! If you treat everyone like an ass, if you treat God's bondsmen with contempt, that is something else. You will be stuck like an ass who has wandered out on the ice, unable to take a step on a frozen river.

If in your time you are the most learned of all men in the world and everything in it, master of these transient appearances, know that this world passes away. Your knowledge, if you have any, only appears to be so for the short span of your lifetime. But after you are gone, and for the afterlife, your worldly knowledge, even if it be worlds full of knowledge, is worth nothing.

So . . . We have told you the story of the grammarian to remind you of the way to become naught, in short, to remind you of the knowledge of annihilation.

O true friend! Work to find the jurisprudence of jurisprudence, the sense of sense, the grammar of grammar, in short, the knowledge of knowledge, and learn the science of truth before you leave this world. Know that:

The water in the jug which the desert Arab carried was a measure of the knowledge we and all of humanity possess. Because he had not yet seen the Tigris River, he supposed that the water collected in his own rain ditch and his own jug was the most valuable and sweetest water there is.

Soon he will see the Tigris and be amazed. The knowledge we have is just that much, while the Caliph's knowledge is as great as the Tigris. And just imagine, there are vast oceans into which the Tigris, and so many other rivers like it flow.

We should know that it is asinine to bring water to the Tigris in a jug. If we cannot learn that, we will not only be asinine, we will be asses.

In one respect, the Arabi man should be forgiven for being proud that he is able to bring a jug of water to that great gate. For he has never seen even a small stream in his live, let alone the Tigris. Because he is an Arab of the desert, even one drop of water is valuable to him.

If the Arab knew as much about the Tigris as you do, he would not have carried water across the desert to the Tigris. If he had even heard about the Tigris, he would have stopped somewhere and shattered the jug against a rock for the pleasure of giving a drop of water to the thirsty desert sands.

****

How the Caliph accepted the Gift and bestowed Presents although He had absolutely no Need of the Water or the Jug

> When the Caliph saw the gift and heard his speech
> He filled up the jug with gold and gave increase
> He delivered the Arab from misery
> He granted him robes of honor and money
>
> 2895. Saying, "Place into his hand this jug of gold
> Take him to the Tigris on his way back home
> He came by land through desert on his way here
> To return by water will be easier."
> When the Arab saw the Tigris from the boat
> He kept bending and bowing in self-reproach
> "The bounteous grace of that Shah is wondrous!
> That he accepted the water, more wondrous!
>
> 2900. How did that ocean of generosity
> Accept such corrupt coin from me so quickly?"
> All the world's a jug that's filled up to the brim
> Know this, O my son, with beauty and wisdom
> It's a drop from the Tigris of His beauty
> Which no skin can contain for all its plenty
> It was a hidden treasure so full it burst
> Making earth than heaven's spheres more luminous
> It was a hidden treasure so full it rose
> Making earth a sultan clothed in satin robes
>
> 2905. If he'd seen a branch of the Divine Tigris
> He'd have destroyed that jug, he'd have destroyed it!
> Those who've seen it are always beside themselves
> They've hurled a stone at the jug, beside themselves
> You who've thrown stones at the jug in rivalry
> The jug is the more perfect for shattering

The jar's shattered, the water has not run out
It is shattered, yet a hundred times more sound
Each piece of the jar dances in ecstasy
To partial reason it is absurdity

2910.   In this state neither the jug is manifest
Nor the water; consider; God knows what's best
Knock on meaning's door, and you will be let in
Beat the wings of thought, be made a shah's falcon
The wing of your thought is heavy and clay-stained
Clay for you seems like bread, because you eat clay
Eat less of bread and of meat, for they are clay
That you may not like clay in the earth remain
When you become hungry, you become a dog
Brutish and bad-tempered and come of bad stock

2915.   You're a dead carcass when you've eaten your fill
With neither awareness nor feet, like a wall
So one moment you're a dog, then a carcass
In the path of lions how will you run fast?
Know you have no tool for hunting but the dog
So do not throw so many bones to the dog
For when the dog eats its fill, it's arrogant
How will it run in the good chase and the hunt?
What drew that Arab on was the want of food
Until he saw that court and found that fortune

2920.   In the story we spoke of the Shah's favor
Toward that needy man who had no protector
Whatever a man of love says, scent of love
Springs from his mouth towards the abode of love
If he speaks theology, it's poverty
From that sweet discourse comes scent of poverty
Scent of religion comes from his blasphemy
If he speaks doubt, it turns into certainty
False froth upon the sea of sincerity
Is set out there by a source of purity

2925.   Know that its froth is pure and that it is fit
Like abuse which comes from the beloved's lips
Falsehood coming from that quarter seems the truth
O falsehood that would adorn even the truth!
If out of sugar you make a loaf, like bread
You will taste sugar when you eat it, not bread
If a believer finds a golden icon
Will he abandon it to those who bow down?
No, he'll throw it in the fire and destroy it
He'll destroy its form, borrowed and transient

2930.   So the idol-shape will not remain in gold
Because form's a hindrance and thief on the road

The gold's essence is the essence of Lordship
The idol-stamp on gold coin is transient
Do not burn a rug on account of a flea
Don't let the day go because a fly's buzzing
You worship idols if you remain with forms
Look at the meaning and put aside its form
If you'd go on Hajj, seek a hajji for friend
Whether he be Hindu, Arab or Turkmen

2935.   Don't look at his form, the color of his skin
Look at his purpose and determination
He may be black, but he's in accord with you
Call him white, he is the same color as you
This tale's topsy-turvy, like what lovers do
It's been told with neither a head nor a foot
It has no head, for it is pre-eternal
No foot, for it's always been post-eternal
It's like water, every drop there is therein
Is both head and foot, and neither one of them

2940.   Attend well! God forbid, this is no fiction
It is the very coin of our condition
Since the Sufi has strong will and intention
What is in the past will never be mentioned
We are Arab, jug, and king, we are all three
Those led into falsehood are those who would be[158]
The husband is reason, wife, greed and passion
Two dark deniers; the bright lamp is reason
Now hear whence the source of denial arose
There are many various parts to the whole

2945.   Parts are not parts in relation to the whole
Not like rose-scent, which is a part of the rose
The grace of leaves is a part of the rose too
Part of that nightingale is the ring-dove's coo
But if I'm busy solving difficulties
How should I then give water to the thirsty?
If you're wholly perplexed, in straits, have patience
The key to obtaining relief is patience
Abstain from anxious thoughts, practice abstinence
Hearts are forests, thought the lion and wild ass

2950.   Abstinence is superior to all cures
For to scratch only makes an itch become worse
The basis of cure, certainly, is to abstain
Behold the power of the spirit: abstain
Become like an ear as you take these words in
So that I may make for you a gold earring
As a ring in the ear of the goldsmith moon

158. Koran 51:7-11.

You'll ascend to the Pleiades and the moon
First, listen; for the diverse created beings
Are diverse, from ya to alif, spiritually

2955. Among letters there is doubt and confusion
Though in one view, they're from head to foot all one
One way unified, another, opposites
In one view joking, another, serious
Resurrection Day will be the greatest view
Those with will and intention want to be viewed
For him who's like a double-dealing Hindu
Exposure comes on the day of greatest view
Because he does not have a face like the sun
All he wants is night to serve as a curtain

2960. Since his thorn does not have one single rose-leaf
The spring season is his secret's enemy
If a man's all rose and iris end to end
Spring is like a pair of shining eyes to him
The thorn without inner meaning seeks autumn
So it may seem fellow to the rosegarden
To hide the rose's beauty and its own shame
So the color of each one will seem the same
Therefore autumn is spring and life to the thorn
A limpid ruby seems the same as a stone

2965. The gardener even in autumn knows this
The whole world can't see as well as one eye does
The world is that one person, a simpleton
The stars are all parts of the moon, every one
So every image and fair form is crying
"Good news! Good news! Behold, here arrives the spring!"
So long as blossoms like a coat of mail shine
How should fruits display their bodies on the vine?
When the blossom falls, the fruit comes to a head
When the body breaks, the spirit lifts its head

2970. Fruit is the meaning, the blossom is its form
The blossom is the good news, fruit its reward
When the blossom's shed, fruit becomes visible
When this decreases, that becomes plentiful
How shall bread give strength if it is not broken?
How shall grapes yield wine unless they are crushed in?
If myrobalan's not mixed with medicines
How shall health be increased by the medicines?

When the Caliph saw the Arabi man's gift and understood the state he was in, he realized how pure the desert Arabi's spirit was. He filled his jug with gold. He gave other gifts to this bondsman of God who had come to his gate. He gave him a robe. He told his men, "Take our guest back to his country by way of the Tigris. It will be shorter by water than by land."

His intention was to show him the Tigris, in exchange for the water he had brought. And just so, when the Arabi man saw the Tigris he lost his mind. Never in his life had he seen such a mighty river, such a vast amount of sweet water. He realized what he had brought and to whom. He understood better the greatness of the Caliph's spirit. He immediately prostrated himself to the ground.

To himself and out loud he said, "What a great Padishah he is, to have accepted my jug of water when he has a whole Tigris of sweet water. He gave me so many presents for such a humble gift. He gave me gold for my worthless coin. He did not hesitate. My God, what greatness is this!" Now, O son! That jug is a parable and a parable of this world. There is gnosis and beauty in that jug. But this jug full of beauty and wisdom is not even one drop compared to the beauty and wisdom of that great Padishah.

God said in a sacred hadith: "I was a hidden treasure and I loved to be known." One of the most sublime of that hidden treasure's qualities is beauty, and so sublime a beauty cannot stay hidden, could not. And this is the mystery of the created universe.

Divine being and beauty was full of such superior qualities, and so full to overflowing, that its need to overflow rent the veils of the Unseen encircling being, and its magnificent light struck this realm and this earth. Thus it created earth more luminous than the heavens.

For the most honored of the creatures God created was man. And the first human, Hazret Adam, was created from earth. It was with the self-disclosure of God Himself in the human that, spiritually, earth became more luminous than heaven.

At the same time, what is intended with this earth, which God dressed in satin robes, overflowing from His hidden treasure, is not only vast steppes, green valleys, magnificent deserts and mountains stretching far as the eye can see. The essence of earth and all created things is man.

To be sure, if the desert Arab, who in this story represents the intellect, had seen the Tigris, which is the self-disclosure of divine being and divine beauty in the form of water—or even a branch of the Tigris, any body of flowing water—he would have shattered the jug of his body. His regard for his body [*vücût*] would have been erased and he would have risen up and flowed like the Tigris to be united with the single and absolute being [*vücût*].

Such has been the adventure of many a spirit. Many spirits have forsaken their own being after seeing one branch of the Tigris of divine beauty. They have shattered the jugs of their bodies on the rock of not-being. O mature spirit! You who have shattered the jug of your body on the rock of not-being! Let me give you the good news that the jug you have shattered has gained its real value by being broken. In fact it is with this annihilation that it achieves union. The jar is broken, but its water is not wasted. It has not spilt on the ground but ascended to the sky, mixing there with the divine ocean of being and becoming immortal.

Do you understand? This shattering is such that real wholeness is born from it.

Partial intellect may not understand it, but the truth is exactly this. Each particle of every shattered jar comes alive and begins to dance in infinite ecstasy around divine being and beauty.

****

One must understand the meaning of these words. Once spirit is freed of the bonds of body, neither jug nor water remains . . .

Still one must know that only God knows best the truth of every thing.

If you doubt and wonder how and wherefrom I know all these secrets, what you must do is scratch at the door of meaning. If you want the door to open, you must knock. Those who hear that you are at the door will open this door to you.

The value of a person is measured by his effort. A person ascends on the wings of thought and effort. You must spread these wings and transcend the horizons of partial intellect so that there will be others to take you higher, to the heavens of universal intellect.

But how will you ascend if your wings of thought and effort are caked with mud and heavy? In the swamp into which you have fallen, who can see that you are anything other than mud?

For worldly desires are really nothing but a swamp. Those things you feel passion for and are sunk in were all created of earth. The essence of even the bread you eat is earth. Eat as little as you can of these. Do not be greedy for the delights and riches which draw you to the world, so that your body may not grow heavy by eating much of them and prevent you from rising up.

If hunger makes you thrust for every bone and bounty like a dog, and when you fill your belly you cannot move because you have eaten so much, and you become motionless as a corpse, without eyes for any kind of wakefulness, how will you find a way to escape these worldly passions and burdens and ascend to the skies?

Don't throw so many bones to the dog of the body, so that it will not stuff itself and become unruly. A dog that stuffs its belly will not be able to hunt beautiful prey.

What drew the Arabi man up to higher levels was his poverty. Because he was not soiled by worldly filth, not stuck in the mud, not burdened by heavy matter, he was not left at the bottom but rose up high.

The Caliph gave him gifts because he saw the purity of spirit in him. The story of the desert Arab which I have told you is not the story of a mean life; it tells of contentment, sincerity, and the levels ardor and love may raise a spirit. The mysteries of union and unity are in this story.

It is enough for you to know that it is not a fairy tale, but a tale of wisdom.

For this story is the story of love, and you have heard it from the tongue of a lover.

Consider that only the language of love rises from each word you hear from the tongue of a lover. The fragrance of love spreads everywhere.

If a lover speaks of jurisprudence, everything he says will pertain to poverty and not-being. This poverty means to be poor in worldly passions, and this not-being, to be free of the body's transient fantasies.

If a lover blasphemes, all who are gnostics will understand his meaning to be faith.

Many thought it was blasphemy that Mansur Hallaj's said, "I am the Truth." But he was saying, "I am not, for there is no being other than God." Even if a saying such as this, which declares the reality of God, be considered blasphemy, it is faith itself.

If the ocean is the ocean of purity and rectitude, what does it matter if the waves and foam that come from it are awry? When the wind and waves die down, what is left in the sea is its own purity. When the gale subsides and the waves are still, nothing is visible to you but beauty and goodness.

Let us say that Ibn Arabi, Juneyd Baghdadi, Beyazid Bistami or Mansur Hallaj said something irregular. But they were in ecstasy when they said it. There were storms and waves on their pure, bright waters. See the truth in their words when the waves die down.

And know that even in storms, their foam is pure, clean and precious.

Suppose that your beloved scolds you with such words, so what? It is the one who loves you most who says them. Love is a stormy state, the lover is intoxicated. And without doubt, he speaks in intoxication. That is why words of love are daring.

So, while love is askew, intellect is straight. If you are a gnostic, see the shining intellect in the waves of love. And know that intellect is a self-disclosure of light, but the infinite light which illuminates creation is found only in love.

Look not to form but to essence, Suppose that you melt sugar, make dough, and knead it into the shape of bread. When you eat it, you will taste not bread but sugar.

In the same way every mortal whose body is kneaded with the dough of love is like sugar kneaded into the shape of bread. That is why there is the taste of sugar and the luminosity of light in bitter, dark things said by the friends.

And suppose that a Muslim finds an idol made of gold. Will he throw away the gold because it is in the shape of an idol? If you melt the gold idol, there will be nothing left of the idol form, but there will be gold left.

So, the goldness of gold is God-given. Let us say that a kafir makes a cross of gold, or an icon, a statue, or some other form—whatever the form, it is still gold.

To burn a comforter because of one flea, or ruin your day because of the buzzing of a fly, is not an intelligent thing to do.

External appearances fool the intellect. If someone who sees a golden statue supposes it to be a statue merely, and doesn't see the gold, he sees only the form. But that statue is made of gold. To see gold as merely a statue is just idolatry.

Go on the hajj with a companion. Your companion may be an Arab, an Indian, or beautiful as a Turk. Do not regard your companion's color and fret that he is Indian, or dark-skinned. Consider, that man with a dark-skinned face is a hajj pilgrim like yourself.

Whether his external color is black or yellow, every person's inner color is the same as yours.

We have let this story go all over the place. Like anxious lovers and their thoughts, it has neither head nor foot.

That's what a lover's thoughts are like. Like the sublime beauty they love, they have neither beginning nor end. There is no time in this love and the thoughts born of it. It is not limited by time; past, present and future are all the same to them. Because a lover's heart is set on fire in pre-eternity, it is pre-eternal, and because the beauty he loves is post-eternal in quality, the hearts of lovers too are post-eternal.

Let us say that what I have related here, told with such a love, is water pouring out from a sea of oneness, drops pouring down from such a sea. A drop has neither beginning nor end.

But this is neither parable, tale nor history. In reality it is our state; your state and mine.

For the Sufi is a powerful spirit progressing continuously forward along a path by which he will never return. For him there is neither past nor future. The Sufi is continuously in a "state." That state is the state of being with Him, in Him, and annihilated in

Him.

That is why the story I have told is our story. The Arab in the story, the jug, the water in the jug and the Padishah he brought it to—they are all us.

As it says in the Koran: "By the sky with numerous paths, verily you hold discordant doctrine, by which are deluded those who would be deluded" (51:7-9).

This means: "You who deny! Sometimes you call Hazret Muhammed a sorcerer, sometimes a poet, sometimes an oracle and sometimes a lunatic. Thus you show that you are unaware of the path shown by the greatest of Messengers, and you talk nonsense." The Gracious Koran relates a great truth, that opponents of Hazret Muhammed called him a sorcerer and a poet, slandered him and accused him of merely telling stories. Thus every spirit must do away with its inner doubts and see that the verses of the Koran rule all creation and the vicissitudes of all beings.

The heat's eyes of those who want to see it this way are opened by God. Those who stubbornly insist on not seeing will surely end by into the abyss.

That is why you must know the man in this story as intellect, and soul and its greed as woman. You will take into account that the one leads to light, and the other to darkness. But whether spirit is male of female, when it finds the right path, soul and intellect will reach the truth, reach light, by supporting each other.

If you ask the reason for denial, consider that the whole has various parts. Among these parts many are opposites of another. Light and darkness, verification and denial, are among such opposites.

What is fundamental is the whole. Although the part is of the whole, it is not the entire whole. The rose is the whole, its scent is its part. If the voice of the nightingale means the most beautiful of all voices, then the melodies of other birds, such as the dove, should be considered parts of the nightingale's voice.

The absolute and whole being of God the Truth self-discloses in various parts. God's manifestation in the form of majesty means the self-disclosure of divine power and grandeur. God's overwhelming power becomes evident in his majesty. When God self-discloses with the attribute of beauty, He fills creation with grace, mercy and divine generosity. God has these attributes and many more like them, some of them opposites, but is with all of them one pre-eternal and post-eternal whole.

The human was created in the form of a self-disclosure of divine power and divine qualities. That is why, for example, soul and intellect in a person are contraries and separate forces in conflict. But just as divine qualities become one whole when they take on the color of unity, such parts of the human as soul and intellect too take on the color of unity and thus become whole.

But if I try to put forth all difficulties and provide answers, when will I give those thirsting with the fire of love the wine of love they thirst for, how will I satisfy their thirst?

The wisdom we seek here is wisdom of the heart. Let some understand it from what I say, and others from my silence.

If you are anxious, wondering how you will get out of the difficulties you are in, first try patience. For patience is the key which frees the bondsman from every affliction. Then avoid longing for the world and worldly delights, and avoid worrying about anything other than God. Abstain from such anxieties! For in the forests of the heart, thoughts are the lion and anxieties, the wild ass.

As is the case with many physical illnesses, the cure for spiritual afflictions like fear, anxiety and worry is abstention.

Just as there is a diet for each kind of disease, there is a diet for the disease of thought and anxiety. For example, the abstention proper to scabies is abstention from scratching. Because the more you scratch, the more you itch. In diseases of thought and anxiety, affliction increases by increase of doubts, questions and difficulties.

I have told you so much about the mysteries of unity and the states of love. Now I will fasten golden rings to your ears. But in order for me to do that, first you must have the ear to hear these mysteries.

Be one of those who works the gold of gnosis, like the moon that works in gold all night long! Rise like the moon and become an earring in the ear of the crescent moon. May your spiritual station be high as the moon, or the stars of the Pleiades. Dive into the spiritual realms of the heavens and wander the divine realm [*lâhut alemi*]. This is now my wish for you. Let me see you perfected in the path of God.

Pay attention to all the letters of the alphabet, from alif to ya. They appear as different lines and forms, and they have various different sounds. So it is with spirits in the world. Each is different from the other.

But if you pay a bit more attention you will see that those letters you thought different from one another all come from the same letter alif, that is, from the single line of alif in variations and forms. So the roots of all the letters unite in alif. But not really in alif either, for alif is a line formed from the uniting of several points. It is a beautiful and meaningful line.

But because of the countless variety of ways in which the letters born of that same alif can be combined, what meanings they acquire, how contrary they become, one to another!

Sometimes they form satire, or useless sentences, significance wasteful of the beautiful being of words and statements. Sometimes they unite like soldered gold to form the blessed names of God, Koranic verses, or hadiths, becoming single in the most beautiful and sublime of meanings, becoming all goodness.

Sometimes they write of the brightness of light, sometimes they put the darkness of infidelity in the form of black writings. It is these letters which bring forth the pages of the Gracious Koran from divine speech. Yet the same lines make of deceptive books containing the spiritual darkness within kafirs and deniers.

So all this speech arises from a single letter alif, and although born of the same source, that is, although fundamentally single and one, can in self-disclosure and appearance be separate words and sentences too numerous to count.

And so it is with the spirits who break away from the same sublime source to become on earth beautiful, ugly, good, bad, transient or eternal. They differ from one another as do the forms which the line of alif takes on with bends and twists.

****

It is these varied spirits who will give account of their actions on the Day of the Greatest Viewing, the Resurrection, and will be treated differently and accorded different rewards.

There are spirits who long heart and soul for what we call the Day of the Greatest Viewing, the day when the spirit presents itself to the greatest Beloved and chooses to annihilate itself in His being. Because on that day the spirit will be joined with that greatest Beloved. Because that spirit has prepared all its life for that day and waited for that day, its interior is filled with goodness and beauty, and its light has become a brightness full to overflowing.

On such a day of course those spirits whose faces are black like Indians will fall into disgrace. They do not want to see daylight. They wish to remain hidden in the darkness of night, which covers all their faults. Only such darkness can compete with their infidelities and sins.

A rose cannot bloom on a tree made of thorns. But the brightness of spring is like two bright eyes for pure and clean spirits who bloom like roses and irises. Spring displays all the beauty and splendid colors of such spirits. Both the afterlife and Resurrection are for such spirits a matchless springtime displaying all their purity and beauty.

Spirits who don't have a rose and iris-like beauty to be seen wish not for spring but for autumn. Because autumn is the season of thorns and branches ugly as thorns. Autumn is like a darkness which removes the difference between rocks and rubies. Because roses do not bloom, it is a time when thorns remain hidden.

But it is only thus for eyes that do not, and can not, see the truth. If you ask the gardener which is the rose and which is the thorn, he knows this in autumn as clearly as in spring.

The gardener who grows the various roses and other flowers of the universe, who does not withhold His mercy either from thorn-like or rose-like spirits, is always aware of the ugliness of thorns, just as he is aware of the beauty of the rose.

Every star in the sky appears to be a piece of the moon. In the same way, every gnostic on earth is a piece of the full moon-like perfect friend. In fact, the world consists only of that "one person," and that "one person" is unaware of any ugliness and far from all evil. There is no place in his heart for ugliness, evil, or darkness.

That is why in both the worldly and the spiritual realms every branch, every tree, every rose and every flower that has no fear of spring is full of joy when it arrives. First the trees are clothed in a raiment of flowers, and the leaves don robes of honor. Then these flowers take off their clothes, like bodies in the sun, shedding petal by petal. In short, when every spirit strips itself of the petals of flesh and reaches the point of being pure spirit, that is when the awaited fruit arrives.

The flowers fall and fruits begin to appear. So it is with the spirit freed of the bond of flesh. The flowers which appear so beautiful and colorful at the beginning of spring, that is to say, all bodies, will one day be shed. It is enough that underneath this body's flower there be spiritual fruit.

So, meaning is the fruit. And the flower is a beautiful appearance which hides that meaning for a time. But every flower is in reality a fruit, that is, it announces the good news of a meaning. Do not grieve that the flower is shed and gone, that the colorful, fresh beauty is erased from sight. Its task is in fact to bring forth the fruit, which is the greatest bounty; to prepare the conditions under which the fruit may mature.

Just as one must break bread in order to eat it, in order to drink the wine which makes a person lose consciousness of self one must squeeze grapes and obtain their juice.

If you want to find the cure for what ails you, if you want to put salve on your wound, you crush myrobalan and mix it with other medicines to prepare the elixir you want. That is how medicine is made to improve one's health.

****

CONCERNING THE PIR'S QUALITIES AND OBEDIENCE TO HIM

Husameddin, ray of truth, take a few sheets
To add description of the Pir's qualities
2975. Though the strength of your slender body is done
For us there can be no light without the sun
Though you're thin as candle wick and lantern glass[159]
You're the thread's end, the heart's under your command
Since the thread's end is in your hand, at your wish
The beads of the heart's necklace are yours to give
Write of the states of the Pir who knows the way
Choose a Pir and know he's the same as the way
The Pir is summer, others autumn season
They are like night, and the Pir the moon within
2980. I gave the name of Pir to fortunate youth
Fortune is not aged in time, but in truth
It is so aged, it has no beginning
There is no rival for a pearl so unique
Surely potency grows stronger in old wine
Especially if it is knowledge divine[160]
Choose a Pir, for without a Pir this journey
Is full of fear, danger and calamity
Even on a road you've traveled many times
You can become distracted without a guide
2985. Don't go alone on a path you've never tried
Beware! Don't turn your head away from the guide
If his shadow's not protecting you, O fool
Your head will spin with the crying of the ghoul
Who will toss you into ruin off the path
There've been many smarter than you on this path
Hear from the Prophet about their perdition
What evil-spirited Iblis did to them
Taking them a hundred thousand years' away
He left them naked and sinning where they strayed
2990. See their bones and hair—all that remains of them
Take example, don't drive your donkey toward them
Seize your donkey's neck and draw him toward the path
Toward the good men who guard and who know the path
Don't take your hand off him, don't let him run free
For a donkey's love takes him where grass will be
If in a heedless moment you set him free
He will go for parasangs to find green leaves
The donkey's mad for grass, a foe to the way
He's brought to ruin many who go his way

---

159. Koran 24:35.
160. "We taught him (Khizir) knowledge from Our own presence" (Koran 18:65).

2995.   Whatever he wants, if you don't know the way
Do the opposite, that will be the right way
"*Consult females* and *do the opposite* then
He will not be ruined who disobeys them"
Do not be a friend to appetite and lust
For what leads you from the path of God is this
To break this passion there's nothing in the world
Like the company of fellow-travelers

O Husameddin, reflector of divine light! Now get a few sheets of paper and I will tell you of the qualities of the Pir.

True, you are tired out. There is no strength left in your frail body. But just as we have no light without the sun, we are left in the dark if the sun of your spirituality does not illuminate our surroundings.

You know the chapter "Light" of the Koran. It says there (24:35): "God is the light of the heavens and the earth. The likeness of His light is as if there were a niche and within it a lamp, the lamp enclosed in glass; the glass like a brilliant star, lit from a blessed tree, an olive, of neither East nor West, whose oil is well-nigh luminous though fire does not touch it. Light upon light! God guides whom He will to His light."

O Husameddin! You are a like a crystal lantern in which God's light shines like that. Although because you are human, your glass is very fragile, from the point of view of spirituality you are a spirit charged with taking light from the self-disclosures of the sublime and spreading it to the people of the world. You lead men of heart, you are the first among them. You are a person for them to emulate.

Since you have the end of the thread in hand, since you are putting the pearls of heart and language of these *Spiritual Couplets* on the threads of written lines, the pearls, rubies and emeralds of this heart-necklace are your bounty too.

So, O Husameddin! Write the story of that Pir who knows the way to God. First find that Pir and know his path as he does. A Pir who knows the way is like the summer season, like the sun in springtime, and the people are like autumn. As long as the hearts of the people are not lit and illuminated by the light of such a Pir, a spiritual spring producing fruits and crops will not manifest in their hearts as nature, after knowing autumn and passing through winter, comes alive with the sun of spring and gives forth leaves and fruits.

O Husameddin, know that the people of this world are a dark night! Think of the Pir who illuminates them as a moon sparking in the sky of that night.

I have likened fortune that is young like you to the Pir.[161] I call it Pir. But it is a Pir of intellect and gnosis because of the maturity God has bestowed upon it, not because of the years it has lived. It is mature in the level at which it finds and sees God. It is not old in months and years.

There is no measure of time for the tarikat Pir. The arrived of God have no beginning or end. Their beginning and end is the same. Time is not for them. He is an arrived person, unique in time and in his time. He is a matchless pearl.

An arrived person is someone who has been living since pre-eternity. In that sense he is like an old wine. Old wine is much stronger than new wine. And this is a wine

---

161. *Pir* also has the meaning of "old."

which provides the delight of God's divine knowledge. That is the wine which provides the pre-eternal and post-eternal joy of the universe. Every spirit who has known the joy of pre-eternity will certainly drink that wine before others who sought it later.

Find that Pir who knows the way and shows the way. For without him, the journey you are on has a thousand and one terrors and dangers. Take the path Hazret Muhammed indicated when he said, "First the friend, then the road." Because when there is no perfect and arrived guide to the way, it is not given to every bondsman to complete the journey.

Even when a person is on a road he has traveled many times and is used to, he may sometimes seek someone to give him directions and make it easier for him. Since that is the case, how will you travel a road you've never taken alone?

If you behave stupidly and set out down this sublime road without a guide, know that the voices of soul-devils [*nefis devleri*] will defeat you, they will make you turn back from the path of God. People who supposed themselves to be far more intelligent than you have trusted in themselves and taken this path, and far from completing their journey, came to mischief somewhere along the road.

If you want to know how those who follow their noses have taken detours and gone astray, read the Gracious Koran! There you will find many a story of those who went astray and fell into error.

You will learn from the word of God how Satan separated them from righteousness and kept them off the path for a hundred thousand years. You will find there the story of those who conformed to Satan, doffed the robes of religion and were left utterly naked.

All that is left of them is a few pieces of bone and some hair. Regard those bones and hair, do not drive the donkey of your soul down their path. Grab hold of the donkey's neck! Turn its head in the right direction. Take it in the direction of the beautiful travelers, those who are aware and know the path of God.

And beware, don't let the soul's mount wander on its own! Turn it away from the path of its own appetites. For if the soul goes for what it knows, it will go bad. Struggle with it constantly, be awake. For the gardens where nature's mount [*tabiat merkebi*] wants to go are the gardens of the soul's desires and passions. If you become heedless and leave it on its own even for a moment, you will see the donkey go to the meadows of the soul's passions, far, far away from you and the path you must travel.

For the soul's donkey knows nothing of the path of God. It hates the path of sovereignty [*melekût yolu*]. It adores fresh grass. It loses its way. There are those with heads like such mounts who are slaves to their donkeys and hasten to follow them. They come to mischief running down the path of caprice and desire, the path of the stomach and fresh grass.

You may at first be one of those who does not know the right path. If that is so, ask your soul where it wants to go. Be smart and go in the opposite direction! For if a person is able to stay on a path contrary to the one his soul desires, it means he has found the right path. Remember the hadith, *Consult females . . .* Talk with your soul,[162] ask it the way, ask what it thinks, but whatever it says, do the opposite. For all those who have not chosen a way contrary to that of their souls, but rather conformed to them, have been

---

162. The Arabic hadith phrase in fact begins, "Consult them," where "them" is grammatically feminine, and the Arabic word for "soul" used here, *nafs*, is also grammatically feminine. So the hadith is interpreted as meaning: "Consult your souls (and do the opposite)."

separated from the path they should follow and been destroyed on paths of error.

A person grows distant from spirituality to the degree he consorts with material and bodily interests. While he busies himself with such material and bodily things, death comes early and extinguishes all hopes. He falls into a realm so foreign to him that his eye has no power to see the light of that realm. There he is deprived of the beloved and doomed to loss.

That is why the most trustworthy support is the arrived of God, who from the start of the journey disarm the caprices and desires of the soul and free a person from their seductive power and encourage him on the right path. Their support is the guidance they give.

****

THE LEGACY OF THE PROPHET, PEACE BE UPON HIM, TO ALI, MAY GOD HONOR HIS FACE: "ALL SEEK NEARNESS TO GOD THROUGH SOME ACT OF OBEDIENCE. SEEK NEARNESS THROUGH FELLOWSHIP WITH INTELLIGENT AND ELECT BONDSMEN SO THAT YOU MAY HAVE PRECEDENCE OVER ALL."

The Prophet said, "O Ali, lion of God
You are a mighty hero and full of heart
3000. But do not put your trust in ferocity
Come under the protection of hope's palm tree
Under the shade of an intelligent man
Whom no one can carry away from the path
His shadow is like Qaf Mountain on the earth
And his spirit is the high-soaring Simurgh
If till Resurrection Day I sing his praise
Don't expect end or final verse to his praise
In the human creature the sun veils himself
Seek to understand; and God knows what is best
3005. O Ali, of all devotions in the path
Choose the protection of the bondsman of God
Everyone flees into some act of worship
And sets up some kind of salvation in it
Flee into the shade of the intelligent
From the foe who wars against you in secret
Of all devotions this is the best for you
You will be ahead of all ahead of you
When the Pir accepts you, take heed, surrender
Go like Moses under command of Khizir
3010. Bear whatever an unveiled Khizir may do
So he will not say, 'Here we part, me and you!'[163]
Although he scuttles a boat, remain silent
Though he slays a child, do not tear your hair out[164]
God has said that his hand is as His own hand

---

163. Koran 18:65-82.
164. Koran 18:71,74.

> He said, '*The hand of God is above their hands.*'[165]
> God's hand causes him to die and come alive
> How alive? He gives him everlasting life
> If rarely, someone has gone alone this way
> The Pirs' hearts have befriended him on the way
> 3015. Those not present are not beyond the Pir's grasp
> The Pir's hand is but the handle of God's grasp
> Since they bestow such a robe on the absent
> The present are better off than the absent
> Since they give such provision to the absent
> See what bounties they lay before those present
> Where is one who takes up service face to face
> Compared to one who remains outside the gate?
> Once you've chosen a Pir, don't be faint of heart
> Weak like water or like clay crumble apart
> 3020. Though every blow may leave you full of rancor
> Without polish how will you be a mirror?"

One day Hazret Muhammed said to Imam Ali:

> O Ali! You are the lion of God. You have a brave heart and are a hero with the strength of a great champion. You are heroic in your spirituality, able to resist the desires and passions of the soul with an iron will. As you are outwardly, you are inwardly; your heart and your will are as strong as your arms, perhaps stronger.
>
> Yet do not trust in your lion-like strength, hasten into the shade of the tree of hope, take refuge in the spiritual support of a great murshid, a caliph of God who will always show you the right path, the path of God.
>
> Achieve the spirituality of that intelligent person whom no one and no worldly speech or worldly desire can cause to stray from the right path. That perfect human has reached the level of oneness and there is nothing left for him to ask from God, neither for the world nor even the afterlife. He has become the divine life itself—go to him.
>
> His shadow on the ground is like Mount Qaf, it encircles the world. His spirit is an Anqa perched on Mount Qaf, he is a Simurgh of Mount Qaf, and his spirit flies way beyond the peaks of that mountain, way, way up high.

In that great century, O Husameddin, the sun of truth here described was Hazret Muhammed himself. He was the intelligent man. The caliph of God, and Mount Qaf, and the bird of fortune perched on that mountain—he was all of them.

And Hazret Muhammed went on sharing mysteries with God's lion Ali; the sun of truth, the light which dazzled his own eyes, was hidden and veiled in the human body [*insan vücûdu*]. The attributes of God are hidden in his qualities. He was telling Ali to understand this and know that God knows best the truth:

> O Ali! Know this truth, that the most sublime worship to be performed in the path

---

165. "Those who swear fealty to you do no less than swear fealty to God. The hand of God is above their hands" (Koran 48:10).

of God is to be in the shadow of spirituality of a murshid whom God has sent to His bondsmen; to emulate him. Every spirit in this world takes a different path in worship. Everyone seeks a road to salvation, a way to reach God. You must put aside all those paths and chose the embrace of that intelligent murshid, so that within it you may be completely freed of that hidden foe who opposes you.

Such worship is for you above all other forms of worship. With this worship you will be at the head of the caravan traveling to God. You know the story of Moses and Khizir told in the eighteenth chapter of the Gracious Koran. Now let me remind you of that story with verses from the Koran. One day Hazret Moses said to Khizir: 'May I follow you, so that you may each me the true knowledge which was taught to you?' Khizir said: "You will not be able to bear seeing what I do."

Moses promised him, "God willing, you will find me patient. I will not object to anything you do." Khizir replied: "In that case, you must conform to me and not ask me about anything I do until I explain it to you." Moses promised him and they went off together.

They got into a boat. But Khizir made a hole in the boat. Moses objected, saying, "Have you scuttled the boat in order to drown those inside it? What you have done is incredible, truth be told." Khizir reminded him of his promise: "Didn't I say you would not be able to bear with me?"

Moses apologized: "Do not scold me for forgetting. Do not expect from me more than my strength allows."

They continued on their way.

They came across a boy. Khizir killed the boy. Moses could not contain himself and said, "You have taken an innocent life. He was an innocent who had never hurt anyone, you have truly done a wrong."

Khizir gave the same answer: "Didn't I say you would not be able to bear with me?"

Moses apologized again: "If I ask you about anything again, abandon your friendship with me, let this be my last apology to you."

They continued on their way.

They arrived at a town where the people gave them nothing to eat and did not give them hospitality. There they saw a wall which was crumbling down. Khizir repaired the wall, preventing it from falling down.

Moses was shocked by this as well and said: "If you had asked, you could have been paid for doing that."

Khizir: "This question of yours means we will have to part. Now I will tell you the inner meaning of those things you were impatient about:

"The boat was owned by several poor people who worked at sea. I wanted to make it in need of repair. For there was in that country a ruler who seized every seaworthy boat.

"With regard to the boy I killed, his mother and father were believers. But if that boy had grown up, he would have become a kafir and led his parents astray. I did not give the boy a chance to seduce his parents and lead them into denial. I asked God to give them a purer child, one who would have more compassion.

"As for the wall, it was the property of two orphan children. The children were boys. There was a treasure buried for them under the wall. Their father was a good and honest man. My Lord wished the boys to grow up and find their treasure with their own hands, as a mercy from God. So if the wall had fallen down while they were still children, the treasure would have been exposed and taken by whoever found it.

"As you see, I did none of these things by my own will. I fulfilled the command of my God. This is the inner meaning of the events you could not bear."

So, O Ali! Bear patiently with the actions of Khizir, who knows no hypocrisy and acts only by the command of God. So that he may not say to you, "Begone! You and I must part," as in the story. For the story in the Koran of Moses and Khizir is the story of how a murid must behave toward his murshid, with perfect acquiescence and submission. So should you do. When you find the Pir, submit yourself. He will take you to truth and goodness.

If he scuttles a boat, do not take it amiss; do not be angry if he kills a child. Do not forget that God said, "His hand is under My hand."

And also remember these verses from the forty-eighth chapter of the Koran (48:10):

"Those who pledge their fealty to you do no less than pledge their fealty to God. The hand of God is above their hands: then anyone who violates his oath, does so to the harm of his own soul, and any who fulfills what he has covenanted with God, God will soon grant him a great reward.

"Consider, if God's hand should kill that child, it can also bring him back to life again. And what of that, when He can give the child eternal life.

"A perfect friend of God, a true murshid, is the Khizir of your time. If that Khizir shatters a boat into pieces, do not object. Nor tear out your hair if he kills a child!

"Sometimes it also happens that a person who never meets a Khizir, who has no murshid, takes the right path and reaches God. Such people receive secret support from all the Pirs, the friends. Whether in the East or in the West, if a heart is bright and full of light like a clean mirror, the sun of truth surely shines upon it.

"Although the aid of a visible murshid gives greater peace of mind, murshids sometimes invisibly guide spirits so that the sun of truth shines upon a heart.

"Since the hand of the Pir is in reality the hand of the Creator, He can dress a bondsman in a robe of arrivedness from the Unseen as well, if He wishes.

"Although such robes of honor are given to those who are absent, those who are present are without a doubt much more fortunate. They have the felicity of being able to see the hand stretched out to them and the robe put upon them with their own worldly eyes.

"If God's friends give robes and nourishment to the absent, what all do they not give to guests who are right there before them, what bounties do they not offer them? Would they not make them fly and reach sublime stations of rank?

"Those who reach the presence of the friends of God and stand at the ready before them are of course more fortunate than those outside the door.

"If you have been deemed worthy of such a murshid, if you have been fortunate enough to receive his support, be faint-hearted no longer! Do not pour like water or scatter like earth. Do what you are told to do so that your spirit may ascend and your soul be reformed. Keep your word and continue on your path. Burn in the fire of love, in the crucible of ardor, and become pure gold.

"In order to make a clear, bright mirror out of metal, what fires they expose it to! What pressures they bring to bear upon it! If you feel such pain from every fire and every wound, how will you be polished?"

****

How the Man from Qazvin tattooed the Figure of a Lion on his Shoulders and regretted it on Account of the Needle Pricks

Listen to this tale storytellers relate
Of the Qazvini people's customs and ways
On their bodies and their shoulders and their arms
They have tattoos pricked in blue to ward off harm
At a barbershop said a man from Qazvin
"Give me a tattoo and do it artfully."
"O valiant sir," said the barber, "what figure?"
"A ferocious lion," the man then answered

3025. "Leo's my ascendant, tattoo a lion
Exert yourself, prick plenty of blue dye in."
"Where shall I tattoo you?" he asked. The man said:
"Prick the icon's design on my shoulder blade."
Then as he stuck the needle in his shoulder
The pain of it settled into his shoulder
"O sublime barber, what are you tattooing?"
The man began to moan, "You are killing me!"
"Why, you told me to do a lion," he said
"What limb did you begin with?" the other said

3030. He replied, "I have started out with the tail."
"O my own two eyes," he cried, "leave out the tail!
My breath's cut off by the lion's tail and rump
My windpipe is closed off by the lion's rump
O lion-fashioner, let it have no tail
For the needle's pricking has made my heart quail."
The barber began pricking another place
Oblivious, merciless, and without haste
"Which of the lion's members now?" the man cried
"It's his ear, my good man," the barber replied

3035. "O Doctor," the man said, "let him have no ears
Let us keep this business short, omit the ears."
The barber began to prick another spot
Once again the man from Qazvin gave a shout
"On this third place now what part of his body?"
"My dear sir," he said, "It's the lion's belly."
"Let the lion have no belly," the man said
"What need when the picture's already sated?"
The barber became amazed and bewildered
He stood for a long while biting his finger

3040. Then the master flung the needle to the ground

He said, "When has this happened to anyone?
A lion without belly or tail or head—
Whose seen one? None has by God been created!"
O brother, endure the pain of the lancet
That you may escape your Magi soul's lancet
For the sky and sun and moon bow in worship
To those who've escaped bodily existence
Anyone in whom the Magi self is dead
Sun and cloud obey what he has commanded

3045.   Since his heart has learned to make the lamplight burn
The light of the sun will never make him burn
God mentioned how the rising sun *turned away*[166]
To the side as they were sleeping in *their cave*
For the part heading to the universal
The thorn will become entirely beautiful
What is it to honor and exalt the Lord?
To know yourself to be of earth and abhorred
What is it to learn God's unification?
To be burned up in the presence of the One

3050.   If you wish to shine as bright as the daylight
Set fire to your existence dark as the night
In His existence which fosters all being
Like copper in alchemy melt your being
You have fastened your hands tight on "I" and "we"
All this ruin is caused by duality

Cities have strange fates. They are sometimes famed for their brave and good, and sometimes for their wicked. Generous folk congregate in some regions, and in others, stingy persons; in some, honest folk, in others, cheaters. Later this can change, the good can go bad and the bad become good.

Now I will tell you an old story about a man from Qazvin, listen: In order to ward off ill fortune, the people of Qazvin used to make a custom of having their bodies, their arms and shoulders, tattooed with blue ink.

One of these Qazvinis went to a barber one day and asked to have a design tattooed on his body: "Give me a tattoo and make it beautiful, make it attractive."

"As you command, valiant sir," said the barber. "But what kind of tattoo do you want? Which design shall I tattoo on your body?" he asked.

Without hesitation the Qazvini told him what he wanted: "Tattoo the picture of a roaring lion on my body, for my astrological sign is the sign of the lion, and my heroism is the heroism of the lion. I only ask that you prick the needle in deeply and use a lot of blue ink, so that time may not erase the lion."

Then the barber asked: "Where on your body shall I tattoo this formidable lion?" The Qazvini said: "Between my shoulder blades."

When the barber took needle in hand and pricked his skin, the Qazvini could not keep himself from shrieking, and moaned, "Master! You have killed me! What kind of

---

166. Koran 18:17.

design are you tattooing on me?" The barber: "You asked for a picture of a lion." The Qazvini: "Yes, but what part of the lion have you begun with?" The Barber: "Its tail." The Qazvini: "Forget the tail, my dear! Let it be a lion without a tail. For the tail of that lion is stopping my breath. It is ruining me. You are tattooing the picture of a lion, but be fair and don't draw the lion's tail!"

So the barber left off doing the tail and moved on to the head, pricking the Qazvini's skin deeply with the needle as he had instructed.

The valiant Qazvini couldn't tolerate this either and began to wail again: "What part of the lion are you doing now?" The barber said: "The ear, my hero." The Qazvini moaned: "Mercy, be fair! Do the lion without ears as well. Make it an abbreviated picture of a lion, without ears or tail. Give up on the ears and keep this business short."

In the same way neither the lion's head, nor its belly, nor its mane could be depicted. Finally the barber through his needle on the ground and shrieked:

"No one has ever had to deal with such disgrace. Does one do a picture of a lion without ears, tail, head and body? God never created a lion like that. A lion without head, feet and tail is a lion that has never been born. You are telling me to do the picture of a 'nothing.'"

So, my friend! bear the pain of the needle so that you may be free of that infidel soul of yours and its needle pricks.

It is to the heroes of the path of God who are freed of the body to such a degree that they feel no bodily pain, in whose hearts there really is a lion lying in wait, that all the heavens and its moons and suns bow down.

Moon and suns go into an ecstatic trance, whirling about them, and lay their foreheads on the prayer mat of service to them. They lit by the fire of union with God in the hearts of those heroes.

Clouds pouring down rain and suns illuminating the universe with light are joyful under their command.

The sun cannot burn those whose hearts are burning with the fire of divine love. No torment of this transient world can affect those whom love of God and divine ecstasy have made unconscious of self, those who are free of the soul, and such spirits have no fear of those external threats.

In the Gracious Koran God related this mystery with regard to the Companions of the Cave (18:16-17): "'Go into the cave, that your Lord may shower His mercies upon you and dispose of your affairs in comfort and ease.' You would have seen the sun rising to the right of their cave and setting to the left, while they lay inside the open space of the cave. This is among the signs of God. He whom God guides is rightly guided."

Thus because the sun had no permission to enter the cave, those inside continued to sleep while the sun was outside, remaining unconscious of their selves in ecstasy, in divine love, in peace and quiet. The sun struck the right side of the cave while rising and the left side while setting, and did not burn the Companions of the Cave. They were under the protective hand of God. The lovers of God also are not burned and destroyed by the majesty and beauty of the sun of divine Greatness [*Kibriya*]; for they subsist [*bâkî*] in God and are freed from their selfhood, they are the arrived who have seen The Truth as The Truth.

If a particular takes the road to the universal, even the thorns around that particular become roses head to foot. The thorns of selfhood and being within those burned with the fire of love for God the Truth become roses of kindness and mercy which are part of the universal.

To comprehend the greatness of God is to sense the divine power within the human and know the incapacity of the soul and its lowliness. But what knows this is the spirit, which sends its sublime feelings of glorification to God.

To learn to establish God's unity [*tevhit etmeye öğrenmek*] means that a person burns up and destroys himself before the oneness of God and takes the path to becoming The Truth with The Truth, and on that path makes naught all his bodily desires [*vücût hevesleri*] and ties of the soul, in short, his existence [*vücût*].

If you want to be illuminated like the sun and become pure light, set alight your soul dark as night with an ecstatic fire. So that there is no trace of duality left in you and you may subsist with God the Truth.

Melt your mortal being in the elixir of that eternal being, as copper melts in alchemy and becomes gold. Become pure gold.

Do not fasten your hands on the door of such words and illusions as "I" and "we," which stink of selfhood; do not get yourself in such a state that you cannot do without them. If you exist [*varsan*], you are in His great being [*varlık*], which means you are not [*yoksun*] and only He exists [*var*]. You are one of the infinite motes which make up the universal, and at the moment when you are able to forget even your mote-ness, you will comprehend that you are in Him and in that universal.

If you want to hear the story of those who find themselves at the edge of the abyss, unable to break free of "I" and "we" in this transient world, let me tell you the tale of the wolf and the fox who went hunting in the service of the lion.

****

HOW THE WOLF AND THE FOX WENT TO SERVE THE LION IN THE HUNT

> A lion, wolf, and a fox went off in quest
> In pursuit of prey to hunt in the mountains
> That by giving support to one another
> They might bind up their prey tightly in fetters
> 3055. And the three of them altogether might seize
> Much rare and fine prey in the wilderness deep
> The fierce lion was ashamed to be with them
> Yet he treated them kindly, as companions
> To a shah like that soldiers are troublesome
> But community is mercy: he took them
> For a moon like that the stars are a disgrace
> He stays with them for generosity's sake
> The Prophet received the command, *"Consult them . . . "*[167]
> Though there is no counsel like his opinion
> 3060. Barley can be weighed in the scales beside gold
> But that is not because barley is like gold
> Spirit has become the companion of form
> For a while a dog may guard the palace door
> When the hunting party went to the mountain

---

167. Koran 3:159.

At the lion's stirrup, majestic and grand
They found a wild ox, a goat and a fat hare
Their enterprise was proceeding quite well there
He who chases a lion's heels in the fight
Will not fail to eat roast meat by day or night

3065.   They brought their catch from the mountain to the wood
Killed or wounded and dragging in streams of blood
Wolf and fox expected the share they would bring
Would be according to the justice of kings
The reflection of their greed struck the lion
The lion knew what that greed was based upon
One who is lion of mysteries and prince
Knows everything that passes through the conscience
O thought-seeking heart, be wary, be on guard
When you're with him keep evil thoughts from your heart

3070.   He knows and drives on his donkey in silence
He smiles to your face to conceal his own face
The lion knew the evil thoughts in their minds
Yet was kindly and said nothing at that time
But he said to himself, "O you mean beggars,
I will show you the treatment that you deserve
Is my judgment not then sufficient for you?
Is this what you think my bounty amounts to?
You whose wisdom and judgment derive from mine
From the world-adorning bounties that are mine

3075.   What can a picture impute to the artist
Who has bestowed thought and awareness on it?
Is your opinion regarding me so base?
You who are of all time the shameful disgrace
If I don't cut off the heads of those who hold
Evil opinion of God,[168] my fault's untold
I will deliver heaven's wheel from your shame
So this tale will ever in the world remain."
While thinking thus, the lion displayed a smile
Do not be confident of a lion's smile!

3080.   The wealth of the world is like the smiles of God
It's made us drunk and arrogant and worn-out
For you poverty and pain are better yet
O lord, for that smile drags you up in its net

One day a lion went hunting, taking a wolf and a fox with him.

Let us say right away that all three are symbols. The lion was a traveler of gnosis and guidance annihilating his existence [*vücût*] on the path of unity. The fox represents intellect and love, and the wolf, the soul.

All three set out together promising to help one another in hunting and catching their

---

168. Koran 48:6.

prey. Before their eyes they saw plentiful, fat prey. To be sure, the lion needed no companion on this journey. But he displayed greatness and showed his companions various kindnesses and gifts. For the great accompany the small in order to bestow bounty on them and show them generosity. It is of course unthinkable that so many friends and prophets of God, having earned degrees of intimacy with God, should for sake of personal gain befriend or converse with persons who have taken themselves into the soul's abyss. They enjoy the pleasure and good reward of bringing to the path those who lag behind. That is why they do not keep fallen spirits and materialists from their grace.

Traveling with soldiers is not easy for such a shah. But the lion did not leave them because he believed there is mercy in community. The lion was like a shining moon, and the animals with him like extinguished stars, and the brightness of the lion's light shined more gloriously among these extinguished stars, attracting eyes and hearts.

Hazret Muhammed took his light, his inspiration and power from God and had no obligation to seek counsel from anyone. Yet despite that, it is written in the Gracious Koran (3:159):

> It is part of God's mercy that you deal gently with them. Were you severe or hardhearted, they would have broken away from you. So overlook, and ask forgiveness for them, and consult them in affairs. Then, when you make a decision, put your trust in God. For God loves those who render their trust.

Gold is weighed in the scales, but in order to weigh gold, they put barley beside it. This does not mean that barley gains the value of gold. Here the function of barley is to bring out the value of gold.

If spirit is now in a form, what does it lose of its spirithood? A palace does not become a hut because a dog guards its gate for a while. What will one day reach divine union is not the flesh, but the spirit. But because the dog Qitmir served the Companions of the Cave, its name was mentioned in the Koran.

The lion, the wolf, and the dog went as a group to a mountain where they caught a mountain ox, a mountain goat, and a rabbit.

Certainly those accompanying a lion will have much to eat. And so it was this time. They chased their fat, fresh prey into the forest. The mouths of the wolf and the fox were watering for their prey, their passions aroused, their avarice increased. It drove them wild to see thick, bloody pieces of meat. This did not escape the lion's notice. The Shah of mountain and forest divined the secrets of his companions. Just as what passes through hearts of murids is not hidden from a shaykh, so did the lion know the thoughts of his companions.

You who have feelings and thoughts alien to the great path, you who approach the shaykh with dark hearts thus! Empty your heart of ugly, alien desires! If your shaykh does not mention to you the secrets you keep, do not suppose that he does not know them!

If all of people's sins, all their shame, were thrown into their faces by their betters, life would be much more difficult. Of course that lion of the path knows yours thoughts and feelings. But far from telling you your secrets, he finds it right to pretend not to know, not to sense them and smiles at you, wishing those shameful thoughts to be veiled by a smile and shed by the sinner and become naught.

So did the lion. He knew what they were thinking. But he did not confront them. He said to himself: "You greedy beggars, I'll soon give you the lesson you deserve."

"You don't find my power, my rule, enough? You do not consider how much more I am able to bestow? Is this much all that you can grasp?

"You are like some sort of picture. It is through my will that your bodies move or come to rest, I give to you what you eat and drink. Every bounty given to you is part of my world-adorning beneficence.

"How can a painting revile the painter who made it? How can it think evil thoughts about its artist? Although a painting may appear to feel, think, and criticize, who other but the painter gives it that appearance, that effect? It is the painter who, while making the painting on a tablet, works all his feelings and thoughts into it and decorates it with all his skill.

"Shame of the world! Is this how you were going to think of me?

"God said in the Gracious Koran (48:6): 'That He may punish the Hypocrites, men and women, and the polytheists, men and women, who imagine an evil opinion of God. Upon them is a round of evil; the wrath of God is upon them; He has cursed them and readied Hell for them; evil a destination it is.' If I now do not cut off the heads of those who have evil opinion of God, I will have committed the crime and sin itself.

"You who recognize neither bounty nor power! Let me free this wheel of the world from the shame of your existence [*vücût*], so that as long as the world lasts this story will be known and told and people may take warning from it."

Worldly position, wealth, glory and rank are God's smiles to His bondsmen who chase bodily desires; first they leave those who are fooled by them and take the wrong road drunk and proud, and then ruin them.

O bondsman valued in the sight of God! What suits you in this world is to be poor in existence [*vücût*] and to feel the torment of longing and loss you should feel toward divine unity. To laugh in this world, in this worldly filth and passion, is to weep in the end.

For the divine smile is the divine smile of amazement and sorrow at the heedless who love the transient desires and beauties of the world instead of His sublime being, His love and His beauty.

****

HOW THE LION TESTED THE WOLF AND SAID, "COME FORWARD, O WOLF, AND DISTRIBUTE THE CATCH AMONG US."

> The lion said, "You divide the catch, O wolf
> And thus mete out justice renewed, O old wolf
> In this distribution be my deputy
> So the substance you possess be seen clearly."
> "O shah," the wolf replied, "the wild ox is large
> He is your share, you are fat and strong and large
3085. The goat is middling, and so will be my share
> O fox, there's no mistake, you shall take the hare!"
> The lion said, "How can you speak thus, tell me
> Where I am, how can you talk of 'you' and 'we'?
> What a dog a wolf must be to speak of self
> Before such a peerless lion as myself!

Come forward, approach, O ass of self-regard!"
When he did, the lion mauled him with his claws
Since he saw in him no seed of right conduct
He tore the skin off his head as punishment

3090.   "You did not renounce self at the sight of me
Such spirit as yours must die miserably
Since you did not pass away in my presence
It was best to sever your head from your neck."
"Every thing is perishing except His face"[169]
Don't seek existence, since you're not of His face
To all those who perish in our face and die
"Every thing is perishing" does not apply
They've arrived at the *but*, they've gone beyond *not*
He who is in the *but*, he perishes not

3095.   He who knocks saying "I" and "we" at the door
He remains in *not*, turned away from the door

"Hey, old wolf," the lion roared, "Divide this prey among us! Let us see the virtue of the years you have lived and the experience you have had, do right and show justice in this division!

"Be my deputy in this work of apportioning. So that we may see what sort of substance you are made of."

The wolf approached and said, "O great Sovereign! Among these prey the one worthy of you is this wild ox. It is fat and stocky. You too are great and powerful. I find it worthy of you.

"That wild goat should be my share. It's size is appropriate for me. It is neither too large nor too small.

"As for the rabbit, let us give it to the fox. Thus the fox too will have a share according to his size." And he added:

"O Padishah, I believe there is no flaw in this apportioning of mine. This is a division of perfect justice."

But for the lion what was important was not the division of the spoils but the wolf's claim to selfhood. "O wolf!" he shouted. "How could you say such a thing. How can you make such a claim to selfhood in my presence, using words like 'I,' 'you,' and 'we'? What a dog a wolf must be to speak up in the presence of such a matchless lion as I and seek a share, planning a division according to size. Instead of requesting whatever I see as appropriate for him, he brazenly tells me to my face what division he thinks proper."

And the lion called out to the wolf: "Approach, you conceited ass! The wolf had no choice but to approach him, and the lion tore him to bits, killing him with one blow of his paw, and stripped him of his skin.

"Since being with me and being able to see me was not enough for you; since you did not give up your own selfhood in my path but strolled through my great court in conceit, death is what you deserve," he said.

God said in the Gracious Koran (28:88): "And call not upon a god other than God. Every thing is perishing but His face. To Him belongs the command, and to Him will

---

169. Koran 28:88.

you be returned."

Since everything but God's being will become naught, and since you have not attained the mystery of not-being in His being, that is, of being immortal with Him, do not seek other being. God has said, "Every thing is perishing."

But He also gave the good news that spirits who are immortal in God are not included among those to be destroyed.

Such spirits transcend in annihilation the degree of "There is no . . . " and arrive at the rank of "but God."[170]

All who knock at God's gate, but who make the sound "I" or "we" with the doorknocker in their grasp, will not have His door opened to them. Such people curl up like a lâ ["There is no . . . "][171] and fall into the emptiness of not-being.

****

THE STORY OF THE MAN WHO KNOCKED AT A FRIEND'S DOOR AND THE FRIEND ASKED WHO HE WAS, AND HE SAID, "IT IS I," AND THE FRIEND SAID, "SINCE YOU ARE YOU, I WILL NOT OPEN THE DOOR, I KNOW NO FRIEND WHO IS 'I'"

> A man came and knocked at the door of a friend
> "Who are you, O trustworthy man?" asked the friend
> "It is I," he said. The friend replied, "Begone!
> A table like this is no place for the raw."
> Who'll cook the raw, save them from hypocrisy
> Other than the fire of exile and forfeit?
> For a year of traveling that wretched man
> Burned in fire of separation from his friend

3100.
> He burned and was cooked, and then he came again
> To pace up and down by the house of his friend
> He knocked with a hundred fears and great respect
> Lest his lips let slip a word of disrespect
> His friend called out to him, "Who is at the door?"
> He said, "O heart-charmer, you are at the door."
> Said the friend, "Since you are me, enter, my self
> There is no room for two I's in this palace."
> A thread with split end is not for the needle
> Come on through this needle if you are single

3105.
> There's a relation between thread and needle
> The needle's eye cannot take in a camel[172]
> How should the body of a camel be slim
> Save by the scissors of asceticism?
> For that the hand of God is necessary
> *"'Be!' and it was"* of impossibility
> It makes possible all things impossible

---

170. A reference to the Muslim profession of faith, "There is no god but God."

171. The Arabic character for "l-a" is curled.

172. "For those who reject our signs and treat them with arrogance, there will be no opening of the gates of Heaven, nor will they enter the garden, until the camel pass through the eye of the needle" (Koran 7:40).

By fear of Him wild things are made tractable
What of lepers and the man who is born blind?
That great One's spell brings even the dead alive[173]

3110.   And the not-being that's more dead than the dead
When He gives it existence, it is compelled
Read: *"Each day He is engaged in some affair"* [174]
Do not suppose that He has no work and care
The least of His works on each and every day
Is to dispatch three armies upon their way
One army from the loins of men to mothers
So that inside the womb the leaf may mature
And one army goes from the wombs to the earth
So male and female may populate the earth

3115.   One army to death's appointed hour from earth
So that all may see the beauty of good works
Come and hasten, for this discourse has no end,
Back to those two sincere and devoted friends

This well-known story is based on a hadith which is related in Baghawi's work *Masâbih*. Amr ibn Abdullah al-Ansari said: "One day I knocked on Hazret Muhammed's door and he called out, 'Who is it?' I said, "It is I." I heard Hazret Muhammed inside saying, "I . . . I.." in a tone showing he was not pleased with the answer."

As in that true story, a man knocked at the door of friend and heard a voice call out from inside, "You who trust in yourself, who are you?"

"It is I," the man cried. Now the voice which replied from within was not soft and kind as before. It said:

"Go away! My house and my table are not the place for raw, immature people."

Only the fires of separation and exile cook such raw spirits. Only such fires can free them from the illnesses of discord, duality and selfhood.

The man who was sent away understood the wrong he had done. He understood that he must stay away from the person he most loved and burn in the fire of separation, yellowing like a dry reed until he became mature like a scorched flute. For a year he gave himself up to this trial of separation. Thus he wandered from land to land, burning in torment, until he returned to his friend's door.

Filled with fear and apprehension, he banged the doorknocker. He kept himself under strict control so that no disrespectful or inappropriate word might escape his lips. Again that voice came from within, asking, "Who is it?" The lover who'd knocked at the door answered in a weak voice, "It is you, O friend! For there is no being in the world but you."

This time the door was opened, to a man who had gained maturity in the fire of exile. The friend within said, "Since you and I have become one, now come in! For in the sanctuary of my home there is no place for two separate 'I's.'"

In the same way, a thread with a split end cannot even pass through the eye of a

---

173. "And I heal those born blind, and the lepers, and I quicken the dead by God's leave" (Koran 3:49).
174. ". . . every day He is engaged in some affair" (Koran 55:29).

needle. All the fibers of a thread must be joined and be one so that it functions to pass through the eye. O beloved, you have been melted in the fire of exile until you are thin as a thread, come and pass through the eye of this needle without any difficulty!

It is no easy thing for a body [*vücût*] to melt in the path of God, becoming spirit to such a degree that it can pass through the eye of a needle. But it is not difficult for a thread which is not split to pass through. But God said in the Gracious Koran (7:40): "For those who reject our signs and treat them with arrogance, there will be no opening of the gates of Heaven, nor will they enter the garden, until the camel pass through the eye of the needle."

This means that as long as those who chase after greatness, conceit and selfhood do not melt away from their own transient selfhood and souls in the path of God, they do not earn the right to enter God's paradise of oneness. When such people learn the judgments of the shariat and the ways of the tarikat and follow them, and can take a great person's medicine, the gate of the heavens will be opened to them.

Don't imagine a camel as thin as a thread, wondering how the body of a camel can pass through the eye of a needle! As long as this camel of soul and selfhood is not whittled down by love, not-being, and the sword of "no" [*lā*], so that it is put in the state of "no thing" [*lā shay*], that is, nothingness, of course body cannot pass through the eye of the needle.

The power that can whittle down the camel of being and soul and put it in the state of nothingness is the power of God.

Just as God can by his will and command make the most "impossible" things happen, and can create so many beings out of nothing, he can give the reward of not-being to those who appear to be.

He can make naught countless camels, not just one camel, and pass them through the eye of a needle and free them.

If He wishes, those born blind can see. If He wishes, He can turn those whose bodies are rotted by the disease of leprosy into beauties with rose-like skin.

Put aside these possibles—if God wishes, He can even revive the dead. If He wishes, not-being, which is deader than a corpse, comes to be. Bodies considered beings take on forms and the world is filled with countless things He brings to be out of nothing.

Again in the Gracious Koran it says (55:29-30): "Every creature in the heavens and the earth seeks everything from Him. He disposes of creation each instant. Then which of the favors of your Lord will you deny?"

The Lord's smallest work is to send three armies to the world each day. These armies of people are born from their fathers' loins into their mothers' wombs, and from their mothers' wombs into the earth. At the same time each day armies and armies of people take the road to the appointed hour of death and go to give account to God.

But there is no end to this discourse, O friend. Let us return to the story of those two sincere friends!

****

CONCERNING THE ASSERTION OF GOD'S UNITY

> "Come in, you who are wholly me," said his friend,
> "Not different like rose and thorn in the garden."
> The thread has become single, do not now err

If you see that *kaf* and *nun* are two letters[175]
Like a noose, *kaf nun* bring attraction to bear
Drawing non-existence into great affairs

3120. Thus the lasso must be double in its form
Although in their effect the two are as one
Whether feet be two or four, the road is one
Like the two shears of scissors which cut as one
Look at those two fellows who are washing clothes
One appears to be to the other opposed
The one throws cotton garments in the water
And the clothes are dried by the other partner
Then the first one douses the dry clothes again
As if willfully thwarting an opponent

3125. Yet seemingly at strife, the two opponents
Act with one heart together in agreement
Every prophet and friend has his own doctrine
But each brings you to God, all are really one
While the audience was taken off by sleep
The millstones were carried away by the stream
The course of this water is above the mill
It is for your sake it flows into the mill
When your need for the mill no longer remained
He fed it back to the original stream

3130. The rational soul comes to the mouth to teach
If not, there's a separate channel for that speech
It goes without sound, without repetition
To the rosegardens *beneath which rivers* run
O God, reveal that station to the spirit
Within which discourse without letters exists
That the pure spirit may run upon its head
Toward the vast expanse of non-existence
An expanse very broad and very spacious
Nourishing our imaginal existence

3135. Space is narrower in the imaginal
Which is why pain comes from the imaginal
And even narrower still is existence
Which is why there full moons become like crescents
Existence in the world of sense and color
Is a narrow prison, even narrower
Narrowness comes of number and compounding
The senses incline you toward compounding
Know the unity of God through sensation
If you want the One, drive in that direction

3140. The command *"Be!"* [*Kun*] is one act, and *Kaf* and *Nun*
Occur only in speech, while meaning is pure

---

175. The letters *Kaf* and *Nun* spell *Kun*, "Be," as in "'Be!' and it was."

This discourse has no end, go back now so that
We may see what befell the wolf in combat

The friend who was sought out called to the one seeking him, "Come, come inside! You have annihilated your soul in one year! You are no longer the contrary of the rose, like a garden thorn. You are now a rose with the rose. Don't be fooled by the apparent duality, you are now at oneness."

The two forks of the thread have joined. Now it is easy to pass through the eye of the needle. The Arabic word "*kun*" = "be" is formed of the letters *kaf* and *nun*. Although these two letters are apparently separate, when they are joined they make up the command "Be!" This is the command which brings beings out of nothing.

The command "Be!" is the word brings from nothingness into being all the beings hidden in the sea of not-being, the Throne, the Footstool, the skies and the stars, the tablet upon which fates are written and the pen that writes them, all the spirits and all the jinn and humans.

Although the eye may see "duality" in a rope woven of two layers, the function the rope performs is "one."

Whether the number of feet a creature has is two or four, look to the direction they are going. They end up in the same place. You know the Koranic verse, "Guide us to the straight path." For centuries all believers have said this to the Creator. Thus a countless number of people all try to take the same path. Don't be fooled by the number of people, look to the singularity of their path.

Many a prophet and friend of God has come to the face of the earth and each one has founded a separate path and brought a different religion. Do not be fooled by the differences of these paths and the separateness of this religions. For they are all united in bringing people to same right path, to the same God. They point to the same God and the same truth.

It is enough that those listening are not heedless or asleep. Once the eye of the community is veiled by sleep, the waters will carry away the millstone. O son of Adam . . . Actually, the water that flows over the mill is for your sake, that is, it passes through the mill as a kindness in order to guide you and send you to God. Know that God's friends are like that. In order to free people of creaturely passions, they put up with the trouble of their company. If your heart is inattentive to those you guide you, who show you the way to God and tell you the mysteries of God, if your ears do not hear and your eyes grow sleepy, at the moment of sleep the rivers flowing by will take off the millstone as well.

The mill is for you, it is for your grain. If you have no grains left to mill, the miller will change the direction of the water. He will cut off the water flowing to the mill and give it back to the river.

The words of the friends are like that water. If there is a customer at the mill and if the customer has grain, they change direction and flow to the mill in order to grind their wheat. If there is no work at the mill, or the customer is asleep, they have many places to go and will not stop there anymore.

On the path of God words take the form of sound in order to say things to those who have ears, in order to teach the truth. If not, the water of speech has other channels. This stream bed is the path of spirit and the channel of the heart.

Speech knows how to flow silently down this path. If the hearts listening have no comprehension nor ear, it cuts off its voice; it makes it way silently, without repetition or rhyme, in its own spiritual river. It moves on to rosegardens under which flow rivers of meaning and truth.

My God, You show us that place where Your speech is heard without clothing of speech and with need for sound. Pure spirit runs the vast wilderness of annihilation in You not on foot, but on its head.

Whatever there is in reality is in that limitless realm of not-being. This world of imagination [*hayâl âlemi*] we see, these appearances of mortal bodies, are all nourished by that realm of not-being. Our universe is not-being's dream, its imagination. But these seemingly infinite images are nothing compared to the reality in that realm of not-being. Or very narrow, and the spirit is in torment because of that narrowness.

The divine realm is so vast compared to this world of bodies, it is not easy to comprehend it and its mysteries. That is why Hazret Muhammed said: "The intellect was created in order to render the bondsman to God. Not to comprehend the Lord's mysteries."

So, mysteries cannot be comprehended by the intellect. O spirit, you will reach those mysteries through gnosis, insight, feeling, and finding the Creator within yourself.

That which is in the realm of imagination is naught in the realm of not-being. Because the realm of imagination is born of not-being, imagination is narrow as not-being is vast. Imagination is born of not-being, and existence [*vücût*] born of imagination. So existence is even narrower than imagination. That is why in this realm of existence many a full moon appears slender and narrow as a crescent moon.

Finally, the realm of color and sense in which we find ourselves is utterly narrow, compared both with not-being, imagination, and being [*varlık*]. The world and everything in it—the flesh, the soul and its passions—is tiny and dark as a prison compared to the realms prior to it.

The narrowness and darkness of this realm is caused by composition and number. For number is evident, it is measurable; composition is limited by color and form.

Our five senses, our passion for color, form, sound and taste, continually drives us in the direction of composition, distracting us with number, color and form. Look to the spiritual with the senses bestowed upon you, not the material. Learn about the unity of God with those senses, not the world. If you really want to go forward, go forward toward God and the truth.

For this realm of color, form and duality brings together many a contrary like rose and thorn. These things which appear to be contraries unite only in meaning. Since the basis of all number, of millions and billions, is one, the basis of the colors, forms and pluralities which fill up the world you see is also one.

Like *kaf* and *nun*, the function of the two-letter command "*Kun*" is single. Even if letters of the word "Be!" can be counted, their meaning cannot be counted or divided.

Neither do the plurality of numbers and colors cast a shadow over the unity of God, nor is God's unity an obstacle to the limitlessness beyond count of numbers, colors, material and spiritual beings, delusions and images. At the same time, no matter how many the number of things you see, feel and touch, they are one in meaning, and on the day when there is an end to the things constantly ceasing to be in this realm of generation and corruption, that "one," that is, that "meaning," is all that will be left.

Thus if you wonder what unity is, want to learn it, to reach it, leave forms behind! Squeeze out of the press of matter! Attain meaning and unity!

But let us return again to our story. Let us tell of what happened to the greedy wolf. Perhaps you will understand better the moral to be gained from the tale.

****

HOW THE LION DISCIPLINED THE WOLF, WHO SHOWED DISRESPECT IN DISTRIBUTING THE SPOILS

> That proud-headed lion tore off the wolf's head
> There'd be no difference nor two-headedness
> O old wolf, it's *"So on them we took vengeance"* [176]
> Since you were not dead in the emir's presence
> And then the lion turned to the fox and said:
> "Distribute them now so we may eat breakfast."

3145. He bowed to the ground, "O chosen Shah," he said
> "This fat ox will be your food at your breakfast
> And for the victorious Shah at midday
> This goat will serve as a portion stored away
> And this hare will make a nice stew for nightfall
> Served for the most gracious and bountiful Shah."
> Said the lion, "O fox, you've made justice shine"
> Who taught you to make a distribution so fine?
> Where did you learn how to do this, O magnate?"
> "O Shah of the world, I learned from the wolf's fate."

3150. The lion said, "Since you're pledged to love of me
> Collect the others and take your leave, all three
> O fox, since you have become wholly for me
> How should I do you harm, you have become me
> I am yours, and yours all the beasts of the hunt
> Set your foot on the seventh heaven, rise up!
> Since you've taken warning from the wolf so vile
> You are not a fox, you're a lion of mine."
> The wise man is he who takes warning from death
> Of friends in trials which could have been prevented

3155. "Thanks to the lion," the fox thought gratefully
> "That he summoned that wolf before he did me
> Had he bid me first and said to me, "Divide!"
> Who is there who could escape from him alive?"
> Praise be to Him who brought us into the world
> Following after all our predecessors
> So that we have heard of how God did chastise
> Former generations in preceding times
> That we too, like the fox, may watch ourselves more
> Pondering the fate of wolves of days of yore

3160. On that account God's prophet, faithful in speech
> Called us a people "on whom God has mercy"
> Behold those wolves clearly, their bones and their fur

---

176. Koran 7:136; 15:79; 30:47; 43:35, 55.

> And take admonition from them, O masters!
> The wise put aside this existence and wind
> They've heard how Ad and the Pharaohs met an end
> And if they do not, others will take warning
> From what befell them because of their straying

The great lion tore of the head of the shameless wolf so that there should not be two heads, two separate reigning powers.

In four chapters of the Gracious Koran, God makes known why and how He punished the disobedient who did not listen to the messengers He sent to his bondsmen. He declared the end of those who do not conform to His messengers with the phrase, "So We took vengeance on them," and with, "See what became of the deniers," showed Hazret Muhammed, and by means of this final Messenger, all His bondsmen the right path.

That was how the lion punished the wolf for not abandoning his selfhood before the greatness of God, for not dying to self.

What happened to the wolf is a sign for wolf-like people who have not annihilated themselves, not died to self by their own will and choice, not freed themselves from duality, before God's being and unity.

So, after the death of the wolf, the lion turned to the fox, who represents persons of experience in affairs who have been given a share of divine intellect, and repeated his command: "Come, O fox," he said, "Divide these spoils we hunted for together!"

First the fox prostrated himself to the ground. Then he said: "O sublime padishah, let this fat ox be yours; let this mountain goat be your mid-morning stew. And eat this rabbit for your evening meal."

The meaning of this division was clear. Whatever there is in the world, great and small, all are reflections of God in the mirror of not-being, all are manifested from Him, and when He withdraws from the mirror, they will return to Him again. That is, they were naught in the lion, they were nothing but images. To desire them would be a futile desire, like wanting the image in a mirror or the sunlight hitting a wall. Since everything in the universe, every color, every image, will return to God, the intelligent thing to do is grasp that divine unity, to work for that, on that path.

So thought the fox, and that was what he said.

The lion asked: "O purely-created fox! You have brightened the lamp of justice. How did you learn to apportion in this way, from whom did you learn?" Without hesitation, the fox replied:

"My Sultan, I learned this now, from observing what happened to the wolf. I understood that everything in the universe is yours; everything consists of you. It is an error to insist on duality at the level of your being, to make claim to selfhood and feel vain pride."

The lion said: "O fox, since you have learned our divine unity, given thanks for our unity and not laid claim to selfhood at our sublime court, your thoughtfulness and service are accepted by me. Take all three of the captured animals, eat them in good health! And suffer no anxious thought!

"Since you have found the end in me, have become me and understood your not-being, how could I now hurt you, how could I not protect you from all pain and trial, when you are me.

"Remember the guidance of Hazret Muhammed's saying, Whoever is for God, God will protect him." Consider that, for those annihilated in God, there is no fear of selfhood or duality. Feel the delight of being among those arrived thus, set your foot upon the seventh heaven and ascend.

"O fox! Since you have taken warning from that selfish wolf, you are no longer a fox, you are my lion, you are me, you are the lion in me! Surely a person who learns courtliness from the ill-mannered, who takes a lesson from the avoidable trials suffered by people around him, is intelligent."

The fox listened to these flattering words, and inwardly thanked God. "Thank God that the lion first proposed to the wolf that he apportion the spoils, and then to me. If the lion had first proposed it to me, who would now save me from the lion?"

Yes, thank God that brought us into the world after those who came before us. With His books he taught us about all the right and wrong actions of those who came before us. We learned how many a people who did not listen to the counsel of prophets and friends were punished by God.

We have seen how many, despite all the good and right propositions made to them, chose the wrong path and hastened into disaster.

Great God wished that we should know the stories of those old wolves who lived in the past, and that we should take warning from them.

So that is why the final Messenger of God called us "The Community of Mercy." He made us known as the people upon whom God had mercy and compassion.

O all dear people sent into the world after so many have come and gone, be aware of the good fortune of your arrival in the world! Consider the tribes and peoples who have come and gone, take lessons from what happened to them!

You have learned the stories of those who followed Pharaoh and of the Tribe of Ad, and many others like them, so you know how they strayed from the right path and lost both worlds.

Now you will either take example from others and choose the right path, or you will mistake the right way and be considered a lesson to those who come after you.

For those who descend from the divine realm to this realm of trial, there is no other way.

****

How Noah, peace be upon him, threatened his people, saying: "Do not wrestle with me, for I am a veil; in reality you are wrestling with God within it, O forsaken people!"[177]

> Noah said, "O rebels, I've died in spirit
> I'm not I, I live by the spirit's spirit
3165. Since I am dead to Adam-like perception
> God is my hearing, my sight and perception
> Since I am not I, this breath I breathe is His
> Only kafirs breathe a word in its presence."
> There is a lion in the form of this fox
> One should not advance boldly upon this fox
> If you don't pledge yourself to him in this form

---

177. Koran 71:2-28.

Then you will not hear from him the lion's roar
If Noah had not had a hand from the Lord
How could he have set the world into discord?

3170.   He was myriads of lions in one form
He was like fire, and the world a stack of corn
He launched against that stack such a burning flame
Because the stack did not pay the tithe due him
He who like the wolf opens his mouth to speak
To this hidden lion disrespectfully
The lion will tear him, like the wolf, to shreds
And recite to him, *"We took vengeance on them"* [178]
Like the wolf, from the lion's paw he'll take blows
Before a lion, only a fool is bold

3175.   If only those blows fell on the flesh alone
So that heart and faith would remain safe and whole
My power is shattered when arriving here
How ever shall I make these mysteries clear?
Make little of your bellies' needs, like that fox
In His presence do not play tricks like a fox
Lay the whole of your "we" and "I" before Him
The kingdom is His, give the kingdom to Him
When you have become poor in the righteous way
The lion will be yours, and the lion's prey

3180.   For He is pure, by "the Exalted" described
He has no need of fine things, kernel or rind
All the plunder and the wonders that there are
Are for the sake of the bondsmen of that Shah
The Shah covets not, happy he who discerns
He made all of this empire for his creatures
Of what use should be possession of empire
To Him who made the two worlds and all empire?
Watch your heart when you are near the Exalted
So you are not shamed by thoughts disaffected

3185.   For he sees the inner self, thought, and desire
As one sees a strand of hair in milk that's pure
He whose clear breast is devoid of imagery
Is a mirror for the Unseen's imagery
Without doubt he is our true secret-sharer
For believer is mirror to believer
When he strikes the touchstone with our currency
Then he can distinguish doubt from certainty
When his spirit is the touchstone of all coin
He will distinguish the true from the false coin

Hazret Noah said to his tribe: "O people without understanding, do not think I am one of

178. Koran 7:136; 15:79; 30:47; 43:35, 55.

you and try to abuse me. I am not I. I have become free of animal spirit, alive with the Beloved and eternal with Him. And so God has become my hearing ear and my seeing eye: The breath filling and emptying my chest is His breath. The voice I am instrumental in bringing to your ears is His voice. Although I appear like you to be in human form, in reality, what has taken on this form and showed you the way to reach Him is not me, it is Him. Those who do not believe this, who do not understand the truth in these words and actions, are deniers, kafirs."

The form which appears to you may be a fox or a sheep. But within that fox's fox appearance and hidden under that sheep's coat there is a lion. One can't pretend to bravery before that image of a fox or that sheep's coat.

That is how it is, God's messengers and God's arrived may in form and appearance be small, weak and unpretentious. But in the mirror of their hearts there is the lion of being and unity. With this light which shines in their hearts they are more powerful than the most magnificent of beings.

Let us say that you look at their appearance and cannot comprehend the lion within. You to whom God has given an ear to "hear," do you not hear the lion's roar in their voices?

If Messenger Noah had not had in him the hand of God' power, how could he have re-established creation in the world? When he cursed them, all the faithless on the face of the earth died. With one lion's roar he set the world and the creatures of the world against one another. Noah was not a lion, but behind the veil of body he had countless truths, and most importantly of all, he became the lion of divine power. He was like a fire, and the world and all the creatures in it like a haystack. When the haystack did not give him even his rightful share of one tenth, he knew that the haystack was good for nothing but burning and he let loose such a fire into the world that everything burned to ashes. The fire Noah let loose was water. But it was such limitless water that it did the work of fire in the world.

If the wolf who spoke before the lion about the division of the spoils had known his limits and not tried to do it, if he had known to say only, "Let it be as you command," he would not have fallen prey to the lion who had taken him with him as a friend on the hunt. He would not have lost his head, he would not have suddenly been smitten by divine revenge.

All those who before a hidden lion sent to the world are like wolves with their mouths hanging open and do not know their limits will sooner or later be punished. For only fools pretend to bravery in the presence of a lion.

But if only it were just the human body torn and broken in the claws of lions and panthers . . . If only kafirs and hypocrites attacked like wild animals only to break the human body . . . and not the heart, faith and heart, with perversion . . . If there were not such an end as to take the paths of denial, stubbornness and infidelity before God lions, the friends and prophets, and break off from Islam and faith . . .

How shall I tell this secret? Let us say that there is much to be said, whether about Heaven or Hell. But there are mysteries it is not easy, even impossible, to put into words.

At the same time, I may recommend that you be like the fox. This is to not have recourse to trickery in the presence of the lion and to not think of your self. As the fox left the division up to the lion, so do you as well. To think of yourself first will make you, as the wolf did, forget rank and respect.

The property you claim is yours is actually His. It belongs to the pre-eternal and post-eternal owner. Do not make contrary claims before him, saying "This is my property." Abandon words making claim to selfhood like "I" and "we." Know that in His path your existence [*vücût*] is naught, and that reaching such nothingness will take you to being. You will be freed of not-being and taste the delight of being on that day.

If you ask, "Which is the right path?" know that it is that taken by those devoid of claim to selfhood. If you walk that path, all the prey caught by the lion—all divine bounties—will be offered to you. God created these bounties for you. For you to find them is pleasure for Him, and grace for you.

Know that God has no need of the bounties He creates, especially the things which worldly people know as bounties. That great Padishah has created al good and beautiful things, all kingdom [*devlet*] and felicity, only for His bondsmen.

Kingdom belongs to His bondsmen who understand the meaning in creation, who know how to look upon the universe with an eye which takes warning. They keep the mirror of the heart pure of filth that will destroy its shine.

The Exalted [*Sübhan*] means God who is pure and exempt from any lack and flaw, and especially creaturely qualities. Know that God is the Exalted. So that you may not fall into a state to be ashamed of before Him and in His sight. God the Exalted knows all your secrets and all your thoughts. Every dark feeling, thought and action is known to Him, like a black hair in white milk. For God is all-knowing, all-aware.

Hearts that are kept far from worldly filth, clean and pure, are the hearts which reflect divine mysteries. The mysteries of God, wishing to appear in them, leave their own hidden realm and find self-disclosure in such hearts or in a realm such hearts see.

That pure-hearted person is a person who at that moment knows our secrets, knows the sides of us that can reach God and those which can't. When his heart's mirror is so illuminated that God mysteries can be seen, a place is found there for the heart of all believers, and this is one meaning of the saying, "Believer is mirror of believer." For in this beautiful saying the "believer" is both God and the bondsmen . . . One of God's beautiful names is "Believer." Thus divine light self-discloses both in the friend of God and in the murid who gives his heart to him. The friend is mirror of the murid and God is mirror of the friend to the extent that the friend is God's mirror.

If our heart's wealth, our love of God, the divine light self-disclosing in us, strikes the touchstone of that pure-hearted friend, that touchstone will immediately separate truth from doubt. Whether or not our hearts are pure gold is evident in the touchstone of his heart. Only that touchstone which is the mirror of mysteries knows the pure from the corrupt heart's gold.

Thus do the friends know all the faults of those whose hearts are filled with worldly images, worldly colors and worldly filth, like corrupt gold. And in those whose hearts are pure like pure gold, which can be mirrors for divine light, they taste the profound delight of seeing the reflections of that light.

****

How Padishahs seat gnostic Sufis before themselves, so that with them their Eyes may be Illumined

3190.   The custom of Padishahs, you may have heard

If it may be that you now will remember
Is to keep warriors standing at their left
Because the heart in the body's on the left
Chancellor and secretaries at their right
For the right hand's work is to keep books and write
They place the Sufis facing them, like mirrors
For they are mirrors of spirit, and better
They polish their hearts in thought and memory
So the heart's glass takes in virgin imagery
3195. He who is born fair from the loins of nature
Placed in front of him there should be a mirror
A beautiful face is a mirror-lover
The hearts' fear of God and spirit-polisher

The great old padishahs had a custom. If you have not heard of it, let me tell you about it. If you have forgotten, let me remind you.

Champions, heroes and courageous men sat to the left of those padishahs, and by having powerful warriors seated at his left, the padishah alluded to the power of the heart, located on the left side of the body.

Finance officers, accountants and all those who held the pen would sit at his right when they came into the assembly.

Because writing on paper, whether words or figures, is done with the right hand, the padishah would ensure their righteousness and honesty in this manner, reminding them that one absolutely must write for goodness and righteousness.

But he would seat directly across from him those who know God the Truth, those Sufis who have the light of God in their hearts and faces, knowing that they have spirits brighter than even the purest mirrors.

Sovereigns saw the light of God in the arrived of the age and took from their light the power and inspiration to govern their states and peoples.

For it is the friends and Sufis who polish their spirits with thought and remembrance of God [*zikir*] so that the purest and most transparent figures may appear on the mirrors of their hearts. In other mirrors there appear only things with bodies, forms and colors. But in the heart-mirrors of Sufis there shine the most diaphanous feelings, thoughts, mysteries and divine light. Of course one should hold a mirror up to a person who has come into the world through the loins of *innate human nature* [*fitrat*], that is, born beautiful and beloved and illuminated with God's love by birth. So that he should see his own beauty and, and this beauty should be reflected for the eyes of others. That is why every beautiful face is in love with mirrors. And every beauty wants to see itself in the mirror. It seeks an eye to see its beauty and a heart to love. God is the beauty of beauties and such also is the mystery of His creation of the universe and mankind. That is why God said, "I was a hidden treasure and I loved to be known."

And that is why God's light shines in every reflection of beauty in a person's face. Beautiful faces give polish to the spirits of those who look at them, and arouse a fear of God and a love of God in their hearts, because they erive their light from that divine source.

****

HOW A GUEST CAME BEFORE JOSEPH, PEACE BE UPON HIM, AND JOSEPH DEMANDED OF HIM A GIFT AND PRESENT

> From distant horizons came a loving friend
> To visit Joseph, the true and righteous friend
> For they had known each other well as children
> Reclining upon acquaintanceship's cushion
> He recalled his brothers' cruelty and envy
> "I was a lion, and that a chain on me

3200.
> A lion is not dishonored by a chain
> Of the destiny of God I don't complain
> Though the lion have a chain upon his neck
> He is prince over all the chain-makers yet."
> "How were you in prison and the well?" he said
> "Like the dark moon before it waxes," he said
> If the new moon is bent double in that time[179]
> Does it not at last become full in the sky?
> Though the seed-pearl in the mortar's ground up fine
> It looks aloft as a salve for heart and eye

3205.
> They cast a grain of wheat underneath the earth
> Then they raise up ears of grain out from the earth
> Then they pulverize it with the mill again
> Its value increases as life-giving bread
> They crush the bread with their teeth, and it becomes
> Mind and spirit of comprehending reason
> And when that spirit is overcome by love
> It then *rejoices the sowers*[180] who have sown
> There is no end to this discourse, come back then
> To learn what that good man said to Joseph then

One day a guest came from far away to visit Hazret Joseph. They had been friends as children. The visitor's heart with filled with a profound love for Joseph. They were acquainted with one another from pre-eternity.

This guest began to speak of Joseph's brothers, of their envy and their unjust, destructive actions. Joseph's judgment of his brothers was not vengeful. He believed they had been an instrument of divine destiny and thought:

> They were a chain of iniquity and torment. I was a lion. It is no shame for a lion if he is in chains. It doesn't occur to me to complain of God's measuring-out and destiny. Our glory can bear trial, it is content with destiny. In short, it gives thanks for every state which comes from God, for every event.

Pay attention when a chain is put upon a lion. A lion does not serve those who chain it,

---

179. *Muhâk*, the period of three nights during the lunar cycle when the moon is invisible.

180. "This is their similitude in the Torah, and their similitude in the Gospel is as a seed which sends forth its blade and then makes it strong, then it becomes thick and stands on its own stem, filling the sowers with wonder and delight" (Koran 48:29).

on the contrary, they become its servants.

The faithful friend in this conversation represents the intellect of return [*maâd aklı*]. Joseph was the spirit in the well of body [*vücût*], the lion spirit. To be sure, this lion was bound by the chains of several internal and external senses. But far from being ashamed to be bound by the senses in the well of body, he felt a kind of pleasure in it. He would not stay long in that well anyway, and he would rise up to the degree that he was able to bear that chain. This chain completed the image of Joseph's magnificent beauty like tresses which increase one's beauty.

Joseph's friend asked him: "What did you feel in the Egyptian prison and in the Canaan well?"

Joseph gave the expected answer. He said: "I was like the moon on the last night of its cycle. For after it waxes as a full moon, it wanes like a crescent and is finally invisible; but the moon is not advancing toward nothingness in this way, it will again become a crescent and wax full. I too was invisible at first, whether in the Canaan well or the Egyptian prison. But then my crescent moon sparkled. Because the light of guidance came to my rescue, I spread light over Egypt. Here I became a just padishah.

Let me tell you parables. They crush pearls in a mortar and make a powder. Let us say that the pearls feel pain at the moment they are crushed, but in the end the pearl powder is mixed with kohl, and when applied to the eyes of beauties helps them see beings better, more illuminated. Or they mix the pearl powder with honey and eat it. In that case the pearl powder gives strength, expansiveness and peace to the heart.

The wheat buried in the earth, which spends its lifetime in the prison of earth, at first seems to have been destroyed. But in time that same wheat raises its head from the earth, grows green, gets tall, produces seeds, and the seeds fill the granaries. And as if that were not enough, they grind the seeds in the mill to make flour and bake in the oven to make bread.

The story does not end here. Teeth grind the bread, chewing it up, and wheat that was once under the ground gives life to the body, nourishing its root, spirit, for which it thirsts. In humans wheat becomes intellect, comprehension and understanding. It becomes a casket to keep the human spirit in, full of the love of God.

Finally when spirit is annihilated in the love of God, the wisdom of the last verse of the forty-eighth chapter of the Gracious Koran is realized: "Their similitude is as a seed which sends forth its blade and then makes it strong, then it becomes thick and stands on its own stem, filling the sowers with wonder and delight. By thus multiplying their number and strengthening them, God enrages the deniers. God has promised those who believe and do good deeds forgiveness and a great reward." So, every seed sown in the path of God amazes with its fruit even the sowers. But let us return to the story of Joseph.

****

How Joseph asked the Guest for a Gift

3210.   Joseph said, after he'd told him his story,
"Now, what traveler's gift have you brought for me?"
To come empty-handed to the door of friends
Is like setting out for the mill without grain
At the Resurrection, God most high will say,

"Where is the gift you have brought for Judgment Day?[181]
You have come to Us and *alone* without food
In the same manner as We created you
Now what have you brought to Us as a present
For the day when you are raised up from the dead?[182]

3215.   Or had you no hope you would return again
Did the promise of today seem to be vain?"
If you deny you will one day be His guest
From His kitchen you will take ashes and dust
And if you do not deny, with empty hand
How do you set foot in the court of that friend?
Spend a little less time sleeping and eating
Make this the present you've brought for the meeting
Be *little in sleep among of those slumbering*
Be one of those who at dawn *are repenting*[183]

3220.   Make a little movement like the embryo
So you'll be granted senses which light behold
And then you'll be outside of this womb-like world
You'll be in a wide expanse beyond the earth
Know the saying, *"God's earth is wide,"*[184] refers to
The expanse that the friends have entered into
The heart's never straitened by that expanse fair
The fresh boughs of the palm do not dry out there
You are burdened by the senses at present
You are falling headlong, weary, exhausted

3225.   Since when you sleep you not burdened, but borne
You are free of pain and your fatigue is gone
Know you have a mere foretaste in time of sleep
Of the state of the friends when they are carried
The friends are Men of the Cave, mendacious lout!
They sleep while rising up and turning about
Without need to act and without consciousness
God is drawing them *to the right and the left*[185]
What is the right side? Good and beautiful deeds
What is the left side? It is bodily needs

3230.   These two kinds of actions proceed from the friends
Though, like an echo, they're unconscious of them
If an echo makes a sound lofty or base

---

181. "You come to Us bare and alone as We created you the first time, leaving behind you all that We bestowed on you . . . " (Koran 6:94).
182. "Take provision for the journey, but the best of provisions is right conduct" (Koran 2:197).
183. "They were in the habit of sleeping but little by night, and praying for forgiveness at the hour of early dawn" (Koran 51:17-18)
184. "Spacious is God's earth!" (Koran 39:10).
185. "You would have thought them awake while they were asleep, and We turned them on their left and on their right sides" (Koran 18:18).

The mountain is unaware in either case

Joseph told his old friend of all the things that had happened to him. Then he said, "O friend! Tell me, have you brought me a gift? If so, what is it?"

For one doesn't come empty-handed to the door of a friend.

Joseph had no need of a gift. But his asking for a gift is reminiscent of the murshid's expectation of a gift from his murid. For on that path dedicated to God, every murshid expects from his murid a heart purified by exile, asceticism, trial and various tests. When those who have not been able, with purity of heart, to walk the path shown by the murshid come again to his door, it is like coming to the mill without wheat. What he expects from all his dervishes is that they be in good temper and do good deed on the path to eternal felicity.

And so, on the Day of Resurrection God will say: O My bondsmen! What beautiful, good deeds have you brought Me as a gift? For what and to what end have you spent your lifetimes? I gave you bounties, what did you do? I gave you powers, to what end did you expend them? I gave you intellect, in what way did you use it?"

The terror that will meet a faithless spirit who comes empty-handed on Resurrection Day, without the gifts of faith, deeds and love which should be conveyed to God, is great. To be sure, God, who creates countless bounties and kingdoms for both worlds, has no need of a gift from His bondsman. But the spirit's need for wealth in worship and faith when it ascends to God's presence is great.

In order to repay the debt and give thanks for having been created as a human, one's pouch must not be empty on the day of accounts. We cannot return to God's presence as we were first created, naked and empty-handed. Those who do not believe they will be God's guests one day can only get fire, ashes and earth from His eternal kitchen. What can a person who has not avoided sleep and gluttony to store up spiritual provisions, who has taken no delight in worship and had no share of the abandonment and expectation of fasting present as a gift to the afterworld?

In the fifty-first chapter of the Gracious Koran it says (15-19): "Those who fear God will be in the midst of gardens and springs their Lord has given to them. They lived a good life. They were in the habit of sleeping little by night, and in the hour of early dawn they prayed for forgiveness. And in their wealth was a portion for the needy and poor, and they gave it."

In that case, sleep little! And be one of those who begs forgiveness from God at dawn!

Be one of those who stir like babes in their mother's womb, so that the power to see the light may be given to you.

In a sense, this world is narrow and dark like the maternal womb. To die as a good and mature spirit is to be born happily into the divine realm, the vastest and most lasting of all realms.

In the thirty-ninth chapter of the Gracious Koran it is said that the people of Heaven and Hell will be driven in groups to those realms (10).

And: "O you My servants who believe! Fear your Lord, good is for those who do good in this world," and "Spacious is the world God has created!"

That vast world is of course not this world where you are now, and will remain for only a few days. That realm is a unique realm where prophets and friends of God go. In that world there are people who have found themselves in God and know God with God. The place where one strives to find oneself in God and know God with God, however, is the world where you are now. In this world you bear the burden of the senses which have been given to you. If you weary and lose the strength to bear the burden, the realm you will tumble down into headlong is not a realm where you will find God. The divine realm is a universe of expansiveness where fresh young date palms never grow old and dry and there is no narrowness of heart.

Consider sleep! While asleep you are not a bearer of burdens. Sleep is the time when you are freed from the burden of the senses and ascend to the heavens. At that moment there is no fatigue, no weariness, only rest and the lightening of all heavy burdens.

But know that the greatest of all comfort and ease you enjoy only at the moment when you are in the dream of spiritual feelings, asleep to the light of day and creaturely feelings, is the state of God's friends even when they are awake to worldly lights and worldly events.

Because they are free of the weight of worldly filth and worldly feelings, they have the ease of sleeping and dreaming even while they are awake. They are free of worldly ties and unfettered by the limitations tying spirit to matter.

They are the Companions of the Cave who seem to you to be awake, who are asleep to creaturely burdens even while they walk, see and speak. As it says in the Gracious Koran (18:18): "You would have thought them awake while they were asleep, and We turned them on their left and on their right sides."

That is how it is. God turns left and right the apparently awake arrived, without their knowing.

What is "the right"? Without doubt, good deeds, worship and spiritual actions. What is "the left"? Bodily desires, physical passions. Eating, drinking, wearing clothing, and doing all these in order to satisfy bodily passions.

The first conditions for such "left" actions is that one be a slave to the body [*vücût*], aware of the body and under its command.

But the bodies [*cisimler*] of God's arrived have become light, their bodies have with divine love and attraction transcended the requirements of their own materiality and have entered a state of pure spirituality although they appear to be bodies.

They have become sites of manifestation for divine self-disclosure, they have passed away from self with the vast delight of seeing God and the truth in every beautiful thing. They are like echoes, not like matter. Just as a sound echoes from mountain to mountain, while the mountain is unaware of it, they are unaware of what they do, whether spiritually or bodily. For the power manifest and moving in both their material and spiritual being [*varlık*] is the divine power itself. They are the mirror of that power.

****

How the Guest said to Joseph, "I have brought you a mirror as a gift, so that whenever you look into it, you will see you own fair face and remember me."

Joseph said, "Come, now, and take the present out."
He was shamed at this demand and wailed aloud
"I so often sought to find a gift for you,"
He said, "but no worthy gift came into view.
Shall I come to the mine bearing grains with me?

Shall I bring a drop of water to the sea?
3235. I will bring cumin to Kirman if for you
I surrender my heart and my spirit too
There is no seed that is not found in this well
But for your beauty, which has no parallel
I saw fit to bring as my present for you
A mirror like the light of the breast for you
So that you may behold your fair face therein
You who like the sun are the lamp of heaven
I have brought a mirror for you, O bright face
So you'll think of me when you behold your face."
3240. From within his vest he brought out the mirror
The business of fair ones is with a mirror
What is the mirror of being? Not-being
If you're no fool, bring the gift of not-being
Being can be seen only in not-being
The rich show to the poor generosity
The hungry man truly is bread's pure mirror
The mirror of flint that sparks fire is tinder
Not-being and lack, wherever they appear
Are for excellence of all arts the mirror
3245. When a garment is elegant and stitched well
How should then the tailor exhibit his skill?
Trunks of trees must be unhewn in order that
The carpenter may cut into stem or branch
The doctor who sets broken bones goes to where
A person with a broken leg is found there
What shall manifest the art of medicine
When there is no one who is injured and thin?
If the vile baseness of copper were not known
How could the power of alchemy be shown?
3250. Lack is mirror of perfection's quality
That baseness mirrors God's power and glory
Contrary is manifest by contrary
It's through vinegar that honey is perceived
He who sees and recognizes his defect
Races at full gallop toward being perfect
He who supposes himself perfect to be
Is not flying toward the Lord of majesty
There is no worse malady of the spirit
O vain charmer, than to think yourself perfect
3255. From your heart and from your eye much blood must weep
That you may be rid of this complacency
Iblis's fault was to think, *"I am better!"*
This disease is in the soul of all creatures
Though he see himself as among the humblest

411

There is dung under the clear water's surface
When he stirs it up to put you to the test
The water turns the color of excrement
There is dung, young man, in the bed of the stream
Though it appears to you to be a pure stream

3260.   It's the Pir who knows the way, who's sagacious
Who digs channels for the streams of soul and flesh
Can dung by the water of the stream be cleansed?
Can man's knowledge sweep away soul's ignorance?
Is a sword able to fashion its own hilt?
Go, show this wound to a surgeon to be healed
Flies gather around the mouth of every wound
So that no one sees the foulness of his wound
Your thoughts and your possessions are like those flies
Your wound is the darkness of your states of mind

3265.   And if the Pir applies a salve to your wound
At once the pain and lamentation are soothed
So that you suppose the wound has gone away
When the salve has shone upon that spot a ray
You are wounded in the back, know it's the salve
It's the ray that has healed you, not your own self

Joseph's faithful friend paused when Joseph asked him for a gift. He was pained. He was filled with sorrow that he had not able to bring a gift worthy of Joseph.

The guest said to Joseph:

Beautiful and beloved Joseph! I searched much for the gift you mention. But I couldn't find a gift worthy of you anywhere. Whatever I could bring you would be like bringing a drop of water to the sea.

If I had brought you my life and my heart, it would have been like bringing cumin to Kirman. For there is always cumin in Kirman. Its hinterland is filled with cumin, from one end to the other.

There is nothing of value in this world that you do not already possess in ocean-like abundance. I thought about it, what would be a gift worthy of your matchless beauty?

I found it appropriate that it would have to be a mirror. A mirror in which only you would be able to see the most beautiful self-disclosure in creation. Only you can see, when you look in a mirror, divine light self-disclosing in the human face. Because you are the most beautiful, the brightest, of all who have been created so far.

And the guest took a mirror out of his vest. He gave the mirror to Joseph, saying "Always remember me as you look into this and see yourself, and in your own beauty the One who created you!"

For beautiful people, looking in the mirror is a pleasurable thing. God views the most superior of the beauties He has created in the faces of beautiful people, especially people with beautiful spirits. He loves this viewing. For He sees His own beauty in their faces. This means that beautiful people and God's arrived are the mirrors of God.

No one has ever seen his face in muddy water. But if water is clean and transparent, he who looks into it sees himself as illuminated as an image in water.

The mirror of being [*varlık*], that is, of divine body [*ilâhî vücûdu*], is not-being. God saw His own image in the limitless mirror called not-being. That which we think of or see as being in this universe is the self-disclosure of that image.

If you want the self-disclosure of divine beauty, and especially divine being in the mirror of your face and heart, choose not-being. Understand the mysteries of not being in being, find them so that beauty may find the pleasure of self-disclosure in your pure mirror too.

If you seek other proofs that being appears only in not-being, pay attention to how the rich are in need of the poor in order to exhibit their wealth. In the same way, without light we would not know what darkness is. In fact everything you see in our world, a realm of limitless darkness, is because the sun casts light upon this world.

The mirror of bread is an empty stomach, the mirror of flint is tinder. Every power [*kudret*] in the universe seeks a mirror to display it, every beauty, every goodness, every action [*hareket*] becomes evident when it finds its mirror. So that in this same universe there are so many powers, and beauties, unknown to us because they have not yet found their mirrors.

Wherever there is lack, wherever there is not-being, wherever there is need, that place is definitely the mirror of an art. Because in order for an artist to display his art, that art must be lacking there, or at least done insufficiently and badly. When there is such insufficiency and lack in the environment, the artist finds a way to put forth both his art and his knowledge. Many are the useless things languishing in need and privation which change form, meaning and even quiddity in the hands of that artist and become useful.

In order for a tailor to show art, he must have in hand cloth that has not been cut and sewn. There is nothing for a tailor to do with a well-sewn piece of clothing.

If wood has been well-seasoned, carved and polished, there is no more need for a carpenter. A master carpenter makes beautiful furniture from raw wood. What should a bonesetter do with someone whose ankle is not twisted, dislocated or broken? His art is to heal dislocations, breaks and twists.

In the same way, if a person is not sick, weak and suffering, what malady can a doctor save him from?

A doctor can only display his art of healing and curing by treating the sick, the suffering and the invalid. Hazret Jesus reunited the blind, not the seeing, with the light. He brought back to life not the living but the dead. In the same way Hazret Muhammed made streams flow from his fingers for his thirsty companions during the battle. There would have been no need for this miracle if the lips of those warriors of God had not gone dry at the moment of battle, if they were not burning with thirst due to the harshness of both the battle and the sun.

If copper were like gold a pure, inviolable and stainless metal, would alchemists have worn out their lives to turn copper into gold? If human hearts were not rusted, stained and befuddled with varied worldly filth, what messenger or friend of God would have taken up the duty of guiding them to the right path?

If reflections of divine power are seen in the friends and prophets, and if these great spirits, these superior humans, with their spiritual and intellectual superiority, are able to show persons devoid of humanity, it is because of these varied insufficiencies and erring ways in the people they encounter.

So the mirror of perfection is lack. That is why a person who does not find in himself any fault, any need for unity, attainment and wholeness, does not remember or seek God. The poor wretch believes he is whole and perfect. He has no awareness of his helplessness, let alone his not-being. He believes he exists. Because he exerts no effort to remove this not-being and reach being, to become eternal in the One who really is, because he does not make his spirit mature in this field of the world, when he one day realizes that he truly is not, it will be too late.

It is a reality that every thing becomes evident through its opposite. If not for the bitter, the value of the sweet would not be known, if not for vinegar, honey, if not for plurality, oneness.

How should the heart which does not suffer the pain of separation from God, of distance from divine goodness, beauty and being, know the sweetness of union with the most beautiful of all? In order to make one's horse prance on the path of perfection, one must first understand the necessity of prancing to a perfect human and feel the need for this. The moment a person feels this need, he leaps into the right path with nine extra horses and crosses distances in an instant like the wind.

The great malady in people is their error in thinking themselves perfect. This is the most harmful of all spiritual diseases. To remain a stranger to diving power and become arrogant and proud in the illusion of one's won power.

May this malady of self-conceit leave you, and you be freed of the most powerful of maladies. If you wish, weep blood not only with your seeing or visible eye, but weep with your heart, so that at the price of torment and tears your spirit may fill with the expansiveness and comfort of freedom from claim to selfhood.

Satan's great malady was to see himself as higher than Adam, whom God created superior to the angels. "I am better than he," Satan said. That is why he refrained from bowing down to Adam. He opposed the divine command and was cursed with the name of Satan.

Many, many people have this satanic spirit which is manifested in seeing one's self as superior to everyone and everything. Beware of such thoughts and of such people.

Such people sometimes show false humility, pretending they feel lowly and prostrating themselves. They make a habit of worship and behave as if they are among those who are pure, clean and believing.

Know that the humility of such people, who do not submit themselves to a murshid, is arrogance! They are like rivers whose flowing water appears pure and clear on the surface but have dung and varied filth accumulated below. They do not show you the filth in their spirits.

If your soul is the kind of water which is filthy at the bottom, and one day someone stirs up this water of your soul with a visible or invisible stick to test it, at that moment you will see your water cloud up and take on the color of the filth at the bottom.

Beauty! There is dung at the bottom of the river. Don't be fooled by its pure, clear appearance! There is no trick people have not invented to leave their souls in the enjoyment of error and transient pleasures and passions. The soul's errors are the hardest of all addictions to renounce.

The soul is like water flowing atop black clay, that is, over a dark and filthy bed. The arrived of God, who know the ways to reach God, clean this water with the aid of the wisdom they possess and connect it to the sea of purity with a channel, making it flow with the beauty of a pure and clean river. They make the water of their guidance and forgiveness flow from the sea of God's knowledge, and when they make it reach the dirty gardens in the depths of your soul, all that filth finds a channel to not-being and flows out. You are left pure and clean.

A stagnant river does not know the filth at its bottom. It cannot clean its own bed of filth. A human hand is needed to make the river clean. In the same way, many people are unaware of the filth in the riverbed of their own souls. It takes a friend of God to see that filth and the hand of a murshid to clean it. They see the filth at the bottom, like birds who fly high above. With the power bestowed upon them by God, they see the riverbed of the soul in the human body. They wish to clean it of filth, this is their duty and their pleasure. If you too want to be a traveler on that great path, let a pir who sees the stains in the depths of your soul taste that pleasure.

Have you seen a sword carve its own hilt, giving it a more beautiful shape? If everyone tried to cure his own wound, illness would become more grave. Run to submit a pus-filled boil to the surgeon, and remember the proverb, "A knife cannot carve its own handle."

Flies buzz around a wound so that no one can see how bad it is. Those flies are your bad thoughts, your property, your wealth, your passions. Your wound is the spiritual darkness within you.

If an arrived person, a Pir, a murshid, spreads the salve of love, friendship and guidance on that raging wound of yours, the thrill of feeling God, of being in love with God, will free you of the wounds of your self and soul. You will be filled with a light of God you have not known, and whose limitless delight you could not have known before reaching that state. You will find yourself free of anxiety for this world and the afterlife.

Sometimes it happens that when the slave is applied to the wound, the patient thinks the pus is gone and becomes heedless, suddenly feeling that he is better. But this is only the shining of light on the wound. In order to be healed, to be a spirit exactly as God whishes, the treatment must continue. Do not abandon the murshid! The path he will show you is not just the beginning of the path. One must walk this path to the end.

Your wound is on your back! Do not be heedless of that salve. Realize the seriousness of the wound you cannot see with your eyes. In order to heal the soul's boil with the salve of love, friendship and divine light, and offer you the pre-eternal and post-eternal health of self-disclosure, dive into the murshid's light of the grace! Do not suppose, the moment you begin to heal, that the delight of convalescence is your own power. Do not fall into the pit of arrogance and pride, do not again veer off into the heedlessness of Satan, saying, "I am better than he," do not abandon the mushid who heals you and will make you better still!

****

HOW THE RECORDER OF DIVINE REVELATION BECAME AN APOSTATE BECAUSE THE RAY OF REVELATION STRUCK HIM AND HE RECITED THE VERSE BEFORE THE PROPHET DID, PEACE BE UPON HIM, AND HE SAID, "SO I TOO AM THE SITE OF REVELATION."

> There was a scribe before the time of Uthman
> Who took care in writing revelation down

When the Prophet dictated revelation
Upon a leaf he would write down that portion

3270.   The beams of revelation would shine on him
And he would discover wisdom inside him

It was that wisdom itself the Prophet read
Just writing it down made that fool lose his head

Thinking, "That which the illumined Prophet says
That truth is within me in my consciousness[186]

The ray of his thinking then struck the Prophet
The wrath of God descended on his spirit

He abandoned both writing and religion
A sworn foe of Mustafa and religion

3275.   Mustafa said, "If the light was from you, then
How have you turned black, O obstinate pagan?

If you had been divine revelation's fount
You would not have let this much black water out."

He did not want his good name bandied about
By all and sundry, and that kept his mouth shut

He was burning up inside and, wondrous that
For this reason he could not bear to repent

He was sighing, "Ah!" but "Ah!" brought him no gain
When the sword arrived and stole his head away

3280.   God made good name a hundred maunds' iron weight
O so many are bound by an unseen chain!

The path is so blocked by denial and pride
That he can't make manifest even one sigh

God said, *"shackles, so that their heads are forced up"*[187]
Not from outside are those shackles put on us

"We've covered them," with *"a barrier behind"* [188]
Uncle doesn't see the bar fore and behind

That bar has the color of open country
He does not know it's the bar of destiny

3285.   Your lover bars the beloved's countenance
Your murshid is a bar to the murshid's sense

Many kafirs have a love for religion
Some chain holds them back, pride or reputation

The chain's hidden, but it is worse than iron
An ax may cleave in two a chain of iron

It is possible to lift an iron chain
None knows the cure for an invisible chain

If a man is pierced by the sting of a bee

---

186. "Who can be more wicked that someone who invents a lie against God, or says, 'I have received revelation,' when he has received none, or says, 'I can reveal the like of god has revealed'?" (Koran 6:93).

187. Koran 36:8.

188. Koran 36:9.

The man can extract the sting from his body
3290.   But since the wound is caused by your existence
The pain does not cease, it hurts with violence
The explication of this springs from my breast
But I fear it may occasion hopelessness
No, do not despair, but make yourself cheerful
Call out for help to Him who answers the call
Saying, "You who love to forgive, forgive us
You who cure old incurable wounds, heal us!"
Wisdom's reflection drove the Prophet's scribe down
Do not let conceit trample you underground
3295.   Wisdom is flowing into you, O brother
From the Substitutes, it's borrowed from others
Although the house has found a light within it
It shines forth from a neighbor bestowing it
Give thanks, never show conceit, do not be vain
Listen attentively and do not disdain
Hundredfold pity and grief, this borrowed state
Has kept communities from communal state
I'm slave to him who does not think he's arrived
Each time he comes to a caravanserai
3300.   Many hostels must be left along the way
So that a man may arrive at home one day
Though the iron is red hot, iron's not red
The color's a kindling ray that is borrowed
If light has filled up the window or the house
Don't think aught but the sun to be luminous
"I am luminous," every door and wall says
"These are all mine, I have no one else's rays."
Then the sun says, "O you who are incorrect
It will all be obvious when I have set."
3305.   "We are green in and of ourselves," the plants say
"We are laughing and tall in stature and gay."
"O my people," the season of summer says
"Look upon yourselves when I have gone away."
The body boasts of its goodness and beauty
While spirit, concealing its plumes and glory
Says to it, "Who are you then, O you dung heap?
You have life for a day or two through my beams
The whole world can't contain your pride and disdain
Wait till I abandon you and spring away
3310.   Those who loved you ardently with dig your grave
And make you a morsel for insects and snakes
One who so many a time in your presence
Would die for you will hold his nose at your stench
The rays of spirit are speech and eye and ear

The ray of fire's in the boiling of water
Just as spirit's ray upon the body shines
So the Substitutes' ray on my spirit shines
When spirit's spirit from the spirit retreats
Know spirit becomes like spiritless body

3315.   I lay down my head upon the earth for this
So on Judgment Day she may be my witness."
On Judgment Day *"when the earth quakes mightily"*
Then she will bear witness to all that has been
For *"she will declare all that she knows plainly"*
On that day earth and rocks will begin to speak[189]
The philosopher in thought denies it all
Tell him to go and dash his head on this wall!
Speech of water, speech of clay and speech of earth
Are sensible only to the men of heart

3320.   The philosopher denies Hannana's[190] speech
He's estranged from the friends' sensitivities
The ray of melancholia, he opines
Brings many images into people's minds
No, reflection of his infidelity
Casts upon him this disbelieving fancy
The philosopher denies Satan exists
While at the same time he is by Satan transfixed
Look at yourself if you have not seen Satan
The brow is not blue without madness from him

3325.   If a man's heart is filled with doubt and torture
He's a secret philosopher in this world
He professes firm belief, yet now and then
That philosopher's vein makes his face blacken
Pay attention, O Faithful, that vein's in you
There is many an infinite world in you
All the seventy-and-two sects are in you[191]
Alas if they gain the upper hand in you
Everyone who has the power of this faith
Out of fear of this is trembling like a leaf

3330.   You have laughed at Iblis and other satans
Because you regard yourself as a good man
When spirit turns its coat inside-out at last
The religious will cry out "Ah, and alas!"

---

189. Koran 99:1-8.

190. The blessed moaning pillar made from a date palm against which the Prophet used to lean while delivering a sermon before a pulpit was built.

191. The Prophet quoted God in a sacred hadith as saying, "The Jews and Christians have been divided into seventy-two different sects. My community will be divided into seventy-three sects. All but one of them will go to Hell." The Companions of the Prophet asked, "Which one is that, Messenger of God?" He replied, "The path walked by myself and my Companions."

On the counter all that seems gold's smiling bright
For the touchstone to test it is out of sight
O Veiler of Faults, don't raise the veil from us
When we are subject to the test, protect us
The false coin jostles against the gold at night
While the gold is keeping watch for the daylight
3335. With the tongue of its inner state, the gold says
"Just wait, tinsel coin, for the clear light of day!"
Damned Iblis, for hundreds of thousands of years
Was a Substitute and prince of believers
He boxed with Adam because of his disdain
And like dung in the morning light was disgraced

Hazret Muhammed's scribe before Hazret Uthman was a man named Abdullah ibn Abu Sarh. As soon as Abdullah heard from Hazret Muhammed the revelation which came down to him, he would write the verses out on paper, executing this blessed duty with utmost seriousness.

It made the scribe emotional to write down revelation, sensing himself being illuminated with the light of revelation. He would abandon himself to the sound and meaning of the verses and feel their wisdom within him.

One day when his heart was filled with the light of revelation, the chapter "The Believers" came down to Hazret Muhammed. The following sentence suddenly fell from Abdullah's lips: "We created man from a quintessence of clay, then We placed him as sperm in a place of rest, firmly fixed; then we made the sperm into a clot of congealed blood, then of that clot We made a lump, then We made bones out of that lump and clothed them in flesh, and then We constructed it with a different creation; so blessed be God, the best to create!" [23:12-14].

Then Hazret Muhammed said, "Write! What you have spoken is a verse of the Koran which has just now come down."

Abdullah ibn Abu Sarh was stunned.

At first he thought excitedly, "So I also receive revelation?" Then he fell into the dark doubt, thinking, "Revelation comes down to Muhammed because he is a messenger of God the Truth and takes his light from God. But if what I said, that is, what arose within me, is also a verse of the Koran, then I also receive revelation. In that case either I too have become a prophet, or Hazret Muhammed is making up these verses."

The mysterious rays of this doubt and anxiety were reflected onto the spirit of Hazret Muhammed. The instant that the Messenger of God sensed the clouding of his scribe's spirit, and the reasons for it, the wrath of God descended upon the scribe's spirit.

Abdullah lost his function as scribe as well as his religion and faith. Because of that he became an enemy to Hazret Muhammed and joined with those who rejected him.

Hazret Muhammed said: "O stubborn kafir! If the light of revelation has descended upon you and revelation from God come, why does it not continue? Why are you now left in the dark? Would a person whose spirit was touched by revelation flail around in such ignorance? If you were the the source of the divine river, would you now open the way to this flood of infidelity and error?"

The scribe of revelation was completely confused. On the one hand, he supposed that he was a man of honor and reputation, and was ashamed; on the other, he couldn't open his mouth to say anything to anyone, fearing his supposed honor would come to nothing and his name be ruined.

He couldn't even repent anymore, he was burning up inside. The sword had fallen and the head was severed. The sighs filling him were no longer heard. For although a person may repent in solitude, if he continues to behave outwardly in pride and Pharaoh-like stubbornness, his repentance has no effect. At most he will deceive himself and be inwardly confused.

For arrogance a pride so block a persons path that even if a kafir finds in his heart a sigh and a longing for the light, it will not be projected outwards.

And in the thirty-sixth chapter of the Gracious Koran, God the Truth said of such people (36:8): "We have put yokes around their necks up to the chin, so that their heads are forced up." But don't you object, saying you do not see such shackles around the necks of kafirs! These shackles are not outwardly fastened upon their necks.

In the same chapter, God said (36:9): "We have raised up a barrier before them and a barrier behind them, and furthermore We have veiled them so that they cannot see." What they cannot see is the divine oneness and beauty, the light of God.

The obstacles set up on the paths of such people are as wide as deserts. They think this broadness is wealth, plenty and ease.

They cannot tell that such deserts of position, fortune, wealth and lust are actually insurmountable walls of steel, and that all these obstacles have been set up according to the requirements of the measuring-out and destiny.

The human bodily eye cannot see these obstacles and imperfections pertaining to the soul, each of which is a trap. These are the dangerous blocks which can only be detected by seeking the aid of a friend of God and learning from him the visible and invisible barriers which block one's way on the path to God. As long as a person does not do so, his life on earth is lived in vain.

As long as you fall in love with the beauty that is beloved of your soul and stay in love, you cannot see the light of the spiritual beloved. As long as you plunge into the pleasure of worldly delights and worldly bounties, and give your ear and heart to the voice of the guide belonging to your soul, you cannot hear the voice of the true murshid who shows you the ways to reach God.

There are kafirs who burn with a longing for faith. But since they stubbornly suppose themselves to possess honor and reputation, pride and similar feelings prevent them from taking a spiritual path. Worldly ties rise up before them like an insurmountable wall.

To be sure, these walls are invisible. But they are stronger than steel. For an ax, or any tool, may undo iron chains. But who can break apart these invisible ties, and how?

If a bee stings a person, the body mobilizes all its powers to get rid of the pain, poison and evils which result from the sting. Pain and swelling is ameliorated by salve applied externally.

But if the bee that stings your body does not come from outside, but is produced within you, in your constitution [*bünye*], you do not have the power to get rid of it, to get rid of the hidden wound it has opened inside your body. You feel burning pains within you, but you neither know what is wrong nor how to cure it.

I feel the desire within me to explicate this further. I want to further illuminate this truth. But I am concerned that what I say may plunge you into despair.

But while there is God, one cannot despair. Know that God definitely answers every call, rushes to help all who ask for help, and He is the Merciful and the Compassionate, and do not fail to ask from Him everything that is appropriate. He is the Creator who, if He wishes, will in an instant bring you from darkness to light, from infidelity to faith, from mourning to peace of mind and the greatest of all hopes.

O Lord! You are God who knows forgiveness to be the greatest pleasure and felicity of sublimity, higher than all; forgive us. O great Physician of those whose hearts are calloused, of callous-making maladies, even of those whose calloused wounds are ancient and hardened! My God, who covers all faults and removes them! Forgive us! Keep us from erring illusions and ugly acts of arrogance! If we are in denial, teach us to love You, to seek You, to find you!

The reflection of God's wisdom upon his heart took that scribe of revelation Abdullah from the right path. It brought that Muslim who was swept up in erring conjecture and strayed into error to join the incurable kafirs. The reason was that the scribe of revelation Abdullah saw himself as on a par with Hazret Muhammed, supposing himself of the same stuff as Hazret Muhammed.

O brother! Beware, do not be one of those who sees himself everywhere. Do not let your view of yourself raise the dust of plurality and duality in you. O brother! God's wisdom is flowing over your spirit and your understanding. But this wisdom flowing over you flows from the light of the being [varlık] of God's Substitutes, that is, from perfect humans, it flows from their riverbeds. The arrived of God have destroyed their own materiality and come near to the divine realm; they are spirits who have been freed from the darkness of body and reached the light of unity.

If you see a light reflected from them in yourself, do not mistakenly suppose that the light comes from you! To be sure, you are tasting the delight of finding illumination in the house of the heart. But do not forget that the illumination overflows from a neighbor's house, which spreads light everywhere around.

If a ray from that light falls into your house, be thankful! But do not be proud of it. For the first step toward error and denial is pride and arrogance.

Pity the person who becomes the site of manifestation of divine grace and supposes that the light of God reflected in him, the illumination of a prophet or friend, comes from within himself, and becomes proud; he makes claim to selfhood, or like the scribe of revelation Abdullah turns off into darkness again, just as this state of the soul has distanced many a community from the felicity of being the community of a messenger.

I am slave to those who do not suppose they have the right to sit at the head of the table at every caravansarai.

For if those who cross distances on the spiritual path suppose when they arrive at a station and stop there that the journey is over and they have arrived at their goal, if they suppose they are seated at the table of truth, they are duped in vain.

For spiritual stations, like caravanaries, are not the property of those who stop in them. One stays there for a short time, enjoys hospitality there for a short time, and sets out on the road again.

A person must stay in many inns and caravasaries in order to reach his home or final destination. The art is to not stay long at inns, to be able to get back on the road and cross distances on that road without tiring.

Although an iron heated on the fire turns red in color, red is not the color of iron itself. Neither that redness nor that sparking appearance is really a property of iron. Both the color and brightness of red-hot iron are transient. Iron takes that color and light from the oven in which it has been placed.

If at sunset the windows of homes and palaces burn bright, do not suppose this is the inner light of the homes and palaces.

Every house unaware of the rays of the sun, supposing the light burning at sunset in windows of homes and palaces to be its own, may be swept up in an illusion like: "This brightness is my own light. This light is reflected from my being."

The sun, with a dignified manner, says to those house and palace windows proud of the light reflected from it: "Just wait a little. You prideful ones of little understanding! Let me get behind that mountain or that sea. Let me withdraw from the horizon. Then it will be very easy for you to understand if those windows burn with your light or if the light is reflected from me."

The language of plants in spring is like that as well. They suppose they are fresh and green by their own art. For days and weeks they brag proudly of these fresh, green colors. For days they live in the delusion that their color comes from themselves, and that is why their gaiety and beauty is beyond measure. They flatter themselves on how slender their bodies are and how beautiful their faces.

The the days of spring and especially the summer months call out to them in their own language to them: "O greenery, O plants, be not proud! Just wait until we have passed. Then you will see that these colors and this freshness do not belong to you. They are the products of our good-spirited breath, our breezes, our heat and our rains.

The body lives under both the illusion that it exists and that it is beautiful. To boast of its being and beauty is its nature. But spirit is invisible; it is not visible to the eye even as a transparent body. It conceals from the eye the power and strength that keeps it its body [*vücût*] alive, colorful and beautiful.

Spirit says to the body: "O creature made up of a handful of clay and a few sweepings, what are you boasting about? Is it not I who keeps you fresh and alive? If I were to go, how would you be, left behind? What would happen to you?

"O body! O mortal shadow, your temporary dwelling! O bodies of those considered to be the most beautiful of all! Do you not know that those who love you, who love you enough to worship you while I am with you, will when I have left you dig you a home not in the embrace of their arms but in the embrace of the earth.

"The best of those you leave behind will read the Fatiha[192] not for you, that is, not for your body, but for me, that is, your spirit. Your lovers who said they would sacrifice their lives for your beautiful face and elegant form will leave you when you become a spiritless body starting to rot and stink, and will not even dream of you, of the moments when you were alive and beautiful, anymore."

As long as the spirit is in the body the most beautiful of words, the warmest and most faithful, fall from rose-colored lips. Every word takes on the character of a beautiful melody rising from an instrument. The ear hears these beautiful words and the eye is awed by the beautiful person who says them.

The seeing of the eye, the hearing of the ear and the speaking of the tongue are evidence of spirit, like boiling water is of fire.

---

192. The Fatiha, the first chapter of the Koran, is recited as a prayer over the dead.

Just as the body is beautiful, and kept illuminated from within and alive, because spirit strikes it like a ray of light, the light of God's friends illuminates my spirit in the same way.

Just as the body takes its life from spirit [*can*], spirit [*can*] takes its life from the spirit of spirits [*cânan*]. The spirit of spirits is the friends, and if they were to withdraw their divine brightness from my spirit, I would die like a body whose spirit [*rûh*] has flown. For the friends, like spirit, bring one to life or cause one to continue to live. Once any spirit [*can*] has been illuminated by their light, it can no longer be called spirit if it is deprived of them for an instant.

I put my forehead of worship to the earth feeling with all my being my nothingness and not-being before the divine power, and I want this earth to bear witness that my spirit burns with the light of the friends.

Do not ask how senseless earth can bear witness to the purity of my spirit and the profound respect and love I feel for the arrived! In the ninety-ninth chapter of the Gracious Koran it says that on the Day of Resurrection the earth will bear witness to our every state (99:1-8):

> When the earth quakes mightily and throws forth her burdens, and man cries out, 'What is wrong with her?', on that day she will declare her tidings: for that your Lord will have inspired her . . . Then whoever has done an atom' weight of good will see it, and whoever has done an atom's weight of evil will see it.

The dust, thorns, plants, trees and everything on earth will conform to that divine inspirations and speak, and tell every word, every secret, every piece of information with profound openness.

I do not see the need to describe to you here the greatness of Resurrection Day and the terror of that day. Real gnosis is that a person should find the ways to die to his own self before dying, and thus be born to that day of accounts as one of the arrived of God.

If you ask the philosopher, he will accept neither the signs of Resurrection Day not the death before death. He does not believe that stones and trees will speak. Tell him to go and bash his head against those stones he believes will never speak, so that he may gather his wits! Tell him:

Only men of heart understand the language of water, earth, roses and plants. When after years and years of ascending through the joy of naughting themselves they reach the degree of being able to comprehend all truths, they see how mineral and vegetable, birds and all animals speak in remembrance of God. Others do not see and hear what the prophets and friends see and hear because they are still blind and deaf under the command of self and matter inside the body.

When Hazret Muhammed used to give sermons before a pulpit had been constructed for him, he would lean his blessed body against a pillar made of a date-palm trunk. Can the philosopher understand what that date-palm felt, how it trembled in awe and moaned deeply? Certainly he is unaware of the reality of the mysteries and meanings which the prophets and friends have seen up close and know. Because he is unaware, he tries to resolve these mysteries and meanings according to his own intellect.

The philosopher says that people affected by feelings of love create all sorts of conjectures and fantasies. The rays of creaturely love prepare the imagination of people so that such feelings, thoughts and beliefs arise. To suppose that wolves, birds, stones and trees are beings that can feel and think, believe and speak—such delusions are the result of these fantasies.

One day Hazret Ali said to Hazret Muhammed: "O Messenger of God, when I go out to the desert from Mecca, I do not see one stone or tree that does not greet me." To be sure, the philosopher does not understand the truth of that. In fact the reflections of his states of mind far from faith, his corruption and infidelity, lead him into such doubts and conjectures. He concludes that things he sees and imagines are illusory, and supposes that the friends and prophets have the same corrupt fantasies.

The philosopher rejects the existence of jinn, devils and satans. He thinks these are all fantasies created by conjecture, and does not know that he is in the hand of the Satan he rejects even while he rejects him. He has become Satan's toy, his fool.

If you, O philosopher, cannot see Satan, look at yourself in a mirror. Observe the bruise on your forehead. This bruise occurs on the faces of those who bash themselves on stone after stone, rushing off day and night after pleasure and crazy behavior.

Look and see that color on your face, and since you are a philosopher, that is, since you are able to think, at least think about the mystery and the reason for this.

Even if people who have such doubts and darkness in their hearts hide themselves and pretend to be Muslims, the philosophy of denial is coiled in their hearts.

O believers! Don't be like the philosophers, like those who have lost their way! For there's a philosopher's vein in almost everyone. Almost everyone has moments of doubt. Within you too there are so many limitless realms you do not know of yet.

If you abandon the way of the friends and prophets and dip into the branches of philosophy, the philosophers' paths all contrary to one another, at the end of the road you will meet only disappointment.

Every heart in which there is doubt and belief in error instead of perfect faith will tremble like a leaf in autumn on the Day of Resurrection.

Because you suppose yourself to be a good person and think that "superior people are distinguished by their rejection of the invisible"—that is rejection of what you cannot see, you laugh at devils, satans and jinn. But to suppose that what you do not know and cannot see does not in fact exist is the clearest expression of ignorance and error.

If one day the spirit turns the sheepskin it wears inside-out, turns you inside-out, and the truths you have not seen dazzle your eyes like the sun while the invisible satans within you are spread out under the light of that sun, then look and see what groans will be heard coming from so many of the religious people, including yourself, who supposed themselves good men while in the world. Those groans arising when those who suppose themselves good people see the wretchedness of their inner selves are certainly heart-rending.

But as Hazret Muhammed said: "In whatever state a bondsman dies, whatever quality is dominant in him while he dies, when he is raised up again he will be raised up in that quality."

All the gilded things in the shop of the world are joyful and laughing with the pleasure of seeming to be gold. Those who sell them are bold because they can sell copper as gold to all who come along. The reason for this is that there is no touchstone around, or rather that the touchstone is hidden where eyes cannot see it.

So it is with people's behavior and beliefs, they are either of copper or gold. If the spirit and touchstone of gnosis which distinguishes the false from the pure gold of such belief and behavior is hidden behind a curtain and unable to function, people can be so mistaken as to think their own copper is gold.

And so: O God who covers faults! Do not raise the veil which conceals all our sins! Do not see and do not show our inner selves visible in all their ugliness behind the veil! Save us from them, give us a spirit of pure gold! Cleanse our spirits of all else but You! In short, pity us! Help us, for we have and will have no refuge but You!

However much false gold may swagger in the darkness of night, in the same shop side-by-side with pure gold and shiny as pure gold, pure gold does not mind. It laughs at the boasts false gold can make only in the darkness of night, and waits in dignified patience for the light of day, and speaks thus to the false metal beside it in its own language:

"O pitiful liar! Do you think night lasts till Resurrection Day? Morning will come tomorrow anyway. Then you will see for yourself how you are bright red and I have the yellowness of gold."

Do you not know that the angels bowed down for hundred of thousands of years to Satan, whom God cursed. Satan, proud of being created of fire, had been for ages the teacher and commander of the angels.

But out of that same pride, disdain and arrogance, one day he engaged in contest with Adam, who was created of earth. He was so bold as to say to God, "I am better than he."

Later when he lost the contest he engaged in with Hazret Adam in the presence of the angels, the filth within him was exposed, in the way that the odors of dirty, filthy things are brought out when the light and heat of the sun strikes them. He became the laughing-stock of the angels who had bowed down to him. Now, so that you may better understand this disgrace, I will tell you the story of Bal'am son of Ba'ur.

****

HOW BAL'AM SON OF BA'UR PRAYED, "MAKE MOSES AND HIS PEOPLE TURN BACK FRUSTRATED FROM THIS CITY THEY HAVE BESIEGED."

> All the world was slave to Ba'ur's son Bal'am
> For he was like to the Jesus of his time
> They bowed in prostration to no one but him
> The spells he cast made the sick be well again
> 3340. He boxed with Moses from pride in perfection
> You've heard the story of what became of him[193]
> But there have been, whether hid or manifest
> Hundreds of thousands like Bal'am and Iblis
> God caused these two to become notorious
> So that against the rest they might bear witness
> He hung these two thieves up on the scaffold high
> Though there have been many subject to His ire
> He dragged them by their forelocks into the town
> But the victims of His wrath are beyond count

193. The Koranic account of Bal'am son of Ba'ur is famous: "Tell them the story of the man to whom We sent Our signs, but he passed them by; so Satan pursued him and he went astray" (Koran 7:175)

3345.   You are God's favorite, but within your bounds
        Oh God, oh God, do not go beyond those bounds
        If you box with someone more loved than yourself
        You'll be dragged to the depth of the seventh earth
        Why is the tale of Ad and Thamud told of?
        So you may know how the prophets are beloved
        The earth's swallowing, thunderbolts, hurtling stone
        Are signs of the might of the rational soul
        Kill all animals for the sake of mankind
        Slaughter all mankind for the sake of the mind

3350.   What is mind? The universal intellect
        Partial intellect is too, but not perfect
        All the animals that do not obey man
        Are inferior to those who're tamed by man
        For mankind their blood is made lawful by God
        They have no manifest intellect, they're wild
        The dignity of the wild was damaged when
        They were hostile in opposition to men
        What honor, O marvel, will be yours at last
        When you have become like a *"frightened wild ass"*?[194]

3355.   The tame ass should not be slain, since he's useful
        When he becomes wild, his blood becomes lawful
        Though the ass has no knowledge restraining him
        The Loving One makes no excuses for him
        How then should man be excused, O noble friend
        When he shies away from the voice of reason?
        Kafirs' blood is lawful necessarily
        Like arrows and lances shot at a wild beast
        Lawful too are all their wives and their children
        Because they shy away from august reason

3360.   Intellect that flees intellect's intellect
        Becomes animal instead of intellect

The people of the world loved Bal'am ibn Ba'ur to the point of worshiping him. They so believed in his spiritual superiority that they bowed down to no one else. Bal'am's breath did really heal the sick and make them well.

With time Bal'am himself came to believe that he possessed spiritual power and superiority, to the extent that he began to compete against Hazret Moses and tussle with him.

What was the result? You will learn of that. But you should know that there are there are hundreds of thousands of such Satans and Bal'ams in the world. They too told those who praised them that they possessed spiritual virtues and grew arrogant before those who bowed down to them, coming to believe in their own lies.

For that reason they were cursed by God and driven away by God.

---

194. "What is the matter with them that they turn away from admonition, like frightened asses fleeing a lion?" (Koran 74:49-51).

God the Truth made Satan and Bal'am renowned so that with their mistakes and the errors they made they might be an example to others and other bondsmen might take lessons from what happened to them.

That is why God hung those two bandits high on the scaffold of infamy. For there are so many bandits in the world who meet with divine punishment quietly and, wretchedly defeated by their own souls, plunge headlong, without hands, without feet, into the abyss of error. As in the fifty-fifth chapter of the Gracious Koran, where it says (55:41): "The sinners will be known by their marks, and will be seized by their forelocks and their feet," God caught those two by their hair and raised them up high. They were raised up, their scalps aching in pain. But there are so many others who have met with God's wrath that it is impossible to know and count them all.

For there is a way to tread the path of God and a courtesy to the love of God. If a person becomes confused on the path and supposes he has arrived when he has not, donning the tunic of the arrived when he is not one of them, in short, if he does not obtain the grace of a friend of God or murshid, he may one day fall into an irremediable state.

Hazret Muhammed said: "God has mercy on those who know their measure and do not transgress their bounds."

You may be accepted by God and preciously brought up. But you are still forced to fear God and not transgress bounds with Him who loves you so. If you err and engage in combat with someone superior to you in God's sight, God will distance you from His light as he did Iblis and Bal'am.

The stories of the Ad and Thamud tribes were not told in vain. These stories show how preciously favored the prophets are in God's sight. Those who cross God's messengers as Ad and Thamud did end in destruction.

You can read in the chapter "The Spider" of the Gracious Koran how the earth swallowed up Qarun, how stones rained down upon the Tribe of Lot, and how the knees of the Madyans loosened and caused them to collapse on the ground. All were disasters which arose because these peoples crossed the prophets who were sent to them.

For all of these are proofs of the force and sublimity in the sight of God of those possessed of rational soul [nefs-i nâtıka]. The rational soul is a spiritual force which self-discloses in humans as gnosis, comprehension, and capacity for speech, and which is a great kindness and a gift God presents to his prophets and friends and His bondsmen precious and favored in His sight.

The animate beings [cânlılar] on earth are not limited to humans. God also gave spirits [cân] to animals too various and numerous to be known. He made them sites of manifestation of life [hayât] also. Yet still it is obvious that for the sake of humans He sacrifices the other animate beings He created, that he kills them and has them killed so that humans may live.

For the good of humans God sacrifices so many animals, and so many humans are sacrifice for the sake of one prophet or friend possessed of the intellect of return [akl-ı maâd].

What is intellect? Certainly, what is meant here by intellect is the superior intellects of the prophets and friends, that is, universal intellect. To be sure, partial intellect is a part of intellect or a part intellect, but that is what it is, part intellect.

The animality degree of wild animals is inferior to the animality of domesticated animals. In animals who do not flee humans there is hidden a superiority relatively nearer to the human.

But it is permitted for humans to sacrifice, slaughter and kill every type of wild animal.

At the same time, if you are hunting prey, first kill your own soul! Rather than killing the animals outside, in the desert, in the wilderness, in the wild, swimming in the sea and flying in the sky, annihilate that soul monster, so much more dangerous to you, hunt down its animal qualities and remove them so that you may be really human.

Don't be like a wild ass fleeing a lion. For the wild ass to flee the lion means for a person to flee the prophets and friends who are the lions of men. In this regard remember verses 48-51 and 54 of the seventy-fourth chapter of the Gracious Koran: "Then no intercession of intercessors will profit them. What is the matter with them that they turn away from admonition, as if they were frightened asses fleeing a lion? . . . Nay this is surely an admonition."

So, it is a sin to kill asses as long as they work in service of men. But if an animate being is both an ass and becomes wild, its blood is lawful.

You may ask what sin it is for an ass to behave that way at first, since it has no intellect, no knowledge or insight to free it from wildness. But God did not make it a sin to kill the ass He did not give insight to, on the contrary, He made it permitted.

So, O sublime beloved! O friend! If a human to whom intellect and insight has been given becomes wild like a mountain ass, a stranger to and uncultivated by the sacred words which blow like breath from the divine breezes of the prophets and friends, why and how should God forgive him?

Far from it being a sine to declare war on those who deny God and His books and messengers, it is God's command, it is a religious requirement, it is a good deed. To make war in this way is an obligation. As those kafirs enslave their God-given spirits at the hands of their souls, losing them, it is a laudable duty, merely as a punishment given by the command of justice, to bring their wives and children among the ranks of the believers and enlighten them with faith. This duty has a laudable goal—to save their in fact innocent wives and children from error.

On the other hand, like the flowing of streams and rivers into lake and seas, the intellects of humans must flow across the friends and prophets who are the intellects of intellects. The goal of every intellect should be to reach the greatest of intellects, that is, universal intellect. For human intellect to flee this path of progress means for it to become animal.

The intelligent act is to take the path of the friends and prophets. One must work to see every person on the good path, without condescension, without cursing and scolding those who have lost the way.

Only such action frees a person from losing his way on the path of God. Beyond that, you may be as beloved as Bal'am, you may be an angel, but if you oppose God's prophets and friends and try to vie with them, you too will be among those who lose their way. Such action also brings you far from intellect and universal intellect.

Those who look with contempt upon people and consider themselves among the high, who stick out their tongues and raise their hands against the divine commandments and God's messengers—even if they be angels, like the angels Harut and Marut—they will be struck down with worldly punishments and be lost.

That is why I will now tell you the story of the angels Harut and Marut who trusted in their angelic natures and tried to rule over the people of the world and for that reason came to mischief and were lost.

****

How Harut and Marut relied on their own Chastity and tried to mix with the People of the World and came to Mischief

Like Harut and Marut who in arrogance
Were struck by the blow of the poison-tipped lance
They put confidence in their own sanctity
If buffalo trusts lion, what will that be?
Although he thrusts with his horns a hundred times
He will be torn limb from limb by the lion
Though he become all horns like a porcupine
The buffalo's always killed by the lion
3365. But while the Sarsar wind uproots many trees
It makes each blade of grass glisten with beauty
That harsh wind has mercy on the puny grass
O heart, do not trust in your own strength and brag
How should the axe fear the branches of a tree?
Though they're thick, it will hack them down piece by piece
But against a leaf it will not beat itself
An edge strikes only a sharp edge like itself
If there's lots of firewood, does a flame weep?
Does a butcher flee a multitude of sheep?
3370. When compared to reality, form is weak
The sky is kept upside-down by its meaning
Take analogy by heaven's wheel; wherefrom
Does its whirling proceed? Directive reason
The whirling round of this body like a shield
Proceeds from, O son, the spirit which is veiled
This wind's motion comes from its reality
Like a wheel captive to the flow of the stream
This breath's in and out, the ebb and flow of it
Whence does it come but from desiring spirit?
3375. Now it forms the letter *jeem*, now *dal*, now *ha*
Now it turns breath into peace, now into war
In the same way our Lord made the Sarsar wind
Become for the people of Ad a dragon
While for the believers He transformed that wind
Into peace, safety and consideration
"The Meaning is God," said the Shaykh of Islam
The sea of meanings of the Lord of all realms
All of the tiers of the earth and of the sky
Are chaff on that sea of spirit flowing by
3380. The jumping dance of chaff upon the water

> Comes of the agitation of the water
> When the sea wishes it to struggle no more
> Then it tosses the straw and chaff on the shore
> When it draws them back into the waves at last
> It does to them what the Sarsar does to grass
> This topic has no end. Hasten back, O youth
> Return to the tale of Harut and Marut

The wish of the angels Harut and Marut to descend to the world from the spiritual realm of the angles was a cause of disaster for them. What dragged them into the world was again the evils of mankind. Seeing the tragedies flowing across the face of the earth and how men were helpless at the hands of their various passions, these angels made complaint to God and asked that an end be put to what they had seen.

God the Truth told the angels: "If you possessed the lust of Mankind, you would have committed the same sins.

The angels maintained that was impossible and requested they be given the job of reforming the world. So God imbued them with the lust of mankind and commanded them to go down to the city of Babylon. Harut and Marut began serving as judges in Babylon. But one day they were confronted by a very beautiful woman and fell into her trap.

Both of the angels fell in love with her. The woman proposed that they murder her husband or worship idols, or at least drink wine. She said there was not other way that she would not yield to their desires. The angels thought about doing one of the three things she proposed. They thought the least harmful would be to drink wine.

But when they drank wine, they recited God's greatest name and taught her the secret of ascending to the heavens. The woman used the secret and ascended to the heavens and God turned her into the planet Venus. He had the angels hung upside-down over the pit of Babylon and left them in worldly torment.

The disaster that befell Harut and Marut arose from the abundance of trust they put in their own selves. They trusted overmuch in their angelic nature. It was like the water buffalo's trust of the lion. To be sure, the water buffalo can do many things with its horns. But if the lion wishes, it can shred those horns like dry branches.

Man was created by God and has many weapons, and an intellect, to protect himself from danger. But if it is the lion of God's measuring-out who comes to face him, what can man do?

A person who trusts overly in his own will, even if every hair on his body, let us say, like a porcupine's, be a weapon protecting him from danger, divine destiny will still find a chink in his body to insert judgment. The art is to accept from the start that one has such chinks and not be swept up in vain pride.

A strong wind does not strip away fine blades of grass. They bow before the wind and straighten up, becoming in a sense more beautiful. But the same wind uproots fallen trees trusting in their own thick, strong and grand stature. It tears off their limbs and puts them into a state which can please only woodsmen who come at them with axes.

That strong wind takes pity on the delicate, weak appearance of the grass. Far from breaking and tearing the grass, it caresses the grass as it passes by.

So, my heart! Awake! Know that the divine destiny and measuring-out have mercy! Destiny and the measuring-out is harsh to those who claim selfhood, trusting in their own transient power and grandeur.

It treats with compassion those who show it understanding and know their own state confronted by its sublime power.

No ax is frightened by the multitude and thickness of trees and branches. It cuts them down and shreds them to pieces. But an ax never strikes a blade of grass with its sharp edge. The only things it gives an ax joy to cut down are great trees and thick branches.

Does a burning fire care if a pile of wood is small or great? Once it begins to burn, the greatness of the pile only increases the power of its flames.

A butcher doesn't care if sheep are many. His job is to butcher them. Butcher and sell them. The butcher wants there to be many sheep to butcher and sell. Think of the world we live in as destiny's slaughterhouse where many a strong ram is cut down. God the Truth's almighty blade destroys all the sheep pretending to be rams on the face of the earth.

What are shape and form before the power of meaning? It is spirit and meaning that keep the body alive and make it move.

Keep your mind on the meaning of how the dome of the sky stays hanging over our world like an inverted bowl. Try to understand the mystery of this.

What force turns the heavenly spheres that embrace our world in dome upon dome, along with all their stars and suns? Stop to consider this grandeur, this mind-stopping speed! The power that establishes and turns these heavenly domes many times greater and more numerous than we can imagine is intellect, universal intellect. Intellect is the meaning of these skies, and these skies are the appearances of that meaning.

O son, in reality every body is the shield of a meaning, it is the form in which a meaning is hidden. All the movements of the body and the activities of the spirit hidden within it.

The wind, whose being [varlık] is invisible, may blow lightly or violently. All of the wind's movements and the effects it has on things arise from its meaning. That meaning is God's power. The wind brings forth intellect in the state of motion. The creator of intellect is God, Creator of all beings.

The paddles of the mill appear to be captive to the water of the river. We suppose that the paddles turn because the water is flowing. In reality what turns the mill is the divine wisdom which gives the river water the property of fluidity. In short, it is the same meaning which makes the mill turn.

The taking in and releasing of breath in a person's chest is the action of the spirit which possesses the power to live or the love of living.

The spirit is a divine breath in a person. Breathing in and out comes of the spirit's being. So where does that breath you and taking in and out come from? Consider that.

But the spirit sometimes makes the breaths of the chest the letter *jeem*, sometimes *ha*, sometimes *dal*. So with the breaths it takes in and out, spirit sometimes makes peace and sometimes war.

But whether the words coming from spirit's mouth are for peace and love, or make the subject conflict and war, the mouth and the tongue are forced to execute spirit's commands. The cannot resist spirit.

Spirit keeps the mouth and tongue under its command. Sometimes it moves them to the left, sometimes the right. Sometimes it makes them sing of rosegardens, sometimes it speaks of the wounds thorns have made in the body.

On some days the words that come out of the mouth, with the life given them by spirit, smell of roses and cry out like reed flutes. On some days the spirit makes those words bitter like biting snakes and stinging scorpions.

You know how when God sent the wind, which flows around us like the human breath and gives us life and air, upon the people of Ad, He put it in the shape of a dragon.

God again made that wind perform a function that gave life to His believing bondsmen, that cooled them and spread mercy upon them.

The Shaykh of Religion, whom God sent into this realm as a sea of meaning, said: "The meaning is God" [*mânâ Allah'tır*][195] By this he meant to say: God, who is visible in the created world only through His manifestations and who is the meaning of all these phenomena, is a sea of divine spirits. Each level of the earth and sky is like a piece of straw swimming in that limitless expanse of meaning.

All this chaff on the surface of the water dances in the water and the waves. It rises up as if in the whirling dance when that sea is in a state of unrest and torment.

If that sea did not rise up and make waves, how would the chaff on its surface dance with such pleasure?

If you understand the pleasure and joy of chaff on the surface of the sea, know also that when the sea of meaning wants the chaff quiet, it throws it on the shore.

Although the chaff is made up of beings who think themselves alive, they too leave the sea of life and hit against the shores of death and silence.

When, on the contrary, God takes them from the shores of silence and death and put them into the wives of life and motion, chaff-like animate beings faced by the divine will remain within the setting of the measuring-out and destiny, as if moved by w violent wind that lays them down, lifts them up and sends ripples streaming through them.

Now let us return to the story of Harut and Marut.

****

THE REST OF THE STORY OF HARUT AND MARUT AND HOW AN EXEMPLARY PUNISHMENT WAS INFLICTED UPON THEM IN THIS WORLD IN THE PIT OF BABYLON

3385.   From Heaven's window was to them visible
The sin and wickedness of the world's people
They began to bite their hands in sore offense
But their eyes did not perceive their own defects
An ugly man perceives himself in a glass
And enraged he turns his face away from that
When a conceited man sees someone in sin
A fire derived from Hell appears within him
He calls it defending religion, that pride
He does not see his soul's arrogance inside
3390.   Defense of religion's sign is otherwise

---

195. It cannot be known with certainty whom Hazret Mevlana gave the titles "Shaykh of Religion" [*din şeyhi*] and "Sea of Divine Meanings." Some have said he referred to Muhyiddin Arabi or Sadrettin Konevi this way. It is possible that Shamseddin Tabrizi was the shaykh who said "The meaning is God," of that Mevlana's father Sultan al-Ulema Bahaeddin Veled said it. It is possible that it was said by Muhakkık-ı Tirmizi or Fariduddin Attar, and that all these possibilities may be confirmed by a study of the works and anecdotes attributed to these persons.

A world becomes flourishing green from that fire
"If you are polishers," God said unto them
"Do not look down on heedless, black-deeded men
Render thanks, O soldiers of God and servants
That you have been freed of lust and woman's cleft
If I impose that kind of meaning on you
The heavenly sky will no more accept you
The chastity that you have in your bodies
Is reflected from My care and chastity

3395.   Beware! See that it is from Me and not you
Lest the cursed Devil prevail upon you."
Thus the scribe of the Prophet's revelation
Thought wisdom and light of logic was in him
He thought he sang along with the birds of God
When an echo-like whistle was all he had
Though to mime the song of birds you may aspire
How will you know the birds' object of desire?
Though you may learn the nightingale's warbling notes
What do you know of what it has with the rose?

3400.   And if you try by analogy to guess
You're like the deaf who watch moving lips and guess

The two angels began to see clearly the evils of human temper and every sort of corruption and sin at every turn.

What they saw made them so angry that they bit their hands. But while their eyes saw the evils and sins of the people of the world, they could not see the faults asleep in their own selfhood.

When an ugly man who has never looked in a mirror sees himself in a mirror for the first time, he finds the image before him incredibly evil and ugly and cannot believe the ugly man in the mirror is his own image.

When a conceited person sees the sin and error of someone else he gets angry and flies into a rage as if the fire of Hell had kindled within him. He scolds the other person harshly and tosses all his sins in his face.

And he flatters himself that he does all this out of religious zeal.

He lectures those around him on morality and public spirit. But because his eyes do not see his own inner corruption, because he does not notice what he himself does, he does not realize his own infidelity.

The signs of true religiosity are different, however. The entire world is illuminated by the true light of religion. Its sun gives life to the universe and dresses it in greenery.

God the Truth called to Harut and Marut and said:

If you are pure angels created of light, do not blame sinning, suffering humans who were created of earth and sunk into the filth of materiality and lust, do not look upon them with contempt.

It befits you to give thanks for your own state. God created you free and pure of all passions, distant from matter and materiality. Know that this is the greatest occasion your being has to give thanks.

Consider, if I gave you lust and body as I did humans, in a short time you would become like them, and the heavens you left behind would no longer accept you. You would fall headlong into a sewer like the pit of the seven spheres of earth, the lowest of the low. Your heads would be heavier than your feet. You would be unable to ascend to the heavens, you would be captive in the hand of the soul, the soul whose owner is sublime as long as he rules it, but execrable when captive to it.

You beings created of light are in reality transparent mirrors. The purity, chastity and honor in you is in reality the reflections of these qualities of Mine in your mirrors. Beware of falling into the error of seeing these as values put forth by your own selfhood. Beware lest the satans of arrogance and selfhood delude you. Neither regard faults in others nor have regard for yourselves. Do not stray, like Hazret Muhammed's scribe of revelation who thought Koranic verses came down to him also, into the heedlessness of thinking you are peers of My Messenger.

That scribe of revelation was mightily deluded, thinking he was a nightingale in the garden of unity; he fell into the error of supposing that the nightingale song he heard was his own voice. The voice he heard, however, was nothing but an echo from one mountain to the other of My cry to My Messenger. To suppose an echo to be the original voice itself is to be far from every kind of gnosis.

A person may imitate the songs of birds. But with those songs birds are expressing love to one another, expressing feelings and intentions. Do you suppose that when you imitate the voices of birds, you express, let alone understand, those intentions?

Even if you learn the nightingale's song and succeed in singing like a nightingale, is it possible for you do achieve what its heart exchanges with the rose?

Don't suppose that you have arrived at the meaning of those sounds, that beating of wings and expansion like the blooming of a rose. That is like the state of the deaf who watch the lips of a person moving and suppose they have understood what he said.

If you like, now I will tell you the story of such a deaf person.

****

How a deaf Man went to visit his sick Neighbor

A man rich in heart said to a man who was deaf:
"You have a neighbor who is on his sickbed."
"Being hard of hearing, what," the deaf man mused,
"Will I understand of the words of that youth?
Especially as he's ill and his voice weak
But I must go to him, there's no remedy
When I see that his lips are making movements
I'll draw analogies to guess what he says
3405. When I ask, 'O suffering friend, are you well?'
He will say, 'I am fine,' or 'I'm pretty well.'
I will say, 'Thank God! What have you had to drink?
He will say, 'Sherbet,' or 'Broth of kidney beans.'
I'll say, 'I wish you health! Who is the doctor
Treating you?' He will say, 'Such-and such doctor.'

I'll say, 'He is known to bring blessings with him
Things will go well for you now that he has come
The luck of his foot is something we have tried
Wherever he goes, what's needed is supplied."

3410. Having got ready these likely responses
That good man came into the patient's presence
"How are you?" he asked, the sick man said, "I'm dead."
"Thank God!" he said, and the man was offended
Thinking, "Why thanks? He's in fact my enemy."
The deaf man had made a guess, and guessed wrongly
"Poison," the sick man said, when he asked his drink
"May it bring health," he said—the man's wrath increased
Then he asked, "Which is it of the doctors who
Is in attendance to find a cure for you?"

3415. "It is Azrael," he replied, "now begone!"
"His foot is blessed, be joyful," said the deaf man
Then he left, saying to himself happily:
"Thanks to God for that, now I will take my leave."
The invalid thought, "This man's my mortal foe
He's a mine of viciousness, we did not know."
He sought a hundred terms to vilify him
So to send a letter full of all of them
As when one has eaten rotten food, and it
Turns the heart over until one can vomit

3420. Restraint of anger is this: don't vomit it
So you may have sweet words in reward for it[196]
Since he had no patience, in torment he writhed
Crying, "Where is that cuckold dog catamite?
That I may pour down on him what he gave me
For the lion of my thought was then asleep
One visits the sick to give heart's peace to them
But this was rather an enemy's revenge
So he should see that his foe was thin and weak
And his own treacherous mind should be at peace."

3425. Many are they who do works of devotion
Hoping for acceptance and reward for them
But this is hidden sin in reality
It is foul, that which they think is purity
Like the deaf man who thought he did a kindness
When in fact the result was the opposite
He sat down pleased, thinking, "I've rendered service
I've given my neighbor the respect rightly his."
But in the sick man's heart he lit for himself

---

196. Those who spend, whether in prosperity or adversity; who restrain anger and pardon men. God loves those who do good. . . . For them the reward is forgiveness from their Lord, and gardens with rivers flowing beneath, and eternal dwelling . . . " (Koran 3:134, 136).

A blazing fire that would burn up his own self

3430.   *Beware of the fire that you have kindled, then*
For truly you have increased yourselves in sin
The Messenger instructed our Bedouin
"Pray, for you have not really prayed yet, my man."
So that for these dangers there'd be a recourse
Each ritual prayer contains the phrase, *"Guide us."*[197]
Meaning, "O God, do let my prayer be mixed
With the prayers of those who err and hypocrites."[198]
Reasoning by analogy, that deaf man
Rendered a friendship of ten years all in vain

3435.   Avoid especially analogies drawn
By worldly sense to boundless revelation
Though the letter is grasped by your ear of sense
Know that your ear for the Unseen world is deaf

A man aware of the states of others told a deaf man that his neighbor was ill. The deaf man thought to himself:

> Let's say I go to see how he is. But with these deaf ears of mine, how will I know what that young patient is saying?
>
> And a sick person's voice is very weak, inaudible. But the man is a neighbor and it is my duty to go and see him. I must ask how he is and win his heart.
>
> I will pay attention to the movements of his lips while he is talking and try to understand what he is saying.
>
> I will say to him: "O my suffering friend, how are you?" And without doubt he will answer me something like this: "Thank you, I am well." I will say: "Thanks be to God!" and ask him what kind of soup he has had. He will doubtless tell me the kind of soup. I will say, "May it bring you health." Then I will ask him what doctor he has looking after him. Whatever the doctor's name, I will praise him and give him courage and confidence. "Wherever that doctor sets foot, he brings good fortune with him,' I'll say, and comfort him: 'Since he has come to you, everything will turn out fine."

The man was as naïve as he was deaf, and rehearsed what he would say like that. He prepared the sentences he would say. He thought out what his neighbor would say and planned how he would comfort him, and having encouraged himself thus set off to visit his neighbor.

"How are you?" he asked. "O mercy, I am dying," the sick man said. The deaf man did not hear this answer and continued with the sentences he had planned. He did not forget to say, "Thanks be to God." The poor sick man did not expect to hear this and, very offended, answered his neighbor's question about what he had taken to eat by saying, "Poison!" He became even more angry when the deaf man responded by saying, "May it bring you health!" When the deaf man asked what doctor was treating him, he answered, "Azrail!" The deaf man said, "Oh, that's very good, his foot is very lucky,"

---

197. Koran 1:5.
198. Koran 1:7.

and thinking he had pleased his neighbor, bade him farewell and left.

The sick man began to feel profoundly sad. "It seems this man is my mortal enemy," he thought, "the man is a fountain of evil!" Then he thought of doing something to him, of insulting him, sending him a message full of cruel words.

Like someone who has eaten nauseating food and can only find relief by vomiting, the sick man wished to expel from his spirit the pain he felt and the words that had clouded his heart, sending them back to their owner.

But the right thing here would have been not to become angry, to overcome his anger. Evil words and angry actions, like vomiting, is unpleasant behavior. Some part of what comes out of your mouth will surely get on you and you will soil yourself.

But the deaf man's sick neighbor was not mature in that way. He could not overcome his rage. He muttered to himself, "Where is that dog, that son of a whore? While he was here my illness prevented me from throwing his words in his face. The lion of my thought, of my intellect, was asleep at that moment," and he continued:

One visits a sick person in order to give comfort, to say things to make him well, to win his heart, ask how he is. But that man exploited my illness and weakness, he actually took pleasure in seeing me prostrate like this. His evil heart rejoiced at my wretchedness and felt ease.

****

There are many people who perform their duties of worship in the expectation of getting something back from God. They expect to be rewarded for it, believing that if they worship God they will be accepted in His sight and He will pay they for that worship.

In reality, they are not afraid to commit all sorts of sins after they perform such worship. They suppose that the worship they do, the ritual prayers they perform, will exonerate them of past and future sins.

In reality such worship is no different from sin. It is a hidden kind of sin committed by people who mix trickery with worship.

Like that deaf neighbor who thought he had done good but was unaware that he had hurt his neighbor and broken his heart.

But he made the sick man completely ill. He lit a fire in his heart that would never go out, but he was burned up in the same fire. That is exactly like the state of people who worship as a show for others. They suppose that with this fake worship they will some-day benefit from the bounties of heaven, the beauties of heaven and the beautiful spirits in heaven. But they are mistaken and have distanced themselves from the God whom good spirits will reach one day, and they have burned themselves up in the most painful fire of separation in the universe.

"Beware of the fires you light! For you aggravate these fires with your sins and with your sins make them impossible to put out." The great majority of these fires are states and behavior of yours which you think excusable.

God's command, "Do not approach prayer when you are drunk," does not, as many think, refer only to the drunkenness that arises from drink.

You cannot perform the ritual prayer at moments when you are drunk with heedlessness or material or spiritual lusts as well. That is the greatest sin that can arise from not being able to tell in whose presence you are. One only goes into the presence of God pure and with a heart full of the love of God. It is those who can enter His presence completely without body, with a purity and cleanliness that consists simply of spirit, who are in a true state of worship.

That is why Hazret Muhammed said to a hypocrite who had just finished praying, "Pray, for what you did was not prayer!" For Hazret Muhammed also said, "Prayer performed without perfect peace of heart is not prayer."

In every ritual prayer the recitation of the Koranic "Fatiha" chapter, and especially the verse "Show us the straight way," is required so that a person who enters the presence of God may say it with all heartfelt sincerity, and if he finishes the chapter, saying, "The way of those on whom You have bestowed Your grace, not those with wrath upon them, and those who have gone astray," believing what he has recited, the doors of divine mercy and divine light are opened to him. In this regard prayer is the state of the spirit in union with the true Beloved. The total beauty of that great Beloved's manifestation is displayed to the human spirit in such prayer.

The deaf man was left deprived of his ten-year friendship with his neighbor because he acted out of his own conjecture and analogy merely. Now, O efendi, if the conjecture and analogy a person may fall into occurs facing God most high, so that it distances you from His friendship, know that although your sensory ear may hear sounds and words, your spiritual ear is deaf to sounds which come from the realm of the Unseen.

****

THE FIRST TO BRING ANALOGY TO BEAR UPON REVELATION WAS IBLIS

> The first who drew these paltry analogies
> With regard to the lights of God was Iblis
> He said, "Fire is without doubt better than earth
> I am made of fire, and Adam of dark earth
> Judge the branch by analogy to its source
> He is of darkness, and we, light shining forth."
3440. God said, "No, but there will be *'no relations'*[199]
> Honor's prayer niche will be pious abstentions[200]
> This is not bequeathed us by the fleeting world
> Through relations, no, it is spiritual
> No, these things are bequeathed to us by prophets
> They are inherited by devout spirits
> The son of Abu Jahl was, as clear as day
> A believer, while Noah's son went astray
> The child of earth is illumined like the moon
> Your face is black though you're child of fire, begone!"
3445. Learned men use such analogies to find
> Which way to pray on cloudy days or at night
> But when the Kaaba's before you in the sun
> Don't investigate and draw comparisons
> Don't pretend you can't see it, don't turn away

---

199. "When the trumpet is blown, there will be no further relations between them on that day, nor will they ask after one another" (Koran 23:101).
200. "Verily the most honored of you in the sight of God is the most righteous of you." (Koran 49:13).

Based on what you've reasoned—God knows best the way
When you hear the calling of the bird of God
Like a lesson you memorize but its sound
Then based on yourself you draw analogies
Supposing essential what is mere fancy

3450.   The Substitutes have a terminology
Of which words themselves do not know the meaning
You have learned the sounds of the birds' language,[201] but
Kindled a hundred analogies and lusts
Hearts are wounded by you, as was the sick man
The deaf man thrilled at the success of his plan
Revelation's scribe heard the voice of the bird
And supposed he was a partner to the bird
The bird struck him with its wing and blinded him
Plunging him to the nadir of death and pain

3455.   Do not you, too, fall from heavenly station
Because of some echo or vain opinion
Though you are Harut and Marut, and outrank
Those on the roof of *"We who are ranged in ranks"*[202]
On the bad deeds of the wicked have mercy
Do not indulge in selfishness and conceit
Lest God's rivalry spring from ambush, beware
That you don't fall headlong to the earth's nadir
"O God, Yours is the command," said both of them
Where can safety be without Your protection?"

3460.   So they said, but while they said it their hearts beat:
"How should evil come from such bondsmen as we?"
The two angels' desire kept on pricking them
Until the seed of conceit took root in them
They said, "You who are of the four elements
Ignorant of the purity of spirits
We will draw curtains of light across this sky
We will come to earth and raise canopies high
We will worship God and set up a just reign
And every night fly up to Heaven again

3465.   That we may become the wonder of the world
And establish security on the earth."
This analogy to earth from heaven's state
Conceals a difference; it is not accurate

Satan was the first creature to pursue the path of analogy by comparing his own nature with that of Hazret Adam in opposition to the speech of God, which as the light of God illuminates spirits and the universe.

The reason for this was that Satan refrained from bowing down to Hazret Adam,

---

201. Koran 27:16.
202. Koran 37:165.

although the one who commanded all the angels and Satan to bow down to Adam was God.

When God asked Iblis, "What is preventing you from bowing down to the human I created with my own hand?", Satan said: "Certainly fire is superior to earth. I was created of fire. Since Adam was created of earth, I compared fire with earth and reached the conclusion that I am superior to Adam and cannot bow down to black earth. For what is original is light. What is subsidiary, that is, secondary to the original, is darkness. Since earth is dark, how can it be that light should be subject to earth?"

God's response was: "Relations and ancestry are not considered; those who abstain from what God has forbidden and worship God with perfect sincerity of heart are the prayer-niche of virtue."

In fact if Satan and Adam were to really be compared, relative to the light of the fire from which Satan was created, the light forming Adam's essence [*cevher*] is as superior and luminous as the light of the sun relative to night. For the spirit breathed into Adam's body kneaded of earth is a part of the divine light.

Worshiping God, loving God, is not for this transient world, that it should be right to connect it with relations and ancestry. Love of God is a virtue which spirits acquired only at the gathering in pre-eternity at the moment when they were with Him. But this can only be the inheritance of God's messengers. Those who understand His messengers are those who comprehend their superiority of spirit and the spiritual values they have brought to mankind. While they live in the world they take the spiritual food which nourishes a sublime spirit and acquire the comprehension which enables them to turn toward and prepare for the post-eternal realm.

If one ascended to such spiritual heights by means of ancestry, the son of Messenger Noah would not have been among the deniers and lost his way. If it were simply a matter of relations, the son of that rebel of rebels Abu Jahl would not have been a believing Muslim in every sense of the word.

The illumination with divine light of man who was created of earth, making him sun of the heavens of spirituality, is God's great gift to mankind. As for you, O Satan! Although you were created of fire, you are devoid of divine light. You cannot illuminate, you can only burn, and for this you have been thrown out, for this you have been cursed.

Such analogies are appropriate for those searching for the direction of Mecca on dark cloudy nights in the desert. But when the sun is up and the Kaaba is before you shining in all its beauty, it is unreasonable to keep searching for its direction.

Do not diverge into the intellect's errors of analogy and intransigency, pretending not to see the Kaaba shining in the sun! Do not turn your face away. Do not forget that only God knows best in all things.

The divine bird sings with its entire beautiful voice. If you perceive the inspiration arising from these calls, and the verses which come like musical phrases from that inspiration, in their external form merely, memorizing them like lessons without reaching their internal meaning, you will have learned nothing.

Then you will draw analogies always based on such external views and become completely deluded.

The arrived of God have statements such that the words and phrases within them are unaware of the meaning there.

You hear only the sound of the language of the birds taught to Messenger Solomon. So you think you have learned much, and by analogy extract from these sounds many meanings in error.

In the sixteenth verse of the twenty-seventh chapter of the Gracious Koran, God said:

And Solomon was David's heir. He said: 'O people! We have been taught the language of the birds and been given of all things. This is indeed grace manifest.

Solomon was David's heir because he had the power to understand from the speech of birds the hymns David sang with his beautiful voice and played on the flute, and because he could address birds with the most beautiful of sounds.

That is also why Fariduddin Attar gave the title Language of the Birds to his book Treasury of Wisdom. That language is the one heard and spoken by those who understand what the divine bird who conveys inspiration is singing, and the divine meaning in each of its songs.

For that reason the statements of knowledge made by scholars in *medrese* seminaries teach you many things, but you will only learn divine truth from the language of the birds heard and interpreted by the friends of God. So do not commit an error, like the deaf man who offended his neighbor, and break their hearts!

If you remember, it was this bird song of which I speak that the scribe of revelation heard also and, content merely with the sound he heard, pretended to be the peer of Hazret Muhammed.

So, Harut and Marut! Do not you too suppose such reflection, that is, the light of divine self-disclosure, comes from you, and thus fall from your place in the heavens!

To be sure, you are Harut and Marut. You reside in the Realm of Sovereignty [*melekût aleminde*] and declare, as it says in the Gracious Koran (37:164-166): "Not one of us but has a place appointed. And we are surely ranged in ranks, and we are surely those who glorify God."

Stay in these ranks of yours and remain pure as you are. Do not leave your appointed place. Do not fall into arrogance and pride and try to see the faults of others, especially humans, and blame them.

On the contrary, take pity on mankind. Curse their evil deeds, their selfhood which drives them to evil and their arrogance which makes them think only of themselves.

Be vigilant. So that the divine rivalry will not stir from its realm of the Unseen and hang you upside-down in the depths of the earth.

Harut and Marut responded by saying: "Our great God! It is Yours to command. If You did not bestow Your bounty and protect us, how would be find other bounty and protection?"

They said this, but they felt within themselves a profound desire to descend to earth and rule mankind. Their hearts fluttered with this desire and they trusted in themselves, thinking: "How could we be evil, when we are God's angels?"

Both of the two angels were extremely uneasy at heart in their desire to rule the world. Gradually the seeds of arrogance, pride and trust in self grew in their selfhood and bore fruit.

Finally they descended to earth by God's command. And they called out to the people of earth, "You who were created of water, air, fire and earth, and who live unaware of the spiritual and bodily purity and cleanliness of the angels in the realm of sovereignty! We are creatures of the realm of light. We stretch across the face of the sky curtains woven of the light of worship of God. And descending to earth, we cast the shadow of divine justice over the world.

"We have come to earth for the sake of justice. Every night when our daily duties are done, we will ascend back to our stations in the skies. There we will live again in our own purity the realm of light.

"We will continue in this function until perfect morality and justice is established in the earth and with the justice we display we will be an example to all creation and be renowned."

But what happened on earth did not conform to what the angels said. For the Realm of Sovereignty is one thing, and earth is another. The people of earth had a body different form that of the angels, a material body. There was passion and lust, in sum, human nature. And the great majority of humans had not reached a degree where they could be free of that human nature.

Although if humans throw off the burden of soul in them and become pure spirit, their level can be superior to that of the angels, the number of them who are able to dedicate themselves to God and become free of worldly filth is always small. And most of those who do keep it secret from the crowd of men. Divine love cannot be known to all or told to every ignorant person. One must keep great secrets from those not intimate with them. Now, speaking the language of Hakim Sanai who hid behind the veil, I will tell you about the need for lovers to keep themselves hid from the ignorant.

****

EXPLAINING THAT ONE MUST KEEP ONE'S STATE AND INTOXICATION HIDDEN FROM THE IGNORANT

> Listen to what Hakim who stayed hidden said:
> "Wherever you drink wine, there lay down your head."
> When the drunken man strays out of the tavern
> He's the laughing-stock and plaything of children
> He falls into the mud wherever he goes
> Every fool laughs at him lurching down the road

3470.
> While he's like that, the children who badger him
> Know nothing of wine or the state he is in
> Except he who's drunk on God, all are children
> None's adult but he who has escaped passion
> God said: "This world is a sport and play, and you
> Are all children." And indeed God speaks the truth
> You are a child if you don't abandon games
> Without strong spirit how will you be ablaze?
> Know, O youth, that this lust here pursued by men
> Is like the sexual coupling of children

3475.
> What is children's intercourse? An idle play
> Not like that of a Rostam and Muslim brave
> They're like wars between children, these wars of men
> Without meaning, brainless and beneath contempt

All their battles are fought but with swords of wood
All the hostilities they launch are no use
They all ride on reed-stick horses, and they cry:
"This is our Buraq,"[203] or "This has Duldul's[204] stride!"
They carry their mounts, raised up in ignorance
Fancying they ride the mounts that carry them

3480. Wait till the day when those borne aloft by God
Will pass by the nine tiers galloping abroad
"The spirit and angels shall ascend to Him"[205]
Heaven shall tremble at spirit's ascension
Like children, you all are riding on your skirts
For a horse you take the corner of your skirts
"Conjecture does not prevail"[206] is what God said
When has conjecture's mount run to the heavens?
Preferring the stronger of two opinions
Do not doubt you see the sun when it's shining

3485. When that time comes see the horses that you ride
You have made of your own foot a horse to ride
Your conjecture, thought, sense and comprehension
Know they are like the reed-stick rode by children
The sciences of men of heart carry them
The sciences of men of flesh burden them
When knowledge shines on the heart it is a friend
When it shines on the body, it's a burden
God said: *"Like a donkey carrying huge tomes"*[207]
When it's not from Him, knowledge is burdensome

3490. The knowledge which is not directly from Him
Like the paint on a bride's face is not lasting
But when you carry this burden patiently
He will take it and give you felicity
Don't carry in vain this burden of knowledge
So that you may ride on the steed of knowledge
So that on that steed you may be the rider
And then the burden may fall from your shoulder
How will you escape desire without His cup
You who by His name alone have been filled up?

3495. What is engendered of attribute and name?
Fantasy, which indicates union with Him
Have you seen a sign without a signified?
If there is no road, there will be no ghoul's cry
Have you seen a name without a thing it names?

---

203. The Prophet's mount during the Miraj.
204. The Prophet's mule.
205. Koran 70:4.
206. Koran 10:36, 53:28.
207. Koran 62:5.

Have you plucked a rose which is spelled "ghoul" by name?
You've pronounced the name, seek what it signifies
Know the moon's not in the stream but up on high
If beyond letter and name you wish to go
Purify yourself of self, quick, at one stroke
3500.   Lose color like iron and be colorless
In abstention be a mirror without rust
Make yourself pure of the attributes of self
So you may see the pure essence of your self
And in your heart the sciences of prophets
Without teachers, without tutors, without books
The Prophet said: "Of my people there are some
One with me in essence and aspiration
Their spirits behold me by a light the same
As the one by which I too am seeing them."
3505.   They see him in the Water of Life they drink
Without hadiths, scholars or the two *Sahihs*[208]
Know the secret of *"At night I was a Kurd."*
And of *"In the morning I was an Arab."*
For a parable of hidden knowledge, read
The story about the Greeks and the Chinese

When Sanai, the treasury of wisdom, said, "Wherever you have drunk of the wine of divine love, there lay your head," he meant to tell you that whichever arrived person has made you feel divine love, whichever murshid, whichever sage of the tavern has served you this wine with his hand, abandon yourself to his instruction; and do not tell others who will not understand of the great love you felt. Especially if you are in ecstasy, if you are in a state of intoxication, do not let others see you. Beware of people who will ridicule you and make fun of you! For the thing ignorant people make an object of ridicule is the greatest of pleasures and felicities.

You know how when a drunkard too intoxicated to see what's in front of him leaves the tavern he cannot find his way home. He doesn't know what to do or where to go. He staggers along the street. In the end he becomes an object of ridicule for street children.

Neither, of course, can the state of those who have passed away from themselves in divine love be understood by childish people who do not know the taste of the wine of divine love.

For those who have not drunk that wine of love are like street children, however old they are. They have not achieved a maturity of spirit or perfection of salvation from the soul. Their spiritual character has not yet come of age.

For them the world is a place of fun and games. Involved in worldly delights and desires, they are both players of games who show off for those watching them, and they are spectators who laugh at those who like themselves are ridiculed by all the world.

That is why God has said in the Gracious Koran: "Know that the life of this

---

208. The two *Sahih*s (*Sahîhayn*) are compilations made by the scholars Bukhari and Muslim of hadith reports of things the Prophet said and did. The books are called *sahih* (sound) because of the extreme care and accuracy the two scholars practiced in making the compilations.

world is but play and amusement, pomp and mutual boasting and rivalry in multiplying riches and children. Here is a similitude: How rain and the growth it brings forth delight tillers; soon it withers, you will see it fade and then it dries up and crumbles away . . . And what is the life of this world but goods and chattels of deception?" (57:20). And God best tells the truth.

In this life it does not matter if you are a child or sixty years of age. You are cheered only by toys, like a child.

If your spirit does not burn in the fire of love, if it is not cooked, if it remains raw, you are doomed to become chaff like the greenery nourished by those rains; your spirit must be washed so that you become clean.

Children play at entertaining guests, cooking, they play house, based on what they have seen or heard. They play at being man and wife. They take this game of man and wife even as far as something approximating the reality. But the pleasure they feel is mere imitation. They do not feel the real pleasure of marriage. The false food they cook in false pots, like food cooked of weeds and chaff, has no taste and is false.

But is the pleasure felt by a Rostam, or any hero of war, when he returns to his wife like that? It is both pleasure, and brings them a child, it brings one or several people into the world. None of this happens when children play house.

Thus is the delight taken in the world by hearts which do not feel divine love empty. It is only those spirits overflowing with divine love who give beauty even to the body in which they are concealed. They taste while awake even the most superior and divine of pleasures others taste only in dreams.

Beyond this, struggle with the world is in vain. The wars like this fought by the people of the world are like the wars of neighborhood children or their war games. Mounted on horses made of tree branches, brandishing wooden swords, children who play the game of war sweat blood and tears in vain. They drive on the horses they mount, running along in the illusion that they are riding horses. they think the horses carry them when in fact they are carrying their horses.

Now, you who stay children all your lives! You whose eyes are enchanted by the show of this world! Wait until you see the horsemen God has mounted. It is they who will gallop their horses beyond the nine heavens.

On that Day spirits purified of worldly filth will like angels "ascend unto Him in a day the measure of which is fifty thousand years" (Koran 70:4). On that Day they will rise to God the Truth. But while even the angels cannot approach God beyond a certain degree, beyond the Sidre tree, the miraj of the spirits will pass beyond that degree as Hazret Muhammed did. This ascension of God's friends will make the heavens tremble.

But you who do not consider these things ride on a wooden horse, thinking you hold the reins like children holding up the edges of their skirts. Your little intellect is like the edge of a skirt, your conjectures and fantasies are like a wooden horse.

Great God has said in the Koran: "But most of them follow nothing but fancy; truly, fancy can be of no avail against truth" (10:36; 53:28). Since this is the case, how can it be possible to race to the heavens on the mount of fantasy and fly to the Throne?

You know what conjecture is! Usually you will have two or more conjectures, and you will think to yourself that one of them is the case while the other seems more logical, and you will not know which is true but be forced to choose one in doubt.

But just as all your doubts disperse when the sun rises, just as you see its brightness and the realities it illuminates, you will see the truth on the Day when you will have no more need of conjectures and analogies.

When the life of this world comes to an end and eyes are opened to the truth you will see in amazement and terror how you have supposed your own feet to be a pure Arab steed and you have been riding nothing but the horse of your own body. You will understand that your conjectures and vain thoughts, your false sense and understanding are all like that wooden horse, and it will be put before you with convincing clarity how childish you have been all your life.

Why do those people of the heart, those travelers in God, fly as if winged beyond the delights of this world? Because their bodies [*vücûtları*] are carried not by their feet but by the knowledge of truth. It is they who fly upon the pure Arab steed of knowledge. It is the people of body and soul who are crushed under the burdens they suppose to be knowledge.

Knowledge is beneficial if it is illuminated by the light of the heart, if it is illuminated in the path of becoming knowledge of God. Yunus Emre said:

My Yunus Emre's a poor man
His neck is brushed by death's own hand
He reads from the book of the heart
He never took up pen in hand

That he found it necessary to say this explains the point. But when knowledge makes people prisoners of the transient body, and becomes a burden for that body, it has no benefit even if such people are surrounded by God's friends. Scholars of that false knowledge find fault in every one of God's friends and get into such a state that under the burden of that knowledge they cannot see beyond the world.

That is why God the Truth has said in the Koran: The similitude of those who were charged with the Torah but subsequently failed in it is that of a donkey which carries huge tomes. Evil is the similitude of those who falsify the signs of God. And God guides not people who do wrong" (62:5).

The phrase "which carries tomes" in this gracious verse indicates whose who received the Torah but did not put into practice that divine book of the religion of Moses. God the Truth likened them to donkeys which carry books of knowledge and law. Donkeys who do not understand even one word of the books they carry on their backs, and are unaware even that they are carrying books.

For knowledge which does not come directly from God is like beauty which does not come directly from God. It is like the paint put on the faces of brides by their attendants. The paint which swiftly fades away shows the real face of the ugly girl.

Only if you know how to bear the burden of divine knowledge, understand the value of carrying it, will God teach you what you do not know. It is such a peace of heart that it will relieve you of the burden of all knowledge, transform all the evils of your life and the ugliness around you to goodness and beauty, and you will be one of the saved and attain to the truth.

Do not continue to carry the worldly knowledge burdening your shoulders for the sake of the desires of your soul. Abandon it, so that you may see the treasury of true knowledge in your heart. Every stone in that treasury will illuminate your darkness like jewels and emeralds. This knowledge of the heart, this gnosis, is not like any other, and the day you mount the well-paced horse of this gnosis you will see the burden of all that is other than God fall from your shoulders and see that you have so become spirit and light that you can fly.

You who are content with the mere form of the word "He"! What you call "He" is not just a word. "He" is God. "He" is one of God's beautiful names. He" is a crystal cup containing the wine of divine love. If you do not drink of that wine, if you do not see the color of that wine with which a divine hand fills that cup, if you do not taste its delight, then what you have in your hand is just an empty cup. For the entire secret and entire beauty of that cup is in the wine within it.

And if you chant "He! He!", if your "He"s remain on your lips and do not give you the delight of the divine treasury, in short, if you stay merely with the form of "He" and do not taste its meaning, do not imagine it, then your chanting and thought are in vain.

This divine word, this beautiful name, will bring your imagination to life. You will see God in its letters, its written form and its sound, and its image will bring you to union with the Beloved every moment that you speak it. The divine name and attribute will be proof of such union. Have you ever seen a signifier which does not signify a thing?

Have you ever heard a name which has no owner? Every name is definitely the name of a being or a meaning. What might the letters "he" and "e" ["ha" and "waw"][209] say to you? If a "He!" consisting merely of sounds were not a call to you from the owner, Beauty of beauties, of this name, if it did not create a meeting between you, what value would it have beyond a useless sound? You know the letters contained in the word "rose," and you have learned to place them side by side to spell the word. But can this knowledge, this spelling and pronouncing, give you the scent of the rose, can it show you the rose's color? What good is the name to you if you have never smelled a rose in your life? Let us say that you keep repeating the word "honey." Will you mouth taste sweet?

Given that you pronounce the divine name, that you call out His sublime name, go and find the owner of that name! Search out the ways to reach Him and be united with Him. Although this path goes through your heart, run and seek a murshid who will show you the path of your own heart! In reality, the bright moon is in the sky. In order to grasp the moon you see reflected in a flowing river, do not throw yourself into the river or into a well. You will reach the divine light not by descending to the depths of the earth—that is, by staying with names and attributes—but by taking wing to the heavens, that is, by abandoning being [varlık] to arrive at the essence.

Know that there are limitless mysteries hidden in every one of God's names. The Merciful, the Compassionate, the Powerful, the All-Subjugating—all these names are pronounced by virtue of the lining up of letters or sounds. If you pronounce only the letters when you write or say these names, then you are not attaining to these mysteries.

If what these letters and sounds brought us to know were only themselves, our mouths would burn when we say "fire," and thorns would pierce our tongues when we said "thorn." If iron is not polished, it rusts. It loses its own color and takes on the color of rust.

Be like polished iron. Free yourself of rust. Then you will behold yourself as a bright mirror in which all things are reflected.

The only way to such illumination is to free your spirit of the attributes of soul. So extinguish your soul, liberate yourself from slavery and subjection to it, so that Beauty

---

209. The Arabic letters *ha* and *waw* spell *hu*, meaning "he."—Trans.

who owns your spirit may appear in your mirror.

In such a heart's mirror there may appear and be known all the knowledge brought by the prophets, the science of truth, and gnosis, without books, without aids, even without a teacher. It is enough that you mirror be pure.

Hazret Muhammed has said: "There are some in my community whose substance and effort shares in mine." Such are the greats in whose heart's mirror shines the Muhammeden reality. Whatever their status and work in society, they are the great hearts characterized by the character of Hazret Muhammed and qualified by the divine attributes he bears.

That is why Hazret Muhammed has said: "They see me by the same light I see them." They are not separate from Hazret Muhammed for each one of them is qualified by our Messenger's qualities and illuminated by the same light. According to the principle that if two things separately become the same as a third thing, the two things also become the same as each other, the great intimacy, indeed the identity, between Hazret Muhammed, in whose essence shines the light of God, and the arrived of God, in whose essences that same light shines, is obvious.

That the Messenger said this himself was perhaps not out of humility, but out of his own reality.

You know that the name Sahîhayn was given to the works of Bukhari and Muslim, who expended limitless efforts to collect the hadith of Hazret Muhammed with perfect correctness. Because these works contain the hadiths of Hazret Muhammed, they offer him and his reality to those who read and understand.

But people of the heart may see and find all realities in an eternal source, that is, in their own hearts, without reading these books.

Bayazid Bistami expressed this by saying: "Your knowledge goes from dead thing to dead thing. We take our knowledge from the sole Living who does not die."

Know the mystery of Shaykh Abul Vafa Hazret's saying, "In the evening I was a Kurd," and understand the meaning of his saying, "In the morning I was an Arab."

Abul Vafa, who was an ancestor of Chelebi Husameddin, was an illiterate Kurd and said this to a gathering of people who wanted him to give a sermon. He had promised to give a sermon, and the night before saw Hazret Muhammed in a dream. In the dream Hazret Muhammed gave him the good news that he had been taught divine knowledge [*ledün ilmi*]. The next day the Kurdish shaykh kept his word, and began his sermon with this sentence.

So, *divine knowledge* can be taught to one whose heart is pure, even if he be illiterate.

If you wish to know what this secret knowledge is, let me tell you the story of the Romans and the Chinese:

****

THE STORY OF THE CONTENTION BETWEEN THE GREEKS AND THE CHINESE OVER THE ART OF PAINTING AND PICTURING

> "We are the better artists," the Chinese said
> "The power and glory are ours," the Greeks said
> Said the Sultan, "I will put you to the test
> To determine which of you may be the best

3510. The Chinese and the Greeks made themselves prepared
The Greeks were in knowledge the better aware
The Chinese said, "Set aside for us a room
Special to us, and another one for you."
There were two rooms whose doors faced one another
The Chinese took one and the Greeks the other
The Chinese asked for a hundred colors then
The Shah opened up the treasury for them
Every morning colors from the treasury
Were portioned out to the Chinese in bounty

3515. "Only the removal of rust," the Greeks said
"Is worthy of the work, not color or shade
They returned to polishing and closed the door
They became clear as the firmament and pure
There's a way from two hundred colors to none
Color is like clouds, and clarity a moon
What you see in clouds as illumination
Know it comes from the stars and the moon and sun
When the labors of the Chinese were all done
They were happy enough to beat upon drums

3520. The Shah saw the pictures when he came inside
The encounter with them robbed him of his mind
Afterwards he went across to see the Greeks
A curtain was raised up by one of the Greeks
The reflection of the Chinese works now fell
Upon the walls the Greeks had purified well
All he'd seen in the first room seemed better here
The eye was robbed right from the eye-socket here
The Greeks are those Sufis without need, O son
Of books, art, and study by repetition

3525. But they have polished their breasts and made them pure
Of lust and greed and stinginess and rancor
That mirror-clarity is, without a doubt
The heart which receives images beyond count
From it Moses possessed within his bosom[210]
The Unseen's infinite form without a form
Although all Heaven cannot contain that form
Nor the Footstool, nor the world's fish nor the Throne
Because all of them have number and limit
Know the mirror of the heart has no limit

3530. Here intellect is silent, or mistaken
For the heart is with Him or the heart is Him
No reflected image shines on forever
Except in the heart, with and without number
Forever, each new image that falls therein

---

210. Koran 7:108, 20:22, 26:33, 27:12, 28:32.

Is displayed without any imperfection
Heart-polishers have escaped color and scent
They behold beauty without fail each instant
They've set aside knowledge's formality
They've raised the flag of *the eye of certainty*[211]
3535. Thought is gone, and they've found luminosity
They've found the core and source of intimacy
Death, which so terrifies all these other men
Is but an object of derision for them
Over their hearts there is none that can prevail
Hurt falls not on the pearl but the oyster shell
Though they've let go grammar and jurisprudence
They've taken up poverty and effacement
Since the eight paradises have been shining
The tablets of their hearts have been receiving
3540. They are higher than Throne, Footstool and the void
Firm upon *the seat of the truthful* of God[212]

Painters from Anatolia and China entered into a competition with each other. Each side claimed that their art of painting and ornamentation was superior to the other's. The Padishah told them to stop squabbling and produce works of art.

They agreed to do so. First the Chinese asked for a studio of their own. They said they did not want the Anatolian painters to see their work, and asked for them to be kept away.

The Chinese painters were afraid the picture they were making would be copied. The Padishah assigned each group of painters separate rooms. The two rooms were separated by a thick curtain.

The Chinese requested various paints from the Padishah. He opened the treasury to them and they took what they wanted.

The Anatolian painters did not ask for much. They took what was necessary in order to clean the rust off the walls and polish them. The Roman painters preferred colorlessness to color; they understood the value of colorlessness.

The work went on for a long time. Both groups worked silently in their rooms. The Chinese were gratified that the painters of Rome did not see what they were doing, and they applied color after color of paint; they painted designs which dazzled the eye with the number and beauty of their colors.

The painters of Rome held different ideas. They believed that the end of so many colors was colorlessness, and that art was not in the plethora of colors but the manifestation of colorlessness, in the same way as the clouds in the sky and the waters in lakes have no color of their own.

What gives them color upon color is the sun in the heavens.

When the work was done the Chinese were overjoyed. The beat upon drums and danced. With their joyful noise they announced that their work was finished and the vic-

---

211. Koran 102:7.

212. "The righteous will be in the midst of gardens and rivers; upon the seat of the truthful, in the presence of an all-powerful King" (Koran 54:54-55).

tory was theirs.

The Padishah saw their painting and was awed. He was struck in spirit and heart by the sovereignty of color and beauty of form.

When it was the turn of the painters of Rome, they simply asked that the curtain between their room and that of the Chinese be raised. The walls of the room were so highly polished that they were like brilliant mirrors, and when the curtain was raised and the works of the Chinese were reflected there they were much more beautiful in reflection than in the original. Like reflections on water, every beautiful thing in the room was combined with the beauty of polish and mirroring, so that it was more charming than the original.

O son! Here the works of the painters of Rome are the Sufis who have no interest in lessons to be repeated, in books, or in showing off their art. That room is the heart of the Sufi which is pure of all dust and rust like the most brilliant of mirrors. The truest of beauties is reflected in such mirrors. It is in such mirrors, that is, in the hearts of such advanced Sufis, that divine self-disclosure occurs.

If you ask what it is they clean away to bring their hearts into such a state, it is rage, arrogance, selfhood and hypocrisy, lust and passion.

God commanded Messenger Moses: "O Moses! Thrust your hand into your vest! Let it come out pure white, as one of the nine miracles sent for Pharaoh and his people!" Moses obeyed the command, and his hand appeared "white and shining like the sun of the world." For the mirror of Moses's heart reflected the endlessly vast and formless form of the Unseen. This means that when Moses placed upon his breast the hand he had withdrawn from the vision of everything other than God, it appeared as a pure white hand shining with the lights of self-disclosure.

In reality the limitless form reflected in the heart of Moses does not fit into the heavens or the earth, not in the oceans or the fish hidden therein. For these are all countable and manifestations of limitation. But it is impossible for what has no limit to fit into something limited. It is only the heart's mirror divested of all worldly filth which can be a mirror, a reflector, of that self-disclosure of essence and attributes without limit. For the mirror of the heart, like the beauty reflected in it, has no limit.

Here the partial intellect must fall silent or be silent in awe. The reason for this is the limitlessness of the heart's mirror. For is it the heart that is with God, or God who is with the heart? The heart can resolve this, but not the intellect.

Only the heart is eternal with Him. The hearts of God's arrived are mirrors of both unity and plurality. The only mirror to reflect all those images is the mirror of the heart. That is why, from pre-eternity to post-eternity, every image reflected in the heart appears there divested of all veils.

Those who polish their hearts with the love of God see a different kind of beauty shining there each instant; each instant they are witness to another of God's infinite beauties. For them the colors and scent whose beauty we embrace do not exist; they have risen beyond color and scent.

For they are the ones who know God. They have abandoned the images in the rind of worldly sciences and raised the flag of the eye of certainty, and as a result they have reached the level of the reality of certainty and see the divine beauty.

That is why the Gracious Koran says: "You will see it with the eye of certainty."

For there are degrees to the levels of certainty: the knowledge of certainty is to reach

God by way of knowledge, to learn of God through knowledge.

The eye of certainty is the transformation of this knowledge into vision. At this level the heart succeeds in seeing God. But there is a superior degree, its result, which is the reality of certainty: to be annihilated in God, or to become God the Truth with God the Truth. This is the reality Hacı Bayram Veli described as knowing, finding, and becoming:

> Bayram knew his own essence
> There he found knowledge's sense
> The finder became his self
> You too know yourself, yourself

Those who attain the degree of the eye of certainty are freed of thought and reach the light. It is they reach the sea of familiarity and join the immortals [*ölmezler*]. For them death, which all fear, is a sport. To be freed of the body and reunited with the beloved is a festive holiday for them. That is why the arrived of God laugh at those who fear death and at the fear of death. It is possible to tear their bodies to pieces, to hang them by the neck like Mansur, to skin them alive like Nesimi. But these torments do not seem hard to them. They don't even feel what is done to them. They are like Abraham, who was thrown into the fire.

The torment and loss we think we have inflicted upon them is at most inflicted upon their shell. No calamity can be inflicted upon their hearts, which are the mirror of God and remain sound like a pearl within that shell. And perhaps such calamities are another kind of joy for such hearts.

They are those who have abandoned the strictures of grammar [*nahiv*] for effacement [*mahiv*], that is, annihilation in God; they have chosen poverty [*fakr*] over jurisprudence [*fikh*]. And the annihilation and poverty they have chosen is in reality being [*varlık*] itself. In their hearts shine the images of the Eight Paradises, not the images made by the Chinese painters. They choose fidelity and the right path, and the level they reach is the level of God. They rise to a station beyond the Throne, the Carpet [*ferş*], and the Footstool [*kürs*].

****

How the Prophet, peace be upon him, asked Zayd, "How are you today and in what state did you rise?" and Zayd answered him, "*This morning I awoke as a believer, O Messenger of God.*"

> Said the Messenger to Zayd one fine morning:
> "Pure companion, how did you wake this morning?"
> Zayd replied to him, "As God's faithful bondsman."
> He asked, "Where's the sign that's bloomed in faith's garden?"
> Zayd said, "I have been thirsting all through the day
> At night the pains of love have kept me awake
> So that I have passed through the days and nights here
> As through a shield passes the point of a spear
3545. For over there all religions are the same
> A hundred thousand years and one hour the same
> Pre- and post-eternity are unified

The way there cannot be searched out by the mind."
The Messenger said, "Show me the traveler's gift
Sign of the way of that fair land, where is it?"
Zayd said, "When the people see the firmament
I see the Throne and the ones who dwell in it
I see eight paradises and seven hells
Clearly as idolaters see their idols

3550.   I distinguish among people, one by one
Like barley from wheat upon the milling stone
Who is for Paradise, who estranged from it
Is as clear to me as a snake from a fish."
The birthday of all peoples, Roman or Black
Is *the Day when faces will be white or black*[213]
However flawed the spirit was before this
It was in the womb and from the people hid
The wretched are wretched in the mother's womb
All of them will by the marks of God be known

3560.   Bodies carry the spirit-child like mothers
Death is the pangs and the throes that come with birth
All who have passed wait in anticipation
To see in what state that spirit will be born
"It's one of us," the Ethiopians say
"No, it's not, it's beautiful," the Romans say
When it's born in the realm of spirit's expanse
There's no more quarrel over the white and black
If it's black, then the Blacks carry it away
And if white, then the Romans take it away

3560.   Until born, it is unknown to everyone
Very few are they who can know the unborn
It is *by the light of God* that such are blessed
For they have a way to see inside the flesh
Semen is white and sweet in its origin
Spirit shines Roman or Ethiopian
It honors *the most beautiful in stature*
And carries to the lowest depths the others[214]
There is no end to this topic, hurry on
Lest we be left behind by the caravan

3565.   *The Day when faces will be white or black*, who
Will still feel reverence for Turk or Hindu?
In the womb, who's Turk and who Hindu is hid
When they're born, one sees who's strong and who wretched

While Zayd ibn Haris was still a child he left home one day with his mother to visit a

---

213. Koran 3:106-107.

214. "We created man in the most beautiful stature, then we abased him as the lowest of the low" (Koran 95:4-5).

relative. On the road an enemy tribe grabbed Zayd from his mother and sold him at the market of Ukaz.

He was bought for Hazret Hatija by her nephew, and after she married our Messenger she put Zayd at his service.

Much later Zayd's father learned that he was with the Messenger of God and went to Mecca to ask for him. Hazret Muhammed said: "It is up to Zayd whether he stays or goes. Ask him to decide." But Zayd said: "O Messenger of God, you are my father and my uncle. There is no one on earth I could prefer over you," and chose slavery with the Messenger over freedom without him.

One morning Hazret Muhammed asked Zayd: "O pure-hearted friend, how did you pass the night, and how did you awake in the morning?"

Zayd answered: "As a believing bondsman." The Messenger said: "If flowers have bloomed in the garden of faith, where is the sign of this, show me a sign." Zayd told him:

> For so many days I wandered in the desert thirsty. I burned in fire during the nights and could not sleep. I passed the days and nights as a spear passes through a shield. With that speed I reached the degree of oneness, that mystery of the reality of certainty, where all religions, all schools are one. Every visible thing was in a state of the various self-disclosures of that One who is single. Time did not exist there. A century was the same as a day, even the same as an hour. Neither morning nor evening existed there; pre-eternity was joined with post-eternity, the beginning and end of the universe had become the same. Partial intellect is insufficient and lost on the way there, it could not reach that realm of not-place and not-time.

Then Hazret Muhammed asked: "O Zayd, once you rose to the sublime realm, what happened there? Tell me, did you bring a gift from that realm appropriate to the intellect and understanding of this world?

Zayd said:

> I was the Throne and those at the Throne as clearly as those on earth see the heavens. Just as an idolater see the idol before him, the Eight Paradises and the even Hells were clear to me. Just as I separate wheat from barely in a mill, I can separate the people of the world in the mill of the heavens. I know which of them is good and which evil. They appear to me as those who will go to Heaven and those who will go to Hell. I can distinguish between them as I distinguish between a snake and a fish.
>
> God the Truth has said in the Gracious Koran (3:107): 'Those whose faces will be white, they are in God's mercy. Therein they dwell forever.' The people of certainty know whose faces will be white on Resurrection Day, who will be beautiful, joyful and happy; and whose faces will be black and their spirits remain in darkness. O Messenger of God, is the light of faith or the darkness of denial in people's faces? I have become one of those who see them before Resurrection Day. But the whiteness or blackness of faces will be known only on Resurrection Day.

Although the wretched are wretched in their mothers' wombs, the signs of this invisible wretchedness which become visible only after the spirit enters the body are known to those who know. For the body is in a sense the mother's womb within which each spirit matures. Whether the body is white or black, every state that will come forth on the day of death occurs in the spirits while they are in the womb called the body. In other words, when a spirit penetrates a body it gives to the body the form of its own preparedness; it becomes the spirit of that body. In another sense the spirit bows to the judgment of destiny and the measuring out. It travels from the gathering in pre-eternity to this world as a flawed spirit. But because its shame is hidden under the veil of the body, it is not visible to those whose eyes do not see it.

And all during a lifetime the body is pregnant with the child called spirit. The body carries it in its womb for the space of a lifetime, nourishing it, and death is the pain of the spirit's birth into another realm.

Azrail was created from a unique light called the power of conjecture. It seizes each spirit according to the nature of that spirit. It appears to some spirits in its pure being, and at that moment the spirit binds itself with profound love to the One who wishes to take it; the spirit leaves the body and lovingly throws itself into the arms of the Beloved.

The power Azrail has to subjugate all spirits comes from the power of the light of conjecture in him:

When a spirit enters into a body, it does not leave its station in the realm of spirits. It is joined to the body like a ray of light which is not separated from its source. In fact the connection the spirit makes with bodily form is for the purpose of gaining the character that will please God, in order to reach the meaning of creation. Either it gains this character and ascends with it, or it acquires an animal character and remains in the prison of nature, never reaching the sublime realms.

Azrail approaches such spirits with a terrifying face, not with his own beautiful face. He makes them tremble in terror and seizes them that way.

When a spirit leaves the body in order to be reborn in the realm of spirits there is a struggle between the white faces, that is, the Romans, and the black faces, the Ethiopians. The Ethiopians represent the wretched spirits, who are bad-natured, vicious and envious, in short black. They become excited, thinking that spirit is one of them. The Roman spirits, high-natured, enlightened and white, want the newly arrived spirit to be one of the good ones as they are. And when a spirit which has separated from a body is born at last into the afterworld, the conflict between the black and white spirits is over. Whether the spirit is white or black becomes obvious to the entire spirit realm.

If the spirit is one of those bound to darkness, lust and animal nature, the blacks take it; it is surrounded by angels of torment who take it to the realm of darkness to which it belongs.

If it belongs to light and is one of the good and beautiful spirits, angels of God's mercy and good news take it and bring it to the station of which it is worthy.

It is not easy to raise the veil of the body which covers the beauty or ugliness of a spirit and know, before it is born from the womb of the body into the spirit realm, which group it belongs to. This is only known to the friends of God who recognize the states of its body, its actions, even its colors and smells, before it is born.

Because the friends of God the Truth have attained the secret of gazing with the light of God, they find the way to see beyond the veil to what is inside skin and flesh. The human being, the drop of water presented to the mother's womb, is in fact sweet and white. Regardless of whether it comes from a person whose skin is black or white, this drop of seminal fluid is at first the same color at first.

But when that same drop mixes with the reflection of the white spirits, the light of the white spirits gives it the color of the most beautiful in stature. It is enlightened with all the beauty and superiority creation manifests in the human. If the same drop of seminal fluid is struck by the darkness of the blacks, that is, the animal-like spirits, it becomes the lowest of creation. Thus it becomes enslaved to the darkness of soul and passion. While every newborn child must in fact be pure of all infidelity and denial, it takes the black or white path with the spirits which bring it into the world.

But this discourse has no end. We must hurry on if we are not to fall behind the caravan and lose sight of it. We must come to the point and learn the mysteries Zayd spoke of before too long.

For the day when faces are white or black will come. Are you Ethiopian, Indian or Turk? Are you beautiful like a Turk? It will all emerge before all the groups of spirits on that Day.

It is not clear in the hidden womb of this world who is an Indian and who is a Turk. Because this is not a matter of the outward color of the body, not a matter of external blackness or whiteness. The issue is whether your spirit is dark like an Indian or white like a Turk. This is not clear in the mother's womb. But whether the spirit is strong or weak, mighty or base, emerges once it is born.

****

HOW ZAYD ANSWERED THE PROPHET, PEACE BE UPON HIM, SAYING, "THE STATES OF THE PEOPLE ARE NOT HIDDEN FROM ME."

> "I see them all plain as Resurrection Day
> Men and women, as they shall be on that Day
> Shall I tell it all, or shall I stop my breath?"
> Mustafa bit his lip, as to say, "Enough!"
> "O God's Messenger, shall I tell the secret
> Make that Day in this world today manifest?

3570.
> Allow me, that I may raise up the curtain
> That my inner jewel may shine forth like a sun
> That the sun be eclipsed by me, when I show
> The difference between date-palm and willow
> Let me display Resurrection's mystery
> The adulterated coin and the sterling
> The people of the left who have their hands cut off
> The color of blasphemy, color of fraud
> The seven abysses of hypocrisy
> By moonlight which has no eclipse or waning

3575.
> Let me show forth the hair-cloth of the wretched
> Let me make heard the kettle-drums of prophets
> Before the eyes of the kafirs let me bring
> Heaven and Hell and the barzakh in between
> Let me show the pool of Kawsar splashing there
> Wetting bright faces and ringing in their ears
> Let me name, one by one, and say who they are
> Those who are running in thirst around Kawsar
> Their shoulders are rubbing against my shoulders

I can hear their distraught shouting in my ears
3580.   Out of free choice, the people of Paradise
Are hugging one another before my eyes
In each other's honor they make pilgrimage
Plundering kisses from one another's lips
This ear of mine is deaf from cries of 'Alas!'
Shouted by the disappointed, 'Oh, Alas!'
These are only signs, I would go much deeper
But I fear I may offend the Messenger."
He talked on like this in drunken abandon
The Messenger pulled him by the collar to him
3585.   "Beware," he said, "draw the reins, your horse is hot
God is not ashamed[215] has struck and shame is gone
Your mirror has jumped from inside its cover
Where has falsehood been spoke by scale or mirror?
Where have mirror or scale feared to speak ever
For the sake of anyone's hurt or honor?
Noble touchstones are mirror and weighing scale
If for two hundred years you will serve them well
Saying, 'Cover up the truth and show for me
More than there is, do not show deficiency.'
3590.   They will say to you, 'Don't be ridiculous
Scale and mirror, then deceit and artifice?
Since God raised us up so by means of us two
One might be able to come to know the truth
What will we be worth if that does not occur
How will we adorn the faces of the fair?'
But if God's self-disclosure has made your breast
A Sinai, then put the mirror in your vest."
"Shall sun of truth and eternity," Zayd said
"Then fit into a felt case inside a vest?
3595.   It will burst both the armpit and the pretense
Nor madness nor mind remains in its presence."
He said, "If you lay a finger on the eye
You will see the world now of the sun deprived
The tip of one finger is veil for the moon
And this indicates God's veiling of things too
He may veil the whole world with a finger tip
By means of a splinter the sun is eclipsed."
Close your mouth and gaze on the depths of the sea
It's to man that God has subjected the sea[216]
3600.   As are Salsabil and Zanjabil fountains
Controlled by Paradise's exalted ones
We control the four rivers of Paradise

---

215. Koran 33:53.
216. "It is He who has subjected the sea . . . " (Koran 16:14; 45:12; see also 17:70).

By the command of God, not by our own might
We let them flow wheresoever we desire
As magic works by a magician's desire
Just as these two eye-fountains are kept flowing
Ruled by the heart and by the spirit's decree
If the heart wants, they flow toward poison and snake
And if it wishes, then faith is given weight

3605.   If it wishes, they flow toward sensory things
If it wills, they flow toward represented things
If it wills, they flow on toward universals
And if it wills, they stay with particulars
In this way the five senses, like threading spools
Move according to the heart's will and are ruled
Whatever direction the heart points them in
All five senses go, trailing their skirts with them
That hand and foot are under the heart's command
Is evident as the staff in Moses' hand

3610.   If the heart wills, it makes the feet start to dance
Or makes them flee lack and go toward abundance
If the heart wishes, it makes the hand confer
In order to write a book with the fingers
The hand is in the grip of a hidden hand
Which keeps the body under its own command
If it wills, it smites the foe like a viper
If it wills, befriends God's friend as a helper
If it wishes, it's a ladle serving food
If it wills, a battle-axe of ten maunds hewed

3615.   What is the heart now telling the body's limbs?
It's a wondrous hidden cause, this connection
Has the heart obtained the seal of Solomon?
It is able to rein the five senses in
Five external senses are easy for it
Five internal senses are controlled by it
There are ten senses and seven limbs, and more
Count for yourself what has not been mentioned here
O heart, since you are in empire Solomon
Cast your seal's spell upon fairy and demon[217]

3620.   If you are free of deceit in this domain
Three demons will not take the seal from your hand
After that, your name will conquer all the world
As your rule your body, you'll rule both the worlds
And if the demon takes the seal from your hand
Your fortune will die and your kingdom will pass
Then "O sorrow!" will be your doom, O bondsmen[218]

---

217. Koran 38:35-38.
218. "Alas for those bondsmen . . . " Koran 36:30.

Till the Day when you are gathered up again
If you deny your deceit, how will you save
Your spirit from the mirror and from the scales?

Zayd said to Hazret Muhammed: "O Messenger of God! I see the secrets within people as clearly as they will be on Resurrection Day; just as I see who is a woman and who is a man, I see who is for light and who is for fire, I see it absolutely clearly.

"Now, command me and I will tell this secret. If you do not find it right, set a lock upon my lips and I will be silent."

Hazret Muhammed bit his lip, signaling him to be silent, and said: "O Zayd! A sign is sufficient for the gnostic."

But Zayd had not yet awoken from the sate of ecstasy he was in. He did not notice our Master's signal and continued speaking excitedly:

O Messenger of God, let me put before you today the Day of Resurrection people think of as happening in the future. Let me reveal all the mysteries of Resurrection. Command and let me rend the veils of these secrets. Let the jewel of divine wisdom within me shine like the sun in the heavens. Let me so shine that the brightness of my light will make the light of the sun invisible, just as the stars become invisible when the sun rises. O Muhammed, let me show which trees will bear fruit and which will not. Let me show forth which people are laden with faith like trees laden with fruit, and which have no awareness of the fruit of divine wisdom, like trees which bear no fruit.

Command! Let me now declare which gold is pure and which false, as it will be known to all on the Day of Resurrection. Let me make plain which people knew how to remain pure like pure gold amidst worldly filth and worldly passions, and which were rusted with the dark or red rust of infidelity in the same crucible of the world.

You know those who in the fifty-sixth chapter of the Gracious Koran are called "the companions of the left hand." In this chapter you brought, God the Truth has said: 'Alas for those whose registers are given from the left!'[219]

And similarly in verses 25-29 of chapter sixty-nine.[220]

Command, O Muhammed, let me expose the color of infidelity and deceit. Let me show, in the light of your prophethood which cannot be eclipsed let alone fade away, the seven abysses of hypocrisy.

What forms do the spirits of the wretched take on in the afterworld? Let me show forth what ugly sacks they wear. And what sounds do the durms of the prophets make? What news do the words the prophets bring from God to man give? Let me interpret them.

Let me show, with the complete clarity of the sun shining in darkness, Heaven,

219. "The companions of the left—alas for those companions of the left! n the midst of a fierce blast of fire and in boiling water, and in the shades of black smoke; nothing to refresh nor to please. For previously they were wont to be indulged in wealth and persisted obstinately in supreme wickedness. They would say: 'What? When we dies and become dust and bones, shall we truly be raised up again? And our forefathers of old?'" (Koran 56:41-48).

220. "But he who is given his register on the left will say: 'Ah! Would that my register had not been given to me! And I had never known of my account! Ah! Had this made an end of me! My wealth has been no profit to me!' (Koran 69:25-29).

Hell and the barzakh to those who deny them.

Let me make those kafirs hear the sounds of the rollicking flow of Kawsar. Let me show how the people of Paradise are cooled by that holy water, and reveal the scene of the torments of Hell where the people of Hell writhe burning, with their parched lips and cries like fire, around Kawsar without drinking it.

At this moment I feel their shoulders rubbing against mine. The cries of their suffering ring in my ears. They are horrifying enough to make me deaf. At the same time I see the spirits of Paradise hugging one another. They grasp one another's hands. They visit one another at their stations in Paradise, embracing and kissing happily. But all I have said and tried to show is only an indication of the scene which is clear to me. I would speak of it more plainly, go more deeply, but Hazret Muhammed will not permit me. I fear offending the Messenger.

Zayd was swooning in ecstasy and had lost his mind, getting into such a state that he would reveal all secrets. At that moment Hazret Muhammed felt the need to wake up his slave. He took hold of his collar, pulled on it and said:

Zayd! Get hold of yourself! Horseman of the realm of sovereignty! Stop! Rein in your tongue, for you are in such a state that you are saying things which must not be said. It is for God to reveal truths. Surely God is not ashamed to strike parables concerning a fly, or larger creatures, in order to reveal truth. This is announced in the second chapter of the Gracious Koran. And God has said in verse seventy-three of the twenty-second chapter: 'O mankind! Here is a parable set forth, listen to it! Those other than God on whom you call cannot create a fly, even if they all gathered together for the purpose!' Remember that! Do not forget that for the prophets and friends, the revelation of secrets is a result of not having digested them. Do not forget that one of God's beautiful names is the Curtainer, and do not, because you do not properly digest secrets, sacrifice the felicity of being able to become a person qualified with that attribute!

The mirror of your spirit has leapt out of the body's case. In such a spirit mirror, everyone sees his own form. For neither mirror nor scales can lie. Have you ever seen a mirror which shows ugliness as beauty, or scales which show the heavy as light, because the ugliness or the crime weighing heavy in the scales will shame others?

Mirror and scales are measures which tell the truth. Neither mirror nor scales will stray from its path, even if you serve them for two hundred years and beg, 'O mirror, O scales, for my sake, for the sake of the two hundred years I have served you, hide the truth! Show me as beautiful, do not show me as ugly. Show my good works as plentiful, not wanting.'

They both will tell you, in the language of their states:

"How ridiculous you are! You call us mirror and scales, yet you expect qualities from us which do not pertain to mirror and scales. All we do is show things as they are and weigh them correctly, we can not do otherwise. For God created us as instRomants for the revelation of certain truths. He gave us the qualities of showing and weighing rightly. Not only do we display the flaws of the ugly and the crimes of the deceitful, we are instRomants by which the beautiful are rewarded for beauty and the good are rewarded for justice. For we display them to themselves with complete rectitude, just as we do the ugly and sinning."

But, O Zayd! If the light that struck Mount Sinai has struck your breast, if self-disclosure has occurred within you, hide the mirror in your vest. Do not reveal the mysteries of the divine realm to the extent you have seen them. Conceal them in words as I do, so that you may both declare the truth and the spirit able to understand that profound meaning may do so. One of the greatest aspects of the wisdom of the divine Being and the divine mysteries is that they are not apparent to every eye and every heart. It is not for you or I to act contrary to this. Continue to tell mysteries by way of words and make them felt by way of intuition so that the people of perfection may see the truth. Let those who have not reached maturity find in this concealment the courage to continue to pray. For it will destroy the courage of most people to see their end clearly. They will think they cannot change their bad end and become completely evil. But there is no evil which cannot be changed into good by way to prayer to God. For God is the Merciful, the Compassionate.

But Zayd was still intoxicated with the same spiritual excitement:

O Muhammed!" he cried, "Can the sun of God, that pre-eternal and post-eternal sun, be hidden in a vest?

You know better than any of us that nothing can stand in the way of the manifestation of that light. Neither deceit, nor falsity, nor vest. Everything is shattered before it. Neither reason remains nor madness. What is shining in me is the ray of that light. Can anyone who sees this mystery have any will left?

Hazret Muhammed responded by saying: "You are right, O Zayd. But know this also, that the smallest point can shut out the whole of creation for a person. What can you see if you put the tip of a finger upon your eye? Will not the sunny world appear dark to you at that moment?"

Consider! When you put your finger over your eye, you can see neither moon nor sun. But they remain in their places, shining with the same glory. It is you who do not see. There are so many arrived of God whose hearts are illuminated and who keep suns hidden within them. Their bodies are a veil hiding their reality from those who look upon them. This is a likeness of God's attribute The Curtainer. If God wanted everything to be seen, no light would ever be concealed. But if He appoints a particular time for the appearance of a thing, you can try all you want to reveal it, and even believe that you have, but no one will see it.

The Curtainer is such that His most evident state like being veiled. Even so, eyes that see, especially hearts that love, never have any difficulty in seeing that light.

Close your lips! Be silent, and gaze into the depths of the sea. Sounds, waves and the noise of life are all on the surface of the sea. Once you have descended to the depths, you will be in perfect silence and peace. This state of the sea is like divine knowledge. Those who view it from outside, those who have not yet penetrated its depths, roll and crash like waves with the first excitement of knowledge of God. But those who dive into that knowledge are covered with the calm, sober silence of the divine realm.

God has said in the Gracious Koran that the springs of Salsabil and Zanjabil in Paradise will be under the control of the people of Paradise. Just as the people of Paradise can make use of the waters of those springs, to that same extent the prophets and friends of God obtain grace from the mysteries of divine knowledge in this world. The drink divine mysteries and the wine of divine love as they drink of the waters of the rivers of Paradise they possess.

This means that for the people of heart, there are varied paradises in this world of bodies as well. It is possible for them in this world also to see the rivers of Paradise, derive grace and light from them, to attain a self-disclosure and see the divine Beloved sparkling in varied manifestations.

If we wish, we can control the flow of those rivers of Paradise like the forces magicians bend to their will. But we can do so not by virtue of our own power or magic, but because God has command it.

The people of heart can make the rivers of Paradise flow in the direction they wish just as sometimes the springs of your eyes, flowing with the love of God like rivers, pour out pearls on your thirsty cheeks when you weep, or may gaze in the direction you wish, pouring out the light of your gaze instead of tears.

If the heart wishes, the light of the eye which flows like water will pour out in the direction of evils like snake poison.

But when the heart wishes to understand mysteries and secrets which give example, the eyes gaze in that direction. They gaze into the depths of the world of the afterlife; and if the heart takes pleasure in worldly forms and colors and the realm of plurality, the eyes will surely see nothing else.

Not only the gaze but the springs of the other four senses of taste, hearing, touch and smell are like the light of the eye under the heat's command. Like five separate faucets in an ablution fountain, they flow into the grooves the heart desires.

The hands and feet of the human body are under the command of the heart like the staff in Moses's hand. If the heart wishes, it can make that staff into a dragon, or adorn it with color and flowers like an erguvan tree.

If it wishes, it makes the feet dance, or moves them to whirl. If it directs them, they go toward poverty and lack, or toward plenty and perfection.

By its command the hands do accounts or write books.

You know that the heart is hidden and controls the body, the hands, the feet, the eyes and ears as an invisible power. From this you can understand that there are forces in the universe which control the hands and feet of creatures in the same way, although you do not see or know of them.

It is the heart which is a snake to enemies and a helper to friends. It is the heart that serves up food to the poor, and the heart that beats the enemy over the head like a ten-maunds club.

What kind of command is it the heart gives to all these bodily members and invisible and visible forces, and what kind of promise does the heart make, that no bodily member, no force, can resist it? The bondsmen follow its command like slaves. Is it union the heart promises them, or something else? Can it have found Solomon's seal? It has made the body and its members like the obedient realm of Solomon. What magic ring does the heart use in order to become the Padishah of the forces of soul and spirit?

The five external senses and the five internal senses in the form of comprehension, imagination, thought and memory [sic] are all under the heart's command.

These ten senses, internal and external, and the seven limbs—the head, two hands, two feet, abdomen and back—all, all in this bodily clime are under the command of the heart Padishah.

In explication of this Hazret Muhammed said that each person is the ruler and Solomon of the country of his body.

****

Now, O heart! Since you are the Sultan of such a clime, know the value of your domain! Be a righteous judge in your country as Solomon was! If you do not want fairies and demons to steal your seal, if you do not want your country to fall victim to tyranny and darkness, gladden it with spiritual and angelic forces, and by means of them rid the land of corrupting and satanic forces. In short, rule over fairies and satans by means of that ring upon your finger.

If you do, the satans will not be able to steal your ring. Your fame will conquer the world. And someday your justice and state will rule not only your own body but both of the two worlds.

You know that the human body is a symbol of the divine image [*ilâhî görünüşünün bir remizi*] and God's site of self-disclosure [*tecelligâh*]. You should also know the value of having and ruling such a body. Be a Sultan who rules justly over the domain you possess. If you do not, if you allow Satan to steal the ring on your hand, if you enslave that mighty talisman to the soul, your entire sultanate, your good fortune and your prosperity will be wiped out.

So, you who lose the greatest of all pleasures, felicities and bounties to the satan of the soul and the pleasures it promises, what you are doing means that your heart will continue to be stabbed full of holes with the dagger of sighs until the Day of Resurrection. If you wish proof of this, read chapter thirty-six of the Gracious Koran. There you will find the disappointments and sighs of those who take the wrong path made plain.

And if you take an even worse path and say that you are on the right road, that you are not blaspheming and denying, and even though you are, delude yourself, you will be even worse off than they.

For the scales which you have not employed in the path of God and goodness will weigh your state one day.

****

HOW SLAVES AND FELLOW SERVANTS THREW SUSPICION UPON LUQMAN, SAYING THAT HE HAD EATEN THE FRESH FRUIT THEY BROUGHT

3625.   Luqman was among the slaves of his master
        More despised in body than all the others
        The master would send his slaves to the garden
        So that for his pleasure they'd bring fruit for him
        The slaves despised Luqman like a parasite
        He was spiritual and dark-skinned as the night
        His fellow servants ate the fruit, all of it
        Happily in the most extreme greediness
        They told the master Luqman had eaten it
        The master was bitterly displeased with him
3630.   When Luqman had inquired what was the matter
        He opened his lips to reproach his master
        "O master," said Luqman, "in God's presence

463

A treacherous slave cannot be accepted
Put us all to the test, O benefactor
Require us to drink our fill of hot water
Make us run out upon the steppe after that
Riding on your horse while we remain on foot
You will see which of us has done the bad deed
See the art of Him who reveals mysteries."

3635.   So the master gave the servants hot water
For them to drink, and they drank it out of fear
After that he made them run out to the fields
And they ran along the rows of the sown fields
They began to vomit in their affliction
The water brought up the fruit from out of them
When Luqman vomited what he had within
Nothing but pure water came from inside him
If Luqman's wisdom can show forth in this way
What will the Lord of Being's wisdom display?

3640.   *On the Day when inmost thoughts will be searched out*[221]
What's latent and you don't want seen will come out
When *they shall be given to drink hot water*
All veils will be torn from that which you abhor [222]
The torment of infidels is done by fire
Because the proper test of stones is by fire
Often we speak gently to our stony hearts
Giving counsel of which they will take no part
A severe wound requires severe remedy
A donkey's head is worthy of a dog's teeth

3645.   *Wicked women for wicked men* is decreed
Ugly is for ugly mate and deserving[223]
So whatever you desire to mate with, go
Die in it, take on its quality and form
It it's light, to receive light prepare yourself
If it's distance, be far and absorbed in self
If from this ruined prison you seek escape
Bow and draw near [224] to the Friend, don't turn away

Luqman was despised both by his master and his master's other slaves. This reason for this was his pathetic physique and very dark skin. Luqman was an Ethiopian and the slave of a Damascene Arab.

But underneath the blackness of his skin he was one of the exceptional creatures who carry a white light within them. He paid no attention to the ill treatment he received, and

---

221. "The Day secrets will be tested" (Koran 86:9).
222. "Can they be compared to those who will dwell forever in the Fire and be given boiling water to drink, so that it tears up their bowels?" (Koran 47:15).
223. Koran 24:26.
224. Koran 96:19.

he tread the path of goodness and virtue with sure steps.

One day his master sent Luqman along with his other slaves to the orchard to bring him some fruit. The other slaves ate the fruit the gathered and said Luqman had eaten it, wanting to put a black mark upon him. The master became angry with Luqman and spoke to him bitterly.

When Luqman had understood the reason for this anger, he said to his master:

Honored master! A treacherous slave is not only unacceptable to his master but to God Himself, and cannot gain God's approval. I do not want to remain accused of guilt. O great master, come and put us to the test! Have all the slaves drink a large quantity of hot water. Then bring us into the open country and let us run there while you ride on your horse. Then you will understand who it is that has done wrong, and you will see the works of God who brings secrets out into the open.

The master accepted his slave's proposal. He did as he had said. Forced to drink hot water, the slaves began running, and vomited up all they had eaten. But only the water of bile came up from Luqman's stomach.

Consider! If Luqman's wisdom could display this secret and this evil, what secrets are there that God will not bring out on the Day of Judgment? What crimes will me not bring out into the open?

God has said in the eighty-sixth chapter of the Gracious Koran: "Surely God is able to bring him back to life on the Day that things secret will be tested. On the Day man will have no power and no helper."

That day many a man will be made to drink hot water as Luqman's fellow slaves were. God has said in the Gracious Koran: Will the state of those who will delight in the bounties of Paradise be like that of those who will drink the boiling water of Hell and be disgraced?"

The torment they will feel when that water of Hell tears apart their bowels will be great, and their secrets will come out. The heart of a kafir is hard an unfeeling as stone. Just as one must light fires around hard stone and pour vinegar on it in order to break it, it is fitting to throw the heart of a kafir into fire in order to test it. This is the method God has chosen in order to soften and melt stony hearts. For time after time what gentle words have been said to those hearts like stone, what sweet counsel has been given to them, yet they have not been able to understand the meaning of those beautiful and gentle actions.

It is said in the twenty-fourth chapter of the Gracious Koran: "Impure women are for impure men, and impure men for impure women." That is why all evil creatures are for evil creatures, and why it is said that a dog goes to its tooth and a pig to its hide. Learn from this parable why the people of Hell are considered worthy of the Fire.

And so whatever you wish to posses, wish to resemble, wish to be, run for it and seek it out. If you wish to be one of the chosen community, find that community and give up your being in that community's being.

If you wish for light, prepare yourself for light to set itself upon you! If you wish to reach God, seek the ways to become The Truth with The Truth!

If not, if your intention is to be distant from God, be selfish! Work only at the command of your self. Keep away from God and from humanity!

And finally, if you are among those who hear the invitation of God in chapter ninety-six of the Gracious Koran, "Bow down in worship and come near to your Lord!" and you struggle to be free of the prison of the body, let the only voice to which you run be the voice of the invitation of God the great.

****

THE REMAINDER OF THE STORY OF ZAYD AND HIS ANSWER TO THE MESSENGER, PEACE BE UPON HIM

<blockquote>

This discourse has no end. "O Zayd, now get up
Bridle the faculty of speech of Buraq

3650. Faults are exposed by the faculty of speech
It tears apart the curtains of the Unseen
God desires for awhile to remain unshown
Drive away this drummer and close off the road
Do not gallop, draw the reins in, veiled is best
For each to be glad with his conceit is best
God desires that those who have no hope of Him
Not avert their faces from worship of Him
So that by worship they may be ennobled
Occupied with pious acts and be humbled

3655. They are ennobled even by just one hope
For a few days they may run by its stirrup
He wishes that mercy should shine upon all
On the bad and good, mercy universal
God wishes that every prince and every slave
Should be hopeful and be fearful and afraid
That this hope and fear remain inside the veil
So that they may be fostered inside the veil
Where are fear and hope when you have rent the veil?
To the Unseen belong might, glory and trial."

3660. At the water's edge there stood a brave young man
Thinking, "Our fisherman here is Solomon
But if so, why is he disguised and alone?
And if not, why does he look like Solomon?"
He remained of two minds until the time when
Solomon became shah and sole sovereign
The demon had fled his kingdom and his throne
That devil's blood shed by sword of his fortune
When upon his finger he placed the seal ring
Armies of demons gathered there and fairies

3665. The men of the land came in order to see
Among them was the youth who had been deceived
Solomon opened his hand, he saw the ring
All at once vanished his anxious wondering
When a thing is hid there is anxiety
Attention is on the thing which is not seen
Fancy of the absent grows thick in the heart

</blockquote>

When it becomes present, thought of it departs
A bright sky does not mean that it will not rain
Nor the earth's blackness it won't produce again

3670.   "I require *'those who have faith in the Unseen'*[225]
So shut the window of this palace fleeting
If, as on the trumpet's Day, I opened it
Could I say, *'do you see any flaw in it?'*"[226]
So that they may make efforts in this darkness
Each turning his face in that way and in this
For a while things will be as in reflection
Thief will be able to hang the night watchman
Many a sultan and man of lofty mind
Will become enslaved to his slave for a while

3675.   Service done in absence is genteel and good
Keeping the absent master's command is good
How is it to praise the Shah in his presence
Compared to not losing shame in his absence?
The commander of a fort on the border
Far away from the Sultan and his order
Who defends the fortress against every rout
And will not sell it for riches beyond count
Who though on the frontier, in the Shah's absence
Remains loyal as he'd be in his presence

3680.   To the Shah he is better than all the rest
Ready to give up their lives in his presence
Thus half an atom of duty in absence
Is better than hundred thousands in presence
Faith is praiseworthy now, and obedience
They will be spurned when all is clear after death
"Since the Unseen, veiled and the absent are best
Close your mouth, for us to be silent is best
Withdraw your hand away from speech, O brother
God Himself will make divine knowledge appear

3685.   The sun's face is proof enough that the sun is
Is not God *the greatest of all witnesses?*"[227]
"No, I will speak, for they join in asserting
God and the angels and the men of learning
God and the angels and those in knowledge versed
Witness there is no Lord but Him who endures."[228]
Who are the angels, when God has testified
That they should partner in what is testified?
It is because ruined eyes and hearts can't bear

225. Koran 2:3.
226. Koran 67:3.
227. Koran 6:19
228. Koran 3:18.

The sun's radiance and testimony clear
3690.   Like a bat who relinquishes every hope
Because he cannot stand up to the sun's glow
As are we also know the angels are friends
Of the splendor of the sun in the heavens
Saying, "We have from a sun derived our light
Upon the weak like vicegerents we shed light."
Every angel has its rank in light and worth
Like the new moon or three days old moon or full
Every angel according to its degree
Has that light *in pairs of wings, two, four or three*[229]
3695.   Like the wings of intellects of human beings
Amongst which there is much difference in between
Hence the partner of each human good or ill
Is that angel who shares in the same measure
The dim-sighted who can't tolerate moonshine
It's in order to guide them that the stars shine

Because of what Zayd had said, Hazret Muhammed spoke again and said:

> O Zayd! The secret of oneness and nearness to God realized during the moment of prostration cannot be strung upon the string of speech. For the sake of the degree you have attained and the bounties you have seen, get up and prostrate yourself again! Put a bridle on the Buraq of speech. Do not use your tongue to reveal secrets that should not be revealed!
>
> For speech can expose faults as much as it tears the veils of the Unseen.

It is not without reason that God has chosen to remain in His own realm of the Unseen until the Day of Resurrection. It is God's greatest wisdom to not be seen, to not appear before every eye and heart. Stop the drummer, so that you may hear the beautiful sound of silence on this path. Next to the beauty of the concealment and silence of divine wisdom, what is speech but a drummer who bursts the eardrums?

The steed of speech should not be driven on with all speed. Draw in its reins. To reveal what God wishes to be concealed is not gnosis. It is better for mysteries to be kept hidden and for everyone to be gladdened according to his opinion and degree of understanding.

God wishes to remain concealed behind the veil of the Unseen and for His bondsmen to pursue hopes and goals and to worship Him with hope. The bondsman's hope is either for the afterworld or for this world. The gates of supplication are open to the hopes of both. This means that the hopes and goals of both those who seek the afterworld, which is to say spiritual delights and pleasures, and those who go after worldly pleasures and desires, form a bond between them and God. Knowingly or unknowingly, every bondsman is bound to God by hope and anxiety.

Hope and anxiety are the veils of the realm of the Unseen. When the veils are torn aside one day, those who stand before them seeking God's compassion, whether through hope or fear, will see that realm emerge with all its glory.

---

229. Koran 35:1

When the veils are torn aside neither fear nor hope will remain, because everything will be out in the open. At that moment a person will either meet what he most fears or see that his good-intentioned supplications and wishes to reach God have been accepted, and will receive the reward of Paradise which God promised. If this were not the case, if every bondsmen knew while in the world what his end would be on the Day of Resurrection, the worldly and the thief would be distraught and the believers would live in happiness. But divine wisdom would have no authority. For God wants not only the believer to have hope in Him, but the thief as well, and even the kafir. And who knows, perhaps one day a person who walks toward the precipice as a slave of his soul while still in the worldly realm of body will awake from his heedlessness for a moment, and if he begs God for help and goodness, let there be no doubt, God is so great that He will forgive him and not hesitate for an instant to accept him among His good bondsmen.

You will remember the story of Solomon and the youth:

One day Messenger Solomon went to bathe and gave to his wife the seal ring which made him ruler of all the world. A demon took on Solomon's form and got the ring from the woman. Now with neither ring nor kingdom, Solomon went to catch fish in order to earn his living.

It was then that the youth saw Solomon there by the river's edge dressed as a poor fisherman and was amazed. The youth thought to himself how much the fisherman resembled Solomon and wondered, if it really was Solomon, why was he dressed as a fisherman, and if not, who did he so resembled him.

The youth returned every day in doubt and hesitation and was amazed to see the same scene. Finally Solomon slit the belly of one of the fish he caught, found his ring inside, and defeated the demon. He destroyed the demon and returned to his throne. The armies of demons and fairies were again under Solomon's command.

When Solomon was seated on his throne he told the people what had happened to him. The people came in droves to see him. Among those who came there was also the youth who had seen the sovereign dressed as a fisherman, and when he saw the ring on Solomon's hand, he no longer had any doubt.

Here Solomon represents the traveler on the path of God and the youth represents rational thought. The river is the water of gnosis. The fish is God's wisdom and art. The demon who steals Solomon's ring is the soul, worldly desires. Solomon's seal ring is his love of God, the love which keeps a person continuously tied to God and His path, the state of ecstasy.

So, Solomon became inclined toward the world for a moment and paid a heavy price. The youth who represents the intellect and thought was plagued by indecision, suspicion and anxiety when he saw Solomon dressed as a fisherman occupied in the hunt for God's wisdom and art.

For suspicion and anxiety overcome a person when what is sought is hidden; when it is invisible and what it is cannot be known. When what is sought appears, suspicion and doubt are gone and the spirit is face to face with reality. When the truth self-discloses, the spirit seeking to see God's beauty reaches its goal. Those who bow to their souls and go astray suffer the punishment of their suspicions and opinions.

If the sky is clear and the heavens blue and full of light, that does not mean it will never rain. And if the ground is black and without vegetation, one cannot think that the earth will never bring forth greenery again. As long as God commands it, the heavens will not be without the blessing of rain and the dark, bare earth with become green again.

A person is close to God to the extent that he believes the Unseen will one day satisfy his wish for rain from the sky and vegetation from the earth.

In the second chapter of the Gracious Koran it says: "This is the book having no uncertainty in it, guidance for those who fear God; those who believe in the Unseen, who are steadfast in prayer, and spend out of what We have provided for them. And who believe in the revelation sent to you, and sent before your time, and who have assurance of the hereafter. They follow true guidance from their Lord, and it is they who will prosper." These verses say that God is pleased with those who believe in the Unseen. And this is the wisdom in God's having closed the window opening from this mortal world onto the Unseen. For faith is beautiful while realities are hidden, while they are not visible, but reached by way of comprehension, thought and intuition.

And God has said in the sixty-seventh chapter of the Gracious Koran: "He who created the seven heavens one above another. No want of proportion will you see in the work of the Most Gracious. So turn your gaze again: do you see any flaw?" And He asked how He should split the heavens at the center and open them up, bringing forth all the hidden realities; and will ask you, after the heavens are split and everything comes out, if you see any flaw. Thus is explained the greatness and value of having faith without having seen the realities behind the heavens.

God has done this for the good of mankind, so that humans may achieve a level of humanity at which they may find the truth themselves, and for sake of the happiness of be able to see His bondsmen achieve such a level of humanity.

So that people may open their eyes wide in order to find God; so that they may not give up searching even if the skies be cloudy; so that they may not suffer the terror of the veils that do not reveal the divine realities to their eyes, saying, "There is no cloud in the sky, what is this smoke?"

The world is sometimes confusing. A thief may put a judge upon the gallows. So many people are helpless before their own slaves and become slaves of their own souls. They make the members of the body, which are prepared to carry out all actions when commanded by the spirit, give orders to the spirit which satisfy only their own brutish passions; they use the spirit as a slave to their lusts.

A person pleases his Lord when through intellect and insight he finds the ways to become a slave not to his passions but to God.

God is pleased by those who love Him and find Him while they do not see Him and He is yet in the Unseen. A person who bows to the ground in the presence of a sovereign is sincere if he is loyal to the sovereign with the same respect and glorification while far from him as well. Soldiers who protect and defend a country from its frontier forts die in battle loyal to a sultan they often have never seen.

Guards who are loyal like that do not sacrifice the forts of the sultan for sake of anything, material or spiritual. They refuse all bribes offered to them and serve sovereign and state with perfect sincerity.

Those who thus defend far-off forts with complete sincerity and noble loyalty, even giving their lives in this way, are certainly more valuable to a sultan than those nurtured with mercy and bounty in his own palace. Their service is superior to the service of those who work in within sight of the sovereign and hear his commands in person.

Like the loyalty of the heroes on the frontier, worship of God and faith in Him is only acceptable prior to the day of death.

To be sure, the faith of the faithless at the moment they see God in person on the day of death and grasp His greatness at the Resurrection will not be acceptable to Him.

O friend, since the Unseen, since being veiled, is so valuable and meaningful, hold your tongue! On this subject only silence is beautiful. The right to reveal divine knowledge [*ledün ilimi*] is special to God alone.

Know that just as you understand the sun exists when you see the sun, you will understand the existence, oneness and greatness of God by knowing God and having faith in Him. For as it says in the sixth chapter of the Gracious Koran, there is no greater witness to the greatness of God than God Himself.

Zayd was overflowing with the mysteries of divine oneness and felt the turbulent sea within his spirit was very far from being able to fit in the container of his heart and tongue. He needed so to tell the secrets overflowing within him that he virtually begged Hazret Muhammed:

> Do not forbid this lover who has lost his mind, this lover of God, from telling the secrets within him! For not only I but God, the angels, and learned men join in revealing this truth.
>
> God, the angels, and those learned in divine knowledge who have achieved the degree of knowledge of truth, all bear witness that other than God there is no existent [*var olan*], no being [*varlık*] whose existence [*varlık*] is eternal, no life, and no beauty.
>
> Has not God said in the third chapter of the Gracious Koran: "There is no god but He: That is the witness of God, the angels, and those imbued with knowledge, standing firm in justice. There is no god but He, the Exalted in Power, the Wise."?

By "those imbued with knowledge" here is intended the friends of God who know the mysteries of God. Great and just God called out to the spirits at the gathering of Alast, "Am I not your Lord?" and they testified, "Yes!"

The learned of that gathering of Alast are those who see the divine beauty, who know the divine oneness. In achieving God-knowledge they are even more advanced than the angels. True, both the angels and the learned have drunk the wine of oneness. But the cup remained in the hands of those who posses divine knowledge. And once God has borne witness to His own being and His own oneness, who are the angels to share in such witness?—do not ask! The function of the angels here is a great one. For there is no eye and no heart which can see and love the light of the sun of oneness, its brilliance that dazzles eye and heart, without being ruined. The angels soften that infinite brilliance in the light of their own transparent beings. For if eyes and hearts are dazzled by the light of the angels, if the light of the angles is like that, who knows how heart-searing that will find that of God. The messengers able to see the light of the angels, and the friends of God, gazed at the divine light and the mysteries of oneness through the veil of the angels. Moses did not have the strength to see the divine light in all its glory. Hearts ruined by His love and His light are like bats who cannot even stand the light of day. So that the human intellect, which faced with the light of God is no different from the eyes of a bat, should not give up hope of seeing that sublime brilliance, God sent it the help of the angels. And in the same way, He sent His messengers and friends to help mankind. Just as the moon, which takes its light from the sun, is proof of the existence of the sun, so are the messengers and friends witnesses of the divine light.

That is why a divine gleam, like a light reflecting in a mirror, burns in every heart which says from the depths of the heart, "I bear witness that there is no god but God and Muhammed is His messenger." Sometimes it burns with such strength that such hearts feel that all spirits are filled by the reflection of that light with a pleasure which cannot be described.

There are different kinds of angels. Some are slim as a crescent moon, some appear like a three day's moon, and some are at the final line of light like a full moon. These angels, some more mature, more bright than others, bear witness to the divine light. The angels of the heavens and the friends and prophets on earth are ranked in degrees, just as people on earth have different degrees of intellect, thought, understanding, beauty and maturity.

The different degrees of angels are given wing as are the intellects of men. Just as people's conjectures, fantasies, capacities of comprehension and thought are like wings with which they ascend, so are the numbers of pairs of wings angels have sometimes two, sometimes three or four, and they perform their functions carrying different lights in their wings.

Angels of evil serve the evil of men and angels of goodness serve the good. Only the arrived of God see those angels and the flames of divine light in their wings. It is they whose eyes of the heart are opened to the heavens by divine power and wisdom.

But those whose eyes of the heart are too weak for any light, even the light of the moon, find their way by the stars. Those who do not have the power to see the sun with their eyes, who cannot bear the moon or the light of the moon, look at the stars.

Those who cannot see for themselves the divine sun shining in prophets and the friends run to those who have and have taken light from them. Those who gather around the friends of God in eras when there are no messengers on earth, and fill their bowls at the fountain of one of the friends, help those who can partake of light cup by cup or drop by drop. The road they travel by the stars of guidance and the tarikat, not by the sun of guidance and the tarikat, will one day surely reach the sun itself.

****

HOW THE MESSENGER, PEACE BY UPON HIM, SAID TO ZAYD, "DO NOT SPEAK THIS MYSTERY MORE PLAINLY THAN THIS AND PRESERVE CONFORMANCE."

> The Messenger said, "My companions are stars
> Lamp to travelers, to devils, meteors
> If everyone had that eye and had that might
> To receive from the sun of heaven that light
> 3700. No moon and no star would be necessary
> To perform for the sun as testimony
> What need is there for a star, O little man
> To be proof of the existence of the sun
> To earth and cloud and shade the Moon is saying
> "I'm a man, *like you,* but *it's revealed to me*[230]
> Like you I was dark in nature and cloudy

---

230. Koran 18:110, 41:6.

The Sun's revelation gave this light to me
I have darkness in comparison with suns
I have light for the darkness souls have within
So that you may possess the strength, I am faint
You are not the man for the Sun radiant

3705.   I am woven like honey and vinegar
To find the way to sickness of the liver
O hostage, since you've recovered from disease
Leave the vinegar and keep eating honey
Free of lust and prospering is the heart's throne
The Merciful God is seated on His Throne [231]
After that God rules over the heart directly
Since the heart has achieved this affinity
There is no end to this discourse. Where is Zayd
So I may counsel him not to seek disgrace."

"Since the light of every eye and heart is not able to bear seeing the brightest thing; since eyes and hearts must approach light only to the degree they can see it, O Zayd, do not show people a brightness they cannot bear to see! Be patient in making them accustomed to light. For so many people the space of a life, sometimes many lives, is not enough to see divine light.

"O Zayd! My companions are the stars of the sky of guidance. They hold up a light for travelers in truth. And for satans and satanic spirits they perform the function of meteors.

"For those who leave the path they are stones which work their way into the liver, but for those who walk the path I show them they are full moons. The sun of truth which I have brought illuminates them. That is the reason why, O Zayd, your duty and the duty of those like you is not to reveal secrets before their time but to hold a light up for people.

"Consider, if everyone had the power to see directly the light of that sun of oneness, would there be any need for stars, which take their light form the sun and prove the existence of the sun?"

This means that companions of Hazret Muhammed like Zayd had no need of the stars' help in order to see the sun. The companions achieved the felicity of seeing that light of truth in the being of Hazret Muhammed himself.

True, the arrived of God who would live in this world after Hazret Muhammed were never going to meet him face to face. But spiritually they too were companions of Hazret Muhammed.

They would witness the divine light every instant in the beauty of Hazret Muhammed visible only to them. That is why Shazali Hazretleri said one day: "If the Messenger of God were invisible to me for even the blink of an eye, I would not count myself among the Muslims."

On the other hand, Hazret Muhammed said to those whose hearts are dark and hard as earth and whose eyes are veiled with the clouds of heedlessness: "Yes, I too am like you a man created of flesh and bone. I too like you have need of water and bread in or-

---

231. "The Merciful is firmly established on the throne" (Koran 20:5).

der to live. But the point where I am different from other men is that revelation comes to me."

What is meant by this is that whether a person is arrived, whether he is a believer, a kafir, it is the same, there is no difference between them. But the gates of spirituality are not opened by material and human means. In order for the gates of gnosis and truth to open and the light of oneness to be visible, the revelation or inspiration filling the hearts of the prophets and friends is necessary. In order for someone to be a mirror of revelation, he must be a prophet, and into order to be site of inspiration, of love, he must be one of the arrived of God.

"O Zayd, in my nature too there was the darkness of body and matter. But the sun of Messengerhood dispersed my clouds. My body was filled with light. But just as the moon is less bright than the sun, so surely am I compared to God. With respect to shedding light upon people I have the brightness of the moon in the heavens. For my light is less than the sun's; as long as I am in a human body I can only bear that much light. More than that would burn my spirit, and I would not be able to perform my function in the world. On the other hand, O Zayd, the people I am charged to bring to the right path do not have the strength to see directly the light of that sun of suns.

"In order to bring health to the sick liver, I have in my compound not only honey but vinegar as well. Just as oxymel is made by mixing honey and vinegar, and is given to the patient and heals his liver, in order for me to be of use to humans made of dark earth I must not be simply light. That is why I was made of a mixture of dark and light.

"For the power that will cure men is such a mixture. Not the eye nor the heart nor the nature of mankind can tolerate a spiritual light which is not darkened with even a little of the dross of matter. It is for that reason that the friends of God enter among the communities of mankind with both lordly [*rabbânî*] and human qualities. For it is not possible for mankind to feel close to, let alone believe, a murshid who in no way resembles itself.

"Now, O you who are caught in the grips of disease! Since you have been freed of human bonds and the soul's veils, the disease of darkness is gone from you. So there is no longer any need to add vinegar to honey. Abandon vinegar." Taste honey alone, like the arrived man of God who said:

> Yunus, you have said it sweet
> Ate vinegar and honey
> Found the honey of honey
> Let my beehive plundered be

"Drink the wine of love. Be pure spirit, so that without veil and without intermediary you may see the light of the Muhammeden Reality and the sun of oneness.

"When the human heart achieves that degree God rules that heart directly. As it says in the twentieth chapter of the Gracious Koran in the verse, "The Merciful is firmly established on the throne," God rules the Throne He has created in the human being. All that is in the heavens and earth and between them and under the earth is His.

"Speak openly if you like. Surely He knows what is hidden, and the hidden of the hidden.

"Yes, God in on His Throne in the Unseen. But the Throne in the heavens is not apparent to every bondsman. That is the place circumambulated by the angels in the heavens. It is the great prayer niche for the supplications of humans on earth. At the same time, the hearts of the friends who have ascended to the level of oneness are the throne on earth. Those on earth who can see with their eyes and their hearts know that throne. For the heart throne is where the sun of God rises and the realm where the moons which are His qualities shine.

"Thus the hearts which God rules directly are those hearts of the arrived where the divine realm shines with the suns and moons within them. But this discourse has no end. Where is Zayd? Where is he, so that I may address him and tell him not to do as those who seek fame do, not to reveal the mysteries of the Unseen and be disgraced."

****

RETURNING TO THE STORY OF ZAYD

3710. You will not find Zayd here now, for he has fled
    He has dropped his shoes and from the shoe row leapt
    Zeyd can't find himself, so why should you find him
    Like a star illuminated by the sun
    You will find neither a mark nor trace of him
    Not a straw on the Milky Way's straw-strewn beam
    Our senses and finite reason become naught
    In the knowledge and wisdom of our Sultan
    Their inner senses and their intellects
    On the waves of *they're assembled before Us*[232]

3715. When night comes it's time again to go to work
    The stars which have been hidden now go to work
    God gives consciousness back to those without sense
    With rings in their ears, troop after troop of them
    Dancing, waving their hands in praise of the Lord
    Crying, *"You have brought us back to life, O Lord"* [233]
    All that skin and that bone which had become dust
    Now become horsemen who're raising up the dust
    To bodily form from non-existence they come
    Grateful and ingrate, at the Resurrection

3720. Why pretend not to see, turn your head away?
    In nothingness did you not first turn away?
    You planted your foot in nothingness and said
    "Who is there who will uproot me from my place?"
    Do you not behold what God's artifice did
    When it dragged you by the fringe on your forehead?[234]
    Until into these different states He drew you
    Of which no thought or dream had occurred to you?
    That not-being is His constant slave always
    Work, O demon! Solomon's alive always

3725. The demon is making *pots like water-troughs*[235]

---

232. Koran 36:53.
233. Koran 40:11.
234. Koran 11:56.
235. Koran 34:12-13.

Not daring to answer back or make rebuff
Look at yourself, how with fear you are trembling
Know that not-being too is always trembling
And if you reach out for relations worldly
It is from fear too you suffer agony
But love of most beauteous God, everything
Though like eating sugar, is spirit-razing
What is it to raze spirit? To lose one's life
To not grasp the water of eternal life

3730.   Upon death and dust people fix both their eyes
They've a hundred doubts for the water of life
Strive to turn those hundred doubts into ninety
Go by night, for night will leave you if you sleep
In the black night of darkness seek out that day
Led by intellect which burns darkness away
There is much good in that evil-colored night
The mate of darkness is the water of life
How can you manage to lift your head from sleep
While you are sowing sloth with a hundred seeds?

3735.   Dead food is allied as the friend of dead sleep
The night-thief works when the merchant is asleep
Don't you know who it is bears you enmity?
Those of fire are foes of those with earth bodies
The foe of water and its children is fire
Just as water is the enemy of fire
Water kills fire, for fire is the enemy
And the hateful foe of water's progeny
And this fire is the fire of concupiscence
Which has the root of sin and error in it

3740.   The external fire is one water may quell
But the fire of lust is bringing you to Hell
The fire of lust cannot by water be spent
For like Hell its nature inflicts sore torment
For the fire of lust what is the remedy?
Religion's light—*your light puts out kafirs' fire*
What can put out this fire? The light of God can
Take as your master the light of Abraham
So that from the fire of your Nimrod-like soul
So that body of yours like to kindling wood
May be freed from the soul's fire like to Nimrod

3745.   Indulgence does not make fiery lust grow less
Make it do without and then it must grow less
How long will you heap up kindling on a fire?
How can one who brings kindling bring death to fire?
When you hold back the kindling, then dies the fire
For fear of God carries water to the fire

The face of the good that wears rose-colored rouge
From the hearts' fear—can fire blacken it with soot?

You will not find Zayd now, for he has fled this world. He has reached his God. He has kicked off the weight of the world fettering the foot of his spirit, escaped the body and material form, and ascended to the spiritual realm.

Never mind your finding him, Zayd is in such a state that he cannot even find himself.

As a star becomes invisible when the sun rises upon it, so has Zayd become invisible in the light of the divine sun rising on the star of his spirit. He has achieved the degree of invisibility while yet in a body. This is one of the evident degrees one achieves in being the Truth with the Truth. Just as God is invisible, so are they who achieve the mystery of reaching Him, being with Him, and being in Him. They reach a state in which they do not even see their own bodies.

It is not possible for those who have not yet reached that degree to know and see the state of those who have this attraction and ardor in the way of God. That is the secret of why you do not see Zayd.

Zayd has transcended the limits of our senses of touch, hearing, sight and smell. The pre-eternal and post-eternal light of our one and only Sultan, Creator of the Universe, has made our senses and our speech invisible.

According to the gracious verse, "They will be brought before us," in the thirty-sixth chapter of the Gracious Koran, the senses and intellects of people who are invisible in the light of that sun of gnosis, that God-knowledge, dive at the slightest summons into the oceans of eternity and are lost to their own existence. This is a state of attraction, of ardor, of passing away from the body. When that state of attraction and ardor is withdrawn from those annihilated and lost in the light of God's existence according to the degree of His summons, the limitation of body begins again. It is like when the stars appear after the sun has gone. The stars of sense and thought shine once more in the dark night of humanity, and worldly burdens and worldly difficulties recommence within humans.

The lover spirits God attracted thus return to consciousness, troop after troop. But rings of gnosis appear in the ears of their spirits and they awaken knowing various sciences and truths.

In their joy they clap their hands and thank God and say, as in the fortieth chapter of the Gracious Koran: "Our Lord! Twice You have killed us, and twice You have given us life! Now we have recognized our sins: Is there any way out?"

This supplication, this faith, this dying and coming to life again are the meaning of the verse in the second chapter of the Gracious Koran: "You were without life, and He gave you life; then He will cause you to die and again give you life, and again to Him will you return."[236]

On the Day of Resurrection the rotted skin and bones will rise up like the dust raised by galloping horses, and hasten to give their accounts.

This is what the state of the arrived of God, who burn with the love of God in this world and pass away from self through an attraction, is like. While they are dead and rotted away, become dust and invisible, God returns them to the world and they find body and life.

---

236. Koran 2:28.

With one difference, that on the Day of Resurrection all spirits, Muslim or kafir, will be clothed in a body.

But those who hasten to the divine summons while still alive, who pass away from self with the wine of love and the light of God and die and come to life again on that path, are the arrived of God who have gained God.

Now, you who do not believe! Why do you turn away from these truths? Pretend not to see, not to know, the divine power which is as plain as the sun? Once you were in non-existence. There you had the same lack of insight. You thought you would always stay there and did not believe you would come from that not-being to this world of visibility. You stood fast in the vastness of not-being, saying, "Who, what power, can make me budge?" But with one "Be!" of His you became a leaf blown by the wind. You left the vastness of not-being and invisibility and appeared in this transient world of being and manifestation.

What power was it that took you by the hair and threw you into this realm of humanity? You will find this in the eleventh chapter of the Gracious Koran. If you have the insight to understand, hear the words addressed to the tribe of Hud: "I put my trust in God, my Lord and your Lord. There is not a creature that moves but He grasped it by the forelock."[237]

This means that He is the one who grasped you by your hair and brought you from not-being into existence. By leaving His path of righteousness you will show how small you are and you will become smaller as time goes by. Those who grow greater are those who do not lose the right path and walk on to Him alone. The One who brought you from not-being to existence and while you exist brings you from color to color, from form to form, from one life to another life, is always the same God. Know this. Consider that the not-being you were in before coming to the world is always under His command.

It is said in the thirty-fourth chapter of the Gracious Koran: "And to Solomon We gave the wind, which takes a month's journey in early morning and a month's journey in the evening; and We made a fount of molten brass flow for him; and there were jinn who worked before him, by the leave of his Lord, and if any of them turned away from Our command, We made him taste of the penalty of the burning fire. They worked for him as he desired, making arches, images, basins as large as water-troughs, and cauldrons fixed in place."[238] Thus have the powers of the soul, of conjecture and imagination, been put under the command of the spirit in every body, which is the Solomon of that body. Neither the demon of the soul nor the jinn of conjecture or imagination, neither satan nor angel, nothing in fact has the power to escape the command of the sultan spirit. With the one condition that the spirit remain sultan of the body and keep the enchanted seal in its hand away from the demon soul and not become its captive.

O human beings, do you all the time you live fear becoming nothing, trembling with that fear? But know that even not-being fears God.

Why do you embrace worldly position, advancement and wealth? Why do you embrace things you think sound, like possessions? Is it not because of the same fear of becoming naught? It is an agony for you not to realize that you so embrace the world you will one day abandon anyway.

Those who escape that agony, which invisibly clasps all people in its embrace, are

---

237. Koran 11:56.
238. Koran 34:12-13.

the lovers of God. Because they are not attached to the world and wish only to be annihilated in God, they happily give up everything they have.

Everything but love of God, even if it be all the bounties of the two worlds, is nothing but agony. If you ask what agony is, it is not to reach the love-water of life, to be deprived of that.

Those who look with eyes full of fear upon the earth which will one day clasp their fragile bodies to its breast are blind, deprived of the ability to see the truth. If they could see, they would see the love of God, which is the water of eternal life their spirits have longed for since pre-eternity.

If you doubt the existence of that water of life, look to overcoming that doubt. For the water of life is not some water you drink from a mountain spring. You will drink that drink of light not with the lips of your mouth but the lips of your spirit. Walk on from the night of humanity to the dawn and the sun of annihilation in God!

There is much good in dark nights. Think of the life of the world as a long, dark night! If you are among those who wait in this night for the sun of truth which rises with the sincerity of the heart, you will drink of the holy water.

For once a person's spirit is embraced by lights, what does it matter if it is night or day? You who kill time sowing seeds of heedlessness in the earth dark as night, if you do not have enough strength to lift your head from empty things and the sleep of heedlessness, it is because you incline overmuch to earth.

Death-like, heavy sleep plagues those who eat unlawful food. The heaviness of the food they eat brings on sleep and nightmares. Once these sleepers have closed their eyes, the sun rises on thieves. For thieves work at night and rob those whose sleep is heavy. Jinn and satans work while those whose spirits are heedless of the truth, heedless of knowledge of God, sleep the sleep of heedlessness. Satans, who are created of fire, are the enemies of humans who believe themselves superior to them even though they are created of earth. For humans are created of water as well as earth. Just as fire is enemy of water, Satan is the enemy of humans, who are created of water. For Satan is the child of fire, and human beings are the children of water. The great advantage water has over fire is that it can extinguish fire. This means that humans are by their nature armed against the satanic forces that belong to fire and wish to trip up their spirits. The fire that wishes to pull the human soul to the paths of the left hand, to drag it along and burn it, is the fire of lust. It is the fire of profound attachment to and seduction by worldly passions. Beware of lust, which is the wish awoken in the human soul for any kind of sin or transient desire. For beginning with the denial of the One who created you, to cheat others, to embrace position and wealth, in short to burn with an insatiable feeling of hunger for anything material and for materiality—all are manifestations of the same lust.

This fire is that fire difficult to extinguish. While your may put out the fire that burns wood with a glass of water, your water will often not be enough to put out the fire of desire and passion which burns the logs of evil. The nature of Hell is dominant in the fire of desire and passion. Water is not effective against it. On the contrary, it rages all the more water touches it.

Such fires must be put out not with water but with light. For fire too has light, but divine light extinguishes satanic fire. People whose spirits have become mirrors of God's light and self-disclosure no longer have any fear of fire.

Think of Abraham! Nimrod had him catapulted into a fire so violently hot that no one could approach it. In such a fire a human body should have burnt up in an instant like a piece of kindling.

Abraham did not burn in the fire. The light of God within him saved him from Nimrod. The fire he was propelled into appeared to him as a rose garden. He gathered great big roses there and left.

The soul in the human being is like Nimrod, and in the violence of fire of the soul the human body burns up at once. Do not put fast-burning dry wood on the fire of lust and denial, for then you will not be able to put it out. It is the duty of fire to burn. As long as you give it wood, saying, "Take it, burn!" it will not go out.

Even when a fire has reached its greatest violence, if you do not put new wood on it, it will not continue to burn. It will exhaust itself, becoming coals, and then ashes. What will give you the strength to stay away from things that feed and fan the flames of soul fire is the love of God and light of God within you.

Most people are fooled by the rose color of fire. They suppose that the secret of pleasure, felicity and beauty is in fire. When they burn in the fires they throw themselves into with this supposition, their faces become black. the black color of evil and kafir-hood is reflected on their faces. The rose color they expect becomes invisible.

By contrast, the flame within all who are illuminated by the light of faith and whose hearts are filled with fear of God makes their faces pink. Look attentively at people who are filled with the love of God and illuminated by this love, and you will see their faces grow more beautiful and pink with every passing day.

The light of faith which beautifies people inwardly, not by means of colors applied from outside, is the light of goodness and beauty. A person becomes beautiful to the extent he feels goodness in his spirit and practices generosity all of his life, in a word, to the extent that he continuously walks the path of God.

****

THE FIRE THAT BROKE OUT IN THE CITY DURING THE TIME OF UMAR, MAY GOD BE PLEASED WITH HIM

> In the age of Umar a great fire occurred
> It devoured stones as if they were mere wood
> 3750. It burned on and on through houses and buildings
> Until it struck the nests of birds and their wings
> Half the city was caught up inside the flames
> Water itself feared the fire and was amazed
> Prudent persons were throwing upon the fire
> Sheepskins filled up with water and vinegar
> But the fire kept on increasing out of spite
> Supported by the One who is infinite
> People came running to Umar, crying out:
> "Water can in no way make our fire die out."
> 3755. "That fire is one of the signs of God," he said
> "It's a flame from the fire of your wickedness
> Put aside water and apportion out bread
> If you're my people put aside stinginess
> "We have opened up our doors," the people said

"We've been men of chivalry and generous."
"You opened your hands not for God's sake," he said
"According to custom and rule you gave bread
For pride and for glory and ostentation
Not in fear, piety and supplication."

3760.   Wealth is seed, don't plant it in every marshland
Do not place a sword in every bandit's hand
Distinguish enemies from religion's friends
Seek the one who sits with God and sit with him
Everyone shows preference to his own folk
The fool thinks he's really done a piece of work

Let me tell you a story. In the time of the caliphate of Hazret Umar there was a fire in Medina such had never been seen before. The horrific fire licked the entire city with its flames. It devoured not just plants, trees and wooden buildings but also rocks, as if they were dry weeds. Rocks split into pieces from the heat of the fire. Birds flying in the sky and nests at the tops of great trees scorched and burned.

The fire became more violent every minute and approached Hazret Muhammed's tomb. Only there did it calm and stop, while it kept on burning the other parts of the city.

Intelligent, experienced elders in the city took various measures against the fire. But neither water nor vinegar was of any use. The fire seemed not of this world, as if its flames were coming from the Unseen realm.

At last the people appealed to Umar. "O Caliph of Muhammed!" they cried. "What is the remedy for such a calamity?" Umar told them:

Although this fire is a worldly calamity, its function is to show you the power and violence of God, in a word, His name The All-Subjugating. For this fire, O Medinians, was lit by the fire of the malady of avarice which has been apparent in you for some time. It has become your nature to hoard wealth, to not help the helpless, to sew up the mouth of the wallet of generosity.

But generosity is one of the fundamentals of Islam. To help the poor. To avoid being tied passionately to worldly possessions. Muslims are Muslim to the extent that they work not only for their own bodily comfort but for the felicity of other Muslims and to rescue them from poverty.

I can relate to you many hadiths from the tongue of Hazret Muhammed regarding the evil of stinginess and how it makes a person one of the people of Hell. But there is no time for that. Do not pour water or vinegar on the fire which is burning you. Pour bread and aid on the fire of poverty that is burning the poor of the city. This is the only way to save Medina from these flames you see.

The Medinians objected to this:

O Commander of the Faithful! How can that be? We are not stingy. There must be an error. Our doors are open to the poor. We have never neglected to distribute bread to the poor.

Umar said:

You are right as far as appearances go. But regard your inner selves. Have you been opening your doors to the poor out of love for God and for the acceptance of God, or for sake of reputation and ostentation? Has what you give to the poor been given with the perfect power of faith, or in the effort to appear a bit more Muslim?

In sum, the aid given with a heart pure as brilliant mirrors upon which no dust has fallen is, to be sure, very acceptable. The charity sullied by the dust of reputation, ostentation, position and hypocrisy has no value.

Know that possessions and wealth are seed. If you scatter this seed on parched ground, on sand or on rocks, it will go to waste and bear no fruit. Aid given without sincerity of heart is like that. The wealth God has given to you in plenty is in fact still God's wealth and belongs to the community of people whose hearts are tied to God and who open their palms to the sky.

Do not remain distant from the good work of giving, heart and soul, your wealth to its real owners.

Do not forget that although religion [din] and hate [kin] may be similar in sound they are opposites. One is the expression of perfect goodness, the other of perfect evil.

When you give charity and distribute wealth, do not favor those who open their hands to you and not to God. Do not give your wealth to hypocrites who surround you. They are people devoid of purity and cleanliness who will make you sin rather than perform good works.

Worship is for God and bounty for His people. When there is even the slightest feeling of self-interest and its pleasure in something you do, it is no longer a good work. I want to explain this to you by a greater example. Why did Ali, the Lion of God, not spit in the face of the foe he battled but rather put aside his sword? I will now tell you that story so you may know the meaning of true sincerity:

****

HOW AN ENEMY WARRIOR SPAT IN THE FACE OF THE COMMANDER OF THE FAITHFUL, ALI, MAY GOD HONOR HIS PERSON, AND HOW ALI DROPPED THE SWORD FROM HIS HAND

From Ali learn sincerity in action
Know God's Lion was pure of all corruption
In battle with infidels he overcame
A warrior and drew his sword and made haste
3765. The warrior spat in the face of Ali
Every prophet and friend's honor and glory
He spat on that cheek before which the moon's face
Bows in prostration in the prostration-place
Ali threw his sword down all of a sudden
And desisted in making war against him
That champion was amazed at this action
And the mercy and forgiveness he showed him
He said: "You lifted your keen sword against me
Why did you then toss it aside and spare me?
3770. What did you see better than combat with me

That you slackened your efforts in hunting me?
What did you see that quelled such anger as yours
That such a bolt of lightning flashed and recoiled?
What did you see that the sight reflected here
Made a flame in my heart and spirit appear?
Beyond space and creation what did you see
Better than life, that you granted life to me?
You are the Lordly Lion in bravery
Who knows who you are in generosity?

3775.   In that you are the desert cloud of Moses
Out of which arrived matchless bread and dishes."
The clouds bestow wheat which mankind by toiling
Prepares and cooks and makes as sweet as honey
The cloud of Moses spread the wings of mercy[239]
Giving cooked, sweet food without difficulty
For those who ate of the bountiful cooked food
Its mercy raised up a banner in the world
For forty years that provision and bounty
Did not once fail that hopeful community

3780.   Until they too, on account of their vileness
Rose to demand leeks and green herbs and lettuce
O people of Ahmed, you are noble men
That food will abide till the Resurrection
In the Prophet's "*With my Lord I pass the night,*
He gives me food and drink." alluded to that
Accept this saying without anagogy
So it goes down your throat like milk and honey
Anagogy is the return of bounty
Since it sees literal meaning as faulty

3785.   This view arises from our weak intellect
It's rind, the pith's universal intellect
Anagogize yourself, not prophetic hadith
Defame your nose, not the rose's scent so sweet
"You are all intellect and sight, O Ali!
Relate a little of that which you have seen!
Our spirit is split by your clemency's sword
The water of your knowledge made our dust pure
Relate! I know that these are His mysteries
For to kill without the sword is His doing

3790.   He who fashions without limbs or instruments
Who bestows these invaluable benefits
Makes consciousness taste a hundred thousand wines
Unbeknownst to the two ears and the two eyes
Relate! O falcon of the Throne, fine hunter
What you now are seeing with the Creator

239. Koran 2:57; 7:160.

483

The Unseen is comprehended by your eye
While others present have fastened shut their eyes
One man sits beholding a moon manifest
While another sees the world all in darkness

3695.   And another beholds three moons all at once
All three men are sitting in the same place, yes
Their eyes are open and their ears pricked, all three
They're petitioning you, while they flee from me
Is this the grace of God, or eye-enchantment?
You've the form of a wolf and I, of Joseph[240]
Though there be thousands of worlds, more than eighteen
Not every eye can hold captive those eighteen
Ali, chosen by God, reveal mystery!
After an evil fate you bring goodly ease

3800.   Either you tell what your intellect has seen
Or let me say what has shown forth upon me
It shone on me from you, how should you hide it?
Without tongue, like the moon you send rays of light
But if the disc of the moon could speak and say
It would sooner guide night-travelers to the way
They'd be safe from error and oblivion
The ghoul's cry by the moon's shout be overcome
Since the moon shows the way even without speech
It would become all gleaming rays should it speak

3805.   Since you are the gate of knowledge's city
Since you're the beam of the sun of clemency
Be open, O gate, to those who seek the door
So that by means of you husks may reach the core
O gate of mercy, forever stay open
Threshold of there is *'no one like unto Him.'*[241]
Every air and mote is a site for vision
But who says, "There's a door," if it's not open?
An idea in the heart never will stir
Until the doorkeeper opens up a door

3810.   When the door is opened a man is surprised
He grows wings and on that idea he flies
A heedless man found treasure in a ruin
After that he rushed to search every ruin
If you have not got the pearl from one dervish
How seek out the pearl from another dervish?
Though conjecture run with its own feet for years
It won't get by the cleft of its own nostrils
Do you see anything but your own nose, tell me
And if you turn up your nose, how will you see?

---

240. Koran 10:4 and following.
241. Koran 112:4.

It was a day in battle. Hazret Ali had knocked an enemy soldier onto the ground, and was about to raise his sword to deal the final blow. The soldier, amazed that he was at the mercy of such a champion as Ali, did the most disgusting thing one can do in a war and spit in the face of the hero of Islam.

It was obvious how confused a creature that man must have been in order to be able to spit at a person with such a beautiful and blessed face as Hazret Ali.

Hazret Ali was aware of the divine essence [*cevher*] he carried within his body and was among those who'd said "Yes!" at the gathering of Alast. He'd found the light of self-disclosure in his spirit; he had said, "I am the one who raised Joseph out of the well!" He was called the Lion of God in Islam. The sword he held in his fist was the gift of the greatest Messenger.

But Ali was fighting in the way of God. The man he'd knocked on the ground was a kafir champion and for Ali it would have been nothing to sever his head from his body with one blow.

But even so, Ali suddenly stopped and decided not to kill his enemy.

The champion lying on the ground was completely amazed. At that moment, especially after having done the disgusting thing he did, he thought he was sure to lose his head. He thought Ali would be enraged and put an end to his life with an even more terrifying thrust than the one before.

It was unimaginable to him that he would ever see the great champion of Islam spare his life at such a moment. In profound amazement, he asked Hazret Ali:

O Ali! After throwing me on the ground, Why have you stopped still just at the moment when you were about to cut off my head? Why did you throw down your sword? Why did you leave me alive?

O Ali! What appeared to your eyes better than destroying me, that you suddenly went from the greatest anger to calm? You were striking like a lightning bolt when you suddenly settled down like calm weather.

What light shown in your eyes that I was left in the dark? You no longer see me, you cannot.

O Ali! What light of faith is the light that appeared to you at the most triumphant moment for a blow?

What did you see superior to all creatures, more beloved than life, that you spared my life? Tell me! O Ali! It is as if something like that light you saw has shown within me as well. It is as if I have become aware of the faith and moral character that has you spellbound. My spirit is filled with a profound delight such as I have never known or felt before.

In heroism you are the Lion of God. I knew this. But what are you in kindness, in greatness? What is your place, what is your measure? I am not capable of grasping this.

Just as Moses's cloud miracle created an oasis of shade, blessedness and greenery in the Tih Desert; just as it gave forth bounty never before seen and rained down bread from the sky, in the same way your manly generosity spared the life of a defeated foe with the sword of Ali pressed to his throat.

As the clouds in the sky sate the thirsty earth with water, mankind works, struggles, plants seed in the black earth, and from each seed that is planted harvests hundreds of blades of wheat. And then the people of earth grind that wheat, cook it and make it into sweet foods.

But Moses's cloud was not like that. When it spread the wing of God's mercy over the earth the miracles told of in the Gracious Koran appeared.

Yes, with his miracle Moses showed his tribe what kind of prophet of God he was. They received bounty for exactly forty years. But when one day Moses went up Mount Sinai to bring forth the Torah, the corrupt people of the tribe once again deceived those whose fondness for corruption was greater than their fondness for God and they worshiped the calf instead of the God Moses had told them of.

When Moses returned and confronted them with the sin of what they had done, there were those who had hundreds of thousands of regrets and, because God commanded it so, war broke out among them. The sword of those who knew to worship God was mightily sharp. Thousands of those who worshiped the calf fell by the sword.

Yes, and the halva of power also rained down on the tribe of Moses in the Tih Desert. Huge clouds appeared in the sky over the desert so that the sun should not burn those who believed in it. But this tribe had grown tired of eating just one kind of food. They wanted other bounties, for example leeks and green herbs and lettuce. If God, who makes the impossible possible, had wished, he would have given them these things too. But once again God showed his anger to those who think only of their stomachs instead of giving thanks to their Lord. Once again they set out into the torment of the limitless, waterless, cloudless desert.

Yes, Moses found water and halva in the desert for his tribe. Jesus too asked for dishes of food from heaven and the skies brought that wish to fruition.

When it came the turn of Hazret Muhammed, on the night of the Miraj he asked God for mercy and forgiveness for his community and great God said, "Whatever you wish is accepted by Me. Your community will always have three groups: Those who rebel, those who obey, and those who long for their God as people thirsty in the desert long for water . . .

"I will send my mercy and forgiveness to your rebellious bondsmen. I will give My paradises to those who obey. As for the felicity of beholding My infinite beauty, I will offer it to the thirsty."

Hazret Muhammed said: "O my Lord! That which Moses and Jesus asked for, You gave to their communities right at that instant. Why do you Keep my community waiting?"

God's answer was this: "O Muhammed, your community is the greatest of all communities. I made your community thankful for My bounties but patient with My trials because sooner or later they will dive into the sea of My mercy.

"Whatever the tribes of Moses and Jesus wished for according to their preparedness, they saw it. But your community is made up of those who wish for My spiritual realm, the divine power I bestow upon spirits, in a word, the path leading to Me. I will give them My Friends as examples so that they may go straight on the path they wish for."

For the community of Muhammed, the most virtuous of all communities, all the bounties of God will abide eternally until the Resurrection.

And just so, that Messenger of God said: "I pass the night with my Lord. My Lord feeds me and gives me water." For some of his companions chided Hazret Muhammed for fasting many days at a time without eating at all; they said it would make him weak and he should not do it. It was then that Hazret Muhammed said the above hadith and revealed a mystery. The statement God feeds me and gives me water was an allusion to eternal, spiritual nourishment. The reflections of God's varied self-disclosures and His light from the Unseen realm were nourishing Hazret Muhammed's spirit to such a degree that he felt no need for material nourishment. This was such delightful food and fulfilling water of life that only a messenger of Hazret Muhammed's measure could taste it.

At the same time, if you feel that you want to taste such bounty also, you should embrace this hadith as it is. You should know that the water he drank, the food he ate, was real nourishment exceedingly superior to worldly delights and bounties. You should know and believe that a person whose spirit is filled with light by God will be completely sated of earthly nourishment.

The one path that will deprive you of such delight is the giving of a different meaning to that reality, that is, the path of anagogy. For a person who strays into such anagogy sees reality in error.

For anagogy is to the rejection of God's graces and gifts. Once the way to anagogy has been opened, no truth remains in the world. It is the people of partial intellect who stray into the path of anagogy. But the partial intellect is not capable of knowing truths. The partial intellect is the skin of things, it is form and appearance. The universal intellect is "essence" [öz]; it is true and great intellect. Those who possess universal intellect are aware of the spiritual realm. Such mysteries of reality cannot be known without awareness of that realm.

If you are interested in anagogy and suffer from the infirmity of having to give another meaning to truth, first try to see the reality you least understand. Anagogize your self.

If you anagogize yourself correctly, assimilating your spirit to the divine reality, you will be freed from the opacity of matter and dive into the realm of light. But if you cannot smell a rose garden, do not blame the roses. Understand that it is your own nose that is unable to detect scent.

The kafir soldier found faith because of Ali's clemency, tolerance and gentleness, and begged him:

O Ali, you are all intellect and sight! O Lion of God, you see before you eyes what we cannot, as if it were shining in the sun! Speak! What did you see? Tell me what you saw, even if just a little!

I have collapsed before your sword wielded by your lion's paw, but that hard sword has not cut me. Now my spirit is torn to bits before the sword of your gentleness. My inner self is washed in your knowledge of truth.

The earth of my body has been washed clean by the water of your wisdom. O Ali! My body you did not slay with your sword has been killed by the sword of your clemency. Your faith has freed me from that iron cage. But to kill a man without a sword is something belonging only to God. It is God's work to kill the soul in a person and ensure his spiritual life. God is the One who creates without instrument or means and plunges us into limitless bounty.

The great Creator makes the human intellect taste the delights of countless wines, and does so in such a way that the neither the eyes, ears, nor lips of a person have any awareness of the wine cup. O Ali, now I understand why the world loves you so much, I understand the wisdom in that. You are the shadow of God on this earth, you are on His path.

O you who open up the mysteries of pre-eternity! You are the interpreter of God's revelation, the guardian of the treasury of God's knowledge, the gate to the path which leads to God.

O falcon who hunts sublime prey at the Throne of God! What all have you seen in the spiritual heavens where you take wing, in the realm of the Unseen? Tell me this secret! God existed before this heaven and earth were created. God created a Throne for Himself; what was He and where was He before He created that Throne?

You who comprehend the mysteries of the Unseen realm! Your eyes are accustomed to seeing the beauty in oneness. But not every bondsman is favored with this felicity. How shall everyone understand that there is oneness in the vastness of plurality?

O Ali, think of three people, one of whom sees the moon in the sky shine as brightly as it does. For the second, even the world seems dark. There is infirmity and calamity in his eye, and that is why he is deprived of the gift of sight. As for the third, his gaze is so sharp that he has the power to see three moons at the same time.

But you know that the eyes of all three men appear to be open. Their ears hear. O Ali, you know their secrets while I do not. However much each of these three kinds of people believes they are on the path of God, what is their relationship of nearness to you? How will they return to God? O Ali! God gave you the secret of knowledge of divinity, He has shown you the external and internal states of every kind of bondsman. For you there is nothing hidden or mysterious about them. So, O Ali, you know these three types as well. What path are they on, what way-station have they reached?

The soldier bowing to the feet of Hazret Ali's spirituality saw those degrees on the path of God but did not know the secrets of them. In reality, those of the three groups who saw the world as dark were at the station of dispersion [*fark*] and difference [*tefrika*]. Their comprehension knows only their own selves. Those who saw one moon shining in the sky were at the station of coincidence [*cem*]. There is nothing but God in their consciousness.

Those who saw three moons in the sky were at the station called coincidence of coincidence [*cemü'l-cem*]. They have achieved the secret of seeing God in three states at once. The three states of God are the states of essence [*zât*], creator [*hâlik*] and creature [*mahluk*].

The knowledge of divinity God gave to Hazret Ali was such that through that knowledge he knew, as origin [*mebde*], as return [*maâd*], as high [*ulvî*] or low [*süflî*], the preparedness [*istîdâd*] of those in these stations and to what state and quality fundamental in them they would return.

The champion lying on the ground continued begging:

O Ali! What is this state? Is this an enchantment of the eye, a kind of magic belonging to the Unseen realm, or a hidden kindness, a grace of God's?

At this moment it is as if you appeared to me in the form of the enemy, and I appeared to you in the form of a friend beautiful and beloved as Joseph.

As you know, when Joseph's jealous brothers asked their father for permission to take him with them, Messenger Jacob did not want to give permission and said he feared that a wolf might eat his Joseph. What he feared then happened; a wolf did not eat Joseph but the brothers threw him in a well.

This is like my own condition. At first you appeared to me in the form of an enemy. I was so afraid of you and I mistreated you badly. But in your eyes I appeared young and beautiful like Joseph. You loved me and you spared my life. This is my good fortune. For if I had died by your hand I would have been deprived of the honor of Islam. Now thousandfold thanks be to my God that you blessed actions have made me a Muslim.

What difference if the worlds are eighteen thousand or more? What does it mean to those who cannot see the creatures and the wisdom in creation if the starts are countless in number? There are eyes which cannot ever see eighteen of them. And there are eyes which can, just by looking at one of them, see the eighteen thousand worlds and their great Creator. Without any doubt, it is the friends of God, the arrived and perfect, who see and attain the mystery in what they see.

Now, O Ali! O chosen bondsman of God! O beautiful fate and destiny, which has sprung up before me like Khizir after the evil destiny written on my brow, that of being a kafir! You who are, in a word, the source of faith! Reveal to me the mystery which God conceals behind so many veils of meaning and makes manifest only to those who can see!

For if you do not reveal it, I will. I have so embraced the light overflowing from your spirit in these few moments, I have so abandoned my own selfhood and kafir soul, entered into the states of seeing divine mysteries, and seen them, that if you insist on not revealing them, I will now tell what I have seen; I will declare the truth which has dawned in my heart like a light.

This light filling my heart is from the sun of your gaze. I now understand you and your function on earth. Although the moon which takes its light from the sun has no tongue; although it does not tell secrets, does not tell from whom it takes its light, it has no need of language to declare those secrets. It has attained the degree of telling those secrets with the language of light.

God's friends take their light from God. Divine mysteries fill their hearts as light which dazzles the eye and heart. And like the moon in the sky, they remain silent, preferring to relate with the language of state the wisdom they have attained. But if the moon also spoke and showed the way to those lost, as it does with its light, what great bounty that would be for those who have lost their way.

This means that if the friends would speak, if they would make people aware of mysteries and truths, surely there would be fewer lost in the world.

If the training [*terbiye*] given by way of gaze and sight were also given by way of language, those hearing the beautiful voice of one who shows the way would surely abandon listening to the horrific voice of the soul monster. In short, if the moon which shows the way without speaking were to speak also, the light seen by those who look at the moon would surely be even more magnificent.

"O Ali! You who are the gate to the city of knowledge and the light of the sun of clemency. Since the city of knowledge, and the sun of truth and clemency Hazret Muhammed brought, is Hazret Muhammed himself, those who wish to enter that city and take spiritual power from that sun must surely pass through your gate. For Hazret Muhammed himself said: 'I am the city of knowledge and Ali is its gate.'

"O beautiful gate! Open to those who wish to pass through, remain open! So that those outside may find the possibility of reaching the truth.

"O God's gate of mercy! Remain open! By means of the path of shariat, you show the people of knowledge the way. In the path of tarikat you are guide to the people of gnosis. Your light is a window opening onto God's realm of oneness. If you will not be the means, not help; if you conceal your light, neither gate nor view nor window can be opened from the spiritual realm onto our spirits.

"O gate of mercy, O entrance to "And there is no one like unto Him,"'remain open forever."

Every air, every mote, every breath displays the oneness of God. But as long as the gate to God's truths remains hidden and closed, who can say there is a gate there?

If a friend of God who sees truths does not open that gate, though there be those who knock, what bondsman will not doubt that there is a gate opening to God? What bondsman could even know that there is a gate?

But if gates are not shut tight and a bondsman sees a gate of ecstasy and love opening in his heart, he will be awed by the beauties he sees for himself. In that state of awe he will see his entire being become spirit and the birds of doubt and soul flying away. The bondsman will take wing to the sky of spirituality through that gate.

You have heard how a heedless person found treasure in a ruin. He supposed that all ruins were filled with treasure.

Then he wandered from ruin to ruin looking for treasure. Just as a person who suddenly finds a treasure in a ruin is deluded by the fantasy that all ruins are filled with treasure, a heedless person who meets one of the arrived yet is unable to acquire pearls of spirituality will derive no benefit from the jewels of other great ones.

And it is also the case that if a person cannot find the dervish essence in his heart, if he cannot conquer his soul, free his spirit of passions for material things and the chains of the world, and moisten his lips with the delight of subsistence in God [*bekâ*], what good will it do him to be surrounded by a hundred thousand dervishes?

A person in pursuit of thought and faith does not feel this faith in himself, and if he does not acquire faith and spiritual training from one of God's friends, he will not find what he is looking for anywhere; he may run after the thought for the span of lifetimes but will never get further than his own nose.

If your nose does not catch the fragrant scent of the Unseen realm, will you be able to see anything but your own nose? Acquire all the thought and virtue you like! If your spirit does not catch the scent of the beauty of oneness and does not taste the delight of burning in the fire of love, can your virtue be more than worldly virtue?

****

HOW THAT KAFIR ASKED ALI, MAY GOD HONOR HIS PERSON, "HOW COULD YOU THROW ASIDE YOUR SWORD WHEN YOU TRIUMPHED OVER ONE SUCH AS I?"

3815.   "O Commander of the Faithful, speak," he said
          "So spirit, like embryo, may stir in flesh.

The seven stars, taking turns determinate
Wait upon every embryo, O spirit
While the embryo is still ruled by the stars
How should it move on to the sun from the stars
When the time comes for it to receive spirit
At that time the sun becomes helper to it
The embryo's brought by the sun to movement
For the sun quickly endows it with spirit
3820.   It received from the stars only an imprint
As long as the sun had not yet shone on it
By what path did it achieve a connection
While inside the womb with the beauteous sun?
By a hidden path far from our perception
Many are the paths of whirling heaven's sun
There is the path for cultivation of gold
The path whereby a stone becomes emerald
The path for giving red color to rubies
The path for making horseshoes flash like lightning
3825.   And the path whereby fruits are brought to mature
And the path for heartening those distraught with fear
Speak, O falcon whose wings are with light ablaze
You who on the arm of the Shah have been trained
O Shah's falcon who hunts down the Anqa, speak
You who without aid of troops vanquish armies
You're the people, you're one and hundred thousand
Speak, I am the fallen prey of your falcon
Why is there this mercy in the place of wrath?
To give a dragon a hand—whose path is that?"

When least expected, the enemy champion had seen the light of Islam, seen The Friend shining in the mirror of Hazret Ali's spirit, and was now experiencing the profound joy of Islam. It was in that spiritual intoxication that the champion called out to Hazret Ali:

O Commander of the Faithful! Explain this beautiful mystery to me that my spirit may come alive like the babe in the mother's womb. For the making of a body out of the seed which brings forth a little human being in the mother's womb, with a heart, lungs, head, brain, bones and flesh, occurs under the influence and guidance of the seven stars [planets] in the sky.

The lights of life streaming from Saturn, Jupiter, Mars, the Sun, Venus, Mercury and the Moon[242] one by one affect the babe in the mother's womb, each of them cultivating life in it for the period of one month. This process continues for seven months. In the eighth month the babe remains again under the influence of Saturn, and in the ninth, of Jupiter.

In order for it to become a human being it must receive the cultivation of these

---

242. According to the Ptolemaic scheme observed here, the sun and moon are among the seven "stars" revolving around the earth.—Trans.

nine star beams while in the mother's womb.

Life is quickened in the babe during the fourth month during the influence of the light beams of the sun. The body is penetrated by the spirit during the turn of the light of the sun.

And since it is during the fourth month while a person is still in the mother's womb that he senses the sun, and his body is quickened by that light, O Ali, by the light of your sun I too now feel a new spirit in my body, like a babe in its mother's womb. This spirit is striking me from the sun of God's oneness and the bright mirror of your spirit.

For the babe in the womb can receive only a body, a shape and form, from all the other stars. What give life to this body is the sun. How does the life-giving sun, one of the great self-disclosures of divine power, find the way to the babe hidden in the mother's womb? How does the sun illuminate it with divine self-disclosure while yet in the fourth month? And how, knowing what wisdom, does the babe in the mother's womb produce a connection with the sun? By what mystery does it learn the way out of the first prison it has fallen into and find the sun?

This secret, this wise finding of the path, is still today beyond our perception and knowledge; it is hidden and concealed within divine mysteries.

If you ask what path this is, if you wish to think of something like it, I can say a little. It is the path by which among the minerals under the earth only gold takes secret nourishment from the sun in order to find that noble yellow color and value of gold.

This is the path full of mysteries whereby emeralds and rubies acquire that green and red color, that incalculable value.

It is the same path whereby the peach is given its palate-cooling taste, the apricot its fragrance which spreads in the mouth, and every lovely fruit the maturity proper to it.

This is the same path whereby the horseshoes on the feet of fleet horses strike lightning flashes. The lightning flashes of God's attraction and guidance leaping from horseshoes bring humans to the heights of maturity in the end and bestow upon them the form of the perfect human.

This is the path which brings into the light those who sorrow at being left in darkness, their hearts deprived of light on dark nights, and fear the bandits of passion who convey their souls to evil. The same enchanted path is the one which takes them from fear to fearlessness, which gives their hearts divine courage; which makes these hearts believe, despite all who are straitened, in the existence and unity of a merciful and compassionate God in His Unseen realm at His Throne; which gives these hearts the taste of love of God and brings them to attain the mystery of illumination by God's light.

Now, O you whose wings are illuminated by the light of intimacy with the greatest Padishah, you who have passed away from self in the delight of perching on his forearm! Tell me that secret!

However much you appear on the surface to be one person, one single individual in Muhammed's community, there are hundreds of thousands of divine qualities gathered together in your being and in the meaning of your being [*varlık*]. For you are one of the grand-scale [*mücellâ*] mirrors which exist on the face of the earth, and for that reason you are not a single individual but an entire community all on your own.

O sultan who has snared the bird of my slavish soul with your falcon's strength, reveal the truth!

Speak! Why did this never before seen will, pushing you from rage to kindness, to gentleness, come to you precisely at a moment of wrath, precisely at the moment when your sword was about to destroy a kafir? To free, with the most beautiful forgiveness in the world, a snake ready to kill you, right when you are about to crush the head—what virtue is this? Whose path is this?

****

HOW THE COMMANDER OF THE FAITHFUL ANSWERED, EXPLAINING THE REASON WHY HE DROPPED HIS SWORD IN THAT CASE

3830.   He said, "I wield the sword for the sake of God
        Flesh does not command me, I'm servant of God
        I'm Lion of God, not lion of passion
        My action bears witness to my religion
        I am *you did not throw when you threw* [243] in war
        The sun is the wielder and I am the sword
        I've put the baggage of self out of the way
        All other than God is not-being, I say
        I am a shadow, my master is the sun
        I'm doorkeeper, not a veil concealing Him
3835.   I'm like a sword bejeweled with pearls of union
        In battle I quicken, I do not slay men
        Blood does not take the sheen of my sword away
        How should the wind bear my cloud off from its place?
        In mildness, justice, patience, I'm a mountain
        Not a straw; when has fierce wind stole a mountain?
        It is chaff that can be borne off by the winds
        For many are the infelicitous winds
        Winds of lust, winds of greed and winds of anger
        Sweep away those who do not perform the prayer
3840.   I'm a mountain and my being's built by Him
        If the wind blows me like straw, that wind is His
        My affections do not stir but by His wind
        No one but love of the One is my captain
        Rage is shah over all shahs and is my slave
        I have put under the bridle even rage
        Clemency's sword smites the neck of my fury
        The rage of God comes upon me like mercy
        I am plunged in light although my dome is cracked
        I am a garden though I be Bu Turab
3845.   Since what is other than God has come between
        It behooves me to put my sword in its sheath

243. Koran 8:17.

So that my name may be *he loves for God's sake*
That my desire may be *he hates for God's sake*[244]
My generosity, *he gives for God's sake*
And my existence, *he withholds for God's sake*
My stinginess is *for God*, my gifts *for God*
I belong to no one, I am all *for God*
What I do for God is not conformity
It is vision, not conjecture or fancy

3850.   I am liberated from effort and search
I have fastened tight my shirtsleeve to God's skirt
If I'm flying, I keep in sight where I soar
If I'm circling, the axis where I revolve
If I'm dragging a burden, I know where to
The sun leads me as my guide and I'm the moon
To say more than this to people there're no means
In a river there is no room for the sea
I speak humbly, in measure of intellect
This is the Prophet's practice, it's not defect

3855.   Hear a free man's witness, of self-interest free
Slave's witness is not worth two grains of barley
In the shariat the witness of a slave
Has no value for the judgment of a claim
Though they offer support in your case, by law
A thousand slaves' witness is not worth a straw
In the sight of God the slave of lust is worse
Than eavesdropping serving boys and prisoners
They can be freed by a word from their master
While lust's slave lives sweet but dies sour and bitter

3860.   The slave of lust can have no release at all
Except by special favor and grace of God
He has fallen into a bottomless pit
By his own sin, not by force or injustice
He has thrown his own self into such a pit
I find no rope to reach the bottom of it
That is enough; if I multiply this speech
Never mind livers, even hard rocks will bleed
If livers bleed not, it's not because they're tough
It's their mania, confusion, and bad luck

3865.   They will bleed one day when their blood is no use
Bleed at a time when blood's not thrown back at you
Since a slave's witness is not acceptable
His witness is approved who's no slave to ghoul
'We sent you as a witness'[245] says the warning
Muhammed was free of creaturely being

---

244. A hadith.
245. Koran 33:45.

Since I am free, how should enmity bind me?
Come in, nothing is here but God's qualities
Come in, for the grace of God has made you free
For precedent to His wrath is His mercy
3870. Come in now, for you have escaped the peril
You were stone, alchemy made you a jewel
You've escaped unbelief and its thorny grove
In His cypress forest blossom like a rose
Glorious man! I am you and you are me
You are Ali, how should I murder Ali?
Better than any piety was your sin
In an instant you passed over all heaven."
Most fortunate was commission of that sin
Is it not from a thorn that the rose-leaves spring?
3875. Did not Umar's attempt to kill the Prophet
Convey him to the court of divine consent?
Was is not the sorcerers' magic that made
Pharaoh call them, and fortune come to their aid?
But for their magic and denial of Moses
Who'd have brought them to wayward Pharaoh's presence?
Would they have seen his staff and miracles then?
Sin became piety, O people of sin
The Lord has struck off the head of hopelessness
For sin and mischief became obedience
3880. Since He changes the shape of evil doings
Making them piety despite whisperings[246]
Thereby Satan the Stoned is pelted with stones
Split into two parts, by envy burst and torn
He engages in struggle to foster sin
And drags us into a pit by means of sin
When he sees sin has become obedience
For him comes round an hour infelicitous
Come on in! I have opened the door for you
You spat on me and I gave a gift to you
3885. Thus I repay those who treat me cruelly
Bowing when they put the left foot against me
What then do I give to those who are sincere?
I give everlasting kingdoms and treasure

Hazret Ali answered, saying, "I wield my sword not for my own pleasure but at the command of God. I cut off the heads of kafirs and hypocrites by the command of God. I am the Lion of God, I am the sword not of my own soul, my own arrogance and pride, but of God.

"I perform the command of my faith. My actions and behavior prove and bear witness to what kind of religion I believe in.

---

246. Koran 25:70.

"As verse seventeen of chapter eight of the Gracious Koran attests, the God whom you have only now come to believe in said to His Messenger at the Battle of Badr, 'You did not throw, I did.'"

The meaning of the complete verse is: "It was not you who slew them, it was God. When you threw, it was not your act, but God's, in order that He might test the believers with a gracious trial."[247]

During the Battle of Badr when the Hypocrites came to kill the Muslims, Hazret Muhammed leaned over and took a handful of sand and stones and threw it at the kafirs.

The confusion caused by the sand thrown in their eyes caused the kafirs to run away and led to their complete rout. It was then that God told His Messenger, with the intention of announcing that Muhammed bore divine quality and carried out His command, that the action of throwing mentioned in the gracious verse had been His.

So it was this event of which Hazret Ali reminded his opponent who begged him to reveal mysteries. And he said to him:

In reality I am not I. I am one of those who has attained the degree of annihilation of his soul in the path of God. For me there is no other being, including myself, other than God. The power and invincibility of my sword is not due to my skill. It is not my sword, it is God's sword, and that is why I use God's sword only for those purposes God wishes.

I am a shadow, I am the shadow of God. But since I am not a black, dark shadow but the shadow of oneness, I am illuminated and a shadow made of light. My function is to raise the veils between the bondsman and God, and for that reason I am not a veil but a remover of veils.

I am a sword of God encrusted with jewels, and I quicken, I do not kill, those who meet me in battle. My removal of the selfhood pertaining to the soul and the world of those who war with their souls in the path of God appears to those viewing it from outside to be a kind of death. But those aware of the reality of the situation see that those freed by my hand from selfish and satanic qualities attain eternal life when they shed their bodies.

My sword is never dirtied by the blood of oppression and injustice.

No wind issuing from the soul, from desire or anything other than God can carry off the cloud of my body, which is a shadow or flame of the divine sun.

I am not a piece of straw. Perhaps I am a mountain produced by the accumulation of clemency, patience and justice. How should cyclones of soul move such a mountain?

The soul and desire have opposing, contrary winds which only weak, straw-like people cannot resist.

The winds of violence, lust and passion sweep away like dry leaves those who are not always and only in the court of God.

A body built by God like high mountains which knows that it is built by God and enjoys the pleasures of intimacy with God cannot be shaken by greed, lust or violence.

That is how my body is. When I am carried away by the wind like a piece of straw, know that what blows me away is not one of the worldly winds I have men-

---

247. Koran 8:17.

tioned. Only His wind, the cyclone of God's attraction, can carry me away.

The commander of the army of my body is God, no power but the wind blowing from His being can move my arm and sword.

Now, O champion, since you have asked me why I have not slain you, listen:

What defeats my violence is the sword of my clemency, not my wrath. However much the roof of my visible body may collapse, I am plunged in light, I have found eternal life; however much I have been called Bu Tarab,"[248] I have become a garden and orchard. And I am the earth which brings forth and decks with color the fruits of gnosis of the gardens of oneness which blossoms with giant roses.

My body, made of this earth of God, battled with you for the sake of God alone. I was not fighting for my own sake. I am among those who love battle for the sake of God and do battle for the sake of God. Everything I have, all my generosity, is for the sake of God. If I put a limit on my generosity, it is only because God's approval requires it.

Nothing I do for the sake of God is conformity or fantasy or suspicion. Everything I do, I do it knowing and seeing. On the path of God I am flowing water, not just one drop. The sea is the destination for the rivers of divine love. What attraction and ecstasy is in the rush of all flowing water to the sea, so is the oneness and effervescence in the union of every drop of light separated from God with that divine light.

In that level of oneness and effervescence, I have wings. There is neither conjecture nor doubt, nor judgment nor seeking. I have taken hold of God's skirt in order to escape all these states and see clearly the beauty in oneness.

Do not suppose I am like everyone else. When I take wing I see the realm of divinity, and when I revolve, I see the point around which I revolve.

I know where I will take the burden I carry. It was the greatest of prophets who loaded me with that burden. My burden is the light of guidance and the human trust of divine vicegerency. I can deposit these two great values only with a friend of God who like me is able to be a perfect mirror to divine light. In sum, I am like the moon in the sky and my guide is the sun.

Now I am at the farthest limit of what I will say to you. One goes no further than this in revealing mysteries to people. Neither do I have permission to say more than this. For just as an ocean does not fit in a river, the sea of the lights of oneness and divine secrets does not fit into the rivers of language and the comprehension of people.

What I say is measured to what the intellects of listeners can take in. For me to do thus and stop at that point or be silent is no fault or shame. For this is the measure of all that cane be said to a community, of what Hazret Muhammed took from God and conveyed to the bondsmen. The final and greatest Messenger of God did not have permission to reveal more of the divine mysteries to people than this.

I bear no resentment toward anyone nor have I any hidden self-interest. I am free of that malady special to mankind. This means that you are speaking with a free spirit. You are hearing his testimony. As you know, the testimony of people who are

---

248. One day Hazret Ali had gone to the Garden of Mutahhara and lay down on the ground. Our Messenger saw him there and called out kindly to him, "Arise, O Abu Tarab," which means "Father of Earth." Thus Hazret Ali's nickname became "Abu Tarab."

not free, of prisoners or slaves, especially if they are slaves to their own souls, is not worth two grains of barley.

That is why the testimony of slaves is not regarded in cases and decisions of Islamic law.

If your witness be not one but thousands of slaves, Islamic law will not count their testimony as worth a straw; it will not hear such testimony. Consider: if the testimony of the slave of a master is not heard in court, who will value the testimony of someone who is slave to his own soul? Every miserable spirit who is prisoner of his own lust and slave to the transient passions of the body is in the sight of God worse than the bondsman who has fallen prisoner in war.

If the occasion comes for a slave and he is steadfast in loyalty, a couple of words from the lips of his master will make him free. The instant he hears the phrase "I have freed you," he is no longer a slave. But by whom and how can the spirit who is prisoner to his own soul, who is smeared in the filth of the world and slave to his passions, be liberated from all that filth? Those who cannot liberate their hearts from worldly filth give up the ghost with difficulty; they cannot easily leave this world.

In fact to be able to abandon the lethal poisons of worldly delights and lusts is, to be sure, the art of spirits who are not heedless and ignorant of their own spirituality.

Those who are slaves to their lusts cannot be freed of the slavery which seeps into their bones until a special grace from God rains down upon them.

These prisoners of soul, these slaves of base lust have, God forbid, fallen into a bottomless pit so deep there is no exit from it. Because as one falls through this pit there are varied delights, lusts and sins of which one never can have one's fill. It is almost impossible for the duped spirit to give these up and do without them. Only God's infinite forgiveness and mercy can liberate such spirits from the swamp they are buried in.

In short, those misguided ones have thrown themselves into such a pit that my mind can find no rope to save it. This dark pit like the pit of Ghayya in Hell is the dark pit of the soul.

So true freedom is not the freedom given to you by a master or whoever controls you but to be free of your own oppressive and despotic soul, to find the path of mercy and virtue and take wing to the skies of spirituality.

But now I must stop talking. For if I were to continue just a bit longer even marble, let alone the human liver, would not be able to stand it and would bleed.

If a heart stands up to all these mysteries and still does not bleed, know that this is because it is harder than stone, made of a mortar of heedlessness, ignorance and evil. That heart is so sunk in worldly filth and so plunged in worldly desires that darkness flows within it and its veins instead of blood.

But on such a day such blood will flow from their hearts that no force but God will be able to extinguish the burning greed in that blood and save them from the torments of Hell.

May the blood flowing in your heart be of benefit to you. May that blood bring you to goodness and nobility. While blood flows in your veins, use it well. Ask Jesus for your cure while he still walks the earth. Once he has withdrawn to Heaven, your request for a cure will have no effect.

In a place where the testimony of slaves is not valid, do not take slaves or seek liberation from slavery. Your testimony will be accepted only if you are not a devil of lust and not the slave of Satan whom God has cursed, if you have not lost all your will under the command of your soul and in service to it.

In chapter thirty-three of the Gracious Koran groups that opposed Hazret Muhammed are mentioned, the kafirs and Hypocrites: "O Prophet! Fear God and do not hearken to the kafirs and Hypocrites! Follow that which comes to you by inspiration from your Lord! O Prophet! Verily We have sent you as a witness, a bearer of good tidings and a warner, and as one who invites to God's grace by His leave, and as a lamp spreading light."[249] For that Sultan of messengers is as free as possible from all worldly ties. My freedom comes of my having taken light from him and attaining the good fortune of being close to him in every way. That is why I, who am illuminated by the light of the Muhammedan Reality, am both free and happy. Given that I am free, by what power could violence or anger make me its slave? There is no quality in me other than God's qualities that I should be slave to other than God.

Now, O champion whose heart has been illuminated by the light of Islam and the rays of guidance! Come and approach me. Give thanks that God has liberated you from the darkness of infidelity and called you to the virtue of light!

For by that invitation you are liberated from all your evils and evil qualities and become free. You see in your own soul that God's mercy is superior to His wrath.

Pay attention to the truth that God's mercy is superior to His wrath and understand immediately that on the path of God being an instRomant of God's mercy is also superior to being an instRomant of His wrath.

Come to me, for you are finally liberated from fear and danger. You who until just a few minutes ago were a rock of error and ignorance. But at this moment the elixir of my spiritual support and my love has transformed you into a jewel turned onto the right path. You were a stone of blackest black and became a light illuminating all around you. You are liberated from infidelity and its forest full of thorns. Now you can bloom like a rose in the garden of God. The flame of faith has found its candle in your lamp. The darkness wrapped around your spirit and your surroundings is filled with light.

O you who have attained the most magnificent of all felicities! There is no longer any duality between us. Just a moment ago you were a stranger, and I was Ali. No there is neither you nor I. You are now as much me as I am you. How can I, Hazret Muhammed's companion Ali, slay Ali?

You committed a crime superior to any good work or act of worship. For because of that crime, you attained guidance. You came to know the oneness of God and gave thanks for that oneness.

From earth you reached the skies. As the rose petal grows from the thorn, flowers of faith with faces as beautiful as roses bloomed from your crime.

You know about Hazret Umar. He was going to commit the gravest crime of his life. The crimes of hundreds of thousands of sinners were piled upon every step he took. For he intended to slay the Messenger of God because Abu Jahl had said to him one day: "You sister believes in Muhammed, she has left her faith. If you had the slightest bit of rivalry in you, you would not have let her."

Umar immediately felt jealous and took up his sword the intent to kill his sister

---

249. Koran 33:1, 2, 45-46.

and Hazret Muhammed.

But when his sister came home he felt his heart would stop. For he heard a voice. The voice was in fact his sister's, but she was reciting the Koran. She was reading verses of chapter "Tâ Hâ," which Umar had never heard before which were too sublime and divine for him to have heard, in a divine voice appropriate to them.

Umar realized that these verses were not, could not be, the words of men. But he did not want to overcome his rage, he could not convince himself to turn away from the path he'd taken. He was thinking it would be easy to kill the girl and would go kill Muhammed first. So he ran in a rage to where Muhammed lived. Others told Hazret Muhammed that Umar was coming and he said "Let him come." He rose to his feet to embrace Umar. At that moment Hazret Umar's spirit was cleansed with the light of faith. He said to the man he had intended to kill: "O Messenger of God, please call me to Islam," and he became a Muslim.

And so it was with Moses and the sorcerers. Thinking Moses was a sorcerer like themselves, they told Pharaoh they could defeat him. For this they were going to receive a great reward.

They performed various acts of sorcery in the presence of Moses and Pharaoh. But when Moses put forth his staff, it became a serpent and swallowed up all their spells and the illusions they had performed. At that point the sorcerers understood that this was not like their spells. They realized it was a miracle and all at once they believed. Pharaoh threatened them with death, and he killed them. But the sorcerers did not renounce their faith, and they became martyrs in the path of God.

If the sorcerers had not committed a great sin and set out to defeat Moses in the presence of Pharaoh, what force and what coincidence could have brought them into Pharaoh's presence and made them taste the wine of martyrdom?

That is why, O workers of sin and rebellion, these stories are good news for you. Your sin can bring you to good works and to God. It is enough for you to see the greatness of God who forgives all sins. Is it not because of these sins which take the place of worship and good works that God has destroyed the despair in people's hearts?

That so many sins are thus transformed into good works make Satan explode with rage and tears him into a hundred thousand pieces.

Satan wants to dupe humans and have them fall into the deep and dark pits I have just told you about. For this he invites you to sin. He makes sin seem to be a pleasure one cannot do without. You are fooled and run fast as the wind straight toward sin. But when these sins to which you hasten are transformed into good works by the grace of God, that is the most infelicitous moment for Satan.

For as Gabriel announced to Hazret Muhammed, God in His mercy first forgives sins, and then in His infinite greatness turns all evils into beauties.

That is why, O champion whose past was as a kafir, and whose present is as a Muslim, I have opened to you the gates of the city of knowledge. Come in through this great gate! Be washed in the light of love awakening in my heart for you.

Consider that you wanted to enrage me. If I had been swept away by rage because you spit in my face, I would have killed you for the sake of rage alone, that is, for a reason not worthy of me, following the commands of my soul. But I was engaged in battle not in order to satisfy my pride but for God's sake.

I also could have killed you for God's sake. But when you spit in my face you opened the possibility of my killing you for my own sake. Of course I did not take that way, and your sin was transformed by God into good work, taking you on to the light. If I, as an instRomant of the great Creator, can give a sinner like you such felicity, consider what glad tidings and treasures He, and without instRomant, will not bestow upon His bondsmen!

How could it be that He would not set before the bondsmen who love Him madly treasuries of spiritual gems and gnosis full of goodness and beauty and eternal life, and Himself?

O new Muslim, this is the divine treasury whose gates I have opened to you.

****

HOW THE MESSENGER, PEACE BE UPON HIM, WHISPERED IN THE EAR OF THE STIRRUP-HOLDER OF THE COMMANDER OF THE FAITHFUL ALI, "I TELL YOU, ALI WILL BE SLAIN BY YOUR HAND."

> "I'm a man whose draught of kindness will not be
> Poison in wrath even for one who slays me
> The Prophet whispered in the ear of my slave
> That he'd sever my head from my neck one day
> The Messenger by inspiration of the Friend
> That my death would come by his hand in the end
> 3890. He said, 'Kill me first, so that this hateful deed
> Will not be able to issue forth from me.'
> I said, 'Seeing that my death will come from you
> How can I seek to make destiny the fool?'
> He fell down before me, 'Noble man,' he said
> You must cut me in two for the sake of God
> So that this malicious end will not be mine
> And my spirit not agonize for its life.'
> I said, 'Go, *the Pen is dry*, and by the Pen
> Many are the banners that are upended
> 3895. In my spirit there is no hatred for you
> For I do not see this as coming from you
> God is the agent, you are His instrument
> How should I oppose and strike God's instrument?'"
> "Then why retaliation?" the champion said
> "That's from God, too, a mystery," Ali said
> "Although at His own action he take offense
> He causes gardens to grow from His offense
> For Him offence at His own act is seemly
> Since He's one in subjugation and mercy
> 3900. He is the prince in phenomena's city
> In all kingdoms He is king of devising
> If He breaks His own instrument, He will mend
> Whatever it may be that has been broken."
> Know the allusion, "*With better We replace*

"The verse we make forgotten or abrogate"[250]
Every shariat He has abrogated
He removed grass and put roses in its stead
Night abrogates occupations of the day
Behold inertia which sets the mind ablaze

3905. Again the light of day abrogates the night
Consuming that inertia by burning bright[251]
To be sure, that sleep and rest are a darkness
But is not the water of life in darkness?[252]
In that darkness are not intellects remade?
Is not the pause a good voice's stock-in-trade?
Contrary is by contrary brought to light
In the heart's black speck He made eternal light
The Prophet's wars became the axis of peace
Those wars were the source of these latter days' peace

3910. By cutting off hundreds of thousands of heads
That heart-ravisher made safe all peoples' heads
A gardener lops off the harmful branch so that
The date-palm may acquire healthfulness and height
The expert cultivator digs up the weeds
So that his orchard fruits smile succulently
And the physician pulls out the rotten teeth
To spare dear ones distress and infirmity
Many advantages are wrapped in defects
For the martyr there is life wrapped up in death

3915. When the throats that swallowed daily bread are slit
"They are nourished, rejoicing"[253] is delicious
When an animal's throat is severed justly
Man's throat grows, and its excellence is increased
How then when a man's throat is cut, consider
Judge this by analogy with the other
A third throat is born which will draw nourishment
From the lights of God and His divine sherbet
The throat that's been cut drinks sherbet, but only
When it dies in the *yes* and is of *not* free

3920. O stingy short-fingered man, now make an end
How long will your spirit live only by bread?
Like the willow, you've no fruit because you've spent
All your dignity for the sake of white bread
If sensory spirit can't leave bread alone
Find alchemy to turn your copper to gold
If you want to have your clothes freshly laundered

---

250. Koran 2:106.
251. Koran 17:12.
252. Koran 25:47; 78:9-11.
253. Koran 3:169-170.

Do not turn away from the bleacher's quarter
Although bread has broken your fast, cling to Him
Who binds up all that is broken, and ascend!
3925.   Since it is His hand that binds what is broken
Surely His breaking must be restoration
If you break something, He'll tell you to fix it
And you will have nor hand nor foot to fix it
For He alone has the right to break a thing
For He knows how to repair a broken thing
The one who knows how to sew, knows how to rip
Whatever He sells, he buys better than it
He turns a house upside-down, leaves it a wreck
Then makes it even better in an instant
3930.   If he severs from a body its one head
He raises at once a hundred thousand heads
If He had not ordained retaliation
Had not said, *"There's life in retaliation"*[254]
Who could on his own stomach raising a sword
Against one who's slave to the decree of God?
Because all whose eyes have been opened by God
Know the slayer is forced by the measuring-out
Anyone who's collared by that destiny
Would strike off the head of his own progeny
3931.   Go, fear God and do not rail at evil men
Know your impotence before divine judgment

There was a man who held Hazret Ali's stirrup while he mounted his horse. He was Ali's groom and stirrup-holder. He was one of ten men invited from Yemen to join in battle against the kafirs. His name was Ibn Muljam. One day while Hazret Muhammed was telling Ali about famous bandits, he said that the worst of bandits was he who killed a man who had been generous with him, and he added:

O Ali! Your martyrdom will come at the hand and sword of a bandit who will come from Yemen named Aburrahman Ibn Muljam.

And so, when soldiers were called upon to come from the four quarters to fight in the war against the Kharijites, ten soldiers came from Yemen, and one of them was named Ibn Muljam.

Each of the ten Yemeni men kissed Hazret Ali's hand presented him with gifts. Ibn Muljam wanted to give him a sword. But he was a man with such a mean and evil spirit that Hazret Ali did not even look him in the face and did not accept his gift.

Ibn Muljam begged to be admitted into his presence and fell down at his feet. "You accepted the gifts of my friends, O Ali, why did you not accept mine? For the sword I have brought you is worth ten Arab swords," he said. Ali said: "How can I accept that sword when you are going to kill me with it." Ibn Muljam was amazed at this and cried: "No, such a crime would never issue forth from me. I have come to lay down my head

---

254. Koran 2:179.

for your sake." Ali replied: "Yes, you came with that intention. But soon discord and defiance will fill your spirit instead of loyalty and love, and you will commit this act."

This was the story Hazret Ali told to the champion on the ground before him and said:

I am such a champion of God that I saw no need to slay my own murderer. I know whom God will employ as the instrument of my death. For Hazret Muhammed told me. He whispered the same thing in the ear of my groom Ibn Muljam, the one who will kill me.

When Ibn Muljam heard about this from me and from the Messenger of God, he came to me and begged forgiveness and repented hundreds of thousands of times. He said:

"O Ali! Please kill me! At least cut off my hands, so that I will not have the power to commit this most heinous of actions!"

I said to him:

"O Ibn Muljam! How should I change God's measuring-out? How could you encourage me to seek a trick to escape God's destiny?"

But he was groveling before me in torment and continuing to beg:

"O Ali! For the sake of God, free me from this ugly body of mine! Clean the rust of my body from the mirror of the world, so that my spirit will not burn in Hell for the worldly sin I will commit! Let me not be God's most despised bondsman!"

I said to him:

"Go away, Ibn Muljam! The judgment written on the tablet of destiny is not like that written on the tablet of the measuring-out. God's command must be carried out in the way God wishes. Whether we wish it or not, the divine command will come to pass as it was commanded. The Pen of destiny has already written that my martyrdom will be by your sword. The ink of the Pen has dried. Many are the banners which have been upended by the writing of the Pen, and states destroyed.

"Give thanks and keep your heart at ease that I bear no anger nor enmity nor resentment toward you. It is not you or your sword that will kill me. In my eyes you are an instrument of God. And you will carry out your function. Whatever God wills, He wills it well. Whatever He wills, it is the most beautiful of measuring-outs. Every suffering He gives us, every trial, is like a boon. In the hand of God's will and power you are steel and I am a wooden stick. You are a sickle and I am the harvest. My Lord will throw me or cut me down, not you."

Then Ibn Muljam asked:

"O Ali! If that is so, then what is the reason for retaliation? Why does God use me as an instrument to kill a great friend of His like you, a champion who is the pride of creation and of Islam? I want to be an instrument in service to you, in good and beautiful works in your service."

I said to him:

"O Ibn Muljam! Retaliation too is God's destiny. It is His command. That command is such that the human intellect does not have the power to understand it."

Only He has the power to change what He has done. For if God wishes to change something He has brought about, it is because there is another divine wisdom in it. His will, which dries up the world and turns it to desert with a wind, also uses another wind to turn it into a paradisiacal garden adorned with limitless greenery and giant roses.

God is one in subjugation and kindness. All the wrath and kindness we encounter is His work, in fact both are bounties no different from each other. The power to do the exact opposite of what He has done is His. That is why God is evident in invisibility and hidden in manifestation.

He is the sole Sultan in this realm of events and creations. He is the one master and ruler of all continents, all countries and thousands of cities and millions of bondsmen.

If God uses a bondsman who is the instrument of His command as an instRomant of retaliation, and the bondsman is injured thereby, he raises that bondsman to a higher and more felicitous life than before. For what creates, slays, destroys and quickens is only the hand of His power.

God has said in the second chapter of the Gracious Koran: "None of Our revelations do We abrogate or cause to be forgotten but We substitute something better or similar. Do you not know that God has power over all things?" Truly, God is engaged in perpetual action, bringing the signs of existence [*vücût ayetlerini*] He has engraved on the face of the universe which He created from one state to another, from one manifestation to another, turning them from one direction to another, or wiping out completely their original states and substituting for them others which are the complete opposite or similar or far superior and beautiful.

That is why many a lack is transformed into a plenitude, many sins into good works, many infidelities into Muslim-ness, many depravities into the most beautiful morality. And if God wishes, He will transform these again, into other or their opposite states.

Whenever God has abrogated the judgment of a shariat, He has swept weeds or thorns from the garden of being and put giant roses in their place.

What transforms wild roses into the most beautiful of cultivated roses, and makes grass, flowers and even trees grow from walls of stone, is His power and judgment alone. By His judgment the nights follow the days and the days the nights. His gift of night to His bondsmen is not the withdrawal of light from their surroundings but the apportioning of a time for rest and the delight of sleep. The state of sleep presents His tired, exhausted bondsmen with a new and vital life.

When night comes to an end and creation is again illuminated with His light, the world smiles on His bondsmen with the dawn. Spirits awaken again to life, to the greatest meaning of life, work, sight and worship. To be sure, sleep is a state of rest and darkness. But consider that the sacred water which gives the spirit eternal life is found in this darkness. Even those plunged in the sleep of the grave which has no awakening will on the Day of Resurrection rise again to life and motion as if they have sipped the water of life.

The nights are a bed of heedlessness for those asleep to divine wisdom and the oneness of God, but for those whose spirits are close to their God, a mysterious mirror where divine beauty is self-disclosed.

Those who recite the Gracious Koran in beautiful voices, or sing to music, pause in order to take a breath and thereby increase their voices and continue the music.

Creation is a realm of opposites. White is brighter when set beside black, light is more beautiful set against shadow. The human eye sees God's light not with the white of the eye but the black pupil of the eye. In the same way, the flame of divine love which sheds light upon all creation burns in the black speck in the heart called "the greatest blackness" [*sevâd-ı azam*].

You know of the wars of Hazret Muhammed. Whether kafir or believer, many bondsmen died in those blessed wars. But those wars brouht peace to the world. Moreover, this peace is eternal for those able to comprehend and to see the light of Muhammed. This means that ware is fundamentally a manifestation of divine subjugation [*kahır*], but its result is kindness, goodness and beauty.

The gardener cuts the boughs of the date-palm so that it may bear more and better fruit. Hearts who boughs and branches are not cut in the path of God by the sword of the measuring-out and destiny will certainly never be able to taste the fruits of gnosis, that is, knowledge of God, and the light of God. The expert gardener also pulls out the wild weeds at the roots of fruit trees so that they will become stronger and more beautiful. The physician pulls his patient's rotten teeth to free him of suffering, and the surgeon must not hesitate to cut off a gangrenous limb in order to save his patient's life.

The bodies of martyrs and all those who pass away in the path of God die in this world, but this is not death, it is resurrection to eternal life. Their worldly nourishment is cut off, they have begun an eternal fast from the bounties which your Lord gives to the people of the world.

God has said in the third chapter of the Gracious Koran: "Do not think of those slain in the path of God as dead. No, they live, finding their sustenance in the presence of their Lord. They rejoice in the bounty provided by God. And with regard to those left behind, who have not yet joined them, they wish to say there is nothing for them to fear nor will they grieve."[255]

The bounties God expends upon them are superior to every value, every delight and beauty.

This is true not only for human but for the other living creatures as well. If an animal is slain or sacrificed according to the shariat, humans derive sustenance from its flesh. Thus the bodies of animals attain the degree of annihilation in man; their virtue increases. If an animal's virtue is increased by death according to the shariat, what might the attainment of a human not be who gives up food in the path of God? If a human, while still in the world, resists the worldly delight, lust and passion he desires and hungers for and rises to a spiritual degree in which he is liberated from his soul and finds the ways while still in the world to attain the bounties God has promised to those who die in His path, there is no measure for the pleasures he will taste and the bounties he will receive.

The Gracious Koran, which is a sea of divine pearls and a limitless treasury of wisdom, is the book which gives the good news of these bounties to spirits on the path of God.

The Gracious Koran announces the good news of bounties which encourage a person on the path of God, not of delights tasted on the path of worldly desires. After all the bounties and delights which pass down the throats of animals and men, when the human throat is closed to worldly delights, a third throat comes into being, and the spirit is then nourished by the lights of God which pass down that throat.

Such a divine light is the sherbet of martyrdom, the sherbet drunk with infinite delight by the throats of believers whose blood is spilt on the ground by the swords of kafirs in battle.

The throat which drinks that divine sherbet must be free of "not" and taste the delight

---

255. Koran 3:169-170.

of annihilation in "yes." For "not" is everything other than God. "Yes" is the answer given by the spirits at the gathering of Alast to your Lord's question, "Am I not your Lord?"

You who see the sustenance of the spirit only in meat and bread! You whose support for others is scant and your vision short! How long will the food of your spirit be worldly delights alone? How much longer will you remain deprived of and distant from tasting the delight of the light of divine love? Like the willow tree, you will be devoid of fruit. Are you going to live unaware of the taste of the spiritual food of your Creator, spending your human power on eating and drinking, pursuing only worldly desire, delight and lust? The world and everything in it is mortal like you. The taste and infinite delight that is not mortal is to attain immortality in that great Creator.

Lust and passion are minerals like copper. If you cannot get rid of your hunger for material things and persist in drinking worldly delights, look to changing that drink. If our belly hungers only for bread of wheat, make a change in what you eat. Drink the elixir which an arrived person can give you. With him taste the delight of spiritual nourishment! So that the copper you have expended your life for may be turned into gold.

If you want the clothes you wear to be clean, do not avoid launderers!

To be sure, bread relieves your hunger. But take care that this does not lead you into addiction to material things and prove an obstacle to the ascension of your soul. Try to liberate yourself from the bonds of nature and animality, take hold of God's mercy and forgiveness and ascend.

The hand of mercy which bandages and heals broken limbs may when necessary break old fractures, which have not healed well, again in order to repair them. When He breaks something, He does so in order to make what He breaks better and stronger than it was before.

But if you try to break your hand and foot, He will tell you to fix what you have broken, and there will be nothing left to you but frustration and the loss of your hand and foot.

People break things supposing they are doing something important, and are not even aware that they have broken anything. What great sin it is when those who have no art and have not yet reached the point where they can make things try to repair the fractures of others and, thinking they will make things better, leave them even worse than before.

So, run to the greatest Maker! Leave yourself to His sublime art, and distinguish well His deputies in this world, for if they are His true deputies they will both repair what is broken in you and show you the ways to ascend to the presence of the greatest Physician.

It is in order to repair broken spirits that the arrived of God are God's deputies. Only he who knows how to sew fabric should cut it. He who will buy better should sell things.

God has said in the second chapter of the Gracious Koran: "O you who believe! The law of retaliation is prescribed to you in cases of murder: the free for the free, the slave for the slave, the woman for the woman. But if any remission is granted by the brother of the slain, then grant any reasonable demand and compensate him with handsome gratitude. This is a concession and a mercy from your Lord. Whoever exceeds the limits after this shall be in grave penalty. In the law of retaliation there is life for you, O men of understanding."[256]

If God had not said there was life in retaliation, what bondsman by what power could smite a bondsman of God's with the sword? For every believer whose eyes have been opened by God knows very well that to kill or be killed is the necessity alone of the measuring-out and destiny which come to all.

Anyone who hears the command of the measuring-out and destiny may, as the instRomant of God, willing or no, become the murderer even of his own child.

So go! Fear the wrath of God! Known your impotence before divine power! All who trust not in God but in the soundness and righteousness of the path they have taken are plagued by pride and deficient.

****

HOW ADAM, PEACE BE UPON HIM, MARVELED AT THE ERROR OF IBLIS AND THOUGHT HIMSELF BETTER

One day Adam looked at Iblis the wretched
Judging him as false and worthy of contempt
He behaved conceitedly with arrogance
Thinking Iblis the accursed ridiculous
Came a shout of God's rivalry, "Sincere one!
You are ignorant of mysteries hidden
If He were to turn the sheepskin inside-out
He would rip up from its very root the mount

3940.   At once tear the veils of a hundred Adams
Make of a hundred Iblises new Muslims."
"I repent of that bad regard," Adam said
"I will not think so arrogantly again
You who aid those who call out for help, lead us!
There is no pride in knowledge or in riches
Let not stray a heart You've guided by Your grace
Keep the evil the Pen has written away
Drive evil destiny from off our spirits
Keep the brethren of resignation with us

3945.   Naught is bitterer than Your separation
Naught but torment in loss of Your protection
Our worldly goods rob the goods of our spirits
Our bodies rip the clothes off of our spirits
Since our hands devour our feet, can anyone
Survive but by safety of Your protection
And should he bear off his life from grave danger
He'll bear off a stock of bad luck and terror
For without the Beloved spirit shall be
Blind and blue alone for all eternity

3950.   If You give no way, though he may save his life
A spirit is dead that without You has life
It is fitting for You if You scold Your slaves

---

256. Koran 2:178-179.

You who succeed in all things You undertake
And if You say that the sun and moon are chaff
And the stature of the cypress bent in half
And the Throne and heavens worthy of contempt
And the mines and seas of all value bereft
That is proper to the perfection that's Yours
Power to perfect all that's mortal is Yours

3955. For You are pure, maker of non-existents
Of danger and not-being independent
He knows how to burn that causes things to grow
For when He tears a thing, He knows how it's sewn
Every autumn he causes gardens to burn
He makes the rose grow again with its color
Saying, "Withered ones, come out, be fresh again
Come, be fair and of fair renown once again!"
The narcissus eye went blind, He restored it
The reed's throat was cut, again He fostered it

3960. Since we are products of craft and not craftsmen
We are nothing more than humble and content
We are all of the soul and do soul-like things
If You do not call us, we are Ahrimans
We have been delivered from Ahriman thus
Because You redeemed our spirits from blindness
To all they that possess life You are the guide
What is a blind man without a staff and guide?
Except You, all that's pleasant or unpleasant
Is the essence of fire and burns man to death

3965. He who finds protection and support in fire
Is a Magian and a Zoroaster
Everything is vain but God and verily
His grace is a cloud that rains incessantly

One day Hazret Adam regarded Satan with hatred and contempt. Regarding that accursed creature, he was engulfed with pride, thinking of his own high station. He began to laugh at the state Satan was in. But the rivalry of God would not accept this. God addressed Adam and said: "O simple man! You do not know the divine mysteries. And it is natural that you should not. For it is not possible to know Our mysteries without Our consent. The goal of the creation of yourself and all the people who will descend from you, and this universe you see, is the self-disclosure of our one and absolute being in the realm of manifestation. Our subjugating and majesty has been self-disclosed in this realm, as has Our beauty. While the friends choose Our self-disclosure of beauty, Iblis displayed majesty, accepting Our pain and trial.

Abandon self-reliance and take refuge in Our unity. Do not forget that the force which drives you to disobey and eat the forbidden fruit is also Our destiny and measuring-out.

If God turns the sheepskin inside-out, that is, if He shows His wrath and majesty instead of His mercy; if He sees the error of a person's ways and feels it necessary to make the power of His subjugation known; even if that person is apparently in a state of profound faith and worship, the power of God will rip that immovable mountain of faith up from the root and turn it upside-down. He will send the one who ascends the seven heavens like Satan down to the bottom of the seven layers of earth. In an instant He will tear the veil of faith of hundreds of Adams and bring hundreds of satans to a new Muslim's level of faith and purity.

Messenger Adam came to himself at that moment and said: "My God! Again I have fallen into error. I felt pride at being one of your chosen bondsmen. But I repent, may I never again look at anyone with eyes which see evil; may I never fall into inappropriate thoughts." Now:

My Lord, You who send Your grace and guidance to those who seek help; who cry from their hearts, "O my God, come to our aid!" Show us the path which leads to You. Guide us to your grace and do not show us the way that does not lead to You.

Do not make us proud of these transient riches and humble knowledge! Do not make us among those who boast of these.

Do not separate from the path those who have set down Your path. Take us far from every evil destiny has written for us! Do not deprive us of friends who love their God, who are on His path, follow His command and love Him! Make us joyful only by union with You, and my God, do not scorch us in the intolerable fire of separation from You.

We know that for the spirit there is nothing more bitter than separation from You. If You do not annihilate this transient being of ours, if You do not deem us worthy of the felicity of being in You, we will be left in endless torment and complexity.

Our worldly goods seek to plunder our spiritual wealth. Our bondage to the world seeks to sever our tie to Your divine realm. This visible body of ours struggles to hinder us from reaching our true being, which is invisible like You. Our bodily garment wishes to destroy our spiritual garb and leave us naked without Your robe of honor.

If when our foot wants to go toward the good and true, our own hand prevents it, if our own souls do us the greatest wrong, how should we save our spirits from that devil of error without Your liberating aid?

As long as a person who has with obedience and worship saved himself from the dangers of evil has not saved his spirit from such dangers into which the soul tumbles as duality and selfhood, neither can he be saved from the misfortune into which he has fallen.

In a word, as long as the spirit does not find the spirit of spirits, it has condemned itself to eternal blindness. Such a spirit must suffer an infinite fire of separation and inexhaustible mourning.

If You do not raze the wall of duality between the spirit and the spirit of spirits, if You do not show the way to the spirit separated from You and submit it to a murshid, its state is no longer separation, it is death. The spirit thus separated from You is eternally dead, even though it appear to be alive!

If You are angered at Your bondsmen and scold them, Your anger is not wrath but grace for those who understand. For such spirits feel the greatness of Your mercy and grace even in your reproach. You scold the bondsman for his fault, but you do not reject him. This is proper for You. For in all the universe only You are flawless.

You can say that the moon and sun have no light. You may find a straight path crooked or not like a beautiful cypress. You may look down on the Throne, which is the highest level of the heavens, You may find the earth devoid of gold and the seas poor in fish and even water. For Your perfection is superior to all of these. To see and to create more beautiful, better and flawless things is Your art, Your skill alone.

For You are far from all defect, You are safe from any kind of danger and especially have no fear of destruction. It is You who give being to nothingness. I is You who when there was nothing at all, created everything that exists so that Your bondsmen should know You and find You. It is enough that all You have created out of nothing should sooner or later attain the felicity of finding You and understanding You.

For You also have the power to destroy and wipe out those You have created. Only He who can sew has the right to tear, only He who can make more perfect has the right to destroy.

Each autumn You set the garden ablaze with hues of red, yellowing and withering. Then when the day comes, You send Your mercy to the same garden and make pink roses bloom within greenery, leaving the world You withered in a sultanate of color and harmony.

With all of this You wish to say to the spirits: O spirit who comprehends nothingness and death! O body rotting beneath the ground! Walk! Come to existence from nothingness. Just as this rose you see has attained being in spring after a winter of nothingness, you too must shed the realm of nothingness which is this world, be purified of worldly passion and filth and hasten to be annihilated in Me, the One true Being.

The narcissus flower fades and its beautiful eye goes blind. You power opens those eyes again. The reed is cut, it's body dries out. The hand of art caresses it, giving it spirit and breath. The dried-out reed becomes a flame-voiced flute which sings of You, telling Your story and giving voice to the suffering of separation from You.

We are not creators; we are the accumulated creatures. We are among those who have seen their flaws, their impotence, and their nothingness before Your sublime power with the eye of truth and submitted to Your command. Our only wealth, our only pride, is to have been created by You, to taste the delight of being spirits to be disciplined in a body in order to return to You.

We have been made slave to a soul. We all cry in error, "My soul! My soul!" We think only of our own souls and cannot see beyond our own noses, and if You do not call us to You with Your beautiful voice, we will all remain at the nadir of the black earth like red devils.

Your grace has rescued us from blindness and the misfortune of not being able to see beyond the veil. With the eyes You Have opened for us, we have seen that there are satans on earth. And again, it is Your grace which has saved us from the satans.

You are the sole guide of spirits which have taken on a bodies so as to know You and come to You. For it is You who have said: "O My bondsmen, you tread a path other than the path I have shown you, and you are all in error; seek the right path from Me, I will grant it."

For that is what Your Messenger told us. And so we ask you for the path. We request a staff and aid. Would you leave us with no staff, without aid and without eyes?

We know and believe that whether beautiful or ugly, bitter or sweet, everything other than You is empty, transient and most difficult of all, burning fire.

Whether a person comes close to raging fires and worships, with a bright red face, the fire he supposes is You, or worships at the temple of the fire of lust he cannot forgo, both are the same thing. He is both a Magian and Zoroaster. Whether he bows down before lust, before the soul, or before the pleasures of nature, he worships other than God and is on the wrong path.

In sum, as the Arab poet Labid said, know that all is vain but God. Hazret Muhammed said that was the truest thing Labid ever said. As for those who see nothing other than God, for them nothing is in vain.

The grace of God is a cloud raining down mercy from the skies without cease.

****

RETURNING TO THE STORY OF THE COMMANDER OF THE FAITHFUL ALI, MAY GOD HONOR HIS PERSON, AND THE TOLERANCE HE SHOWED TO HIS MURDERER

> Return now to Ali and his murderer
> And the great kindness he showed his murderer
> "Day and night I see the murderer," he said
> "With my own eyes, yet feel for him no hatred
> For death has become sweet as manna to me
> My death holds resurrection tight as can be
>
> 3970. The death without death is made lawful for us
> Rations without rations are bounty for us
> Apparently death, it is life inwardly
> Hidden subsistence while cut off outwardly
> Birth to the embryo nestled in the womb
> Is a going out, and in the world it blooms
> Since I love death and long for it intensely
> The forbidding '*don't cast yourselves*'[257] is for me
> Only the sweet berry is prohibited
> What need for sour ones to be prohibited?
>
> 3975. Berries that are sour in both kernel and flesh
> Prohibition is in that very sourness
> The berry of death has become sweet to me
> '*No, they live*'[258] was revealed on account of me
> *Slay me, trusted friends, as if I were to blame*
> *For me eternal life is in being slain*
> *Truly, my life is in my death, O young man*
> *How long shall I be parted from my homeland?*
> *If my staying here were not separation*
> *He would not have said, 'We return unto Him.'*"
>
> 3980. He who returns comes back to his own city
> From the turning wheel of time to unity

Let us return again to the story of Hazret Ali. There is great wisdom in the tolerant way Ali treated the man who was trying to kill him. It tells us how a friend of God behaves both in the face of death and in the face of destiny.

---

257. Koran 2:195.
258. Koran 3:169.

Hazret Ali continued:

I have no enmity toward a person charged with the duty of killing me. I see him night and day, but feel no anger or reproach toward him within me. For death is to me as sweet as manna. I sense the good news of one who informs me of the resurrection God will bring about after death. I have faith that this resurrection will be another, eternal life. I feel happy thinking that death is the bondsman's going to God. I have faith that this is a beginning not an end; that it is immortality.

The baby migrating to this world from the mother's womb blooms like a flower. In the same way, the spirit in the case of the body in this world wishes to bloom in the other world. It feels the job of joining the giant and eternal roses of the paradisiacal gardens there.

I feel love and longing for death. In the second chapter of the Gracious Koran God has forbidden His bondsmen from hastening to death with the prohibition: "Do not cast yourselves into danger with your own hands."[259]

In fact death is sweet and perhaps for that reason God has forbidden death to humans by saying they should not kill themselves by their own hand. If death were a bitter thing, why would He forbid them to kill themselves? For it is the things which seem sweet but are in fact not that are forbidden. People are not told to abstain from eating bitter fruit. For even if told to, people will not eat it. The fact that both the rind and inside of a fruit is bitter itself means that God has forbidden people to eat it.

The friends of God who know the truth do not fear death, on the contrary they thirst for it and seek it. They are those who comprehend the meaning of God's verse, "Do not think suppose that those who die in the path of God are dead, they are alive in the presence of their Creator."

Mansur Hallaj would say one day: "O my trusted friends! Kill me like a villain! For my true life is in my death. For my homeland is there, it is that greatest, that most beautiful One Himself. So tell me, O Friend! O Beloved! How long will I be far from my homeland?

"If my true homeland, my home and everything of mine were in this world, if I were not separated and in exile from my real homeland by being in this world, would God have said in the second chapter of the Gracious Koran, 'We belong to God and surely to God we will return.'"

The return is that act by which a person goes back to the place from whence he came. Here "return" has no other meaning but to go back to one's origin. So death is the return to the true homeland of we who have broken away from God and been in exile so many years.

Both material and spiritual death and very different for God's chosen bondsmen that for the common run of people whose measure of feeling and comprehension has not developed. For lovers of God both material death, which is the annihilation [fenâ] of the body, and spiritual death, which is the disciplining and reformation of the soul, are sweet and delicious. For they know that, as it says in the gracious verse, for those martyred in the path of God there is the bounty of resurrection to a new life. Spiritual death gives them immortality in God [bekâ] and the felicity of opening their eyes in the realm of subsis-

---

259. Koran 2:195.

tence [*devam*] and becoming eternal in the infinity of that pleasure and joy.

But those who are uncooked and undeveloped have a fearful resistance and aversion of the kind felt for unknown things to both material death and spiritual death. For they are incapable and deprived of comprehending the good news that awaits them beyond the veil of both deaths.

****

HOW THE STIRRUP-HOLDER OF ALI, MAY GOD HONOR HIS PERSON, CAME AND SAID, "FOR GOD'S SAKE, KILL ME AND DELIVER ME FROM THAT FATE."

"'O Ali, kill me quickly,' again he said
'That I'll not see that bitter hour and moment
I make it lawful for you, now spill my blood
So my eye won't see that dread resurrection.'
I said, 'Should each atom be a murderer
And go to attack you wielding a dagger
None could cut the tip of one hair off of you
Since the Pen has writ such a line against you
3985.   But I will intercede for you, do not grieve
I'm master of spirit, not the body's slave
This body possesses no value for me
Without it I am manly, son of manly
Dagger and sword are like sweet basil to me
My death is my narcissus bed and my feast
He who tramples on his body in this way
How should he covet princedom and caliphate?
Outwardly he seeks position and power
So he may show emirs the way to power
3990.   So he may give fresh spirit to emirate
And fruit to the palm tree of the Caliphate.""

Hazret Ali related to the man whom he'd defeated but not killed because he spit in his face that the stirrup-holder came back and begged: "'Ya Ali! Kill me! As soon as possible, save me from the shame of being your murderer, this greatest punishment of all! So that I may not see that moment when I kill you! Do not hesitate! Shed my blood! May my blood be lawful for you! So that my eye may not look upon you wrongfully. May the eye that looks upon you wrongfully go blind.'

"I said to him: 'O Ibn Muljam! Do not suffer in vain! We do not have the power to change this destiny and measuring-out.

"'Know that if every atom of all beings were to come alive and all become blood-shedding arrows or swords and leap upon you with the intent to kill, not even one of them could bring you death. They could not even harm one of your hairs, let alone kill you.

"'For the Pen of the measuring-out has written thus in your case. You cannot be killed without your having carried out that command. But do not feel sorrow for this, it will also be me who intercedes for you when we reach the other world tomorrow.

"'In fact God, who has charged you with the task of killing me, knows your suffering much better than I do. And do not forget that in striking me, in shedding my blood, you will kill the me whom you see. You will not kill the real me. You will tear apart the cage of my body and free my spirit. That is your task. You will kill my form, not me. For do not forget that in fact you cannot kill the me expressed by:

There is inside me an "I" within my "I"

No person and no power can kill it. For it is the only immortal being in these visible and invisible realms.

"'My real manliness and heroism is not in this visible body of mine. I am a manly man completely outside of this body. Sword and dagger are my basil, my flowers. Death is my feast of fellowship and felicity, my garden of Paradise filled with narcissuses.

"'Can there be greed for emirate and caliphate in someone who treads his own body thus underfoot?

"'My duty in caliphate and emirate is to show the way to caliphs and emirs and to be an example of the spirit, faith, justice and manner in which caliphate and emirate should be carried out.

"'Emirate and caliphate gain me nothing. I possess emirate and caliphate in order to bring a new spirit to the rank of emir and to make of the sapling of the caliphate a great tree which will bring forth fruits of truth, justice and faith.'"

****

EXPLAINING THAT THE MESSENGER, PEACE BE UPON HIM, SOUGHT TO CONQUER MECCA AND BEYOND MECCA NOT OUT OF LOVE OF WORLDLY DOMINION—FOR HE SAID: "*THE WORLD IS A CARCASS*"—BUT ON THE CONTRARY, AT THE DIVINE COMMAND

And the Prophet's struggle for Mecca's conquest
How can he of love of this world be suspect?
On the day of trial[260] he shut his eyes and heart
To the treasures the seven heavens impart
When the horizons of each of the heavens
Were filled with houris and jinn who gazed on him
They had adorned themselves for the sake of him
So where is his care for other than the Friend?

3995.   He was so filled by the majesty of God
He did not give way to those nearest to God
"*Neither prophet sent nor angel nor spirit
—do you understand?—can be contained in it*"[261]
"Our eye did not rove,[262] unlike the crow," he said
"We are drunk on the Dyer, not flowerbeds."
Since treasures of the heavens and intellects
Appeared as straw to the eye of the Prophet
What should Mecca, Syria and Iraq be
That he would long for them and show bravery?

4000.   That conjecture belongs to the hypocrite
By analogy with his own mean spirit

260. Koran 53:1-18.
261. A sacred hadith.
262. Koran 53:17.

When you make a yellow glass veil to look through
All the light of the sun seems yellow to you
Shatter that blue and yellow glass, so you can
Come to distinguish the dust from the horseman
The horseman is enveloped in rising dust
What you fancy a man of God is but dust
Iblis saw dust; "This offspring of clay," he said
"How should he rival me with my fiery head?"

4005.   As long as you see those dear to God as men
Know that view is a legacy from Satan
If you're no child of Iblis, O malcontent
How did you receive that dog's inheritance?
"I'm no dog, I'm God's Lion, I worship Him
The Lion of God is he who escapes form
This world's lion hunts down prey and provision
The lion of the Lord seeks death and freedom
Since in death he sees hundredfold existence
Like the moth he burns away his existence

4010.   Desire for death is a necklace for the true
A desire which was made a test of the Jews[263]
God said in the Koran, 'O tribe of the Jews
For the sincere death is treasure and a boon
Even as there is a desire for profit
There is a desire for death better than that
O Jews, for the sake of your reputation
Put this request in speech uttered with the tongue.'
Not one single Jew had so much bold vigor
To speak when Muhammed raised up that banner

4015.   'If they should utter this with their tongues,' he said
'There'd not be in the world one single Jew left.'
Then the Jews brought property and tax on land
Saying, 'Do not put us to shame, O bright lamp.'"
To this discourse there's apparently no end
Give me your hand, since your eye has seen the Friend
From this dunghill come to a bed of roses
Since you have seen the torch burning in darkness
Don't stop but keep going quickly step by step
Toward Iram's garden from this bottomless pit

Consider: The Messenger of God waged war on the kafirs, battled for the sake of God and conquered Mecca. Could he have taken Mecca out of love of the world and desire for command?

God had already tested him on the night of the Miraj, spreading out before him the treasures of the seven heavens. This truth is related in the fifty-third chapter of the Gracious Koran:

---

263. Koran 2:94-111; 62:6-7.

By the star as it descends, your companion is neither astray nor is he misled. He does not speak out of his own desire. It is no less than inspiration sent down to him.

For indeed he saw Gabriel again while coming down, near the Sidre Tree. There was the paradise to be reached.

There Muhammed's eye neither swerved nor went beyond bounds. For truly did he see the greatest of the signs of his Lord.

This means that while Hazret Muhammed was on the Miraj the treasures of the realms of sovereignty and domination were displayed to him, but he did not incline toward any of them, neither with his heart nor his eye, he only requested the command of his Lord, performing his duty of relating His commands to His bondsmen and avoiding everything which draws the eye and heart.

The spirits of the seven heavens ran to see him and along with the houris filled up the heavens.

God put before him all of His beauties, so that he could see and appreciate them. But Hazret Muhammed was not in a state to look at anything but the one and single Friend. God was his sole beloved.

His heart was filled with the mightiness and majesty of God. Even the arrived of God who have beheld the gleaming of the divine light and are plunged in it could not reach the station He did.

Was it not the Messenger himself who said: "In the station of unity we have attained there is place neither for a messenger of God nor angel of the Throne."

Truly, neither Gabriel nor the angels closest to God nor any messenger has been able to reach the realm of oneness and beauty he reached and was accepted into.

That is the place where his eye which saw and love none but that Beloved saw nothing but God and did not swerve. This station is the station of annihilation in God [*fenâfillah*] described in Koranic verse and sacred hadith.

He who is drunk on God and reaches that station cannot become drunk on just any garden, or even notice one.

For the eye of Hazret Muhammed, even the treasures of the heavens seemed as worthless as a piece of straw. Mecca, Damascus, Iraq—could these lands for him be worth fighting wars to possess them?

Those who suppose that Hazret Muhammed was pursuing worldly desires and sultanate and those who see the world through their own eyes. In fact it is not possible for those who view the world through the window of their own inner vileness to see it any differently.

For example, someone who puts a yellow glass before his eyes will see the world as yellow. For him now the light of the sun is yellow, and the blueness of the heavens is yellow. But what is desired is to be able to see the sun of oneness not in the colors of plurality but in the color of its own colorlessness.

You must now break the yellow or blue glass before your eyes so that you may see the horseman who is enveloped in a cloud of dust, that foremost rider of all creation, in his own color. The spirits of God's prophets and friends are horsemen enveloped in the dust of the body; you who see only dust, when will you see the horseman galloping within it?

When Iblis saw Adam he could not see the light of God and spirit of God within that body created of clay. He saw even the body enveloping that light as clay in the form of a body, and therefore did not bow down to Adam, thinking, "How could clay be superior to a being like me created of fire?"

Ali, the Lion of God, said to his future murderer Ibn Muljam:

Although I am known as God's lion, the lion I resemble is not the lion you know, on the contrary, it is the lion of immortality [beka] in the state of a spirit liberated from all majestic appearance and form, separated from the body, roaring only for God.

The worldly lion seeks food. It attacks in greed, burning with the passion to take possession of the entire forest, all creatures.

But the lion of spirit has no need of material nourishment. Its sole and inexhaustible nourishment is love of God.

A lion filled with the love of God wishes to be liberated from majesty, mane and claw and subsist in God. It wishes to escape slavery to the soul die to the qualities of the body.

For once such a lion has died its body is destroyed, like the body of a moth which goes up in smoke, burned in the flame of a candle. But the flame was worth it, its spirit has become light itself.

To be able to want death is a desire as profound as that of true lovers for union with the beloved. For in that death lovers will attain the mystery of being able to see divine beauty. But this same desire for death was a harsh test for the Jews. For regarding the Jews who disbelieved in Islam, "Claiming that they are superior to all other humans and that the entire world, and the bounties of the afterworld and Paradise, were created by God for them," God sent his most beloved Messenger these verses:

Say: "If the other world be for you especially and not for anyone else, seek death, if you are sincere."

Say: "O Jews! If you think you are friends to God to the exclusion of others, then express your desire for death, if you are truthful."

"O Jews! Death to the body is inexhaustible treasure and infinite gain for those who are true."

Since you enjoy the pleasures and passions of great gains in the world, why do you not seek the greatest of all gains? You do not seek death from the depths of your hearts and spirits, but could you at least lie and seek it with your tongues and say, 'If only we would die.' Even if just from the corner of your lips, could you make a request for your own death?

When Hazret Muhammed made this invitation according to God's command, not one Jew dared to reply. It was as if they had sensed the meaning and result of this great proposition, for Hazret Muhammed said: If even one among the Jews had said this and dared, even if only with the tip of his tongue, to ask for death, there would not be one Jew left in the world.

Then they asked Hazret Muhammed for asylum. They brought property and tax, and said: "O great Messenger! We are among those who know the righteousness of your prophethood. But because of our ignorance and passion for money and worldly avarice, which has become a tradition for us, we cannot come to the right path. For that reason do not ask us to seek death, do not disgrace us before the people by asking us to say something we cannot do and will not say."

Thus the Jews became a clear example of those who cannot abandon worldly desires and passions and who, defeated by their own souls, cannot attain high spiritual degree.

They remained in the position of those who know the truth, sense he danger, yet are so helpless before their own souls that they cannot abandon the world.

There is no end to the subject of love and friendship and desire for death and hope for union. O spirit! Since your heart's eye has seen the beauty of the Friend, come, give me your hand so that you may reach the path of God! You who although in your body are buried in bodily darkness, have succeeded in scattering that darkness to see the light of oneness. There is no value in staying in the bottomless pit of nature. Come out of the well! The gardens of Paradise await you.

****

How the Commander of the Faithful Ali, may God honor his person, said to his Companion, "When you spat in my face, my soul was stirred and there remained no Sincerity of Action; that was what prevented me from killing you."

4020.   The Commander of the Faithful told that youth
      "In the hour of battle, O champion, when you
      Spat in my face, the soul's passions were aroused
      And the temper of my disposition fouled
      Half was for sake of God, half for passion's sake
      In God's affair one must not associate
      You were fashioned in form by hand of the Lord
      You were not made by me, you're the work of God
      Break a form God has made, but by God's command
      Take up the Friend's stone to cast at the Friend's glass."

4025.   Hearing this, in the heart of the infidel
      Such a light appeared that he severed his belt
      "I had sown the seed of injustice," he said
      "I had imagined you to be different
      You're the scale balanced according to the One
      No, you are of all balancing-scales the tongue
      You are my family, kin and origin
      The blaze of my candle and my religion
      I am the slave of that lamp which seeks the eye
      The lamp from which your lamp's radiance derives

4030.   I am slave of the wave of that sea of light
      Which conveys such a pearl as this into sight
      Offer me profession of the faith, for I
      Regard you as most exalted of this time."
      Nearly fifty persons of his tribe and kin
      As lovers turned their faces to religion
      So many throats, multitudes, Ali redeemed
      From the sword by the sword of his clemency

Clemency's sword is sharper than a steel sword
It wins more victories than a hundred hordes
4035.   With only two mouthfuls of food, O alas
Thought's exhilaration has been frozen fast
By a grain of wheat Adam's sun is eclipsed
As the Dragon's tail blocks the full moon's brilliance
See the heart's subtlety—one handful of clay
And its moon chases the Pleiades away
When bread was spirit, it was beneficial
When it becomes form it stirs up denial
Like green thistles a camel eats and derives
From them a hundred benefits and delights
4040.   Those same thistles when they're dried up and withered
And eaten by a camel in the desert
What a pity such nourishing rose's leaves
Become a sword to cut its palate and cheek
Bread is like the green thistles when it's spirit
When it becomes form, then it is dry and thick
With the habit that you used to formerly
Eat of it, O delicate Husameddin
After that same scent, you're eating this dry crust
Although the spirit is now mingled with dust
4045.   It now cuts flesh, it is dry and mixed with clay
O camel! Abstain now from eating that hay
The words coming now are much too soiled with mud
Cover up the well, the water's fouled with mud
So that God may again make it sweet and pure
So that He who muddied it may make it pure
Patience brings the object of desire, not haste
Have patience—*and it is God who knows what's best*

Finally the Commander of the Faithful said to the enemy champion before him:

O champion, while we were fighting you were defeated. As my sword was about to take your life you spit in my face in confusion.

This was an action I never expected in a moment of combat, and it was very hard for me. But I was not fighting with you for myself, in order to satisfy myself or win honor. I was fighting the infidel. I was fighting in the path of God, in order to obey His commands and punish those who disobey those commands.

If I had been swept away by my soul and killed you, it would have been half for God's sake, and half for my own.

But to think of any duality in the path of God, who created us and gave us permission to reach Him and fight for Him, is no to be worthy of Him.

On the other hand, how could I kill you for my own sake, for you too are human. You too are a form appearing in God's earthly realm. The form made by God can only be broken by God's hand. Only His stone can shatter His crystal. A bondsman has no power to strike a stone against that matchless crystal.

Now do you understand everything?

When the infidel champion heard this, such a light enveloped his heart that he severed the belt around his waist, the belt worn by fire-worshippers, and threw it aside. Thus the tie which bound him to infidelity was broken.

In short, he came to faith and said to Hazret Ali:

O Ali! What a pity that I had not understood you. I thought you were among those who do battle for soul and desire. But know I know that you are a balance-scale with the just and fair nature of God, that is, right and just like He is. Your character is the character of the Creator.

The light which now fills me came to me from your light. You have given my spirit the profound delight of faith. This light is your legacy. So you are my origin, my tribe and my relation.

You found your Lord, who seeks eyes to see His light and hearts to love His beauty, by means of His greatest messenger. Now I too am bondsman and slave to the same Messenger, who offers the light of God only to eyes which see.

O Ali! Teach me the Profession of Islam [*Kelime-i Şehadet*]! Pronounce it and I will repeat it. I want to hear the faith in God and His Messenger from you and affirm it. O Ali, you are the pride of time and crown of all heads.

When Hazret Ali put his steel sword in its sheath and struck his enemy with the sword of clemency, he made the divine light burn in his spirit and caused fifty other people related to that champion to become Muslims. They all became believers treading the path of God.

For the sword of clemency is sharper than the sword of steel. It wins victories superior to those won by hundreds of soldiers.

****

Unfortunately we became hungry and ate a few morsels of food. After eating, our power to continue with the *Spiritual Couplets* has flagged. The wisdom of Luqman has been affirmed. Luqman used to say to his son, "O son, thought slumbers when the belly is full."

He who eats too much is always left in the darkness of nature. The superiority of fasting to other kinds of worship is in its virtue of keeping the mind awake while fasting and causing it to ascend to God. The dictionary meaning of *savm*, "fasting" [*oruç*] is "sublimity." "Fasting" is called *savm* because it is the most sublime of all kinds of worship. He who wishes to knock at the door of the realm of sovereignty [*melekût alemi*] takes recourse to hunger and thirst. He who wishes to shut down the paths of the satans rectifies them by hunger and thirst. One should consider that Messenger Adam's sun was eclipsed when he ate one single grain of wheat.[264] The shadow that fell between sun and moon darkened the light of the full moon.

Behold the fine, transparent beauty of the heart! A handful of clay, a few morsels, have left the heart's moon in darkness. The subtlety of spiritual comprehension is so delicate that the world and thought of it extinguish that comprehension. However much food is necessary to live, it can be an obstacle to feeling, thinking, and especially to burn-

---

264. The reference here is to wheat as the forbidden fruit eaten by Adam and Eve.—Trans.

ing with love of God.

Because food is for the world and what is intended here by "morsel" is the human condition [*beşeriyet*], the desire of the soul.

If only it were possible for us to always take spiritual nourishment. When food is spiritual, it has many benefits. For spiritual bread is knowledge of God, gnosis. The spirit nourished by it finds immortal life [*ölümsüz hayat*].

This spiritual food is like, for example, green thistles. If a camel eats the thistles while they are still green, it derives a hundred benefits from them. Its coat is beautified, its disposition is calmed, its milk becomes nourishing, its foals become sweet and fat. But if the same thistles dry out and become hard and a camel in the desert eats them, its mouth and the insides of its cheeks are torn. The camel will complain and sigh: "What a pity that such a well-cultivated rose has become like a sword without flavor or spirituality; it is a thing tearing up the mouth and throat."

So, Husameddin, while the nourishment we tasted together was spiritual, it never tired us, it gave us profound pleasure. We have considered together the ways to reach God. We have tasted the delight of divine love. We narrated the adventures of Sultan Spirit. We saw what becomes of the lion of soul.

We have known the truths of Hazret Muhammed. We have set down the paths leading to divine mysteries. We have lived in the realm of days and nights woven of delight, pleasure and joy.

In short, while what we ate was such spiritual nourishment, like green thistles it brought us hundreds of spiritual pleasures and benefits.

O beautiful man! O dear Husameddin! What you have tasted at my table has always been that spiritual food and you became accustomed to those morsels of pleasure and joy.

Now you are trying to eat this dry bread according to the same custom, with the same delight. But that spirit and taste is no longer in the bread. The meaning in your pure and stainless spirit-mirror has become clouded with dust and dirt not from the food of oneness but the food of plurality.

The thread of speech is broken and fallen on the ground, stained by dirt and mud. The pearls of speech are scattered. They can't be seen for all the dust and dirt. The clear water that mirrored the Lord you saw is now cloudy. The pure water we drank is mixed with human dregs.

What is that meddling worldly morsel which has clouded the pure water of the heart's well? Before we take it in, come, let us cover the mouth of the well.

So that the water may become clear again. For the spiritual water we drew from the heart's well is clouded, dried up and gone. Wait! Let the pure, sparkling waters of gnosis come into the well again by the secret ways of God and His sublime springs.

O body, that with two morsels of worldly food reaches material comfort! Take your rest! The eyes of Husameddin are clouded by the tears he has wept over the loss of that lover, that gnostic, that beloved wife of his! Open and beg mercy for she who has been reunited with God!

And you, Jalaleddin! Be silent until the waters are purified and display the sublime mysteries beneath. For God who clouds waters will purify them again.

You know that all comes with patience. Great wishes are not attained with haste. Patience is half of faith and the way to the greatest of victories. True gnosis is to know when to speak and when to be silent.

How many mysteries we have told. But far from saying everything all at once, in order to speak mysteries at the proper time and to those who understand, how often have our lips remained closed like stubborn rosebuds. The God to whom we have given our hearts is just and created all things with justice and measure. And thus He rules. None of his creatures, be they living or no, be they events or thoughts, is without account and measure. Come, let us conform to that measure.

He knows that we have given our hearts to Him. For it was He who gave His heart to us first of all, He created His bondsmen in profound love. The bondman's love is the manifestation of God's love. Now let us reflect upon the meaning of being one of God's beloveds and be silent a while.

Let us know that only God knows and performs the best and most righteous of works.

Listen! Commentary on *The Spiritual Couplets* of Mevlana Rumi

Glossary

Abu Bakr or Abu Bakir – The first "Rightly Guided Caliph" or successor to the Prophet Muhammed.

Abu Hafs – Abu Hafs al-Haddad, Sufi d. 880 in Nishapur.

Ahmed – Variation of the Prophet's name, Muhammed.

Aisha – A wife of the Prophet Muhammed.

Alast – Literally "Am I not . . . ?" in Arabic. The phrase refers to an event in pre-eternity when God gathered the spirits of all mankind and asked them, "Am I not your Lord?" and they replied, "Yes, we testify" (Koran 7:172).

Ankaravi, Rüsuhi Ismail – Ottoman Mevlevi shaykh and author (d. 1631) who wrote the most widely-known commentary on Mevlana's *Spiritual Couplets*.

Anqa – A mythological bird, often identified with the Simurgh, sharing characteristics of the phoenix and dwelling on the Qaf Mountain range which encircles the world.

Aşık Paşa – Anatolian author (d. 1311) of the Turkish *Garibnâme* (Book of the Stranger).

Azrael – The angel of death.

barzakh – Literally "isthmus," an intermediary region which serves to connect two realms.

besmele – The ritual formula, "In the name of God."

bey – A Turkish commander or nobleman (in today's usage, simply "Mr.").

bondsman – Any human being as a creature dependent upon God.

Buraq – One of two creatures the Prophet Muhammed rode during the Miraj.

Chelebi Husameddin – Husameddin was Mevlana's deputy and, at the time Mevlana composed the *Spiritual Couplets*, his secretary. "Chelebi" is a polite title.

destiny – Destiny [*kazâ*] is an event or form in which the pre-eternal "measuring out" [*kader, takdîr*] is manifested in the world.

friend – When the word "friend" is used is an abstract manner, as in "the friend," rather that "my friend," etc., it is a term meaning "friend of God" [*velî*]. When capitalized it refers to God.

Fuzuli – A poet renowned among the Ottomans who wrote in Turkish, Persian and Arabic. Author of the most famous Turkish *Leyla and Majnun*. Died 1555.

gem – The word "gem" sometimes denotes a jewel, and is sometimes a term for "substance."

Gülşehri – Anatolian author (flourished 13ᵗʰ-14ᵗʰ) of the Persian *Feleknâme* (*Book of the Firmament*)

hadith – An account, having an established chain of transmission, of something the Prophet Muhammed said or did. When the hadith is a direct quotation from God, it is called a "sacred hadith."

Hazret – An honorific, meaning "Presence of," when preceding names of God (for ex., "The Truth") or persons of spiritual distinction, which as a sign of respect distinguishes them from others with the same name.

Hazret Ali – The Prophet Muhammed's cousin and son-in-law; the fourth of the first four, "Righteously Guided," Caliphs; the first of the Shiite imams.

Huma – A mythological bird whose shadow bestows sovereignty.

Humayra – A name of Aisha, wife of the Prophet Muhammed.

Husameddin – A disciple of Mevlana's who helped him write *The Spiritual Couplets*, taking dictation from Mevlana. Mevlana sometimes addresses Husameddin in the work.

Iblis – See Satan.

Ismail Ankaravi – Author of the most famous commentary on Mevlana's *Spiritual Couplets*.

Israfil – The angel who blows the trumpet for the Resurrection.

jihad – Although often translated as "holy war," jihad means "struggle," and the word is used in many varied contexts.

kafir – Someone who refuses to recognize the truth of Islam.

Kawsar – Name of a river in Paradise.

Khaybar fortress – The exploits of Prophet Muhammed's cousin, son-in-law and successor Ali in conquering this fortress near Medina are legendary.

Khizir – Mentioned in Koran 18:65-82, Khizir served as Moses's spiritual guide and is widely believed to be an immortal who rescues those in need.

Majnun – The famous lover of Leyla; literally, "lunatic."

measuring-out [*kader*, *taqdîr*] – In pre-eternity, the bestowal by God of certain amounts of certain attributes to each thing He creates; predestination in this sense.

messenger [*resûl or peygamber*] – A prophet sent by God with a specific message, for example, scripture; "the Messenger" is the Prophet Muhammed. Moses and Adam are also referred to as "messengers."

Mevlevi order – The dervish order founded in the name of Mevlana Jalaleddin Rumi.

Miraj – The "journey by night" on which the prophet Muhammed ascended through the heavens to meet God.

Mount Qaf – The legendary mountain range which encircles the (flat) world.

morning draught – Wine drunk in the morning to cure hangover.

murid – An aspirant guided by a murshid.

murshid – A spiritual guide.

Mustafa – A name of the Prophet Muhammed.

mystery, secret – The term *sırr* can mean a secret or a mystery, but it also denotes the invisible, inner meaning, state or reality of something, particularly of a human being; thus it can mean "consciousness," "mind," the private thoughts and emotions of a person, and more generally, the truth or fact of something.

namaz – The five-daily ritual prayers.

Neşati – Ottoman Mevlevi poet (d. 1674).

padishah – Sovereign ruler; used interchangeably with "shah."

Pir – Murshid; sage; person in whose name a mystical path is articulated.

post-eternity – Eternity without end; the eternity which ensues after the end of the world.

pre-eternity – Eternity without beginning; the eternity prior to the creation of the world. "The gathering in pre-eternity," also referred to as "the gathering of Alast," is where God asked the spirits of humankind, "Am I not your Lord?"

prophet – See "messenger."

Rafraf – One of two creatures the Prophet Muhammed rode during the Miraj.

rising verse – The first verse of a poem.

Rum – In the context of Mevlana's work, the Seljuk domains in the Christian West; the old lands of the Roman or Byzantine empires.

Salsabil – A spring in Paradise.

Saqi – The cupbearer at a feast, and by metaphorical extension, a spiritual guide who passes around spiritual felicity.

Satan – Iblis, a jinn who consorted with the angels. When God commanded him to bow down to Adam, he refused and God banished him from heaven. In lower case, a "satan" is a demonic creature.

secret – See "mystery."

shariat – Muslim law and rule; any revealed system of law.

Shaykh Ekber – "The Greatest Shaykh," Ibn Arabi.

Siddiq – A name of Abu Bakr, a companion of the Prophet and the first Caliph.

Siddiqa – A name of the Prophet's wife Aisha, daughter of Abu Bakr.

Sidre tree – A tree in heaven past which the angel Gabriel was unable to accompany Muhammad.

Sinan Pasha – Ottoman poet (1437-1486).

Simurgh – See Anka.

soul – The soul [*nefis*] is what arises when the spirit enters the body.

Substitutes [*abdâl*] – Human beings at a high spiritual level capable of taking the place of the Axis [*kutup*], who is at the highest level.

Süleyman Çelebi – Author (flourished 14th-15th century) of the Turkish *Mevlid* (verse work on the subject of the prophet Muhammed's birth).

sultan – Ruler; sovereign or subordinate to a caliph.

tarikat – A spiritual "path" having a founder and custom and rule.

Umar – Second of the four Rightly-Guided Caliphs who succeeded the Prophet Muhammed as leaders of the Muslim community.

the Unseen – The realm of the invisible, which is the realm of meaning, truth, reality and mystery.

wind chimney – An Iranian-style chimney for the purpose of bringing air into the house.

Yahya Kemal – Turkish poet (d. 1958).

Yunus Emre. – Turkish poet (c. 1238-1320).

zahid – A proverbial type of figure who believes religion consists exclusively in performing prescribed worship and who is quick to find fault in others who do not agree; a person who takes things too literally.

Index